S. M. EISENSTEIN
BEYOND THE STARS

Eisenstein in 1928

S. M. EISENSTEIN
Selected Works

Volume IV
BEYOND THE STARS: THE MEMOIRS OF SERGEI EISENSTEIN

Edited by
RICHARD TAYLOR

Translated by
WILLIAM POWELL

BFI PUBLISHING
LONDON

SEAGULL BOOKS
CALCUTTA

S. M. Eisenstein
SELECTED WORKS
General Editor: Richard Taylor
Consultant Editor: Naum Kleiman
Volume IV: Beyond the Stars: The Memoirs of Sergei Eisenstein
Edited by Richard Taylor
Translated by William Powell

First published in 1995 by the
British Film Institute
21 Stephen Street
London W1P 1PL
and
Seagull Books Private Limited
26 Circus Avenue
Calcutta 700 017
India
Copyright © Seagull Books Private Limited 1995
        © annotation: Richard Taylor 1995
British Library Cataloguing in Publication Data
Eizenshtein, Sergei *1898-1948*

ISBN 0 85170 460 3

Typeset, printed and bound in India by Seagull Books, Calcutta

Contents

Acknowledgements

The preparation of the English-language edition of Eisenstein's memoirs in this fuller version has been a long and complex process. The typescript upon which this edition has been based was prepared by a team of Soviet (as we would then have said) scholars and experts, advised and assisted by many friends and colleagues of Eisenstein and this translation preserves all the idiosyncrasies of language and punctuation. We should like first and foremost to express our gratitude to them. In first place we must name Sergei Yutkevich, the President of the Commission for the Creative Heritage of S. M. Eisenstein; Naum Kleiman, Director of the Central Film Museum, Moscow; Leonid Trauberg, the veteran film director; Natalia Volkova, the director of TsGALI (the Central State Archive for Literature and Art of the USSR) and her colleagues Galina Endzina and Yuri Krasovsky; Isabella Epstein, of the USSR Union of Cinematographers; Lydia Podgug, bibliographer at the USSR State Lenin Library; Leonid Kozlov and Viktor Listov, film scholars at VNIIK (the All-Union Research Institute for the History of Cinema); and Vladimir Dmitriev and Valeri Bosenko of Gosfilmofond, the State Film Archive of the USSR.

While these people were responsible in varying degrees for the production of the Russian typescript, we must take the joint responsibility—and, where appropriate, also the blame—for the presentation of that typescript to the English-language audience around the world. We have tried, as far as possible, to retain Eisenstein's often eclectic paragraphing. For this edition we have, despite Naum Kleiman's arguments for the title *Yo!*, chosen to call this volume *Beyond the Stars*, which we, like Eisenstein himself, believe aptly distinguishes his approach to cinema from that of Hollywood (see p. 439). Our friends at Seagull Books have been understanding and supportive to the point of indulgence and we have also received valuable encouragement from Ian Christie and Paul Willemen of the British Film Institute.

William Powell was responsible for the translation. He would like to thank Richard Taylor for his constant support, which

ix

made the task a much lighter one, and for elucidating many of Eisenstein's elliptical remarks and cryptic passages. And equally freely offered was the energy he demonstrably devoted to the annotation which has turned this autobiography into an encyclopedia of late Western civilization! He would also like to thank Professor Ted Braun, University of Bristol, and Tony Pearson, University of Glasgow, for their time on questions concerning early Soviet theatre. The Reed International Books Library provided valuable assistance, swiftly furnishing books that were otherwise unobtainable. Most of the passages translated by Eisenstein therefore appear in the original English.

Richard Taylor was responsible for the annotation. He is grateful to William Powell for restraining him, on the whole, from flights of pedantry that Eisenstein would not have been ashamed of, and for labouring with such perseverance and good humour to produce a lively and highly readable translation of an original that all too often seemed unsalvageably impenetrable and self-indulgent. He greatly appreciates the assistance given to him by the staff and less human resources of both the Library and the Computer Centre of the University of Swansea and by the secretarial staff of the Department of Politics at the same institution. He would also like to thank specifically the advice and assistance received from Dr Julian Graffy, University of London; Professor Jeffrey Richards, University of Lancaster; Professor Richard Shannon, Dr Julian Jackson, Dr. Jeremy Jennings and Dr Paul Garner of the University of Swansea; and Alan Bodger for the usual advice on really intractable problems. Richard Taylor would also like to acknowledge gratefully the contribution to Eisenstein studies of Rosemarie Heise, formerly of the GDR Academy of the Arts, who had already solved for the German translation many of the most irritating problems associated with the annotation of the autobiography, and thus saved him valuable time and energy.

Last but not least, we both owe the usual massive debt to our respective families and friends for their support, advice and sympathy throughout the course of this considerable undertaking.

R.T. & W.P.

The History of Eisenstein's Memoirs

Foreword by Naum Kleiman

Every unfinished work presents its own peculiar difficulties to those who study it. When preparing a manuscript like this for publication, everything individual, unique and idiosyncratic assumes primary importance: the prehistory of the author's way of thinking and the way in which he committed his thoughts to paper; the actual circumstances of the work; the degree of its completeness and the state of the manuscript's preservation; the link between this text and others the author wrote, earlier, concurrently and later . . . Not the least important is the extent to which the author's legacy has been assimilated: i.e. the entire biographical, historical and aesthetic context of the published work. Sometimes the editor comes up against contradictory and even insoluble problems, where any decision means losing something. But it is impossible to avoid interfering with the text: it is up to the editors' intuition and conscience to draw the line, before initiative descends into distortion and even (albeit unintentionally) falsification. In such circumstances, the editors' guiding principle must be honesty with their readership.

The reader should know that the composition of this book is not uniform. The 'memoirs' proper make up the basis of the text: Eisenstein wrote them between 1 May and 12 December 1946. The chapters of this manuscript, kept in the archives, are of extremely uneven quality. Finished passages, reworked by the author himself, may be followed by fragments and sketches which peter out into terse outlines. Some parts of the text were too rough to be included, although it was our ambition to include as much as was possible. At the same time, pieces of text were included (both between the chapters and within them) which were written during the four years preceding that: from 1942 to 1945. These conjectures and interpolations were most often dictated by the author's marginal notes or blanks in the manuscript. But some earlier texts have been inserted on supposition. The sequence of chapters is also hypothetical in some cases and it is quite certain that the reader should not regard the general composition of the book as 'authoritative'. The whole thing is conditioned by the state of the basic manuscript and results from the way Eisenstein's autobiography came into being.

The prehistory of the 'memoirs' begins, I think, in March 1927 when Eisenstein conceived his book *My Art in Life*. The title of this project was in direct opposition to another book that had just come out, the memoirs of Konstantin Stanislavsky: *My Life in Art*.[1] The work planned by the twenty-nine year old director was to be seen of course as an anti-memoir. The programme was set out in the sketch 'My Art in Life: The Aims and Tasks of the Book':

> The hardest thing is not to solve, but to pose a problem. Knowing how to set a problem is the greatest skill. Questions about their art always flummox young practitioners. And the answer always resides in the question being posed incorrectly . . . Ten years of working on 'damned' problems. On coordinating them in sum to one method. *Si non è vero ma ben trovato . . .*[*] To stop the brains of the younger generation becoming clogged up with incorrectly set problems. Every discipline is a part of our speciality. And each one exists individually inside our heads. Defining the moment of their intrusion—and by what part—into the theory of my key work is my second task . . . I am not afraid of theoretical 'truisms'— it is a *textbook* I am dreaming of, not a manifesto . . . Autobiography and practical examples can make a high-flown theoretical abstraction concrete. For the younger generation must progress from this textbook to practise what it thinks and how it thinks. The structure of thought and attitude towards things—that is what I should like to convey.[2]

The realisation of this plan began six years later, when Eisenstein started reworking the shorthand notes of his lectures at the All-Union Cinema Institute, VGIK, for the academic year 1933/4 for his textbook *Direction: The Art of Mise-en-scène*. In order to

---

* Italian: 'It may not be true, but it is a happy invention.'

demonstrate the generally acknowledged rules of creativity, Eisenstein slowed down the directing process for his students and readers, working on the treatment of a single study. But, for all his attempts at an 'objectivisation' of method, he did not shrink from using examples from his own work: he talked about how this or that scene from one of his films was achieved, elucidated how some of his concepts and ideas came to be, drew on his memories and analysed his own creativity or that of his colleagues and friends. Some of these 'digressions' could be considered as 'memoirs'. Other projects of the 1930s were even closer to that genre. So in 1932, soon after his tragic return from Mexico, Eisenstein tried to write about the countries in the Old and the New Worlds, through which his three years of travel had taken him. To judge from the drafts, it was not his intention to jot down his 'tourist's impressions' so much as to attempt to explain the reasons for his social, psychological and artistic inability to work in the conditions that prevailed in the West. Apparently, his wounds from clashes with film-makers in Western Europe and Hollywood were still too raw and the work went no further than working notes and cursory 'drafts'.

Also unrealised was the plan for 1933, 'Things Not Done'. This was a projected collection of screenplays that he had not filmed, accompanied by the author's commentary on the circumstances which led up to them, the advances in cinema they represented and the drama of their fate at production. From this idea emerged the plan for a completely different book. In the spring of 1940 Eisenstein began compiling a collection of his major theoretical articles: from his first manifesto 'The Montage of Attractions' (1923)[3] to his recently-begun research, 'Montage 1940'. He was going to call the book *Close-Up*, explaining the title thus:

> I have always acted with the greatest modesty. I took this or that feature or aspect of a cinema phenomenon and tried to take it apart as comprehensively as possible. I took it in close-up . . .

But this was to have been neither a chance collection of 'features' and 'angles' which the researcher would visit, in no particular sequence; nor a substitution of some concepts of cinema with others he had allegedly become fascinated by once more—which was what many of Eisenstein's critics thought at the time. In order to show the logic of his development and the system of ideas he advanced, the director decided to write semi-autobiographical, semi-theoretical 'linkages' between the articles. These preparations and clarifications began *post factum* to grow—perhaps to the astonishment of the author himself—into memoirs about the events which were to turn out to be epoch-making, and about the motives (often purely personal)—which hardly anyone knew of—that had led to a shattering hypothesis or a recognised cinema discovery. The collection of articles began naturally to evolve into a book, given the rather hackneyed title *Method . . .* For the introduction to the new book, Eisenstein chose as an epigraph Pushkin's semi-ironic words:

> To write your memoirs is alluring and pleasant. You love nobody, you know nobody as well as yourself. The topic is inexhaustible.

So on 15 May 1940 the word 'Memoirs' appeared on the manuscript . . .

It occurred again two years later in Alma-Ata, the capital of Kazakhstan, where the Mosfilm studios had been evacuated during the war. On 17 October 1942 Eisenstein wrote a small article *Mémoires posthumes*[4] as a preamble to his reminiscences 'about a Europe that has gone and an author who survived.' It is hard to say how he envisaged, at that moment, his 'posthumous memoirs': did he want to confine himself to his peregrinations around Europe, or was he intending to let his thoughts return to his childhood and youth? Perhaps he had in mind all forty years of his life—up to the start of the Second World War. In any case, in Alma-Ata—'the heart of Asia'—his memory repeatedly brought him back to distant Europe and the past. Even in the summer of 1942 he began an article about the great singer Yvette Guilbert and slid, imperceptibly and unintentionally, into memories of his Papa. A year later, in October 1943, he returned to his essay on Guilbert and straight after that, as if they wrote themselves, there followed sketched memoirs about Otto 'Aitch' Kahn, patron of the arts and Meyerhold, his teacher—texts full of grief, irony and nostalgia for a bygone age.

Eisenstein began filming *Ivan the Terrible* at the start of 1943; in the brief intervals between shooting he rewrote *Method*. In contrast to the first version, the manuscript of which remained in Moscow, he did little more this time than quote old articles (sometimes in fact fairly comprehensively), pride of place going to all the ever-lengthening 'connecting passages' and the 'history of ideas' which were here and there interrupted by reminiscence, portraits, sketches and intimate self-analysis . . .

It should be noted *en passant* that this semi-autobiographical style was not a genre peculiarity of *Method*, nor a consequence of the nostalgia which dogged Eisenstein in 1943, a tragic year for him. Even by the end of the 1930s, there can be seen in many of his works a tendency to include memoir-like mini-novels and self-portraits within the context of his theoretical thought. Then there is the series of articles about his friends and comrades-in-arms with whom he fought for his art (Tisse, Mayakovsky, Dovzhenko, Malevich, Prokofiev and others), where the 'literary portrait' of the protagonist was limited by the evident or unconscious effort at self-portraiture. Eisenstein perceived the serious heart attack he suffered on 2 February 1946 as the point at which his life ended. While he was still in the Kremlin hospital, he confessed to Prokofiev: 'My life is over; only the post-script is left.' The composer's wife, Mirra Mendelson-Prokofieva, recounted: 'Sergei Sergeyevich was deeply saddened by his friend's illness and fully understood that it meant he could not carry on with what he loved most. He fervently began persuading Eisenstein to write his memoirs, partly so that the post-script would be finished and partly because Eisenstein did indeed have something to remember and it would be a useful and interesting achievement.'

The history of the actual 'memoir' manuscript begins on 1 May 1946 when, still in hospital, Eisenstein wrote a short chapter on his childhood, later sketching out plans for the future chapters and the theoretical 'blocks'. He turned to the foreword by the end of the first week. Even at this early stage one can see the stylistic peculiarity of the new book: the flights of his thoughts and his pencil were completely free. At some time in 1928 he had trained himself (influenced to an extent by Joyce, the Dadaists and psychoanalysts) for 'automatic writing'—for self-analysis. Now he wrote avoiding the extremes of experiment, but allowing himself to follow each fleeting association, freely digressing from the plan he had set himself earlier. Sometimes even he could not see where a chapter he had begun might finish, and several times he comments humorously on his meandering 'stream of consciousness'.

One of the problems that interested Eisenstein as a theoretician of art was the question of the artist's self-portraiture in his work as, for example, in his book *Nonindifferent Nature*, where he remarked that the most lifelike, the best self-portraits by El Greco and van Gogh were their landscapes![5] When working on his memoirs he noticed quite early on that the book would be a 'book about itself', not only in terms of material, but also of style. On 18 May 1946, writing out a quotation from *Uncle Tom's Cabin* for his textbook *Direction*, he found, *en passant*, the title for his 'life-story': *Yo*. '*Yo*' is Spanish for 'I'. Possibly, using Spanish in the title gave an ironic distance, diluting its 'concentrated egocentrism'. There were definitely echoes of his longing for Mexico, where Eisenstein had been really happy, 'himself' and where he had learned to speak and understand Spanish. And of course there were reminiscences: he must have thought of Mayakovsky's poem 'I' and his autobiographical sketch 'I Myself' . . . The more so as the points of departure for Mayakovsky and Eisenstein coincided in the genre of memoir: the first declared: 'I am a poet, which is why I am interesting', the other also did not want to fix the chronological, external events of his life, but intended to answer the question 'How to become an Eisenstein'—a director, a creative personality—with complete honesty.

Anyway, a few chapters in the manuscript are marked 'MEM' and others '*Yo*'. June and July 1946 were months of especially intensive work on the *Memoirs*; that was when Eisenstein was convalescing in the Barvikha sanatorium, and then living in his dacha at Kratovo, not far from Moscow. Despite the doctor's warnings, he wrote a great deal and frantically. However in August 1946 his mother, Yulia Ivanovna died. The half-diary, half-memoir sketch, *After Thursday's Shower*, which records his mother's last day and her demise, turned out, by all appearances, to mark the end of his regular work on the chapters of the memoirs.

However, even at the start of the summer, Eisenstein began to research colour in cinema: he returned to *Nonindifferent Nature* and started preparations to complete the first volume of his text-book *Direction*. The theoretical works drew him ever further from his memoirs. On 14 October, two studies appeared: *Layout* and *The Vixen and the Hare*. Initially planned as the final chapters of his textbook, the element of memoir in both these (especially the former) was so strong that they began to gravitate towards the new book. Analogous cases had arisen earlier: texts which began as a part of *Colour* or *Method* finished up as chapters of memoir. Apparently Eisenstein himself hesitated as to which would be the better context for these studies. For even in the Foreword to his memoirs he promises that he will *demonstrate* his creative process for the reader. So the studies, which are dated 14 October 1946, became the final chapters of the book about himself. After that, only the article *P.S.* was written, two months later. If we go by the heading of this chapter, can we suppose that Eisenstein had put the finishing touches to his book and that it only remained for him to fill in the gaps, put the chapters in order, dot the i's and cross the t's? I think this would be an over-hasty conclusion. We have only to remember the previously cited admission that the director made to Prokofiev, that the *P.S.* should not be taken as the end of the memoirs. More probably, Eisenstein was intending to write only one more chapter about knowing that one's life is about to end and the penalty of fame in one's own lifetime. This is supported by an article dated 12 December 1946 in his 'working notebooks': 'Today I began writing a portrait of the author as a very old man.' This chapter was a play on the title of Joyce's first novel *A Portrait of the Artist as a Young Man* and Eisenstein wanted to call it *O.M. [Starik]*. Paradoxically, that had been his nickname since Proletkult. He was not yet forty-nine.

Eisenstein, though, did not write the chapter *O. M.* He was busy throughout 1947 with theoretical works (*Colour*, *Pathos*, *Nonindifferent Nature*, *Method*, *Pushkin and Gogol* and others), lecturing at the Cinema Institute, organising the Department of Cinema in the Institute for the History of Art . . . Clearly he was not going to be able to write his memoirs. Eisenstein died suddenly on 11 February 1948. And the book *Yo* was found among his incomplete works.

The publication of Eisenstein's memoirs is attended by even greater problems than preparing his theoretical books for publication. He himself admitted that he was writing about himself, not adhering to his earlier plan, and not impeding his train of thought. So the compositional principle of the text could be neither biographical chronology (being broken consistently within each chapter) nor unity of material (on every page it is extraordinarily varied). But the considerable charm of this book resides in this freedom, and it must be preserved at all costs. Apart from that, the conditions in which he worked on the manuscript exerted an influence on it. When Eisenstein touched on this or that event in his memoirs, or on a person or an experience which he had written about earlier in his largely unpublished books and articles, he did not always rewrite his memories but left a blank for the corresponding existing text. But when he was in hospital, in the sanatorium or even at his dacha he did not have the old manuscripts to hand. There were consequently many gaps left, and the manuscript breaks off at the point where a fragment was to be inserted from another source.

Finally, when Eisenstein re-read the chapters he had already written after a break in the work, he did not confine himself to stylistic corrections, but wrote inserts or more developed versions of the various passages. All this made the general picture of the manuscript extraordinarily complicated. Its publication required a preliminary study not only of the corpus of manuscripts for 1946, but all the manuscripts Eisenstein had left. However, publication of the memoir material began a long time before such a colossal undertaking was possible.

In 1960 when the journal *Znamya* [The Banner] (nos. 10 and 11) first published fragments from Eisenstein's memoirs, it was far from clear how things stood with the book. At that time only a part of the director's archive had passed into the safe-keeping of the state and it had been catalogued only in a preliminary way. Most of the hand-written notes from the last period of his life were kept by Eisenstein's widow and heiress, Pera Atasheva, and had not been scrutinised by scholars. The publication in *Znamya*, undertaken at the initiative of Atasheva, was intended to draw public attention to Eisenstein's life and creative personality: his films were then undergoing a revival. This publication was composed of various fragments and chapters in a purely adventitious composition, with the general title *Pages from Life* and laid no claims to scholarship. But even the version in the journal caused great interest and was immediately translated into many languages.

In 1964, the six-volume series *Selected Works of S.M. Eisenstein* began to be published in Russian.[6] A large part of Volume 1 was taken up with memoirs bearing the title 'Autobiographical Notes'. But even that publication proved incomplete: some chapters, in Pera Atasheva's keeping, were completely new to researchers; some were compiled from parts of other works (and, conversely, part of another book was attributed to his memoirs); the manuscripts from the war period, from which Eisenstein was planning to take many extracts, had been simply disregarded—the author's 'methodology' for his work on this book was still unclear. One serious problem the editors faced therefore was the composition of the material. The numerous lacunae and lapses in the text, the vagueness of dates and sequence of chapters resulted in cutting and pasting and setting the material picked for publication in the chronological order of the *events* described, as far as that was possible. This meant that even chapters that were preserved complete were disjointed. The Editorial Committee however could claim justification: by the start of the 1960s there was still no published monograph in Russian on Eisenstein and it was important to give the reader an idea of the different stages in his life and creativity.

It was only in 1973, after the completion of the research on the director's manuscripts by colleagues at the TsGALI (Central State Archive of Literature and Art of the USSR), and the members of the Commission for the Creative Heritage of S. M. Eisenstein, that it became possible to study his principle writings—including his memoirs—systematically.

Work on compiling the new book *Yo* was substantially complete by December 1979. The point of departure was the dating of the chapters written in 1946 in order to preserve the author's whimsical but always well-grounded chain of thought. It then became clear that the date on the manuscript could not be an utterly reliable guide: sometimes the date referred to the time the chapter was written; sometimes to the time it was re-worked or stylistically corrected; while some chapters were not dated at all. The guiding principle was to try to establish, as far as possible, the logical development of the manuscript. Compared with the 1964 version, the sequence of chapters was not the only thing that changed: the arrangement within many of the chapters was also different. This became possible during the reorganization of the archive, as pages that had been separated at an earlier stage were discovered and re-united. Links between separate fragments were discovered, and the mysteries of many of the gaps were solved. Studying other works by Eisenstein clarified the sense of the marginalia and concise sketches in the manuscript of the *Memoirs*, where the author intended his earlier sketches to go. So the chief omissions were supplied (all the interpolations and insertions that had been made during compilation are shown in square brackets), which helped to restore the cuts unwittingly made earlier. In addition, a few rearrangements had to be retained, where the concise text did not seem to have a more developed equivalent, or where Eisenstein seemed to have planned to write connecting passages but had not managed to.

At the same time, it should be remembered that fragments from other works (*Direction, Montage, Method*) were brought into the *Memoirs* in accordance with the author's notes, in minute quantities, just as much as was necessary to meet the demands of the fluency of the narrative. This decision was taken in relation to early essays which Eisenstein wanted to rework for this book. Only those essays marked with 'MEM' are included in the main body of the memoirs—for example, *The Twelve Apostles* (in the first version), *Charlie Chaplin, Comrade Léon.* There is, however, a series of articles whose theme corresponds to the chapters promised in the foreword to the memoirs, but which were not actually written. Eisenstein promised to include in his memoirs descriptions of his encounters with Gorky and Mayakovsky, José Climente Orozco and Jimmy Collins; his friendships with Prokofiev, Tisse, Glitser, Dovzhenko and many other outstanding contributors to the cultural world. He wrote earlier essays or short pieces on many of them, but not only were these manuscripts not prepared for the book, they were not even signalled as needing re-working. Such texts could only have been included in an appendix—under the general heading *Profiles*.[7]

The composition of the text that results from this work cannot of course be considered academically definitive, or final. It is possible that other fragments relevant to the memoirs will come to light or be identified. The order of the chapters might be ascertained; in some cases it is adventitious because there are no direct authorial indications or indirect marks. But we hope that the book in its present form corresponds most closely to Eisenstein's plan— at least insofar as we today understand this plan to have been.

EUROPEAN RUSSIA AND
NEIGHBOURING STATES IN 1922

Part One

Eisenstein with a *calavera*, 1931, Mexico. (Photo: Jimenez)

About Myself[1]

'*Visse, scrisse, amo . . .*'

    I would like to be able to sum myself up with such economy—three words.

    The actual words would be different from the three that Stendhal used in this brief account of his life.

    Stendhal's will stated that these words—'I lived, I wrote, I loved'—were to serve as the epitaph on his tombstone.[2]

    True, I don't suppose that my life is over. (And I fear that there are still many struggles ahead.)

    Again, I am not sure that three words would be enough.

    But of course, three words could be found to meet even this case.

    For me, they would be:

    'I lived, I contemplated, I admired.'

    And let the following serve as a description of how the author lived, what he contemplated and what he admired.

Foreword[1] *

First of all I must warn you.

These notes are completely amoral.

And I must at this point disillusion anyone who is expecting a series of amoral episodes, seductive details, or indecent descriptions.

There is here nothing of the sort: this is not Casanova's diary, or the history of a Russian film director's amorous adventures.

In that vein, no doubt, Frank Harris's autobiography *My Life and My Loves* (1923) is the most amoral of contemporary lives.

This highly unpleasant, caustic and importunate author set down his life and the catalogue of his affairs with the same distasteful candour and tactlessness that characterised his relations with most of his eminent contemporaries.

Did anyone escape the pen of this man with the moustache and wide-set eyes of a blackmailer?!

I read three volumes of his autobiography in the USA—naturally, bought 'under the counter'—in an 'unexpurgated' edition, where, for convenience's sake, everything that the censor had cut from the usual edition was printed in a different typeface—'for the convenience of its readers'!

And?

Of all the indecent episodes I cannot remember a single one!

In fact, out of all the three volumes, only one scene has remained in my memory—and that is of dubious veracity. Someone, I think it was one of the young Harris's first 'bosses', was overcome by a nervous laughter of such intensity that he shook for three days solid. He died afterwards, because his flesh had begun 'to come away off the bone' (!) from all the shaking.

So, although love and hunger are considered the strongest of our instincts, we must conclude that when it comes to autobiography they do not leave a very strong impression.

---

* In English in the original.

4

This is probably the case when these emotions have finally been sublimated. Which is why there will not be much about them here.

There will be even fewer shocking details and passages.

These notes are amoral in a completely different sense.

They do not moralise.

They have no moralistic aim or didactic purpose.

They prove nothing, explain nothing, teach nothing.

I have spent my entire creative life writing dissertations: I have proved, explained and taught. Here, I want to stroll through my past, as I loved strolling through flea markets and the second-hand shops of Petersburg's Alexandrovsky Market, or along the bookstalls on the Paris embankments, or through Hamburg or Marseilles, at night, and through museum galleries and halls with waxworks.

I have never enjoyed Marcel Proust.

And that has nothing to do with snobbery—deliberately ignoring the terribly fashionable interest in Proust.

More probably, it is for the same reason that I dislike Gavarni.

I always used to be shocked when people mentioned Gavarni in the same breath as Daumier.[2]

Daumier was a genius. His greatest pictures can be hung beside works from art's greatest epochs. But Gavarni was no more than an elegant *boulevardier* of a lithographer, for all that the Goncourts[3] sang their friend's praises.

In the twenties and thirties, it was popular to mention Proust and Joyce together.

Joyce is a veritable colossus, whose stature rises above fashions and the squalid *succès de scandale* caused by some too explicit pages in *Ulysses;* the censor's ban; a subsequent lull in fashion and temporary neglect. Marcel Proust, on the other hand, enjoyed only a brief reign, to be succeeded in later years first by Celine, then by Jean-Paul Sartre.[4]

It is probably my dislike of Proust which explains the circumstance that I do not recall very clearly whether the critics' surprise at the unusual title referred only to *Du Côté chez Swann* [Swann's Way] and *A l'Ombre des jeunes filles en fleurs* [Within a

Budding Grove]; or to the general title *A la Recherche du temps perdu* [Remembrance of Things Past].

My attitude to Proust has changed little, although now this title makes me shudder with particular violence.

It holds the key to that insanely ornate thoroughness which characterises Proust's descriptive prose, as he lists each immutable autobiographical detail as if palpating or caressing it, trying to hold the past in his hands, although it has been hopelessly lost . . .

Now that I am approaching fifty, an acute, tormenting desire wells up inside me to seize the time I have lost, to keep hold of it as it slides into the past.

One Anglo-Saxon put it very well when he said that we all live as if we have a million years ahead of us . . .

People live in different ways, of course.

Some husband time.

Others spend it wisely, or squander it.

A third kind lose it.

The famous *'Verweile doch, du bist so schön'** (Goethe, *Faust*). Our epoch is somehow even more deprived than was Goethe's, when only a genius could have guessed at this central drama of twentieth-century man . . .

In February of '46 I had a heart attack.[5]

For the first time in my life, I was forced to a halt, confined to bed.

My circulation was weak.

My mind worked slowly.

There was no prospect of the situation changing for several months to come.

But I relished this.

I thought I would at last be able to take my bearings, look back, take stock.

And understand everything: about myself,
about life,
about the forty-eight years I had lived.

I will say straight away: I understood nothing. Nothing about life. Nor about the forty-eight years of my life.

---

* German: 'Stay awhile, thou art so fair'.

6

Nothing, except maybe for this:
that life has gone by at a gallop,
without looking around,
always changing trains,
as if chasing one train from another.
My attention fixed permanently on the second hand.
To arrive there on time.
Not to be late.
To arrive here on time.
To get away from here.

While fragments of childhood, a slice of youth, and layers of maturity fly past the windows of the carriage.

Bright, motley, spinning and colourful.
And suddenly, the terrible realisation!
That none of this has been held on to,
nothing seized;
only sipped.
Nowhere drunk to the bottom.
Occasionally, swallowed whole.

Going up a staircase, you feel you have already in your mind's eye descended it.

Unpacking a suitcase, you have already thought about packing it again.

Setting books out on a shelf, I have fallen to thinking about who will take them from their places when I am dead.

And when I kiss a pair of lips, new, unfamiliar, for the first time, I am already thinking of how the farewell kiss will rest upon them.

Peer Gynt goes through the typhoon of dry leaves—thoughts he has not pursued, deeds not accomplished.

Thomas de Quincey writes about how he would take lodgings, set out his books, then drop everything and escape to a new place where he could start again.*

I made the acquaintance of King Gillette, the inventor of the safety razor, when he was about sixty.

---

* I did not find these details in the author's autobiography, *Confessions of an English Opium-Eater*. So much the worse for the autobiography, and so much the better for the idea! (E's note)

7

He was obsessed with building villas in desert regions.

A house—a palace—would rise above the sand; he would plant orchards around it; but then the builder would dash off to a new part of the desert to construct a new palace, and so on and so on.

I have lived in much the same sort of way, in relation to the events in my personal life.

Like a pack animal or horse that has a sheaf of corn hanging in front of him which he chases, headlong, hopelessly, for ever.

I remember one thing from the long months of my confinement to bed.

And that was the unstoppable flow of memories of countless past hours, which came in response to the question I posed myself: 'But was that a life?'

Or was it merely a journey at breakneck speed, pulled by a team of racers, to the nearest ten or twenty minutes, day, week or month?

That was a life, it turns out.

And it was lived acutely, joyfully and in torment,

and even bright in places,

unquestionably colourful,

and one that I would not wish to exchange for any other.

And that was what I madly desired to grasp, hold back, make fast by describing those moments of 'lost time'.

Moments, always knowing they are awaited,

remembered

and a certain impatient perseverance in living through them.

I passed through a staggering age.

But I do not want to write about this age at all.

What I want to set down is how an average person can pass through a momentous time as a completely unexpected counterpoint.

How someone can 'fail to notice' a historical date as he blithely passes it.

How someone can grow absorbed in Maeterlinck while overseeing the construction of trenches during the Civil War, or in Schopenhauer, while dossing down in the shadow of the armoured trains.[6]

How someone would walk upon the Filmland of Hollywood.

How someone would behave, when being interrogated by American policemen, as opposed to French.

How someone would scale the thousand-year-old pyramids of Yucatán, or sit intently at the foot of the ruins of the Temple of a Thousand Columns, pensively waiting until the familiar outline of the constellation of the Plough sinks (upside-down according to our perceptions) behind the Soldiers' Pyramid.

How someone would sit intently with the aim of fixing this moment in the future stream of memories, just as sailors navigate by the same stars.

Or how someone would engrave on his retina images of his first . . . lesbians' ball, witnessed in Berlin twenty years ago.

Any line of any picture or person stands out as if branded on one's visual memory.

I can believe that absurd popular myth that the murderer's image can be fixed on the victim's retina as clearly as on photographic film.

This ridiculous notion is the basis of the substantive proof of the black murderer's guilt in *The Clansman,* which described the Ku-Klux-Klan phenomenon and inspired Griffith's *The Birth of a Nation.*[7]

The first time in the theatre as spectator.

First time as director.

First time as producer.

First impression of cinema: in Paris, 1908, on the Boulevard des Italiens.[8]

The famous coachman by that genius Méliès, who drove a carriage pulled by the skeleton of a horse.

Mr Hartwick the butcher in his glossy black cuffbands, who owned the dacha on the Riga coast that my parents used to rent when I was a child.

Mesdames Kevič, Koppitz and Klapper, who owned summer pensions where we lived after Mama and Papa had separated.

Grandma, Vassa Zheleznova[9] *sui generis* of the Marinsky system of the Neva barge network.

Childhood walks in the Alexander Nevsky monastery.

Top. Ivan Ivanovich Konetsky, Eisenstein's grandfather Iraida Matveyevna Konetskaya, grandmother. *Below.* Yulia Ivanovna Konetskaya and Mikhail Osipovich Eisenstein

The silver shrine of the saint whom I was destined to glorify in film after his country had made him a national hero.[10]

The stupefying aroma of fermented maguey juice filtered up from the *pulque* (the Mexican type of vodka) distillery, which was lit by candles and with a tawdry madonna, and permeated my temporary sleeping quarters on the first floor of the Tetlapayac hacienda.

It was a real hacienda, after *Doña Manuela's Hacienda,* an adventure story which once captured my imagination, on the pages of *Mir priklyuchenii* [The World of Adventures].

Real Mexico, ten years after it had been conjured up in my first work in theatre.

People.

Khudekov, the proprietor of the *Peterburgskaya gazeta* [Petersburg Gazette], and the story of how I sold him cartoons in 1917.

Gordon Craig, who summoned me from Italy to 'drop everything' and meet him in Paris to loaf about the bookstalls on the Seine embankment for a while.[11]

Shaw, who caught up with me on the Atlantic with a radiotelegraph, granting permission to film *The Chocolate Soldier,* if I so wished, in America, on the understanding that the text was left untouched.

Stefan Zweig,[12] working on *The Complete Scoundrel* (he wanted to 'fuse', combine, every element he found personally unworthy, into the one person (letter from the time he was writing *Fouché*).

The living Himalaya of old man Dreiser[13], sitting at a table with me in Chistye Prudy,[14] or in a basement bar in New York during the Prohibition Era, or chopping firewood in a lumberjack shirt in the wilds of his country estate on the Hudson—the fireplace downstairs and the 'Pompeiian' friezes in the upstairs room (where I slept). The unusually deep-chested voice of his young wife, which to me demonstrated that mixed blood is the ideal condition for genius to thrive.

The gallery of America's 'film bosses'.

Profiles of my colleagues working in film lodge in my consciousness for a short while: von Sternberg, Stroheim, Lubitsch,

11

King Vidor.[15]

Profiles . . .

America has the delightful custom of writing profiles, cultivated in particular by the *New Yorker* magazine.

They are then brought out in anthologies (chiefly by Knopf).

A few biographical facts,

some career details,

a well-known piece of slander,

a drop of venom,

a few anecdotes and some gossip . . .

I do not intend writing any profiles here.

If only I could mentally fix the curve of someone's brow, the corners of his mouth, the way his eyes narrow or how he smokes cigars.

But I am no journalist trying to insert into the columns of a profile the portrait of a fascinating businessman, a popular female playwright, a match king or music-hall idol.

I am not writing about them; how they spent their time and energy.

I am writing about my own time.

And they are at best a brief encounter, a stream of images; I dwell upon them only fleetingly before time hurls me onwards.

Sometimes it is just a brush with my elbow. At other times, it lasts days, and sometimes years,

but something always remained—not proportional to the length of time, but to the strength of the impressions, the amusement the meeting brought, personal reasons . . .

An old reporter could of course say more about journalists.

An old stage-hand has memories more valuable than my impressions—a touring director at the Bolshoi Theatre. The guardian of the Volkovsky Cemetery, or Merkurov the sculptor,[16] who made plaster-casts of eminent people after their death, or simply a morgue watchman would have a greater stock of impressions of the dead than I do. I have never fought in any war.

But would a stage-hand also have gasped from the heat while filming a bullfight on the sand of the arena in distant Mérida, between the Gulf of Mexico and the Caribbean Sea?

Would the old reporter have had to ward off such a hail of questions from the floor as beset me after my lecture at the Sorbonne?!

And I doubt that the morgue watchman would have had occasion to go down the narrow alleyways of a disreputable quarter of Marseilles and be confronted by the funereal window-dressing of the butchers' shops, where the gilded head of the traditional bull rose ghost-like from the black velvet drapery decorated with a silver border. On either side of the shops were posters shrilly advertising films; or brothels. And the funeral the next day? The hearse-driver's top hat, as he sat on his bench, was as high as the first-storey window. And as he rolled over baskets of ripe vegetables, crushing them in his progress down this more than merely narrow street, he scraped the children's dresses, which were hanging ready, off their hooks with the small angels on the carriage.

Under his arm he carried a pith helmet which had a long black plume of protective lace.

A cruel mistral provided cover for the coachman's exit from the side street, but he had to take the corpse—the grandmother of three butcher brothers, who led the cortège bellowing in drunken grief—far out of town.

The helmet replaced the top hat as twelve girls, from an orphanage, sang a lament.

And just round the corner there stood a life-size copy of the Lourdes grotto, with models of the Madonna and Bernadette painted to look life-like. The innocent virginal orphans stared at the little saint, from whose life story on the screen, as told by Werfel,[17] Hollywood, commercially minded as ever, has garnered so many dollars. This was where the inhabitants of this Yoshiwara[18] of Marseilles could come to pray for forgiveness for their nocturnal transgressions, and the next morning viciously fight around the stone pool, used for rinsing out the washing, away from the entranced gaze of Bernadette Soubirou and her secret cave.

Marseilles can only bring to mind another Yoshiwara, not the one in Tokyo where everyone has been now. But Monterrey.

That apart, I now observe another curious fact.

There is another contradiction in this piece of writing.

There is as much reading as there is writing!

Beginning a page, or a section or a phrase, I have no idea where it will take me as it develops.

It is like flicking through a book: I do not know what I will find on the other side of the page.

No matter that the 'material' is mined from the 'depths' of my own resources; never mind that the 'factual' material is the product of my own experience. There are whole new tracts of utterly unexpected territory whose existence I never dreamed of, much that is completely new. Juxtaposition of material, conclusions reached from these juxtapositions, new aspects and 'discoveries' which flow from these conclusions . . .

More often than not, these pages are the purest specimens from the quarry; they emerge, in the actual process of writing, in quantities no smaller than do the foregone conclusions and intentions, when some element demands with unexpected intensity to be set down on paper.

For this reason, this is not only an adventurous and exciting 'journey' through the pictures and images of the past; it is also a disclosure, on this path, of such conclusions and juxtapositions. And—but for juxtaposition—the separate and uncoordinated facts and impressions had neither the right nor the grounds to claim their place here!

These are not literary characterisations.

All this is no more than two jaws of young teeth sunk deep into the overripe peach of approaching life.

Going into the actual encounter too hurriedly,

but savouring the taste, aroma, and amusement for many years to come.

Mayakovsky, and how friendship failed to take root.[19]

The heavy-jowled deacon at my cousin's christening, and the need to engage Father Dionysus in conversation in the hours preceding little Boris's immersion in the font.

And the walk in the garden, a twelve-year-old godson on the right-hand side of the venerable elder who wore spectacles on his nose and had in irrepressible desire to name the species of every tree that we passed . . .

Much to my surprise, I can remember one name to this day: alder.

Is this of any use to anyone apart from myself?

That no longer matters. I need it, above all.

Apart from 'didacticism'.

Apart from 'edification'.

Apart from 'the historical fresco'.

Apart from 'man and his age'.

Apart from 'history refracted in consciousness'.

But simply as a possibly new loss of time, incurred while pursuing time lost in the past.

If it is necessary, it will be printed.

If it is not necessary, it will be found in my 'literary legacy'.

But perhaps it is necessary.

Because virtually all of this is highlights from prehistory, the antediluvian years preceding the era of the atom bomb.

And perhaps for another reason.

I once asked my students what lectures they wanted me to give during an Institute course.

I was not expecting any particular answer.

Someone shyly (but not unctuously) said: 'Don't talk about montage, or pictures, or directing. Tell us how to become an Eisenstein.'

It was terribly flattering, if not very clear who could want to become one.

But here it is nevertheless.

Here is precisely how I became what I am.

And if anyone finds the result interesting, then he will find scattered notes as to how this process works.

The Boy from Riga (An Obedient Child)[1]

Not a mummy's boy.

Not an urchin.

Just a boy.

A boy aged twelve.

Obedient, polite, clicking his heels.

A typical boy from Riga.

A boy from a good family.

That's how I was aged twelve.

And that's how I was when my hair turned grey.

At twenty-seven, the boy from Riga became a celebrity.

Doug and Mary[2] travelled to Moscow to shake the hand of the boy from Riga—he had made *Potemkin*.

In 1930, after his speech to the Sorbonne, the combined forces of Premier Tardieu and Monsieur Chiappe were not sufficient to expel the boy from Riga from French territory.

For the only time in his life, his hand shook as the boy from Riga signed his name—on a contract in Hollywood worth $3,000 a week.

When they tried to expel the boy from Riga from Mexico, twelve US senators signalled their protest. Instead of expulsion, there was a triumph: I shook hands with the President at one of the countless celebrations which take place in Mexico City.

In 1939, the boy from Riga was snowed under with cuttings from American newspapers saying that *Alexander Nevsky* was given a screening in the White House, at Franklin Delano Roosevelt's special request.

1941 saw the first edition of the American Film Index come out: a conspectus of the first forty years of cinema. According to the foreword, it turned out that the boy from Riga came fourth in terms of the amount of column-inches devoted to him. First was Chaplin, then Griffith; but our boy from Riga came straight after Mary Pickford, who was in third place.

Little Sergei Eisenstein with his father. Riga 1904

At the height of the war, the boy from Riga published a book about cinema; the American and British editions sold out instantly.[3] The post brought a pirate edition, in Spanish, that had been printed in Argentina. And after the collapse of Japan it turned out that a translation had been printed there during the war . . .

Because all this time my country was lavish with medals, orders and titles.

But the boy from Riga is still twelve, as before.

This is the cause of my sadness.

But my happiness also resides in this, I think.

It is not a new idea to say that few people perceive themselves as they are in reality.

Everyone sees himself as someone, something.

The interesting thing is not that, but the fact that this conception is much closer to the precise psychological make-up of the gazer, than is his objective appearance.

One sees himself as d'Artagnan. Another as Alfred de Musset.[4] A third as Byron's Cain, at least, and a fourth, being more humble, is satisfied with his position as being the Louis XIV of his region, his district, his studio, or his family circle—on his mother's side.

When I look at myself in complete privacy, the image that most readily springs to mind is that of . . . David Copperfield.

Delicate,

thin,

short,

defenceless,

and very timid.

This sounds funny after the list of names given above, perhaps.

But funnier still is the fact that perhaps it is precisely because of this self-perception that I assembled this welter of personal details, which so intoxicate my vanity, and fragments of which I have listed above.

The character of Don Juan is open to many hypothetical interpretations.

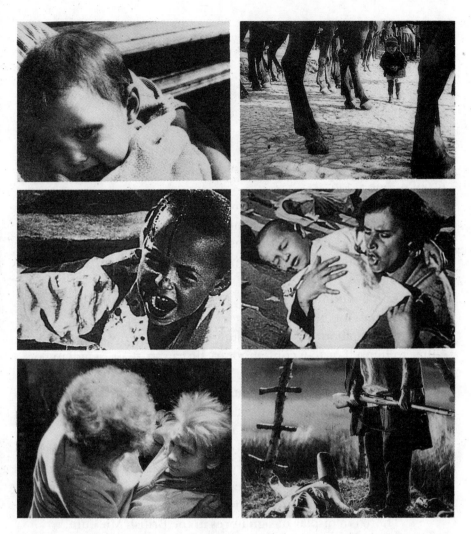

The martyrdom of children in Eisenstein's films. *Above. The Strike. Middle. The Battleship Potemkin. Below. Bezhin Meadow.* 'It would seem that the time had come to see myself as an adult'.

Some are probably just as valid as others, for various cases of actual Donjuanism.

But in the light of Tynyanov's brilliant hypothesis in 'A Nameless Love',[5] there is an alternative approach to the favoured semi-psychoanalytical interpretation, to Pushkin's 'list' (or Chaplin's hordes).[6]

This latter interpretation posits Donjuanism as a fear for one's own potency. It sees each successive conquest as yet further proof of one's potency.

But why admit Donjuanism only in sex?

It is a much stronger impulse in other areas, especially those where the important questions are to do with 'success', 'recognition' and 'winning', which are no less important than sexual conquest.

At some point, each young person begins philosophising, assembling his personal views on life,

talking about his various judgements on general questions, either to himself or to a contemporary he can trust, or to a diary, or more rarely, in letters to friends.

As a rule, these judgements are of more than dubious value to humanity. The more so as their originality lies not in their actual invention, but in where they were taken from.

But there is always a hint of something touching and amusing, such as you might find in a child's first drawings, sometimes well executed; suddenly—with the advantage of hindsight—you see the embryonic features of what is to come.

There is a display of signatures in the British Museum.

In one corner there is a letter from Queen Elizabeth I, teaching a moral to her beloved sister Mary Stuart, who was complaining about the lack of comfort in her dungeon where she was imprisoned. The Virgin Queen's virile writing echoes, in strange form, a small drawing (from a slightly later period) pinned to another corner of the display.

It is no more or less than the *mise-en-scène* for the execution of the unfortunate—but far from innocent—Scottish queen, which was advocated by a lord at the behest of the 'redheaded maiden Bess', as Ivan the Terrible referred to her.

Immediately adjacent, on a sheet of graph paper, you can

read a few words in the childish hand of the future Queen Victoria.

The fourth is much the most exciting. It was written by a young, dark-skinned French Commander-in-Chief, of Corsican extraction.

Shortly before this, he had shouted (in the words of the heroic legend) about 'the many centuries looking down from the summit of the pyramids upon his soldiers' who had fought none too willingly in recent operations. The young commander led them in their landing on the arid sands of Africa. Victory was piled on victory and the words of the young military genius resounded across continents, together with the name 'Bonaparte'.

And what message, on that torn scrap of paper, did the young Corsican send to his brother from his tent?

'I have tasted everything. Grief and joy. Successes and routs. Only one thing is left: to become a self-absorbed egotist.'

This is not from Onegin's diary, but from the thickets of the barely charted areas of Napoleon's life . . .[7]

Napoleon came to mind here for a reason.

It is to him, and nobody else, that the boy from Riga referred in his first analogous note, as he tried to make sense of reality:

'Napoleon did everything that he did, not because he was talented or a genius; he became talented so that he could do everything that he did . . .'

If it is axiomatic that notes like this one written by fifteen-year-olds or twenty-year-olds (I was then seventeen) can be treated as immature ambitions (the words of the Corsican general are not just Childe Haroldean pessimism or anticipation of what Stendhal expertly played upon subsequently—there is also a certain principle, brazenly brought to life—egoism!) then the image of a David Copperfield from Riga is perhaps not so unexpected after all.

But why belittle myself?

I had no experience of poverty or deprivation in childhood, nor any of the horrors of struggling for existence. Further on, you will encounter descriptions of my childhood—for the time being, take it on faith!

In the Proletkult.

Why I Became A Director[1]

Every normal child does three things: he breaks things; he gets inside dolls or watches to see what is there; and he torments animals. For instance, if he does not turn flies into elephants, he turns them into little dogs, at the very least. This involves amputating the middle pair of legs and the wings. The fly cannot leave the ground and scuttles about on four legs.

That is what normal children do. Good ones.

I was a bad child. I did none of these things at that age. I have not one tormented fly, nor one vase smashed with evil intent on my conscience . . . And that, of course, is very bad. It is precisely for that reason, I suspect, that I was driven to become a film director.

It is a fact that good children, such as those I described initially, satisfy their curiosity, primitive cruelty and aggressive self-assertion in relatively inoffensive pastimes, like those listed above.

The urge passes with childhood. And in adulthood none of them would even dream of doing anything like it again. It is quite otherwise for the 'good boy' than for the generally accepted 'little terror'.

In childhood, he does not maim his dolls, smash crockery, or torment animals. But let him grow up and he will be irresistibly drawn towards diversions of this nature.

He will hunt feverishly for an outlet where it is safest for him to indulge his appetites.

And ultimately he must become a director. Then he will be in the best position to realise all the potential denied in childhood.

Watches that I failed to take apart at the right time led to my passion for rooting around in the recesses and springs of the 'creative mechanism'.

Dinner services that were not smashed when they should have been were reborn as respect for authority and traditions.

My cruelty, which did not find an outlet with flies, dragonflies and frogs, coloured my choice of theme, method and the credo of my work as director.

In fact, people in my films are gunned down in their hundreds; farm labourers have their skulls shattered by hoofs, or they are lassoed and buried in the ground up to their necks (*México*); children are crushed on the Odessa steps (*Potemkin*); thrown from rooftops *(The Strike)*; are surrendered to their own parents who murder them (*Bezhin Meadow*); thrown on to flaming pyres (*Alexander Nevsky*); they stream with actual bulls' blood *(The Strike)* or with stage blood (*Potemkin*); in some films bulls are poisoned (*The Old and the New*); in others, tsars (*Ivan the Terrible*); a shot horse hangs from a raised bridge (*October*) and arrows pierce men lying spreadeagled on the ramparts outside a besieged Kazan (*Ivan the Terrible*). And it seems no coincidence that it was none other than Tsar Ivan Vasilyevich the Terrible who ruled my mind and was my hero for very many years.

Not to mince my words, I am hard on my characters. But it is interesting that there, in the actual screenplay for *Ivan,* I have concealed my defence.

And I do mean the screenplay, since various ideas planned for Ivan's childhood did not make it into the film.

The screenplay shows how the sum of childhood impressions can lead to the forming of socially (or historically) beneficial matter: when the emotional complex that these impressions have created coincides in feeling with what the adult has to accomplish in the course of rational and determined acts. In other words, there is a series of striking impressions from childhood, and feelings that accompany them: 'Watch out for poison, watch out for the boyars', from the lips of his poisoned mother as she dies; the pathos of the fallen Russian towns on the Baltic coast (which the nurse sings about); the venality of the boyars near the throne of the Prince of Muscovy—these themselves define that passionate, emotional colouring of what the mature Ivan will have to achieve in the name of national progress (the abolition of feudalism and a foothold on the Baltic coast).

When the emotional impact of a series of childhood traumas coincides with the problems that the adult comes to face, then it is a blessing in disguise.

This was the case with Ivan.

From that point of view, my life was very fortunate indeed!

I turned out to be necessary for my time, in my work, in exactly the same way as my individuality was defined.

I forgot to add that I was very obedient as a child. In later years, this could only become the sharply accented 'naughtiness' of an adult.

Here, disrespect for adults turned out to be exceedingly useful in the self-determination of those paths which our cinema had to take, and which completely opposed the traditions of a cinema older (more adult, senior!) than the Soviet.

But the originality of our cinema does not lie only in its form, scope, or method.

Form, scope and method—these are merely the result of the basic peculiarity of our cinema. It is not a pacific medium: it is a fighting force. Our cinema is a weapon, first and foremost, to be used for combating hostile ideology; and primarily it is a tool whose principal task is to influence and recreate.

Here, the art is self-consciously aware that it is one aspect of violence,

that it is a tool of terrible force when used 'for evil' and a weapon that can smash, whose invincible idea will forge a way.

The years of my life have been years of untiring struggle.

And years of such titanic struggle are bound to call to life an art that is similarly aggressive in all respects; and also an idiosyncratic 'operational aesthetic' for appreciating it.

And the applications of aggression in my work have gone far beyond the limits of the situations in a film or the methods by which a film exerts influence, according to the director's credo of a volitional basis for the construction of a shot in a film; of a volitional basis that bends the viewer towards the theme.

Questions about how to direct the viewer's mind have led inevitably to a growing familiarity with the internal mechanisms for exerting influence.

That was how people began to experiment.

And on several occasions, there was a paradox: pictures that were experiments in the methods of exerting influence, forgot to influence!

The watch, reduced to its component cogs, no longer worked!

A director always has his particular favourites out of all those elements which make up a spectacle. Some love crowd scenes; others, intense dialogue; others, the decorativeness of life; others, the play of light; others, the living truth of verbal balances; others, the reckless exuberance of the action in a scene.

Most of all in theatre, I loved the *mise-en-scène*.

Mise-en-scène in the narrowest sense of the phrase: the conjunction of spatial and temporal elements in the interactions of people on stage.

I was always fascinated by the way independent lines of action with their detached regularity interlaced with the rhythmic tones of their patterns and the spatial displacements in the one harmonious whole.

The *mise-en-scène* remained not only my favourite: it became a constant point of departure not only for setting a scene, which evolves from the *mise-en-scène*, and goes on to affect all the component parts—but it went much further than this.

Through analysis of the conflicting play of motifs, rendered by the graphic flourish of the *mise-en-scène*, I reached a definition of expressive movement being a *mise-en-scène* built around a person.

Translated into a new medium, from theatre to cinema, the *mise-en-scène* was resurrected into the popular *mise-en-cadre* (by which you must understand not only juxtaposition within a shot, but also the interaction of different shots in a sequence), and I came to a new object of fascination: montage.[2]

In its more complex aspect, this was the audiovisual counterpoint of sound cinema. In a different aspect, *mise-en-scène* developed into playwriting: the same interlacing and intersections were defined between different characters or the different features and motifs of one character.

Orthodox, graphic *mise-en-scène*, a cuneiform of the simplest spatial outlines, which were subordinate to the strict network of rhythmic calculation of time—this was always to be the initial prototype for movement through the most complex counterpoint passages, which are especially complex in cinema because they have to bind together elements that have no common denominator, starting with the contradictory pairing of depiction and sound.

Where did those first sensations come from, which were to transport me forever with a love of audiovisual constructs and temporal-spatial conjunctions?

Izhora.[3] The River Neva. The College of Ensigns of the Engineering Corps. The pontoon bridge.

I remember the heat as if it were yesterday,

the fresh air,

the sandy bank of the river.

An ant-hill of raw fresh-faced recruits moved along measured-out paths with precision and discipline and worked in harmony to build a steadily growing bridge which reached hungrily across the river.

Somewhere in this ant-hill I moved as well. Square pads of leather on my shoulders supported a plank, resting edgeways. Like the parts of a clockwork contraption, the figures moved quickly, driving up to the pontoons and throwing girders and handrails festooned with cabling to one another—it was an easy and harmonious model of *perpetuum mobile*, reaching out from the bank in an ever-lengthening road to the constantly receding end of the bridge.

The inflexible period allowed for the construction was divided into seconds of separate operations, rapid and slow, which dovetailed and interwove; it was as if the circuit of a racecourse had been marked out according to a rhythmic time scale, but staggered, depending on the time allowed for the separate operations which made up the whole. All this fused into the marvellous, orchestral, polyphonic experience of something being done, in all the variations of its harmony.

The bridge grew longer and longer.

It hungrily squeezed the river beneath.

It stretched out towards the opposite bank.

Men scurried about.

The pontoons were rushed here and there.

The second hand raced round . . .

Hell, it was good!

No: it was not patterns from classical productions, nor recordings of outstanding performances, nor complex orchestral scores, nor elaborate evolutions of *corps de ballet* in which I first sensed the rapture, the delight in the movements of bodies racing at different speeds and in different directions across the graph of an open expanse: it was in the play of intersecting orbits, the ever-changing dynamic form that the combination of these paths took and their collisions in momentary patterns of intricacy, before flying apart again forever.

The pontoon bridge which extended across the immeasurable breadth of the Neva, towards the sandy shore of Izhora, opened my eyes for the first time to the delight of this fascination that was never to leave me.

It is easy to see why the impression was inescapable: I became aware of it at precisely the same time as my fascination with art was undergoing a certain shift.

This shift was decisive: from fascination with the perception of art, to the vague attraction of actually producing it myself.

A few especially sharp impressions in the theatre not long before this (*Masquerade, Don Juan,* and *The Constant Prince*[4] in the former Alexandrinsky Theatre), the social shift from the February to the October Revolution and the complete jettisoning of one set of notions seemed to suggest the possibility of a voluntary change of career plans (I had joined the Engineers) and my unexpected and profound involvement in little-known and unexpected fields of art (Japanese, J. Callot,[5] Hogarth and Goya)—all these factors pressed me urgently to test my strength in a new direction. For the time being on paper, in thoughts and daydreams.

And in this period each new impression insinuated itself into the developing character of one moving into work in art. Some impressions were to do with an interest in form; others with an interest in thematics.

The melting pot of the Civil War and military engineering work at the front made me acutely aware of the fates of Russia and the Revolution and gave me a fascinating sense of history in the making, which had made a deep impression with the broad canvas of the fates of nations and epic ambitions, and was then realised in the thematics of future films 'of monumental scale'.

Strong, profound impressions put off for years.

Spontaneous ones were interwoven in the actual process of emergence. In those conditions the natural tendency toward regularity and harmony—to a degree of ardent passion—could be inflamed by the essentially ephemeral impression of the construction of the pontoon bridge.

Perhaps I was so fascinated by the spectacle of the bridge because I had not by that time seen the similar regularity and idiosyncratic harmony of the historical process, in the chaos of Civil War?

For there are points of view according to which a savage will see an ornamental design, born from his incomprehension of a reality lying beyond his grasp. It is the first attempt at imposing order on the surrounding confusion.

One way or another, the 'shift' caused by measured collective actions governed by a strict graph proved permanent.

For that is how the stars move, not touching one another,
how tides ebb and flow,
how day succeeds night, and summer, spring . . .
That is how people pass through others' lives,
determining each other's fate . . .

And I think that the first draft of a script I wrote for a mime told the story of a wretched young man who travelled amongst friends who had no choice but to move along predestined orbits at speed, forever.

Some zigzagged, others went in figures of eight, still others followed the curve of a parabola flying from the unknown on to the stage, only to hurtle off into the unknown once more, after a brief collision with the hero. Particularly heartrending was the fate of his lover: at the very moment of intimacy, she was whisked away along her preordained curve, 'according to the equation'.

The most terrible part was the hero's dawning realisation that his path, whose straightness had been a source of inner delight as it cut through the restless sinusoidal curves and geometrical equations of his partners' paths, was not one of his own devising. It was merely an arc of very long radius, and no less predestined than anyone else's.

The mime ended with a universal transformation scene of intersecting paths and the hero quietly going mad.

What played the greatest role in this? The pontoon bridge, or Schopenhauer's pessimism (in those years I read his philosophy) or Hoffmannesque fantasy? One thing is evident: that it was the seemingly abstract geometry that first of all tried to serve the sense and emotion of the theme.

I cannot remember when I became superstitious.

It interferes greatly with life.

A black cat crossing my path . . . I must not walk under ladders . . . Friday the thirteenth . . . don't put your hat on the table or you'll be poor . . . don't start things on a Monday . . .

So much more to worry about in life!

But if you think about it, it is very much like the appearance of a crucial feature within a work. Perhaps it is even the precondition for this very feature to arise?!

What do these superstitious beliefs have in common?

One circumstance: namely, that the subject, or the phenomenon, apart from the fact of its spontaneous happening, has a certain meaning.

Thirteen is not simply the sum of thirteen units; it is of itself an entity, invested with a peculiar power to influence.

A black cat, running across one's path, is not just a furry mammal pursuing its natural needs; it is a complex combination of a graph's intersection: your path, multiplied by the colour and read off against a complex of (ill-omened) associations, linked from time immemorial with gloom and foreboding.

They quarrelled with me a great deal. For a very long time, and at every opportunity. How I wrote screenplays, worked with actors, or cut the film.

They left me in peace mostly when I was looking at shots and composing them. They took a more lenient line with me in this.

And I think this was because I always set up my shots according to the principle of . . . a black cat crossing my path.

In subject and composition, I try never to limit the frame solely by the way things appear on the screen. The subject must be chosen thus, turned this way, and placed in the field of the frame so that, besides mere representation, a knot of associations results that mirrors the mood and sense of the piece. That is how the dramatic style of the frame is created. That is how the drama interweaves with the canvas of the work. Light, camera angle, the cutting of the shot—everything is subordinated not merely to representing the subject, but revealing it in that conceptual and emotional aspect, realised at a particular moment by means of the specific subject that is before the lens. 'Subject' here is to be taken broadly. It is far from simply 'things'; but may in equal measure apply to passions (people, models, actors); buildings and landscapes; or skyscapes—mare's tail, or other types of cloud.

The fan of cumulus cloud around Ivan the Terrible as he stands at the gates of Kazan is at the very least a depiction of meteorological conditions. Primarily, it is an image of tsardom, and the massive distorted silhouette of the astrolabe above the Tsar of Muscovy's head at the very least can be taken as a trick of the light; the chance intersections of the circles makes it look more like a cardiogram, showing the meditative statesman's train of thought.

Here it is visible and palpable, but you can take almost any frame and, having chosen it, prove that the crossings and re-crossings of its graphic form and the interplay of tonal areas, texture and outline, tell their own imagistic story which transcends the problem of mere portraiture. Here it is good to observe how such a tendency dates back to the best examples of the Russian classics.

I have had to talk and write a fair amount about the similarity between montage in our cinema, and the traditions of Pushkin's writing.

What I have to say here with regard to the dramaturgy of a shot distinctly echoes what, in works by Gogol or Dostoyevsky, may be defined by the term 'the subject in details'.

Andrei Bely coined this term and one of the most astonishing chapters of *Gogol's Mastery* [6] is dedicated to the stunning abundance of examples of ambiguity (ambivalence) of the subjects and images that seem to lie in ordinary, routine narrative. I think that, starting with Mitenka's thumbnail when he is arrested on Mokraya Street, right up to the imagistic concept of the novel in its entirety, we can place *The Brothers Karamazov* in the same category of phenomena as Gogol, in Bely's skilful exegesis.

E. T. A. Hoffmann's Lindhorst [7] could be briefly glimpsed somewhere between the one and the other, probably; his bizarre existence as king of the elves, behind the banal exterior of an archivist, the burning lilies become a gaudy dressing-gown.

Ivan the Terrible on the Kazan campaign. Eisenstein's drawing for the film. Alma-Ata, 29 April 1942

Still from the film *Ivan the Terrible,* Part One: Ivan at Kazan

The imagery of the scene has a complex pantheon of precursors, as we can see.

And the nearest is the fascination with the ambiguity of the movement of the *mise-en-scène*—grotesquely tangible (and grotesque precisely because of its tangibility!) in the small 'geometrical' mime described above.

But usually, in a creative economy, there is no waste.

Even a small mime can be resurrected.

In 1932 I was full of ideas for a comedy.[8]

And one of the pivotal movements occurred when the tangle of human relations and situations grew so involved that there was no dramatic solution.

The camera pulled back.

The black and white tiled floor was like a chessboard. On the alternate squares stood the tired characters, looking for a way out of the utter mess of the action. And above the board, tugging at their hair, sat the writer with the director, trying to make sense of these labyrinthine human relations.

A solution was found!

The action proceeded.

The paths of the characters converged and diverged fluidly.

Relations converged and diverged.

The comedy moved on.

No film was shot . . .

And perhaps that is the very reason that many years later in *Ivan the Terrible* another chessboard figures on the screen.

The Tsar's wise plan for avoiding the blockade of the Baltic by sailing across the White Sea is illustrated by a journey across a chessboard. A board which the Tsar sends as a present to 'redheaded Bess', the Queen of England, Elizabeth I.

But chess is much more fully representative of the type of journey that the plot of *Ivan* makes through the screenplay.

The Tsar counters each of the boyars' moves.

The boyars counter each of the Tsar's moves.

The Tsar's moves are noble, free of self-interest and directed at preserving the interests of the state. They are blocked by every shade of ambition, self-interest and envy (Kurbsky), generic greed (Staritskaya), embezzlement (the aging Basmanov), Pimen's possessiveness, and so on.

As for the praise and the criticism the screenplay received, it is curious that both admirers and critics alike fix upon one and the same image.

Some praise it for presenting the viewer with a completely accurate game of chess, which leads unerringly to a solution of the problem as set out.

Others say that it is brilliant chess—but nothing more.

It must be that both are right.

(There's another funny thing: I've never played chess, and I'm quite hopeless at it.)

Each of us has, probably, been allocated a definite number of passions that balance one another.

Chess is an especially accessible way of turning these pipe-dreams into reality.

I spent my ration on the sound montage of a film, on the counterpoint of interrelating human acts, on the patterns of *mise-en-scène*.

The laurels of Lasker and Capablanca[9] do not bother me.

But since I've started complaining . . . A little earlier, I was complaining about black cats.

But the problem is far more serious.

It is not only a spider, at morning, noon or night; not only a coffin, or a white horse, which God himself decreed shall be a harbinger (the gipsy frightened Pushkin with 'Beware the man in white', and d'Anthès' military uniform did indeed turn out to be white!)[10] that trouble the peaceful current of my life.

Anything that is almost a mundane event, becomes generalised, laden with import.

Saving electricity, I turn off the light. But for me there is much more to it than that. Turning off the light is 'Departure into Darkness'. Unplugging the telephone is 'Disconnection from the World'. A delayed payment (and how often that happens to me!) is the 'Shade of Beggardom'. And all this is with a capital letter.

And everything is full of the most acute sensations.

Any trifle becomes a generalisation almost instantly.

If a button is torn off, I feel a scruff that moment. If I forget a surname, I already fear 'lapses of consciousness'—I have amnesia and so on. An observer would probably find this very amusing.

But it is very disconcerting having to live with it.

But in my profession, this has defined:

my ability to choose, from all possible details, that very one in which the generalisation resonates with particular clarity;

my deftness in selecting that detail which throws the image of the whole into especially sharp relief.

The pince-nez aptly comes to stand for the 'whole' of the doctor in *Potemkin*, and the actual phenomenon of *pars pro toto* is of great significance when choosing and rationalising the methods of working in art.

And this fact is characteristic: something frequently observed momentarily becomes a generalisation, leading to the desire to establish general rules for which the one particular common occurrence is one of the possible manifestations of this general rule.

As I say, this is very inconvenient in life.

I derive some consolation from the fact that Tchaikovsky and Chaplin both had an analogous complaint.

I have read that it was enough for something to be planned for one evening to send Tchaikovsky into a flurry of nerves for the whole of the day leading up to it.

And personal experience has taught me that the slightest worry about money caused Charlie terrible anxieties and fear of possible ruination, destitution.

If I mention here also that I once spent an entire winter working only by night, always wearing a dressing gown, and draining cup after cup of black coffee, all because my imagination had been fired by the similar behaviour of . . . Balzac, then that is one more characteristic trait which defined my route to art.

That the concept of *comme il faut*, in the sense in which Tolstoy himself used it,[11] was a sacred one during my youth and everything above, is quite clear.

One glance at my photo with the slanting parting, my thin little legs in a balletic pose, is enough to show that such 'achievements' are only possible if the parents are of a sufficiently tyrannical bent, and the governesses rule with an iron hand.

Such a system is bound to foster rebellion.

With a sufficiently menacing father, such a rebellion

typically takes the form of internal single combat with any superior. This is where the fighting against religion comes in: I did my bit.

The curious stimulus arises: how am I any worse?

The attraction to art, the need to work in art, the vocation —these probably run somewhere deep down.

The external stimulus was the motto: it's not the gods who fire the pots.

I have lectured in every language and in very many countries abroad. And it was all because he once was hurt that someone active in our society was able to express himself equally well in any language.

When my career was still in its infancy, I was hurt by the four weighty albums, with their grey canvas covers, in Nikolai Yevreinov's[12] library in Petrograd; four albums, full of cuttings and reviews of his productions and works.

I would not be able to rest until the volume of excerpts about me exceeded those four grey albums.

I did not rest until the publication of my book *The Film Sense,* which set out a fairly comprehensive appraisal of systems of ideas in cinema.

Finally, I piled up mountain upon mountain of conclusions and observations I had made on method in arts, for, of course, if I did not have my own system in this field, I would hardly consent to rest in peace in my grave!

Which here is the greater?

The words of Rémy de Gourmont:[13] 'to formalise the fruits of our own observations is the inevitable aspiration of man, if he is sincere.'

Or what the amazing eighteenth-century British poet William Blake wrote, in his poem 'Jerusalem': 'I must Create a System, or be enslav'd by another Man's.'

Whichever it is, the impulse is strong, but I mention this here again to show how even this particular, in a completely unexpected way, is reflected not in the choice of activity, wilfulness of habit, or innovative drive (as a means of iconoclasm) but in the actual features of handwriting, and manner.

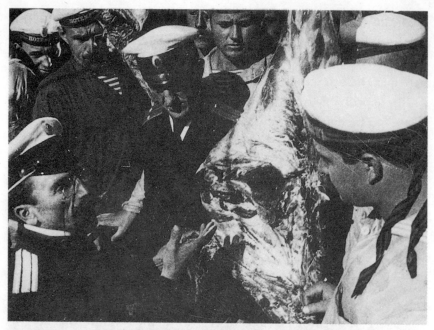

The doctor and his pince-nez. Stills from *The Battleship Potemkin*·

The fact is that this intense stimulus doubtless has its own inhibitors.

Any 'achievement' is not only (or perhaps, so much) a solution to a practical problem set before one; each time, it is a 'struggle with the ghost', a struggle for freedom, from some 'injurious' item from the outside.

These forces are by no means unknown: we generally have a pretty good idea of where they come from and indeed their precise identity!

Nevertheless, it is always a bit like Jacob's struggle with the angel in the Bible.[14] It is personal, happens at night, counts its dislocations of legs (which the angel did not occasion Jacob) and takes place somewhere behind and away from the principal solution to the problems of one's time that one sets oneself.

I treat my creations with uncommon carelessness. Once I have achieved my goal—which is often on my internal account, defeating my internal enemy—authority, which wounds me—the angel!—then the matter leaves me of its own accord, and what happens to it on the outside bothers me far less than might be the case.

So I can cut it up without pity. But the interesting thing is not that, but that this peculiarity of 'my palette' finds reflection even in a certain specific character of the composition, inside the things themselves.

The weight of their impact comes not from the explosions, but from the process of laying the charges.

There may be an explosion. Sometimes, it is on the level of intensity of the previous charges; sometimes it is not; and sometimes it is barely detectable.

The chief efflux of energy is used up in the process of overcoming: hardly any time is spent on the achievement, for the process of overcoming has become the moment of freedom. Which is why in my films it is the process of laying the charges that is the most memorable.

The pressure of the soldiers' feet on the Odessa steps. And the roaring lions (*The Battleship Potemkin*).

The siege and subsequent storming of the Winter Palace (*October*).

Waiting for the drops of milk from the separator (*The Old and the New*).

The attacks of the 'cavalry wedge' in *Alexander Nevsky*.

Ivan, at Anastasia's grave, and the 'You lie!', the explosive atmospheric pressure as he resigns himself to his fate, etc.

As regards the actual stimulus of, 'How am I worse?', he was lucky.

The whole country took up the cry: 'Catch up and overtake'.

And the personal impulse interweaves with the phrase and impulse of the time. Inattentiveness to the essence, resulting from an attempt at coming to terms with old, harmful experiences, is of course a game purely for the imagination.

The author who puts his name to this writing is the author 'of his subject'. And although it might seem that the subject matter of his works jumps, during a two-decade period, from Mexico to a cooperative of peasants working in a dairy, and from a mutiny on a battleship to the coronation of the first tsar of all the Russias, and from *Die Walküre* to *Alexander Nevsky*—it is still one and the same theme.

And one should know how to extract from anything the material which is consonant with what one's time and epoch demands; the evergreen, original aspect of your own personal theme. This will ensure that you will tackle the theme of each new work with burning enthusiasm.

This is a source of creative good fortune.

It is only necessary for the theme to take its place in the structure of the themes of its time, country and government.

But I have covered the theme of my work elsewhere.

The limits of this article are set by another theme: the theme of how the writer became a director.

I have already broadened the scope of this theme when I tried to describe incidentally how the author came across some of the peculiarities of his directing.

What the author did when he already was a director will be set down in a more appropriate place.

The Riga coast. Photo: S.M. Eisenstein, 1912 (?)

Souvenirs d'enfance [1]

My first childhood impression was . . . a close-up.

My first memory is of a branch of cherry or lilac, coming in through the window of my nursery.

On the Riga coast. The Baltic Sea.

In the dacha. At Majorenhof.

Very long ago.

That is, in my early childhood—at two or three years, to judge by the fact that, according to our family records, we spent 1900 and 1901 in Majorenhof.

I have vague recollections of various toys lying on the floor and patches of sunlight on the nursery walls.

But I can clearly remember the branch.

There are also memories that clearly belong to when I was six.

There was also a dacha on the coast.

And it was doubtless in 1904.

When Uncle Mitya came to say goodbye—he was my father's younger brother. He was killed at Mukden, in the Russo-Japanese War.

Apart from my uncle, a young but manly officer who had an awe-inspiring gleaming curved sabre, I remember the blood-red wood-shavings that were scattered on the path, and the white-washed stones that edged it.

Also I remember the lady next door.

Someone very elegant, with black parted hair.

But I remember most of all her swirling Japanese kimono, in purest azure and pink hues (a trophy from the war?—her husband was also fighting). I have an impression of her small head at the top, and the rest of her consisting of streaming material.

Especially the sleeves. I remember the sleeves so well because in one of them she carried a tiny puppy.

I also remember the lights in the garden, on Olga's birthday —in honour of a cousin.

An amateur show, where they put on *The Butler Did It*,[2]

which must have been my first ever play. As well as delight, I can remember a certain element of terror at another uncle's charcoal moustache—it was Uncle Lyola, my mother's younger brother.

I also remember a gramophone with a massive pink fluted horn which sang hoarsely:

'On the wall a giant gna-at
Then I swat it with my ha-at
Oh what fun!
Oh what fun! . . .'

And from the road to the dacha came the insistent voice of an old Latvian woman, who mixed up the Russian:

'Norget-me-fots—flowers, norget-me-fots!'

Finally, a balloon-seller:

'Come on, come on, lovely balloons—*Luftballons!*'

I remember most distinctly some fabulously tasty pears in a sweet sauce, like Italian *zabaglione.*

I was to eat such *zabaglione* with Pirandello,[3] in the distant future, in a small Italian restaurant in Charlottenburg, Berlin. But this was much later—twenty-five years away!

Otto H. and the Artichokes[1]

'Fiery Angel—Pir-andello . . .'[2]

The old chap was greatly pleased by such an etymology for his surname.

But I cannot take my eyes off his waistcoat.

It is the combination of waistcoat and soft collar usually to be seen poking out from under the waistcoat.

And a soft tie.

Zabaglione defies linguistic analysis. But this wondrous invention of beaten egg yolk, sugar and one of those dazzling southern Italian wines, speaks for itself.

Pirandello entertains me in one of the tiny Italian restaurants on one of those less frequented Berlin side-streets.

(The day before we were in a Japanese restaurant. Small chafing dishes on the table. Raw fish. And two Japanese cinema executives returning the courtesy after a visit to Moscow. Three days before, it was an Indian. Rabindranath Tagore's[3] nephew was repaying his hosts for a reception in Moscow. One dish looked like a sweetmeat, a fruit syrup. It tasted like a Gillette blade.)

Paramount had invited him.

I have not been invited yet. Actually, that was the purpose of our meeting.

He. I. A colleague from the trade delegation.

And someone else too.

Although this someone was the most important figure at that meeting, I have forgotten his name.

And strange though it may seem, his face too.

I think he had a forked beard, and wore pince-nez. I may be mistaken.

But I remember the important bit.

This someone was a good friend of the mysterious and all-powerful Otto H.[4]

Otto H. was the means for arranging a contract in America.

It was down to the representative of the trade delegation to make the necessary contact.

He was a curious man.

With curly hair and a soft hat.

He put an aitch in front of surnames where there should not have been one and he dropped it when there should. 'Heine' became 'Eine' and so on.

In addition he was married to the daughter of a brilliant mathematician.

My interest in the commercial side of the business meeting was slight.

I was much more preoccupied with the image of the 'Fiery Angel' sitting in front of me.

Although the angel was here chiefly for the entourage of the business discussion.

Anyway, I was not an admirer of his.

If I were 'in search of an author'[5] I would hardly turn to him.

He is too *fin de siècle,* somehow, as people were once too Regency at the start of the nineteenth century.

There is an element of the yellow waistcoat in the wearer.

I now have a distinct memory of yellowing photographs with waistcoats just like that one.

He did not make the move to Paramount.

Although this thought was, as he said, intriguing.

The screen and the projection box exchanging insults.

The people on the screen have no wish to be subordinate to the will of the projector, conveyed to them by the rays of light.

How tedious! Old-fashioned! What self-plagiarism!

His face was wreathed in wrinkles.

The soft waistcoat.

The soft tie.

I must remember how he looked.

The Fiery Angel of life-giving ideas had long since departed.

And soon the Fiery Angel—Pirandello himself—left this sad world.

The *zabaglione* cooled.

The *zabaglione* waited.

And *zabaglione* continued to be served even when Pirandello, the Fiery Angel, was no more.

Now the mysterious and all-powerful Otto H. has also left *ins Jenseits.**

So, he was not able to clinch the right deal with the 'Almighty'.

I got to know him, only *post factum.*

After I had joined Paramount,

where I wound up without the assistance of this patron of the arts, this Maecenas . . .

Otto H.

An Italianate *palazzo* on Fifth Avenue.

A millionaire. A banker. And a financial director of Paramount.

Four Gainsboroughs hung on the walls of his up-state house on Long Island.

The head of a bearded man, above the fireplace in the *palazzo.*

'Recognise the brush-work?'

I did not.

'Only a Jew can paint a face with such subtlety,' Otto H. proudly exclaimed. And he added as if in passing, 'Rembrandt.'

Rembrandt is not a divinity in my pantheon. But I pretended that I was looking at an El Greco . . .

Artichokes, artichokes!

Artichokes proved to be the most memorable thing.

But that was at another meeting.

At lunch.

I experienced for the first time how inconvenient a butler can be if he stands behind your high-backed chair.

In the Hotel Adlon in Berlin, these men walked up and down in their light blue coats and whipped the unfinished plates of steak away, shoving a salad before you, suddenly covering a dish that you were barely familiar with, with a dressing you weren't expecting. They seemed irritated, annoyed.

Here, appearing out of nowhere, these hands paralysed your oesophagus.

To make matters worse, there was an endless array of count-

---

* German: 'for the other world.'

47

less forks and smaller forks, spoons and teaspoons, knives, bread-knives, and smaller knives still!

And on top of all that, artichokes!

The company was small, select.

Horatio Liveright, the grizzled publisher, was there.[6]

He published books of scandalous notoriety.

Indiscriminately, be they political, social, morally dubious or plain immoral.

In any event, they were sensational.

A law suit.

An injunction.

A successful appeal.

The public campaigned against the court's decision.

Everything thrived on sensation.

Apart from ancient erotica and radical theoretical psychologists, Horatio also published early Dreiser, which caused a stir.

And one of the dazzling trophies adorning his list was *An American Tragedy*.[7]

Horatio Liveright turned up as my supervisor on *An American Tragedy* about six months later. This was a project which Paramount offered me.

It was only much later that I learned that Paramount always offered this patently undistributable (because of the nature of the subject matter) film to foreigners.

But Paramount's proposal caused such an outcry that, after Paramount and I parted company, *An American Tragedy* was nonetheless filmed. By Sternberg. He drew its teeth, and the result was tiresome, poor.[8]

But artichokes . . .

Artichokes, according to Webster's *Dictionary* . . .

But to hell with the genus! To hell with the entire family!

This malignant produce of the earth appeared on the table at the very moment I was called to the phone!

It was Alexandrov.[9]

He was speaking from the Isle of Tears.[10]

After being stuck in Paris for a month, he only caught up with me in New York that day.

There was something amiss with Grisha's visas.

He was not allowed ashore.

With a group of Soviet engineers, he surveyed the distant New York skyline through a barred window. It was bisected by the Statue of Liberty, so suspiciously near the Isle of Tears.

I was persuaded to go round to this latter-day 'prisoner of Chillon'[11] as soon as I had finished lunch.

. . . Meanwhile, all the guests had finished their artichoke.

I sat down.

There was a butler behind me.

Horatio Liveright was opposite.

On one side, Otto H.'s white moustache.

And on the other, the smiling friendly face of his daughter.

At least his wife was absent, thank goodness!

I had, just once, and briefly, seen this strangely twisted woman in a cape.

I suspect that her husband's radical circle of friends did not enjoy her blessing. She was more concerned with exiled monarchy.

While I was on my first visit, I learned that Mrs Otto H. had entertained some great prince, princess, or consort the day before.

The absence of this lady did not make my task any easier.

The gleaming silverware, the exotic flowers (were they camellias? orchids?) and the guests' dinner-jackets diverged in a blur of concentric circles. The buttons on the footmen's coats gleamed, faintly menacingly.

On the dazzling whiteness of the table-cloth, it sat before me.

Alone.

The art-i-choke.

To look at, it was like the cupola of an Orthodox church.

I mean the general outline, and the way its individual leaves, the smallest nearest the top, resembled the chequered criss-crosses of the cupolas of St Basil's or its inadequate imitation, the Church of the Sacred Blood on the Catherine Canal.

The similarity is so close that later I offended the painter, Roberto Montenegro, who rendered my likeness on a mural, at the Mexico City Pedagogical Institute.

My face, like Cortés the conquistador's, was painted against two baskets of pineapples and artichokes.

Montenegro was deeply hurt.

Those were not baskets at all.

They were walls.

And they were not pineapples, or heaven forbid, artichokes.

They were church cupolas, rising above the walls of the Kremlin.

A thousand pardons!

But the artichoke was still sitting on the table in front of me.

Silence.

And I sensed (or maybe I did not?) everyone staring at the small grey-green dome that was standing on its saucer before me.

For those of us with so-called creative natures, spontaneous impressions of life have the habit of storing themselves up in a stock of memories.

And to explode as a living sensation, in a quite unforeseen way, at that very moment when the emotional experience is necessary.

Why was it on that day, precisely there in Alma-Ata, that I should think of the artichoke and Otto H.'s tablecloth?

Was it because exactly two weeks previously I was filming the scene of the capture of Kazan, the famous scene with the candles?

One candle burned underground, right next to the gunpowder which packed the mine.

The other burned above.

That is how all the various songs about the taking of Kazan tell it.

The flame of the second candle indicated how much time remained before the explosion.

They should burn out simultaneously.

Having more oxygen, the second candle would burn out more quickly, of course.

There was no explosion.

(The first candle had not yet ignited the powder.)

Ivan was furious.

'Bring me the gunners!'

The gunners stood with a noose around their neck—but it was an invisible noose that strangled me when I saw a new kind of vegetable.

Eisenstein and Otto H. Kahn, New York 1930

I remembered the artichoke by association with the scene I had just filmed, with the candle at Kazan.

The candle was rammed on to the spike of the helmet, whose outline recalled the ominous *cynara scolynus* [artichoke], which in turn seemed to have been copied from a blueprint for a church cupola.

The gaze of the Tsar and Malyuta, the gunners and Tartars, Kurbsky and the clergy, were fixed on that candle for what seemed an age.

Another question involuntarily springs to mind.

Perhaps the system of tense close-ups, transfixed in expectation, the rhythm of the tension,

and the very fact of ramming the candles on to the actual domed peak of the helmet—had as their emotional basis that long-distant but as we have seen, insistently acute rhythmic sensation that stuck in my memory—the memory of the artichoke, at Otto H.'s banquet!?

After all, the first half of the scene (before the charge detonates) can be summed up in one word:

'Discomfiture'!

So the stock of rhythmic memories of a past sensation nourished the present.

But my reminiscences have led me away from my discomfiture at the artichoke.

. . . I omitted to mention the most important thing.

My embarrassment derived from not knowing how to eat this strange vegetable,

whose leaves form a cupola and end in a small spike that sticks maliciously upwards.

Or more accurately, from not knowing how this is done in the company of millionaires.

You learn in childhood that tsars eat only chocolate, and every dish comes with sugar.

But how do millionaires eat artichokes?

Does one just eat the fleshy pulp at the base?

Or do they,

like common mortals, suck out this base separately from the torn-off leaves?

I felt hot and cold at the thought of having to perform this operation, not unlike sucking out the flesh from a crab, in full view of the company which had finished the operation some time ago, and was waiting to see how this Russian barbarian would extricate himself from this difficult situation.

The meeting on the Anichkov Bridge. Still, taken by Eisenstein, for his film *1905*. (Cameraman: Alexander Levitsky)

Millionaires I Have Met[1]

Red Indians wearing feathers.

Kings.

And millionaires.

You know about them only from books.

Fenimore Cooper: Pathfinder and Chingachgook.

I used to play at Red Indians.

And I saw the Tsar when I was little.

I have never met a king.

I had only second-hand knowledge of millionaires.

Baker Street, Madame Tussaud's (the waxworks, founded when Monsieur Tussaud brought two wax models of the severed heads of Louis XVI and Marie Antoinette to London).

But I did see one king, in fact, albeit a brief profile. He was in his black, covered carriage, driving to the theatre one evening.

It was just long enough to compare his likeness with that of Nicholas II, whom I had seen twice before, and in greater detail.

Once in Riga.

And again at the unveiling of the Alexander III memorial. That notorious 'bump on a hump on a lump', by Paolo Trubetskoy ('My father and grandfather were executed', by Bedny, and 'Many would like to see this granite pedestal as a plinth for a guillotine, but I won't allow it', by Kerensky, or *à peu près*).[2]*

I watched the Tsar from a house on the corner of the Fontanka. (I saw the window recently, bricked up, the embrasures 'looking out' on to the still missing bronze horses—a legacy from the siege of Leningrad.)[3]

In those days, the window was one of Kitayev's—he was tailor 'by appointment to His Majesty'.

Mother had had her dresses and outfits made at Kitayev's since she was a young girl, and on this 'ceremonial occasion' Kitayev generously made his windows available to his particularly loyal *clientèle d' élite*.

---

* French: 'words to that effect'

Here, tea and petits-fours accompanied His Imperial Majesty's progress down Nevsky Prospect.

For some reason tea and petits-fours always accompany the passage of ceremonial processions honouring a crowned head.

There is a brief—but very effective—scene in Noël Coward's *Cavalcade* where the children become so busy fighting over the pastries that they forget to go out on to the balcony to watch the procession. Their father, bedecked with medals, is marching in it. Kitayev interlarded the petits-fours (so called because they are a quarter the size of conventional pastries) with additional delicacies: little gems, about the Tsar's private life.

I remember the story of how the Empress (Maria Fyodorovna) once brought in Alexander III's frock-coat, 'to turn it into a riding habit'.

The giant Tsar's clothing would be ample for this (as his bed in the palace at Gatchina testifies!).

But Kitayev, of course, 'substituted some material for the frock-coat', and kept it as a relic.

But no stories, cups of tea or petits-fours could spoil our view of the unimpressive figure that the thin, khaki-clad colonel, bearer of the royal regalia, cut, as his right hand toyed shyly with the gauntlet on his left.

Otherwise, the scene is a familiar one from a painting by Serov.[4]

Serov comes to mind here because one of my friends—Shurik Verkhovsky—saw this portrait during the Revolution, impaled on the railings of the Winter Palace, and left flapping upside down.

It was also at that time that vodka bottles clinked under Catherine's chin (opposite what had been the Alexandrinka) and Alexander III's beard. They held small red flags in their hands.

Nevsky Prospect resounded with shouts. 'Tell us about the Tsaritsa Sashka, and that lecher, Grishka,'[5] 'Shame on Tsar Nicholas' etc. etc.

I feverishly hoarded everything of that nature that I could get my hands on.

My notion of the Revolution was interwoven with the most romantic elements of the Great French Revolution and the Paris

Commune.

Pamphlets! Goodness, how can one get by without them?!

To be honest, I should say that, for my picture to be complete, there ought really to have been a guillotine on Znamenskaya Square, where Paolo Trubetskoy's monument stood . . .

How did it come about that a boy from 'a good family', whose father was a bulwark of tsarism, could suddenly . . .

Little Sergei with an album, Riga

The Christmas Tree[1]

I remember the Christmas tree. Decorated all over with candles, stars and gold-painted walnuts. Interweaving strands of golden tinsel fell like rain from the topmost crowning star, and there were festoons of gold paper-chains. These are the only chains a middle-class boy of that tender age knows about, as his parents lovingly decorate the tree for him. They, however, cannot think of chains without also thinking of the small chains on doors which enable them to see who is there before opening the door. Chains are to keep burglars out. Burglars are heartily disliked in middle-class families. And this dislike is instilled in the children at a very early age.

But there was the child himself: curly-haired, wearing a small white suit and surrounded by presents. I cannot instantly remember whether on that occasion there was a tennis racquet, or a child's bicycle, a train set or skis, among the presents. Anyway, the eyes of the child glowed—probably with joy, rather than reflected candle light.

The yellow spines of two books stood out among the presents and, strange though it may seem, it was these that gave the child the greatest joy.

This was a special present. One of those on the 'list' common to middle-class families. This was not just a present—it was a dream come true. The curly-haired boy was very quick to get stuck into the yellow books, as Christmas Eve guttered and flickered in the candles and crystal.

The curly boy was me, aged twelve.

The yellow books were Mignet's *History of the French Revolution*.[2]

And so this is the scene of my introduction to the Great French Revolution: Christmas Eve, amidst the tree, walnuts and cardboard stars.

Why? Why this complete dissonance?

It would be no easy task to reconstruct the entire chain, to say what planted in my curly head the desire to have precisely that book as a Christmas present. Probably my reading Dumas. *Ange Pitou,* and *Joseph Balsamo* of course had long since enthralled this 'impressionable little boy', to use a cliché from biographies.[3]

But the unsavoury trait of curiosity and inquisitiveness had already made its presence felt. It was to spoil so many pleasures for me by turning them into merely superficial perceptions. Instead of pleasures, this inquisitiveness brought me many delights. I was no longer satisfied with knowing literary flights of fancy based on great events: I wanted to know the underlying history too. It was quite by chance that my thirst for knowledge led to a fascination with the French Revolution, and this was long before I showed any interest in my own country's past.

The history of France was one of the first things to make an impression on me and when further layers of impressions settled upon the first, this first chance happening virtually became the rule.

By some miracle, the 'impressionable little boy' stumbled upon more historical works in his father's bookcases. They seemed out of place there, in the library of this upright citizen who had successfully worked his way up the ranks.

But I found 1871 and the Paris Commune there, in a handsomely illustrated French edition. It was kept next to albums about Napoleon Bonaparte, who was my father's ideal—as he was of any 'self-made man'.[*]

My fascination with revolutions, especially French ones, dates from that tender age. First of all of course it was because of their romance. Their colour. Their rarity.

I greedily devoured book after book. The guillotine enthralled my imagination. I saw amazing photographs of the columns toppled in the Place Vendôme. I was fascinated by the caricatures by André Gill and Honoré Daumier. I was excited by figures like Marat and Robespierre. I could hear the crack of rifles—the Versailles firing-squads—and the peal of the Paris tocsin. In short, I felt the same thrill at these associations with my first impressions that I received from descriptions of the Great French Revolution.

---

[*] In English in the original.

Victor Hugo's *Les Misérables,* at the start of the nineteenth century, was the third strand of the Revolution. The romance of the fighting on the barricades was informed with elements of the ideas being fought for. Naive though it may be as far as the profundity of its social programme is concerned, Hugo's sermon on social injustice is nevertheless expressed with passion and pitched at just the right level to inspire anyone young and just beginning to think about life, with similar ideas.

Such was the curious cosmopolitan tangle of the impressions of my youth.

Living in Riga, I spoke German better than Russian. But in my thoughts I lived French history.

But things developed.

Interest in the Commune was bound to lead on to curiosity about 1852 and Napoleon III. Dumas' epic works, which were so exciting when I was twelve to fifteen, gave way to Zola's epic Rougon-Macquart cycle which gripped not just the youth, but also the embryonic—still unconscious—artist in its talons.

An Unremarked Date[1]

Arkadi Averchenko 'himself'[2] spoilt it—my drawing.

Haughty and superior, he tossed it away carelessly with the words:

'Anyone could have done that.'

He had black hair.

An olive complexion.

A puffy face.

Did he wear a monocle, or did he wear his pince-nez as if it were one?

And a small button-hole.

. . . The drawing really wasn't up to much.

It showed Louis XVI's head shining in a halo above Nicholas II's bed.

Caption: 'Lucky devil!' (I could not find a one-word Russian translation for *veinard*).

Arkadi Averchenko—and consequently *Satirikon*—and the subject of the drawing date this episode accurately.

It related to this very time.

It was at this very time that Alexander Kerensky was fulminating against those in favour of erecting a guillotine on Znamenskaya Square.

I considered this a direct personal attack.

I frequently passed the Alexander III memorial, and I used to imagine that Doctor Guillotine's 'widow' stood on top of the granite pedestal . . . I wanted so much to be a part of history, but what sort of a history was it, if there was no guillotine?!

But my sketch really was poor.

It was sketched with a pencil.

Then gone over in ink.

In a broken outline which had no dynamic, or any expressive spontaneous flight of thought or feeling.

It was rubbish.

I would hardly have admitted as much to myself then.

It did not occur to me to 'put it down to politics', by way of consoling myself.

I put it down to 'genre', and switched over to 'everyday life' [*byt*].

'Everyday life' required that I apply elsewhere.

So there I was, in the foyer of the *Peterburgskaya gazeta* [Petersburg Gazette].

The entrance was on Vladimir Street, next to an old grey building with Empire columns.

This was later to house the Vladimir Gaming Club.

The hallway was narrow and done out in white tiles like a bathroom, or a fishmonger's.

It was in this gloomy, smoke-filled foyer that I first saw journalists in their natural environment.

An impeccably dressed man, like a wolf dressed as a footman, furiously defended his exclusive rights 'to the Mirbach story'.

Mirbach's assassination was the very latest sensation.[3]

Someone had dared to poach this subject for his own piece.

In the middle stood an old man with aquiline features.

He looked just like a photograph I had seen of Liszt.

A mane of grey hair.

Deep-set blue eyes.

As distinct from Liszt, his collar was soft, grubby and, furthermore, not at all clerical, nor were there any of those pimples with which nature had endowed Liszt so generously.

He stood out strikingly against the tobacco-coloured small fry.

I learned later that this was X, a very famous character in journalistic circles.

Famous for being beaten about the face more than any of his colleagues.

His speciality was blackmail.

Of the most petty and low sort, at that.

But I was called into the sanctum.

Into the office.

To see himself.

Khudekov.[4]

He was tall.

Quite immobile at his desk.

Reconstruction of the events of 1917 for
the film *October*

A corona of grey hair.

Puffy, reddish bags beneath bluish-white eyes.

Narrow shoulders.

A grey suit.

He had written a thick book on ballet.

The drawing offered was bolder than the previous one.

I used a pen straight off. No pencil and rubber this time.

The subject was a free-for-all. Policemen and housewives.

'What is it? Gangsters?'

'No, the police, restoring order.'

The policemen wore armbands with G.M.* on them.

I wore an armband like that in the first days of February [1917]. Our Institute was converted into a centre for law and order and assigned to the Izmailov regiment.

Khudekov nodded.

The cartoon ended up in a tray on his desk.

Then on a page of the *Peterburgskaya gazeta*.

I was very pleased. Just think: I had seen this paper every day, ever since I had been a boy.

Before it was taken to Papa, I would greedily devour the sensationalist headlines of the *feuilletons*, and the 'diary'.

Now I too was on those cherished pages.

And ten roubles better off.

My first wages in the field of . . . etc.

A second cartoon followed.

The subject: how the people of St Petersburg have got used to the . . . shooting.

(There was then firing in the city. More than enough of it.)

Four cartoons led up to a punch-line.

The last one had:

'You would appear to have been hit by a shell.'

'You don't say! Do I really?'

Half a shell stuck out from his back.

Profound?

Funny?

Hmm . . .

---

* i. e. *Gorodskaya militsiya* or City Militia. (Trans.)

But—accurate!

I remember being caught up in gunfire on the street once.

Banners were moving down the Nevsky. Demonstrators.

I turned off up Sadovaya.

A sudden salvo.

A rout.

I dived under the arches of Gostiny Dvor.[5]

The street emptied immediately after the shooting.

The pavement, the road—it was as if a jeweller's had been turned out on to the street.

Watches. Watches. Watches.

Fob watches on a chain.

Watches with pendants.

With bracelets.

Cigarette cases. Cigarette cases. Cigarette cases.

Tortoise-shell and silver.

Monogrammed, and with dates. Plain ones even.

I saw people quite unfit, even poorly built for running, in headlong flight.

Watches on chains were jolted out of waistcoat pockets.

Cigarette cases flew out of side pockets.

And canes. Canes. Canes.

Panama hats.

It was summer—July. (Either the third or the fifth.) The corner of Nevsky Prospect and Sadovaya Street.

My legs carried me out of the range of the machine-guns. But it was not at all frightening.

Force of habit!

These days went down in history.

History, for which I so thirsted, which I so wanted to lay my hands on!

I resurrected them myself, ten years later, for *October*, Alexandrov and I stopped the traffic for half an hour, at the junction of Nevsky and Sadovaya.

But I was not able to film the street strewn with hats and canes, in the wake of the fleeing demonstrators. (Even though there were people in the crowd who were there for the purpose of strewing things.)

Some economically minded old men who took part in the crowd scene (I think it was the one involving the workers from the Putilov factory) diligently picked them all up as they ran, no matter where they had landed!

... Anyway, the cartoon caught the way people lived.

Was it profound or funny?

It doesn't matter.

Before my eyes, a miracle happened.

Tall,

elegant,

A crown of grey hair,

immobile, like a rock,

pale eyes with red puffy bags,

the author of a thick book on ballet.

Himself.

The proprietor.

He suddenly burst out laughing.

I was startled, actually.

This picture brought me twenty-five roubles.

Too little!

Ten and twenty-five—it would never add up to forty.

Lukomsky's *The History of Ancient Theatres* cost forty roubles exactly.

And those thirty-five wouldn't last long.

I borrowed forty from my family, bought the *History*, and planned a wide range of work.

I was advised to go to ... Propper.

Birzhevka.

I walked towards *Ogonyok* [The Flame].

That was the name of the weekly supplement of the *Birzhevye vedomosti* [Financial Gazette].

Pierre-O (Zhivotovsky) managed the cartoon division (his authority however was undivided).

He was a terrible jumble.

And it was most unfair that he was a jumble ... that was one and indivisible.

Anyway, I was at Propper's.

I had sneaked off that day, from the Engineering School

which was on Furstadt Street, in the old *Annenschule.*

A few days before all hell had broken loose at that School.

Classes were either being cancelled, or severely disrupted.

After the enjoyably intense training period at camp—night picket duty in the rain and bad marching weather on the road to Petrograd during the parlous days of Kornilov's attempt to seize power had given it a romantic quality —

after the tension of mid-term examinations and drilling (pontoon-bridge construction, mining, mechanics, etc)—

there suddenly descended a protracted period of incomprehensible stagnation and fatigue.

But that morning, nobody was allowed through the gates.

It was too much!

I knew of an access yard on to Furstadt Street.

I just vanished into thin air . . .

Rather than skulk in the corridors, I went to see Propper.

I don't remember the foyer at all.

Probably because I was admitted almost immediately.

A very small office.

No Empire windows, set high behind curtains of dark damask.

A cigar between his teeth.

Not a big one:

thin,

not very expensive.

Nothing like Nero. (Khudekov might have been compared with the Emperor, except that he was much thinner.)

A bit like a dentist.

A small, pointed beard.

A doctor's white overalls.

With bandages all down his back, starting at the neck.

And I do not remember there being any desk.

Everything was moving.

The knots of the bandages.

The small beard.

The cigar.

An uncontrollable torrent of words.

I held a file of quite vicious cartoons, aimed at Kerensky.

Eisenstein demonstrates Lenin's gesture on the platform. Rehearsing for the last shot of the film *October*

Propper clearly found the subject matter embarrassing.

But he apparently liked the artist.

His words tumbled out.

'You are young . . . of course, you need money. Come back in two days' time . . . we'll settle it all then. I will pay you in advance . . . ' Etc, etc.

I left, slightly deafened, agreeing on every point . . .

And I do not remember where the editorial offices were.

Or where I caught the tram.

Or how I ended up opposite the Admiralty.

Opposite Alexandrovsky Park.

I have always liked the view of the square in front of the Winter Palace as I ride past, before it vanishes behind the first buildings on Nevsky.

Bare branches rose above Alexandrovsky Park.

Many years later, when I was working on the screenplay for *1905*, a detail lodged in my mind: according to one of the veterans of Bloody Sunday, little boys had sat in those trees 'just like sparrows' and, when the first volley was fired upon the crowd, they jumped. 9 January happened here.

14 December happened somewhere near.[6]

I know these dates, of course, but in those days they were somehow remote, of no particular relevance to me.

It was the square's architectural ensemble that I found interesting.

It was still light.

There was some shooting in the town.

But who paid it any attention?

There was even a cartoon about that in *Petersburgskaya gazeta*, signed by Sir Gay.[7]

The tram went down Nevsky.

I sat, tired but satisfied, behind a pile of articles which I had collected the last time I was in the public library, thinking of Propper deftly rolling his cigar from one corner of his mouth to the other, and of how Propper himself rolled from one corner of the small bright room to another.

There was an article about the eighteenth-century engraver, Moreau the Younger.[8]

His bright engraving of *La Dame du palais de la reine* was mine for a tenner—I found it in a grubby folder in one of the most decaying antiquarian dealers in the Alexandrovsky Market.

It was soon joined by a series of other sheets.

And the sheets were joined by articles, which I had assiduously collected from catalogues of engravers, in our ancient library . . .

An aunt by marriage, Alexandra Vasilyevna Butovskaya, inherited from her blind husband, a general, one of the best collections of engravings. They had built it up over a lifetime and the fragile old lady introduced me to the charm and subtlety of Callot's work (she had the complete Callot), della Bella (she had the complete della Bella), Hogarth, Goya (I do not have room for those artists not completely represented!).[9] Roughly a year later, my aunt *par alliance* [by marriage] decided in an instant that my 'sheet'—was not a sheet at all, but a leaflet—a reproduction from an engraving in the Louvre . . .

During the period I am writing about, I was still full of illusions, and I would run my hands over the engraving with all the rapture of a true collector caressing a genuine treasure.

I spent about an hour ordering the articles on the eighteenth-century engravers.

Then I went to bed.

There seemed to be more shooting than usual coming from one part of the town.

But it was quiet in our house in Tauride Street.

Before going to bed, I pedantically wrote the date on the cuttings to show when they were put into order.

25 October 1917.

By evening, that date was already part of history.

I distilled that missing part of history in my autobiography when I filmed in the Winter Palace.[10]

Le Bon Dieu [1]

For some reason, I conversed with God in the French style: He and I were on *vous* terms. 'O my Lord, do You . . .'

'Do You grant me Lord . . .' was rather like '*Cher Jésus, ayez la bonté* [Dear Jesus, in Your bounty], or '*Sainte Cathérine, priez Dieu pour nous*' [St Catherine, pray to God for us . . .], as the French have it.

In English, 'you' has long ago lost its meaning of '*vous*'. It is even used in such expressions as 'you dirty skunk'. 'Thou' has been preserved for talking to God. Like the German: '*Du lieber Gott*' [Thou, dear God].

I am not writing a list of instructions, or anything of that sort. It is rather a medical history.

I do not wish to lay down norms, but to list the occurrences, coincidences and events which have made me what I am. The last thing I want to write is a guide to becoming a film director.

Things, for example, like the question of religion.

I think that the religious element in my life was a considerable advantage.[2]

But religion has to be kept within limits, appropriate to time and place.

And to be of the right sort.

Dogmatic religious education is damaging: it is a 'stifling'* of the living origins as they struggle to find a way out.

Catholicisme pratiquant [practising Catholicism] is also not necessary.

It is worth taking the 'fanaticism' out of religion: it can later be separated from the original object of worship, and be 'displaced' to other passions . . .

'You have to have this experience',* or, to avoid generalisations, I shall say of myself that 'I had to have!'*

Holy Week in the Suvorov Church, my last confession in (?) 1916.

---

* In English in the original.

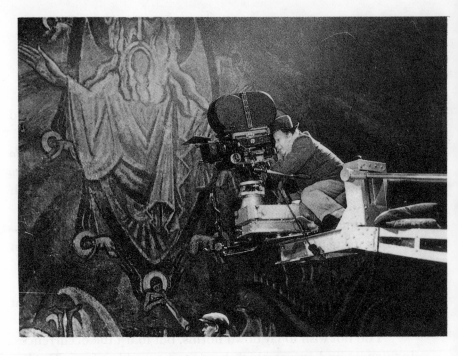

Filming the scene of Ivan's repentance for *Ivan the Terrible* Part Three

Every church acknowledges a pope as law-giver and primate in the affairs of the world.

And every church has the opposite extreme: a St Francis, who goes barefoot and embraces lepers and wretched holy curs (*domini canes*).

Curiously enough, the same two threads run through Russian Orthodoxy, and they are equally irreconcilable.

I did not trouble myself particularly over that until I began work on *Ivan the Terrible.*

And I investigated it for a special reason.

When I had 'created' Pimen,[3] a figure about whom little is actually known (apart from his conspiracy and how Ivan punished him, having him carried back to front on a horse between Moscow and Novgorod), I suddenly had grave doubts.

Post factum (as in almost the whole screenplay) I began to look for justifications. And it was the sixteenth century that provided just such a pair in Russia too.

Joseph of Volotsk[4] and the Josephites were a Russian order rather like the Jesuits 'with political aims'.* (The metropolitans' correspondence about France and Spain.)

And Nil of Sora—the Russian St Francis.[5] (Dostoyevsky's Elder Zossima and The Grand Inquisitor [*The Brothers Karamazov*] are, to an extent, a continuation of this pairing. Although the real models for Zossima were Serafim of Sarova and, even more so, Tikhon of Zadonsk.)[6]

I think that the tendency of this second sort—the ecstasists, dreamers, 'meditators'—can be harmful, in a certain dosage, to one's creative life.

If it does not suck away at religion permanently!

But Josephites —they are another matter.

I remember a brief but intense impression of Nil's following.

The priest of the Suvorov Church on Tauride Street.

He went through Holy Week as if suffering the Lord's Passion.

I remember him in tears of torment at vigils of incessant

---

* In English in the original.

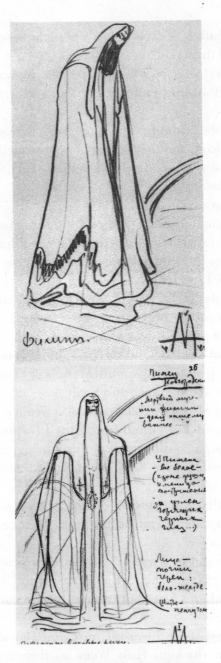

Above The Metropolitan Philip.
Drawing by Eisenstein, Alma-Ata, 4
April 1942 *Below* Archbishop Pimen.
Drawing by Eisenstein, Alma-Ata, 11
January 1942

prayer, in the press of people, whispered confessions and the absolution of sins.

I have forgotten his name and surname.

But it was something close to those impressions that I was to hear crying out from El Greco's ecstasies.[7]

From the monstrous, terrible and awesome pages of Holy Week in Joyce's *Portrait of the Artist as a Young Man*.

From the painting by the Le Nain brothers, 'The Ecstasy of St Francis'.[8]

In his hands, confession was an act, a laying bare of the soul in contemplation, or an expression of suffering, either moral or physical.

This is not a dispassionate litany, the questions and answers of the *Prayerbook*.

(I also had a look at this part of the book for the first time in connection with Ivan, the scene of the Tsar's confession—this list of the norms of physiological and social self-defence in a primitive society which branded as sin everything that might jeopardise its biological and early social vitality.)

If I had been told that—I think I have remembered his name!—Father Paul's forehead exuded droplets of blood in the candlelight when he read the Acts of the Apostles—I would never have ventured to swear that this was not so!

This is probably one of the reasons why El Greco's 'In the Garden' in London's National Gallery, affected me so profoundly: it was as if I had already *known* it, seen it somewhere.

The beautiful legend of 'Take Thou this cup' became, in its earliest form, one of my impressions in the little church from the distant village of Konchanskoye (Suvorov's place of exile), reverently translated to Tauride Street, and lovingly clad in the 'stone chasuble' of the edifice destined to safeguard it.

The scream of colours in El Greco's 'In the Garden'.

Father Pavel 'had to be an experience'* and, as soon as I had undergone this 'experience'.* I practically left the domain of these emotions and ideas, while preserving them in my stock of useful memories.

---

* In English in the original.

It was at Tsar Ivan's confession of course that this knot of personal experiences, which always flickered weakly in my memory like the dull glow of an icon lamp, burned at their strongest.

But living impressions piled up on one another.

The next powerful and consummate impression on these lines was . . . Rosicrucianism.

Unimaginable! Minsk. 1920.

The height of the Civil War.

Minsk, just after we had liberated it.

We, and the Political Administration of the Western Front, were almost the first troops in.

I had painted agit-trains while still in Smolensk. In Minsk I built a mobile stage. I painted the backdrop for Gorky's *Lower Depths*. The morning after working. Chocolate behind the church, with its frescoes depicting the life of Christ (in twentieth-century dress, *en continuant la tradition* [so continuing the tradition]).

And in the midst of all that there was a poster advertising a lecture by Professor Zubakin on 'Henri Bergson's Theory of Laughter'.[9]

I attended. 'Not very much impressed.'*

'More impressed by himself.'*

Not so much by the lecture; more as he was the following day.

Imagine a statuette.

Clearly in ecclesiastical attire.

A long black overcoat looking in silhouette like a soutane.

A black hat.

A black beard, trimmed short, surrounding an extraordinarily pale face like a funeral border.

Grey-blue eyes.

And gloves of black cotton.

Standing on the corner of the street.

With a small black book, open,

immersed in his reading.

Amidst the din of lorries.

Ordnance.

---

* In English in the original.

Ivan's repentance, still, Part Three. (Photo: Viktor Dombrovsky)

Horses.

Barbed-wire barriers and *chevaux de frise* around the tempo-rary tribunal buildings.

Military formations.

The clatter of boots.

And the diminutive figure in black was not unlike Chesterton's Father Brown, immersed in his book in the middle of the commotion of soldiery in this newly liberated western city.

The book was not a prayer book.

But the last thing I had expected to find—Maupassant's short stories.

Nor was the diminutive figure a father.

But strange as it might seem—according to *their* hierarchy —one much higher up: a bishop!

But not a canonical bishop.

A . . . Rosicrucian bishop.

Bogori the Second, whose 'worldly' name was Zubakin, a professor of literature and philosophy (?), then the cadre's instruc-tor and lecturer.

I will never forget the premises of the Minsk 'lodge'!

There was a single-storey building in an access yard, which the Red Army had taken over for billeting the troops.

It had a few rooms with some simple beds, gaiters, puttees, an accordion and a balalaika.

There were some troops, worried about something and thoughtful.

Further on, there was a small door.

Behind it was something that might once have been a study, with a writing desk without a lid.

We went inside—there were a few people there.

A gigantic Russian aristocrat with a German surname, de-generate and a former anarchist. A failure—the son of a second-rate Russian composer. Smolin, the actor, with the troupe touring the front. Between playing Mirtsev in the play *Vera Mirtseva* (the play which begins with a shot fired in darkness, the prosecutor's wife killing her lover, and depicts the prosecutor gradually becoming convinced that the murderer is his wife), he cured migraines by lay-ing-on hands and gazed into a crystal ·ball for hours in his hotel

Lecture: 'The Problems of Irony', Minsk, 14 August 1920 (Drawing by Eisenstein)

room.

Someone was strumming the balalaika behind the door.

There was a clattering of pans—supper time in the field kitchen in the yard.

But then the long-limbed anarchist threw a white tunic over his army shirt and leggings and knocked three times on the floor with a rod.

He imparted the message that 'Bishop Bogori is ready to receive us'.

An ablution of the devotees' feet at the hands of the Bishop himself.

There was a strange brocade on the mitre and he wore

something like a cape.

Some words.

And we, linking hands, walked past a mirror.

The mirror sent our union into the . . . astral.

Behind the door, the accordion succeeded the balalaika.

The empty pans clattered . . .

The troops were already cheered.

They had been subdued by their wait for supper.

But by this point we were already . . . knights.

Rosicrucian knights.

And the Bishop had only a few days previously begun initiating us into study of the 'Cabbala' and the 'Arcana' of the Tarot.

My ebullient enthusiasm was of course ironic, but I was able to hide this for the time being.

Bogori led us through the most ancient mystical rites, like Dante his Vergil.

Into the last 'seals of mystery'.

Discussions of the 'Arcana' often made me sleepy. In my half-awake state, the phrase would hammer away: 'Nothing could be plainer to a flea than the "Arcana"'. It was in the second half of the saying that I dozed off.

I believe that it is only the most interesting part of the study that I stayed awake for. The study constantly revolved around divinities, God, and divine revelations.

At the very end it became clear that the initiate was being told that 'there is no God for God is He.' Now that was something I liked.

And I very much liked the systematised textbook of 'Occultism', where the written exercises began practically with a selection of 'seeds' (useful both for educating one's observation according to Konstantin Sergeyevich's 'Method',[10] and for the preliminary steps to becoming a spy—remember the children's games in Kipling's *Kim*!) and ended with a practical achievement . . . elevation.

I bought this 'textbook' by the ruined walls of Kitai-gorod[11] a few years later—now there are no walls, nor ruins—for three roubles. Now it is in my library, next to Eliphas Levi's *The History of*

Magic[12] on shelves allocated to the 'imprecise sciences' (magic, cheiromancy, and graphology, of which more elsewhere!).

In the autumn of 1920, military duties took the 'knights' to Moscow with the exception of the lanky one and the actor-cum-healer, who were lost somewhere.

Mikhail Chekhov and Smyshlyayev[13] were among the new disciples. We had conversations in a cold hotel, where I slept on my trunk.

They took a rather Theosophical turn. Rudolf Steiner was mentioned with increasing frequency.[14] Valya Smyshlyayev was trying to accelerate the growth of his carrot seedlings by suggestion. Pavel Andreyevich was fascinated by hypnotism. They all muttered mantras. Mikhail Chekhov alternated between fanatical proselytising and blasphemy.

I remember one conversation we had about 'the invisible lotus' which flowered, unseen, in the devotee's breast. I remember the reverential silence and the glassy eyes of the believers fixed on their teacher.

Chekhov and I went out on to the street.

A thin covering of snow. Silence.

Dogs frisked playfully around the street lamps.

'I have to believe there is something in the invisible lotus,' said Chekhov. 'Take these dogs. We cannot see anything and yet they can scent something under each other's little tails . . .'

Cynicism of this order often goes hand in hand with belief. Such was Chekhov.

I alone remained in possession of my wits.

I was by then ready to die of boredom one minute,

or to burst out laughing the next.

I was finally declared a 'knight errant' and released. I tried, on my errands, to put as much ground as possible between myself and the Rosicrucians, Steiner, and Madame Blavatskaya.[15]

Another page of impressions in the past . . .

Novgorod—Los Remedios[1]

A jet of water four storeys high pumped out of the ground.

It looked like a picture of a geyser in a geography book.

It gave off a faint smell of sulphur . . .

And it reminded me even more vividly of textbooks, with their aroma of printer's inks, in those days when they were still interesting, on that first evening when I leafed through the only-just-purchased book not in search of tedious spiritual nourishment but as a . . . bibliophile.

On evenings like this, textbooks, especially geography ones, send such tempting glimpses your way that later you will have to see them for yourself. Everyone has seen the picture of the mail van driving through a tunnel hewn out of a vast tree trunk. We will know no peace until we too have been able to drive through such a gigantic sequoia, in an American national park.

So it was in my case.

It is worth noting that the family of trees is called sequoia after the Indian chieftain, whereas the individual giants are named, for the most part, after Civil War generals, although the majority of them were no more than a couple of short planks' worth.

The tallest sequoia bears the name of General Sherman who razed Atlanta to the ground.

The column of water that pumped out of the ground went some way towards dispelling the *idée fixe* of another picture, showing a geyser in Yellowstone.

Perhaps this fountain was responsible for my not going to Yellowstone but being content with Yosemite.

. . . The rays of the sun were diffracted in the fountain during the day.

And in the evening the fountain glowed in the multi-coloured floodlights.

It played before the *Kursaal.* There were crowds of confused people swarming in front of it.

For some reason, I spent that summer, the last before I finished the *Realschule*, not with Papa on the Riga coast, but with

Mama, in Staraya Russa.

The fountain played before the *Kursaal* of Staraya Russa.

And people were dashing hysterically this way and that because it was 1914 and war had just been declared.

In the *Kursaal* galleries, complete strangers threw themselves into each other's arms, sobbing.

A colonel sat weeping in his wheelchair, covered by a tartan rug; he wore dark glasses and had doffed his forage cap, showing a scanty head of hair . . .

People threw themselves into each other's arms in that same way three years later, when Petrograd suddenly buzzed with the news that Rasputin had been murdered.

In 1917, he was an invisible presence in every home, every mind, the subject of every piece of scandal.

Only the *Vechernyaya Birzhevka* [Evening Financial Gazette] managed a line about the murder, and that had to go on that edition's contents page.

The edition was confiscated immediately.

And I am the proud owner of a copy somewhere, which by a miracle fell into my hands on that memorable day.

. . . But the panic now is greater, of course. They even had to turn some people away from the station, it was so crowded.

It was impossible to leave Staraya Russa by train.

Someone had the brain-wave of sailing across Lake Ilmen, down the River Volkhov, and then taking the train to Tikhvin.

That summer brought me three forceful impressions.

Before war was announced, in the July heat, there was a church procession on a patron saint's day, at the recently reopened church in Staraya Russa.

The vivid impressions I received from that informed the procession in *The Old and the New*.

The second key event was my first ever 'literary encounter', when I met Anna Grigoryevna Dostoyevskaya.[2]

But the strongest impression of all was 'a trip'.*

Small white churches jostled one another like saints in ikons who wear white robes and virtually merge into one.

---

* In English in the original.

Filming the scene 'the Novgorod Assembly' for the film *Alexander Nevsky*

The Church Spas-Nereditsa in Novgorod, 1944, after being destroyed by the Germans (Newsreel shot)

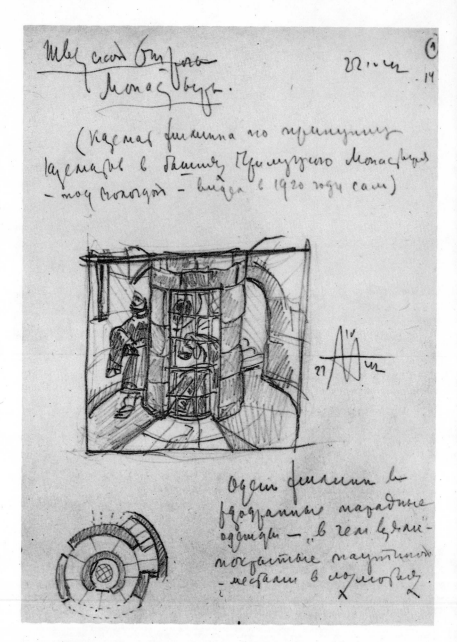

Eisenstein's drawing for *Ivan the Terrible* Part Three. The explanatory text above the picture reads: 'The Tverskoi Otroch Monastery' (Philip's solitary cell, on the principle of the solitary cells in the towers of the Prilut monastery near Vologda, which I myself saw in 1920). Text below reads: 'Philip is attired in his torn vestments "in which he was seized"—covered in cobwebs and tattered in places.' Alma-Ata, 22 April 1942

Because of the war, I sailed through one of the oldest parts of our country—a journey that was fabulously beautiful.

But otherwise the war affected me little that year.

During that last academic year, we went on several street demonstrations.

We shouted until we were hoarse.

We carried portraits of the Tsar and torches, which blackened our nostrils with soot.

Papa donned his military uniform, with a general's brassards . . .

In the spring of the following year, I saw my first evacuation —civil servants' families leaving the city of Riga.

This coincided with my leaving for St Petersburg, where I enrolled at the Institute.

My transfer from Papa to Mama was painless, natural and even by official transport.

But that was a year later. For the present . . .

The journey was by steamer, from Staraya Russa to Lake Ilmen. 'The Marble Sea' at nightfall.

A white belfry stood on the opposite shore, like a white lighthouse.

We sailed slowly down the Volkhov, past Novgorod, bathed in moonlight. Dazzling white churches, too many to count, in the still night air. We glided silently past.

A magical night!

Where had these temples come from, that appeared to have come down to the stately river? Had they rolled, like whitecurrants, to drink the water? Or had they come to moisten the hems of their white garments?

I visited Novgorod many years later, when I was preparing to film *Alexander Nevsky*. That time it was not *en passant*; I stayed there.

I had not forgotten the vivid image of a white mass of churches crowding on the banks of the Volkhov.

They seemed to have been strewn all over the town. In the Torgovaya district. In the Sofiskaya. In the outskirts. Everywhere at a distance.

If I were a poet, I would probably say that on moonlit nights the churches of Novgorod come down to the banks of the Volkhov, from either shore, to communicate with one another, as once, long ago, the prelates crossed half Russia to meet—Sergius of Radonezh from the Trinity monastery to see Dmitri of Prilutsk, at Vologda.

An old monk explained this meeting to me as he showed me the antiquities of the Prilutsk monastery (in 1918) and the terrible stone oubliettes in its corner towers.

In the middle of the round space on the top floor of the tower was something like a hollowed-out stone shaft with a grille at the top. Refractory sons of the church would be imprisoned in these upright stone coffins, to serve out their sentence. (Then the monk went on in the same voice to complain that the ration cards given them were not category A but B, even though it was they, the monks, who did all the work.) Roughly a decade later I was astonished to see cells of exactly the same kind, in the old part of Sing-Sing, which was to be demolished and modernised after 1930.

A two-storey stone dungeon, formed from stone containers placed on top of each other with a grille door at one end. There were no windows. And the large stone roof over the rectangular building was like a box, open end down, containing the small stone cells and the windows on to freedom.

But I am a film director, not a poet and so, as I wandered around ancient Russia, I was just as amazed by the builders' skill in choosing the sites for the churches and belfries which were dotted across the landscape.

Alexander Nevsky did not only take me to Novgorod; he took me to Pereslavl which looks like a lovely little toy town because of those square churches and their onion domes. They might have come from the toymakers' warehouses in the monastery of the Trinity and St Sergius.[3] As if a thief had dropped the tiny churches in his haste to get away from what is now Zagorsk, on his way to ancient Pereslavl which was where Alexander Yaroslavich grew up; and half a millennium later, on that very lake, the young Peter tried out his toy fleet.*

---

* According to legend, the hills were formed when the Devil fled from the holy face of the Cherubim, and dropped *en route* clods of earth stolen from the Holy City.

In reply, I think, prelates dropped cloisters and little churches on these

But these churches were not placed at random. They were positioned with great wisdom. And the white belfries, like lighthouses for vessels at sea, rose above the green sweep of the Russian plains, celebrating and marking the route for countless numbers of pilgrims, who travelled hundreds of miles to bow down before the holy relics.

Go back a distance of five, ten, fifteen, twenty kilometres. The road twists, scaling hills and vanishing into valleys. Look around you and the bell towers are still visible. And you can see the streams of pilgrims along the route, taking their bearings from belfry to belfry on paths marked by a director of genius.

And what forethought went into that last stage of the journey upon the White Sea, for those aiming for the relics at Solovki!

Barges carried the pilgrims from the shore to the islands.

The holds were full of pilgrims, thrown together in a heap.

Stuffy. Dark. Gloomy.

The barge was unmoored.

She began rocking.

She pitched from wave to wave.

There was howling and wailing coming from the darkness of the hold,

as they suffocated,

languishing as if in the underworld.

But then, before dawn, the monastery appeared in the distance.

To the accompaniment of shouted canticles which rose above the noise of the storm, and the deacon's bass proclamations, the hold crashed open.

Utterly deprived of their senses, they gulped down the fresh air.

The wind before dawn filled the sails. Lifted the waves. A towering image of the Saviour rose up from the deck. In the light of candles fanned by the wind. In the smoke of the censers, swung by the strong arms of the monks on the White Sea coast. In the deafening volume of the singing. Beheld by those emerging from

---

elevations which were born of Satan's greed and cowardly haste. (E's note)

under the monastery's cupolas and towers.

And it is as though the torment of this Vale of Tears was ended and before us lay the Promised Land.

The pilgrims lay prostrate; and when the sun rose they descended, trembling with awe, upon the consecrated soil of the monastery.

The Catholic churches in Mexico were sited with equal skill.

Here, for dozens of miles, you can see the domes of Santa Maria Tonanzintla from the approaches to Puebla, or the flashing crosses of the Virgen de los Remedios at the gates of Mexico City.

But this is no credit to the Catholics, particularly. It was not they who chose the sites.

These were the locations of ancient pyramids, which were once crowned by Aztec and Toltec temples.

The real wisdom of the Catholics lay simply in building their churches on the foundations of the temples they had pulled down—on the summits of those pyramids, so as not to spoil the pilgrims' chances of finding their way by the pyramids as they had done for thousands of years, crossing the land from all directions as they headed for the foot of these very pyramids.

Large groups of pilgrims seem an anachronism nowadays.

The strange apparel of the priests who dance from dawn to dusk without pausing for breath, repeating the single changeless steps in honour of the Madonna, is partly responsible for this. Who knows whether it is in honour of the Madonna, though? Perhaps it is for an older divinity, the mother of gods who has lost her place to a new rival—the mother of the Christian God—but who has remained unchanged for succeeding generations descended from those who initiated her cult. The priests peered through their fingers—when, that is, they were not employing them for receiving gifts. Not that they care whom the pilgrims come thousands of miles to pay tribute to. As long as the gifts can be converted into money, and streams of gold flow in torrents to Rome. The repetitive melody of the dance was stupefying. There were the cries of the pilgrims' children. Mothers put them to breast. The tones of the organ. The fumes from the candles. Heat and frenzy.

And the steady flow of human figures, bathed in sweat, crawling on their knees from the base of the pyramids to their consecrated summits.

Their knees were bound with rags. Some had tied cushions to them and these were torn to shreds.

Often outlandish headwear fashioned from feathers (the brotherhood of the *danzantes*). Cloth over the eyes.

Streams of sweat.

Old ladies among the pilgrims carried someone in pain in their arms; they wore cheap blue shawls.

Panting, they reached the last step.

The binding was ceremoniously removed.

After the darkness and torment, the suffering man saw before him the wide-open doors bathed in the ruddy candlelight of the temple of the Madonna de Guadelupe, de Los Remedios, the Cathedral of Amecameca, and a grey trunk stripped bare of its leaves standing before it.

The Citadel[1]

The word 'citadel' is now not so fashionable.

You rarely come across the phrase 'the citadel of capitalism'.

And almost never find 'the citadel of fascism'.

The Citadel can only mean King Vidor's film, or A.J. Cronin's novel.[2]

But during my childhood in Riga the citadel was a reality.

Both as the Castle, the governor's residence.

And as the Citadel, a landmark of the old part of the city, the Powder Tower with three stone cannonballs to one side.

The military administration of the garrison was quartered in the Citadel.

There was an exercise ground. A barracks chapel, where I would be taken to Father Mikhnovsky for confession in my pre-school years.

A flag, fluttering in the breeze.

Striped sentry boxes.

Under the flag loomed a two-storey building—the official residence of one the highest-ranking officers of the garrison—General Bertels.

Alyosha Bertels and I became friends before the General retired.

I remember the Citadel because it was the scene of my extreme rudeness to an odd gentleman who was visiting the General's family at the same time as my mother was.

I took a hearty dislike to him.

I forget the exact form my rudeness took—of course, it was on a smaller scale than the trick I played on Madame Reva, a friend of Mama's: I released a dove under her fashionably long skirts.

Picture my horror when, a few days later, that same gentleman in gleaming military dress suddenly appeared at one of my classes at the *Realschule*. He turned out to be the warden of our educational district, no more or less: Prutchenko.

Horror turned to amazement when he not only recognised

me, but he even said something complimentary about having had the pleasure of meeting my mother and me when out visiting.

I remember a precisely analogous situation in Mexico, where the combined authority of three of us ejected a swarthy individual from my bunk. He had no right to be there. His eyes flashed fire.

Barely had we set foot in the Promised Land of Mexico City, when we received a summons to go directly to the Chief of Police.

There was no semblance yet of ill will: it was merely a formality.

You can imagine my astonishment when we saw, standing next to the Chief of Police, that same swarthy chap who turned out to be . . . the Chief's brother!

In Spanish: 'We have already met the señor.'

A smile revealed a semicircle of white teeth against the bronze of his face . . .

A horse ride with Papa at Edinburg on the Riga coast, 1911

'The Knot that Binds' (A Chapter on the Divorce of Pop and Mom)[1]

The biggest stationer's in Riga stands on Kaufstrasse. This street is curious for being 'as wide as it is long' (I think this is the description of one of the characters in the 'original' *Pinocchio*, which I read when I was very young, before there were 'versions' like Alexei Tolstoi's, or Alexander Ptushko's—and Disney was probably younger than I was).[2]

Kaufstrasse, with its regular flagstones, was wider than it was long.

This fact was especially obvious since all around it were the narrow little streets of the old part of the city.

On the left of the shop stood the bookstore Jonck und Poliewski; diagonally opposite was Deubner; and opposite was the huge drapers, Chomse.

Above the shop, there was a signboard: 'August Lyra, Riga'. Lyra was written with a 'y' (what we call 'igrek' [*upsilon*] and the Mexicans *'la i griega'* [Greek i]. For some reason, this letter is very popular over there. I remember there was a small bar on the outskirts of Mexico City called that, and it had a big Y on its signboard). We were taught to pronounce 'y' as 'u', hence 'August Lura, Riga'.*

This shop was a paradise of stationery requisites: it had every sort of crayon, ink of every hue. The blotters to be found there! The pens, the corrugated card (for flowerpots), the erasers, envelopes, penknives, folders and files!

There were postcards in another section.

Photographic postcards were fashionable then.

Black-and-white photographic reproductions (printed on startlingly contrasty paper) showing famous or popular scenes.

An angel, guarding two children as they walk on the edge of a precipice.

---

* The cyrillic 'y' is the Latin 'u' (Trans.).

A suicide pact: two lovers bound with ropes and about to throw themselves into the abyss.

A maiden dying of consumption, gazing into the rays of sunlight streaming into her room . . .

These postcards were collected like stamps and, like stamps, they were painstakingly mounted in albums.

(Perhaps it was these pictures that fed my dislike of 'subject' and 'anecdote' and marked the start of my career in cinema?)

Also there were larger-format pictures. And with a border, to boot.

In those years, America seduced England and Europe with a girl of a certain type.

She was a strapping figure, with jutting chin and dreamy eyes gazing out from under a towering pompadour, or else her hair would be in a chignon (normally drawn in with a hatching pen) and she wore a long skirt—she was the creation of a man called Gibson and was the famous 'Gibson Girl'. Her image swamped humorous magazines like *Punch* in London and the *New Yorker* just as, during the Second World War, everywhere the American Army went was crowded out with the so-called Varga girl—a half-naked girl painted by the South American artist Varga who pioneered the creation of the 'pin-up'.[3]

These pictures appeared as inserts or centrefolds in almost every magazine that was posted to the front line.

The soldiers would carefully cut them out and stick them to the walls above their beds in their shelters, dug-outs, barracks or field hospitals.

The former were as well-bred as the latter were loose.

I can clearly remember one of the pictures of 1908 or 1909; it was, for its time, quite sensational. It was in the style of Gibson.

Entitled 'The Knot that Binds',* it depicted a large black ribbon tied in a bow at the middle.

On the left, was the traditional profile of the Gibson girl. On the right, the profile of the no less typically Gibson young man. All the Gibson girls had the same face, and the young men all seemed to be their brothers, they looked so alike.

---

* In English in the original.

And in the middle of the bow, facing the viewer, was the little smiling face of a child.

This image cut particularly deep into my memory.

Why?

Probably because at the time I saw it, I myself was 'the knot that bound'.

But I was a knot that was unable to bind the family together and keep it from breaking up:

my parents were divorcing.

Actually, nobody should be interested in the fact that my parents divorced in 1909.

It was a sufficiently common occurrence in those days, just as 'theatrically arranged' suicides were to become extremely modish a little later.

But it was to have a very profound effect on me.

These events poisoned the family atmosphere at a very early age. They corrupted both my belief in the foundations of the family and the charm of the family hearth, driving them from my imagination and emotions.

To use literary historical jargon, 'the theme of the family' vanished from my frame of reference when I was very young.

The way it vanished was quite agonising.

And now it appears in my memory like flawed film, with sections missing and continuity errors, a film only thirty-five per cent of which is suitable for showing.

My room and that of my parents were adjacent.

All night long I heard the bitterest exchanges of insults.

How many times did I run barefoot through the night to my governess's room, to fall asleep with my head rammed into a pillow. And no sooner had I dropped off than my parents would come rushing to wake me up and say how sorry they were for me.

Another time, both parents believed it was their duty to open my eyes to the faults of the other.

Mama cried that my father stole.

Papa, that Mama was an immoral woman.

Court Counsellor Eisenstein did not shrink from using more precise terminology.

Yulia Ivanovna, the daughter of a merchant in the first

guild, accused my father of worse yet.

Then a hail of names: all the big-wigs of the then Russian colony in the 'Baltic provinces'.

Papa had duelled with someone.

Papa had not actually duelled with someone.

One day—and I remember it as if it happened yesterday — mother, in a beautiful red and green checked silk blouse ran hysterically through the flat to throw herself down the stairwell.

I remember Papa carrying her back; she was writhing in her hysteria.

I know nothing about the 'suit'.

I picked up fragments that Ozols, the messenger, had testified as a witness; something to the effect that the cook Salome (it took a great many years to dissociate her name from spinach and eggs, and to see it in its Wildean light!) had 'revealed' something .

Then there were a number of days when I was taken out to spend the whole day walking around town.

Then Mama, her face red from crying, bade me farewell.

Then Mama left.

Then the removal men came.

Then the furniture was taken (it had been Mama's trousseau).

The rooms became vast empty expanses.

This was actually fun.

I began waking up refreshed after a night's sleep.

But during the day—I used to ride around the empty dining and drawing rooms on my bicycle.

What was more, the piano went too, and I was released from my music lessons which I had just started having.

I do not smoke.

Papa never smoked.

I always followed my father's example.

From the cradle I was destined to become an engineer and architect.

Up to a certain age I competed with my father in everything I did.

Papa went riding.

He was very corpulent, and only one horse from the Riga

Tattersall* could carry him: it was a massive draught horse, with a bluish wall-eye.

I had riding lessons too.

I did not become an engineer and an architect.

Nor a great horseman.

After that lunatic of a horse dashed off full-tilt along the Riga beach, with me on its back, and crashed into a breakwater somewhere near Bullen, I somehow lost interest in it.

My next attempt was in Mexico, when a horse of equal insensitivity bore me through a maguey plantation, around the Tetlapayac hacienda.

Nowadays I ride only in cars.

Similarly I do not play the piano; only the radio or the wind-up gramophone.

Yes. And I do not smoke because I did not permit myself to grow fond of tobacco at that age.

First, the ideal: Papa. Second, my irrational submissiveness and obedience.

Perhaps that was why I so hated all those features in Upton Sinclair, because I have known them since I was a babe in arms?

Pieties![4]

Lord, how much they weigh and have weighed upon me— for better and for worse.

Trotzkopfiges [wilfully] not recognising the obligatory: often very *hardi* [impudently]—Mayakovsky, during the period of the first 'Lef'.[5] Ch[arlie] Ch[aplin]—if to be quite sincere!*

And morbidly unhealthy: *en avoir aussi, en avoir autant* [to have the same, to have as much].

In the slightest, most trivial matter.

Yet, it can be an active stimulant:

it made me a director (*Masquerade*).

It drove me towards fame* (Yevreinov, and the cuttings), even to public speechifying, lectures abroad (Anatole France's journey to Buenos Aires for a thousand dollars 'and travel expenses'!**).[6]

---

*   i.e. stud register. (Ed.)
** In English in the original.

Stefan Zweig in Moscow, for the centenary
celebrations of Lev Tolstoy's birth, 1928.
(Newsreel shot)

'A Family Chronicle' (Stefan Zweig, Ernst Toller, Babel. About Freud. Meyerhold and K. S.)[1]

Today I stumbled upon the last notes Stefan Zweig ever made, in the *Gazette littéraire*.[2]

Stefan Zweig . . .

I think it was [Herbert] Spencer who declined an introduction to Alexander II.

He explained this by saying that personal acquaintance all too often shattered the far pleasanter impression that one could form from someone's reputation in literature.

This is frequently the case.

But sometimes only partly.

After Dreiser and Dos Passos[3] it was Stefan Zweig's turn to dine with me in my book-filled room, at the table with its waxed tablecloth on Chistye Prudy.

Dreiser later noted in his book that I had the biggest bed in Russia.[4]

Dos Passos stuffed himself with gooseberry pie while commenting that prisons smell the same the world over.

But a little later, on returning to Austria, Zweig described this room in a piece called 'The Heroism of the Intelligentsia'.[5] He ascribed to it . . . a washbasin that it had never contained.

I greatly liked his Dostoyevsky and Nietzsche, Stendhal and Dickens.[6]

He had come for a conference commemorating Tolstoy.

We met at one of those 'international receptions', where you could spend the whole evening talking to someone looking like the archetypal German. In French, for some reason. And suddenly, just before leaving, you would hear him say to his wife in Russian, 'Marusya, let's go to bed!'

Zweig proved very popular.

And we drank tea with a Frenchman. Towards the close of evening, he turned out, of course, to be a Russian, a Professor

Ivanov. Ivan Ivanovich, at that!

A few days later, Zweig was at my flat.

I met him with a bombshell, an eruption of Vesuvius—at any rate with the unexpected:

Confusion of Feelings[7]—was that autobiographical?'

'Ach no, it was about a childhood friend.'

It did not ring true.

I deeply regretted asking, and quickly helped him out of his embarrassment.

I knew he was close to Freud. (Otherwise of course I would not have struck him dumb with such a potentially tactless question!)

And I turned the conversation into an enquiry about the great man from Vienna.

His 'Freud', 'Mesmer' and 'Mary Baker-Eddy' were yet to be written.[8]

And I heard him speak of much of what came out later in the book.

More than that.

He conveyed very vividly the particular patriarchal atmosphere that reigned over that oval table on Thursdays[9] bonding the idolised professor and his ardent disciples.

It was impossible to describe the atmosphere of the first discoveries, which were perceived as revelations. The unbridled flow of thought set off by mutual contact. The wild surge of creativity and the triumph. But the darker side of this fresco was equally significant; this neo-Athenian school where a latter-day Plato and Aristotle were merged into the one overwhelming personality of a man with a Wagnerian name.[10]

There was mutual suspicion and jealousy between the disciples. Among them were Stekel, Adler, Jung.

And there was Freud's even greater suspicion of them.

The suspicion and jealousy of a tyrant.

Merciless towards anyone who was not steadfast in the doctrine.

Especially towards anyone who tried to follow his own deviations, in the context of his own ideas which did not coincide with those of the teacher in every respect.

The surge of rebellion against the Patriarch-Father.

Corresponding accusations of renegadism, of perverting his teaching. Excommunication, anathema . . .

The Oedipus complex, which has been blown up out of all proportion to its place in Freud's teachings, is discernible in the strife within the school itself: the sons who encroach upon their father.

But it is more of a response to the tyrannical regime of the father who, like Saturn, devours his children, than to Merope's[11] innocent husband, Laius.*

Adler and Jung were already breaking away; Stekel was leaving . . .

It was all uncommonly vivid.

But surely this image of the internal life of a small group of talented fanatics, revolving around their bearer of learning, is exactly as you would expect it to be? Surely the story in the Bible is right, which embodies in Judas the inevitable spectre of suspicion that hovers before the eyes of the founder of the doctrine?

Surely this is no less eternal or true an idea, than the image of the uncertain proselyte who wants everything factually verified, to be palpably proven true—Doubting Thomas?

As for the situation itself, surely that gives rise to the image of the horde devouring the eldest of the species, itself an image inseparable from Freud's teachings?

And perhaps it is the actual situation of him being surrounded that leads to the inevitable 'resurrection' of forms of behaviour common when life is set in the analogous atmosphere of a closed clan, in a virtually patrimonial order?!

. . . But why do I grow so heated when I talk about the atmosphere within a group of scholars that broke up so long ago, and who are so distant from any of our present struggles?! And Father Saturn has rested from battles and skirmishes for quite long enough.

The reason of course is this: after introducing this descrip-

---

* In fact, the more vicious tongues of the ancients have brought us extraordinarily unexpected and curious details of the reasons and causes of Oedipus' encounter with his father, which we know of otherwise only from Sophocles' version. (E's note)

tion, I abandoned the subject of Freud and his inner circle of friends; these last few pages have been devoted to a situation that is similar in every respect, but with different names and which I left to plough my own furrow.

A similarly grand old man at the centre.

A master of similar charisma, but a man of wily treachery.

As distinguished by the stamp of genius, but also by an equally tragic fall and a discord in the original harmony, that characterised the profoundly tragic figure of Freud. And how strongly this stamp of individual calamity is impressed upon the whole outline of his teaching!

The same circle of fanatics, drawn from the students around him.

The same intolerance of any symptoms of independence.

The same methods of 'spiritual inquisition'.

The same ruthless destruction.

Rejection.

Excommunication of those whose only crime had been to speak in their own voice . . .

Of course, my description of Freud's curia had switched subjects earlier: I am now describing the atmosphere in the school and theatre of the grand old man of my youth, my leader in drama, my teacher.

Meyerhold![12]

A combination of creative genius and treacherous personality.

The countless agonies of those like myself who selflessly loved him.

The countless moments of triumph as we witnessed the magical creativity of this unique wizard of the theatre.

How often did Ilyinsky leave![13]

The agonies Babanova suffered![14]

What purgatory—short-lived, fortunately!—I endured before I was expelled from the Gates of Heaven, from the ranks of his Theatre, when I 'dared' to set up my own collective elsewhere—in the Proletkult.

He adored Ibsen's *Ghosts*.

Times without number he played Osvald.

Konstantin Stanislavsky and Vsevolod Meyerhold, at a rehearsal in the opera studio, 1938

He produced it many times.[15]

He often showed me how he acted him, playing on the piano when he was in contemplative mood.

I think he was attracted by the theme of repetition, which so amazingly permeated the story of Mrs Alving and her son.

And how often would he revisit his split with Stanislavsky[16] upon his close friends and students, resurrecting a part of his own creative immaturity, craftily manoeuvring the necessary pre-conditions and settings like the director he was.

His love for K[onstantin] S[tanislavsky] was amazing—even in the bitterest years of struggle against the Art Theatre.

How many times did he speak of K. S. with affection, how highly did he value his talent and skill!

Where was it, in which poem or legend did I read how Lucifer, the first among the angels, led a rebellion against Sabaoth and, being 'cast down', continued to love him and 'shed tears', not because of his destruction or banishment, but because he was no longer able to gaze upon his countenance?!

Or was it from the legend about Ahasuerus?*

---

*   i.e. the 'Wandering Jew'. (Ed.)

Alexander Levshin, Isaak Babel, Eisenstein, Olga Ivanova and Alexander Antonov
at the dacha in the village of Nemchinov Post, summer 1925

A picture taken by Eisenstein for the episode 'The Railway Strike' for the film *1905*. (Cameraman: Alexander Levitsky)

There was something about Lucifer or Ahasuerus in my teacher's rebellious countenance: and he was an incomparably greater genius than the universally acknowledged and 'canonised' K. S., but he completely lacked that patriarchal composure, which was taken as harmony but was rather limited by philistinism, of which, Goethe said, every creative personality needs a certain amount.

And who better than that high-ranking official of the Weimar court has proved, by his own life, that a degree of philistinism guarantees peace, stability, deep roots and sweet recognition: whereas its absence condemns an overly romantic nature to perpetual casting about, searching, failures and flights, vicissitudes of fortune and, frequently, to Icarus' fate, which brought the Flying Dutchman's life to its conclusion . . .

His pining for K. S., that patriarch who basked in the glow of second and third generation idolators and enthusiastic devotees, recalled Lucifer's tears or the ineffable yearning of Vrubel's 'Demon'.[17]

And I remember him towards the end, when he was preparing himself for a *rapprochement* with K. S.[18]

It was touching and profoundly affecting to see this imminent *rapprochement* between these two elderly men.

I do not know how K. S. felt: he had been betrayed in the last years of his life by the change in the creative direction his own Theatre had taken. It had turned its back on him, and looked to the new generation—that perpetual source of invigorating creativity—for the fresh ideas of eternally young talent.

But I remember the gleam in the eyes of the 'prodigal son' as he spoke of a new reunion that would 'obviate' all tendencies superfluous to true theatre. The one had foreseen them at the beginning both of the century and of his creative path, and had nothing to do with them; the other had renounced them some decades later, when Nemirovich-Danchenko's assiduous cultivation of these non-theatrical tendencies threatened to stifle the founder of the Art Theatre himself.[19]

Their closeness was not to last long.

But it was not internal collapse or discord that led to the break this time.

One was finished by the tragic consequences of his internal discord which had its roots in his unbalanced temperament—the other died.[20]

But in those long years, when I had put my personal trauma behind me and made peace with him, and counted him my friend, it always seemed that in his relations with students and followers he was playing out that same personal tragedy of his own break with his first teacher . . .

In those rejected, he felt his own gnawing bitterness anew. And, by rejecting, he became the tragic father, Rustum, who struck Sohrab as if seeking justification for what had happened in his youth, without malicious intent on his 'father's' side; it was simply the result of an independent creativity of spirit on the part of the 'prodigal son'.

That was how I saw him in this drama.

Perhaps this is not objective enough.

Perhaps not 'historical' enough.

But then this whole business is too close to me: I am too much a part of it—it is too much a 'family chronicle'.

Because on the principle of 'grace descending' through the laying-on of hands of the older man, I am in a sense the son and grandson of theatre's departed generations.

. . . During my meeting with Zweig, I did not of course think of any of this; I listened to him attentively.

Then I entertained him with stills from *October.*

He was transported with delight and praised them unreservedly.

He did so in a strange, almost tearful voice, slightly singsong.

He wanted to take one, at least, as a souvenir.

'Oh, they really are good! Oh, very good!'

I offered one—of my choosing.

'Oh, they really are very good! Really good!' (And in the same sing-song rhythm) . . . 'I would like another,' (and again) . . . 'Very good . . . really . . . if you're sure you can spare it . . . '

Of course I could.

I liked him very much.

Although I did find *Amok* a disappointment.[21]

Which was not surprising. Before reading it, I heard a most detailed account of it from . . . Babel.[22]

And heavens, what a pale reflection of this striking story did the real *Amok* turn out to be!

I heard the story one evening at sunset, on the upper floor of the dacha at Nemchinovka. I worked on the upper floor with Agadzhanova, writing the screenplay for *1905*, and on the lower floor with Babel, on the screenplay for *The Career of Benya Krik*. . .[23]

In the intervals I stuffed myself with stewed apples. Their aroma and the chill from the little icebox carried right out into the garden.

Why *The Career of Benya Krik?*

My enterprising director, Kapchinsky,[24] suggested that, since I was working in Odessa filming the southern scenes for *1905*, I might as well film . . . *The Career of Benya Krik!*

In the summerhouse in the corner, I drank *zubrovka* vodka with Kazimir Malevich, who was down from the city on a trip.[25]

Resting his chin on his fist as he lay on the grass, he spoke in awe of the phenomenal potency of donkeys.

But of course Babel's stories were the most amazing.

Some people lead charmed lives!

Who else but Babel would come across a bonfire on his way to the dacha from the station at Nemchinovka?

By the fire there was a Jew . . .

A solitary Jew, playing the cello . . . by an open fire . . . in a coppice near Nemchinovka station . . .

Babel then told the story of *Amok* in his own words and brought it all to life so that one could picture it: the dazzling tropical moonlight shining on the deck; the fascinating woman and her abortion; the gangway collapsing into the water taking the coffin with it; and the terrible despair of the doctor in his far-flung practice in the Indies.

It was there also that I scribbled away at *The Bazaar of Lust* [26] whenever I had a spare minute. I submitted it to Proletkino, under the pseudonym . . . Taras Nemchinov. Nemchinov—that needs no explanation.

But Taras was a sort of protest at Grisha, who had called his son Douglas (he is now a lanky World War Two lieutenant), whereas I had insisted on Taras!

As for the story about Babel's *Maria*, we never exchanged so much as a word about it. But that was much later.[27]

Here, at the dacha in Nemchinovka, I first heard of Stefan Zweig from Babel.

Then I received a letter from him about his work on *Fouché*.[28]

Next, an invitation to meet him in Vienna, and visit Freud with him.

I was not able to make it.

We never met again.

We lost contact with each other.

In 1942 he committed suicide in Brazil. He and his wife gassed themselves.

Toller had hanged himself in 1939.[29]

I first met him in Berlin in 1929.

Mass Man never appealed to me.

Although I think that *Eugene the Unlucky* was a great work.

I embarrassed Toller as I had Zweig.

He received me in his two small clean rooms which were a little effeminate in their floral decorations.

Gesturing grandly, he said, 'Take whatever you would like for a memento.'

What should I take? Taking nothing might have caused offence.

On the wall hung two early Daumier lithographs. Not particularly good ones. They were in narrow gilt frames.

A cup, perhaps?

One of the little vases?

I was looking for things in these two rooms which he had a pair of.

There *was* something!

A Mexican horseman made of wickerwork—a toy which, in its style and method of weaving, looked like Russian bast-work.

I took that.

A little later—terrible embarrassment.

The horseman had belonged to Elisabeth Bergner.[30]

Oddly enough, later I spent fourteen months in Mexico!

The straw horseman that Ernst Toller gave Eisenstein. (Photo: Davlat Khudonyazarov)

But the only wickerwork toy I brought back was Toller's horseman . . .

And also a crocodile which I gave to Kapitsa.[31]

He used to collect crocodiles of every shape and size—something Rutherford[32] also did.

Pulgas vestidas[33]. Woodcuts by José Guadalupe Posada,[34] and much else besides. But the only wickerwork toy I took was the Toller-Bergner horseman!

Toys[1]

Firecke's corner-shop was a child's paradise.

Nuremberg tin soldiers in boxes made from bark.

Hindu soldiers.

Jungle men.

Red Indians.

Napoleonic soldiers.

A special delight was the large crate of odds and ends, which you could buy individually.

Model landscapes. The most involved manoeuvres could be planned using these models.

Favourites: a Red Indian, swimming (a half-figure)— Pencrow.

The Humpty Dumpty Circus. Toys with jointed limbs were special favourites. A donkey and a clown who could be made to adopt any position.

Andrei Melentevich (Andryusha) Markov was the son of Melenti Fyodosovich Markov, who ran the Riga-Oryol railway line.

Friendship in Riga.

They moved to St Petersburg.

Their residence in the Nicholas Station.[2]

Near the exit arch on the left (towards the Old Nevsky) there was a large room with a gallery.

The gallery was completely covered with sand and there was a broken but stunning toy train set.

Points. Signals. Bridges which crossed rivers of glass over blue paper. Stations. Lights.

I had never been much taken by machinery.

I had never opened up a watch.

Probably because I was so taken by machinery in another context—art—and so loved to open up psychological problems to do with art.

Playing with Andryusha, I was always a comical passenger (using the first toy to come to hand) who invariably missed his train, fell beneath the wheels, got the signals wrong and tried to

116

catch up with the express train by running along the rails. Everything that could go wrong, did.

Another friend, who was French, and whose name and surname I have forgotten, was the son of the owner of the pen factory.

I will never forget the rhythm of the machinery as it mixed the prepared nibs with the grinding oil, so that the finished product would not rust. This is why new 'greasy' pens do not write straight off: they do not hold the ink.

The father, the owner, was a ginger-haired, stout and unshaven character who resembled a very much fatter and more unkempt version of Zola, in his mature years.

There was a trio of plays we performed on Sundays, with him, Alyosha Bertels, and myself.

The happy ending of one of these plays.

Alyosha *en travestie.**

The French boy was dressed as an English 'bobby'. And I, for some reason, was dressed as a fantastic . . . rabbi (!) who married them.

---

* French: 'in drag'

With Maxim Strauch on the Riga coast

Names[1]

Somewhere, a very long time ago, Chukovsky very wittily defended the Futurists.[2]

He found the same abstract charm in their euphonious nonsense as we find in Longfellow's enumeration of Indian tribes. For us they too are utterly devoid of any sense, and their charm lies solely in the rhythm and phonetic features (in *Hiawatha:* 'Came Comanches . . . ' etc).

Sometimes, when I start remembering things, I lapse into an utterly abstract chain of names and surnames.

The Pension Koppitz.

Igrushcha (the Germanised pronunciation of the diminutive of Igor). And Arsik (from Arseny, a wanton, dumpy, pallid and capricious individual of my age) from Moscow. Frau Schaub, with her little dog—and the ruddy-cheeked, bare-kneed Tolya Schaub.

Esther and Frieda.

Maka and Viba Strauch.[3]

The architect, Felsko, from Riga, with his daughter—an ageing spinster. And Mr Torchiani, who had married her three years earlier. Frau Frisk from Norway, with the strange large earrings, brooches and rings.

Sapico-y-Sarra Lucqui, the Spanish consul.

Рига - Альбертовская ул.
Riga - Albert-Strasse.

The buildings on Albert-Strasse in Riga, designed by Mikhail Osipovich Eisenstein

Muzis[1]

A police superintendent can have a most unusual name.

Particularly if he is in Riga.

Well, who would have thought a police superintendent could be called . . . Muzis.

Nevertheless, he was.

My schoolfriend's father—the police superintendent—was called Muzis.

Muzis was the object of my envy.

Muzis had a fat, grease-stained notebook, crammed full with papers and notes—a notebook, with a rubber-band!

This is probably a hereditary feature for Muzises.

I can picture Muzis's father in my mind's eye, with his grease-stained notebook as he makes an arrest, or is on a search, or 'taking down the particulars'.

My father was an architect.

And when I think of him, it is blueprints, templates, set-squares, protractors and drawing-pens that I see.

Never notebooks.

Notebooks do not run in our family.

How I envied Muzis.

I envy him to this day.

Not because I never had any notebooks.

Even when I was at school, each year I would be given a new notebook with a stamped gold inscription on the cover: Comrade. That was the name of the typical Russian school notebook.

Not only that, but each year the purely Baltic German *Jugendkalender* came out.

The Russian-German mix of cultures was characterised by these two little books, and in the latter there was even a brief poem on this subject.

Strange how the mind can retain all sorts of rubbish.

But this scrap is quite apt here, since it bore directly upon my life:

121

Mikhail Osipovich Eisenstein with his colleagues of the Livonian Railway

I was born in Riga Town.

Erblickte ich das Licht der Welt [I first clapped eyes upon the world],

I was there for a long time,

Weil's mir terribly *da gefällt* [Because I like it terribly there].*

I really did live in Riga for a quite a long time, but not because I was particularly happy there.

It was because Papa worked as a senior engineer in the roads department of the Livonian provincial government, and was busy with an extensive architecture-cum-construction practice.

I think Papa built as many as fifty-three houses in Riga.

And there was an entire street in the crazy *art nouveau* style, which so transported my dear parent.

It was named in both the languages of Riga: *Albertovskaya ulitsa* [Russian] and *Albertstrasse* [German].[2]

Notebooks were disastrous for another reason.

I never could use them—I still cannot.

I never had anything to note or record in them!

This upsets me to this day.

My memory never lets me down.

The essential thing is always to be found in notes in files. I can never think up anything specially to record in my notebook.

Then again, these files are my cross.

They are many.

Endless.

And in each of them is a selection of articles on some sort of basic theme—*Belegmaterial**—some fantastic thought or passing fancy.

It is a common occurrence for a file to tear beneath the weight of demonstrative or instructive (illustrative) material; I pick up the theme, which was the point of a collection that can take a number of years to amass—and I promptly forget about it.

I should compile an 'inventory' of things I have not thought through to the end, or written up in full.

A catalogue, *sui generis*, of my debts to myself.

---

* In the original the first and third lines, and the word 'terribly' in the fourth line, are in Russian; the rest is in German, as here.

** German: 'illustrative material'

Madame Guilbert[1]

'Tu es folle, Yvette!' [You're mad, Yvette!] Sardou told her.[2]

She had a bold idea: she had to sing a song in which the head of a murderer falls from under the guillotine's blade, and she thought of putting a joint of pork into the cap she wears for the song.

'The thud of the meat hitting the stage sounds just like a falling head . . .'

Of course, she did not listen to Sardou. And the public, in an access of delight, leaped to its feet . . .

Paris. 1930. Madame Yvette Guilbert told me about this herself.

Why in Paris?

I was *en route* to America.

Why was I at Madame Yvette's?

Because I was mad with thirst in Paris: fresh spring had turned into dusty summer. Breathers—walks at sunset on the Ile Saint-Louis, past houses which could pass for a *Cyrano de Bergerac* set, although they were real villas like those which were covered in glory by the romance of the Three Musketeers; or the dizzy heights of society, penetrated by Rocambole, the latest paragon for youths.[3]

The *bal musette.*[4]

Since childhood—since my first visit to this marvellous city —I have associated Paris with dust. I was nine then. *Monsieur, Madame et bébé* were travelling—that is, father, mother and my governess.

I remember only one thing from that trip.

Yvette!

I cannot easily pin down when it was you entered the day-dreams of that well-brought-up boy from Riga with the Lord Fauntleroy ringlets and lace collar, but you were a symbol of Paris.

My father, most probably, returned with a picture of you.

Father always went to Paris in the summer. He brought back masses of . . . *articles parisiens* for friends and acquaintances. Postcards of Otero and Cléo de Mérode[5] with albums of photos that showed recognised beauties posing; albums in which slightly risqué and extremely sentimental upheavals in young maidens' destinies unfolded in a sequence of shots—the forerunners of cinema! Albums full of views of Nice, tinted blue at the top and pink at the bottom.

Father, who liked his ties to be brightly coloured.

Father, in the *maison de blanc*,* caught sight of a magnificent ruched tie. He took it to the counter. He did not wish to take . . . two. The question comes: 'And does your good wife have just the one leg?' Only then did he comprehend.

Father was one of the most flowery representatives of that architectural decadence—*style moderne*.**

Father was a reckless follower *de l'art pompier*.***

Pompeux in his behaviour.****

Arriviste.*****

A self-made man.

Owing to chance similarity of the sound of his surname and that of some castle or other, he felt he had pretensions to an Austrian title.

Father was a pillar of the Church and the autocracy. A real State Counsellor of the Dowager Empress Maria's school.[6]

Father had forty pairs of patent leather shoes and a list of their distinguishing features: 'scratched' and so on. His valet Ozols, in his greatcoat, would give him the pair he requested with the aid of the list, taking them from what looked like a multi-tiered rabbit hutch which hung in the corridor.

Father, who placed statues of human beings one and a half storeys high, stretched out as a decoration, on the corners of houses.

Father, who deployed women's arms, made from iron drainpipes and with gold rings in their hands, beneath the angle of the roof. In bad weather, it was fun watching the rain stream down between their tin legs . . .

---

    * French: 'draper's shop'
    ** The term used in Russia for *art nouveau*. (Ed.)
    *** French: 'pretentious art'
    **** In French and English in the original.
    ***** In French in the original.

Father, who triumphantly entwined in the sky the tails of the plaster lions—*lions de plâtre*—which were piled up on the rooftops.

Father himself was a *lion de plâtre*. Vainglorious, petty, too stout, industrious, unlucky, broken—but still he wore his white gloves (on weekdays!) and his collars were perfectly starched. And he bequeathed to me an unhealthy passion for winding layer upon layer—which I tried to sublimate into a fascination* for Catholic baroque and the over-elaborate work of the Aztecs.

Father, who instilled in me the whole melting-pot of petit-bourgeois, petty passions for self-improvement at the expense of others, but who was not able to see that an Oedipal protest would make me hate them even though they were part of my baggage. And instead of being invisibly intoxicated by them, the cold eye of the analyst and tally clerk would break down whatever charm they might have held.

Papa, who hung countless plates on the dining-room walls on wire 'spiders', above colour photographic reproductions of Makovsky's boyar weddings![7]

Papa—but enough!

This is not meant to be about fathers and sons. Nor do I want to present my late father—a typical bully about the house, and slave to Tolstoy's ideas of *comme il faut* [8]—with a list of grievances.

But it is interesting that my protest against what was 'acceptable' in behaviour and in art, and my contempt of authority, were certainly linked to him.

And—my debut in art—on that very day and at that very hour of his death in Berlin![9]

I learned of this . . . coincidence about three years later!

But I am lapsing into blank verse. I must stop.

---

* There is an illegible word here in the manuscript. (Ed.)

MilEngers[1]

Guess the derivation of this place-name: Anzhero-Sudzhensk.*

Give up?

A clue: there was once a town where convicts were made to do the construction work.

The engineers lived in one part, and the convicts in another.

So one can easily understand that these remarks relate to military engineers [*voennye inzhenery*] who in 1918 were called 'Voinzhi', or 'MilEngers'.

I have great respect for a high degree of professionalism.

It might be a barber giving me a shave.

An acrobat on his trapeze.

An expert smith working at his forge.

An experienced nurse tying a bandage.

A good surgeon at work with his scalpel.

I cannot readily say when this love was born in me.

But fascination with the polish of perfection in engineering is doubtless linked to Sergei Nikolaevich Peitsch.

Even the reverse E [Э] of my signature has faint traces in its outline of his dynamic P [П].

And how often did I repeat his instruction when he was confronted by uninspired plans for the defence installations around Gatchina, Dvinsk, Kholm or Nyandoma,[2] fronts which moved with him from 1918 to 1920:

'Just wishing won't make you an engineer.'

---

* A small mining town in western Siberia. The name suggests the Russian words for both 'engineer' and 'convict'. (Trans.)

127

Dead Souls[1]

The detective novel is a form that embraces a whole series of classic typical situations.

One of the most famous is the murder in a sealed room.

The door is locked. The key is on the inside. The window catches have not been touched. There is no other means of exit.

A mutilated corpse lies on the floor, but the murderer has vanished.

This is the situation in Edgar Allan Poe's *The Murders in the Rue Morgue* (or *Rue Trianon*, as he titled it in the first draft in his notebook).

This is also the crux of Gaston Leroux's *The Secret of the Yellow Room.*

And, later, of *The Canary Murder Case* by S. S. Van Dine.

Psychoanalysts ascribe the roots of this situation to our 'memories' of our pre-natal existence.[*]

The number of people in Poe's works who are locked up with no means of escape, sealed in or immured in stone cells is really very large.

There is *The Cask of Amontillado, The Black Cat, The Tell-Tale Heart* (where the old man's corpse lies under the floorboards), *The Pit and the Pendulum* . . .

And they all have the universally scary attraction of terror.

(Let us recall the role that *The Tell-Tale Heart* played in the plot of Dostoyevsky's *Crime and Punishment.*) Otto Rank saw a similar image of 'being locked in the womb' and 'escaping into the light' in the ancient legend of the Minotaur (Otto Rank, *Das Trauma der Geburt* [The Trauma of Birth]).

In the more contemporary derivatives of that legend, it is less the situation of the criminal extricating himself from an 'impossible' situation into the outside world, than the way in which the detective draws the truth out into the open: that is, the

---

[*] See for example the hefty two-volume *Psychoanalysis of Edgar Poe*, by Marie Bonaparte (Denoël et Steele, 1930). (E's note)

128

situation effectively operates on two levels.

In a direct sense and metaphorically—transposed from situation into principle.

At this point we can see that the latter—the transposing of a situation into a principle—can freely exist parallel to the primary, 'original' situation.

Furthermore, in that aspect, as principle, it has its place in every detective novel, for every detective ultimately draws the true picture of the crime 'out into God's daylight', out from the 'labyrinth' of errors, red herrings and dead ends.

And so the detective story, as a variety of genre fiction—in any of its forms—is historically allied to the Minotaur legend and by extension to those primary complexes which that legend serves to express through imagery.

One should on no account forget that the ancient legend is not an allegory. Allegory *consists* of an abstracted representation intentionally and arbitrarily assuming the form of a particular image. The figurative form of the expression is then like a myth—the one accessible means of 'making it familiar' and a comprehensible expression for consciousness. Only later does it attain the level at which it is able to put abstract notions into formulated concepts.

If we recall that a part of the allegory is about *truth*, sitting *in its well* and being raised up into the daylight, then we can see that the traditional image of truth itself lends itself to the same symbolism of birth. This can only confirm our ideas.

So, from the point of view of logic and evolution, it is as well that, historically, the first *pure* model of the genre, *The Murders on the Rue Morgue* (like *The Purloined Letter* by the same author), supplies both the principle and its direct subject-related (situational) realisation, *at one and the same time.*

So the *prerequisite basis* for the action remains in the situation of 'coming into God's daylight' (the 'conclusion'), while the *superstructure* over it is elaborated by the more or less ingenious routes to this conclusion (and it is interesting that even in the term 'disentangling the web' of intrigue we use the idea of the thread with which the hero found his way out of the 'labyrinth'!).

Poe, as is well known, had the murder committed by an orangutan. It could climb up chimney flues: a man could not.[2]

Gaston Leroux, having surrounded the father of the victim, Professor Stangerson, with experiments and problems to do with the 'disintegration of matter' (as if hinting at the criminal's ability to dissolve) provided another extremely ingenious solution.

The criminal vanishes because he is the sleuth, whom he turns into whenever necessary.

Van Dine has the criminal depart earlier, leaving a muffled gramophone playing a record of human speech. The hotel porter thought he was hearing the voices of people in the room when the Canary—a night-club singer—had in fact already been murdered.

As for the trick of the door sealed from the inside, that . . . but let us not give that away. Why deprive those who are thinking of reading the story of the pleasure of doing so?

Especially as everything that has been said of the utter impossibility and hopelessness of situations, which some people nevertheless managed to extricate themselves from, amounts here to no more than a lead-in to a similar situation in practical reality, which I once witnessed. I know the key to the riddle. It had all the savour of a detective story and was centred on a systematic swindle.

In the spring of 1920, the Revolutionary Tribunal heard a case brought against Ovchinnikov, the Senior Clerk of Works. He was a final-year student at the Institute of Civil Engineering; the court was the premises of the former cinema in Velikie Luki, which was where we had played *Marat* and *The Storming of the Bastille*.[3]

In the outlying sections of the military emplacements on the N— front, there was blatant embezzling on a large scale. Financial reserves and the level of social prosperity prevalent in the engineering and technical complement were clearly and demonstrably higher than the modest scaling of pay levels and rationing could have permitted.

There was no particular malice towards the Soviet state implicit in this embezzlement.

They were simply part and parcel of the methods and traditions of making the usual profits from building bridges, roads, state buildings or fortification works, that had yielded a 'natural' profit for the technical and engineering crew, in the days of tsarism.

The young Soviet state held somewhat different views on these traditions.

Especially in the context of the Civil War.

It meant to stamp out such abuses.

And on the initiative of Daude, the storeman, and a junior clerk (who for some reason had an Italian surname, which I have forgotten), a case was brought against Ovchinnikov.

I was sitting at the back of the gloomy hall where the case was being heard.

The 'caste secret' of the 'dead souls' embezzling system was preserved religiously by its initiates.

To the extent that even I, a young technician, was for many months unable to find out what it was, even though my position meant that I always attended when the local workers were being paid for their trench-digging in our section.

The prosecution's case collapsed. Their statements contained errors of fact and the case came to grief on the question of 'bribery' and 'payments' to avoid work.

The ghost of a slaughtered cow hovered, like the shade of Hamlet's father, in the courtroom, calling attention to herself. It was allegedly given to Ovchinnikov as a bribe, to release people from work when they should not have been.

The cow's ghost demanded vengeance.

But it was immediately laid when it was proved that the carcase had been fully paid for.

The anger of the tribunal chairman—a pale, ginger-haired man with piercing deep-set eyes and in a sombre suit—crashed down with such fury upon the shamed prosecution that the question of where the money to buy the cow had come from was never asked.

It was the same story with two sacks of flour, and the young lads who had arraigned their superiors for abuse of funds came within an inch of having to answer charges of slander.

It happened also with the suggestion that warrants had been forged, or imaginary names inserted into the payroll.

By this time I knew how the system worked and, although Ovchinnikov belonged to a different works district, I very much doubt that it was any different there.

It was staggering to see how the case failed through ignorance and how Ovchinnikov, with the friendly approval of those assembled, walked triumphantly to freedom, vindicated.

But what was the system?

First, I should explain the procedure for pay day.

Intended as a safeguard against abuses, it was like an impregnable fortress with doors locked from the inside, and windows too small to admit the passage of a human body, as you will find in the pages of Leroux's *The Yellow Room*, or the hotel room of the murdered 'Canary'.

At the pay session were:

the clerk of works,

a timekeeper,

a technician,

the cashier,

a visiting representative of the government inspectorate, who travelled around the districts and always sat in on pay days, and

two people as witnesses for those being paid.

The order was as follows:

The wages committee sat at the desk.

The cashier counted out the money again.

The sum was recorded.

The paying began.

The workers came up in turn.

There would typically be about a hundred.

Surnames were called out.

The papers checked.

The time-keeper found the surname on his list. He put a tick next to it.

The technician made a tick in a second list.

The man received his money.

He went away.

This went on for five or six hours.

In the same place, they would then calculate how much had been paid.

This figure was registered.

Then the residual money the cashier had was checked.

The figures tallied.

This fact was registered also.

Sergei Eisenstein with his colleagues of the 18th Sappers, Dvinsk, 1919

The clerk of works, the time-keeper, the technician and the cashier all signed the list.

The witnesses added their crosses.

And everything was certified by the representative of the government inspectorate . . .

One might well wonder how anyone could embezzle anything.

Nevertheless, during this one operation, roughly twenty per cent of the sum paid out (it will soon become clear why twenty) passed, unseen, into the pockets of 'interested parties'.

There were two ways of playing it.

With the representative's participation.

Or without.

There were two of them on our sector.

I can only remember the first name and patronymic of one.

Sergei Nikolayevich.

He had been a lawyer in civilian life.

In our play *The Storming of the Bastille*, he acted a red-headed aristocrat who reacted to Camille Desmoulins' fiery rhetoric with sarcasm.

And he refused point-blank to strike any illegal bargain with the engineers.

All I remember the other by was his surname, his pale complexion, grey moustache, slightly curly hair and noble bearing.

He was called Lisyansky.

And he obligingly took part in everything.

The first case is of course the interesting one.

The operation itself requires great skill.

Faultless coordination.

Sleight of hand.

'Dead souls' were scattered among the hundreds of real workers. They comprised about twenty per cent of the total (why twenty, exactly, will become clear later).

The cashier knew the precise sum the 'dead souls' had earned.

It was the job of the time-keeper and cashier to conduct parallel but separate 'second payments' during the paying out, which passed in the feverish activity peculiar to the allocation of money.

In other words.

The time-keeper had to find time to 'insert ticks' between the real surnames and opposite the fictitious ones; the cashier, at the start of the paying out, had to 'pull out' the required additional sum from the total checked for payments:

a phenomenal memory was required of the time-keeper and technician (who held the second list and was also a participant in this), for inserting the 'dead souls' among the living;

and the cashier needed the sleight of hand of a fairground conjurer.

The cashier, Kozello, father to two charming daughters, did this brilliantly.

(He later died of typhoid.)

To avoid disaster, the time-keeper, Dmitriev, inserted the surnames of his school friends into the real list.

It was obvious that everything tallied.

And was there any chance of being exposed?

Of course there was.

Thanks to the Comte de Rochefort. That is not the Rochefort who published his unrivalled *La Lanterne*, a pamphlet aimed at Napoleon III. During my first days in Paris on a visit, I tracked down twenty copies of the first editions of this charming publication in the cellar of a second-hand dealer. Apart from the brilliance of the pamphlet itself, with the unsurpassable play on words of the first line of the first number, Rochefort used the most ingenious routes to send his illicit publication into Paris from Belgium.[4]

Ne plus ultra—referring to the means of despatching the editions of this periodical from Belgium (where it was printed): he sent them inside plaster busts of the emperor himself.*

I do not mean that Rochefort, but the count, the author of the well known book *On Piece Work*.

According to this system, norms were set for the amount of work done (and still are, I believe).

It is enough to check, on the spot, the amount of earthwork

---

* This device was used in a Conan Doyle story. And also, with a famously ironic undertone, in *The Twelve Chairs* by Ilf and Petrov. (E's note)

completed, which in our case was the length of trench dug, to establish the actual number of workers who accomplished it.

However, the trenches on the plots assigned to our managers might be measured by any unit—from the approximate three-pace metre, with a count of one-two-three, to the precision of a tape measure—but the amount of work done always and invariably matched the amount set on the workforce sheet.

Shortfalls of twenty per cent in the length of the trenches (equal to the amount of excess in the register) were nowhere discovered.

So where lay the solution to this 'second line' of the embezzlers' defences, protecting them from the courts?

A shortfall in the work completed would have been too obvious.

It was in that twenty per cent, which I have twice mentioned in my description of the 'plan of action', that the secret lay.

As a result of wartime conditions, the Comte de Rochefort's norms for piece work were officially reduced.

But this reduction was never introduced!

In the accounts, the work was reckoned with the official reduction.

But the previous norms were followed when working.

The difference was the source of the prosperity.

This was the way it worked when the inspector did not take part in the game.

Everything was simplified when the inspector was party to it —it became child's play.

The additional ticks were filled in after the money had been paid out, over a leisurely glass of tea.

All the necessaries were seen to 'on the nod'. Their time was made worthwhile.

Inspectors who refused to comply were 'taught a lesson'— or, more accurately, punished.

Sergei Nikolayevich was driven for miles around the villages, shivering with cold and drenched to the skin though he was. Without any further ceremony he was made to attend the payment session.

He was not offered so much as a drink of tea, never mind supper and a bed for the night.

Cold and wet and stinking of dog he slept in the office on a desk, with only an overcoat for cover and a clear conscience for his pillow!

Dvinsk[1]

On the subject of beds.

World literature has two superlative pronouncements to make on this matter.

One is in Groucho Marx's book, called *Beds*.[2]

It is in this book that you will find that notable chapter worthy of Tristram Shandy, which consists of a heading above a blank page, and the author's footnote to that heading.

It is the first chapter in the book with the general heading: 'On The Advantages of Sleeping Alone'.

The footnote at the bottom of the blank page, which comprises that chapter, says: 'The author did not wish to say anything about this.'

It is easy to guess what the following chapters deal with.

The other one is Maupassant's.

It comes not from a book, but from a small sketch with the same title—'Beds'.

There you come across the charming thought that the bed is the real sphere of man's activities: it is here that he is born, he loves, and dies.

A man's bed is his fiefdom.

And God himself cannot lay claim to this achievement of man's.

For gods, as this sketch continues, are born in mangers and die on crosses.

. . . I slept on the surface of a mirror, in Dvinsk.

There were no beds in the flat—it had been hastily allotted to me after the Red Army had taken Dvinsk. The trestle beds were still not ready.

But a mirrored wardrobe stood proudly in the empty flat.

It was laid on its back.

A straw mattress was laid on top of the mirrored doors, which reflected the world.

And there on the mattress was I.

Lord, I feel I have to find a metaphorical interpretation, an image, in this situation.

But nothing comes.

So I shall leave myself lying on the straw mattress, placed between me and the mirrors of the wardrobe doors . . .

Sergei Eisenstein, the Red Army soldier, Vozhega, 1919

A Night in Minsk[1]

I remember a night in Minsk.

The second year—

the front.

The Political Administration of the Western Front.

The painter, from the mobile troupe of actors at the front, was rolling about on his bed, dishevelled. He had to undertake the most unpleasant task of his life: to take a cardinal decision about what he was going to be, and how. I know how difficult it was: I was the painter.

A sleepless night.

I rolled about on the bed, feverishly.

There was a document on the table next to me.

It was the resolution of the Council of People's Commissars: the students could go back.

It had come that afternoon.

A summons to the Institute in Petrograd.

And that very day I had received permission from the authorities to go to . . . Moscow.

I had earned it (painting the carriages, the collapsible stage).[2]

There—the Institute.

Here—the Department of Oriental Languages. A thousand Japanese words. A hundred characters.

The Institute?

A stable way of life?

I felt a little sorry about the energy I had invested in the Institute. Every branch of higher mathematics was on offer. Right up to integrated differential equations (how much did mathematics teach me about discipline!).

But I felt it might be time to see some Japanese theatre.

I was ready to cram and cram words. And those astonishing phrases from a different way of thinking.

Before that, I wanted to see the theatres in Moscow.

The career that my father had so carefully sketched out for me had been lost.

By morning my mind was made up.

The horse broke his harness.

The die was cast.

The Institute was abandoned.

Call it mysticism.

But my break with the past happened as my father died of a heart attack, miles away.

I learned of the coincidence of the dates when I received the news of his death two years later.

Towards the end of the Civil War that had scattered us (through intervention and collapse) to different ends of the Russian Empire.

Nuné[1]

To this day I am unable to read calmly about the one unique moment in other people's lives. That is the moment which ends with the magical words: '. . . and he woke up the next morning famous.'[2]

Once it was out of day-dreaming and envy. But now . . . I enjoy reminiscing.

Be it in the biography of Zola, who dashed off—still in his bedroom slippers—to the shop on the corner the morning after his first book was published to buy a newspaper—and was dismayed to find there was no review in the usual place. And then light dawned: there was a review. There was! And in the least expected place: on the front page!

'. . . and he woke up the next morning famous.'

Or in the biography of George Antheil—the success of his first concert, or, more accurately, the first success of his concerto.[3]

'. . . and he woke up the next morning famous', comes the constant refrain.

So it was to be with the première of *Potemkin* in Berlin.[4]

The film was shown in a small cinema on Friedrichstrasse.

Vague rumours reached Moscow that it had gone down a bomb [*Bombenerfolg*].

The Germans in those days were busier with bombs of that sort.

Telegrams from Berlin.

Must leave soonest.

Reinhardt ecstatic.[5]

Asta Nielsen.[6]

An evening gala performance was being planned.

The film transferred from Friedrichstrasse to the very centre: the Kurfürstendamm.

Queues.

Queues.

No tickets left.

The film was showing at several cinemas.

Nina Agadzhanova-Shutko in December 1925

Sergei Eisenstein in December 1925

Twelve, in fact.

Newspapers trumpeted: '. . . And he woke up the next day . . .'

I did not make it to Berlin.

I could not get a train for the gala performance.

I could not go by plane.

All because of Kaunas.

The aerodrome in Kaunas was flooded.

The thaw in the spring of 1926 was a fateful phenomenon for air travel as well.

Telegrams. Telegrams. Telegrams.

Then a hit in America.

And again: '. . . And he woke up the next day famous.'

It is a marvellous feeling, waking up famous.

And then to reap the harvest.

Invitations to lecture in Buenos Aires.

To find that one is famous in remote silver mines somewhere in the Sierra Madre, where the film was screened once for the miners of Mexico.

To be embraced by strangers in the workers' districts of Liège, where the film was watched in secret.

To hear from Alvarez del Vayo, before the days of Republican Spain, how he smuggled *Potemkin* into Madrid.[7]

Or suddenly. In a small Paris café, to hear from two dusky oriental ladies, who were sitting by chance at the same small marble table, and were students at the Sorbonne: 'Everyone's heard about you, in Java!'

Or in another ridiculously small club outside the city suddenly to earn a warm handshake from a black waiter as I was leaving, 'a token of gratitude for your work in cinema . . .'

As I approached the tennis court, Chaplin's exclamation greeted me: 'Just seen *Potemkin*. You know, it hasn't aged a bit these last five years? Same as ever!'

And all this was the result of just three months' (!) work on a film. (That includes two weeks spent on the montage!)

It is easy now, twenty years later, to cast my mind over the withered laurels.

To laugh off the three months' work—a record.

It is more important though to recall the period leading up to the plunge, from which our young collective emerged as record breakers.

And in first place, one should remember and remember again Nuné.

So as not to frighten the reader, let me say straight away that Nuné is the Armenian form of Nina.

Nuné is Nina Ferdinandovna Agadzhanova.[8]

The Strike had just been released.

Awkward. Pointed. Unexpected. Unrepentant.

And uncommonly pregnant with almost everything that was to emerge, in maturity, during the later years of my work.

A typical 'beginner's piece' (like Dovzhenko's *Zvenigora* [1928], Pudovkin's *Chess Fever* [Shakhmatnaya goryachka, 1926], *The Adventures of Oktyabrina* [Pokhozhdeniya Oktyabriny, 1924] by Kozintsev and Trauberg, the men who made the classic Maxim Trilogy).[9]

The picture was as tousled and pugnacious as I was in those far-off years.

Skirmishes with the management of Proletkult (the picture was set up under the joint aegis of Goskino and Proletkult).

Writing the screenplay.

During the filming.

After the picture was released.

Finally, a split after five years' work in Proletkult theatre and my first steps in cinema.

A polemic.[10]

An unequal combat between a man and an organisation (it was yet to be dethroned for its claims to have a monopoly on proletarian culture).[11]

At any moment, the matter could turn into 'persecution'.

For my part, I was rather like an impetuous tiger-cub not quite sure of his legs, reared on the milk of theatre, but who had been allowed a small taste of the blood of freedom as a film-maker!

My stance was absurd, dangerous, and not at all advisable for someone who wished to make any progress in his work and creativity.

At moments like this, you need a friendly hand.

Friendly advice.

A word that puts everything into perspective and soothes the unruly and foolish aggressiveness to which you can resort so readily in the heat of the moment. How I missed such a hand later on, in the many difficult and sometimes tragic reversals that beset my later life in cinema . . .

Which is why I am writing about Nuné.

Nina Ferdinandovna Agadzhanova—short, blue-eyed, shy and infinitely modest—was the one human being who extended a helping hand to me at a very critical period of my creative life.

She had been commissioned to write a screenplay for the jubilee of 1905.

She recruited me for this and with a firm hand she set me on the *terra firma* of concrete work, despite all the temptations to carry on polemics and a wilful longing for a fight, while I was threatened with unpleasant things by Proletkult.

Nuné, as she sat next to her small samovar, had an amazing talent for making people pull themselves together. She put countless numbers of people who had suffered a knock to their self-esteem back on a rational and creative path.

She did this selflessly and with great concern, the same way a child might pick up a maimed grasshopper or fledgling fallen from its nest, or an adult bird with broken wing, and keep it in a matchbox, or make an artificial nest from remnants of material and cotton wool.

How many of those damaged and bruised rebels (more often than not Leftists and aesthetic extremists) did I encounter at her comfortable tea table?

This illusion of an idiosyncratic moral ark offering its passengers a temporary refuge from the vicious and harsh winds that raged outside, was strengthened by Beauty, a very high-spirited terrier who would always bound into the room; and by a living 'dove of peace'. I gave it to Nuné after a quarrel, by way of a peace offering. I took it round to her the next day, with a palm frond from the undertaker's that occupied the corner building of Malaya Dmitrovka Street, diagonally opposite the Strastnoy Monastery, before that was demolished.[12]

(Incidentally, two hours after its arrival at the flat on

Strastnoy Boulevard, this dove managed—during its panicky flights from sideboard to screen, from chandelier to telephone, and from the cornice of the tiled stove to the shelf with the complete Byron —so utterly to befoul both rooms that it was almost banished in disgrace.)

Sometimes it was as though we were in Doctor Aibolit's[13] surgery for animals, only magnified—from rabbits with bandaged paws, or hippopotamuses with toothache, right up to adults whose self-esteem had been deflated by life, or whose principles were suffering from a feverish loss of direction, the victims of chance adversities in their art, or people whose lives forever bore the stamp of failure.

The harmlessness of these rabbits with their bandaged paws was most frequently more than relative . . .

It is enough to recall that it was precisely here, at Nuné's, that I first met (and greatly liked) Kazimir Malevich, on the same footing as 'Gabriel', a silvery haired actor who wore a black velvet shirt, or 'Vasya', the morose inventor, who were yet to 'go out into the world in life'. Malevich was indefatigable, stubborn and stood up for his principles. This was during his extremely bitter struggle for the direction of the Institute, which he governed with a fair degree of aggressiveness.[14]

But it is difficult to overestimate the whole moral significance of these evenings for those seekers, who were particularly extremist and therefore frequently found themselves in conflict with the daily order of things, with the generally accepted norm of the arts with its recognised traditions.

The most important thing was that here each could derive strength from the realisation that the Revolution needed everyone. And everyone exactly as he was, in his unique, pointed, individual way.

And what you definitely should not attempt was to take a plane to your idiosyncrasies and smooth them off—which was what the RAPP (Russian Association of Proletarian Writers)[15] bandwagon was making such a song and dance about in those days. No, you had to find the proper way of applying your own particular idiosyncrasy to the task of building the Revolution. And it was most often the case that you had only yourself to blame for failure or adversity, either mistakenly applying yourself to something that was not your bent, or failing through too faint-hearted a quest for that very thing where the full flourishing of individual talent and capabilities coincided with the needs of the situation which you had tackled!

And here, on this path, each realised this and found his own moral support and help. Not only in word.

But often in deed.

That was exactly how I found it.

But Nuné did more.

She not only drew me into a highly estimable project.

But she instilled in me a true sense of the historical revolutionary past.

Her youth notwithstanding, she had herself been a participant—and a crucial one, at that—in the underground movement before the October Revolution.

And so in conversations with her any typical episode of the past struggle became a 'reality' pulsing with life, no longer a dry line in an official history or a dainty morsel for a detective story. (Incidentally, that is the most repellent light in which to view the episodes of the past!)

For her, the question of the Revolution was a domestic one.

A question of routine.

But it was also the highest ideal, it was the ambition of her youth, that she wholeheartedly dedicated to the good of the working class.

The 'incomprehensible' story of the creation of *Potemkin* is well enough known. The story of how this film was born out of half a page of the colossal screenplay for *1905* which Nina Ferdinandovna Agadzhanova and I 'built up' in a joint effort in the summer of 1925.

Sometimes, while leafing through the abundance of your earlier creative work, you come across this industrious 'Titan' with his atavistic thirst, gulping down the immeasurably wide flood of events of 1905 and putting them down on countless sheets of paper.

There is just so much of it!

Even if only in passing.

Even if only an allusion.

Even if only two lines.

It is an amazing sight.

How could two people, in full possession of their faculties, and with proven professional experience, have supposed that all of that could have been set up and filmed? And all in one film, too!

And then you may start looking at all this from another angle.

It suddenly becomes clear that 'this' is far from being a screenplay.

That this voluminous exercise book is a gigantic summary of a fixed and painstaking study of an epoch.

A study that assimilated the character and spirit of the times.

More than simply an array of typical facts and episodes: it was an attempt to get to grips with the dynamism of the epoch, to feel its pulse, the sinews within that connected the different events.

In brief, an extensive summary of that preparatory work, without which the feeling of 1905 as a whole could not pour itself into each particular episode of *Potemkin.*

It was only by drinking this in, breathing it, living it, that the production could talk confidently of 'an ironclad, sailing through the squadron without a single shot being fired.'

Or:

'The tarpaulin separates the convicts at their execution'—

and to the surprise of cinema historians, one short line of 'screenplay' was transformed into an utterly unexpected emotional 'high point' of the film.

And so, line by line, the screenplay became scene after scene. Because it was not the sketchy notes of a libretto that supplied the true emotional depth, but that complex of feelings that blew up like a whirlwind in a series of vivid images at the mere passing mention of the events that I had recently relived.

Chinoiserie of the first water!

Because the Chinese do not value the accuracy of what is said, written or sketched, but the profusion of the concomitant emotions and ideas that is evoked by what has been sketched, written or said.

151

What blasphemy for those who believed in the orthodox forms of 'ironclad' screenplays![16]

How they reproved scriptwriters for daring to express themselves in this way!

We could do with more writers of that school now. People who, on top of all the usual contrivances of their art, could instil in their directors a sense of the historical and emotional integrity of the epoch with the penetration of an Agadzhanova!

And the directors should breathe those themes as freely as we did; freely and unerringly when we were at work on *Potemkin.*

Without being deflected from the sense of truth, we were able to indulge any whim or fancy, bringing it into any event or scene we wished, even if it were not in the original libretto (like the 'Odessa Steps'!), and any unforeseeable detail (such as the mist at the funeral scene!).

But Nuné Agadzhanova did much more than this.

She led me to the historical revolutionary present day via the historical revolutionary past.

Nuné was the first Bolshevik civilian I had met—all the others had sat on military committees (during construction work in the Civil War, in which I served from 1918) or they were 'senior staff' (the First Workers' Theatre where I worked as an artist and director from 1920). She was quite simply a human being.

For an intelligent person who came to the Revolution after 1917, there was an unavoidable stage of 'me' and 'them', before the two concepts merged in the Soviet Revolutionary 'we'.

And Nuné Agadzhanova, this short, blue-eyed, shy, infinitely modest and kind woman was a pillar of strength for me as I made this transition.

And for that she has my warmest thanks . . .

'The Twelve Apostles'[1]

1

I hate it when people say, 'First catch your hare.'

Furthermore, it is quite out of place here.

Having said that, if you want to make a film about a battleship, first catch your . . . battleship.

And if the story of the battleship is to be set in 1905, then no other ship will do, but the type that existed in 1905.

Over the course of twenty years—we are talking now about 1925—warships underwent a drastic change in appearance.

In the summer of 1925, there were no ironclads of the right type to be found in the Baltic Fleet at Luga Bay in the Gulf of Finland—or in the Black Sea Fleet.

Particularly not in the Black Sea: Wrangel[2] had taken the warships, even those of the old type, from there and scuppered most of them.

The cruiser 'Komintern' rocked merrily up and down at her roadstead off the Sebastopol coast.

But she was not at all what we needed. She did not have that distinct breadth of beam, worthy of a circus horse; a quarterdeck; nor the bridgehead, the scene of that famous drama at Tendra which it was our job to recreate . . . [3]

The various parts of 'Potemkin' herself had long since been scattered to the four winds of history, and the heavy plating that had once protected her flanks had vanished without trace.

However, our cinema intelligence network reported that, even if 'Prince Potemkin of Tauride' could not be found, then her sister ship, the once mighty and glorious 'The Twelve Apostles', was still extant.

Moored fast to the rocky shore, held by iron anchors to the unyielding sandy seabed, her once heroic hull stood in one of the remotest inlets of the so-called Sukharnaya Balka.

Sukharnaya Balka was one of the most secret inlets of the Sebastopol roadstead, a restricted naval base.

Photo of Eduard Tisse, dedicated to Eisenstein with the words: 'To dear Sergei Mikhailovich. Mines, twelve apostles, fresh air and water. Funny, wasn't it? Eisenstein. Tisse, 5/10/25, Odessa.'

And for a very good reason.

It was there, among the caves where the convolutions of the gulf extended deep inside the bowels of the cliffs, that hundreds of thousands of mines were stored. At the entrance, like the vigilant Cerberus on a leash, lay the rusty grey rectangular hull of 'The Twelve Apostles'.

But the gun turrets, masts, flagstaffs and captain's bridge were nowhere to be seen on the huge, wide spine of this sentinel whale.

Time had taken its toll.

And only the occasional rumbling from her many decked iron belly came as answer to the knocking of trolleys that carried the heavy, death-dealing cargo from her metal vaults: mines, mines, mines.

'The Twelve Apostles' had become an arsenal.

Which was why her grey hull had been moored so painstakingly tight against the rock:

Mines hate sudden knocks and shun disturbances; they demand peace and quiet.

'The Twelve Apostles' seemed frozen into timeless immobility, as still as the twelve stone statues of Christ's disciples on either side of Romanesque portals. They were grey, still, eroded by winds and worn smooth by storms, like the sides of an iron nave in an iron cathedral, up to its middle in the tranquil waters of Sukharnaya Balka . . .

But the iron whale had to be woken up one more time.

She had to gird her loins once again.

She had to turn her nose—which seemed to be nuzzling against the cliffs—round towards the open sea.

The ironclad lay near the rocky shore itself, parallel with it.

But the 'drama at Tendra' took place on the open sea. It was impossible, either from the side or head-on, to film the ship in such a way that that the looming, sheer black cliffs did not intrude into the viewfinder.

However, the sharp eye of Lyosha Kryukov, the assistant director who had sought out the grand old iron lady among the secret waters of Sebastopol, had seen a means of overcoming even this obstacle.

Eisenstein's assistants, the 'iron five': *[bottom to top]* Grigori Alexandrov, Maxim Strauch, Mikhail Gomorov, Alexander Antonov, Alexander Levshin. Sebastopol, 1925

If we turned the mighty hulk through ninety degrees, the ship would lie perpendicular to the shore; and this way, filmed from the bows, the clefts in the surrounding cliffs would not appear in the background; and seen from the side, she would appear to stand out against the horizon for her entire length!

And so she seems to be on the open sea.

Startled seagulls, used to seeing her as a rocky perch, hovered above her. Their flight heightens the illusion.

Nobody breathed as the iron whale was turned around.

A special dispensation from the Black Sea Fleet Command set the iron titan's nose against the open sea for the last time. She seemed eager for the briny air of the sea after the stale odour of shoreline mud.

The mines, slumbering in her belly, doubtless noticed nothing while this manoeuvre was under way. But it was imperative that no axe should disturb them as the plywood superstructure was being erected on the deck of the real vessel.

We were able to recreate the external features of the battleship 'Potemkin' exactly, from laths, girders and sheets of plywood, using the old Admiralty blueprints.

This is almost a symbol of the film itself: recreating the past, through the medium of art, and on a factually accurate basis.

But not so much as a jerk to the left or the right!

Not one inch must she move sideways!

Otherwise the illusion of the open sea would be lost.

Otherwise the grey cliffs would peer archly into the lens, like the faded beauties looking into the mirror in Goya's etchings: 'And so till death itself'.[4]

The implacable constraints of space kept us in check.

The deadlines were no less implacable.

We had to deliver the picture on the anniversary, and that concentrated the mind wonderfully.

'The perspectives of the imagination', as Yuri Olesha described the irrepressible boisterousness of fantasy, were debarred.[5]

The chains and anchors of the old battleship's hull, rusting in the sea, kept us in check.

Fettered by the constraints of space, and anchored to deadlines, we were prevented from indulging in too much invention and extravagance.

It may be those very factors that gave the film its strictness and elegance.

Mines, mines, mines.

Not for nothing do they keep rolling out of my pen on to the page. All our work was influenced by the mines.

Smoking was forbidden.

Banging too hard was forbidden.

Even being on deck without a special reason was forbidden.

More terrible than the mines was the mine who supervised us —the guardian of the mines. And his name?

Comrade G - L - A - Z - A - S - T - I - K - O - V !*

It is no pun. It is a complete description of the internal substance of this man with the ever-vigilant eye, this Argus protecting the serried ranks of mines, that lay beneath our feet, from sparks, from undue disturbance, from detonation . . .

It should have taken us months to unload the mines, but we had a deadline of two weeks, if we were to complete the film in time for its screening on the anniversary!

Try filming a mutiny in those conditions!

But Russians can overcome any obstacle[6] and the mutiny was filmed!

True, there is a side view of the battleship in the picture . . . but this was taken in the Moorish halls of the Sandunov Baths in Moscow, the grey hull of a model battleship rocking in the water.

2

The mines rolled around in the hold of the ancient battleship, and shuddered as the historical events were thunderously recreated on the upper decks.

And the screen off-shoot caught something of their explosive force.

The screen image of the old mutineer gave considerable cause for concern to the censors, as well as the police and police guards in many European countries.

---

* Meaning in Russian someone who has prominent or large eyes. (Trans.)

Above Alexander Levshin and Eisenstein on the ironclad 'The Twelve Apostles' *Below* Eisenstein made up as the ship's chaplain, ready to replace him in the fall from the gangway.

It was no less of a mutineer in the deep waters of cinema aesthetics.

But, after causing something of a stir in Europe, it set off like Columbus across the Atlantic, to discover America.

Cognoscenti received it very warmly.

But . . . how to get it on the screen?

1926.

The première, in Atlantic City.

Many years after *Potemkin* had been released in America, I had the good fortune to stroll along this new Via Appia, a waterfront revelry of shows and entertainments.

The promenade stretches for miles.

Towering hotels and in front of them, rows of theatres, concert halls and shops.

And a whole strand of 'cinematographs'.

On the day the film was screened—if memory serves me right—this battery of cinemas was firing such massive shells as Fred Niblo's *Ben Hur* [USA, 1926], King Vidor's *The Big Parade* [USA, 1925], James Cruze's *Old Ironsides* [USA, 1926] and Dupont's *Variété* [also known as *Variety* and *Vaudeville*, Germany, 1925].

No easy matter to break through such a squadron!

Furthermore, these films packed out whole rows of cinemas, leaving the venue for *Potemkin* out on a limb; even though it was a large cinema, it was right at the end of the left-hand flank of the battery of cinemas of Atlantic City.

It was a far cry from when *Potemkin* was screened in Cuba, in a bullring for the masses. 'Just one thing had me worried,' the proprietor of the cinema told me later. 'And that was, how was I going to get those people walking about out there to come to my cinema? Once they had got that far they were sure to take a look and, once they had taken a look, they would be sure to advertise the film all along the promenade. But how was I going to get them to come in the first place?'

The day of the première approached.

I grew increasingly nervous.

All the other cinemas had full houses.

What hope did that cinema have, all on its own? What hope for the picture, that came from a remote country, without any big names starring?

Evening came on.

It grew cool.

A thousand holidaymakers left the beaches.

A thousand others who had hidden from the sun poured out of their hotels to take the evening air.

A thousand pairs of feet lazily scraped the endless seafront.

And the owners of even lazier feet were borne in rickshaws by muscular blacks in white jackets and peaked caps.

Peace and quiet . . .

Almost as it is in the film— the scene of tranquillity before the hail of bullets sweeps the Odessa steps . . .

And also as in the film, there came a:

'Suddenly!'

Suddenly there was a penetrating howl of sirens.

One. Another. A third.

And people were already swept to the side, a hasty retreat; they ran off the terraces, leaped out of their rickshaws, and ran along the pavement, colliding with one other.

'Fire! Fire!'

They were not on fire.

There was no building on fire attracting them.

They were driven on by curiosity.

Thirsty for a spectacle.

The fire had broken out on the extreme left-hand side of the seafront. At least, that was where the flashing lights of the magnificent fire-engines were racing towards.

The firemen were headed there.

That was where the desperate wail of the alarm was coming from.

A thousand pairs of feet began running.

A thousand people began hurrying.

A thousand pairs of eyes scanned the buildings on either side with interest.

A thousand noses sniffed the air expectantly, trying to detect the smell of burning.

It was a false alarm.

Someone had broken the glass in error.

And the only spectacle—which could make up for the disappointment—was the figure of the cinema proprietor cursing bitterly as he paid the fine for his mistake: it was in his cinema that a passer-by had set off the alarm, before melting into the crowd.

Not a fire exactly, but still a talking-point . . .

A crowd formed around the pair as they exchanged angry words.

It milled beneath the cinema's awning.

But the argument did not escalate into a fight.

Another disappointment.

But the bored crowd, hungry for another diversion, hit upon the cunningly placed advertising hoardings.

Stills, showing boats of some sort.

Crowds, it looked like, running down a massive flight of steps.

Exactly as that crowd had run when it heard the fire alarm . . .

A huge female face; broken pince-nez; a missing eye . . .

The unusual title: *The Battleship 'Potemkin'* . . .

Without realising it, the crowd was swallowed up by the grilles of the ticket windows and the turnstiles, sucked into the yielding swamp of the carpets in the lower foyer, and was held in the firm grasp of the capacious seats.

The show began . . .

The arguing at the entrance stopped as abruptly as if a wizard had waved his wand.

Out of the corner of his eye, the proprietor noticed that the auditorium was full; that the tickets for the next showing were all sold out too . . .

And the long-wished-for sign hung in the box-office window: 'Tickets for tomorrow's performance on sale now'.

From the next day onward, there was no keeping people away.

'That was done to attract the public's attention,' said the owner smiling. 'And so, occasionally, smashing a small pane of glass can help you break box-office records. The hooligan who smashed that pane which did so much good was me, of course!'

3

'They led an elderly Jew, who was crying, out from beneath the awning of my cinema . . .'

So the proprietor continued.

'The picture often made people cry. But some inner sense told me that something was wrong here.'

He sent ushers after the old man.

They caught up with him.

He shed bitter tears in the director's office.

'Were you in Odessa in 1905?'

'Did you lose family there?'

'Or perhaps you were . . .'—the proprietor's voice cracked with emotion—'perhaps you were among those the Cossacks chased down the steps?'

He waited for the answer with bated breath.

What a stroke of luck! Such great advertising copy falling into his hands like that!

The elderly Jew blew his nose.

Dried his tears.

Heavy sobbing interrupted his story as he told of something quite different.

More remarkable than that.

He did not run down the steps.

He was not sent flying by the Cossacks' whips.

Soldiers did not open fire on him.

Because he was one of them.

Yes.

In those days he had been a volunteer in the tsarist army.

He had served in the Odessa garrison.

On that memorable day he was called out of the barracks along with the others.

Along with the others he was sent to the steps at Odessa.

And, along with the others, he fired round after round.

With the others, he fired into the dark, ill-defined, incomprehensible mass which swarmed at the base of the monumental flight of steps.

And suddenly only now,

after twenty years,

he saw exactly what it was they were shooting at.

Only now did he understand that they were not firing warning shots, but were shooting living people, living flesh.

Sobbing, he gasped in his chair.

It took twenty years and one Soviet film to open his eyes to the tragic paradox of his contribution to the events at Odessa.

On that day twenty years ago, the frenzy of the Black Hundreds began.[7]

The ashes of the sacked port were still glowing.

And in the reflected light of the approaching wave of blood, our man first deserted the garrison's punitive expedition, and on reaching Romania emigrated to America (he had relatives in Chicago).

'This story is of course colourful,' said the proprietor through a cloud of smoke, 'but it was not appropriate for an advert, sadly . . .'

4

Another person who had been there caused a more sensational interest.

His story got into the papers.

And not just the papers.

But even into court . . .

The Ukraine was the epicentre.

As a result, I believe, of the Kharkov or Rostov press.

The film had only just gone on general release abroad, and was shortly to be shown in the Ukraine.

Funny though it may seem, the last place in the world where *Potemkin* was shown was Odessa!

In those days, there was no standard system of film distribution throughout the USSR, and the Ukraine had its own system for the distribution and independent import of foreign films, as well as a more than merely independent commercial distribution 'policy'.

In consequence of various quarrels, Goskino and VUFKU[8] temporarily ceased renting out films to each other, and as a result, the paradox I mentioned earlier came about . . . the Ukraine saw the film last!

But this is beside the point.

The point is the sensation at the time of the film's appearance on Ukrainian screens.

The sensation concerned . . . plagiarism.

It was caused by a certain comrade who called himself a participant in the mutiny.

The gist of his claim was never made completely clear, since he never left anything in writing about the mutiny.

However, as he had taken part directly in real events, he felt he had a right to claim a portion of the royalties due to the author and Agadzhanova.

(Here I might mention that it was precisely because of *Potemkin* that the law concerning royalties on films—as well as plays—was passed at that time.) [9]

The claim was imprecise, and voiced stridently and none too cogently.

But this comrade's assertion that he 'had stood beneath the tarpaulin during the execution on deck' had such an effect wherever it was heard that the case even reached the courts for examination.

The fact that the comrade 'had stood beneath the tarpaulin' seemed irrefutable: the lawyers were on the verge of examining the case of the participant who had been left out of *Potemkin*, when all the strident claims were suddenly dropped, and the whole affair went up in smoke.

One circumstance which even the director had forgotten in the heat of the debate, came to light.

The aforementioned comrade mentioned that he 'had stood beneath the tarpaulin'. . . .

But be so good . . .

If we are going to be historically accurate about this, nobody stood beneath the tarpaulin.

It would have been impossible.

For the simple reason that nobody had thrown a tarpaulin over anyone on the 'Potemkin'.

The scene where the sailors were covered by a tarpaulin was . . . pure invention on the director's part!

I distinctly remember my naval consultant—a former officer in the navy (who incidentally played Matyushenko in the film) clutching his head in despair when I had the idea of covering the sailors with a tarpaulin when they were threatened with execution.

'People will laugh . . .' he had uttered, in horror. 'It wasn't like that!'

And I remember my retort:

'If they laugh, that's what we shall have deserved: it'll mean we didn't do it properly.'

And I gave instructions for that scene to be shot as it now is in the film.

This particular detail, cutting the mutineers off from life, turned out to be one of the most powerful in the film.

The image of a huge blindfold over the eyes of those condemned, the image of a shroud wound round a living body of men, proved sufficiently convincing emotionally to cover up any technical 'inaccuracy' which only a handful of experts and specialists knew of anyway.

People did not find the scene funny.

Which is where Goethe's words ring true: '*Das Gegenteil der Wahrheit um der Wahrscheinlichkeit willen*'*

This proved the stumbling block for our terrible plaintiff who 'had stood beneath the tarpaulin during the execution on deck'. His claim also appeared to be 'the opposite of the truth' and despite all the 'probability' his claim bore, he was covered in disgrace.

It was later discovered that he was no more than a slightly unbalanced adventurer.

The scene remained in the film.

It became the very stuff of the history of those events.

And most importantly:

Nobody, ever, anywhere, has found it funny.

5

Thus two people who, in one way or another, were involved in the

---

* German: 'The opposite of the truth for the sake of probability.'

actual events.

A third—Konstantin Isidorovich Feldman—is now a literary critic and playwright.[10]

In the film he is the student who comes aboard the ship in order to establish a link with the shore.

Thus the student Feldman came—forty years ago now —with the same purpose from the shore to the mutinous battleship.

But the audience wants to know not just about those involved in the events, but in the film itself.

Here are some brief details:

One of the most important figures, structurally, was the Doctor.

The cast hunted long and hard, but in vain: finally, they stuck with a compromise choice.

My film crew, the unsatisfactory choice, and I took a launch to the cruiser 'Komintern', which was where we filmed the scene with the rotten meat.

I sat down disgruntled at the other end of the launch, at some distance from the 'Doctor' and avoided looking at him.

I knew each detail of the Sebastopol roadstead like the back of my hand.

And the faces of the crew.

Involuntarily I began appraising the camera assistants.

One of them was short, puny.

It was the boilerman of the hotel in Sebastopol where we were staying. We killed time there in between shoots.

'Where do they find such weedy people to work with reflectors and mirrors?' My thoughts idly wandered. 'They'll only drop them overboard—or smash them. But that's a bad omen . . .'

At this point my thoughts came to a standstill: the skinny boilerman suddenly appeared in a new light as I reappraised him. I thought of his physical attributes, not *vis-à-vis* the work he has to do, but his appearance.

The small moustache, pointed beard . . .

Shifty eyes . . .

I imagined them behind pince-nez on their little ribbon.

I mentally swapped his oil-stained cap for the hat of an army medic . . .

And at that moment when we got on deck to start the shoot, my thoughts became reality. The ship's medical orderly subjected the infested meat to a cursory squint through the twin lenses of his pince-nez—but a moment earlier he had been an honest boiler-man, hired as an assistant . . .

There is a myth that I played the part of the priest in the film.

Not true.

The priest was played by an old gardener from one of the orchards around Sebastopol. The white beard was his own, although it was slightly combed to one side, and he wore a wig of thick white hair.

The myth sprang from a photograph of a 'working moment'. I was having a beard glued on under the shock of the wig, which stuck out above the cassock he wore in the film. And I was being made up so that I could pass for the venerable gentleman when he fell down the gangway. I was filmed from behind. I could not deny myself the pleasure of a headlong flight!

A third participant in these events, and a key one too, remained anonymous. That did not matter—he never appeared in the film.

Thankfully.

Since he was not an actor, but a furious opponent of the filming.

He was the park keeper at the Alupka Palace.

His down-at-heel boots and baggy trousers almost made it on to film: he sat, resolute, on the head of one of the three Alupka lions, refusing to allow it to be filmed without his special dispensation.

We were saved by the fact that there were altogether six lions on the Alupka steps.

And we ran from lion to lion with our cameras and so confused this severe and abiding guardian of the peace that he finally shook his fist at us and left us to take close-ups of three of the marble beasts.

The 'lion leaping to its feet' was a lucky find we made in Alupka, where we had gone merely to rest from filming on one of our days off.

The ragged trousers of this vigilant guardian would remain forever hidden from view.

Strangely, there was one more participant in this epic making of a film.

He too remained 'off screen' for a time, and it was not until fourteen years later, in *Alexander Nevsky*, in fact, and again in *Ivan* that he involved himself in work similar to that undertaken by others for *Potemkin*.

In the pile of archive material connected with making the film, I found a copy of Minute Two of the session of the Entertainment Commission, of the Commission of the Praesidium of the USSR Central Executive Committee, regarding the twentieth anniversary of 1905, dated 4 June 1925.

Paragraph Three of the Minute concerned the musical score for the film about 1905 that later became *The Battleship 'Potemkin'*.

(Paragraph Two was the decision to adopt N. Agadzhanova's screenplay, which we had written together.)

As for the decision on Paragraph Three, the interesting thing was that it was left to one of the members of the Anniversary Commission, who was going abroad to meet . . . Sergei Prokofiev, to hold preliminary talks about preparing a 'film symphony' as a musical accompaniment to the film! [11]

The lofty peaks of musical genius and bureaucracy could not be reconciled.

And I had the good fortune to share in this notable man's creativity many years later. In 1925 we only dreamed about this.

6

The famous lions were not the only 'lucky find'.

There was also the famous mist.

One misty morning in the harbour . . .

The mist lay like cotton wool over the mirror-like surface of the bay.

And if 'Swan Lake' was being performed not in the Odessa theatre, but among the cranes and landing stages of the harbour, then one could be forgiven for thinking that it was the girls' dresses floating on the water, the girls themselves having taken flight into the distance like white swans . . .

The reality is more prosaic:

the mist over the bay meant simply enforced inactivity—a Black Friday in the calendar of filming.

Sometimes there were seven of these Black Fridays in just one week.

And now, despite this fluffy whiteness, we had a quarrel with this day off.

The black framework of cranes, looming through orange-blossom wedding dresses like skeletons, echoed this inauspicious start.

The dark hulls of boats, barges and trading vessels wallowed in the gauze like so many hippopotamuses.

Here and there, golden needles of sunlight penetrated the lint, burning ruddy-golden holes in the mist.

Then the mist seemed warm, vital.

At other times the sun retreated behind a veil of clouds, as if jealous of its own reflection in the sea that was covered with the swan's down of the mist.

'And how, pray, am I worse than you?'

Anyway, there was no filming.

Inactivity.

A day off.

It cost three roubles fifty to hire a boat.

Tisse, Alexandrov and I sailed out across the misty bay as if crossing an endless apple orchard in blossom.[12]

Three Men in a Boat.

Jerome K. Jerome gave it a subtitle:

'To Say Nothing of the Dog'.

In our case, it was:

'To Say Nothing of the Camera'.

It stayed by our sides like a faithful hound.

The faithful Debrie L rested against a free rowlock.

Like us, it had reckoned on a day off.

Reluctantly it consented to being rocked about in a boat.

And it was quite disgruntled that the persistent energy of

the three boatmen obliged it to set its teeth into the mist.

The mist drifted across the eye of the lens like cotton wool across one's teeth.

'Such things were never meant to be filmed,' its gears seemed to be saying.

If our Debrie really had been a dog, it would of course have snapped its jaws savagely at this point.

Jeering laughter supported the camera's argument:

a shout of 'You must be nuts!' came across the water, from a passing boat.

It was L. who was also in Odessa, working on a different film.[13]

His lean, long-limbed frame, like Don Quixote's, was stretched out languidly in another boat.

Sailing in and out of patches of mist, he hurled us an ironic 'best of luck!'.

Which was what we had.

This encounter with the mist which chance threw our way, and which my mind developed emotionally as we sailed—this assortment of details, the outline of shots taken on the move—were gathered into material for plastic funereal chords.

Only later did the interacting intricacies of montage, at the cutting stage, become evident:

the Funeral Symphony in memory of Vakulinchuk.

This turned out to be the cheapest sequence in the film: hiring a boat to sail across the bay cost us three roubles fifty.

7

The lions. The mist.

The third lucky find was the Odessa Steps themselves.

I always believe that nature, one's surroundings, the set at .the point of filming and even the exposed footage at the point of montage, are all more intelligent than the author and director.

Being able to listen and comprehend what nature, or the unforeseen, is hinting at in the scene that was conceived in your thoughts; being able to detect what the cut film is saying on the splicing table as it lives out its own life on the screen (and this can be at some remove from the parameters of what was intended)—this is a great blessing and a great art . . .

But it demands of the artist self-abnegation and respectful modesty.

And since this is only possible for very arrogant, self-indulgent and egocentric people . . .

But even that is not enough. Something else is needed too.

Namely, an extraordinarily precise intention for the scene, or element of film, in question.

And additionally, you must be flexible in your choice of means for realising the concept.

You must be sufficiently pedantic to know precisely the nature of the desired 'resonances' and sufficiently accommodating to accept objects and means which perhaps were not thought of earlier, but which can transmit this 'resonance'.[14]

In my directing notes, this is shown by a precise accent—from a shot fired from the boat, to the slaughter on the Odessa Steps.

There is the preliminary outline of the means: the rough draft version.

Chance brings a sharper, more powerful resolution, but in the same key —and thus the chance element grows into the body of the film.

Dozens of pages of my directing notes are filled with attempts at working out the mourning for Vakulinchuk, based on the slowly moving details of the harbour.

But through the harbour there floated the details of that chance, misty day and their answering cry was heard emotionally more precisely in the original funereal conception. The unforeseen mist had assumed the central role in the concept.

That perfectly describes the way in which the minor episodes ran together. Gradually they rose to the level of cruelty of the Cossacks' punitive expedition. Outside in the printer's yard; on the outskirts of the town; in front of the bakery. They came to that one monumental flight of steps, each one of which seemed to serve as a rhythmic and dramatic beat in the unfolding of the tragedy stage by stage.

The scene of the slaughter on the Odessa Steps was not

indicated in any of my preparatory notes for the screenplay.

The scene was born out of a momentary spontaneous encounter.

Legend has it that the idea for this scene came to me as I stood at the top (of the Steps) beneath the Le Duc monument, spitting out cherry-stones and watching them bounce down the steps.[15] Picturesque though this legend is, it is pure legend.

The actual 'flight' of steps led to the planning of the scene, and its upward flight set my directing off on a new flight of fancy.

And I think that the crowd's headlong 'flight' down the steps was no more than the material realisation of those first feelings that I experienced when I came face to face with the actual steps.

Anyway, apart from that, only one other thing assisted me: somewhere, in my memory, was a vague recollection of a picture from the magazine L'Illustration in 1905, where a horseman, shrouded in smoke, slashed at someone with his sabre, on a flight of steps.

One way or another, the scene on the Odessa Steps became a crucial scene, the very core of the film's organic substance and general structure.

8

The boilerman, the mist and the flight of steps merely echoed the fate of the film as a whole. It too began life, like Eve, as a rib; it was taken from the endless reams of the screenplay about 1905, which encompassed such a wealth of events.

According to my horoscope, I was born under the sign of the sun.

The sun does not come round to take tea with me, however, as it visited the late Vladimir Vladimirovich Mayakovsky.[16]

But still, sometimes it does me unexpected favours.

So, without Joshua having to hold up his arms in supplication, it obligingly shone for forty days in a row, when we were filming the Battle on the Ice on the periphery of the Mosfilm plot.[17]

But it imperiously obliged us to pack up our things in Leningrad where we had belatedly begun work on scenes for *1905*.

And it made us chase its last rays to Odessa and Sebastopol, and forced us to fish out from the ocean of episodes in *1905* the one we could film in the south.

It is true that the sun had a powerful ally; the director of the Goskino Studio, M. Ya. Kapchinsky.[18]

He would repeat, in every possible way, like the *Three Sisters*, 'To Odessa, to Odessa, to Odessa.'[19]

And he would add with a shrewd smile, 'And don't bother imagining what you are going to film, until you get there.'

We imagined . . .

And so one particular episode became the emotional embodiment of the epic year 1905 *in toto*.

One part that stood for the whole.

And it successfully carried the emotional image of the whole.

How was this possible?

In the heat of war, *Potemkin* was revised in America.

A prologue and epilogue were added.

And a sound track.

It was re-released into cinemas under the title *Seeds of Freedom*.[20]

In this form, *Potemkin* told the story of an old man who had taken part in the events of the 'Potemkin', in the tragic days when Odessa was fighting off the fascists.

Apropos this new version, the magazine *Theatre Arts* recalled the history of the film.

Among much else, the article said this: '. . . it was here that the technique of *pars pro toto* was born . . .'[21]

That is, thinking out the role of close-up in terms of the informational details of 'a particular which can call to mind the whole, and make the audience feel it'. That really has a lot to do with my film.

Such as the doctor's pince-nez which replaced their wearer as appropriate.

The dangling pince-nez stood for the doctor, who was floundering among the seaweed after the sailor had taken his revenge.

In one of my articles, I have equated this method of using

close-up with synecdoche in poetry.[22]

Both are related directly to that psychological phenomenon of *pars pro toto* i.e. the ability of one's perception to reproduce mentally the whole object after having seen only a fragment of it.

But when is that phenomenon artistically viable?

When can that fragment, that particular, or that episode replace the whole, but remain within the framework of the film, and do so comprehensively?

Only, of course, in those cases where the fragment, particular or episode is typical.

That is, when the whole is reflected in condensed form, as if in microcosm.

The image of the doctor with his small pointed beard, his dim eyes and shortsightedness completely fits the characteristics of the pince-nez of the style of 1905, just like the fox terrier with its elegant metal chain behind its ears.

Exactly like the episode in the mutiny on the 'Potemkin', which absorbed, purely historically, countless events (highly characteristic of a 'general rehearsal for October') into its subject matter.

The rotten meat came to symbolise the inhuman conditions that not only soldiers and sailors, but also the exploited workers of the 'great army of labour' had to endure. The scene on deck assembled typical examples of the brutality with which the tsarist régime suppressed any attempted protest, wherever, whenever and however it arose.

And this scene included the no less typical (and, in 1905, frequent) responses of those who received the order to mete out punishment to the mutineers.

The refusal of a few to fire on the crowd, the masses, the people, their brothers, was characteristic of 1905. This was a feature of the heroic past of many of the military units that the forces of reaction sent to deal with the mutineers.

The grieving for Vakulinchuk was echoed by countless cases of burials of revolutionary victims which turned into impassioned demonstrations resulting in extremely violent engagements and reprisals.

That scene encapsulated the feelings and fates of those who

carried Bauman's body through Moscow.[23]

Refusals to fire on the crowd were few and far between and drowned in an ocean of human blood.

The scene on the steps stood for the massacre at Baku, and that of 9 January 1905 when a similarly 'trusting crowd' delighted in the refreshing air of freedom.[24] These displays were also ruthlessly stamped out by the forces of reaction, as when the Black Hundreds went on their orgies of pogroms, and lashed the demonstration in the theatre in Tomsk so thoroughly that they brought down the building as well.

Finally, the finale of the film, which was resolved by the ironclad's victorious passage through the admiral's squadron, a major chord, cutting off the events of the film, stood for the image of the revolution of 1905 as a whole.

We know what later happened to the battleship.

It was impounded in Constanța . . .

Then returned to the Tsar's government . . .

Luckily the sailors survived . . .

But Matyushenko, who fell into the hands of the Tsar's hangmen, was later executed . . .

But it is right that the battleship's descendant, on celluloid, should have finished victoriously.

For that is exactly how the 1905 Revolution, which was quelled so bloodily, has entered the annals of the history of the Revolution. It was first and foremost an objective phenomenon that in historical terms brought victory.

It could be seen as a mighty precursor to the decisive victories of October.

In all the suffering, the role of the great events of 1905 shone triumphantly through this image. And among these events, those on 'Potemkin' were no more than a particular episode, the very one however that could reflect the magnitude of the whole.

9

But to return to the actors who were not credited . . .

Virtually all the actors in the film were unknown and anonymous. There were exceptions. Vakulinchuk, played by

Antonov; Gilyarovsky, who is now Alexandrov, the director; Golikov, played by Barsky who has now stopped directing; and the boatswain Levchenko, whose whistle so helped us while we worked.

What happened to those hundreds of extras who came to work in the film with such enthusiasm and tireless zeal, who ran up and down the steps in the scorching heat, who marched in the endless file of the funeral procession along the causeway to the open sea?

Most of all I would like to meet that unnamed child crying in its pram, before it bounced from step to step on its downhill course.

He would be twenty now.

Where is he—or she? I do not know whether it was a boy or a girl.

What is he doing?

Did he defend Odessa, as a young man?

Or was she driven abroad into slavery?

Does he now rejoice that Odessa is a liberated and resurrected town?

Or is he lying in a mass grave, somewhere far away?

10

But I remember all the names and surnames of the individuals in the crowd scenes on the Odessa Steps.

There is a reason for this.

'Bonaparte's trick' is part of a director's repertoire.

It is generally known that Napoleon used to question his soldiers about one of their comrades-in-arms; and then would astound that soldier with his knowledge of his domestic affairs.

'How is your wife, Louison?'

'How are your parents keeping—the good lady Rosalie, and Thiébault—still working hard is he, near St. Tropez?'

'Your aunt, Justine— got over her gout yet, has she?'

The crowd rushed down the steps.

More than two thousand feet moving downwards.

The first time it was nothing special.

The second time it was even less energetic.

And the third time, laziness had crept in.

Then suddenly from my tower,

through my glinting megaphone,

my shout rose above the clatter of boots and the scrape of sandals, like the trumpets of Jericho:

'Comrade Prokopenko, can't you put a bit more life into it?'

For a fraction of a second, the crowd froze: could he really, from that damned tower of his, see each and every one of them? Did the director's all-seeing eye follow everyone who was running? Could he really put a name to every face?

And with a desperate new surge of energy the crowd hurried onwards, convinced that nothing could escape this demiurge of a director.

Meanwhile the director used his glinting megaphone to call out the name of one member of the crowd whose surname was known to him by accident.

11

And as well as these thousands of extras, there was one more which was in a class of its own.

These uncredited actors caused great disquiet, even on an international level: nothing short of an inquiry in the German Reichstag.[25] This building, its dome smashed and burnt, now resembles a giant mousetrap which the rodents have fled (but not before gnawing away at its façade and corner towers, leaving it like a giant chunk of stale cheese).

There were the unnamed vessels of the admiral's squadron, which intercepted 'Potemkin' at the end of the film.

They were many and threatening.

Their look and number were far superior to the size of the fleet that the young Soviet state had at its disposal in 1925.

This is what caused the agitation in neighbouring Germany.

Did it mean that the information provided by agents and spies was wrong and that they had underestimated the reality?

This led to an inquiry in the Reichstag into the actual size of our fleet.

Fear has large eyes.

And the Germans felt this fear a good nineteen years later, in the spring of 1945 when our victorious troops entered Berlin in response to the wild insanity of German aggression. But in 1926 their eyes were opened wide in terror and blinked at the events unfolding before them on the screen: part of our long shots of the advancing squadrons were no more than archive footage of . . . the old American navy on manoeuvres.

In fact, in one shot you can just glimpse a small Stars and Stripes . . .

The years passed, and the terrible might of our navy became reality. And the memory of that rebellious battleship lives on in the hearts of the pleiad of her steel successors.

But the real American fleet is sailing side by side with ours (as it did once in the picture—in those shots!) and fighting with us for the same goal: the final destruction and extirpation of Fascism the whole world over!

12

And this is the place for me to repay my debt to the main participant—not an anonymous extra this time, but an anonymous creator:

our great Russian people,

its heroic revolutionary past,

and its great creative inspiration, which indefatigably nourishes our artists and craftsmen.

Let me also express here the fervent gratitude of all who create in our land, for the magnificent inspiration that comes from the many millions of people who are the real creators of our works.

Outside the 'Art' cinema on Moscow's Arbat Square, the day *The Battleship Potemkin* went on general release, 19 January 1926. (Newsreel shot)

A Miracle in the Bolshoi Theatre[1]

The Bolshoi Theatre resounded with applause which roared like grapeshot through the semi-circular corridors. I was in a corridor, worried not only for the film's sake, but because of the spit. The last part of the film was held together by spit.

I clambered higher and higher, from the stalls to the dress circle, from tier to tier, as the excitement mounted. I listened anxiously and eagerly for individual bursts of applause.

Until the auditorium exploded with tumultuous cheers like grapeshot—the first time. That was the sequence with the red flag.

A second time—the 'Potemkin's' guns thundered against the headquarters of the general staff in response to the slaughter in Odessa.

I continued my peregrinations of the empty semi-circular corridors.

There was nobody there.

Even all the security staff had gone inside the auditorium. It was a rare spectacle, the first such in the history of the Bolshoi: a film show.

Then there should have been a third blast of grapeshot as the 'Potemkin' sailed through the admiral's squadrons, 'the flag of freedom fluttering in victory'.

Suddenly —cold sweat.

Any excitement I had felt died a death, forgotten.

Spit!

Heavens, spit!

Spit . . .

In the rush in the editing suite we had omitted to glue the end of the last part of the film together.

The splices at the end—the encounter with the squadron— were minute.

To stop them from flying apart and being mixed up, I had stuck them together with spit.

Then I had given them to the editors for splicing and watched the first version. I cut it. I arranged the second—and cut it again.

And then I distinctly remembered: the editors did not have time to glue the final version. The one which had already been wound on to the spool.

The spit had not been replaced by acetone.

And the last reel, to judge by the time that had elapsed and the music, had already started!

What could I do about it?

I ran down tier after tier of semi-circular corridors, which merged into a spiral—and I wanted to vanish into the foundations, drill deep into the earth, into oblivion, on the thread of this screw.

The film would come apart at any moment!

The projector would send fragments flying. . .

The rhythm of the film's finale would be broken.

And suddenly, imagine! A miracle! The spit held!

The picture raced to its conclusion.

We could not believe our eyes later, in the editing suite. Without the slightest effort we separated those minute pieces that earlier had adhered to each other with miraculous strength as they sped through the projector! . . .

Mémoires posthumes [1]

It is the accepted practice to publish someone's memoirs after death.

Usually after the author's death to avoid giving offence or hurt.

But what happens if it is not the author that has died, but that fragment of life and the history that were his contemporaries?

Then one may write posthumous memoirs in one's own lifetime.

These will be of that sort.

About a Europe that has gone.

And an author, who survived.

Epopée [1]

Prologue

1929.

Late autumn, turning into winter.

Berlin.

Martin-Luther-Strasse.

The furnished rooms of the Pension Marie-Luise.

Two king-sized beds.

Massive German eiderdowns.

Friedrich Markovich Ermler lay beneath one. [2]

And I lay under the other.

Friedrich had just arrived that day from Moscow.

He did not care for Berlin.

He found the city bleak.

'What am I going to find to do here?'

He was already thinking about going home.

I had been abroad for several months by that time. I had been on a lecture tour through Switzerland.

I had given a talk in Hamburg.

I knew my way around Berlin.

The next day I would start showing Friedrich Berlin.

He told me what people were thinking in Moscow:

'No word of you has reached Moscow . . . in Moscow, they feel your travels lack impact . . .'

Nobody in Moscow understood, obviously, that to go to Hollywood—the aim of my trip—was a problem fraught with difficulties. Negotiations took up a great deal of time.

Still, in Moscow, in Moscow cinema circles, they felt that my travels—what was the phrase he used?—lacked impact.

'Now if you were to cause a bit of a stir, politically, some-where . . . ,' Friedrich continued, his eyes half open.

I was very open to suggestion.

'Cause a bit of a stir? Lacking impact?'

My breathing came heavily and I rolled on to my side as I

drifted off.

Wait. Let me find a way.

Give me time. Moscow will be happy.

What form would it take? For the present, nobody knew . . .

The light went out.

We both fell asleep.

The Sorbonne

A few months passed.

1930.

Paris.

Mid-February.

I had already returned from a lecture tour to London.

I had been to Belgium, where I had given a talk to workers in a famous Liège suburb.

It was called Seraing-la-Rouge ('the Red'!), which speaks for itself.

To avoid the excessive interest the police had shown in me, I had left Till Eulenspiegel's country with a little more despatch than I had anticipated.

This had prevented me from visiting Ostend, where I had kindly been invited by James Ensor.[3] I was sorry about that as I am a great admirer of his grotesque etchings, where skeletons intertwine with people in the most fantastic arrangements. They carried on the traditions of their bizarre and weird Flemish precursors such as Hieronymus Bosch, bringing them into the twentieth century.

I had given a talk in Holland.

Not without causing minor sensations there.

Ever since my childhood I had been unable to dissociate Van Houten's cocoa, the pointed caps of the ladies, and of course huge wooden clogs, from my idea of Holland.

My first question when I got off the train in Rotterdam (which was where I gave my first lecture) was: 'Where are the clogs, then?'

The next day all the papers carried the banner headline: ' "Where are the clogs (*klompen*, in Dutch), then?" Eisenstein asks.'

On the way to the Van Gogh Museum in the Hague, our taxi almost drove into . . . Queen Wilhelmina.

In those idyllic days the not-so-young Queen could walk about her own capital like any other mortal.

The taxi swerved at the last moment. . .

We took in the world's greatest collection of van Goghs with excitement.

There, hanging next to 'The Gleaners', in the place of honour, was the famous portrait of the postal official with his orange beard. It flashed vivid colour. Streams of chrome yellow, ochre and gold interwove jubilantly in his sharply forked beard, in the same way that the streams of Prussian blue and viridian blended in the upward-spiralling peaks of the cypresses.

That was not where I caused a stir.

Among the newspapers which welcomed me so effusively to Amsterdam there was also an article by a priest—I have forgotten his name.

He wrote warmly about the very wide-ranging manifesto of humanitarian ideas that informs the whole of Soviet cinema.

The next day there was an unimaginable storm raging in the press, lashing the poor priest.

The general tone of this tempest was succinctly expressed by one paper: 'We have not the slightest doubt that Bolsheviks are quite capable of allying themselves with the Devil himself. But to see a man of the cloth offering them sanctuary —that is too much!'

But none of this was particularly exciting or, still less, sensational (apart from for the poor priest!).

And so, as before, Paris.

Paris—bursting with impressions.

But, so far, no sensations.

Talks with America made slow progress.

The diversions of *New Babylon* were loudly trumpeted.[4]

Punctilious observance of the sight-seeing trips that are obligatory for tourists.

The Chemin des Dames and the battlefield of Verdun.[5]

The Musée de Cluny which people visited solely for the metal chastity belt on display there.

The Musée Carnavalet, dedicated to the history of Paris.

But at last, in response to persistent requests, I consented to lecture at the Sorbonne.

Big deal!

A small talk on Soviet cinema.

A screening of *The Old and the New* . . .

Under the aegis of the department *'des recherches sociales'.*

In the Salle Richelieu. A thousand seats.

The Old and the New had still not been passed by the censors.

But a screening inside the Sorbonne counted as a private viewing.

The Sorbonne is extraterritorial.

Such a screening did not need the censor's permission.

A portable projector was set up somewhere near the seated figure of Cardinal Richelieu.

Just as well that it was to take place without the permission of the Board of Censors.

It would never have granted permission to show a film like that, not in the prevailing atmosphere of anti-Soviet feeling . . .

Only recently they had banned our film of one of our latest gymnastics parades.

The only reason given was that the participants were smiling. Did that mean that things were not so bad after all in the Soviet Union?

Soviet propaganda!

Take it off!

As we can see, the French censor is supervigilant!

The British Board was a different matter . . . I had just come back from there. One censor was blind: for silent films? Another was deaf: for talkies? And, while I was there, the third one actually . . . died!

True, none of this was enough to ensure that my films were shown in London although the Board of Censors is not even a governmental body.[6]

What a good thing it was that in Paris, at least, there were still such inalienable rights as freedom of performance!

Blue tickets —invitations—were sent out all over Paris.

Obviously the evening was awaited with great eagerness.

But an act of low treachery ensured that a blue ticket

landed on a certain desk.

It was Monsieur Chiappe's: he was the notorious Prefect of the Paris City Police.

Well, so what? We had no objections even to Monsieur Chiappe's presence in the audience. 'We'll be like the sun' and light up the way for good and evil alike.[7]

But it transpired that things were not as innocent as that.

I arrived at the Sorbonne with half an hour to spare.

I met Moussinac and Dr Allendy, who were to preside over the evening, in a long corridor.[8]

There was a crush at the doors.

The entrance to the building was in uproar.

Of course, this was less to do with me personally than the fact that, during a period of such hostility towards Moscow, a Muscovite had come to talk in Paris.

But . . . Allendy and Moussinac looked terrible.

It turned out that the innocent blue ticket on the Prefect's desk, far from being an invitation for him to attend the viewing, was in fact a ticket converting the private showing into one for the public. That meant that the film had to be approved by the censors. *The Old and the New* did not have that approval.

The police had just ordered Moussinac and Allendy to cancel the performance.

The side door into the auditorium was partly opened for me.

Through a chink, I could see that the audience was still swelling. Many of the seats had been taken.

The statue of the seated Richelieu towered above.

The projector stood at his feet.

And next to the projector stood a policeman, in full dress, with traditional képi and white gloves.

He stood, grabbing hold of the projector-stand convulsively.

'*Quel outrage!*'* This was the first 'flic' to get inside the Sorbonne since the days of Napoleon III!

'He's got a warrant to stop the film. He has the authority to stop the film being shown . . .'

---

* French: 'What an outrage!'

'*Merde!*'* I had already got so used to speaking French that I could swear like a native.

So now what? Go home?

How could I?!

Both the organisers asked me to stay.

I had brought with me an introductory speech I had written: it would last for twenty minutes. I could hardly spin that entertainment out for an entire evening!

A sudden tumult behind the walls.

A sound like a giant champagne cork bursting from a giant bottle.

The crowd had broken through the entrance doors, pressing the ushers to the sides; the human flood poured into the hall.

The organisers looked at me entreatingly.

Couldn't the evening be postponed?

We briskly consulted.

Should we try to show the film?

Contravene the ban?

That, apparently, was just what the police were waiting for.

That policeman would try stopping the projector.

He would probably catch it in the neck from one of the more high-spirited members of the audience.

But other policemen materialised from nowhere . . .

One of the junior organisers rushed in, white as a sheet: 'There are police divisions —in the Sorbonne courtyard!'

'*Quel outrage! Quel outrage!*'

'Watch it, they're squaring up for a fight.'

'There'll be a run-in with the police!'

There were plenty of comrades in the audience—French Communists.

The police would have been all too glad to catch those it wanted in the general confusion . . .

Another explosion.

It was the crowd bursting in through the all-but-useless barriers.

The exits were blocked.

---

* French: 'Shit!'

People sat on the steps.

They stared at the policeman, thunderstruck.

There was a humming like a giant beehive.

How could this be?

Three thousand people and only one thousand seats.

Another young organiser brought even more alarming news: 'There are a lot of people from the *Camelots du roi*, the young monarchists.'

The scene was set for a massive uproar.

We made a quick decision.

I could not make my talk last for more than forty minutes.

And then—what the hell!—we would open up the talk for questions from the floor.

God help me!

The hall filled with mutterings of discontent.

I dived headfirst into the stormy ocean.

The roar coming from the rows of seats could drown the roar of any sea; such was the typhoon of indignation that blew up when Dr Allendy broke the news of the prefect's ban.

The poor policeman changed colour twenty times. From livid purple to deathly pale.

Of course it would be hard to imagine a more favourable atmosphere . . .

There is no point in going into the details of the talk itself.

Apart from the general ideological positions and peculiarities of Soviet cinema, I set out my pet doctrine of 'intellectual cinema'—a cinema of ideas which at that point I was particularly keen on.

All this is expounded fully and in detail in specialist literature.[9]

This doctrine of emotional and intellectual 'overtones' and the plan 'from thesis to image—from image to concept'[10]—I have written about all of this for many years, as I sought to master it, argue for it, fight for it and develop the method.

But I repeat: all this is material for specialist literature and you will find it in any number of articles.

The course of events took a slightly surreal turn—even in Paris Surrealism was fashionable—if 'slightly' is the right word: the speaker was convinced that the audience was doing the precise opposite of what it was meant to be doing.[11]

The most interesting thing would be to describe the dramatic events of the evening, especially as this side was the one never dealt with in my theoretical articles!

In the first place, I hate public speaking.

Paralysis.

But here the wave of incandescent anger from the auditorium that rolled towards me was enough to melt the grip of my paralysis and constraint as though it were wax.

I suddenly felt acute resentment and anger.

You— in the very heart of French scholarship and thought,

the France of Descartes and Voltaire,

the France of the Rights of Man and the Communards,

the France of age-long struggles for freedom.

And now some dirty 'flic' dared to sit (now he was even sitting by the projector!) at the foot of the great cardinal!

Never mind that right now.

Now Paris was all around me.

Paris, whose corridors of power impudently refused to recognise Soviet cinema (despite continuing diplomatic relations).

Paris, which dared in its reactionary blindness to turn its back on the country which had taken the torch of the ideals of freedom from France and raced onwards with it to new horizons.

And so I stood there in that Paris, whose ancient masonry appealed to the best in mankind, and at the same time I was in the grip of reactionaries who permitted the merest sign of freedom to vanish without trace!

(The panel knew that the courtyard was filled with police.)

And in those circumstances, at such a time, when the thousands in the crowd were seething with anger there in front of me, I had the floor; I had the chance to speak.

Were I a man of impassioned eloquence like Dovzhenko or Pudovkin,[12] I would of course have burst forth with the speech of a tribune,

my roulades, worthy of a Calvin or Savonarola, would have made the ancient walls of the Sorbonne tremble.

But for all my solidity, I am less like the 'Eagle of Meaux',

191

the fiery Bossuet—or Gambetta aflame with inspiration, than I am like Henri Rochefort, or to be more honest . . . Gavroche.[13]

And so my weapon against the Goliath of French reaction was not a thunderbolt but explosions of laughter.

Particularly when we came to the part which I referred to as 'a game' of questions and answers.

My choice of weapons turned out the sensible one.

Next day's *Le Matin* (or some such paper) printed: 'Don't worry about Bolsheviks with daggers between their teeth—look out for those with laughter on their lips!'

So there were no grounds for police intervention.

I ask you, what grounds could there be, when a thousand people were being so pleasantly and peaceably amused.

But how they were being amused!

I cannot now recall what answers flew off my tongue in response to the most innocuous and inoffensive questions.

It was the only time in my life, I think, that I have had to give a lecture without having any time to mull over my replies.

Theoretical explanation.

Riposte!

Point of information.

Bull's-eye! There goes the Board of Censors!

Another riposte.

Another point.

Another bull's-eye! This time, the Ministry for Foreign Affairs.

Three more direct hits on the Prefecture.

Great hilarity from the auditorium.

It was held captive, stunned by this foreigner, who had arrived, moreover, from a country considered for some reason to be irrationally authoritarian and quite devoid of any sense of humour (remember the censors vetoing the Soviet film because of all the smiles?), and who spoke so boisterously and instead of bookish academic 'translationese', used extravagantly robust colloquialisms and even, here and there, argot.

These are as alien to the speaker as they are to his environment.

My wanderings about the suburbs of Paris had furnished me

with a choice selection of French humour.

Which is not to say I do not make the occasional linguistic slip.

But in Paris there is a wonderful way of getting out of this: if you cannot find the precise word for the context, it is enough to say *'chose'* or *'machin'* (which also means 'thing' but has a more urban etymology). You may outline the missing subject either by gesture or paraphrase.

You should have heard the audience's delighted enthusiasm as during the inevitable pause after my each and every *'chose'* or *'machin'*, it supplied the missing word.

(Now I may confess that I so liked that game that I interspersed a few spurious *'machins'* and *'choses'* amongst the genuine ones.)

I think it was Mrs Constance Rourke in her book *American Humor* who was the first to enlarge on the idea that laughter is the best means of uniting a large number of people.

The hours I spent in the Sorbonne bore this out.

Where had the *Camelots du roi,* that seam of opposition, disappeared to?

No, there they were. I could see the occasional beret.

And what about that even more hostile element, the White Guards? Weren't they hoping for a little spot of fun during the brawl?

In the general peals of laughter, it really does seem sometimes that it is not only in the Kingdom of God that you find 'neither Greek nor Jew'.[14]

However, it was of course difficult to restrain myself when an official lecturer from a respected Sorbonne faculty cut in with a provocative question. In my reply I used the word *'dépucelage'** in a very vulgar way.

It was in response to someone who asked, 'Do you sincerely believe that the Russian peasant is capable of making useful criticisms of your film?'[15]

I replied that only two sorts of criticism are valuable:

the immediate reaction and criticism from the workers in

---

* French: deflowering, or loss of virginity.

193

respect of their class, for which we make the films,

and the criticism of professional experts;

least of all were we interested in the 'intermediate' criticism of those who had not attained the level of real knowledge and understanding of our work, and at the same time had 'lost their virginity' of spontaneous élan!

On the printed page this does not perhaps seem so witty.

But in the auditorium, brimming over with mirth, with the figure of Richelieu soaring into the air above, and the sweating 'flic' next to the projector and the police surrounding us—the reply burst like a shell.

In exactly the same way as the last answer to the last question: 'Is it true that laughter has finally died in the Soviet Union?'

My reply was an outburst of laughter.

In those days I had very strong, healthy white teeth.

Incidentally, my laughter, which was quite sincere at the absurdity of this idea, did sound quite convincing.

We left the field of conflict.

We crossed the courtyard of the Sorbonne in the twilight.

The police, called out for no purpose, look on dully.

Later I heard that the prefect himself was to be seen wandering amongst them for a while.

This was apparently true.

We walked down the side alleys around the Sorbonne.

We did not see any wounded or dead, although it was explained that a very large number of people were 'driven away' from the entrance doors 'by sheer brute force'.

We walked past the open squares.

We could not believe what we saw!

Lorries full of police were parked in alleys and courtyards.

They were obviously expecting a regular battle.

We finished up in a small restaurant, *'Le Bateau Ivre'* * which took its name from a poem by Arthur Rimbaud.

The restaurant was done up inside like a normal boat. It was the patrons who provided the soupçon of drunkenness.

Then we quietly set off for bed in our small Hôtel des Etats-

---

*   French: 'The Drunken Boat'.

Unis.

Nine o'clock the next morning.

A powerful fist struck the door of my small room.

This could have happened three hours earlier since the police had descended on the hotel at six o'clock precisely.

But the hotel proprietor had blocked the staircase with his body, his chest defending my peace.

'Monsieur Eisenstein got back late last night.'

'Monsieur Eisenstein is still asleep.'

'I will not allow anyone to see Monsieur Eisenstein before nine o'clock.'

What a considerate proprietor!

I am very cross with myself for forgetting his surname.

But a few words about the hotel.

It was narrow, as only buildings in Montparnasse are: it was two rooms wide and five storeys high.

We were trying to make it to the United States.

Our stay in Paris was only intended to be a stop in transit.

Paris we considered as a *'maison de passe'* of a kind, as I would have said were I addressing the audience at the Sorbonne, instead of a blank sheet of paper.

(*'Maison de passe'*—a house of call—is the official designation of those houses visited by men to meet at the appointed time a woman who has made her own way there.)

I was preoccupied with the United States. Which was why, out of all the possible small hotels I might have taken—and of which there were dozens in that area!—I chose the one with the sign announcing the aim of my wanderings. The Hotel United States —Hôtel Etats-Unis!

The hotel comprised ten small rooms, identical in every respect, on five floors.

Below was the office where the proprietors ate. And slept.

The hotel was thoroughly homely.

The proprietors were not even particularly worried about its profitability.

They ran it more as a hobby.

He was an expert on cut diamonds, and had been a fairly successful dealer in Rouen.

He had traded for a long time in semi-precious stones, set them in rings and bracelets, middle of the range affairs, and made a respectable amount. Then at a certain age he had decided to sell not only the stones but the whole business too, and to spend the rest of his days in Paris.

Madame was a stout southerner with black, curly hair and eyes like dark cherries.

Charles, the porter, had a slight squint, fair hair, broad shoulders and wore a striped waistcoat without a jacket. He carried the traditional feather duster of his class.

There were two maids, Bretons more often than not, who succeeded each other with such rapidity that I could never remember their names.

Charles would pinch them with his long bony fingers whenever he came across them cleaning the rooms on the various floors.

And try as they might to stifle their shrieks, they were audible on the ground floor.

'Monsieur' would come out of his 'office' to cough meaningfully into the lift shaft.

The shrieking stopped, only to begin again on a different floor.

There was a night porter, too; he was very well-liked and could always be found in the lower general foyer, snoozing in two armchairs which he had put together for the purpose.

Rue de Grenelle[16]

The ancient stone 'hôtel' (here meaning a large town house) was *entre cour et jardin**; that is, it had a paved entrance yard at the front, with railings between it and the street.

And French windows in the drawing-room that opened out on to the garden at the back of the property.

In those days the 'Rue Grenelle', the Soviet Plenipotentiary's building on the Rue de Grenelle itself, was like a fortress under siege.

You would be admitted through a heavy *porte cochère* on the

---

* French: 'between courtyard and garden'.

left-hand side after a preliminary check through the 'spy-hole', then your documents would be checked while the door was on the chain.

Everyone spoke in whispers. Walked on tiptoe.

Day and night, the staff took turns at the watch; they were armed with guns.

A thick layer of sawdust, scattered on the cobblestones by the conscientious and provident 'archangels' of the Prefect of Police, lent a particularly ominous effect to the whole picture.

At any moment you could expect one of the routine anti-Soviet rallies, rowdy demonstrations by the monarchist organisation, the *Camelots du roi*—waiters who had knocked off for the day and White Guards who had finished whatever it was they were doing (Paris was teeming with White émigrés) or any hooligan element—they were always ready to throw a brick through a window, quite regardless of who might be behind it.

There was always *une bagarre*—a clash—in the offing.

Monsieur Chiappe had nothing at all against an actual clash.

The more the better was his view.

All the more reason to think that the Soviet Plenipotentiary was the epicentre of the city's disturbances, troubles and breaches of security.

But why should police horses break their legs on slippery cobbles?

No doubt what he had read about Napoleon and the sliding hooves as *la Grande Armée* crossed the frozen wastes of Russia on horseback had lodged somewhere in the cranium of that pallid caricature of the puny 'tragic' Pierrot.

As to the idea of unshoeing the police horses, as Kutuzov had done,[17] that was not at all rational, and most unlikely to occur to one whose natural tendency was to keep things clamped up. There was another way: covering the pavement with sand and sawdust. It works just as well.

Rue de Grenelle was on the whole a quiet street.

But if you knew that here again the number of White Guard officers driving taxis was increasing, and that they refused to take fares to that street, then it is not surprising that Rue de Grenelle was silent for hours on end.

In those days silence was ominous.

It was deceptive.

The wind gusted the anti-Soviet leaflets along the sawdust; they were in silent uproar.

Posters and slogans, pasted along the walls right up to the very gates of the building, shrieked inaudibly.

'Throw the 'Soviets' out of Paris!'

'Run them out of town!'

The papers were filled with anti-Soviet shrieks . . .

Le Matin described the oily black smoke that poured out of the chimneys of this 'citadel of Sovietism' in dense clouds at night. 'This menacing one-eyed Arens (the Plenipotentiary's adviser) is destroying the evidence after the kidnap of General Kutepov—the key fact proving the guilt is that he is burning the unfortunate General's corpse . . .'[18]

'Of course it took some doing to choose the very worst time for this case of yours,' our Plenipotentiary, Dovgalevsky, said to me.

He had just concluded the complicated business of finally establishing diplomatic links with Britain.

He was about to become a potential witness to the severing of links with France.

He had a black moustache, like Kipling's or Nietzsche's.

He was a graduate of Toulon University and he looked as though he came from the south of France, too.

I felt sorry for Dovgalevsky.

The 'mysterious matter' of General Kutepov's disappearance had come crashing down on his head.

The reactionary yellow press was accusing the 'Soviets' of kidnapping him . . .

'It would be useless to send a communiqué to Tardieu about you.[19] You yourself must understand that . . .'

Dovgalevsky's moustache bristled.

He took out a piece on the Kutepov affair from a pile of gutter-press newspaper articles. It concerned 'three mysterious Soviet film-makers who recently and for no apparent reason had visited Saint-Cloud in a light blue Hispano-Suiza . . .'

Yes, there can be no doubt whom they are referring to.

A well-to-do representative of Gaumont, a former yellow hussar, who ferried us from London in order to clinch a deal with his firm, as well as for some other diversions, had actually driven us in a huge Hispano-Suiza belonging to a friend of his, a record-breaking racing-driver.

True, the General had had nothing to do with any of this.

From off-stage came the voice of one of Dovgalevsky's aides:

'Why shouldn't you go? Be extradited from France?! What could evoke greater respect than such a stamp in your passport?'

A pause.

It was the first warm days.

The French window on to the garden was ajar.

A ray of sunshine and a light breeze came in to look round the office.

The wind had tired of chasing anti-Soviet leaflets down the Rue de Grenelle.

The ray of sunshine played on the patterns in the Aubusson carpet and the delicate gilt legs of the furniture.

The breeze and the ray had been dying to find out what was going on within these walls.

They were much luckier than the reporters and spies who sat for hours on end with their cameras, filling all the mansard windows in the vicinity as they awaited nervously one of the above-mentioned clashes on the street, or one of those 'mysterious' details surrounding the building that was so loathsome to Monsieur Tardieu's régime.

Expulsion from France would of course carry a certain cachet.

There is however a 'but': security departments the world over follow the rule that the dossier of a *persona non grata* who has been expelled from any major country must be circulated to the intelligence services of all the other countries.

This is called the *'communication du dossier'* and it automatically entails all manner of difficulties when it comes to entering any other country.

And my planned 'campaign' was still far from finished.

America, Hollywood, lay ahead of me.

I asked Dovgalevsky not to take any steps just then.

He was visibly relieved by this.

'We will do it with the help of the French.'

His aide shrugged his shoulders, slightly sceptical.

We parted at that juncture.

And a phantasmagoric kaleidoscope began to revolve.

To paraphrase the famous Frenchman: 'If my extradition papers did not exist, I would have to provoke them.'[20] Never in my life had I felt such an atmosphere as I felt in Paris: such crowds of people, of unimaginable types, *qui pro quo*, such an . . . 'Offenbach' —and I doubt I will see such again!

Friends in Need

Friends in need are friends indeed.

I returned from the Rue de Grenelle to my tiny Hôtel des Etats-Unis.

After my talk with Dovgalevsky the signboard seemed more symbolic than ever—symbolic here meaning 'abstracted from reality'.

There was a small, cramped phone booth in the foyer.

The Paris telephone system was terrible.

It was all but impossible to get a line.

Once connected, it was all but impossible to hear a thing.

That was the case when connected to other Paris numbers.

It was appreciably better over longer distances.

And the longer the better.

I could ring Hollywood from that booth.

My voice has never ventured over a greater distance than from Paris to Los Angeles. And although it was entirely natural that I should gasp on learning that my trip to America had been sorted out, we could both hear each other perfectly. But that came later.

Now, back from the Rue de Grenelle, I squeezed into that stuffy booth.

Again I could hear perfectly clearly.

I was speaking to St Moritz, Switzerland.

Naturally I wanted to speak first of all to someone who could demonstrate (financially) his interest in our stay in Paris.

This was Léonard Rosenthal, the millionaire and 'pearl king'. He had been awarded the *Légion d'honneur* for bringing the centre of the world trade in pearls from London to Paris.

He described the simple device used to enable him to achieve this in a remarkable book with the eloquent title *Let's be Rich!*[21]

A proven expert in human psychology, Monsieur Léonard hit upon the idea of paying the 'pearl fishers' of Indian coastal villages not by cheque but in small silver coins.

Caravans of camels laden with bags of these coins made a great impression. Gradually Monsieur Léonard drew more and more new pearl-producing areas of India into his sphere of influence.

Then (I mean in 1930), his brother spent nine solid months in India each year, managing the pearl business in the territory.

Then he went on a three-month bender in Paris.

While Monsieur Léonard dealt with the sale and export of pearls from Paris to all corners of the globe.

What business could Rosenthal have with us?

It was because of Mara Gris.

Madame Mara was by no means Madame Rosenthal.

She was of much greater significance.

She was Monsieur Rosenthal's friend, and Rachèle, the baby who had been born recently, was proof of that friendship which could not be legally recognised as long as the actual Madame Rosenthal refused to divorce.

Apart from Rachèle, Mara Gris had another daughter, now grown up. When this daughter was still a baby, Mara Gris had collapsed from hunger on the steps of a magnificent villa, the rear of which opened directly on to the Parc Monceau.

But before she did so she had managed to pull the gilt brass bell in the imposing porch.

Thus ended the distressed young lady's disastrous wanderings. She had left the Crimea after Wrangel, and lived in poverty first in Constantinople and then in Paris, where she had starved.

From the moment of her collapse on the steps, Madame Mara's life had been transformed into a fantasy covered with diamonds (and what diamonds! I saw these 'rivières'—waterfalls and streams of diamonds—at a première once).

But none of this would have happened, except that for some reason it was the legendary Rosenthal himself, resplendent in his fiery beard, who came out on to the porch.

He wore his spade beard provocatively: together with his white tie and tails, it created a good and colourful effect.

Rosenthal was captivated by the beautiful young lady, who had fallen senseless near his door.

And the young lady was looked after for many years.

Cinderellas and Sleeping Beauties are not only ballets.

But what has Cinderella to do with us here?!

Quite simply:

Cinderella was our hack-work.

One must live . . .

While I was in London, lecturing, Grisha met Cinderella and her patron.[22]

Madame Mara had a bit of a voice and dreamed of acting in a film.

They were making a short musical;[23] Madame Mara—Mara Gris, now sang songs seated at a dazzling white piano.

Rosenthal, at the other end of the line, was more than evasive.

He clearly had no wish to get involved with any of this.

Also, I doubt if he would even have objected to my hurried departure from French territory.

The more so as it was Alexandrov and Tisse who were making the film.

The police left them alone to travel all over France without let or hindrance, shooting landscape for the short.

They had trouble obtaining permission for their travels.

Of course we were all followed.

Of course the police could not afford the agent's travelling expenses, hotel bills and per diems from Paris to Finistère and from Normandy to Nice.

'Now if messieurs would not mind taking care of all these expenses themselves . . .'

The messieurs agreed with Rosenthal's approval.

And so Alexandrov and Tisse travelled care-free around

France, in the constant companionship of a certain Kurochkin, whom the prefecture had generously assigned them.

Kurochkin was entirely supported by the film crew and spent his free time with two members of the expedition, with whom he shared his innermost thoughts.

Kurochkin had set his sights on a middle-aged widow. Not only was she—not excessively, but quite adequately—loaded; but for some reason she had a motorboat.

Kurochkin had a weakness for motorboats just as Jitter Lester's dissolute and inimitable son has a weakness for cars (in Erskine Caldwell's *Tobacco Road*).

A friend in need . . .

I was still extricating myself from the booth when a young man with curls and a healthy glow rose from his chair to greet me. His cheerful darting eyes would sometimes freeze as he lapsed into thought.

He wore a black hat, black shirt and a black tie. I was surprised that he was not wearing black gloves too.

It would have been hard to find a young man of more radical views and more opposed to the church.

He was my friend and companion, Jean Painlevé.[24]

'My father has already written his letter of protest to the Prefecture.'

'The news has already gone the rounds of Paris.'

Some people have a father like that.

Nevertheless and notwithstanding, he was a former member of the War Cabinet, a renowned mathematician and then president of the Chapter of the Order of the *Légion d'honneur*.

Hm . . .

I would have liked to have seen Monsieur Clout's [*Udar*] face when he saw that letter.

Painlevé and I went out for dinner.

Young though he was, he made fascinating films.

Documentaries.

I had seen one of his films only recently at an independent film festival. It was very interesting and the camera work was first-rate. It was about the underwater life of the hermit crab. His close-ups showing the life cycles of water fleas and his fantastically beautiful film about sea-horses are as involved as an intricate composition by Méliès.

That was the basis of our acquaintance.

Our friendship flourished because of his ardent sympathy for the Soviet Union.

As he tucked into a crab, or some other variety of crustacean which had it been alive would have found itself on his screen, he told of his run-in with the police, laughing.

He said that when he was younger, still a kid, he was in the thick of some political agitation. He had led a group of armed people to storm the Ministry of War.

He knew all its exits and entrances; after all, his father was the Minister there.

Those bizarre incidents were not confined to Paris.

Egon Erwin Kisch, *der rasende Reporter** was one of the best and most merciless of the 'muckrakers'; he told me how, while he was taking part in some revolutionary activities in Austria, he had also stormed—in earnest—and taken control of a government department in which his brother occupied a senior post. (His brother's political convictions were diametrically opposed to his own.) Kisch the revolutionary burst into the office of Kisch the reactionary, which took them both by surprise.

Kisch and Kisch, face to face.

And suddenly the elder brother—Kisch the reactionary— admonished him: '*Egon! Ich sag'es der Mutter*'**

This time, the case of Painlevé the Younger came to rest somewhere between the nursery—the future film laboratory—and father's study.

But more of this later.

Jean Painlevé, resourceful and irrepressible as he was, found a way of taking part in everything that bore even the faintest trace of social protest and disorder.

A particular knack of his was letting himself be arrested, thereby allowing his more 'involved' comrades to make their escape.

For him, arrest was a special treat.

---

* German: 'the raving reporter'
** German: 'Egon! I'll tell mother!'

He got a kick out of seeing the commissioners' panic-stricken faces when he told them who his parents were.

The policemen who detained him would be torn off a strip; they would apologise for causing him such inconvenience; they would salute him and ask him to make his way home quietly.

But not that time!

Jean demanded the same treatment as that accorded the other detainees.

Objecting loudly, he requested that he be taken off to a cell.

He was, and that gave him the chance to threaten the luckless commissioner with dire consequences: the very name of the brat's all-powerful father made him quake.

Only once did someone—a ginger-haired commissioner—get the better of him.

After a long argument with Jean, he muttered his consent and locked him up in a cell.

And then he slipped him two forms under the door, asking him to sign them.

Jean was still so worked up after the argument that he did not bother to read the forms before signing them both with a flourish.

And then a policeman grabbed him by the collar and threw him out on to the street. The whole station resounded with laughter: Painlevé, in his temper, had signed the forms so adroitly slipped to him, thereby conceding that he had been detained (in the first form) and released (in the second).

There is no time here to dwell upon Jean's escapades with men of the cloth, the more so as by that time we had eaten our fill and I was thoughtfully making my way back to Montparnasse.

There was a small sky-blue sports car—a Bugatti—parked by the hotel.

Renaud de Jouvenel[25] jumped nervously out of his chair where he had been sitting in the hotel foyer. He was another friend of mine.

'I've heard all about it. Papa has already sent his letter of protest to the Prefecture!'

Things were getting hotter for Monsieur Clout with every hour.

First Painlevé, now the Senator de Jouvenel!

There was no hint of liberal sympathising here.

Senator de Jouvenel was ambassador to Rome. One of the fruits of his mission was the *entente cordiale* with Mussolini.

I had never seen the senator face to face.

His son was a motor fanatic: even the slim magazine he published, devoted to aesthetics, bore the name *La Grande Route*.

Renaud and I often went racing.

And he asked if he could have one of my articles for his magazine.

. . . There was a phone call for me.

'We're going to see de Monzi immediately!'[26]

It was Tual[27] speaking. He was keen on cinema too, albeit only as a viewer.

'I've made all the arrangements. We'll meet there. Get out there.'

In those days, de Monzi sympathised wholly with the Soviet Union.

Only recently, in fact, he had scored a political triumph: rapprochement with the Soviet Union.

Another old 'hôtel' (meaning a villa).

A yard at the front, a garden at the back.

Diagonally opposite the Luxembourg, I think.

The silver-haired minister who had just retired.

A check bow-tie.

A Basque beret worn at an angle.

And a dazzling background of a screen of burnished copper plates.

He had just closed his door behind the last of an endless succession of visitors which he received daily. Priests from the provinces; retired soldiers with bristling moustaches; businessmen about to retire; ladies in mourning.

'Will they expel you?

'How odd! Why? Anything to do with the *Police des moeurs* [the vice squad]?

'No, it doesn't seem to be . . . we shall make enquiries. We'll see.

206

RÉPUBLIQUE FRANCAISE

PRÉFECTURE DE POLICE

CABINET DU PRÉFET

Sous Direction Administrative

SERVICE DES ÉTRANGERS

REFUS DE SÉJOUR

N° *1-270887*

M *Eisenstein, Serge Mikhaïlovitch*

né le *10 Janvier 1898.*

à *Riga*

de nationalité *Citoyen de l'URSS.*

demeurant *135 Bd Montparnasse.*

objet d'un refus de séjour par *décision Ministérielle*

est mis en demeure de quitter le territoire français à la date du

Dix Sept Mars 1930

Aucune autorisation de déplacement ne lui est accordée, hormis

celle de se rendre à *l'Etranger*

Le présent avis lui tiendra lieu de pièce d'identité jusqu'à son

départ en remplacement des pièces régulières qui lui ont été retirées.

Pour le Préfet de Police
Le Chef du Service des Etrangers,

Le présent avis devra être retiré des mains de l'intéressé à son départ de
France, par les autorités de police de la gare frontière ou du port d'embarquement
et devra être retourné au Service Central des Cartes d'identité 7 rue Cambacérès.

The police notification of Eisenstein's extradition from France, 4 March 1930

'Your twenty-four hours expire tomorrow?

'The first step will be to extend the deadline by a week.'

He rang 'someone'.

And, without having to visit Monsieur Clout, my visa was automatically extended by seven days the following day.

I had to mobilise all my resources during this period.

De Monzi tactfully declined to intervene further personally, but he did refer me to the former director of his ministry —

Monsieur Robert.

'*C'est le pape!*' * the expansive man exclaimed. Built like a peasant, he nevertheless occupied one of the small offices in the maze of corridors in nothing less than the Palais des Tuileries.

I did not have time to learn what his position there was.

'*Pape*' means the Pontiff of Rome, not father.

'You must have offended some Catholics. I can see the hand of the Vatican in this!'

I could feel the thin, bony fingers of Rodin reaching for my throat. Not the Rodin whose statues I found time to admire in the Rodin Museum, between visits to the Prefecture and the Sûreté Generale—no, I mean Rodin, the sinister hero of *The Wandering Jew* by Eugène Sue: the grasping, ruthless agent of Rome.

'You remember!'

Where, when, how could I have encroached upon the omnipotent Vatican and the Pope?

I tried looking at all my activities and comings and goings from the point of view of the vice squad.

Mon Dieu! He was right!

My countless visits to all the famous cathedrals in France.

There had been one to Rheims.

Two to Chartres.

One to Amiens.

Numerous visits to Catholic bookshops.

I had been examining the question of religious ecstasy as a particular aspect of pathos.[28]

In the wardrobe in my hotel room, alternating with works on Lévy-Bruhl's primitive thought were: Saint Jean de la Croix (the

---

* French: 'It's the Pope!'

Spaniard St John of the Holiest Cross), the works of St Theresa; Manresa's guide to the *Spiritual Exercises* of St Ignatius Loyola . . .

I had just recently been surprised to see that those books were not in their usual order; and Jean, the porter in the striped waistcoat, was guiltily avoiding my eyes.

Good heavens, I had only recently visited Lisieux, with Tual, to look at that gaudy monument to the recently canonised 'little prelate', Sainte Thérèse de Lisieux.[29]

Incidentally, the little saint performed a little miracle for us as we were on the way, which was hospitable of her.

Rather, we were given a cautionary tale concerning legends about miracles.

French roads, which have been built well and straight since the days of Napoleon, and are so bright that they gleam at night, are liberally dotted with petrol stations.

Nobody here sets off on a journey worrying about whether there is enough petrol in the tank.

We too drove along unconcerned.

Suddenly the car began to splutter and slow down.

The road went through a forest.

No sign of a petrol station anywhere.

'The pilgrims were overtaken by a disaster on their journey', as the legend would have put it.

'The pilgrims turned to the little saint with a prayer', it would have continued.

The utterances from our lips were of a different nature.

But just as the car was about to come to a standstill, there was a sudden . . .

'Miracle!' as the legend would have said.

The road began to drop away.

The gradient became steeper.

And the car moved freely down the slope, despite its empty tank.

We spoke of the road as if it were animate: 'She's bending down!'

The car coasted along.

And at the very foot of the slope, there was no small saint but something much more important: a robust petrol pump.

'The pilgrims sang a triumphal hymn of praise. . . .'

Go on, tell me legends don't start like that . . .

But Lisieux was of minor importance to me.

I hankered after Lourdes.[30]

I was fascinated by the onset of mass ecstasy as crowd psychosis during 'miracle cures'.

The behaviour of crowds at football or boxing matches.

The races at Longchamps were a disappointment. The French went to the races as if they were going to pick up their salary. They placed their bets and won or lost. No mass hysteria there—not even much excitement over the sport.

I did not make it to Lourdes: my stay in France did not coincide with the dates of the pilgrimages.

On the other hand, I was more than amply recompensed by crowd behaviour at bullfights and the religious performances of the Mexican *danzantes*—the sacred dances.

But this was all to come.

True, I did see the grotto of Lourdes where the miracles were worked and the life-size models of the Madonna and the little Bernadette— but in Marseilles.

This brightly-painted edifice is on the corner of one those small side-streets in Marseilles which consists of nothing but brothels.

More precisely, it is diagonally opposite the big artificial pool which rings with shouted exchanges each morning when the 'ladies' come to wash the more intimate items of their toilet.

A splendid gilt madonna towers aloft over Marseilles on her hill-top, winking at the Château d'If (there you can see what purports to be the sailor Dantès' actual cell—he was to become the Count of Monte Cristo) and at the copy of the Lourdes grotto, across the bay.

One must not wink at the 'houses'.

They have to shutter their windows.

This tradition is so strong that when the red-light district of Verdun, for example, was rebuilt, it was 'rationalised'.

'Houses' that had been destroyed by German shells were rebuilt without windows.

But I have digressed to pilgrimages of a somewhat different

nature. Now a trip to Domrémy is a perfect way to round off the list of purely religious places. To the very spot where the maid of Orleans heard the heavenly voices.

But nobody should be shocked by so close an association between the holiest of maidens and women of easy virtue.

I am not the first to make this association.

Near churches and cathedrals you will always find pictures of saints for sale, along with talismans and votive offerings.

As technology has developed, photographs have begun to replace paintings.

Attractive girls posed in Sainte Thérèse de Lisieux's robes, holding roses, or they tried to model the heavenly or blessed Madonna.

Postcards of girls were on sale in Toulon, for the sailors. Admittedly the subject matter there was a little more frivolous; although being on sale openly, there was nothing evidently actionable.

Nevertheless. . . .

It was striking that both types of pictures were printed by one and the same firm.

And since that firm was economically-minded, it employed the same models in both lines simultaneously.

It was quite affecting to see two copies of this same pretty face, first in the arms of a sailor, wearing the flimsiest clothing, and then in the heavy folds of the saint's robes.

Of course the firm had not done anything wrong.

Could anyone on its board of directors have conceived of someone eccentric enough to go the rounds of tobacconists in Toulon, collecting images from nautical folklore as found on postcards; then going around Notre Dame de Lorette, equally conscientiously seeking out pictures of saints?

The models themselves were the vacuous girl-friends of students and artists.

And as we can see, they had their own 'Notre Dame'—the Madonna!

To get back to the point . . .

Suppose for a moment that even one tenth of my 'spiritual wanderings' were tailed by a plain-clothes officer, or that even some of these trips featured in police reports?

'There, you see?' Monsieur Robert said, in triumph. *'C'est le pape!'*

'Let's go!'

Strange to say, Monsieur Robert was partly right.

It later transpired that amongst the other documents in my file was a memo recording that 'I had made a journey to collect material for use as anti-religious propaganda.'

For the time being that was only a fantastic supposition.

'Let's go!'

Monsieur Robert dropped everything.

Off we went.

Of course, we needed breakfast.

But first we went to the Rue de la Paix.

There was a shop that sold magnificent furs.

While I browsed amongst the chinchilla wraps, sables, stuffed wolves and bears, Monsieur Robert dived into the depths of the shop, to the proprietor's office.

A few minutes later, the owner himself emerged, running out of his office with arms outstretched in greeting.

We took a taxi and raced into the Bois de Boulogne, where we breakfasted *al fresco* at a table with a lovely check cloth.

One of the biggest furriers in Paris was with us.

His pull extended beyond the Prefecture to the Sûreté Générale itself.

'It's an artist they are persecuting!'

This was more than a Frenchman's heart could stand.

*'Monsieur, je suis entièrement à votre disposition.'**

And the monsieur (I have forgotten his name) rushed off to the Sûreté quite forgetting about the furs and other business, in the same effusive way that Monsieur Robert had abandoned all his work in the maze of the Palais des Tuileries—from where Charles IX either did, or did not, shoot the Huguenots![31]

I hurried across the road.

Into the Café des Deux Magots.

The statues of the two Chinese buddhas above the entrance

---

* French: 'Sir, I am wholly at your disposal.'

gave rise to the nickname 'the two buddhas'.

This was the headquarters of the left (democratic) wing of the Surrealists, which had broken away from the Breton faction.[32] They were my friends.

Georges Henri Rivière, in the outer circle of the group, was a curator in the Trocadéro Museum and he took me to meet the Museum's director, who had influence with the Foreign Ministry.

Tual went to talk with the deputy Guernioux, who ran the League of Human Rights—the organisation whose roots went back to the 'Dreyfusards'—the defenders of Dreyfus and Zola.

Maître Philippe Lamour had connections with the young writer, André Malraux[33] through the publishers, 'Nouvelle Revue Française' [N.R.F.]. Malraux *fera marcher** the professoriat (Langevin and the Sorbonne; the Sorbonne after all had suffered the insult of seeing the gendarmerie within its walls for the first time since Napoleon III).

I was introduced to Maître Philippe Lamour by Germaine Krull[34]—a lovely photographer and one of the 'specialists' and 'documentarists' who were especially enthusiastic about the director of *Potemkin* and *The Old and The New.*

She specialised in documentary 'photo-novels' and she, Joris Ivens and I once even filmed some counters in cafés in the suburbs.[35]

Maître Philippe went to Malraux.

Tual went off to see Guernioux.

Rivière and I drove off to the Trocadéro.

It was in the middle of a routine exercise, as various exhibits were being shuffled around.

The current exhibition was to be replaced with displays from the Congo and Australia.

Rivière and I flew down flights of stairs, through galleries and down corridors, and up to the higher reaches, to the director's office.

He and I have also raced down the staircase in David Weil's villa—he was one of the richest men in France.

Georges Henri catalogued this gentleman's collection of

---

* French: 'will mobilise'.

rarities in his spare time, a collection which the Germans plundered with particular zeal during the Occupation.

David Weil was Jewish.

When the Americans discovered them, not one salt mine in the Tyrol still contained his treasure which had been hidden deep within.

It was inside his house that I first set eyes on the most *recherché* of objects that I had ever seen in any collection up to that time. It was more valuable than the Chinese jade* carvings or the Ming and Tang horses; flat, greenish bronze plaques of now quite undatable origin from China. Their value was purely archaeological, and for all my attempts at a comment on their aesthetics, I was stuck for words . . .

This distressed Rivière visibly.

But then we were making our way through forests of African sculptures, masks, shields and spears and into the head curator's small office—he had 'pull' in the Quai d'Orsay.[36]

This 'pull' turned out to be quite feeble.

But he wrote his letter with the best intentions, and I had a chance to admire the African carvings which had been temporarily taken off display . . .

I saw the best examples only at Tristan Tzara's[37] house. He was one of the founders of the celebrated Dada movement. Never to be seen without a monocle, he had a superb collection of masks as well as early Picasso.

I met the close-cropped Gertrude Stein[38] at Tzara's.

But there is no time here to dwell on Gertrude Stein's analysis of irrationality, nor on her advice to me about my trip to America.

Nor is there time to dwell on Dadaism, the latest stage of artistic notions in disintegration, and the retreat not merely to the nursery but to the cradle itself.

Beyond that lay only Tactilism, Marinetti's 1920s firework: art that was tangible rather than visual.[39]

But all of this was over, even by the time of the events in Paris I am describing. Surrealism was still the latest thing: Max

---

* In English in the original.

Ernst's paintings, Buñuel's films (*Le Chien andalou* had been completed; work on *L'Age d'or* had just started).[40]

Also forgotten is the erstwhile popular hypothesis which held that one could discern in Negro sculpture, in its proportions—or rather disproportions—features of the pygmy, the supposed precursors of the other tribes of Africa . . .

. . . But my letter was written.

I took my leave of the treasures and their generous curators.

Which brought me to the Quai d'Orsay.

Mr Marx *(sic!)* was also very generous, but quite at a loss.

He was absolutely powerless to help.

His kind face, as it registered dismay beneath his grey stubble and with his bulging eyes, bore a very strong resemblance, somehow, to the Negro fetishes in the Trocadéro.

Maître Philippe Lamour's mission was more successful.

I was introduced to Malraux in the tiny editorial offices of the N.R.F. with its flaking ceiling. He was still young then.

But even then there was that lock of hair perpetually falling across his face, as it would do for many years to come, as he and I strolled down the streets of Moscow.

He boasted about his truly phenomenal memory, when we were somewhere near the National Hotel.

He knew all of Dostoyevsky by heart.

'I could quote from memory any passage from any novel you want.'

He stopped opposite a baker's and rattled off the first chapter of Prince Myshkin's tragic story [*The Idiot*] (from Hippolyte's letter, I think), then an excerpt from *The Brothers Karamazov*. When he began quoting Raskolnikov [*Crime and Punishment*] I took him by the arm and led him to the hotel.

He stopped again.

'I could remind you of the conversation we had in the N.R.F. editorial office, if you wanted?'

Where could we go? To a café, of course.

All the events of those heady days began in cafés, continued in a café, or ended in a café—if it was not a restaurant or a bistro in the suburbs.

We were talking about Lawrence of *Lady Chatterley's Lover*

215

fame.

Malraux was writing the preface to the French translation.

It was the English original that interested me—it had been banned in America and Britain. But I read it a few months later as I rested after my ordeals in Paris on the deck of the 'Europa', a steamer that was crossing the Atlantic to America.

The 'Europa' was a German vessel and not subject to French, British or American jurisdiction—she was extraterritorial.

And the first thing we had to obtain was a copy of *Lady Chatterley's Lover*, although Joyce's *Ulysses* was also banned in Anglo-Saxon countries.

I had a long-standing love of *Ulysses*.

I had met Joyce in Paris, but it was not at that time, nor in the context of those events, and so I must postpone my description of the meeting until another time.

I found *Lady Chatterley's Lover* very absorbing.

It is amazing how much a poor translation can wreck a good book.

I found a Russian translation of this highly poetic work by one of the best writers in English, published in Riga.

His novels and short stories aside, his 'Lectures on Classical American Literature' provided brilliant sketches of those strange American writers of the mid-nineteenth century, starting with Cooper and Poe and taking in Hawthorne and Melville before finishing with Whitman.

The translation from Riga was sheer filth and pornography.

André did all that was necessary. *'La Sorbonne marchera'.**

Two days later, the professors, headed by Langevin, were ready to protest.

But Tual's endeavours at the League of Human Rights were the most successful.

I was very glad, for him most of all.

His failure to *faire marcher*** Millerand[41] had caused him genuine distress.

This attempt got as far as a very pleasant breakfast with Madame Millerand. It led nowhere.

---

   *   French: 'The Sorbonne will march.'
 **   French: 'mobilise'.

Indeed the most interesting thing proved to be the . . . lift in their flat. It was one of the first lifts to be installed in Paris. Wallowing in the wealth of ridiculous art nouveau trimmings, rivalling our sleeping cars or Maxim's—known to us from *The Merry Widow* [42]—which has kept all its original features, this landmark carried us up to the top floor, two flights up, and took ten to fifteen minutes to do so.

Tual's mission then was the most successful.

I met not only Guernioux, but Victor Basch as well.[43]

He was a delightful old man, in soft collar and black tie done with an old-fashioned knot. He was one of the few surviving Dreyfusards.

Anatole France and Clemenceau were no longer of this world.

It is no easy matter to associate the distinctive features of this ancient imperialist 'Tiger' with his impassioned involvement in the trial of Colonel Dreyfus and, latterly, the novelist Zola.[44]

Incidentally, the 'Tiger' died soon after our meeting in 1930.

And I remember that the windows of bookshops in Paris were filled with his portrait and books about him.

Recalling all this a year later in Hollywood, I taunted Maurice Dekobra.[45] He was the celebrated author of *The Madonna of the Sleeping Cars* which broke all records—in terms of both print-run and banality.

Dekobra had written an equally banal book about Indian rajahs, *Les Tigres parfumés* [Perfumed Tigers].

On the way from Los Angeles to Mexico, we shared a sleeper and I innocently asked him whether this book was in fact about Clemenceau.

This 'Madonna' wrote her books with particular ease on trains, and on sheets of complimentary hotel writing-paper.

I believe the 'Tiger' was buried in his native land, in the Vendée.

And buried upright, as was the custom in that region.

Of course, this malicious and aggressive little monkey could only have been buried standing. He did so much damage to our country.[46]

Quite recently (this time reckoning from 1946) we saw Clemenceau restored to life on screen, in Henry King's film *Wilson* —in the scene in which the 'Big Four' of the Versailles Peace Conference were in session.[47]

Those four were abbreviated to B.F. Colonel House recalled, significantly enough, how he often felt that B.F. stood really for Big Fools.

In the film, the B.F. (take that how you will) confer in that small room in Versailles that was, in 1930, one of the most expensive restaurants anywhere near Paris.

Once, the 'pearl king' treated us to a superb breakfast of rock lobsters there. We sat diagonally opposite the commemorative plaque . . .

All in all, I have been lucky with dead celebrities.

Six months prior to that, Stresemann died.[48]

I remember the Reichstag being decked out in funeral drapes, and the bearing-out of the coffin.

Stresemann's death caused quite a stir in the press.

Raphael Schermann, the handwriting expert, was at the heart of it.

Stresemann was ill.

But one of his colleagues in the Foreign Ministry brought Raphael Schermann a handwritten note, unsigned.

Schermann leaped out of his chair, crying hysterically: 'This man is extremely sick! He must not get excited—he could die of a coronary!'

A few days later, Stresemann disobeyed the doctor's orders and went to the Reichstag.

He had a tussle with someone at a committee meeting.

And . . . Stresemann crashed to the ground. A coronary.

Stresemann had written that unsigned note.

And his colleague in the Ministry had not taken Schermann's advice—the voice of Cassandra.

Much to his despair.

He filled column inches with his despair.

Then Schermann was interviewed.

There followed a lengthy report on the whole affair.

I had never met Stresemann, although Schermann and I

did become quite thick.

He explained that his approach to analysing handwriting was to decode it.

He looked for images and outlines in the lettering that people make subconsciously, when they are preoccupied with an obsessive thought, or are ill.

You always find the shape of a pistol, for example, with potential suicides, and so on.

Stresemann had been worried about his heart condition and the infamous unsigned manuscript was full of 'pictures' of heart attacks (particularly in the unclosed 'o', 'a' and open 'v' and 'w').

'There are more things, Horatio . . .'[49] 'Cheiro' (Count Hammond's pseudonym) wrote in the album of another chiromancer I know of, Oscar Wilde.

Count Hammond read his palm while up at Oxford!

But one thing is beyond doubt.

One trick of Schermann's always worked.

When one went into his office, this bundle of nerves would leap up, pierce you with his gaze and, feverishly drawing his hand across the page, he would start writing . . . exactly as you did!

An exact replica of your hand.

He did this for me too.

And I saw it happen many times.

But I don't intend to go into the relatively simple principles underlying this phenomenon here—suffice it to say that no trickery is involved.

I did not put a single question to Victor Basch. It was enough to see him there before me, and to shake the hand of this living participant in one of the best and most exciting epics I know.

I mean the case of Zola and his fate.

But I assiduously dissociated myself from Dreyfus after he had been conclusively rehabilitated; and this was a position shared by even the most fervent of the Dreyfusards.

This diminutive nobody, this little officer, was the key figure in one of the greatest campaigns and verbal battles in the history of the world. Utterly disregarding the skirmishing over principles between the vanguard of the French intelligentsia and the reactionary

French military machine, he simply daydreamed about whether to take the stamp of an unmerited disgrace off his great-coat.

Lao-tse springs to mind—it was he who observed the way a wheel may spin but there may be a void at the centre; a gap, a space for an axle.

Similarly the spokes spin but the wheel revolves about a vacuum.

Such was the nonentity who figured in history books as a hero, martyred for his principles on Devil's Island, on a par with Silvio Pellico, Vera Figner or Sacco and Vanzetti.[50]

Interestingly, an episode from his family's chronicles casts a very dark shadow over his personal life.

When my epic adventures in Paris were reaching their conclusion and I had signed the contract with Paramount for my journey to Hollywood, the firm's chairman and I examined various possible themes.

One was *The Trial of Zola* (the play was then playing to packed houses in Berlin).[51]

I clearly saw how I could divide this theme up: after the vivid impressions that the epic had left, I wanted to make a split with reactionary France.

To make a transverse cut through the many-layered gâteau of French reaction, splicing original characters from Zola's novels on to my own vivid impressions, and to expose completely the gigantic class struggle that had raged around the trial of my favourite novelist.

And to settle a few personal scores into the bargain . . .

The parameters within which the film was dreamed up and later realised, thanks to the efforts of William Dieterle, never interested me.[52]

I wanted to crown the huge, international protest movement around the 'martyr of Devil's Island' and his defence counsel, Zola, with a minute episode—what the Americans call an anti-climax (anti-apogee, in this case, an anti-apotheosis).

And I learned of this episode from the life of the elderly Dreyfus from one of his descendants, who made no bones about it. It was a family joke.

Short, with a pince-nez and beaky nose, Monsieur Levy ran

a small publishing business which specialised in elegant editions.

A typical example might have been a folio of photographs showing the treasures of the Hôtel de Rambouillet (here 'hôtel' meaning 'palace').

In the 1930s Moussinac worked for him on such editions.

This led to a certain friendship and they went on trips together to the outskirts of Paris with Monsieur Levy and his girl-friend.

The fuss about the court cases had long since died away.

The tempest of public opinion had long since abated.

Dreyfus was a very old man.

He had to be helped in and out of his chair; he could not take off his dressing-gown on his own.

There was a family council.

The patriarch attended, but did not preside.

There was a fierce argument around the table.

The cook was suspected of theft.

Both sides of the story were presented.

The arguments for her and against.

The defence took the floor.

The prosecution launched the attack.

They concluded at length that the *corpus delicti* had not been proven.

They were ready to forget the whole thing.

When suddenly the voice of the patriarch broke the silence.

He had been forgotten in the heat of the argument.

The voice said: 'All the same, no smoke without fire . . .'

And the title: 'The End'.

Devil's Island!

Three hearings in the courts!

Anatole France and Clemenceau! The chief of staff and the enigmatic *bordereaux!** Zola's escape! *J'accuse*! And screeds of newsprint . . . !53

If occasionally I regret not having made this film, that is solely because of this coda.

. . . And even if my meeting with Victor Basch did have

---

* French: 'memoranda'

something aesthetically exciting about it, such as one might experience on meeting Mary Stuart's executioner, or the heroine of Shakespeare's sonnets, or the spy whose reports denounced Christopher Marlowe, nevertheless for my purpose, of course, the meeting with Guernioux was much the more dramatic.

Tual listened as Guernioux telephoned the Prefecture on the League's behalf, promising not to 'pull a fast one with the Italian Fascist' (who was also being expelled) on the condition that 'you don't touch Eisenstein.'

Donnant-donnant * as they say in France.

As if that was not enough, Guernioux told me, 'We will publicly question Tardieu about it, in the Chamber.'

Guernioux was a deputy.

When evening came I could hardly stand up.

But in the hotel (this time I do mean 'hotel') there was a rotund little man awaiting me. He wore a pince-nez and bowler and an umbrella rested between his knees.

It is surprising how people who lose money on your account can still have affection for you!

Paradoxically, this love can be so much greater; like Monsieur Perrichon: he did not love the young man who saved him but the person he saved.

Do you remember Labiche?[54]

That gentleman in the bowler lost a large sum through us.

Not us personally, but all of Soviet cinema.

He used to publish a very respectable film magazine.

It occurred to him suddenly to devote a special edition to Soviet cinema.

After that one edition all the advertisers who had previously bought space in the magazine stopped doing so.

The dear fellow promptly went down the tubes, losing his money and the journal.

Despite this, he was a great fan of Soviet cinema, and one of the first to greet me so warmly on my arrival in Paris. He presented me with a copy of that ill-starred edition.

---

* French: 'One good turn deserves another'.

I met with such overwhelming enthusiasm on two other occasions .

Eugène Klopfer,[55] who lost a large sum when he decided to distribute my first film *The Strike* commercially following the fuss over *Potemkin*. The film naturally never went into distribution . . .

But the owner of a cinema in San Antonio (Texas) treated us in a way we found even more touching.

He found a way of actually losing money on *Potemkin*.

But then what could you expect, distributing *Potemkin* in a redneck area like Texas?

Anyway, the frail greying man came over expressly to see us, when he heard we were stuck in Nuevo Laredo, on the US-Mexican border.[56]

He boasted of his failure with *Potemkin*.

It became clear that subsequent visits were not entirely selfless.

After the second, he began enquiring whether we would like to pass the time in a more interesting way.

Finally he asked point-blank how we felt about shooting scenes relating to the struggle for Texas.

He meant of course the 1846 war and the battles near Palo Alto and Resacca de la Palma, north of the Rio Grande.

America and Mexico went to war when Mexico opposed Texas's voluntary entry to the Union, even though it had been considered a free and independent territory since 1836.

The war ended in September of that year, with the rout of the Mexican army and Zachary Taylor's occupation of Monterrey.

Texas had joined the United States.

'My friends, who own the biggest ranches in these parts, will be only too glad to let you have as many horses as you need.'

We explained to our friend, as tactfully as we could, that first, horses alone would not be enough for a film; and second, there are other ways of losing money than by film distribution.

By making films, for example. Much more can be lost like that.

The old man grunted.

But he came again the next day.

He had a new scheme.

'Señora Montoya!' The idol of Latin America.

'Señora Montoya!'

The old man sang the name out, rolling it around his tongue.

'Señora Montoya!'

She was the Sarah Bernhardt of South America.

He had not heard of Duse.

Otherwise he would have said that she was the Duse.

'Señora Montoya . . . '

Señora Montoya was currently touring.

Señora Montoya would be in Monterrey for a performance in a matter of days. The same Monterrey that Zachary Taylor had occupied.

Monterrey is the first big city you meet as you travel from Nuevo Laredo into the heart of Mexico.

All of twenty-five kilometres or so.

'Imagine a film with Señora Montoya in it! It really doesn't matter what sort of a film it is—anything, with her in it.'

'Do you understand the magic in this name, the effect it would have on the film's success in South America?'

'Señora Montoya . . . '

He had not heard of Réjane either.[57]

Otherwise he would have called her the Argentine Réjane.

I asked him, 'Have you seen her?'

'Who? Montoya? Never! But all the same, Señora Montoya . . . '

He rolled the name around his mouth as if it were an acid-drop.

We decided to pay this marvel a visit.

I did not feel like the ride to Monterrey.

We had passed it en route to the border.

There was hardly anything there worth seeing.

'The Nights of Monterrey', which gramophone records the world over sing of so sweetly.

Apart, of course, from the attraction of the thoroughly individual Yoshiwara, which is beyond the city's outskirts.[58] This crowd-pulling landmark has city walls of its own, and it costs a silver dollar to enter.

There were two night-clubs for dancing, and one small theatre where you could watch the most indecent farces.

The boxes in the theatre were equipped with *arrière-loges* which in their turn have boxes (meaning beds).

The town walls of Yoshiwara housed countless love-nests with girls standing in the doorways and only light woven mats—which billow up in the wind—to hide the girls from passers-by during religious festivals.

Eduard Tisse did not mind where we went, or why, just as long as we went . . .

He went to see Señora Montoya, with the enterprising Texan.

My theatre-lovers returned from the performance late.

Tisse was bent double with mirth.

The gentleman from San Antonio (Texas) spat angrily and suddenly lapsed into the language of his forebears. *'Alte Hure!!'** he furiously muttered through clenched teeth.

The theatre of Señora Montoya could not hold a candle to 'The Theatre of Clara Gazul'.[59]

If the accounts of the victims were to be believed, it was close to a provincial puppet-play, with a hint of *danse macabre.*

I can still recall a sixteenth-century Italian play in which the enterprising spiritual fathers dramatised the Second Coming for the stage. They had set the play in the city's cemetery and used real corpses, taken from the mortuary.

I expect that performance was somewhat similar.

'Montoya!' Our enterprising acquaintance snorted in disgust and drove off to San Antonio (Texas) in his Ford, swallowed up by the night.

We never saw him again.

The next day, the head of immigration control on the American border ran across to our side, to our immense delight. He also used to help us to kill time—and how much of that there was!

'The visas are ready!'

And in an hour or so we were bowling across the Promised

---

* German: 'old tart!!'

Land of America, cutting through Texas.

. . . The short Frenchman in the bowler had come to help me.

He too!

'Don't argue . . . come back to my flat. I live just round the corner from you.'

It was an unusually dirty flat, for a middle-class bourgeois.

It was that particular sort of dirt which the French term *'crasse'*—an expressive word which always reminds me of greasy lamp-black, and there was as much greasy lamp-black here as you could have wished for!

There was an oval table in the drawing room; for some reason it had been covered with a green cloth.

The drawing room doubled as the owner's study.

And it presumably had also once been the editorial office for his journal.

There was a white and gold ink-well on the cloth.

Extremely grimy. And also some small coffee cups splashed with hot coffee.

And small chairs, barely visible in the gloom, chipped gilt Louis Seizes.

Two forbidding, bulky figures in sombre suits were seated upon them.

There was also a woman of slovenly appearance—his wife.

But she did not sit down, or attract attention to herself at all.

This was also a council of war, of some sort.

My portly friend, it turned out, was none other than the secretary of the *Organisation des anciens combattants*—which is like our Veterans' League, except that the soldiers were not actually wounded.

The *Organisation* was very dependable: that is to say, thoroughly reactionary.

And it was in the first *arrondissement*, at that (near Les Halles)—a nest of reaction.

This did not stop him being a very keen and, as his business affairs showed, selfless and sincere ally of our cinema.

He had decided to jeopardise his good name and reputation, and pester some of his friends in the Prefecture.

The two sombre figures, sitting on gilt chairs, helped as best they could, in whatever way they might.

They were brothers, Hungarians. There was a small shop that sold Japanese antiques on Boulevard Raspail, that had a small window display.

I often walked past this shop.

Yamagutsi-san (if I have remembered his name correctly), the owner, also ran the shop; he was a fastidious dresser.

'San' means 'Mr', so there was no point in addressing him as monsieur. That would be as stupid as the way White Guards living in Paris would speak of the Bois de Boulogne wood. 'Wood' is quite tautologous.

The small shop was cold and sterile like a monk's cell.

Some stone carvings—spelled 'netsuke', pronounced 'netske'—lay in the window.

Some ivory.

Inside, two or three bronze vases—*cloisonné*.

I do not care for this variety of Japanese applied art, where differently coloured enamels run into separate pockets, divided off from one another by thin lines of bronze. Since we were in Paris, one couldn't help thinking of *pointillisme*; of Sisley and Seurat.[60]

There too the entire surface of colour is broken up into countless discrete spots of pure colour.

But there it is done taking into account the way the eyes perceive them—that is, as a mixture.

And there the merging of the spots creates a lively, warm play of colour.

But here the different enamels do not merge; it is as though they are nailed down on to the cold surface of the vase. And the barely visible lines of the bronze veins which keep them distinct are like a suffocating web, killing the living play of colour.

The tracery resembles the metal framework of the samurai's self-discipline, imposed without mercy upon the multicoloured clash of emotions.

It was all cold, smooth and soulless.

There, on the wall, hung the darkened scabbard of a samurai sword.

Two or three silk paintings.

The collection was surprisingly small and unexceptional; the quality was low, and the owner seemingly aloof from items which the Japanese usually treat with a respectful warmth.

And it was not surprising, either.

Yamagutsi-san, immaculately attired and of impeccable demeanour, had absolutely no interest in the items in his shop.

There was something of the bronze *cloisonné* about Yamagutsi-san.

And not only the spots of colour in his neat appearance, which seemed contained within bronze interstices.

There, the olive spot of his inscrutable face.

There, the black gleam of his well-groomed hair.

The twin, sharp, dazzling white triangles of his wing collar.

His waisted jacket.

Morning trousers, perfectly pressed.

More than that.

It was as though Yamagutsi-san was also separated from the outside world—from association with people and things—by an invisible bronze web.

Smooth, cold, politely smiling.

Yamagutsi-san was not at all interested in the items in his shop.

Yamagutsi-san only found weaponry of interest.

And by no means antique weaponry.

But only the most advanced sort, of the most sophisticated construction.

However, Belgian companies for some reason were reluctant to sell their rifles to the Far East.

So it was no easy matter buying guns over the counter.

Which was why Yamagutsi-san found it so tiresome in his little shop on the corner of the Boulevard Raspail, and took not the least interest in his flourishing little business.

And the two Hungarian brothers were in contact with the Belgians, generously acquiring the rifles for Yamagutsi-san's remote homeland.

It goes without saying that brothers such as these were bound to have their means of access to the Prefecture and Sûreté.

And that, of course, was via the humblest officials. Such menials, alas, are often the most vital cogs in the biggest machines.

It is they who can write down the data from the appropriate 'covering note', mislay the agenda for a couple of days, and insert the document just when the appropriate dossier is about to be looked at.

A veritable bouquet of such papers had been collected. But the usefulness of 'little people' was discovered on the following evening.

One of the Hungarians had already seen my file!

He could not go into the details. But he muttered something encouraging as he walked past my little table near the La Coupole café.

A camera hung over his shoulder . . .

I think that sometimes he used that camera for a quite different clientèle from Yamagutsi-san's.

For a complete set, only a grandson was missing—the great writer and aristo, of the Proust sort.

But just then Vicomte Etienne de Beaumont appeared as if out of the very ground. (France does not recognise merely 'Vicomte de Bragelonne'!)[61]

Once, he and his wife were in Moscow.

He was interested in the films.

He visited my studio where I did the montage, and the projection box.

I brought him my business card when I was in Paris.

But I never again met that tall, greying, well-proportioned (although slightly stooped) Monsieur Charlus,[62] after he backed out of organising a viewing of *The Old and The New* for a select circle in his small winter retreat.

But in the moment of adversity which afflicted his colleague, the dear Vicomte, who himself did a bit of filming now and then, could never refuse to come hopping (in that way typical of him) to the rescue of *'son cher ami'.**

He himself, of course, could not do anything, but another

---

*   French: 'his dear friend'.

of his '*très chers amis*'* would, of course, be only too pleased.

Jean Hugo.

Hugo?

Yes! Victor Hugo's grandson!

Jean Hugo belonged to our caste—he worked with Carl Dreyer who made *The Passion of Joan of Arc*—one of the most beautiful pictures in the entire history of cinema.[63]

Hugo's grandson!

What more could we need?

A fair bit, it would seem.

But I was reassured on this point—the matter would not rest there. . .

Gance. Colette

People kept saying I should make contact with Abel Gance, the director of *Napoléon*.[64]

He 'ran' two . . . ministers!

True, not in particularly influential departments, but still!

I had met Gance before.

I rang him myself.

He charmingly invited me to drive over to his studio.

He was in the middle of shooting *The Death of the World*, or *The End of the World*—I forget the exact title of his last, grandiose idea. This project swallowed oceans of money, but was even so never completed.[65]

I think he was filming in Joinville.

Or possibly in another studio.

In any event it was at some distance from the city and, I think, somewhere near the Bois de Vincennes.[66]

It was of course impossible to avoid literary reminiscences associated with the wood and the castle, as we drove on our way. Here Paul Féval's heroes were shot, and in the castle languished the heroes of Ponson du Terrail.[67]

Of course, at that point no one could have foreseen that Marshal Pétain would pass his disgraced old age in this very castle.[68]

---

* French: 'very dear friends'.

But of course everyone remembers Mata Hari, who was shot in the courtyard of this palace.

Marlene Dietrich would make herself up for this role, looking at her reflection in the blade of the young officer's sword just before he ordered her execution (she was the precious *trouvaille** of von Sternberg, who was so convincing in his pictures of coarse reality, and so pathetic when he attempted aesthetic work!).[69]

The dark and slender Greta Garbo was to conduct herself more severely as she went to her death in her first film, which I was to see twice in the 'Promised Land', America, after a six-week wait for an entry permit in the border village of Nuevo Laredo (on the Mexican side).

. . . This would be two years later.

The metalled bridge did not so much link the two banks— Mexico and America—together, as hold them apart.

We were stuck on the Mexican side.

For one week. A second. A third.

The immigration authorities did not issue a permit.

Then again, anyone who has seen the film *Hold Back the Dawn* will remember Charles Boyer's confinement to the border.[70]

Three weeks was not so long in Nuevo Laredo. Even four. Five. Six.

People spent months here.

Years, sometimes.

The quota.[71]

And the whole flyblown town of Nuevo Laredo was made up of people, like this, waiting.

They have set up in business.

Shops have sprung up. Restaurants. Petrol stations.

'Businesses.'

There were even old-timers who have spent twenty or twenty-five years waiting to enter North America, the 'land of plenty'.

Most often, they were the parents or distant relatives of people who had successfully settled as émigrés.

The immigration quota stopped them crossing the narrow

---

* French: 'find'.

231

river on to the other side where the neon lights of the skyscrapers were shining; in comparison with the peasant huts of the Mexican side it looked like Manhattan: the cinemas made a racket, and there was even something like a chamber of commerce.*

The children visited their parents . . .

The offspring—their ancestors . . .

But half-way across the bridge arose an implacable, invisible spectre: the result of Hoover's policy, of unemployment and its inevitable henchman, a reduction in the number of workers permitted to enter America from abroad.

This reduction during the years of the Hoover traditions—which had not yet been dispensed with following the recent victory of Roosevelt's Democrats—was enforced extremely simply.[72]

A huge 'black maria'—a vehicle without windows and just a small door with a grille at the back—would drive up to the middle of the bridge.

Turn round sharply.

And stop just long enough to kick all the bewildered 'dagoes' out, returning them to their motherland, Mexico, which treated its own unemployed so harshly.

As I said, I was to see this cheerless picture two years later.

Now I was facing the imminent, similar prospect of flying beyond the frontiers of sweetest France.

We had driven fast, and were already turning into the studio's large driveway.

There was the usual workshop commotion. Complete pandemonium.

Only more so.

They had not yet got to grips with the film's sound-track.

They were still occupied with the fantastical idea of making this film straight off in three languages all at once!

That, at least, was what Gance was doing.

He was making three versions simultaneously—in French, English and Spanish.

Almost all the parts in *The End of the World* were semi-allegorical.

---

* In English in the original.

232

There was even a chaste maiden and something like the devil.

He was played by two actors.

One knew Spanish and French.

The other spoke English only.

There were three chaste maidens.

One for each language.

Another actor in that scene spoke French and English.

For the Spanish part there was a second actor as well.

Imagine it: three consecutive shots in three languages, with a semi-interchangeable cast and countless retakes!

Gance seemed relieved, even, that I had arrived.

So quickly did he tear himself away from this Babel of dialects and accents.

He was unusually responsive even in this small room, screened off somewhere in the heart of his studio, and made detailed notes for a talk with the ministers.

Of course, he could not make any promises. But in passing he related in some detail his own part in his film.

He acted in the prologue. In *Napoléon* he played Saint-Just.

Here he played a carpenter who was playing the role of Christ in a passion play of the sort seen at Oberammergau.[73]

I have never been to Oberammergau, but I have seen a similar play in Washington, performed by an (again) Austrian touring company made up of semi-professional actors.

I no longer recall whether the biblical beards were glued on, or were also natural growth, as in that famous village which also recently played the passion of Christ.

For me the most interesting moment was the taking of the body down from the cross. The body of the actor playing the part of the crucified Christ was very adroitly lowered from the cross by an extremely ingenious system of long towels, passed under his arms.

That was Gance's role in his picture.

He was crucified during the course of events.

And Gance tried to persuade me that he was so overcome by an ecstasy that he began speaking ancient Hebrew.

Is that possible?

PARIS, le 18 Mars 1930

Monsieur EISENSTEIN
Hôtel des Etats-Unis
35, Bd. Montparnasse
PARIS

Cher Ami,

Tout va pour le mieux en ce qui vous concerne. Votre dossier est à nouveau à l'étude, et j'espère que d'ici deux ou trois jours vous aurez une réponse définitive.

Vous pouvez venir me voir au Studio quand vous voudrez, cela me fera toujours plaisir.

Croyez-moi très cordialement vôtre.

Abel Gance

27, Avenue Kléber.
PARIS XVI

Letter from Abel Gance to Eisenstein

Portrait of Abel Gance, with dedication to Eisenstein

'*C'est à prendre ou à laisser*',* as the French say.

Perhaps in the director's performance, even that is possible.

But of course no self-respecting actor would make such demands on himself.

Only recently we recalled the demands Pudovkin made of himself in Alma-Ata, when playing Pimen in *Ivan the Terrible*.[74]

He became so absorbed in the sensation of being eighty-three years old that, rude good health notwithstanding, he suddenly collapsed in front of the camera—he had had a heart attack.

In any case, I kept the photograph of Gance in his crown of thorns, curls, and beard with blood coursing down his cheeks—and the touching inscription in the corner—as a good memento of a very kind person.

The film brought him no laurels—only thorns.

And I remember my first encounter with him a few weeks before.

The setting astounded me.

Mock Gothic and genuine Gothic.

Uncomfortable straight-backed chairs.

And for some reason there was a plaster copy of the 'Androgyne' of Naples—Life-size and taking up half the room.

Incidentally, Alberto Cavalcanti lived in just as idiosyncratic a manner in Paris.[75]

With just this difference: that here early Renaissance, rather than Gothic, arches were built into his apartment as decorations. They were cream-coloured and roughly made. Dark velvet curtains were draped between them, and behind the curtains was an azure background, and a concealed light of similar colouring shone on the pillars and piers.

Next to Gance, in one of the mock-Gothic chairs, sat his financial director, looking like an insatiable chimera. A White émigré called—I think—Monsieur Ivanov. Judging from the look of greed which he gave me, it was clear that his clawed paw was looking for a way to put the business on a different footing.

I think that Gance had already spent his budget three times over, and was looking for new ways of raising capital.

---

* French: 'You can take it or leave it.'

Not long before Chaliapin, by a circuitous route involving a French jeweller from the Rue de la Paix, had tried to woo me.[76]

Chaliapin had conceived the idea of playing Don Quixote, but was terrified of his first encounter with a 'talkie'.

I was deeply suspicious of Monsieur Ivanov's wish to take command in this matter, although he explained it away by saying Chaliapin was backing out and he wanted to start again with his 'own people'.

This notion of 'own people' was of course a more than relative one after 1920, when Chaliapin had left our homeland.

The proposal was left hanging in mid-air.

But many years later I saw Pabst's *Don Quixote* on the big screen and to my shame I could not sit through it.[77]

I remembered Chaliapin as he had been the time I saw him from the balcony of the Marinsky Theatre. He was in *Boris Godunov*, although he was still only a student.

In his memorable last scene 'Away, my child!' or in the scene where he sees the ghost, when, with a trembling gesture of his left hand, he tears the covering off the table.

(I had waited at the box-office all night to buy my ticket.)

I saw him on the screen as Ivan the Terrible in *The Maid of Pskov*, filmed by Khanzhonkov or Drankov, where his nobility, his statuesque bearing and dramatic performance all survived the ridiculous breakneck speed of the sixteen frames-per-second film running through the projector at twenty frames per second.[78]

But what *Don Quixote* showed was something that was so infinitely saddening, so full of a sense of loss . . .

But there is no time to mourn the passing of talents in a distant land. I must maintain the pace and tell of our further mishaps.

Our further encounters.

The kaleidoscopic whirl of people inveigled into the epic tale of my expulsion from Paris.

Colette![79]

Colette!

Paris without Colette is unthinkable, without Colette, the colourful author of *Claudine en ménage*.

Colette, Willy's wife.[80]

Colette—who kept delightful notes of her music-hall days.

(*L'Envers du music-hall.*)

Colette had only recently been the wife of my friend Renaud's father.[81]

But she was unfaithful—with her eldest step-son, Bertrand—Renaud's brother.

Which made it difficult for Renaud to talk to her.

So much so that he drove me along in his speedy little Bugatti, from one end of Paris to the other, to all the rendez-vous to which my epic takes me.

And when I was too tired to stand, or all the excitement proved too much, he drove like the wind to Versailles, where the unique rhythms of the palace staircases and parks and the unruffled surface of the lakes allowed us to recharge our batteries in readiness for the adventures the next day would bring.

An old friend of long standing, Léon Moussinac, took us to see Colette.[82] 'Madame Colette will of course be glad to see you . .'

Colette lived in an unusual place—in a mezzanine of the galleries of the Palais Royal.

The part where the Palais Royal seems pressed into a labyrinth of ancient, narrow alleyways.

Sharply angled streets. Full of entrance ways and recesses.

And in the twilight, characters from *La Comédie humaine* seem to glide down them; or you can imagine the ghost of Gérard de Nerval[83] hanging in the very spot where you now find the prompt box in the Théâtre Châtelet.

Colette had a few tiny rooms above the arcade, with windows facing inwards on to the gardens of the Palais Royal beneath the high-ceilinged apartments of the upper storeys.

What have these small windows not seen in their time, watching from under the vaults of the piers!

Splendid crowds strolling like figures from a Debucourt drawing on the eve of the great events that marked the finale to the eighteenth century.[84]

'Shulamites'*—as the pamphleteers called priestesses of love in those days—once streamed here in garlands.

The lists of their names are still to be found,

---

* The reference is to the song of Solomon (Trans.)

their specialities,

their price-lists.

Then this place resounded with the fiery rhetoric of Camille Desmoulins,[85] and the revolutionary citizens burst out from here on their way to the Bastille.

These arcades and gardens are utterly different from that backdrop we once painted in distant Velikie Luki during the Civil War, for Romain Rolland's *The Storming of the Bastille!*

Later beneath the vaults of this same Palais Royal, the hero of Balzac's *Kidskin* slipped off to the gaming club.

The embrasures of the windows are the same.

They saw:

the Commune.

The siege of Paris by the Germans—once. The liberation of the city.

A second siege. And a second liberation.

Colette's flat was filled to bursting with a collection of glassware.

She was a little late.

Which gave me time to cast my eyes over the marvellous glass, with inlaid flowers, birds and fruit.

Long-necked bottles, with glass figures of saints, monks and angels hovering within.

Colette arrived.

In a man's jacket, and her fringe tousled.

Dark eyeliner.

She will do everything.

On the following day, she was having lunch at a certain house.

Philippe would also be there.

She would have a word with Philippe.

The way I bowed and kissed her hand had something of the Regency period about it.

I felt at any rate like '*un roué*' (elegant bucks, companions of Philippe Egalité).[86]

My surroundings were already having too strong an effect on me.

This effect was finished off by the white wallpaper with

broad *fraise écrasée** stripes.

Philippe—that was Berthelot.

Philippe Berthelot was the all-powerful director of the Ministry of Foreign Affairs—the celebrated Quai d'Orsay, in journalists' shorthand.[87]

Cocteau: 'Forgive France'[88]

In the thick of events, I was suddenly and quite unexpectedly brought a letter from Cocteau.

An irregular pentagram in one corner of the sheet.

The writing looked like drawings, or lacework.

Lines crawled over the page like caterpillars, heading in different directions.

In this letter they did not become word butterflies—the marvellous turns of phrase Cocteau has.

The letter was purely businesslike.

Poor Cocteau—*ce pauvre Cocteau***—was in despair.

He had just heard of my predicament . . .

He begged me to pay him a call.

He wanted to help me.

He was expecting me.

I went to see him.

Cocteau lived right in the heart of Paris.

On the street behind the Madeleine.

Despite being in the middle of the city, this region behind this massive stone edifice with its Greek pediment and colonnades had a bad reputation.

'Madeleine'—'Magdalene', by analogy with the Bible—has a quite precise meaning.

This one teemed with such Magdalenes.

Cocteau liked living in this area.

He felt quite in his element.

And why not?

---

*   French: 'crushed strawberry'.
**   In French in the original.

This was all in keeping with the traditions of French aesthetes.

Once Lautrec, and in my time, Pasquenne, liked not only to visit, but on occasion to spend several days on end at 'Madame Tellier's establishments'.[89]

Poor old Pasquenne! The last man on Montparnasse to wear a bowler. The only way of keeping him in was to cut his hat up. Pasquenne's red-headed wife had several times to resort to this practice.

And poor Pasquenne would sit at home, with no way out until one of his friends bought him a new hat.

Cocteau met me with his usual affectation.

He excitedly held out his hands to me—his massive, thick-veined hands which looked as if they had once belonged to someone much sturdier—*The Hands of Orlac* (if you remember the film with Conrad Veidt?).[90]

He entreated me to . . . 'Forgive France' for the insult she had borne me.

He wanted to help me.

He was in despair.

He could not now use his contacts in the police force.

'That rascal', his valet, a young Annamite,* had just been caught in possession of opium.

Or was it hashish? Or cocaine? All I know is that it was not that wondrous marijuana, which Mexican soldiers stun themselves with.

There is a school of thought which holds that the striking ornamental displays of natural forms in Aztec, Toltec and Mayan architecture are either executed in a marijuana-induced trance, or in a flashback of one. The normal state of consciousness could hardly lead to such extravagances.

Which was exactly how Cocteau's writings and drawings were executed: as his head cleared after the opium.

So this young Annamite—'that rascal!'—had most likely been caught buying opium . . .

---

* Annam was an earlier term for Indo-China or Vietnam: hence an Annamite was a Vietnamese, but there is also an implied association with the word 'catamite' (Ed.)

Jean Cocteau's invitation to the première of *La Voix humaine*

Never mind.

'In France, women are the key to everything . . . will you allow me to do this?'

Mary Marquet was an actress with the Comédie Française.[91]

She was Monsieur Tardieu's—the Prime Minister's—mistress.

Cocteau's one-act play, *La Voix humaine*, was currently on at the Comédie Française.[92]

In the same programme he has included *The Carriage of Holy Gifts* by Clara Gazul.[93]

Mary Marquet was acting in *The Carriage of Holy Gifts*.

'She is making a lot of money because of me . . . she won't object to talking to Tardieu in bed . . .'

That's the stuff!

The last detail was in place.

My case would reach the Prime Minister's bed!

That completes the portrait of France, as far as my case is concerned.

'But you must pardon me. I will now finish earning our breakfast. In fifteen minutes I'll be brought some money. I must complete the order . . .'

The order was a couplet advertising silk stockings, from one of the biggest firms in Paris . . .

Cocteau sat down and poured couplets out on to the paper as though from a cornucopia.

That was not my first meeting with Jean Cocteau.

I had met him before.

Soon after my arrival.

A long time ago I had stuck his portrait to a wall in my flat—it was a round piece of paper which (I think) I had cut out from the magazine *Je Sais tout* [I Know Everything]. He looked thoughtful, his face forming a giant globe and with a body drawn in beneath it wearing a black jacket. One hand held the globe.

I hung up this portrait in honour of his scandalous play *Les Mariés de la Tour Eiffel.*[94]

It broke all the conventions of drama and theatre and caused a scandal.

It was the radio announcers standing on either side of the stage and dressed in Cubist costumes by Picasso.

I even parodied them once, albeit in scenes which never left the paper, for a production in Foregger's theatre; 'Mama the automatic café', and 'Papa the watercloset' for a new transcription of *Columbine's Garter* alias *Pierrette's Veil*[95]

. . . I had been warned.

Cocteau had two ways of receiving guests.

He would either pose as the condescending 'Maestro'.

Or he would play the 'slightly afflicted', admitting visitors lying down, holding forth on his health in a plaintive voice, his huge hands lying across the counterpane. I was received in the latter way.

I was even accorded the highest token of recognition.

In the middle of our conversation there was an unexpected and expressive pause.

And he spake unto me:

'I see you now suddenly filled with blood . . .'

The second meeting was less bucolic.

It was the private première of his play in the Comédie Française. The same *La Voix humaine* which guaranteed his friendship with Mademoiselle Marquet.

This première, in the decent and respectable Comédie Française, also erupted into a scandal.

The scandal was not in response to any 'leftist' trend—quite the reverse—but because of the play's uncompromising rejection of horseplay and the return to traditional theatre—and in its dreariest aspect, at that.

But one way or another, I was the supposed objective cause of this scandal.

In his letter to me, Cocteau wrote that he was not at all hurt by what I had done.

Later on he said that he rather had cause to be grateful to me.

It so happened that I had four tickets for the première.

I had dinner with my friends—four antique dealers with a charming little shop on the Rue des Saints-Pères. Gilt carved madonnas and a whole cellar full of Peruvian pitchers that were shaped like dogs. They were just becoming unfashionable, so it was a buyer's market and there was no longer any sense in dressing the window with them.

Aragon[96] ate with us too. He was a comrade we knew and liked pretty much, although in those days he was still quite taken in by the pyrotechnics of the Breton wing of the Surrealists. And so too did Paul Eluard,[97] who was also a poet and another erstwhile pillar of that same faction.

My relations with this group of the Surrealists, which centred on their leader, André Breton, remained quite cool.[98]

I think that Breton, whose Marxist pose was fairly unconvincing, took offence somewhat when I failed to announce myself to him on my arrival in Paris.

I find it an unrewarding experience mixing with drawing-room snobs who play at Marxism.

But something even worse happened here.

The lame Prampolini, an Italian artist, whose acquaintance

I made at the Congress of Independent Film-makers in La Sarraz (Switzerland) dragged me off to a party largely attended by young Italian painters and poets—Futurists.[99]

The painting may have been bad.

But the poetry was atrocious.

I found myself quite unexpectedly shaking hands with . . . Marinetti.

For my part of course such a meeting could give me no pleasure at all.

As one newspaper put it, in its account of the exhibition's opening, it was only 'piquant to watch one of the prophets of Fascism in the same room as one of Communism's angry disciples'.

Breton could not get over the fact that I had met Marinetti before I had met him.

Although I consider both Futurism and Surrealism equidistant, in terms of ideology and form, from what we have done and continue to do.

It was of course very interesting to scrutinise Marinetti in the flesh.

I never pictured him like that.

Swarthy, with a black moustache, looking like a thick-set policeman or fireman in civvies,

with a beer drinker's paunch jutting out of his morning coat, his coarse and greasy hands.

Such was this 'spiritual leader' of Futurism, Urbanism, Tactilism and, chiefly, chauvinist militarism, in 1930.

He was just as 'colourful' in his French poem which he read with a particularly oleaginous relish.

I can still hear his '*je fl-a-a-aire*'.*

What sort of aroma did the author of this poem drink in?

He wrote the poem in the persona of his dog.

Yesenin only addressed Kachalov's dog, in very lyrical lines.[100]

Not so Marinetti.

He wrote directly as though he were the dog.

And the oily '*je fl-a-a-aire*' comes from that part of the poem

---

* French: 'I can scent'

245

close to the climax, when the hound leaps at . . . human excrement
and stands, quivering, before savouring the odour of his master's
inner essence—his true, mysterious nature . . . Hm. Hm. Hm. *Parlez
pour vous-même,*[*] good sir!

None of this is invention or embroidery.

And this can be proved.

'This' was printed in a collection of *I nuovi poeti futuristi*
(1930) and can be found, with its pompous dedication to me and
my *'grand talent futuriste'*, together with the author's flowery signature, somewhere amongst the purely paradoxical rarities of my
Kunstkammer.[**]

What made Breton still more angry was my close association
with a splinter group, young people of a more democratic outlook.
Its headquarters was in a café which has two Chinese idols above
the doorway—hence its name 'Les Deux Magots'. This group had
none of the arrogance, posiness or snobbery of the 'elders'.

It launched devastating attacks on their blunders. And as it
happens, during that time, a delightful personal attack on Breton
was launched from the midst of that group—a pamphlet, called
'Un cadavre'! . . .[101]

. . . After dinner Aragon dived off somewhere in a rush. The
fourth, spare, ticket I offered to Eluard.

Paul Eluard . . .

The *Larousse Encyclopaedia* used to contain a table showing
the relative heights of the world's tallest structures.

Cathedrals, the Eiffel Tower (I saw Eiffel, when he was an
old man—he was sitting near the gate of his small villa on the road
out of Paris)[102] and the Pyramids—all were there.

Eluard bore a resemblance to Mayakovsky, with the cut of
his suit, his bearing, his shoulders, jaw and challenging expression.
But in the relative scale of people—let alone creative powers!—he
would probably have come somewhere near Notre Dame, if the late
V[ladimir] V[ladimirovich] represented the pyramid of Cheops, or
New York's Empire State Building, which in those days was yet to
find its way on to the pages of the *Larousse*.

'I merely warn you, I shall cause a scandal,' Eluard said.

---

*   French: 'Speak for yourself'
** German: 'cabinet of curiosities'

(The Surrealists detested Cocteau.)

Whether I did not fully believe his words,

or I was curious to witness a scandal—and there was every chance of one—(I had recently passed up the chance of getting into a scandal at a night-club, where a party had had the idea of drinking night-time cocktails in their pyjamas. O happy Twenties!) I had to ignore what he said.

So there we were in the dress circle of the Comédie Francaise.

Starched shirt-fronts. Cuffs. Gold pince-nez. Sleek beards. The women in severe dresses.

Society so respectable it was nauseating.

'The tabs went up', as the older workers in our theatre put it.

A decorous drowsiness settled on all the propriety.

There was only one actor in the play —a woman.[103]

With an imaginary partner . . . at the other end of a telephone.

An endless monologue.

The endlessness slowly drained the scene of any fragments of possible drama.

But my view of the stage was suddenly blocked by the towering four-square figure of Eluard.

A piercing voice:

'Who are you talking to?

'Monsieur Desbordes!?'

The actress dried.

The audience, unable to believe their ears, turned round to look at Eluard.

An unheard of insult!

A two-pronged one, at that.

First, insulting the tradition of the sacred walls of France's leading theatre.

And second, a direct attack on the author—a hint at his all-too-well known proclivities; in this case his name was linked with a young Monsieur Desbordes, a rising novelist.[104]

But Eluard gave the audience no time to come to its senses.

He hammered out with percussive rhythm the classic:

'*Merde! Merde! Merde!*'

Once, when I was reading *Nana* for the first time, I ran up against this word, and spent a long time fruitlessly searching for it in dictionaries.

I was very young and I did not know this French word. And I never surmised that it was one of those words that exist beyond the limits of academic lexicons but are not to be found in dictionaries of slang either because they are so well known.

This word fell like a hammer blow on the heads of the audience.

'*Merde! Merde! Merde!*'

But the paralysis passed.

A hoarse scream from somewhere in the murky depths of the stalls came back in reply.

The scream turned into a roar.

And the roar turned into a stampede; scores of feet ran up to the dress circle.

Gold pince-nez spun off, parting company with their ribbons.

Cuffs shot down as fists were raised, exposing hairy arms.

Starched shirt-fronts of obese men cracked apart as they rushed upstairs like crazed Tartareans.

Bloodshot eyes.

Perspiring bald patches, aglow.

Ladies screamed down from the darkness.

The actress leapt to her feet.

She ran to the footlights.

And in the finest traditions of performances of Racine and Corneille, with an extravagant gesture (her arms were unusually long), she displayed despair alternating with entreaty at correctly judged intervals: her arms were first outflung, then folded across her breast.

In vain! Short, fatty thighs had already rushed up the staircase; short fatty arms had caught hold of Eluard.

Eluard stood still, like St Sebastian with the self-consciousness of Gulliver in Lilliput.

But, flecked with saliva, the Lilliputians dragged him downwards.

The jacket ripped.

Dinner jackets also ripped.

The poet's pallid face sank like a frigate in the unequal combat, then it lunged upwards once more, jaws tightly clenched, before rolling down the massive staircase of the dress-circle, with a heap of other bodies.

A thunderous ovation was directed at the stage.

The play had to go on.

After a display of 'touched gratitude' the actress returned to the interrupted text.

And brought the play to its conclusion with no further interruption.

The end was not far off, thankfully!

The public had not had time to cool off.

And it vented the excess of personal feelings in tumultuous applause.

But . . . the success of Cocteau's work was assured.

'The fire was an enormous improvement to its appearance.'[105]

I do not know if the applause would have been as thunderous had there been no scandal.

But for the incident, would there have been such an ovation?

If it comes to that, could Cocteau have had much reason to complain?

Perhaps he should even have been grateful.

Anyway, I tried to slip out of the theatre without meeting him.

It was no easy matter.

All the side doors were hidden so cunningly that willy-nilly I had to leave via the small foyer, where, nonchalantly propping up the plinth of Molière or maybe Coquelin the Elder,[106] the author was thanking the file of departing patrons for their kind indulgence with a majestic condescension.

At last I found an emergency exit and a few minutes later I vanished down a crack between the house of Molière and the outer wall of the Palais Royal and so into the fresh air.

There!

'There!' said Cocteau, bent double. The couplets were finished.

We had a good laugh at them.

Then the bell rang.

Someone had brought Cocteau 500 francs.

We went out for breakfast.

There were countless ways of making money.

Cocteau sold the chapter-headings of his invariably sensational books to restaurants to be used as names. Recently—since 1930!—these have often been artificially extended.

Such was the case of the famous bar 'Le Boeuf sur le toît' (in memory of a pantomime by Deburau).[107] It was in the cellar of this bar that I met the incomparable Kiki[108] who modelled for all the leading artists of Montparnasse.

Kiki, who belly-danced in Spanish shawls on top of a grand piano, played by Georges-Henri Rivière of the Musée du Trocadéro.

Kiki, who gave me a signed copy of her memoirs.

'Car moi aussi j'aime les gros bateaux and les matelots.*

Finally, Kiki who herself began painting and did my portrait.

Grisha unexpectedly entered during the second sitting.

She squinted her large almond eyes like a well-disposed filly in the direction of Alexandrov and . . . my portrait ended up with the lips of the future director of The Happy Guys.[109]

Les Enfants terribles also made it on to a restaurant signboard—that was the title of his last novel.[110]

This book is signed in his characteristic caterpillar script with the usual flourish of pentagrams: 'A celui qui m'a bouleversé en me montrant ce que je touchais avec les doigts d'aveugle. A Eisenstein son ami Jean Cocteau. Paris, 9.1.1930'.**

We did not however go for breakfast under one of those signs at all.

We left the seething traffic with its roar and hubbub, and everything the French so picturesquely term 'brouhaha' and soared

---

* French: 'Because I like big boats and sailors too.'
** French: 'To the person who astounded me by showing me what I had touched with the fingers of a blind man. To Eisenstein, his friend Jean Cocteau.'

up one of the heights (*buttes*) which girdle Paris.

Those familiar with the geography of Paris will take issue with the fact that the hills do not form a complete circle; but I insist on 'girdle', since a city like Paris can only be partially girdled anyway!

This time, it was not to the heights of Sacré Coeur, which floundered in what are called 'Bon Dieu series'—small medals with Christ's flaming heart, healing ex-votos, flowers, little icons, ribbons, postcards of swallows with real badges sewn to their beaks, witnesses that this devout pilgrim did worship at the foot of this monstrous structure which dates from the time of Napoleon III and which makes a fair stab at disfiguring the face of Paris.[111]

Nor was it to the heights of Montmartre, with its mills or the Place du Tertre, all too well known from paintings, with the bar 'Au Lapin Agile', where once the peerless Aristide Bruant sang his songs.[112]

This time it was a particular delicacy. The heights of La Villette.

There, where the slaughter houses did their work.

Where the butchers toiled.

And where the little restaurants serving rare steaks were just as *recherché* as those to be found down below in the 'belly of Paris', Les Halles.[113] You can get the best cheese and onion soup ever made there; strands of cheese cling to the spoon to be drawn out of the soup like golden seaweed. Or snails, of the highest quality, in other small restaurants. The golden snails' long horns above the entrances would startle us at night.

(You must devote at least one early morning to spiritual contemplation of this shrine to gluttony—caravans of delicacies trail there each night.)

Cocteau and I talked everything over as we ate our rare steaks.

He would talk with Philippe as well as Mary Marquet, as soon as Philippe returned from Geneva.

This was the same Philippe that Colette had promised to have a word with.

And in a few days' time, there was a regular supply of small squares of paper, covered with the microscopic script of the director of the Ministry of Foreign Affairs.

They kept Cocteau abreast of my case.

Cocteau forwarded them on to me.

I kept them as a souvenir.

But before this, I met Berthelot himself.[114]

If I say that, outwardly, Philippe Berthelot reminded me a little of Thomas Mann, then it is much like the stale joke about Maklakov, a Tsarist Minister.

'What does Maklakov look like?'

'Do you know his brother, the deputy?'

'No.'

'Well, he looks nothing like him!'

Each day the epic sent me off to unexpected meetings with people, places, situations. I would have known and seen much less of life but for this!

However, all my running around in connection with it deprived me of a few things.

For example I never made it to the borzoi races or the famous ratodrome, where, according to the defined rules of the game, bulldogs meted out justice to rats.

It even stopped me from even more colourful diversions.

In Paris, apart from Germaine Krull,[115] I formed friendships with a mass of photographers.

Man Ray, Eli Lotar and Kertész, who proposed this diversion to me.[116]

Man Ray received high-society ladies at home in his studio on the small Rue Notre-Dame-des-Champs. (?)[117]

Kertész was received at the houses of high-society ladies.

Kertész said it was hard to find a spectacle more interesting than the sight of these ladies when they had 'lowered their guard'. How they treated their maids, hairdressers; how they moved around in their own homes when there was nobody to inhibit them.

A maid did not count as a person.

One could have a bath in her presence.

And a photographer at one's house was little different.

One could observe, if not physically, then morally a series of scenes worthy of Degas' 'The Bathers', in the 'hôtels' of all these countesses, princesses and viscountesses.

Eisenstein, Richter and Man Ray (Photo: Man Ray)

I was to have worn dark glasses—just in case we should suddenly meet somewhere else later—and dragged cases and lighting
equipment around after him, as if I were his assistant.

I did not make it.

Nor did I make it to the private view of the next season's
fashions at Worth's.

I was also meant to have gone to that with a photographer
—my friend, the Hungarian.

And so my acquaintance with the '*maison de couture*' was cut
off by a certain Madame Lanvin, where dresses for Madame Mara
were made up.

Casting Out the Devil

Everything was stagnating . . .

There was no progress.

Days went by.

My red ticket would shortly expire.[118]

In a few days' time I would be in Berlin.

Had the Party really lost then, and all the passion been
spent on nothing?

A shame!

But I wanted to see Vézelay before leaving France.

It has the most stunning examples of Romanesque architecture, the most intricately figured capitals. The tympanum of the
portal is most severe and, at the same time, fantastical.

We spent a fabulous day in Vézelay (it's twenty-odd kilometres outside Paris).

On my return I could not stop myself sending a postcard to
Dr Erwin Honig in Berlin. He had once come to Leningrad and visited me when I was shooting *October*. He had come as a reporter.
Then he was one of the directors of the huge Ullstein concern,
which had just had a resounding success with its *All Quiet on the
Western Front*—it had a huge print-run.[119] The postcard showed one
of the cathedral's capitals: an angel, taking a devil by its horns and
throwing it out of the ring of palms which surround the gardens of
Heaven.

I informed Dr Honig—we had stayed once in adjacent rooms in the Europa Hotel—that I expected to be in Berlin soon, since the Paris authorities were not unlike this stumpy Romanesque angel . . .

Two days later, the *Berliner Zeitung am Mittag* reached Paris. In the centre spread was my devil being dragged out by the angel— a facsimile of the reverse side of the postcard, and a howl of derision at the French. The epic had acquired an international dimension!

Conscientious workers ensured that another copy of this paper was inserted into my bulging file . . .

This of course did not help matters.

But there was worse to come.

My case was taken up by a small, apparently left-wing rag.

One good turn deserves another: they asked me for an interview.

I was very embittered.

Furthermore, I would appear to have nothing to lose.

The whole affair had clearly failed.

It was not going to come off.

Maître Lamour was in downcast and sullen mood.

Alexandrov and Tisse raced off, with their Mr Kurochkin, to Nice or the Gorge du Loup.

I gave myself free rein in this interview.

'What was your purpose in coming to Paris?'

'I wanted to make the acquaintance of that abbot who brought Huysmans into the bosom of the Catholic church.'[120]

(I remembered that the cheerful Monsieur Clout held the same position in the Prefecture as that once held by the author of *The Abyss* and *Saint Lydwina of Schiedam*.[121] Perhaps he could do the same thing for me? . . .)

'What do you have to say about the incident that has happened to you?'

'I made the mistake of coming to Paris without making a donation to the hospital for elderly and wounded policemen— which enjoys the patronage of Madame Chiappe . . .'

(This was one of the better-known if circuitous ways of slipping Monsieur Chiappe a backhander!)

255

Крупная победа демократической Франции.

Рис. Бор. Ефимова.

ВЫСЫЛКА КИНОРЕЖИССЕРА ЭЙЗЕНШТЕЙНА ИЗ ПАРИЖА.

A caricature by Boris Yefimov in *Izvestiya*: A Great Victory for Democratic France. Eisenstein the film director is extradited from Paris.

And so my retort was double-edged.

There was general laughter the next day on Montparnasse.

In the evening I sat at the last row of tables under the marquee of 'La Coupole'.

My friend, the Hungarian, loomed out of the twilight. It was the photographer [i.e. Kertész].

A few days before (again looming out of the twilight) he had stood sideways on and reported through his teeth, confidentially:

'I've seen your file . . . everything seems to be in order . . .'

But on this occasion he was furious and did not attempt discretion. He shouted:

'Have you gone mad?

'Your interview!

'Everything was all straightened out . . .

'Now it's all wrecked! Finished!'

A lot I cared!

My visa expired the following day.[122]

I had another visit to make to Monsieur Clout.

We would see . . .[123]

[How Monsieur Clout admitted me to his reception hall, and how he greeted me!

'Restez, monsieur, restez!'*

'Ouf!']

Who finally sorted it all out, I still do not know.

And—

And further—reste la question**—was the Prime Minister's sleep disturbed? This remains a secret inter piernitas*** (between the pillow and the blankets) of Mary Marquet.

If this epic had not occurred, it would have been necessary to invent it. This paraphrase of a famous saying by a famous Frenchman is very apt.[124]

The epic revealed before me a dynamic fresco of Paris such as I would never have seen as a mere tourist!

---

*   French: 'Do stay, sir, do stay!'
** French: 'the question remains'.
*** The meaning of this phrase could not be traced.

The Lady with the Black Gloves[1]

From childhood onwards people experience kindly apparitions.

Vague spectres.

Usually female.

Very often this is the memory of a mother one was separated from at an early age.

Sometimes it is a vague premonition of the face of one's future love.

Then people write poetry about them, as did the young Goethe—*an eine unbekannte Geliebte*—to an unknown beloved.[2]

But this is far from mandatory.

Such a romantic image can also penetrate into one's early dreams as a result of a chance impression.

The more so if this impression turns out to be something of a natural inclination, or predisposition in the eye of the beholder.

It is quite remarkable that this Romantic vision is not always lyrical or Romantic, like the translucent bluish vision of a good fairy with its glass bugle hanging above the cradle. It can appertain to another component of Romanticism—to its more bewitching side: irony.

A vision like this of the ironic fairy has hung above my head from my earliest years.

The fairy wears black gloves which reach above her elbow.

She has a real address, in Paris.

Real contracts in the *cafés-concerts* in France.

And she lives, in posters and etchings, with an unforgettable clarity of outline and contour, caught forever by the quick eye of one of the foremost French artists.[3]

What was it about her that first captivated me?

Was it her black gloves?

Or my father's stories—he had heard and seen the immortal *diseuse* during his trips to Paris.

Or the lyrics of her ballads, which I somehow got hold of at an early age?

Or Lautrec's drawings?

Then the memoirs—*La Chanson de ma vie* [The Song of My Life].

Then—*L'Art de chanter un chanson* [How to Sing a Song].

Then—the elusive quality.

She gave a concert in Berlin in 1926, while she was playing Marthe Schwerdtlein in Murnau's *Faust*.[4] And she had left for France only a few days before my departure. In 1929 I was exactly three days late for her concert in Paris.

Fatalité. La Princesse lointaine[*5] in her black gloves—could not be caught.

All the same we did meet.

It was most tedious.

Even though it was Paris.

I was banished from that marvellous city.

Suspected of disseminating Communist propaganda.

Later Berthelot showed me Chiappe's secret report on me.

The most arresting point of my subversive activities (on a par with the fact that all Soviet pictures were made by me!) was the line that Mr Eisenstein, *par son charme personnel*,* was recruiting supporters for the Soviet Union.

It was tiresomely dull in the hotel.

Someone was making a fuss about extending his stay.

Having to wait for telephone messages.

The Boulevard du Montparnasse was yet to turn lilac in the blue of twilight.

The 'Jockey Club' diagonally opposite had not yet come ablaze with lights. 'La Coupole' and 'Rotonde' had still to become magical night-time fairy-tales.

Dull.

Dull, in this Paris of Daumier and Lautrec, Mallarmé and Robida,[6] *The Three Musketeers* and Yvette Guilbert . . .

Tiens! Why not give her a call?

My fairy in black gloves?

Do it directly.

Without any mutual friends etc.

The phone number was no great secret.

---

*   French: 'through his own personal charm'

None of those F.C.s which the bearer of those initials, Fyodor Chaliapin hides behind.

The lady answered the phone herself.

'It's you! Well, I never . . .! Who would have . . .! Of course I know you. I'd love to see you!

I was at her house the next day.

'Money, money. I take lots of money off them. You are going to America: take as much money off them as you can. Fleece them!'

Dame Yvette did not care for America (a case of sea-sickness).[7]

And Dame Yvette loved money.

Her memoirs are full of it.

Battles over contracts. Pay rises. Scandals.

Her salon was virtually a warehouse, a shop, a depot of tangible, valuable possessions.

Small marble tables and lamps.

Small gilt chairs and porcelain.

Bronze vases.

Everything was a little dated but of good quality.

It all needed eight times as much space.

Like the Egyptian Gallery in the British Museum, where the exhibits stand six deep, mummy behind mummy.

The walls were hung with pictures. (Portraits in black gloves).

Similarly decorated is the famous New York restaurant where one may eat tenderloin steaks while looking at walls and ceilings covered with photos showing countless racing accidents.

In fact, not. In contrast to the restaurant, Madame Yvette's ceiling was bare.

Apart from a few chandeliers, scattered here and there in keeping with the variously decorated corners of the room.

Perhaps there were not several chandeliers in the same room at the same time.

Perhaps it was just table lamps and standard lamps whose tasselled shades (popular in the 1890s) brushed against the ceiling.

But thick clusters of lights, as in a shop—that is the image which comes to my mind when I describe it.

Madame was in despair.

She had a cold.

But for that, she would have sung her entire repertoire for me.

And *Dieu sait** I adored her repertoire!

I could easily believe her.

My visit, if not a matinée recital, was undoubtedly dramatic.

An auburn wig.

Self-important.

Inordinately expressive.

Exaggerated tread.

Everything was trumpeted in a declamatory style ill-suited to conversation.

Après-midi—a continuous performance.

Before I went, she bashfully slipped me a copy of Sacher-Masoch.[8] 'Read it on your travels.'

A small volume dedicated to Catherine.[9]

'If you think of placing a bet . . . there is Catherine.'**

Then I understood the show.

Madame was showing something to good effect.

Which was why Catherine in all her aspects passed before me during that memorable *après-midi*.

Madame enjoyed Shaw's one-act play on this theme.[10]

*'Elle est vieille!'*** Madame cried out.

And, masterfully chopping the air with her hand she showed how the Empress's firm grip drew from the ranks of strapping guardsmen the most strapping and handsome.

The overstated gesture of rhetoric.

You saw before you the ranks of men.

Her heavy step paced its length.

You could see the man favoured with the Empress's indulgence.

A strong arm drew the fortunate (or doomed) man towards her.

---

   *   French: 'God knows'
  ** i.e. *Katerinka*; see *Katerinki*, pp 709-11 (ed.)
 *** French: 'She is old!'

'*Mais pas trop vieille,*'* came her husband, Dr Schiller's, weak protest from the depths of his very small chair.

He is so fragile and short.

He foundered like a mouse, ground squirrel or gerbil in any chair, even on a miniature (stylish, high-quality, valuable) grey and gold Louis Quinze.

That sigh summed up the whole drama.

The doctor's waning romanticism.

And Yvette, level-headed, with old-womanly good sense.

'*Sarcey m'a dit . . .*'** [11]

(Good Lord, Sarcey! The siege of Paris. The 70s! She'd be reminiscing about Rabelais or Saint-Simon next?!)

'*Tu es folle, Yvette! On te sifflera!*'***

She told the story about how she performed a piece about the guillotine (probably by Xanrof) wearing a red scarf and a worker's hat as immortalised by Steinlen. [12]

A joint of pork was hidden inside.

And when her head fell from the guillotine into the sand, Yvette dropped this *casquette*, making a dull thud.

'And what do you think? The public were rolling in the aisles!'

Then the upper part of Yvette's face was hidden by a series of half-masks.

All different.

Amusing, portraying different characters.

Sneak previews of the great artiste's ideas were paraded before me *avant la lettre.*****

She prepared several turns in those masks.

The masks were brought to life by her movements and acting. As if it were not Yvette pulling those faces, but they themselves.

Now threatening, now droll . . .

Once Miklashevsky (who I think later became a puppeteer in Italy) [13] gave a lecture on the role of masks on the stage of the Troitsky Theatre (on Troitsky Street in Petrograd). And, snatching

---

    *   French: 'But not too old'
   ** French: 'Sarcey told me...'
  *** French: 'You're mad, Yvette! You'll be hissed!'
**** French: 'before time'

masks out from under the lectern, he put them on and made their expression alter by acting.

At the back was the chairman's table.

Respected. Like the mystics at the start of *The Fairground Booth.*

But, of its members, I remember and see only one.

The others might as well have vanished into the cutouts of their own cardboard busts.

Gone from my memory as they vanished in *The Fairground Booth.*[14]

The one person was—you have guessed it!

God-like. Incomparable.

Me-yer-hold.

I beheld him then for the first time.

And I was to worship him all my life.

The Teacher[1]

A blue crucifix thrown under the polished triangle of the Bechstein.

Colour. The texture of black varnish. Glass. Despite that, it was not a counter-relief.[2]

It was Meyerhold, spread out in his overalls [*prozodezhda*],[3] on the carpet under the piano.

There was a glass in his hands. His cunning, screwed up eyes through the glass.

It was 1922.

On the left were the stout legs of Zinaida, tightly dressed in a black silk dress.[4]

NEP.[5]

I stood at my master's feet.

'Theatrical October'[6] on the stage of *The Cuckold*.

Aksyonov was at my feet, curled up.[7]

Asleep.

Aksyonov, without a beard.

That ginger spade beard which used to flap like an aggressive banner from under the outline of the ancient 'Budyonny helmet'[8] was no more.

He was married to Popova, the Constructivist.[9]

The author in that ridiculous cross between riding breeches and light blue flares which everyone politely called 'overalls'.

The outline of Aksyonov's head looked odd without his beard.

His face was asymmetrical.

The rings of his eyes were inflamed when they were open.

Now they were shut.

And the traces of ginger down that were left seemed to grow out of the bone of his face, which had no other covering.

The master screwed up one eye.

His head fell back.

The glass almost floated in his unique fingers.

'Isadora Duncan told me today that when I'm in overalls I

look like a blue Pierrot . . .'[10]

The confession flew no further than me and no higher than Zinaida's knees.

It remained within those four walls.

Overalls. Biomechanics. Industrialisation of the theatre. Abolition of the theatre.

Theatre introduced into everyday life . . .[11]

For two years the machine-guns rattled around the strident, unswerving slogans.

A rabid polemic against Duncan's visit.

'The Mondays of *The Dawn*.'[12]

Auditoria divided in two.

How many people around him were infected by this youthful enthusiasm.

And it was all nothing more than a chance, newly-donned mask of that same Pierrot.

Diagonally across from the long table of the mystics, Pierrot-Meyerhold sat through the prologue of *The Fairground Booth*.

The blue sketch (by Ulyanov) reminds us of him.[13]

The reminiscences of Nezlobin's associate, old Nelidov, embellished the story.[14]

The pipes. The pipes!

How he played on the pipes.

Standing on one leg.

The other twisted round it like a snake.

The blue Pierrot—who embodied the director's concept—darted out between the long strips of Golovin's curtain in *Masquerade*.[15]

The small pale face between the long dangling sleeves. Sharp reflections of light, spots from the candles.

And a third face.

Blue delirium from the flares and breeches of the girl, Popova.

But he was alone. Immutable. Eternal.

The blue masks were changed round.

So were the reasons for the coffins, lowered from the walls of the besieged cities.

One day Kovalenskaya was supposed to be in the coffin.

Next day, it was Zakushnyak.[16]

And the cities changed as well.

One day, Ceuta was under siege.

Next day, it was Oppidomagne.[17]

One day it was the emotionally elevated recitative of Verhaeren's revolutionary rejoinders.

Next day, the cadences of Calderón's Catholic recitative.

The recitative derived meaning from its context.

But they were essentially all the same.

Lexington Avenue was the blacks' Fifth Avenue.

The central road through Harlem.

On the right stood a dance-hall.

On the left, a Methodist chapel.

There, a brothel.

Here, a house of salvation.

There lustfulness was externalised, in the inimitable rhythm of dancing.

And here divine illumination flowed in the same shuddering of one's limbs.

Ecstasy knows only one way of taking hold of someone.

Whether the intoxication of being possessed comes from God or the Devil, the rhythmic quaking is the same.

The pathos is identical.

And the pathos is, in essence, ultra-black.

By its nature, because of the theme and content.

In one small book, which chance preserved from the flames and was the only one so to survive, are the true discoveries St Ignatius made while in a state of ecstasy: he said as much himself.

First is the Great It.

Then it assumes the form of divinity.

It was not surprising that the Catholic mystery play of the relieved Ceuta and the revolutionary mystical Oppidomagne talked about themselves in a similar register of recitatives!

Furthermore, who could think of comparing them?

People who applauded *The Dawn* do not remember *The Constant Prince*.

Admirers of *The Constant Prince* were unlikely to go to see *The Dawn*.

Meyerhold as the Blue Pierrot. (Drawing by N. Ulyanov)

The idea of blasphemy or any other similar suspicion would hardly occur to people familiar with both plays.

Meyerhold of course was Proteus.

And *The Magnanimous Cuckold*, an evening of interludes at the Borodinskaya, or *The Forest* was always one and the same thing.[18]

Wigs and masks flew up and down.

One day they were that magnificent rarity, 'World of Art'[19]; the next, they were chucked on to the scrap heap of history only to be reborn, two days later, in golden, green, violet, sheepskin wigs in which people choked at the first performances of *The Forest*, with Zakhava as Vosmibratov.[20]

Unprincipled?

Or principled?

Neither one nor the other.

The embodiment of a principle.

The principle of theatre.

Its iridescence.

Coruscations.

Transformation.

Magic.

The master's cunning eye shone through the thin wall of the glass.

Tall and twisted.

Too thin.

Too tall.

Too twisted.

Like its owner.

With plucked eyebrows.

And inked-in wings reaching into the forehead from the bridge of his nose.

A high black collar.

A waist, which seemed even narrower than the collar.

Ludmila Gautier.[21]

A ballerina.

Which gave rise to the same jokes.

Her husband was a boxer.

Too chubby and handsome.

She felt sorry for his face, like Pompey's troops during the

Battle of Pharsalus;[22] like Pompey's troops he was beaten too often.

He was like a steam-roller, that had flattened his wife's terribly slender waist.

'Bring a photographer with you.

'Let the whole world learn of Meyerhold's fate.'

No. 23 Novinsky Boulevard was the premises of our Institute —it was Meyerhold's workshops, the GVYRM.[23]

These two floors, with a mezzanine, were packed with life.

It was as though each wall was made of cardboard and one had only to pierce it and an endless quantity of everyday objects would shower into our rooms: laundry baskets, chairs, wash-tubs, bird-cages.

The master lived in the attic with his family.

In the mezzanine floor below ground level was an empty but chaotic kitchen.

Meyerhold's curls seemed particularly grey on that day.

Perhaps it was in contrast to the clashing brown-green of the ragged coat he was wrapped up in.

The master had a rare facility for dressing up in the most *outré* clothing.

Contriving not to let his slippers drop off his feet, he hopped round the edges of the steps of the tiny spiral staircase and flew downwards.

I could barely keep up with his youthful speed.

I caught him up in the kitchen.

'Call a photographer!'

A pose . . .

I mean: an angle.

(How many heated passions does the divergence of these concepts cause: a frozen slice of movement, as opposed to the dead immobility of a pose!)

The angle was ready.

Shaking, the hapless old man lay on the stove.

Who could have said that this same old man, playing Lord Henry in *Dorian Gray*[24] would embody the irreproachable dandy, rocking in his armchair and staring at his parrot, beak to beak?

He huddled up. Frowned.

His collar reached above his ears.

His jaw was bound in a cloth.

His long fingers were just showing out of his overcoat's cuffs.

'Let everyone know how they treated Meyerhold . . .'

So far, nothing in particular had happened to Meyerhold.

However: the theatre department of Narkompros, which Meyerhold no longer ran, had that day refused the estimate for repairing the theatre . . .

'Send for a photographer . . .'

Farewell[1]

'Poslednii raz ya videl Vas tak blizko . . .'[2]

Why does this cheap phrase, preceding the image of the even more banal 'purple negro' and the trite rhyme with 'San Francisco', come to mind when I want to record the anguish of our last meeting? The pain at the circumstances of that meeting. The pain, perhaps accentuated by the premonition that this meeting would be the last?

Strange to say, probably, the first line occurred to me not spontaneously but because of the next one.

Because of that line, where the 'purple negro' acts as if in a nightmare.

For this 'purple negro . . . is handing you your mantle.'

'Mantle' being the operative word.

The line of quotation arose when, apparently, Pushkin was writing epigraphs: epigraphs, which should be read with a second, silent line added at the invariable prompting of the first, written line.

This peculiarity of Pushkin's epigraphs was examined by that incomparable literary voyeur—Shklovsky.[3] (The definition may not be polite, but it is accurate. 'And I do mean it!'*)

Of course, this was not a mantle.

It was an ordinary dark coat.

A gentleman's coat.

And nothing particular happened in fact to this coat.

One person threw it to one who was somewhat taller than he was.

And the difference between them was such that one held it straight—a little straighter than necessary—and this gave him a challenging aspect.

And the other—noticeably taller—looked broken, and it was as if the coat, which had been flung upon his shoulders, only added to his oppressive burden.

---

* In English in the original

The challenging bearing of the first, who had given the coat, and his arms, which held out this piece of cut fabric, did not leave this impression by accident.

There really was a challenge in how he acted.

The arms shook slightly. From pain. From bitterness.

From the bitterness and pain you feel for one being humiliated.

When another is being humiliated. Someone you love deeply. Adore.

The arms shook.

They shook moreover at the recognition that the second was not worthy to hold the coat out for the first—not worthy even to untie the sandals on his feet . . .

Actually, the latter's feet were well encased in galoshes.

Before, they had stood on the white flagstones which were covered with a red carpet.

The toe of the boots put in to the toe of the galoshes.

And now they sat inside.

Snugly.

But this altered nothing.

The hands shook.

The straps of the sandals were undone in his consciousness.

And under their feet, instead of rectangular paving stones in the heart of Moscow, surrounded by walls, let there lie a dusty road in Syria or Palestine. The young man who gave the coat, probably, would in reverence brush his lips against the prints left in the dust by the firm tread of his stooping teacher. And in his hands let there be a regal purple robe; the disciple would cover the shoulders of his martyred teacher with it and pour soothing oils on the wounds . . . but the cloth is not brocade.

And who said that it was a young man who gave him the coat?

This young man is over forty; of full figure, as tailors say.

And if he could not go on a two-day bender he would start running up the staircase (a bad childhood habit—he always takes stairs at a run) with that inevitable shortness of breath and his heart seething in his chest not from feelings alone. . . .

And . . . *quand même.**

And perhaps: *tant pis.***

This was how Golovin painted the cupolas of cathedrals:

sharply lit from beneath so that the sharp point of the onion domes vanished into the darkness of the night sky.[4]

Ivan the Great was borne off there, piercing the vaults of heaven.

At his feet we seemed particularly minuscule . . .

---

*   French: 'nevertheless'
** French: 'too bad'

The Treasure[1]

Rust.

Dry and reddish, it seemingly covered everything.

Even the scorched grass.

And the petrol tanks, reddened in equal measure by paint which had cracked under the baking sun, and the reddish camouflaging poured over their walls.

And the barbed wire.

And the dusty highway.

And the ridiculous village stores—the bastard offspring of the country supplies' network which had infiltrated the outskirts of Moscow.

Dust. Dust. Dust.

Reddish. Insolent.

Clinging. Working its way into your eyes and throat.

You go hoarse. Your heart chokes.

The car's bodywork was dusty.

And billowing dust pours in through the window like burning lava. Dust . . . Dust.

A big works, painted like a circus or zebra:

camouflaging.

Bombs fell here each night.

And each day there were spirals of red dust.

Dust. Dust. Dust.

Reddish. Insolent. Clinging.

Working its way into your soul.

A tight corner.

Once.

Then again.

There was no dust. No road. No highway.

A soft, green forest cutting.

A soft, green carpet.

Fences of dachas, made from flimsy boarding.

As thin as the fence around a grave.

Behind the fences, silent dachas.

Everyone who could had cleared off for the city.

You don't want to live next door to a factory when there are bombing raids going on at night.

You try to put some distance between yourself and it.

You escape the fiery rain of the incendiaries, carried by pixies at night over the dark-green carpets of the cuttings.

Right away.

Into the chilly cellars of the buildings in town.

The tram's screech calling.

People with wandering eyes hurried to get away from their dachas.

To be succeeded by soldiers imperturbably marching through the red dust.

They quartered themselves in the deserted dachas.

They unreeled the barbed wire and spools of field-telephone wire.

This cutting was particularly quiet.

And the dachas were particularly lifeless.

The sun shone on the short grass.

The wayside grass overhung the unkempt roads.

Its embraces strangled the neglected flowers.

The terrible slant of verandahs.

The floors and steps cracked underfoot.

Chair was set upon chair.

A table stood in one corner.

A broken cup. Children's toys.

An absurdly untidy old man.[2]

Traces of kasha stuck to the stubble on his chin.

These were the remains of his breakfast or . . . to be polite, words of greeting?

A girl, with dark rings under her eyes.[3]

I did not see, in the lumber of the house, the shapely curves of a Javanese puppet. White and gold. Yet there ought to have been one there . . .

I did not venture to ask,

for I would not venture to beg.

O Empress of fabled Wai-Yang.

I remember your slender gold arms, wisely broken at points

determined with mathematical precision for the future limbs to bend.

The long, slender fingers of Eastern craftsmen (I saw their fellows on other islands in the Pacific) make these gilded fragments into limbs. Wooden hinges dreamily moved the golden sticks which came to life in their hands. The dark hands of the masters poured their dark souls into the flashing arrows of the puppets' limbs and these arrows quivered like rays of the sun, separate from the fragile little body of the Empress.

Small. White. Serpent's head on a slender neck.

Two black arrows over the eyes—eyebrows.

Two carmine marks—lips in miniature.

O Empress! You would languidly hold out your arms. Then your elbows would bend as you moved them fluidly over the surfaces of your body, echoing its shape.

Only to shudder once more and change their alignment.

And simultaneously, with a shudder, you turned your head—

And we sailed off on to the enchanted sea.

We had already sensed the marvellous temples behind you, O Empress; they made mockery of the logic of architecture just as the splendid, fabulous vegetation made mockery of attempts to classify it.

And not only plants!

Surely this tree is just as much a jaguar, its clawed paw reaching out for prey?

And this little flower—is it not a bird, fluttering in the virgin forest?

And this liana is a snake that can strangle in its coils, crush in its embraces.

But there were no pagodas or gopurams flashing in the background behind you.

When I first saw you there, behind you were gleaming white, simple kitchen tiles: a white Dutch stove.

Not the patterned tiles of the fairy-tale, 17th and 18th-century Holland.

But the simple tiles of a simple house on Novinsky Boulevard.[4]

Big Dunyasha heated the Dutch stove up, grumbling.

It was no easy task, getting it hot.

It barely flickered with heat and warmth; a gleaming white tiled backdrop for our empress.

Here too the Dutch persecuted her, as they persecuted the islands where she was born. . .

Following the hands of the Javanese craftsmen came the hands of the Javanese puppeteers.

And following them—the marvellous hands of the most marvellous man who ever lived.

There he stood before us; with barely discernible movements of his fingers he poured his soul into the inspired gold and white body of the fabulous Empress.

She lived by his breath.

Shuddered and quivered.

She raised her arms sleepily and seemed to swim before the spellbound gaze of the great master's proselytes.

Somewhere here in the junk and lumber.

Amidst the smashed crockery and cracked basins.

Amidst the gaping holes of the straw-stuffed chairs and faded bouquets of artificial camellias.[5]

She was lying somewhere.

Some sort of embarrassment inhibited my asking the girl with the dark rings under her eyes.

Perhaps it is the same inhibition which dreads shattering an ancient dream merely by touching upon it too abruptly.

Then, when all is dead and altered.

From the back entrance.

In the attic.

Partly under the canopy above the back porch.

And partly in the area between the slope of the roof and the ceiling of the lumber-room.

That same thing for which I had come here at the girl's summons.

It was searingly hot in this attic, which was accessible only by tearing the plywood from the boards, which my driver Lyosha Gadov did with the unrestrained exuberance born of destruction.

The muddy dust lazily drifted over the blue-grey, dead files.

Rays of sunlight shone through the chinks and only flies played above those piles of paper.

'We are worried about them. They could burn.

'We are worried that the dacha will burn too.'

The lady had told me this a few days earlier; but now she was looking apathetically through blue-ringed eyes at the heap of files.

'They've already bombed the area around the factory really heavily . . .'

The dim-witted old man stumped about in the yard—he was her maternal grandfather.

'We couldn't save them anyway.

'They'd only get lost.

'Take them . . .'

Me Too[1]

The Litvinovs had a dog.

But he was not the one who loved it.

Madame Litvinova—Ivy Walterovna—loved the dog, a terrier.[2]

So did the children.

Of course, this is no place for a dog. And if I were as rigorous as Goethe in his old age, who resigned his position as director of the Weimar Theatre because a dog (allowed on the stage during *Saladdin*) had desecrated the great stage, I would have to stop writing now, and put down my pen in pique.[3]

Chide myself for allowing a dog on here, in such a serious endeavour; a mangy dog that, moreover, was not even mine.

This has already happened to me on one occasion.

It was Kachalov's dog that turned to me in my writing, in the form of a quotation from Yesenin.[4]

Then I was defining the effectiveness of a subject on the basis of training a dog.

It is accepted that training is the making use of already existing instincts in order to instil new ones—conditioned instincts.

Effective subjects are those which work on particularly deep-seated reflexes (chasing, *par exemple*, primarily works on the hunter's instinct for tracking down—if you see it from a borzoi's position; or the instinct for making good one's escape, from a hare's point of view, etc).

The Litvinov's dog comes in here for a less important reason.

If you look at it superficially . . .

But I fear that it is much more important if you look at the essence . . .

It is her strange name that leads her to us now:

Me Too . . .

I will not go into the linguistic debris of the origins of this name.

I do not know how to transcribe it accurately.

Eisenstein as Don Quixote: Shooting the joke film *The Battle Between Independent and Commercial Cinema,* La Sarraz, Switzerland, 1929

Is it French, Mitou?

Or Chinese, Mi-Tu?

For me it always had an English sound about it: Me Too.

And transcribed thus it always meant something.

Something perfectly defined:

'I also.' 'And I too.'

Which is why the terrier herself appears on the pages of my notes.

Which is why the terrier is a chapter heading.

Not as a terrier.

But as a name.

And not as a name.

But for what the name means.

'Me too'.*

And that is because the phrase 'Me too' is one of the basic formulae of my behaviour.

To be precise: it is one of the dynamic impulses of my behaviour.

One of the deepest hidden springs which motivated (and still motivates) me to do an enormous amount.

And so: 'Me too!** Us as well!'

---

* In English in the original.
** In English in the original. A pun follows with the Russian for 'Us as well!': *My tozhe!*

The Road to Buenos Aires[1]

Press the tip of a naked blade against my chest or the barrel of a pistol against my temple.

And force me to answer on oath which of my two favourite books has the title heading: *The Road to Buenos Aires*.

Is it the continuation of *Anatole France in His Dressing Gown*, by Brousson, or a collection of sketches by Albert Londres about the white slave trade?[2]

I would have to reach out to the relevant shelf to check.

But I can't be bothered.

My bookcases are in town, and I am at my dacha.

Besides, this is not the important thing here.

So run me through with your blade.

Squeeze the trigger.

Or listen on.

Both books have their place in my life's wanderings.

If I am to admit it with complete honesty then Brousson's book determined (psychologically) my journey overseas.

I have already in these pages bemoaned my blocking indecisiveness in everything extraneous to my wishes at each particular moment when I am working in art.[3]

And I have spoken of the way that many of my actions were determined only by the stimulus of *'y yo tambien'*—'and I too' (I can, I want, I will).

I have never suffered from petty envy.

But I am prone to great, driving and frequently impossibly greedy and inappropriate envy even to this day.

A very long time ago I was struck by the way someone at one of the Comintern conferences—I do not recall which session—made his speech in three different languages in succession.

The dream that I would one day deliver lectures in different countries and in different languages took hold.

This dream became even more urgent when I read in Brousson's *Itinéraire Paris-Buenos Aires* that Anatole France had been invited to lecture in Argentina. His lectures on Rabelais, incidentally, were deadly dull, as later on were the 'things left behind' in the book. The only thing by France I liked was *Penguin Island.*

I would have given anything to be invited somewhere, at some time, to lecture . . .

It is, of course, relatively speaking, less ridiculous and impudent than my just-finished craze for imitating . . . Balzac.

I began to write all night long, wearing a bathrobe, which resembled his white, monastic garb and gulped down cup after cup of black coffee—even though I could do this wearing perfectly normal clothes, in the daytime and drinking an ordinary glass of tea. But this 'playing at Balzac' did have a point of sorts.

I became so prudent that I did not begin writing novels, which I cannot do, but with no less fury I began to get my teeth into theoretical work on my own film experience, which by 1929 had already amassed a fair amount of this and that.

France's 'stimulus' was probably a very strong one.

It is enough to recall that speaking in public at the best of times then (just as now) caused me no end of agony, and demanded a supreme effort to overcome some sorts of inhibitions. Of the many things that I cannot do (and hence hate doing), appearing before an audience is one of the most odious tasks that can confront me.

But, despite that, I gabbled my lectures in three languages in Zurich, Berlin, Hamburg, London, Cambridge, Paris (the Sorbonne), Brussels, Antwerp, Liège, Amsterdam, Rotterdam, The Hague, New York (Columbia University), Boston (Harvard), New Haven (Yale), in the universities of Chicago and California; before blacks in New Orleans and Dorchester, at countless meetings and dinners and in Mexico City I even opened an exhibition by Siqueiros[4] in the premises of the Royal Spanish Club, which had just become the centre of Republican Spain, and for the first time the paintings of Spanish monarchs were curtained off and superseded by paintings by Communist artists.

And finally—finally—before me lay the cherished telegram —an invitation to go from the USA to Argentina and give two lectures in . . . Buenos Aires.

At last!

And I did not even go to deliver them.

Funnily enough my performances were not that bad. I have newspaper reviews somewhere commenting that how the speaker talks is more interesting than what he says, since in many cases that has often already appeared in print.

I treasure these reviews.

For the 'cross' a lecturer has to bear is something like an excess of zeal, voluntarily undertaken to prove to oneself what one is capable of.

But God only knows the labours, the efforts, the self-mastery that are required for this!

How many times have I choked on my breakfast in expectation of the address I had to make between the ice-cream and the coffee!

Afterwards I greedily launched into the ice-cream. But by then it was a pool in the bottom of the bowl—if it had not been taken away altogether.

And only the small cup of tepid coffee was left as a soothing balm for my inflamed soul . . .

How paralysis seizes me on the eve of my performance; I failed to notice almost the whole of my day-long journey through Switzerland, not preparing for my speech, but in a state of nerves before it!

Which lecture was the most terrifying?

Perhaps there were two.

Both were in America.

One was at a convention of Paramount licensees, in Atlantic City.

The other, in Hollywood.

The massive 'Europa', sister ship of the 'Columbus' and the 'Bremen', carried us across the benign serenity of the Atlantic Ocean like a magic carpet.

The ocean was unusually well-disposed to journeys there, as it was to journeys back again.

It only frowned where it had to—where we crossed the Gulf Stream; and it took us by surprise with the strong winds and spray flying higher than the top decks, as high as the captain's bridge.

The contract was signed in Paris.

And we crossed the ocean with our boss—the Vice-President

of Paramount, Mr Lasky.[5]

Mr Lasky began his career in the movies in the orchestra pit.

I think he played the *cornet à piston*, or trumpet.

One of the real pioneers of the film business.

One of the first to tread on the fertile soil of golden California and the first to hit on the idea of inviting theatre stars to act on film sets.

I believe Sarah Bernhardt was filmed in his studio.

Mr Lasky gave me paternal encouragement.

His assistant, Al Kaufman, backed him up. He began as a bouncer at a nickelodeon!

'We arrive in the States one day before the annual licensees' convention . . .'

The convention was to be in Atlantic City (a special train from New York, a colossal hotel, booked for this meeting, a giant room with little flags: Australia, Africa, France, Britain; and the separate states: Buffalo, Kentucky, Virginia, Maryland, and so on, endlessly . . .).

'You'll need to make a presentation for the people who'll be selling your films in the future . . .'

Mr Lasky and I were firmly convinced apparently that we really would be able to reach an agreement on a suitable subject for a film, although even in Paris we could not agree on the treatment of Zola or Vicky Baum's *Grand Hotel*.[6]

'Personal impressions count for a great deal . . .

'Just don't be too serious . . .

'Bring your curls into it somehow . . .

'On the whole, Americans like their lectures funny . . .

'In New York, you must stay at the Savoy Palace . . .

'Your contract gives you no other option . . .

'We have a reputation to keep up, you and I . . .

'When the reporters begin gathering in your hotel lobby . . .'

I thought it was waves rocking the boat.

But the sea was dead calm.

It was just my head, slowly revolving.

And there we were, already at the convention.

Heaven help me, if I can remember one word of my speech!

I only recall that before me, a woman gave a talk; she and her husband had made the first film about elephants—*Chang*.[7]

I vaguely remember that I got down—almost flew—from the platform after my speech.

I remember, as if it were a dream, the terrible blow on my back—the highest sign of affection from the natives—delivered by the towering, thin figure of Sam Katz, the head of world film distribution for Paramount-Public, as it then was.

'I don't know what sort of director you are (this was a typical remark from the trade division of large companies!) but I could use you as a salesman, right away!'

There could be no higher praise . . .

We spent the rest of the day with the Australian delegation, which for some reason warmed particularly towards Tisse and me.

(Alexandrov travelled to America from France on the 'Île de France' a month afterwards, but more of that elsewhere, in a different context.)[8]

. . . The second performance was much more terrifying.

It was in Hollywood.

Over breakfast with all the representatives of the cinema press of Mexico.

It would take just one slip of the tongue, mistake, or the wrong tone, and 400 of the sharpest writers would be against you—for ever!

Almost since my actual entry into the United States, the reactionary press and particularly the emerging Fascist-orientated movement of 'shirt-wearers' under Major Pease, had raised a maddening howl against my invitation, and demanded that I be removed from the American continent.[9] Apparently, my visit was 'more terrible than a landing of thousand armed men'.

My hosts held firm, cheerfully refusing to give in to panic—However, they prudently refrained from causing too great a fuss on the occasion of our visit.

But the press was seething with curiosity.

One should not forget that the three of us were practically the first Soviets in California.

At that time, relations between the two countries were on a

purely commercial footing.

And America in 1930 was the America of anti-Sovietism, of Prohibition; the imperialist America of Hoover, before, two years later, becoming the America of Roosevelt: the America of the New Era and democratic tendencies, which flourished during his second term, and the military alliance with the Soviet Union.

One should take the press seriously . . .

And looking round in alarm at the Hays Office and the first rumours of the Fish Committee,[10] Paramount called the press for a working breakfast at Bird's, which seemed to be a part of the Ambassador Hotel.

I remember at least some scattering of brightly-coloured humming birds, which decorated the walls.

But perhaps this was just the chirping of the large proportion of female reporters, who had flown in for breakfast?

I remember my path to this room.

Like a condemned man to the gallows.

Mr B.P. Schulberg, a Californian who ran Paramount, walked by my side, wreathed as always in cigar smoke.[11]

On the way he had to call in at the hotel's office, and check the boards to see how his stock was faring.

They all gambled.

They gambled on anything.

Pictures. Stars. Contracts. Screenplays. Races. How many points a train would cross in one day. Even greater sums on elections—state, federal, presidential (this gave each electoral college even more excitement in the run-up fever).

They lost fortunes.

Then won them back.

And staked them again.

Another 'Grand Old Man' among the Californians—Papa Laemmle (Universal)[12]—told me that he had staked so much at roulette in California's Monte Carlo—Tijuana*—that he could have bought the entire establishment three times over . . .

---

* Tijuana is across the border, in Mexico. During Prohibition, which banned gambling and drinking, these activities were taken beyond the range of US jurisdiction. There were gambling ships, moored out of America's waters. Gambling and drinking were also hidden from view, in

When we were not allowed back into America from Mexico for six weeks, they bet on us in Hollywood.

They bet on us even when this press call was taking place, although we did not suspect that there was a clash of interests between the New York and the Hollywood parts of the company concerned with us.

I was the protégé of the 'risk-takers', the seekers after novelty and excitement, which I represented in Jesse Lasky's company.

They faced the bankers, who represented financial interests and especially B.P.; they gambled only on certainties, in a cautious and calculating way and, more often than not, were all for repeating winning formulae.

At Paramount, the financial side came out on top; they exaggerated the difficulties of coming to an agreement with us, and on the rebound, said that it was a 'romantic' tendency that had brought us into the country.

In the unequal struggle between these two tendencies within the company, Paramount lost its prime position during those years as MGM (Metro Goldwyn Mayer) emerged with a fanfare, under the inspired 'neo-adventurism' of Irving Thalberg.[13] Instead of following the old lines of 'tried and tested', he continued with his surprising string of successes.

The feudal discord within the group aggravated the naturally difficult agreement we had regarding screenplays.

According to the contract, I had the right of veto over their proposals, and they avoided agreeing to mine.

After six months we had not made a single film.

· We parted.

Which was how it ended—what, taking his cigar out of his mouth, B.P. described as a 'noble experiment'* as he said farewell.

But it was not long before both the 'feudal lords' found themselves out of the company.

---

the fantastic speak-easies, as for example in the heart of New York, behind a concealed door, among the fur coats in the cloakroom, or in Brooklyn, behind the rear wall of a seemingly abandoned and broken-down shop. (E's note)

* A 'noble experiment' was how Americans in those years referred to the Soviet system of state control. (E's note)

[B.P. became manager for Sylvia Sidney (and I believe Clara Bow).[14]

And Jesse Lasky, in his advancing years, ended up as he had begun in cinema, as a freelance producer (and it is worth noting that his films were very accomplished, lively and topical).

But at that time, everything was still full of rosy hope.]

The Works of Daguerre[1]

One's memory retains countless impressions from first meetings.

My first meeting with Bernard Shaw.

My first skyscraper.

My first meetings with Mack Sennett and Gordon Craig.[2]

My first trip on an underground railway (Paris, 1906).

My first meeting with the queen of the platinum blondes, Jean Harlow,[3] against a backdrop of peacocks on a marble parapet, which bordered the blue tinted water of the swimming pool at the Ambassador Hotel in Hollywood . . .

The first meeting with the widow of the great writer—Anna Grigorevna Dostoyevskaya. Specially for this meeting I even read, as a boy, *The Brothers Karamazov* for the first time, so that I would have something to talk to the great lady about. But no conversation took place; the meeting was strictly a meeting; instead of a conversation I had a huge slice of fruit pie (taken from the buffet) and a game of tennis . . .

My first meeting with a film star on American soil. It was . . . Rin-Tin-Tin—the first star we met and made a film with.[4] That was in Boston, where we both made a showing in two adjacent cinemas, each before his own film . . .

The first living writer was my grandfather, the retired General Botovsky, who wrote stories for the *Russkii invalid* [The Russian Invalid].

He was extremely miserly. He died of a heart attack when the war debts were nationalised in 1917.

He was no less mean in his literary craft. He wasted no time, for example, describing nature. 'It was one of those dawns that Turgenev describes so inimitably well . . .' This was but one of the literary pearls to roll off the general's pen.

In his spare time from writing this military man would punch his batman in the jaw till the blood flowed . . .

I can even remember my first film perfectly clearly.

That was also in Paris, in 1906.

At the age of eight, I saw my first film (and it was by Méliès).*

It was typical of his work; I can still remember the intricate evolutions of the half-skeleton horses pulling the carriage . . .

All these first encounters, each in its own way, are distinguished by their own piquancy.

And one of the most piquant in terms of the impressions gained was in America—an encounter with Daguerre's work.

I do not know whether it was because I had never held one before, or never paid them any attention; or, being completely absorbed in the 'photography of the left', I had simply never noticed them.

One of the many film projects I did not realise in Hollywood was a history of Captain Sutter.[5] It was on his estates in California that gold was first discovered.

This film shared the fate of many others . . .

But it enabled me to travel extensively in California.

I even saw Sutter's fort in the capital of California—Sacramento.

In one of the big San Francisco factories—I do not recall what it manufactured—I was shown a relic preserved there:

the saw-blade from Sutter's wood mill, where the first grain of gold was found.

In some of the remoter outposts of California I visited some dim-sighted old ladies who could remember how the 'captain' would pick them up (they were still infants) and dandle them on his powerful cavalryman's knees.

Gradually, from the fragments of impressions and old traditions (in Sacramento for example, they still hold . . . beard-growing contests. The entrants all shave at the same hour of the same day, and meet up after a set period to compare the relative luxuriance of their growth), from customs and habits of the people, I have

---

* And now forty years on, from that same Paris, from the paper *Franc-Tireur* [Free-Shooter] (6 March 1946) comes an excerpt (regarding a screening of *Ivan the Terrible*). It starts: 'For cinema journalists of my generation there are a certain number of leading lights that show us the way as we travel down a long road. Méliès, Chaplin and Eisenstein are landmarks from that era when we were just kids. There are others, but Eisenstein is always among the first few.' (E's note)

built up an idea of the atmosphere in 1848 America; the America of the first gold rush; America, before the Civil War; but also' an America that was already irretrievably enmeshed in a welter of problems which the Lincoln era could only solve by creating others.

These comings and goings took us from the porches of small provincial houses, with the customary rocking-chairs and old ladies sunk in their reminiscences, to harsh landscapes, where soil had been turned over by dredgers to resemble grey hills and mountains, burying the green fields and meadows. The scenery spoke eloquently of the lust for gold devouring the organic joy of nature . . .

Not for nothing were my American hosts perturbed when I chose *L'Or* [Gold] as the subject for a screenplay—Blaise Cendrars' novel about Captain Sutter.

'What? Let the Bolsheviks get at the subject of gold . . . ?' They shook their heads and finally shelved the project with all its ramifications.

Perhaps it was just as well.

Riddled with gold mines, the Californian landscape loudly bewailed the idiotic greed for gold—of which Sutter's life, and the pages of the novel based on his adventurous life, are a howling condemnation.

But following in the footsteps of this colourful captain led me to yet another porch.

The porch of the local museum.

I have forgotten the name of the settlement.

The museum was modest enough.

It held two or three genuine artefacts from Sutter's time— some odd buttons, the brim of a felt hat and, I think, some spurs— here lovingly placed amidst whatever there was pertinent to those years.

Bead bags, candlesticks, cracked cups, samplers, fireside tongs and sugar tongs.

And two or three display cases.

And inside, a revelation.

The first daguerrotypes I had seen comprehendingly.

With Grigori Alexandrov at work on the screenplay of *An American Tragedy*.
Hollywood, October 1930 (Photo: Otto Dyar)

They were small, in parts almost black, and dated back to the time when zinc was used; or they had a smooth surface that winked at me archly—it had to be held at a certain angle for the glass surface to allow you to see the image kept inside the small lockets. They were framed by a ridged border of brass discs as fine as foil.

And there was a decoration stamped on the outside—a bouquet.

And a piece of the living image, like a living fragment of that era, a small picture of the living national character, lay within.

I think that the quantity of material I had read about California's history, the countless stories and, chiefly, the complete immersion in these bygone days, were a magical key: these forebears of modern photography were suddenly able to reach out to me from under the dusty lids of their display cases. They had an intense vitality.

I should say that the epithet 'dusty' is here a purely literary convention—display-cases are invariably dusty, just as all orphans are 'poor, but honest'!

The display case was not at all dusty.

Quite the opposite—it was highly polished, even shiny, as were the linoleum, furniture, and . . . exhibits themselves, which for all their great age, shone and gleamed as if brand new.

There was no place there for 'the patina of time'.

And the museum, with its antiseptic hygiene, rivalled the canteen, drugstores,* filling station* and Western Union* telegraph office nearby.

The past, if not actual antiquity, then another world, another century, looked at me with living eyes from those tiny, opened lockets. One half was slightly shabby with a faded velvet padding, orange, cherry or chocolate in colour; the other contained the portraits: eyes, partings, caps and beards in the Uncle Sam style of countless (and now largely anonymous people). Once they were famous, distinguished: the first inhabitants of their settlements; the agile, business-like and efficient Americans of the 'forties, 'fifties and 'sixties!

---

* In English in the original

There they were.

Their wives.

Children.

Young people, backwoodsmen who had come to the first American towns.

There they were, starting out on their careers.

Wearing their first fob chains across light waistcoats.

Posing slightly stiffly.

The neck stuck out a little too straight, from a very low-cut collar.

The huge, intricate knots of their ties seemed in competition with the interlocked fingers of their huge hands.

You could discern, in the way the fingers bent, their grip on the plough, before these fingers became accustomed to holding not a pen but a goose-quill for making entries in the office ledgers, the accounts books in the banks, the law reports of lawyers and the legal documents of counsels.

There they were, aglow with prosperity.

The lines of their fob chains echoed the diagonal folds of dazzling waistcoats: brocade, velvet, embroidered.

Rotund stomachs creased and stretched their smooth surface.

And the smoothness seemed to find its echo in their steady gaze which no longer betrayed, wide-eyed, the callow adolescence with which they first encountered life.

A comfortable deportment.

And there was something servile in the way the still, plush armchair attempted to arrange its naturally uncomfortable armrests to be as accommodating as possible beneath the elbows of Mr So-and-so,[*] who had achieved riches, recognition and general respect.

Like the throat specialist's small mirror, it reflected a spectrum of colour on to the surface of another daguerrotype, an earlier one. Between the flashes of its surface I could catch the fleeting outlines of a pale plaid.

This is the magnificent variety of checked silk materials in which the wives and mothers of well-to-do gentlemen were attired.

---

[*] In English in the original

The elaborate white ribbed caps, like helmets, enveloped the no less elaborate crimped curls of their hair-dos.

A ribbon or shawl completed the framing of the faces. They all seemed so varied.

Daguerre's and Niepce's[6] ingenious contrivances gradually superseded the early American painter, who journeyed from town to town, from company to company, painting family portraits. Thus the future Douanier Rousseau,[7] who decorated an acreage of walls above fireplaces with familiar landscapes, and introduced pictures of previously prepared paintings of seated figures wearing lace caps, black silk dresses nipped in at the waist, and shawls carelessly thrown on but . . . no faces.

The faces would be painted in, from life: the likenesses of those who had commissioned the works.

The poses in the daguerrotypes were almost as traditional. But heavens, what a variety of faces, what traces of an exciting past, could be discerned in the folds of those faces; the double chins and crows' feet; those who had achieved success looked down their noses at the camera; young, sorrowful faces looked up from under their Confederate caps, as if expecting an imminent death in the field hospitals. These have been so ruthlessly and touchingly described in the pages of notes and diaries of the 'great grizzled poet', Whitman, who eased the last moments for several dozens of them in Washington hospitals . . .

There is a school of thought—and it is probably justified—that the roots of any vice are to be found in even the most respectable of people.

Such as, for example, a tendency to steal.

I do not know how this affects people of absolute morality —I cannot count myself one of these—but I have personally experienced impulsive urges to appropriate what belongs to someone else.

I remember my hands once reaching involuntarily for my penknife to cut out the title page of an old folio edition of a collection of farces by Hans Sachs, so that I could keep an engraving of his portrait.

It was a long time ago, when I first became obsessed as a young man with popular theatre and street farce.

Hans Sachs was, I think, the first author whose coarse dia-
logues I read in the original.

That was also on a first encounter.

And he seemed unique and unsurpassable.

I do not know what vestiges of moral education remained to
restrain me from despoiling the only copy in the Rumyantsev
Library,[8] the repository of my erstwhile idol's portrait.

Probably it was the vague premonition that he was not at all
the unsurpassed perfection I had imagined—as it indeed proved,
when later I made the acquaintance of a host of French, Italian,
Spanish, Japanese or Old English *farceurs*.

. . . A similarly terrible urge ran down my spinal cord like an
electric charge, as I sat in that quiet little room in the small museum in the tiny American village.

Smash the glass panel!

Simultaneously with the wish, my conscience sensed an im-
practicable delirium.

Only my cheeks betrayed the trace of the wish. They flushed
slightly with excitement and my eyes sparkled like a little boy's.

Because little boys do not scrump apples, pears, or nuts
solely from greed—a good three-quarters of the motive comes from
the excitement of the sport!

The panel remained intact . . .

On the other hand, that day marked the start of a greedy,
ransacking-mad lollop among the old antique dealers, bric-à-brac
stores and small curio shops, of which there were so many to be
found, with their intricately wrought signs, if you travelled from Los
Angeles to Santa Monica or Pasadena.

And there, to my great embarrassment, I noticed that the
photographic images of the past which had so enthralled me were
not rated collector's items at all.

At the same time, fairly decent examples, considerably superior to the original selection in the small museum, were very
often exceedingly expensive.

It was because devotees collected not the images but the
hinged cases in which their owners carried them about as they travelled—just as every decent American (up to a certain age) has a
folding wallet of 'Pop and Mom', and (after that age) one with 'wife

and kids'.

Among these lockets there were some very interesting ones indeed: made not only from stamped leather, but also of mastic to resemble carved stone . . . But to hell with all these cases! What I found interesting were the fragments of the living soul of America's past; they were like fabulous djinns, trapped in the valves of these lockets.

I have lovingly preserved a few such djinns in the depths of my bookcases.

Sometimes I take them out.

Blow the dust off.

And it is as though I have let events from America's past out of their cases for a while: they parade before me in my imagination.

Even before I came across Gladys Mitchell's key work* or *Anthony Adverse*[9] these miraculous, glazed zinc discs directed my imagination towards reconstructing America's surprisingly picturesque past. Cities sprang up where buffaloes had roamed, or the tepees of Indian encampments once stood; or around church missions, abandoned amongst the expanses of virgin forests and prairie. Or they arose about moored ships, such as those that had dropped anchor at the mission of St Francis, and never again left that hospitable bay. The gaps between the ships were allowed to fill up with sand; the decks became the ground on which structures were erected; and these became the first houses in San Francisco!

The lid shuts with a click.

The clasp fastened.

The chest's drawer, where it is kept, is closed, or the cupboard door shuts.

And so I lock away, for months on end, my memories of those sights which I gazed at and which transported me back, mentally and spiritually, to the America of Captain Sutter.

---

* *Gone with the Wind* (E's note)

298

My Encounter with Magnasco[1]

It is not always easy to remember first encounters with people whom one will later love.

How did I come to know and love van Gogh?

I think it was because of the Shchukin Museum.[2]

I was hauled off there for the first time—I should say on the second or third day of my stay in Moscow—by one of my Moscow friends who was crazy about Gauguin.

I never much cared for Gauguin.

With the exception of the 'Yellow Christ', which I knew of from a reproduction in a small book by Tugendhold on French art.[3] I read it—someone else's copy—in Gatchina, when I was serving in the sappers. In 1918. Then it was snatched away.

It was a monochrome reproduction.

I only saw it in colour much later.

I found it very disappointing.

I had imagined an entirely different colour scheme—penetrating chrome on a background of ultramarine and cobalt with white spots—the headwear of Breton ladies. In fact it turned out to be some crushed strawberry-coloured, spherical rose bushes, with an emaciated cream-coloured body of Christ. The tone of the landscape was indistinct . . .

This happened after I had used the actual picture of Christ for all the crosses and crucifixes in *Ivan the Terrible.*

The upward flight of the arms of the crucified figure, the inclination of the head and the face, distorted with grief (the twist,* as they say of stetsons!), were exactly what I needed, and I sent my colleagues running all over Alma-Ata trying to get hold of a reproduction.

The Shchukin's collection of Gauguin was better in tone, but it was all the same *confiserie* which looked like a mass of flowerbeds.

And its mannered gaudiness—it was like looking at pink

---

* In English in the original

lobsters entangled in bluish seaweed—immediately drew me to others.

Matisse did not attract me.

I found Picasso intriguing.

The strange, wide-eyed ladies of van Dongen were eye-catching.[4]

But van Gogh was the most arresting.

Meier-Graefe travelled to Spain to pay his respects to Velazquez and suddenly bumped into El Greco.[5]

Velazquez vanished and the captivating maestro from Toledo stayed.

I had been taken to admire Gauguin, but I was instantly overcome with admiration for van Gogh.

As it happened, that was almost how my enthusiasm for El Greco himself began.

There are pictures which become so familiar from reproductions that one cannot look at the original.

Such is the fate of almost all the works in London's National Gallery.

You plough through Muther, Woermann,[6] and similar herbaria, with their dry, incomprehensible and tedious descriptions and 'long shots' of altogether too finicky and over-done masterpieces.

When you see them in real life, they look like enlarged colour reproductions of pictures you recognise from books.

I cannot look at Titian's 'The Birth of the Milky Way'.

Nor can I easily look at Holbein's 'The Ambassadors', with that foregrounded image in exaggerated perspective.

These pictures combine a wearisome effect of over-exposure with an excessively painterly style.

It is equally impossible to look at classical Greek art.

Nor can I look for any period at the Egyptians, who populate the British Museum.

The incisive, unfinished quality of Mexican plastic art, the sketchiness of Peruvian pottery, the shift in proportions in African sculpture—that was what my generation liked.

Which was why of all Titian's works, 'Pope Paul with his Nephews' attracted—and that powerfully!

КДменный крест
около Тверского Отрога монастыря.

'A Stone Cross near the Tver Otroch Monastery', drawing by Eisenstein for *Ivan the Terrible*, Part Three.

But I found my eyelids beginning to droop as I walked around the National Gallery.

The impression I had of the Louvre was quite indistinguishable from that of the Galeries Lafayette and Maison Printemps, the masquerade in Magic City, or the Bal Couture in the Grand Opéra.

Amidst this welter of people and pictures which merge with one another like a flower market or a city station, only the odd painting leaped out at me—Ingres ('Madame and Mademoiselle Rivière'); Daumier ('Crispin and Scapin') and portraits by Clouet. All the rest—including the 'Mona Lisa'—melted into a heatwave of sunspots, figurative art on the ceilings, perspiring tourists dragging their feet . . .

El Greco's 'Agony in the Garden' stands out just as sharply in the dull rooms of the National Gallery.

The dark red of the garment cuts like a razor through the greenery.

Just as the light blue cuts through the yellow in 'St Maurice' or the same blue through the violet in 'Espolio'.

Each colour is a distinct entity.

Not merging into another.

And with no softening of the general tone with thick layers of paint.

The colours cry out like a fanfare.

The form makes a mockery of the theoretical nature of the bodies and clothing, and is constructed by the incisive surfaces of the tone, through which traces of the brush's rapid movements whip like veins.

Figures intertwine, surpassing van Gogh's cypresses in their spiralling movement.

They bend over. Meander.

I met Magnasco in Odessa.

Noisy Deribasovskaya Street.

Pruzhiner's shop signs: 'Primuses repaired'.

The smell of cats; 'feesh' frying.

The smooth set of the flagstones.

Caretaker's white aprons; the town soviet has just decreed they must be issued with badges.

The red plush and the black legs of the infinitely uncomfortable chairs and the three-seater couch in the hotel room.

Cotton curtains.

A dry wind carrying dust.

A feeling of mad longing deep within.

I spent a few days in Odessa on my way to Yalta.[7]

This was not the Odessa pulsing with life that we knew when we were filming *Potemkin.*

Odessa, with the crowd scenes rolling down the steps.

Odessa, traversed by thousands of people filing down the streets to Vakulinchuk's tent.[8]

The Odessa of misty journeys in the harbour.

I was alone in the city on this occasion.

Ahead lay uneasy premonitions about *Bezhin Meadow.*

The thin trees lining the pavements.

The 'Sakhalinchik', the notorious criminal dive, destroyed.

Old-timers talked of the grand commissionaires who used to stand in the entrances of the brothels.

'Le Duc' at the top of the empty steps.[9]

Solitude. Solitude. Solitude.

Longing . . .

A pale yellow building with grey pillars.

The port of Odessa was dead.

As Odessa herself must be dead, and this longing must be oppressive, to drag me to this two-storeyed building.

The building is a museum.

A typical out-of-the-way museum.

Chipped gilt cups and teapots of ill-assorted, Empire china services.

Some Karelian birch.

Copies of paintings.

Breasts turned ruddy brown and darkened landscapes on massive canvases.

Collected from estates in the region.

So in Novgorod it was possible to see in the local museum 'The Italian Comedy' by Benois and Borisov-Musatov,[10]

in Pereslavl, next to brass Buddhas (they were made here, then taken to Mongolia, whence they were brought back as objects of great rarity!) were hung gouaches by Busch and water-colours by Serebryakova,[11]

in the Alma-Ata art annexe of the ethnographical-Darwinian museum, next to the two-headed calves and 'portraits' of nomad encampments, I saw Serov and Dobuzhinsky,[12] somewhat out of their usual environments.

. . . I met Magnasco just as unexpectedly in Odessa.

Who had brought these two small dark canvases here, with their depictions of monastic life?

How did the works of this master find their way to Odessa, precisely? He was drifting somewhere beyond the borders of universal recognition; he had not been accorded general acceptance in textbooks by the clientèle of art history.

I did not know the name, nor had I ever seen his pictures before.

I made a point of remembering this name for the future.

These were probably copies or versions.

It is known that he often repeated subjects and also known that people forged his works.

In fact, I learned all this about fifteen years later when for the first time I got my hands on a monograph by Beppo Geiger *Alessandro Magnasco* (1923).[13]

Magnasco took me into his arms earlier on than that.

And for a reason.

His figures were like El Greco's, but even thinner.

So their ecstatic angularity became even more angular.

For some minutes, this is no movement of a figure caught · by a brush, but a voluntary, affected movement of the brush, hastily disguising itself with the bones and flabby frames of ascetics with outstretched arms, bizarrely folded hands with long fingers.

More often still it seems as though these ornate and fanciful flourishes are scattered among the monks' robes in order to warm up their own swirls and curlicues, loops and intersections, around the hearth.

'Christ Assisting Peter Out of the Water' combines elements from El Greco and Honoré Daumier,

'Beggars and Street Singers' by Jacques Callot,

'Company in the Garden' by Goya or Longhi.

'The Tsar in a monk's habit'. Eisenstein's drawing for the film *Ivan the Terrible*.

Goya's 'Inquisition' is like a fragment from 'The Lesson in the Cathedral'.

Magnasco's satanic monks are a kind of missing link between Greco and Goya, between Goya and Daumier.

Goya, Daumier, Callot, Longhi—all are names I hold dear.

And many paintings by Magnasco lay hidden under these attributions for many years. Apart, it is true, from Daumier, but then again there was a large number of canvases attributed to Salvator Rosa.

Magnasco was born in 1667. He died in 1749.

I find Magnasco interesting because it was his monks, rather than El Greco's, who stylistically determined how my Ivan the Terrible—Cherkasov—should look and move.[14]

Museums at Night[1]

Museums are at their best at night.

Only at night, and particularly when alone, can there be a merging with the display, rather than simply a viewing.

In the Tretyakov Gallery, for example, the professional guides talk in an officialese that can make anything—even icons—seem banal.

Even if the group of visitors trooping in a crowd behind them did not begin the tour blind, the presence of the guide is enough to make them lose their sight.

Not because the guide is a precondition for blindness. But because these unattractive ladies with dried-out hearts and flat, jumper-covered chests ensure that the visitor's perception of the picture is not spontaneous but spoilt by tedious analysis and dull-witted conclusions.

This does not enlighten the mind, and one's vision darkens.

The international bazaars are worse places still to be in the day-time.

The memory of the Louvre makes me shudder.

It was rebuilt in the last years before the war.

But still I remember it in all the bath-house gleam of the galleries—their brightly coloured trimmings and the noise of the profoundly indifferent crowds.

The walls were as densely covered with masterpieces as an envelope might be with stamps. The women on the canvases seemed over-heated in the perspiring animal warmth generated by the milling herds of visitors.

Their corpulent—or ascetic, if by the primitives—bodies glistened with varnish.

It was as if, in this corrupting, market-place atmosphere, these Venuses, Dianas and Europas were ready to climb out of their frames. Just as Degas's unrelentingly porcine women climb out of their baths in his pungent pastels, these subjects might take the inquisitive visitor by the arm and lead him behind the olive, crimson or cherry-coloured curtains in the foregrounds of the canvases they had stepped out of.

If . . . if these ladies of bygone days were not fenced off from the hands of insatiable visitors, behind a grille.

Such is the 'Mona Lisa's' fate after that great unknown lady's notorious escapades at the hands of an international gang of crooks.[2]

The grille and lock are like a chastity belt, put on her to avoid any fresh incidents.

But there is a chastity belt on display in another museum—the Musée Cluny.

It has beautiful collections of artefacts from Renaissance and Gothic France.

Wooden sculptures.

Weaponry.

Everyday objects.

But the hordes of visitors here are all headed the same way.

They have all come with one aim.

There it is.

Lying on a violet cushion,

behind glass.

Toothed and impregnable.

A chastity belt.

This idiosyncratic metal saddle, an iron 'wait for me', assured the ladies' inviolability while their lords spent long years on the arid sands of the Holy Land, on military expeditions . . .

Mischievous tales from the past tell of duplicate keys . . .

Having seen all I wanted to in the galleries, I approached the old curator and keeper.

'There! There it is!' He shouted at me, hoarsely.

I was not able to ask my question.

He was already waving his arms expansively, pointing an index finger at one corner of the room.

'There!'

Poor old man! I was not after that, at all. I did not want to go to the chastity belt (I had already feasted my eyes on that enough!).

But, having seen the visitor approach with a question, he did not consider the possibility that he might have a thought in his head other than the whereabouts of this amusing object.

'There! There!', The ancient Frenchman gesticulated, assuming that I was a typical tourist who did not ask only because I was foreign and could not speak the language.

'There! There!' He must have pointed to that corner a thousand times a day.

But his habitual reply stuck in his throat; this odd visitor was not looking for the notorious belt. All he wanted to know was where the lavatory was . . .

By day, museums put you into a flippant frame of mind.

We lolloped through the museums in the Tower of London.

There was a staggering amount of armour.

In the main entrance, at the top of the staircase, feet planted squarely, stood Henry VIII's suit of armour.

A massive beaten sphere of a stomach, jutting forward arrogantly.

Elbows by his side.

Feet spread apart.

As though the bearer of this suit of armour had just gone away for a moment, and left his impression on the folds of its iron plates.

The armour was like a steel jacket, forever preserving the character and voluptuous habits of its wearer.

Armour. Armour. And more armour.

I walked among it with a wonderful professor of King's College, the ginger-haired Mr Isaacs.[3]

His eyes were kindly, bright, but myopic; his mind ironic (always to be expected of people who are experts on the past, especially —and it is his subject—the epoch of Shakespeare's theatre). He was like someone out of a Dickens novel, with his black gloves, inevitable black umbrella and galoshes all day long, all year round.

He and I rushed down the old streets of Oxford, where every building has its own particular history and era.

And this inexhaustible mine of information, whose frameless glasses concealed derisive slits of eyes, knew every date and all the history of each one of these houses.

But . . . confident though I may be of the way he looked, I

am less so about his glasses. Perhaps he did not wear glasses.

But they so cry out to be included in the ensemble with the umbrella and galoshes that I cannot stop myself from putting them on him, even if only a pince-nez and ribbon!

Glasses and pince-nez held an irresistible attraction for our soldiers in the First Cavalry during the Civil War. Soldiers considered glasses or pince-nez the last word in elegance. Sometimes a young soldier would be jauntily decked out in two or three pairs; he had seen them as an emblem of solidity, or maybe a symbol of learning, but at any rate as something out of the ordinary.

. . . He took me around Hampton Court and Windsor.

There we admired heroic compositions by Mantegna and Rubens's amazing picture, 'The Rape of Ganymede',[4] who was here portrayed as a chubby little boy of six or seven. His mortal fear burst out in a stream he could not contain.

This stream found its way into Russian literature.

It was that very stream which reminded Pushkin of these mountains in the painting's background, when he described the mountains in his *Journey to Erzerum,* because there, through the mists, tumbled streams of mountain waterfalls.

. . . We drew a blank at Windsor.

Only the castle was open.

The museum was closed.

This deprived me of the chance to see Holbein's pencil drawings. A pity.

What was worse, I would not be able to see the collection of da Vinci manuscripts.

I had to content myself with a reverential gaze upon his blackened notebooks in the showcases of another museum-bazaar—the Victoria and Albert in London.

But Eton partly compensated.

The young gentleman, at the very moment of his birth, is entered for this cold prison ten years in advance.

It is the first link in the future English gentleman's education, with all the indissolubility of British traditions.

Properly speaking, you will understand nothing about the composition of a Briton—and a Briton as a civil servant above all—without a visit to the *Penates* of his logical development—Eton,

Cambridge (or Oxford), London with the Tower, Westminster, the gentlemen's clubs and Whitehall.

Eton. Once more, Tudor arches.

Lawns.

The effect 'à la Daumier' of Eton toppers at twilight.[5]

The windows of the schoolrooms are unglazed as they were during the reign of the Virgin Queen.

The inordinately large pillars, running through the heart of the building, cannot compensate for the lack of warmth.

But these pillars are relics of the victory over the destroyed 'Grand Armada'. The 'Grand Armada', read about in history books at a very early age, always seemed a legend—rather like the Flying Dutchman, or the Ancient Mariner.

Here—in these masts, now become pillars and the stout school forms under the victors' descendants—here the Armada is a reality.

Every young boy—whether he is the son of a lord, belongs to one of the best families, or comes from the toiling masses—every young boy has an irresistible urge to take a knife to a desk.

But the desks at Eton are relics.

There are traces of knife-cuts on the very thick boards.

But even these cuts, by virtue of their age, are no less relics.

You cannot make out any recent carving.

Boys' natural impulse to mark their surroundings with the outline of their names has been rationalised at Eton and taken to certain ritualistic lengths.

On the floor above, next to the room with canes which are still in use to this day, is a room with a specialised use.

If the utter starkness of the stone walls on the floor below comes as a surprise, then this smallish room amazes—it is completely clad in wooden panelling.

In this respect it is like the room in Windsor Castle somehow—I have forgotten how—connected with the memory of Cardinal Wolsey.

This room, which is considerably larger than that one, has been set aside for the gratification of the young gentleman's natural instinct.

Here he may give free rein to his impulse: he may engrave

311

the angular outline of his name into the soft wood with impunity.

Which is how he will behave all his life.

Not resisting his instinct's greedy impulse.

But, systematising the situation and its sphere of application, he will rationalise the outward manifestations of his impulses.

All the more relentlessly to get his teeth into the aim or task that lies before him, behaving with wanton ruthlessness, while preserving an outward air of impassivity.

In this respect, British gentlemen are like the famous student in Arkadi Averchenko's short stories.[6]

He decided to go mad.

But, used to student thrift, before he broke something handy he would work out exactly how much it cost.

After which in an 'unrestrainable outburst' of revelry he broke whatever he could afford to.

The 'heat' itself, being brought within strictly-defined limits, was not simply quenched by this. On the contrary: it grew even hotter.

So it is with the English gentleman.

However, for the meantime, at Eton this is no more than carving one's own name (with dates and initials) into the wall's wooden panelling.

Not exactly branding a new acquisition as one's own. Nor even a sign of possession and mastery. A name, and no more.

Columns of names.

Some columns have the same surnames recurring in sequence.

Brothers?

Compare the dates.

No!

Great grandfather.

Grandfather.

Father.

Son.

Grandson.

Great grandson.

Several generations of Shelley.

And some of Byron.

In the museum at Chichen-Itzá

Countless lords.

And from Britain's most distinguished families.

And these columns have been dulled, in varying degrees, by the passage of time; the centuries have left their layer of dust. The proud, severe figure of the British gentleman stands, in the mind and consciousness of other nations, like one vertebra in an erect spine.

. . . But let us return to the Tower.

Before, I had heard Mr Isaacs lecture in the English Literature Department at King's.

Swathed in his doctor's flowing gown, which lent an added brightness to the fiery trim of his shiny, bald cranium, he paid a tribute to his unusual guest by choosing the energy of Elizabethan speech as his subject.

An unstoppable stream of quotations and imagery from this full-blooded, sensual and graphic speech lasted for two hours. The word formations and rich metaphors could, it seems, be kneaded in one's hands like the girls in the crowded parterres of the Globe, the Swan, the Blackfriars or other theatres of that great epoch.

The ebullient character of the uninhibited Elizabethans, magically brought to life by this magus in a doctor's robe, probably came with us on this visit to the Tower.

My learned friend and I allowed ourselves a schoolboy prank.

All the way up the hierarchical ladder—

from the attendant of the hall

to the attendant of the Section,

from the attendant of the Section

to the Keeper of the Department,

from the Keeper of the Department

to the Curator of the Division.

from the Curator of the Division . . .

to the Director—

there was mounting astonishment at the two visitors' (one English, one foreign) official complaint that the public was being misled.

The public was misled by 'the incompleteness of the armour on display'.

The suits of armour were missing a vital detail.

Every man jack of them (if that expression is apt in this situation).

The mystery was cleared up.

The visitors cited the Hermitage, where the armour was displayed in all its glory.

Everyone knows that in those days knights donned each iron legging separately.

Between them was another separate, small (though not always) steel shield, which stuck impudently out from under the steel opening, in the lower portion of the knight's abdomen.

The beautiful forms of the knights' armour in the Hermitage collection silently stand thus in a room in the Winter Palace set apart for them.

The puritanical keepers of the Tower had robbed their steel knights of this essential attribute of masculine aggression.

The Rabelaisian subtext of the protest at the armour's 'inadequacy' first reached the Director,

then the Curator of the Section,

then the Keeper of the Department,

then the attendant in the room,

and even the paunchy armour of Henry VIII.

It seemed to shake with the rich, earthy, Falstaffian laughter, which rolled in guffaws down from the Director's office along the whole chain of command beneath the Tower's vaults, at the protest of the two pedantic visitors—one an English professor of literature; the other a traveller from abroad.

The director of the museum of ancient Mayan culture in the town of Chichen-Itzá (on the Yucatán Peninsula) took it into his head to take me around the museum's galleries by night when there were no visitors.

Museums by night—

especially museums of sculpture—

are amazing!

I will never forget my nocturnal walk through the halls of ancient sculpture in the Hermitage, during the 'White Nights'.

I was then filming scenes for *October* in the Winter Palace; I walked along the passageways connecting the Winter Palace to the

Hermitage just as the light was shifting.[7]

It was a fantastic spectacle.

The milky bluish twilight streamed in through the windows facing the embankment.

And the white shadows, cast by white bodies of Greek statues, seemed to come alive and float in the blue gloom.

. . . It was different in the museum in Chichen-Itzá.

The nights there were pitch black.

Tropical.

Nor did the Southern Cross, only the small tip of which shyly sticks into the night sky over Mexico, provide any illumination. It was too close to the lower border of the magnificent map of the skies which burns above the Yucatán Peninsula and the Gulf of Mexico.

The museum's electricity failed just when we were entering the museum's 'secret section', where the revelry of the ancient Mayan imagination has left its mark on stone artefacts.

The whimsicality, absurdity, disproportion and . . . size of the statues increased as they suddenly leaped out at you from the darkness when the match flame flickered here and there.

Somewhere, Tolstoy (it may be in *Childhood* or *Boyhood*)[8] describes the effect of lightning when you see galloping horses.

The flashes are of such short duration that they light the horses up just one phase at a time.

So they appear motionless.

. . . Here, by contrast, the unexpected flashes as matches are struck in different parts of the room made these still, dark monsters come alive.

Because the angle at which the light burst in altered as the matches burned down, it was as though the stone monsters had had time to change position during the intervals of darkness. They had exchanged places in order to look at the violators of their eternal rest from a new viewpoint—through wide-open, gaping but dead granite eyes.

In fact, for a fully understandable reason, most of these stone monsters who loomed out of the darkness did not have eyes.

But two barrel-shaped pot-bellied gods in particular had eyes. I was led to them by the hospitable candle held by the keeper of these priceless relics, as we moved through the reefs of stone.

Light and shadow alternated.

Followed each other.

But my Virgil's [Dante's] speech flowed continuously as he led me through this dark circle of the underworld of mankind's early beliefs.

Fact about the legends of the gods who possessed the strength of two, flowed endlessly after fact, through this succession of light and dark. The actual succession of light and dark began to resemble the interplay of brilliant reason and the darker depths of the human psyche.

Two spherical, granite gods, who had that complete strength, greeted me with a smile.

Why two?

Each was designed so that he (or she) would have no need of his (or her) partner.

You could only be sure of this by feel.

Not only because it was dark in the hall.

But because the actual object of investigation was tucked away deep beneath the globes of their bellies.

'Don't be afraid to touch,' my guide told me, 'touching was and still is considered to have healing effects, endowing the toucher with a great strength. You can feel how smooth the granite has been worn . . .'

I remembered the famous statue of St Peter, in his cathedral in Rome.

His foot has been half kissed away by the devoted lips of those humbling themselves before him.

Here it was simpler and clearer.

Touching the statues of gods, albeit a symbolic action, was to join with them. By touching their 'double strength' you yourself would acquire part of that superhuman strength.

The miracle-working force suddenly proved itself.

The power abruptly came back on, and we finished our pilgrimage to these gods with all their contradictions in the yellowish glow of electric bulbs.

The mystery was dispelled together with the shadows.

It was scared off by the frank indifference of the feeble

lighting.

The round, wide-open granite eyes of my mysterious acquaintances looked vacant and stupid in that orange-yellow light.

Just as, in the blinding and false electrical light of common sense, everything about them seemed absurd.

But all it takes is for a bulb to blow, or for the dynamo at the power-station to hiccup, and you are completely at the mercy of dark, latent forces and ways of thinking.

The alternation of radiant lighting and periods of darkness allows you, as your imaginings develop, to go on fairy-tale wanderings down mysterious paths of art, like those we went down at the start, through galleries where the chiaroscuro on the bodies of the upright stone monsters moved towards us like Rembrandt's 'Night Watch', but without the beards, whiskers, smiling eyes, or the fine headwear and scarves of the Flemish guardians of order.

Museums should really be visited at night, and alone.

Colleagues. (Hospitals. Grosz. Sternberg. Jannings. Supervisors)[1]

The kindly, grizzled poet Walt Whitman used to visit the wounded and dying.[2]

He would bring them comfort and tobacco.

Kiss them on the lips. Sometimes, more than once.

He wrote letters for them.

He kept strict account and note of all the letters, tobacco, kisses and small change that he gave them.

I was sixteen years old when I went to visit the wounded, in 1914.

I also took cigarettes with me.

I didn't kiss anyone on the lips.

I entertained them with drawings.

I drew for them.

On either side of me were under-officers with luxuriant moustaches.

Medals and crosses on their chests.

I drew, sitting at the table between their beds.

Something along patriotic lines—a caricature.

Kaiser Bills. Franz Josephs. Even Krylov's fables in pictures.

The under-officers politely endured one day. Then another.

On the third, they asked me to draw 'girls'; they commissioned subjects from the popular style of 'lavatory folklore'.

This was George Grosz's[3] term for the murals above urinals; the style, according to his own testimony, that he took as the model for his own drawings.

I was to meet Grosz in Berlin in 1929. I was no forerunner of Varga.[4]

I could not do the 'pin-up Varga girls'.*

News of these drawings reached home. My visits to the hospital ceased.

---

* In English in the original.

The Kaiser and his loyal subjects. Caricature by Eisenstein, Riga 1914

The wounded lay in the Riga Rifle Club, next to the shooting range; our apartment overlooked this, on the other side of the street. They held shooting competitions there for amateurs.

In the winter, there would be skating.

And in the summer, a brass band played on the stand.

I stopped visiting the wounded for exactly thirty years.

It was not until 1944 that I visited a hospital to entertain the wounded.

A particularly idle female worker just landed me with it; she worked in the Department of Mass Propaganda for the Alma-Ata Party Committee.

That time I told the wounded about the wonders of cinema.

Living replicas of my under-officer friends were sitting in the front row. They had the same bristling moustaches and medals.

I had dreaded the visit: the hospital was a special one, for amputees.

I was expecting it to be ghastly.

But I was quite wrong.

The hospital was full of those who 'had served their time in the ranks' and although they were not entire (far from it), they had survived.

Words cannot do justice to the scene: a jaunty soldier hoisting up his dressing-gown to hop across the room and using his crutch as a cue to strike a metal ball in a game of billiards . . .

Mary Pickford[5] has said that when she was preparing to play a blind woman she spent some time living in an institution for the blind to see how they lived.

They were not at all depressed! Quite the opposite.

It was a complete hoot. None of that creeping about.

Never mind the obstacles.

It was all wildly entertaining.

Actually I was not told this by Mary herself, but by von Sternberg, who was to have made this film with her. Mary and I talked about other things.

Sternberg, of course, had a most pronounced inferiority complex.

He had the misfortune to have worked as a film editor in the past.

And, no matter how decadent were the fragments he conceived, showing off in front of Hollywood (for example, *The Scarlet
Empress*),[6] the Hollywood élite would not take him seriously, for all
his posing . . .

We went into the studio during the filming of *Morocco*
[USA, 1930], with Marlene Dietrich and Gary Cooper.

There was a deathly silence.

A crowd scene: a packed Moroccan cabaret and not a
sound.

A platform in the middle of the studio.

He was on that platform, in a black velvet jacket.

A hand supported his head.

He was thinking.

Everyone was silent, holding their breath.

Ten minutes . . . fifteen.

It didn't work.

He was not accepted into the higher circle of Hollywood
society.

He tried to humble 'this Hollywood' by a Europeanism.

He collected leftist art.

But it was not quite the thing.

The names weren't 'right'.

Or, if they were 'right', the pictures were of the 'wrong'
periods.

He commissioned Tom Belling, of course, to do a bust of
him.[7]

It was metal, made from chrome steel.

It was a very voguish material in those days; light fittings in
nightclubs and cocktail shakers—everything was made of it.

Further, the sculpture itself was a mixture of overstatement
and the barely hinted-at.

More precisely: the completely unsaid.

The prominent, shining forehead stood out—even chrome
steel lends itself to flattering a client!—beneath the metal shavings
of curls.

The metal strip of the nose stretched from the forehead
and ended in a hint of a moustache at the bottom.

Beneath the arches of the eyebrows there was nothing.

And beyond the missing eyes, cheekbones and cheeks, sunk in deep shadow, was the inside of what, on the outside, formed the occipital ridge and the top of the neck.

All in all, there was a certain resemblance to the original.

The living original of Tom Belling's sculpture himself was short, greying, with a slightly artistic haircut.

He sported a greyish moustache which drooped unevenly on either side.

He had a passion for jackets and short, square-cut coats.

He was unrestrainedly and apparently quite hopelessly in love with Marlene Dietrich.

He had to go back to square one on three occasions, when his pictures failed.

Each time he climbed back.

He was one of the highest-paid directors.

(Lubitsch alone cost more.) [8]

Even so, nothing helped.

He began his career like this.

He worked as some sort of assistant on a picture.

They finished the picture and the cast disbanded.

The director left.

Suddenly they had to film another episode.

An operation.

They were reluctant to invite the director back. So they decided to do it off their own backs.

Sternberg volunteered to film it.

He did so.

It turned out to be the best of the picture.

He told the story himself. He said he filmed it in the style of Daumier.

I was not convinced.

I think he only mentioned Daumier because he had heard of my admiration for him.

Besides, something else needs explaining.

How can this 'start' be reconciled with another start to his career, which he also told me about?

For a few cents of his own he made a short film in the Los Angeles slums (all on location): *The Salvation Hunters*. [9]

With the rest of the money he bribed Chaplin's technician—a Japanese.

He should 'accidentally' show that reel one evening. When Charlie was going to watch some picture.

If it didn't work, no harm done.

And it might work.

His boss might not shout at him.

He might even watch it to the end.

His boss did not shout at him.

He did watch it to the end.

Not only that: he was full of enthusiasm for it and wanted to meet the author.

He took him by the arm and drove him to the best restaurant.

Sternberg was 'made'.

More than that:

Chaplin took him under his wing.

Charlie himself told me about it, foaming at the mouth in a raging fury: 'I have never met such a disagreeable layabout in all my life!'

Sternberg did not stay with Chaplin's studio.

Which is probably the point of the second start of his career, with the operation and the dubious Daumier.

Snobbery could not hide Sternberg's trauma about his own inadequacy.

Hence, probably, his favouring the higher calibre actors: first Bancroft, then Jannings and Puffy Huszar.[10]

Sternberg called me to Neubabelsberg to meet Jannings and Bancroft as if we were going on an elephant hunt.

Both mastodons were insanely jealous of each other.

One acted 'naturally' (Bancroft).

The other 'actorly' (Jannings).

They were being filmed for some beer advert and raised their glasses in friendly greeting.

Their eyes flashed naked hatred as they did so.

Sternberg and I stifled our laughter . . .

He was filming *The Blue Angel*, and he showed me his rushes: he took each scene about twenty times.

Josef von Sternberg, Emil Jannings, Joseph Bancroft and Eisenstein in Babelsberg, 1929

A predilection for well-built males probably brought Sternberg some compensation.

In Berlin, he even stayed at the Hercules Hotel, across the Hercules Bridge, opposite the Hercules Fountain with its huge grey statue of Hercules . . .

But *The Docks of New York* is a great picture.

The peeling and wind-blown sets of the docks were standing outside the Paramount offices even in 1930. You could tell by looking at them how cleverly the effects had been achieved on screen by lighting and composition.

Young boys were running through them now, headed by the *Wunderkind,* an overgrown lad, my colleague Jackie Coogan.[11]

Jackie had long since lost the unique charm of the 'kid', but he had not yet turned into the repulsive-looking, balding, lanky man that he is now (1946), after returning from the front and working as an entertainer in a Los Angeles nightclub.

Looking at these photographs now, where he took himself off as the 'Kid', fills me with pain and embarrassment . . .

Blasphemy is sometimes unforgivable.

But in 1930 he played Tom Sawyer—quite inappropriately in my view—and ran off to his set leading the other boys.

I cannot imagine Tom round-faced, brown-eyed, plump and well fed.

The first Tom on screen, a silent film, played by Mary's brother, Jack Pickford, had the essential angularity of movement and his cheeks were suitably hollow.[12]

I have in my files somewhere a letter from Fairbanks[13] when I was working on the screenplay for *An American Tragedy.* Doug strongly recommended him for the role of Clyde Griffiths.

He did not play Clyde Griffiths for me.

And not only because I never in the end made *An American Tragedy. . .*

It was Holmes who played Clyde, (and very poorly too) in von Sternberg's production (which was also very poor).

So poor in fact that I could not sit through the picture to the end.[14]

And Theodore Dreiser sued Paramount.

. . . I had already seen Jannings.

Three years before, when I was in Berlin as an 'ordinary mortal', I saw him being filmed in *Faust* at Tempelhof.[15]

They sent Egon Erwin Kisch's visiting card (when he had seen *The Battleship 'Potemkin'* in Moscow), with a very warm recommendation to Jannings; he was posing majestically on a cliff, in the grey cloak of the Prince of the Underworld.

A truly majestic nod gave me to understand that I had had the honour to pass within his field of vision.

In 1929 he fervently persuaded me of the need to film a second Potemkin.

This time, Catherine the Great's lover.

With him in the eponymous role, of course.

'Potemkin had only one eye. If you were to do the film I would gouge out one of mine!'

My first studio supervisor in Hollywood was Bachman, a kind man and a specialist in 'Europeans'. It was he who had taken all the films with Jannings through Paramount and was desperately worried about *Le Petit café* by another Berliner, Ludwig Berger, with Maurice Chevalier.[16]

'When a picture is being made, the supervisior has to work like stink; when it is ready for release, he worries himself sick that the film will bring in less money than budgeted.'

Which was what happened to *Le Petit café*.

Berger sailed back to Europe.

And Bachman flew out of Paramount.

I saw him another three or so months later.

He was still out of work . . .

And I had a most remarkable character, Horace Liveright[17], as studio supervisor.

Horace Liveright used to be a publisher.

Not only a big one.

But one almost invariably linked to scandals.

Scandals are not necessarily political.

It was he who published Dreiser's 'scandalous' novels.

In particular, *An American Tragedy* that I was not allowed to film because of the risk of a political scandal.

The novel was banned for insulting common decency: Clyde and Roberta's adulterous affairs, attempted abortions (and latent propaganda in favour of abortion), and the ensuing murder . . .

The Paramount bosses aspired to make of this 'sensational' novel a run-of-the-mill (just another) albeit dramatic tale about 'boy meets girl'* without conceding on any of the 'superfluous' issues.

These issues, as I saw them, were much weightier.

I was interested at that time in films about society's *mores*, which affected Clyde in everything he did: the ruckus of election fever and his work for the re-election of the governor which broke him.

Once the Niagara of verbiage and description that Dreiser so delights in has been dammed, the novel is a very succinct, very harsh and thorough-going indictment.

Oddly, I have no recollection of Liveright himself.

Not of our first meeting, at Otto H. Kahn's breakfast table.[18]

Nor of our second—a summit meeting at my house in Beverly Hills.

I can only recall the last one because it made me miss (my fault!) meeting Greta Garbo (for the third time!).[19]

Meeting Garbo (on the film set, what is more!) was always a highly problematic affair.

And I am obliged to a mutual friend for the special privilege of such permission—Salka Viertel, wife of the director Berthold Viertel and one-time manager of the Scandinavian star.

I called her Garbelle (by analogy with beau-bel, Gar-beau, Gar-bel).

She called me Eisenbahn (railway, in German).

But this was much later, after we finally did meet.

It was when she and the director, Murnau, were mutual admirers. I remember them both sprawled across the full expanse of a billiard table at Ludwig Berger's house, holding a *tête-à-tête*.

Garbo never permitted anyone to see her while she was being filmed in the studio, because she acted—brilliantly!—purely by intuition without any formal taining.

And, as is known, intuition is not wholly reliable,

---

* In English in the original.

and then work dissolves into tearful hysterics.

For Garbo, acting was a hard way of making a living.

Oddly enough, Chaplin himself worked in a similar way (*all'improviso*); each rehearsal was spent not in perfecting a chosen way of doing a scene, but in different ways and approaches.

Out of a hundred different approaches, a director of genius is bound to come up with several inspired versions; sitting in his famous little black oilskin chair in his viewing room, he picked out the one that worked best.

If there were not enough, back he went to the set.

And if he was not in the mood for filming, he would sail off on his yacht, on the Pacific; only when he felt the inner need again to return to the studio would he come back to the film, camera, set and colleagues who were waiting for him unquestioningly.

Eisenstein, Chaplin and Tisse on Santa Catalina Island (Photo: Grigori Alexandrov)

Charlie Chaplin[1]

Of course, Chaplin is the most interesting person in Hollywood. Some people say that he is unique. That may or may not be the case. Anyway that is not at issue here. I am talking about how I travelled in 1930 from New York to Los Angeles, full of excitement and how, out of all those I was to meet, my meeting with Chaplin was the most interesting. In that distant past I still had not finally sublimated my Formalism,[2] and so I was most of all interested in the question, how, what form would our first meeting take?

The New York—Los Angeles express took four days to do the journey, crossing the sandy plains and flat-topped hills of Arizona. There is absolutely nothing to do on the train, unless you consider buying spurious hand-made artefacts at stops in Indian reservations. My imagination had so much time at its disposal that it conjured up all sorts of future meetings. Fantasy, as ever, began working in analogies: other meetings were remembered. From the earliest to the most recent. From von Sternberg in Berlin, a few months prior to this, to Douglas Fairbanks, a few weeks ago.

How did I meet Chaplin?

I met Douglas twice; after his visit to Moscow we met in New York.

It is well known that the sale of intoxicating liquor was banned in the USA in those distant years. It is equally well known that, for all that, all Americans drink. I do not, personally, but it gave me a perfect opportunity for a jibe.

Travelling to America, you sign a paper undertaking not to break or subvert any of the laws which obtain there. Somewhere, at some banquet, I excused my not drinking by saying I had undertaken not to, which led to gales of laughter in all the papers!

One way or another, Douglas's observance of prohibition was rather to do with the letter of the law. Our meeting in New York took place in the appropriate setting of the appropriate rear premises of an irreproachably decorous hotel where, however . . .

But at this point notions, foresights, memories and analogies came to rest.

331

We were met on the platform of Los Angeles station by the same Sternberg and Fairbanks, who incidentally were not to be reconciled, belonging as they did to different 'castes' of Hollywood society. And that in the 'Promised Land', too.

How would I meet Chaplin?

A few days later we went to see 'Robin Hood', with a return trip to United Artists.[3]

Fairbanks' building was on the left. We were shown into a gigantic office. I think there was a writing desk—not set at an angle, but running the entire length of the office, stretching as far as the eye could see. In scale, only the divan in the palace at Tsarskoye Selo comes near it, and that was three times longer than Alexander III was tall. There were mountains of sketches on the desk, along with open folios and heaps of photographs. Hanging out of this jungle were two bronze panthers. They caught the sunlight. This office was for anything but working in. And really the hero of *The Mark of Zorro* had left just his Mark of . . . Zero. In other words, the boss was out.

We were courteously shown a barely noticeable door on the left. It was the only thing in the office that was small. But as it turned out, the most essential: opening this door, we immediately found ourselves in an atmosphere redolent of the Sandunov baths. This was Fairbanks' own personal, Turkish bath, shining in the resplendent glory of Moorish arabesques.

Sitting on a crimson pouffe in the middle was the 'Thief of Bagdad' himself, surrounded by what looked like ancient Rome: the monumental pink body of Jo 'Schenk, the president of United Artists, draped in a sheet made of towelling;[4] slightly less monumental, olive-hued, was the body of Syd Grauman, the director of the biggest 'Chinese' cinema in Hollywood. Lost among them was the lean Jack Pickford, Mary's brother, and between the wine and the fruit were other people. I also knew Schenk. He had visited Moscow, and to tell the truth, criticised with brilliant incisiveness the plans for the new studio in Potylikha, which he saw as being quite worthless.[5] His idea was that they build it with separate pavilions isolated one from another, rather than have them all enclosed in one 'monumental' Babel, in which everyone would be under everyone else's feet (we still regret not listening to him!). That same

Schenk, by dint of not saying one word, except in English, led everyone to believe he had not the least knowledge of Russian. In consequence people spoke of his person quite uninhibitedly until he crushed everyone by asking them all questions, in Russian, and adding that on his way back he thought he might visit his grandfather in Minsk . . .

The round of handshaking came to an end, and at that moment, with an unimaginable racket, the door opened into the depths. Like the god of Sabaoth, wreathed in clouds of steam, a small wiry figure darted out of the steam section. It looked like the Chaplin of the screen, but it was of course not Chaplin, because even kids know that the Chaplin of the jet-black hair as seen on the screen does not look at all like the real-life grey-haired Chaplin. But this thought is barely formulated; you hardly have time to imagine that this could be Chaplin made-up for *City Lights*, when the man is presented before you: Charles Spencer Chaplin. Charlie cries out in greeting, speaking in broken Russian '*Gaida, troika, sneg pushistyi!* . . . '* Charlie recognised us. And Joe Schenk kindly elucidated: 'Charlie and Pola Negri were close for a year, so he reckons his Russian's fluent.'[6]

Those were the circumstances of our first meeting. Not even my most extravagant flights of fancy had pictured it taking place in the dressing-room of a Moorish-style bath-house.

But that marked the beginning of a very dear friendship, which lasted all of six months while our negotiations with Paramount tried to reconcile the irreconcilable: the subject of a film that satisfied in equal measure my interests as director and Paramount's interests as boss.

---

* Russian: 'Hey there, troika, snow's like powder!...'

Comrade Léon[1]

Is there anyone who did not find the Three Musketeers enthralling in childhood?!

Who did not delight in the bond of friendship between Athos, Porthos, Aramis and d'Artagnan?

Which of us did not take as his own ideal one of those desperate but unswervingly loyal young men who were always ready to use their swords in a noble cause?

Some would like steady Athos the most.

More athletic types would prefer Porthos.

And Aramis was the favourite of those whom the good Lord gave handsome looks, a bushy moustache and an elegant manner.

But d'Artagnan won everyone's heart; he was a selfless, ardent and devoted swordsman and companion who was prepared to risk his life for what he believed in.

Thus: we remember Athos for his murky family relationship with the terrible Milady.

Porthos for his titanic death beneath the pile of masonry.

Aramis from the pages of one of the sequels, where, hauling himself up with unforgettably slow movements, he gained the deck of the frigate that had taken him prisoner and, by casually raising one hand, became the unchallenged captain of the vessel. On that hand gleamed the amethyst ring that had belonged to a general in one of the most powerful secret organisations, to which the vessel's captain also belonged . . .

But we remember d'Artagnan mainly for his moral qualities.

His admirable determination to serve an ideal, to carry out the task set him and to fight for it wholeheartedly, courageously and selflessly.

Which is why d'Artagnan remains the hero of every youngster.

For the Richelieux and the Mazarins, the Buckinghams and the Anns of Austria come and go. They come and go, as struggles and endeavours, ambitions and ideals historically succeed one another.

But striving towards ideals is one of life's constants. That always requires selfless service. And the ideal can be attained only through wholeheartedness, selflessness and fervour.

This is also noteworthy: who can remember d'Artagnan's first name, naturally assuming that d'Artagnan is a surname?

Nobody, I should think.

Is it even mentioned in the book?

I do not have the inclination to leaf through it to find out.

And this is because if I had been told to think up a name for him it would have been Léon.

Léon—in honour of my dear friend Léon Moussinac.[2]

Images often occur to us before we see the completed picture.

Comparisons, before the self-contained description.

There are even government officials who, before introducing definite political doctrines into life, write novels about them.

In this way, by an interplay of living images and characters, they can acquaint the public with their future political programme in its entirety; and, in the experimental political novel, 'roman politique', they can examine the feasibility of these doctrines in practice.

Such are *Coningsby* and *Vivian Gray* by Lord Beaconsfield—Disraeli—where he earnestly expounded, through the characters of the fictional world he had created, the ideas for which the all-powerful minister later fought and argued in Parliament.

I remember an ancient medieval castle.

Mountain ranges in the distance.

Nearby, an impassable moat.

There were embrasures in the walls.

Catapults for lobbing cannonballs were mounted on its towers.

The floors were flagged.

It was set amidst green carpets of lawns.

Using three differently coloured ostrich feathers, a crumpled straw hat and my own striped bath-robe I attempted to transform a moustachioed, laughing Frenchman into the image of Dumas *père's* immortal Gascon.

The immortal Gascon was d'Artagnan.

The Frenchman suffering at my hands was Léon Moussinac. I moulded him plasticly into d'Artagnan long before I noticed the moral similarity between these two magnificent sons of France.

The place of action: Switzerland.

More precisely: the Château of La Sarraz.

The time of action: 1929.

The setting: the Congress of Independent Film-makers, held in the castle of La Sarraz, which the owner, Madame Hélène de Mandrot had generously offered for the purpose.[3]

At that moment, the Congress was not in session.

The Congress was having some fun.

The castle, crammed with relics from the Middle Ages—halberds, pikestaffs, helmets, coats of mail and breastplates—was of course a marvellous backdrop for the screen. Between sessions we used it to show the achievements of the youngest and most advanced of all arts—cinema.

The latest works were projected one after the other on the screen stretched between ancient arches.

The first film to show the building of collective farms (our *The Old and the New*)—the burgeoning socialist system in a state that takes up a sixth of the world's land mass—was shown here after a film which did a thorough-going job in opening up new perspectives of bourgeois consciousness collapsing, in 'Surrealism'—Buñuel's *Un Chien andalou*.

On that same screen were shown the magnificent, tragic image of Carl Dreyer's *The Passion of Joan of Arc* and the abstract bagatelles of Cavalcanti and Man Ray, the experiments of Richter, Ruttmann and Eggeling,

Joris Ivens' latest picture.[4]

The aims of the Congress were not very well-defined.

It took the Soviet delegates a long time to digest the idea that in a capitalist system of government, an 'independent cinema' is the same fiction as an 'independent' press.

The Soviet delegates talked of a different fundamental, key task facing the creative intelligentsia of the West: the necessity for their committed rapprochement with the radical-revolutionary movement in Western states.

The aesthetes and paladins of pure art were, of course, ready for the attack.

But they could be easily smashed.

But there was a more destructive element.

The Congress was international. And among the ranks of French, German and English delegates, who had no political aesthetic, was the limping figure of Prampolini, an Italian, miniature but hostile.[5] He belonged to the belligerent camp of followers and minions of the then fairly active Marinetti, in whom the Italians found a figure of authority. Italian Fascism was increasingly spurring on that herald of militant Futurism, which in those years had long outlived itself. Futurism had long since become shameless militarist propaganda. The few representatives of the two or three far from radical film magazines naturally favoured Prampolini.

Strange to say, something united them with the endlessly polite, taciturn and constantly bowing Japanese delegates.

Even though they were quite abstract, passions rose to the surface just before the resolutions could be passed.

We sat through a practical lesson in the impossibility of apolitical art . . . But these 'Congress resolutions' cannot now be tracked down in memory nor even, probably, in old magazine archives.

And the net result of the Congress, Madame Mandrot's amusement aside (she kindly undertook to pay all the expenses incurred in organising it), was to show little more than that 'avant-garde' Western cinema, outside the main production companies, was riven irreparably with socio-political contradictions, just as were the fields of literature, painting or music. Aesthetes, shocked by the politics, made themselves scarce.

The reactionary wing showed itself in its brazenly Fascist colours.

And the left wing established or reinforced its personal contacts with us; we had heard of one another from articles and films and what had been mere awareness developed into enduring friendship.

We were able to dispense with the completely apolitical character of the Congress's 'conclusions' because of the 'United Front' of the revolutionary and even radical complexion of the groups; and, what was more, to neutralise utterly the anti-Soviet colouring of some of the theses which Prampolini and one of the French organisers of the Congress had tried to insinuate into them.

It was here, face to face for the first time, that we met that potential intelligentsia which gradually assumed the servile livery of Fascism and began assisting in its foul and bloody business.

Next to two very close friends of mine—Ivor Montagu (from England)[6] and Léon Moussinac (from France)—we stood shoulder to shoulder in a phalanx, ranged against them for the first time.

This was my first meeting with Ivor.

He later helped organise the London counter-trial of the Dimitrov who had been tried in Leipzig.[7]

I had met Léon on a previous occasion—back in Moscow.

And his path continued to shine with crystalline clarity; he was an extremely committed member of the French Communist Party during its complex vicissitudes in the French class struggle before the war—he suffered terribly in the concentration camps during the German occupation (but the camps failed to break his revolutionary, Communist and patriotic spirit).

But then . . . but then the war was a long way off.

Even the resolution was a long way off.

For the time being, between sessions and viewings, the Congress was having a bit of fun.

Tisse and Alexandrov had gone to the Congress with me.

The camera came with them—of course.

Who could resist filming a film-makers' congress?!

The plot was already decided upon: the battle between the 'independents' and the 'companies'.

This platform (nominally, even for Italians and Japanese!) was admissible for all (until arguments flared up over the resolutions, among the 'independents' themselves).

Mademoiselle Bouissounouse, with whom, a few months later, I walked down the precipitous steps of Montmartre, was already clad in white, bound with rusty chains found in the castle's cellars and wearing a paper sash with the Independent Cinema emblem. She was chained to the monumental chimneys on the rooftop of the ancient edifice.

338

Eisenstein dresses up Léon Moussinac as d'Artagnan for the joke film at La Sarraz, 1929.

The stout, ginger-haired Mr Isaacs from London, looking like Bluebeard, perspired in his armour as the 'boss' of a film company.

And Moussinac, transformed at my hands into d'Artagnan, headed for the rooftop, to stop poor Mademoiselle Bouissounouse suffering any longer; ancient tiles slid downwards helplessly from under her feet, threatening to cast her and Eduard Tisse's tripod down into the depths.

Jean-Georges Auriol,[8] under the fluttering standards of copies of the *Revue du cinéma* which he edited, manned the machine guns (formerly the Congress's typewriters).

He bore the brunt of the onslaught of villains, with their pikes, halberds and armoury. . . . while in the van Béla Balázs led the attempt to thwart Moussinac's chivalrous endeavours.[9]

The epic was finished by one of the more personable of the Japanese representatives—Mr Moitiro Tsutji, I believe—who generously acceded (in the guise of commercial cinema) to reproduce before the camera the full ritual of traditional hara-kiri (which was what the Congress had been hoping for!)

Madame de Mandrot, advanced in years but 'eternally young at heart', was flabbergasted successively by the treatment of her heirlooms, the sight of her much-trampled lawns and of her distressed geraniums and wild vine, hacked to shreds by halberds.

But eventually this kind lady could hold out no longer: she herself brought out of her ancient trousseau the sheets we needed for a ghost scene, and she gave the armoured troops, who were dying of heat like the crusaders of old, some miraculously restorative drinks.

A year before this, Madame de Mandrot had hosted a congress of leftist architecture. In a year's time there would be a meeting for leftist musicians.

But Madame de Mandrot's familial castle had probably never had to endure such elemental upheavals since the days of belligerent feudalism.

Nonetheless, the *'belle châtelaine'*, as we always called her, was not at all indifferent to the Soviet delegation. As she said her farewells, she told us tragically, 'Ah, Bolsheviks, Bolsheviks—you are the only true gentlemen!'

But the picture was lost, in one of the countless customs sheds which divide the multicoloured and chequered face of Europe into its system of separate states . . .

While I was making Moussinac up as d'Artagnan, I utterly failed to notice that the most captivating features of Dumas' hero also characterised the equally charming Léon.

But it was not simply his daring.

Not only his utter ebullience and lust for life.

Something much more.

Serving the great cause of Revolution informed his entire life.

A difficult, thorny life. The life of a practising revolutionary.

Refined in his tastes, a connoisseur of poetry and himself a poet and a discriminating *littérateur*.

Even an epicure. That was how I knew and remember him in Paris.

He was the talented employee of a publishing house specialising in albums showing French art treasures.

And I knew his employer—the firm's owner—'Little Levy' as he was called. This employer was remarkable for being some kind of illegitimate nephew of the celebrated Dreyfus.

We would drive around the environs of Paris, taking great delight in Versailles, Fontainebleau and Compiègne; and we saw the chateaux along the Loire Valley. Often Little Levy and his love would come with us, but we always went with Moussinac and the latter's dear wife, Jeanne.

We visited Amboise, where Leonardo da Vinci died.

We even once undertook a drive from Paris to Brussels. Another time we drove from the French capital to Marseilles and Nice, via Corrèze, making a detour to Toulon and Cannes to see Henri Barbusse.[10]

Wherever he went, Moussinac proved himself a connoisseur with expert knowledge of culture, past and present, and extremely well-versed in folklore; not a bookish knowledge gleaned from anthologies, but one learned from the living voice.

I listened entranced to the songs (specially the sea-shanties) when he sang duets with the late Vaillant-Couturier after the traditional bottle of 'good red wine'.[11]

Moussinac wrote a huge, monumental volume illustrating the fundamentals of stage decor experimentation during the most turbulent period in Left theatre.

In the pre-war years Moussinac ran the French Communist Party's publishing houses.

And, long ago, he was one of the first to begin writing on Soviet cinema.

Not just writing.

But using his pen as d'Artagnan used his sword, he established a conduit for the West to learn about what was coming from the young Land of the Soviets. And he took practical steps too to ensure the West saw our films.

A chain of Communist film societies, taking advantage of the law concerning 'private screenings' (which could not be censored), was one of the channels through which Moussinac realised his dream on a large scale. He was an inspired man of action, who acquainted France with the cinema of one of the world's most avant-garde countries.

A collection of Moussinac's articles lies before me now.

'Was it so long ago that they rose up, filled with events as exciting as the open sea?'[12]

Now the tempest has abated: the censor's ban; the police raids (as they raided my lecture at the Sorbonne, which Léon Moussinac again organised in 1930); the reactionary attacks; the battles for what was living versus what was dead.

And it is not only we, the elder Soviet film-makers, who still remember the fearless pioneering work—and I do mean 'work'— of Moussinac's indefatigable phalanxes in the early years of our cinema's emergence, when it was just filtering into all of Europe before gaining world-wide recognition.

So Moussinac fought year after year, for culture and for art,
for avant-garde ideas,
for the Revolution.

He fought for France in the same way during the war.

And so he fights now for his country's bright future; an exemplary product of the most progressive Western thought who made the path, on which the Soviet Union stands as a beacon, his own for all time.

Pages from Literature[1]

'. . . Words from the universal book: "Rus".'
V. Khlebnikov, 'Village Friendship'

As the years go by I remember how I would lie on the couch in my father's study—on holidays. Once with Wolf's one-volume Pushkin;[2] another time with Lermontov; a third time, Gogol. The stamped covers with bas-relief portraits were of varying shades of red, like berries: from Pushkin, the colour of ripe cherries, to Gogol, in the soft shades of redcurrants. They were all of the same format. And the passage of years was only sensed by the diminishing distance between my feet, dangling over the edge of the couch, and the floor. The growing boy, whose collection of classics grew from Easter to Easter, from Christmas to Christmas, received 'classics' perhaps at too young an age. I remember how one illustration's caption threw me into a bewildering confusion:

> On a rainy autumn evening
> Walked a young girl all alone,
> Holding in her trembling arms
> The secret fruit of love corrupt.[3]

Dostoyevsky entered my life in 1914, the year World War One broke out. I mastered *The Idiot* 'according to plan', and *The Brothers Karamazov* because of a purely specific circumstance. Mama and her friend were expecting an acquaintance, Anna Grigorevna, the author's widow. This was at the dacha, in Staraya Russa.[4]

This caused an amazing sensation and I anxiously readied myself for a serious conversation with Mme Dostoyevskaya concerning her late husband's work.

To this end I first of all read through *The Brothers Karamazov* in one go. But the conversation never took place. The whole thing was spoiled by . . . blackberry pie. The famous guest was received with honour. They had been baking pies since morning and, to stop me making a nuisance of myself in the kitchen, when they were putting the final touches to the reception, I was paid off with a large wedge of blackberry pie.

This slice proved fatal.

We left to get to grips with it somewhere in the shrubbery at the edge of the resort park. I was with a wonderful girl called Nina, slender and dark, who always wore black and looked at the world with a thoughtful expression from under a shock of curly hair which was cut so that it resembled Pushkin's. In fact, her entire appearance reminded me most of a young monk, hence my name for her: 'Mtsyri'.[5] I called her this to her face, and also behind her back.

In short, we were late for tea with the family and the celebrity. There was no conversation about Dostoyevsky. When we did turn up, panting, Anna Grigorevna had left the verandah. I was just in time to kiss her hand; to hear the reproach, which began: 'What are you doing, young man?'; and to embark on a literary conversation that did not take place. A black straw hat. Crepe scarf and black gloves. And the pale face of an old lady, with traces of authority which reminded me of my own grandmother's despotic character. A heavy gait, and holding something like crutches. That is all I can recall of my first 'literary' meeting. For a long time afterwards I reproved myself for reading *Karamazov* 'for nothing', instead of playing tennis the whole time.

I deliberately dwelt on this question because I suspect I am not alone in this instance. My generation is probably a well-read one: we are the multitude who began conscious life at the moment when the stalwarts of the new Russian classics had just left the stage. Fathers and grandfathers knew the Tolstoys, Dostoyevskys, Ostrovskys and Chekhovs when they were still living, literary figures in society; people whom one might bump into on the street, in one's club, or in the patisserie.

But we caught these people on the point of exit . . . their first complete collected works were just coming off the presses of obliging publishers such as Marx or 'Enlightenment'. And we met their widows in passing . . .

The only living classic, still in circulation, was Gorky—many years after the Revolution.[6] I met Gorky for the first time when he

344

said in delight: 'It's a work of genius, a work of genius! . . .' He had just been told that Shostakovich had decided to write an opera based on Leskov's *Lady Macbeth of the Mtsensk District*.[7]

What is curious in this new phase is the link between a literary classic and tradition on one hand, and the best that post-Revolutionary music could offer, in the works of Shostakovich and Prokofiev, on the other. For example, Shostakovich's early link with Gogol (*The Nose*) and later Prokofiev's with Dostoyevsky (*The Gambler*) and Tolstoy (*War and Peace*).[8] But I came up against perhaps the most curious one recently, while travelling from Alma-Ata back to Moscow after the evacuation.

Taking *The Devils* to read on my journey, somewhere near Ksyl-Orda (or perhaps it was Arys) I came across a long forgotten page from a famous description.

The piece did indeed amuse, having the funny title 'The Franco-Prussian War'. It began with the ominous chords of the 'Marseillaise':

'Qu'un sang impur abreuve nos sillons!' *

You could hear the bombastic challenge, the excitement of future victories. But suddenly, among the masterly variations in the beat of the anthem, somewhere off to one side, below, in the corner but still very close, you could hear the awful strains of '*Mein lieber Augustin*.' The 'Marseillaise' did not notice this: the 'Marseillaise' was at the height of its excitement at its own grandeur; but *'Augustin'* was growing louder, *'Augustin'* was acting with increasing insolence; then the beat of *'Augustin'* began unexpectedly to chime in with that of the 'Marseillaise'. The latter was angered by this; it was at last aware of *'Augustin'* and tried to brush it off, to chase it away like a tiny but persistent fly; but '*Mein lieber Augustin*' had a firm grip; it was merry and self-confident, radiant and impudent and the 'Marseillaise' somehow, suddenly, went stupid and no longer concealed its irritation and hurt.

There were howls of indignation; tears and impreca-

---

* French: 'Let our fields flow with impure blood!'

tions with arms outstretched towards Providence:
'Pas un pouce de notre terrain, pas une pierre de nos forteresses[*]

But now it had no choice but to sing to the same beat as *'Augustin'*. Its tune changed in the stupidest way to *'Augustin'*; it faded and died away. Just occasionally *'Qu'un sang impur'* broke through audibly, only to skip back, utterly humiliated, into the awful little waltz. It surrendered unconditionally: there was Jules Favre sobbing on Bismarck's chest and giving up everything, everything . . . But then *'Augustin'* began to grow harsh; hoarser notes could be heard; you could sense that a vast quantity of beer had been drunk. Acting with gross ostentation, it ordered millions of fine cigars, champagne and hostages; it turned into a frenzied roar . . .

The Devils, Part II, Chapter 5 'Before the Holiday'

This is surely the spur to the unsurpassed power of what was also the work of a great Russian composer, Shostakovich, in his 7th Symphony, which took the whole world of music by storm.[9] And surely it is this page of the great Russian writer's work that lies at the heart of it, continuing the great tradition of fertilising Russian music with Russian literature. You cannot help remembering another phase of a similar cross-fertilisation—this time of painting by music. Repin writes of the inspiration behind 'Ivan the Terrible Murdering His Child':

One evening in Moscow in 1881 I heard a new piece by Rimsky-Korsakov called 'Revenge'. It made an indescribable impression on me. The sounds took hold of me and I thought: can one translate this mood, into which the music has transported me, into painting? Tsar Ivan occurred to me. It was 1881. The bloody events of 1 March had aroused all sorts of passions. A bloody track went through the year. I worked as if demented. I was anxious for minutes on end.[10]

But such digressions take us a long way off the beaten track.

---

[*] French: 'Not an inch of our land, not a stone of our strongholds'

To return to our subject.

Our subject is how the iron arsenal of Russian literary classics, entering our minds and hearts in childhood—by their literary writing—determined and influenced the creation of an original method of Russian Soviet cinema.

The idiosyncrasy of method in Soviet cinema was the fundamental guarantee of our art's unshakeable prestige throughout the cinema world.

What were the factors which caused this?

The October Revolution, which established the Soviet system and opened up new perspectives on the awareness and realisation of phenomena.

As well as bestowing an unprecedented freedom, the Soviet system freed the intelligent mind, equipping it with the ultimate weapon for exposing secrets and lifting veils of agnosticism through knowledge, inspired to infinite courage in exploration, and enthusiastic research and experiment, in all areas where active, constructive knowledge was applied to building firm foundations for life.

Not only that.

But also the fact that the new generation, those who had seen Soviet cinema through its first twenty-five years, stood on the *terra firma* of Russian cultural traditions, an inexhaustible wealth of original and national talent, a repository of the most *recherché* methods of literary writing and experiment.

My encounter with the creativity of the West and America proved catalytic: as in a full-scale firework display above Moscow, the fiery pillars of a young talent's creative urge soared upwards, growing from its foundations set deep in the universal culture and art of the Russian classics.

I am a Westerniser.[11]

I feel at home in Paris.

I feel as though I am walking across the pages of books when I am there.

There is Victor Hugo, there the Three Musketeers.

The Pont Neuf (Tabarin—Bal Tabarin).

'Aux Bonheurs des Dames' and 'Maison Printemps'.

And here cousin Bette ran from embankment to embankment.

Not true—the Russian landscape is no less exciting.

The station at Chern. The town beyond. Granaries on the lower floors. A shop.

Jackdaws in the trees.

Nostalgia:* the jackdaws of the Alexander Nevsky monastery.[12]

Coloured snow. Glasses with eyes—Uncle Grisha's. Orange-blue light shining on and merging with the orange and red paint of the glittering walls.

The Prilutsk monastery.

Vologda.

Vozhega—and the northern plains which I can see as I leave the warm train.

A slice of Russia, from my carriage window between the Volga and Moscow (1943).

*Evocation d'un monde!***

I visited Eton and Windsor,

I saw Cambridge and remembered St Basil's.

'I have been here before,' Priestley.*

I was just as enthralled by Baton Rouge, Natchez, New Orleans and other spots in distant Louisiana; they echo . . . our Empire-style estates.

The same white columns. Staircases. Pediments.

Mexican lacquerwork is like our Mstyora and Palekh. Toys on the Mexican alamedas, like the toys of Sergiev Posad.[13]

José Guadalupe Posada—and our lubok.[14]

The *charro* could be a Circassian.

And the thickset *mestizo* could be a Ukrainian, the hero of one of Gogol's poems or stories . . .

The billowing sails of my imagination carry me across Melville's storm-tossed oceans, across the seven seas of mysterious Ahab;[15] I can catch in my flared nostrils the salt spray of the turbulent Atlantic as I stand on the top deck of the ocean-going giantess taking me from Cherbourg to her New York dock, or I can

---

* In English in the original.
** French: 'The evocation of a world!'

leap across the waves in my small motorboat off the Mexican coast, harpooning turtles.

But I first heard the romance of the surf's roar on the shore of the Baltic; that was the sea whose salt spray I first felt.

That same sea which always held a strong attraction for the wise rulers of Rus; like the traditions passed on down the centuries, this rallying-cry 'to the sea'—from Nevsky to Ivan, and from Peter to our own days—secured a firm foothold on the sea shore, where I was born.

But it was . . . Stanyukovich[16] who made the seas real for me on the printed page; he outdid *Odyssey* and *Iliad* and Coleridge's distant and foreign 'Ancient Mariner'.

And before I read and admired the metaphysical maritime epic of *Moby Dick*, I threw myself head-first into the revolutionary epic of the Russian uprisings of the 'Potemkin' and the 'Ochakov'.[17]

But the first whale I met was not on the pages of that American Odyssey; it stared at me glassily—a stuffed creature, carried around in a wooden booth erected on a barge floating along the waterways of my country, to amaze people living near a river with its huge bulk and menacing look. This was emphasised by the scale of its neighbours: stuffed seals and medium-sized sharks.

Encounters with Books[1]

Birds fly to some saints: Francis of Assisi.

Beasts run to some legendary figures: Orpheus.

Pigeons cluster around the old men of St Mark's Square in Venice.

A lion followed Androcles wherever he went.

Books cluster around me.

They fly to me, run to me, cling to me.

So long have I loved them: large and small, fat and slender, rare editions and cheap paperbacks, they cry out through their dustcovers, or are perhaps sunk in contemplation in a solid, leather skin, as if wearing soft slippers.

They need not be too neat, like suits fresh from the tailor; nor cold, like starched cuffs. But neither must they shine like greasy rags.

Books should be turned over in one's hands, like a well-tuned instrument.

I can steal them. I could probably kill them.

They sense this.

I love them so much that they finally begin to reciprocate my love.

Books burst open like ripe fruit in my hands and, like magical flowers, open up their petals, carrying a fertilising line of thought, an inspiring word, an affirming quotation, an illustration to prove a point.

I am whimsical in my selection.

And they readily drop into my hands.

Fatefully they surround me.

Once only one room was designated for books.

But insidiously, room by room, my flat has filled up with books which loop themselves around things like hoops on a barrel.

So, after the 'library', the study was taken over; after the study, the walls of my bedroom . . .

Chesterton was once asked to read a paper.[2]

'What on?' he asked on arrival.

Eisenstein's flat at Potylikha in Moscow. (Newsreel, 11 February 1948)

'Anything you like—umbrellas, if you want.'

So Chesterton devised a lecture on an expanding subject: hair, which covers our thoughts; hats, which cover hair; umbrellas, which cover everything.

That is how I sometimes perceive my rooms.

Currents flow from the small cells of grey matter of the brain, through the cranium and the sides of bookcases, through the walls of bookcases and into the hearts of the books. Not true! None of the bookcases has sides—I keep them on open shelves, and in response to the flow of thoughts they hurl themselves at my head.

Sometimes the greed radiating towards them is the stronger.

Sometimes the infectious force emanating through their covers is the stronger.

I feel like a latter-day St Sebastian, pierced by arrows flying from the shelves.

And the small sphere of bone, containing splinters of reflections like Leibniz' reflecting monad, seems no longer a cranium but the outer walls of the room, and the layer of books covering the surfaces of its walls are like stratifications extending inside my own head.[3]

Despite all this, the books are not at all uncommon: it is the variety that is unexpected, rather than their second-hand-bookshop collectability or decorative oddness. And perhaps too the unorthodoxy of the collection and the complete absence of what ought to be there!

And often I value them not so much *per se*—a sense of the ideas that surround them—but as a result of an occasional, chance page crushed by indifferent, dull chapters; a separate line lost among pages devoted to quite different questions.

And the density of this aura, of this radiation (or fogginess?) which forms a cloud around the culprits themselves (and which makes them more valuable than the works themselves) almost takes solid form in the shape of a cobweb along which I can slide, even though I fear I might catch myself against it and rip it, like the fine, quivering threads of one's associations. And I feel like one of the wise men from Laputa who was terrified for the safety of

352

his webs.[4]

Sometimes half-sincere well-wishers go to great lengths to prove to me that it is not at all like a cobweb; that instead these are taut strands of barbed wire, bookish wisdom fencing me off from reality.

These well-wishers are half sincere and their assertions are only semi-verifiable.

As is the carping regarding the abundance of quotations.

Quotations! Quotations! Quotations!

Someone once said: 'It is only those who have no hope themselves of being cited who cite nobody.'[5]

Quotations! Quotations! Quotations!

Even Prince Kurbsky, that elegant author of a treatise on punctuation, though otherwise a traitor to his country, reproached Tsar Ivan the Terrible for his quotations.[6]

I quote: 'How many holy words have you taken, and those with great anger and ferocity, not by the line or verse, as is the custom of skilled experts (if one happens to write of something then it is done using short words which evidence great reason)—but excessively, with a superfluity of detail and hostility—whole books, tracts, epistles!'

But quotations differ.

A dogmatist may use a quotation from an authority as a shield, for him to hide his ignorance or well-being behind.

Quotations may be lifeless compilations.

I see quotations as outrunners on either side of a galloping shafthorse. Sometimes they go too far, but they help one's imagination to bowl along two distinct paths, supported by the parallel race.

But don't let go of the reins!

And never—on any account—let quotation follow quotation, in tedious single file!

You will never build or create anything using quotations.

You must build it completely, adhering rigidly to what is concrete, and . . . there! . . . Quotations come of their own accord and fit themselves in wherever necessary—they smooth the passage of the fluent stream.

But not vice-versa, as far as creativity and life are concerned.

Hundreds of people fail to notice quotations, until they find one in their own field: then they see it; it backs them up; or it helps them to see something that before was missing; or it helps them to put something more succinctly.

But vice-versa, and the result is always the same: deathly scholasticism and philistinism—*papier mâché*.

I have quotations.

Not enough of them. I would like to make a montage from the fragments discovered by others, but for a different purpose—mine!

It is like cinema: I don't need to play any part at all. My job is to link all the pieces up.

Books open up at the quotation I need. I used to check—and sometimes I needed nothing before and nothing after, in the whole book.

Here are some syndromes in the pathology of the nervous system. The book opened itself up in my hands, at the very page which addressed the question of the technique of stage movements in Italian comedy . . .

Sometimes a modest-looking booklet with a portrait of Leonardo on the cover (even in childhood I liked reading about him), with the German author's surname and Christian name that had been taken from the Nibelung as a little birdie told me, brings news of the unexpected discovery of an entirely new field which I embark upon even without an expert guide. If I say that the booklet, published by *Sovremennye problemy* [Contemporary Questions], concerns 'Leonardo da Vinci and a Memory of His Childhood' and is by Sigmund Freud, then the significance of the little birdie is exactly in keeping with the description of the kite inside—which Leonardo used to dream about.

Amazing words for a description of a dream!

Thus my introduction to psychoanalysis. I even remember when and where it happened. Only a few days after the official formation of the Red Army (Spring 1918) when I volunteered for the sappers. In Gatchina. Standing in a wagon en route for week-end leave at home. I remember it as if it were yesterday. The carriage corridor. A rucksack on my back. My fur cap stinking of dog. And the quarter-litre bottle of milk I had stood in it.

Later, on the platform of the train, in the mad crush, I was so absorbed in my little book that I failed to notice that some time ago my carton of milk had been completely crushed and the dog-fur of the cap and the khaki rucksack were both saturated.

As regards my sorties through the fantastic jungles of psychoanalysis, which (the sorties) were imbued with the powerful spirit of the original 'lebeda' (as I disrespectfully alluded to the sacred impulse of libido) I shall write of them later.[7]

Let us only recall here that I very quickly assimilated Rank's *The Meaning of Psychoanalysis in Science and Spirit* and the charming Sachs, that shrewd old salamander with the horn-rimmed glasses, whose company I came to enjoy much later on my travels in Berlin.[8]

However, what I found most absorbing in this collection were the quotations from the works of Sadger—on the sexual origins of word-formations.[9]

It is worth noting that after the briefest of shocks at the erotic element of origins (of course, an extremely one-sided and debatable concept), the accent changes very quickly in my case to an interest in its origins—to the history of its development, to the specific emergence of language. This early interest in staring fixedly into the past seems to have had no ill effects. But these we will treat under the heading 'Words, Words'.[10]

We are not now in the world of words, their genealogy, their interdependency of movement and their emergence; here we are not even admiring the necklaces of poetry made of words, or the pattern in the carpet—their linkage in prose. And I will talk of my encounters with prose and poetry elsewhere.

And here it remains only to add that I never actually met Freud, although Stefan Zweig arranged an almost unthinkable meeting with this tragic Wotan who stood in the gloaming of bourgeois psychology; with this Prometheus who could disarticulate his personal tragedy and trauma into the individual links which formed his chain, but was not capable of relieving himself of their weight—not to mention extricating himself from their coils like a Houdini,[11] or to melt them, or simply to snap them. The curse of knowledge that could not liberate him overlies all psychoanalysis. It is beyond analysis. He was successful, sometimes accurate, brilliant;

but so frequently did he come to grief when it concerned the necessity of 'experiencing' or even jettisoning it.

Another old man comes to mind—of an even more fraudulent science. Count Hammond, writing under the pseudonym of Cheiro, published several books about the art of palmistry. I came to know him in Hollywood. Nearby was the strange, indistinct outline of the red-maned Countess Hammond, with words written by Oscar Wilde himself in an album . . . And the strange, pale, myopic figure, dressed in black, frowned painfully at our introduction, when he learned of our departure to Mexico. The fiery red-headed Countess, inclining towards me, explained: the faded little man— she made no attempt to speak *sotto voce*—the little man was slightly hard of hearing; also he was one of the last descendants of Maximilian and Carlotta.[12] I do not have the 'Almanac de Gotha' to hand to establish when and where the last scions of this branch of the house of Habsburg died out, justly and implacably hatcheted by the ruthless Benito Juarez in the foreign land of Mexico, where they went as Emperor and Empress.[13] I think that their marriage was unhappy and without issue (Dieterle's film supports this view, I think)[14] and the strange little man, perhaps, was no more than one of a throng of self-styled descendants of bloodthirsty aristocrats— counts and marquesses, princes and viscounts—which had overrun Califilmia.

He was said to be deaf.

But when I accidentally dropped a coin he jerked and spun round, caught out like the feeblest malingerer falling for the oldest trick in the recruiting officer's book!

But it had nothing to do with him, nor Carlotta, nor Maximilian, nor even with his wife's fiery tresses.

It was all about the 'Count's' right hand.

While he was at Cambridge (or was it Oxford? An unpardonable slip of the pen!), he injured his right hand one boat race and it became paralysed. The left hand is considered the 'control' hand; the secrets telling of great deeds are written on the right.

Paralysis held the right hand in a tight claw—and, though he read thousands of fortunes on thousands of hands, Count Hammond was hopelessly prevented from prophesying his own fate . . .

This linked him with Freud, whose infallible insights were also tied up with the flaws of his own psychological defects—with the disproportionate significance attached to the Oedipus complex. Everyone who has leafed through his works knows of this.

In some respects this is even like certain flaws in Stanislavsky's Method, which emerge so distinctly from a comparison of *An Actor Prepares* with *My Life in Art*.[15] Those flaws contribute greatly to an understanding of the emphases, in places irrational, on details of the system.

So I never met Freud and a small volume containing an autobiographical sketch was sent to me by the great Doctor of Vienna as a souvenir of Zweig's fruitless endeavours. It had his characteristic signature—the capital F of his surname.

And it stands, as if by chance, propped up against the big white oblong of Cheiro's researches into palmistry, with the author's ornate dedication to me in memory of our meeting . . .

Sometimes you do not find something yourself.

But something leads you to it.

And for some reason, you stubbornly reject it.

I can cite two such cases.

D. H. Lawrence, whom later (and even now) I read to distraction, was one.

In 1929 Ivor Montagu valiantly tried to introduce me to Lawrence.

In London. In an astonishing narrow little house (with three windows) on Leicester Square, where he lived next door to the Studio publishing house.

In 1941, in *International Literature*, I saw a photo of London, destroyed by the blitz. The Studio building was still standing, next to a pile of rubble.

On the ground floor was a tiny and 'pretty expensive'* restaurant with a divan running the length of one wall and small tables. It was so narrow that the usual arrangement of tables was not feasible.

Vis-à-vis some sort of 'music hall'.*

---

* In English in the original.

357

I think I saw Carnera[16] inside, before his performance in the Albert Hall in the presence of the Prince of Wales (the one who later abdicated).

Apparently, I found Joyce so real (and uniquely real) in his literature that all other surnames 'had no appeal'.*

After Joyce came Lawrence, on the basis of the . . . censor's banning first *Ulysses* and then *Lady Chatterley's Lover.*

I turned a deaf ear to it.

I bought *Lady Chatterley* on board the S.S. 'Europe' on my way to America.

Not to read it, but out of snobbery.

It was a long time before I read it.

And it was not on board a ship. Nor in the USA. Not even straight away in Moscow.

Why I read it later, I do not even know.

But it completely bowled me over.

Then I ordered *Women in Love.*

I read a malicious attack on Lawrence in *The Doctor Looks at Literature*, which I bought for its article on Joyce.

And later, more: I began to track down every book of inflated 'Lawrenceana'.

I was interested in the affinity* with my views on 'pre-logic'.[17]

He is especially brilliant in his studies on American literature.

It was a roundabout route that brought me to those, too.

I was interested in Rockwell Kent.[18]

I clearly recognised him (amongst the rapidly executed reproductions of his journey across Alaska) from a strange book almost half as deep as it was wide—black with a gold title, and containing his magnificent illuminations, tailpieces and whole illustrations.

It was all about whales.

The title was *Moby Dick.*

There is a very poor film of *Moby Dick,* the one-legged captain played by John Barrymore.[19]

---

* In English in the original.

I saw it once.

Kent's drawings are magnificent.

They interested me for two reasons.

First, for the graphic examples of shot composition (illustrations for a manual I have been planning for a very long time.)

Next to Dobuzhinsky's 'White Nights', Benois' 'Versailles' (while composing vast horizontal landscapes, I came up against this same question when filming the pyramids and the ruined temples of San Juan-Tetihuacán), Degas' canvases (foreground composition), Caravaggio (overwhelming perspectives and figures placed not 'in the frame', that is within the outline, but in relation to the plane of the frame) etc.

The same thing happened with Beardsley.

I bought a play 'by someone called Jonson', because of the illustrations Beardsley did for it.

The play turned out to be Ben Jonson's *Volpone*.

I read it through by chance, and the great Ben left a lasting impression.

So it is now.

I tried to read a bit of the actual book.

I was introduced to Melville and was intoxicated.

Then, by some strange intuition, Jay (Leyda) sent me from overseas Melville's *Omoo and Typee*, admirable constructions (1945!).

Before this, Jay mentioned my name in *The Film Sense* in the chapter from *Moby Dick*—'The Whiteness of the Whale' (apropos my passage about how I used white, contrary to tradition, to denote villainy in *Alexander Nevsky*: the knights and monks).

I hunted feverishly for something on Melville. I find *Moby Dick* interesting even now as possible material for a parody of Lewis Carroll's *The Hunting of the Snark*.

The only thing I have found so far (I found it earlier when I read *Moby* for the first time) was in Mrs Rourke's brief notes in *American Humor* (before the war).

Then I read in *Literaturnaya gazeta* [The Literary Gazette] (1944) that the late Melville's daughter had sent a series of old editions of his works to Moscow.

359

At the same time I read (in Régis Messac's *Le 'Detective novel' et l'influence de la pensée scientifique* [The 'Detective Novel' and the Influence of Scientific Thought] about Melville's *The Confidence Man.*

I looked for it in the Library of Foreign Literature. There was everything under the sun, apart from *The Confidence Man.*

On the other hand there was a wide selection of books on Melville.

Amongst them was . . . Lawrence's 'Studies in Classic American Literature'.

I cannot abide reading in libraries.

Especially in the chill and dirty month of December 1944, in the unheated foreign literature library on the small street off Prechistenka.

But I ploughed through all the chapters on Melville and was left *bouche bée.**

It was so close to the themes of my *Grundproblem*** of Melville *vu par**** Lawrence—utterly astounding.

I received a small volume as a present, via Hellmann.[20]

Then from Jay came *American Renaissance* by Matthiessen and Sedgwick's *Herman Melville* (I was then in hospital, at the start of 1946).

'Revival'**** of the mad attraction for Lawrence.

In December 1943, after my 'breakdown'**** after ninety nights filming *Ivan* in Alma-Ata,[21] I went to rest in the mountains; alone in a small house in an apple orchard near the Central Committee's sanatorium which had been shut for the winter.

In sun and snowfalls I was utterly absorbed in the *Short Stories* etc.

I was interested in the 'animal epic' running through his novellas.

I was occupied by the question of the 'animal epic' in connection with . . . Disney.

Disney as an example of the art of absolute influence—

---

   *   French: 'aghast'
   ** German: 'fundamental problem'
 *** French: 'seen by'
**** In English in the original.

absolute 'appeal'* for each and everyone, and hence a particularly rich *Fundgrube*** of the *most* basic means of influence.[22]

I found the *Short Stories* striking for their abundance of latent action and sheer literary brilliance.

It is curious that *Aaron's Rod* is just as surprisingly poor as *Sons and Lovers,* and perhaps *The Plumed Serpent* too, which I just could not finish! Even though it is 'my "Beloved Mexico"'—perhaps because of 'knowing' the country?!

The second case—although it in fact occurred first—was Vsevolod Emilievich Meyerhold.[23]

In 1915, repeated attempts were made to interest me in *The Love for Three Oranges.*[24]

Having learnt that it was Komissarzhevsky who had made me mad on theatre with his production of *Turandot* written by the same Gozzi at Nezlobin's (not the ghastly pathetic *Turandot* by Vakhtangov).[25]

Mumik (Vladimir) Veidle the Younger tried hard.[26]

In the house on Kamennoostrovsky, where Kozintsev later lived for many years.[27]

With no result. I vaguely recalled the cover by Golovin.[28]

The same one, the original of which is now in my home—my most treasured souvenir of the master.

---

*   In English in the original.
**   German: 'treasure house'

Bookshops[1]

I know a wonderful bookshop.

    I rarely visit it.

    That is probably why it has retained its magical attraction.

    Although I live in Moscow, I visit it in Leningrad.

    It is somewhere between Peski, where I once lived, and Znamenskaya Square, where I can still remember the little local steam train going up and down, bright yellow with clouds of black smoke like a swift vessel on the Mississippi. I remember its route was from the monastery of Alexander Nevsky ('Old Nevsky') to the station and back.

    Somewhere half-way between Peski and the square you turn one way and go down one of those angular Paris streets and come out facing a typical old London shop-front.

    I remember the window display from Berlin.

    It had some of Daumier's unique woodcuts and Epinal's crude and colourful prints.

    And many rare books which I have spent a long time looking for.

    The shop is often closed.

    But I am always allowed in.

    I do not have to hurry in the morning to be there when the shop opens, to make sure of buying the book which I saw in the window the previous evening.

    The shop was shut then. Or I had simply failed intuitively to understand that it was that very book which I needed.

    No need to guess which side the shop-assistant will approach from.

    Or to break out in the cold sweat of horror.

    Is today a holiday? It's already 9.05, 9.10, 9.15, 9.45, 9.50 . . .

    And only at 9.55 do I realise that the shop opens at 10.00.

    Somehow there is no problem with cash.

    Whatever I choose in the shop, I always have enough.

    The first room is lined with books from floor to ceiling—like a mining-gallery.

Whitman's remarkable biography.

Seillière's essays on imperialism (about Nietzsche) which I cannot find anywhere else.[2]

Rochefort merges with the magazine *L'Eclipse*.

A full set of *L'Assiette au beurre*.[3]

The second room with its sloping glass-topped cases. Some amazing Rabelais.

A thick Ben Jonson.

Here are some books, wrapped up. Put under my arm. Strange, the edges are uncut. Gravity does not pull them downwards.

They are seemingly weightless.

Not like Kuno Fischer,[4] whose history of the philosophers I had to drag on to trams, back to Chistye Prudy from the decrepit bookshop on the Arbat, in the 30s.

A scandal. I was visiting someone with eight volumes under my arm.

'Sir! Watch what you're doing with that box!'

And my threatening:

'It's not a box; it's Hegel!'

The magic of unknown words!

A woman selling milk, on the warpath and about to tear me to pieces, suddenly shrank at this new word, and melted into the crowd.

She melted metaphorically, of course, vanishing among the passengers.

But this packet of books, purchased in my favourite shop, really does dissolve in my arms.

Just as the shop's strict English façade melts; just as the small angular Paris street straightens out, and becomes Suvorov Prospect from Znamenskaya Square to Peski.

Then, like an arrow, the railway line from the Nicholas station in Leningrad to the Nicholas station in Moscow; both stations are latterly called October . . .[5]

What is going on?!

The cock has crowed his morning greeting three times to Aurora: not the cruiser which I had towed into the Neva (where it had been in 1917) for the filming of *October* in 1927, and not

'Sleeping Beauty'—but Aurora, the dawn.[6]

I wake up of my own accord.

My wonderful bookshop was a dream.

This is a dream which comes to me rarely, but at least once a year.

It calms all my anxieties about not having enough money, or lacking the decisiveness to buy a book; you find here that *ouvrage,* that book, which once you let slip through your fingers to be bought by another.

A fantastically wide selection of screenplays translated from the Italian smile down at you from their shelves, in the form of a whole eighteenth-century library in French. I could not, as an impecunious student, buy it as I raced back from the front to Petrograd in 1918, although I was delirious about Harlequins, Capitanos, and Brighellas.[7] Bakst is always at my service here; his price always remained beyond my reach.[8]

And how often here do I hold in my hands the full set of Piranesi's 'Prisons'—at home, only three leaves from this book huddle together.[9]

And the wonderful pages of old Petersburg; they were enough to make me salivate when I lacked courage even to go near the richly dressed windows of the antiquarian bookshop on Liteiny Prospect.

The *'splendeur et décadence'* of these shops.

The mahogany and bronze. Green carpets. The corners of cherished folders. Only from a distance. Only through the door. With a shiver of envy.

I did not have the experience or effrontery to walk in and browse. To turn down what I was not looking for. To ask to see something else. And to turn that down, too.

And to leave, albeit after slaking my thirst.

Many years later in Paris, Darius Milhaud and I, strutting along in our broad overcoats, headed for the Galérie Rosenberg.[10]

A 'house' which dealt exclusively in Picasso and Braque.

We walked around the lower halls critically, which always attracts the attention of well-groomed salesman.

We stood before the canvases cavilling, shrugging our shoulders, not in the manner of *épatés bourgeois,* but like Americans sizing up a painting merely to see if it would fit; we are nothing like that type of millionaire who can hang the walls of a room with—or build a house around—a small collection of paintings.

Thus Léonard Rosenthal[11] in his Paris villa which opened straight out on the Parc Monceau and had automatic guns installed in the windows which automatically opened fire if anyone so much as touched a shutter, had lined one room with costly wood and velvet, such as you find inside jewellery cases. The pale light softly illuminated the outlines of a truly divine wooden Bodhisattva, brought from distant India, where Mr Rosenthal's oyster farms had made him his fortune.

Or Otto H. Kahn who designed his dining room in his upstate house on Long Island as a frame for his six Romneys, rhythmically divided by the doors of French windows that reached from floor to ceiling.[12]

After looking at us for a moment, the assistant elegantly enquired whether we would like something a little more finished. As in good brothels, after you have seen the general room, you are asked: *'Est-ce que monsieur désire quelque chose de spécial?'** And you are taken upstairs. We were taken into the small rooms on an upper floor.

Finally, in a minute drawing room, canvas after canvas of Picassos from all periods (apart from those highly prized by museums and private collections) were brought out and shown to us.

The buyers had a taste for the unwieldy.

The salesmen must be all the more attentive.

But soon, with a slight shake of the head, the 'Americans' left, reaching the same decision: the Rembrandt and Géricault offered the day before would be more suitable for the study . . .

So I had a lesson on Picasso, with originals.

Darius enriched my education by a visit to a dentist with a very large practice. His waiting room was hung with one of the best collections of Cézannes.

But we were talking just now about books, and we will leave our encounter with painting for another section.

There are town squares that look like halls.

---

* French: 'Perhaps Sir would care to see something special?'

There are squares that look like boudoirs.

Such were the tiny squares in the small towns of Sicily.

Taut wires criss-crossed above them.

And a lamp hung from the intersection at the centre.

I have only heard of these squares.

I have not been there myself.

Now these squares, of course, have been destroyed by bombs, but they still retain their similarity with halls. It may even have grown stronger.

For the halls were also destroyed. The missing ceiling made them look more like squares.

But I have been on streets that do not look like streets.

Such as the Rue de Lappe in Paris.

It is so narrow, dark and crowded with small but more than dubious bistros that it resembles a gutter. Watch out, or you'll get drenched by a stream of filthy, turbid water that must at any moment come gushing over the slippery stones.

Let's grab this door-handle instead, and seek sanctuary inside the 'Aux Trois Colonnes' and listen to the three accordionists.

The alleys of Whitechapel are like a shop counter.

And, once you have stepped into the maelstrom, you begin to feel that you are not so much a customer as an obedient piece of merchandise, akin to a tie done in a bow, or a celluloid collar such as the one the shop assistants throw to one another.

On a spring evening, the Rue de l'Odéon does not look like a street either.

Too narrow for a normal street, it is more like a wide corridor in a family hotel.

And the shop doors are like doors of furnished rooms.

You expect one end of the street to lead into a drawing room and the other into the kitchen.

It is the utter quiet which creates this illusion.

Not a taxi or carriage to be seen anywhere.

Nor even any pedestrians.

Probably no more than the figures of two women.

They stood in their respective rectangular doorways, diagonally opposite each other.

And they talked scarcely raising their voices, the way people talk if they poke their heads out of their rooms into a communal corridor for a minute.

One of them had grey hair.

In a man's light blue suit with a short skirt.

Above her hung a signboard.

Oddly enough, the presence of the sign did nothing to detract from the illusion of an interior.

Perhaps because its inscription was so odd:

'Shakespeare and Co.'

The other woman was in soft grey. Her skirt reached the ground.

She was Adrienne Monnier.

The first woman was Sylvia Beach.

Mademoiselle Monnier sold French books.

At a tiny counter, the poet Jean-Paul Fargue was signing a copy of his verses for me.[13]

I had never heard of him before.

He of course had never heard of me.

This did not stop him writing, for probably the hundredth time, a nonchalant, inspired dedication on the title page of his slim volume of poems:

A Eisenstein poète Jean-Paul Fargue poète. Paris 1930.

Fifteen years later, in an English edition of *Verve* magazine (no. 5-6) I found some words by Adrienne Monnier about Jean-Paul Fargue:

'Fargue . . . Each of his defenseless hands forms little marionettes.'[14]

These hands were not forming little marionettes, at that moment; they were fluttering above the counter, selecting a volume of their poems.

Sylvia Beach sold English books.

More than that, she published them.

Most crucially, it was she who published James Joyce's *Ulysses*.

Shakespeare and Co., the publishers, elevated Joyce's works to objects worthy of veneration, just as that minuscule shop on the embankment was a repository for editions of Verlaine.

There you could find Verlainiana and anything by Verlaine,

even the banned *Hombres* which was sold there under the counter
. . . quite openly.[15]

Here, it is Joyceana.

Joyce's works.

I greatly loved this quiet street.

I greatly loved this modest quiet bookshop

and the grey-haired Sylvia Beach.

I often dropped in on her.

Sat in her back room.

And gazed at the walls for ages; they were hung with innumerable faded photographs.

An idiosyncratic pantheon of literature.

Can there have been a single writer Sylvia did not know of?

Apart from the moustachioed Frank Harris, Oscar Wilde
was especially well represented in his countless aspects.[16]

Especially in that bizarre suit in which he surprised
America: a velvet jacket, floppy beret, plus-fours and stockings.

Who is coming?

Who is coming?

Who is coming?

He is coming!

He is coming!

He is coming!

Oscar Wilde!

Oscar Wilde!

Oscar Wilde!

The great aesthete!

The great aesthete!

The great aesthete!

The great aesthete's arrival in New York was thus heralded
with posters worthy of Barnum.[17]

I remember this advertising formula very well.

In 1920 I used it for my first theatrical production—for *The
Mexican* (together with the late Valentin Smyshlyayev).[18]

Substituting Danny Ward for Oscar Wilde, and 'great
boxer' for 'great aesthete', these same lines were shouted out by
sandwich men during the intermission, advertising the great boxer
Danny Ward.[19]

While in Miss Beach's shop, I briefly made the acquaintance of a young man with a fringe and slightly powdered cheeks—George Antheil.[20] Until very recently he had lived in a small room above Miss Sylvia's shop. He had just become famous . . .

Wherever I stayed for more than a month, I invariably found such a bookshop. Such a back room. A similarly endearing book enthusiast.

In Mexico City, it was Mizraki the Greek. On my shelves I have many books bearing his label inside: books on the history of Chinese theatre; on the life of Agrippa of Nettesheim; research on Paracelsus. . .

In his shop I came to know Carlton Beals, the author of the creditable book *The Mexican Maze*, and a better one about the political hell in Cuba during the dictatorship (*The Crime of Cuba*).

Carlton Beals had a very famous mother: Carry A. Nation.[21] She was one of those strange, unbalanced women to whom America was indebted for Prohibition. It was she (her photograph has been preserved and printed on several occasions in many publications) who forced her way into drinking establishments on the Bowery or in Brooklyn with an axe or a hammer and smashed bottles and mirrors, window panes and glasses, in the name of the Lord, morality and purity.

She saw the finger of God in her name (Carry a nation) and this fanatical old woman with glasses, long veil and hammer, frenziedly performed what she felt to be her duty.

Her son signed his book regularly; readers would queue up in front of him after buying his *Mexican Maze*.

At the back stood a contented Mizraki—there was a long queue, the book was selling well . . .

In Hollywood, my sanctuary of books was the small Hollywood Book Store.

It belonged to another kindly and quiet man—Stade. He was either a Hungarian Swiss or a Tyrolean Czech. His books were esoteric. And included all the banned editions.

It was at his shop that I picked up a cheap reprint of Vandercook's *Black Majesty* for a dollar; it was about the Haitian Emperor, Henri Christophe, and its potential as a film had long intrigued me.

369

I had wanted to make this film with Paul Robeson.[22]

But Stade, a quiet bookseller immersed in his quiet life of books, among bright dust-jackets, antiquarian volumes and rare editions, had quite a past.

He was writing a book himself.

The hero of the book was none other than Pancho Villa.

And it emerged that this quiet Stade had taken part in the legendary and fantastic campaigns of this *hombre malo** (as his jubilant Mexican supporters called him).

John Reed once marched across Mexico with his detachments.

Ambrose Bierce followed him too.[23]

The figure of the journalist in the film *Viva Villa!* joined together both men, exactly as, contrary to reason, the screen image of Villa joined two utterly different real historical figures together: the historical Pancho and the historical Emiliano Zapata.[24]

The first was a general who staged a putsch, an adventurer;

the second was a leader of the peasant uprising, a hero and martyr.

The positive side of the Rabelaisian monster, created on screen by Wallace Beery, came from Zapata's life. The rest, from the *hombre malo,* as his admirers called him—Pancho Villa's.

At the peak of the Mexican revolution's success, Villa and Zapata stormed Mexico City from two sides and formed a brief alliance.

Then came the inevitable split, Zapata's treacherous murder at the hands of a group of reactionary officers and the other turning-points in Mexico's liberation movement.

There is even a photograph showing the two leaders sitting formally side by side, in gilt chairs in the Palacio Nacional—the 'Winter Palace' of the Mexican capital.

Pancho is in proper military dress. Zapata is dressed as a typical partisan, in a huge sombrero, and festooned with bandoliers.

This fact of course by itself does not support a natural merging of the two into one collective figure!

---

* Spanish: 'bad guy'

There is another misunderstanding, in the image of the journalist, comprising elements of John Reed and Ambrose Bierce.

Johnny remained alive and survived Pancho. That was John Reed's destiny.

The scene of Pancho's death from his bullet wounds, near the butcher's shop, was very well conceived. Johnny composed an impromptu obituary for the dying man, whose passing became a poetic, heroic death.

In actual fact it happened somewhat differently.

Bierce cited instances of Pancho's brutality for his paper.

The reports fell into Pancho's hands.

They did not reach their destination.

And Bierce . . . vanished from his readers' field of vision for ever.

One school of thought held that Bierce's bones lay somewhere along the line of Pancho Villa's campaigns.

I like Bierce and Rochefort very much.

Rochefort's *La Lanterne*[25] (its first twenty editions) was the first work I hunted for in the basement shops in Paris. On the famous *quais* of the Seine.

('Drop everything. Come and spend a month in Paris. It is spring now. We will bury ourselves in books along the Seine.' So Gordon Craig[26] wrote to me many years later from Italy; he was another fanatic about books and bookshops.)

The second book was the classic and now extremely rare volume of Péricaud's research into the Théâtre des Funambules and the incomparable Deburau.[27]

Sometimes I am lucky with books. I should also say that I had exactly the right amount of money for both of these!

I had never dreamed that anything could bring these two, Rochefort and Bierce, together!

Come to think about it, they were sharply contrasted just as much as they were brought together.

They were connected by the title: *La Lanterne*.

And what held them apart was what, at different times, was printed under this title.

Triumphant reaction.

Rochefort was exiled after the fall of the Paris Commune.

And the Empress Eugénie was swept from the arena of history and the fairy-like Tuileries.

But the vengeful lady was not content with the exile of Rochefort—that was not her doing.

Her sovereign hand was itching for vengeance.

Queen Eugénie, herself an exile from France, bought the title *La Lanterne.*

Henceforth, *La Lanterne,* which had ruthlessly (and splendidly) scourged her and *Napoléon le petit,* would heap scorn upon its wretched founder, editor and sole contributor: Henri Rochefort.

She had one of the most jaundiced young American journalists perform this dirty deed.

The idea caught on for one number . . .

The journalist's name was Ambrose Bierce.

. . . Stade had much to say about Mexico.

And the offshoots of my fascination with this country, which took root when I saw some photographs of the Day of the Dead (in a copy of *Kölnische Illustrierte* which by chance fell into my hands) were nurtured by the stories of Diego Rivera, when he had visited the Soviet Union as a friend.[28] I had a burning desire to go there.

A few months later, longing became reality.

Travelling by the train that fourteen months later took me to the land of Pancho Villa and Zapata, I made a stop to say goodbye to Stade.

I left his shop for the last time.

My wallet became fifty dollars lighter.

And my baggage fifteen kilos heavier.

I had just added Frazer's *The Golden Bough* in all its volumes: I had spent many months fruitlessly hunting for it as I travelled through the different cities of Europe.

But, apart from this remarkable, out-of-print work which was so useful in assimilating primitive thought, there lay another, slim little volume. Actually, that is the real theme of these observations.

The book has the light-hearted title *21 Delightful Ways of Committing Suicide.*

This little book belongs to the same category as those

collections of 'nonsense'* done so brilliantly by Lear and Carroll in England and now in America by Perelman, Thurber, Stagg and Saul Steinberg.[29]

It contains some of the most unthinkable ways of taking one's life, colourfully illustrated and described in the most attractive of ways.

There is one man burying himself alive in his own back yard; there is another, smoking a cigar made out of a stick of . . . dynamite; a third, like St Francis, kisses a terrifying monster, green and leprous.

The book ends with the most brilliant, unexpected and, to the point, likely method:

The twenty-first—the last method to be recommended—is suicide by longevity!

The suicide—at an incredibly great age—passes away peacefully in his armchair with a surfeit of years . . .

It is unlikely of course that anyone could improve on this list of ways of doing away with oneself.

But perhaps a more impressive method was demonstrated by George Arliss,[30] dying on screen in a film which I saw roughly a year before I met Hollywood, Stade and the funny book on this dark topic.

It was a film based on Galsworthy's play *Old English.*

And the hero of *Old English*, called Old English (and he was the personification of old England, to the marrow of his bones) was played by Arliss.

Old English—the hero of the piece—was the head of a Liverpool steamship company; a speculator and fraud; an old man half paralysed; 'one foot in bankruptcy and one foot in the grave.' Perpetrating for the first time in his life a swindle with good intentions—to provide for the family of his illegitimate son—he fell prey to another, equally tenacious cheat who had the advantage of youth.

The old despot had amazing force of will, and was utterly unscrupulous—you should see how he manipulated his creditors at a meeting, or made the shareholders of the steamship company

---

* In English in the original.

agree to embark upon an enterprise that was patently not in their interests! He valued independence above all else.

'Only thing in life. Heel on your neck—no matter whose—better dead.'

But the old man could not win.

The next day he would be exposed, bankrupted, ruined.

On the screen this is one of the best scenes.

This is not cinema at all, of course.

The film was made in the early days of sound cinema (I saw it in 1929) and it is, in essence, no more than Arliss's magnificent acting done for the camera, after his countless stage performances.

Arliss's other role is more famous and he has made it his —this is the role of another cheat and villain, but now on state (if not world) level: Disraeli, in a famous play depicting Queen Victoria's omnipotent minister—Lord Beaconsfield—in the midst of the financial speculation surrounding construction of the Suez Canal.

I saw him in this role too, in London.[31]

But perhaps, *Old English* was less pompous; it was even better, more kindly.

Because of that very scene where the old sinner actually takes his life.

In September 1941, after the evacuees, foreigners spontaneously began to leave Moscow like rats leaving a sinking ship.

The pulse of their rushed departure beat feverishly in the little bookshop on Kuznetsky Most.

Before the war, all the buying and selling foreign books was concentrated in this shop. In September 1941 the back room was filled to the ceiling with books sold by the departing foreigners.

The books migrated to my shelves, parcel after parcel.

A lot of books about the Argentine and Peru, which were bound to be close to my 'Mexican' heart.

Mr Steinhard, the American Ambassador, was 'flogging' them.

Books by De Kruif.[32]

Detective stories with garish covers.

And, on the other hand, Sinclair Lewis's novels in their exceedingly modest bindings.

A small volume of Galsworthy's plays.

And among the plays was *Old English.*

I re-read this play year after year, remembering Arliss's performance.

The old man is on a very strict diet.

His daughter keeps a stern eye on this—she is impossibly sanctimonious.

('Um! What's that squealing?' The old man asks.

'I think it's Miss Heythorp singing, sir,'* the footman answers.)

But—keeping it from his daughter who has gone to a Temperance Society charity ball—the old man orders a Lucullan banquet late one evening.

After giving orders for the wine, the old man falls into a pre-prandial sleep. Before this came the scene with his granddaughter and a sharp altercation with Mr Ventnor who had come to blackmail him.

Mr Ventnor is shown the door by the footman.

You would have to see the cunning with which the old man contrives to press the bell at this critical moment.

From the darkness emerged that same room with the heavy furnishings and the heavy portières drawn.

'Old English' is resplendent in his evening suit and white tie. Like a true gentleman, he is in full evening-dress. The lavish meal draws to its close.

'Old English' is lacking all restraint in his gluttony. He drains glass after glass.

The footman's panic.

The daughter's anger when she comes in to say good night to her father, and leaves a bottle of whisky out of the old man's reach.

The old man contrives to rise and seize the bottle as soon as she leaves.

The old man drinks,

becomes drunk.

Memories of the past move before him: racehorses he had

---

* In English in the original.

bet on; actresses he had been keen on; drinking parties, debauchery, the past . . .

. . . Perhaps I was so entranced by this old man because I had met his exact double in reality.

He [Old English] is almost sinking into childhood and was also almost ruined, but he had made everything over to his grandson—the son of his daughter and his . . . groom—the daughter who was forever banished from his home, the daughter to whom the old man had not said one word for over twenty years.

Now this old man (let us suppose that this 'now' is fifteen years ago) muttered almost incoherently, although he presided as before at the long table in the dining room of the impoverished hacienda at Tetlapayac.

We were filming the scenes of the peons' uprising for our Mexican film, on the worldly estates of Señor Saldivar (an extremely kind and courteous man) and his grandfather.

Old Señor Saldivar's eyes lit up at the sight of food and drink—nothing else had that effect.

Having said that, the old man was by no means yet without strength or curiosity.

We filmed, many days running, episodes where the revolting peasants exchanged fire with the landowners' police—the *charros*—in the overgrown cactus palms, or among the sparse foliage of agave bushes. *Charros* wore narrow striped trousers, monumental spurs and felt hats with gold braid.

The acting was unusually realistic.

Because the actors were real peons and real *charros*, retained by the young Señor Julio.

Give both sides a free rein.

Substitute the blank cartridges with loaded ones . . .

The estate manager, Señor Nicolas from Santander, Spain, allowed only the owner, Señor Julio, to shoot off pieces of cactus (in close up, near his face).

The boundless fields of agave were adorned with crosses here and there.

The haciendas lived by a feudal code.

At evening the tall gates were shut.

And no one from the administration block dared to go out into the fields by night.

Stills from the episode 'the execution of the rebellious peons' from the film *Que Viva México!*

The crosses marked the traces of Señor Nicolas's harsh discipline.

Señor Nicolas had recently bought a Packard.

Within a week the Packard was badly smashed up.

Señor Nicolas kept forgetting it was not a mustang he was breaking in.

The Packard leaped across gullies like a horse.

But the hefty bull put an end to the idea of a Packard in the hands of the man from Santander.

The bull regarded the Packard not as a horse but as a member of his tribe.

The powerful horns of this handsome Andalusian twisted the radiator off his unwelcome rival.

The Packard lay on its side.

We were often visited by a strange procession when we were filming.

Two striped *charros* rode at the front.

Then high on his horse, under a parasol, came the elderly Señor Saldivar.

And his personal servant, *'moso'* Matthias at the rear.

(That was how I used to see old man Dzhambul in the outskirts of Alma-Ata;[33] under an umbrella, with glasses and galoshes, riding a steppe horse. He had that same attentive, searching way of looking at you, holding his gaze.)

The scenes were different at night.

The old man called Matthias into his high bedroom.

The old man held a rifle and was sobbing.

He ordered Nicolas to shoot him.

He was ruining his grandson.

He was destroying the hacienda.

Nicolas and Matthias coerced the resisting old man into his bed.

But in the morning he surveyed like a voluptuary the green peppers stuffed with pomegranates and nuts, and the other exotic fare, put before him by the lanky, moustachioed Guadelupe.

The next morning a girl rushed to me in indignation; she played the daughter of the *hacendado*. It turned out that the previous evening the half-mummified old man had made her the most

Eisenstein fresco by Roberto Montenegro.

Eisenstein's set design for Shaw's *Heartbreak House*, 1922.

Eisenstein's costume design for Master Manghan in
Shaw's *Heartbreak House,* 1922.

'Revolution'. Drawing by Eisenstein, 1917.

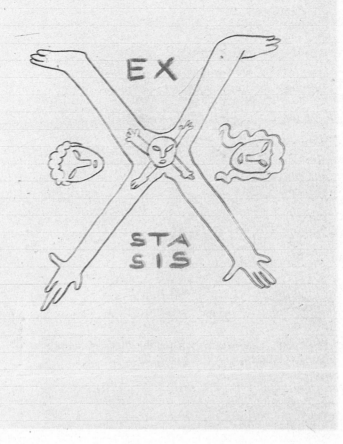

'Ex-stasis'. One of a cycle of drawings by Eisenstein, 1939.

'The Duel'. Eisenstein's draft for the finale of his projected film about Pushkin, *A Poet's Love*, 1946.

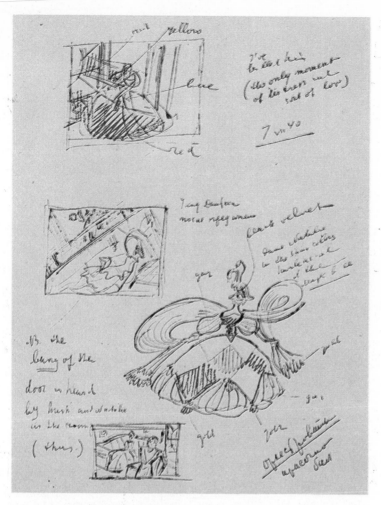

'Natalie', 'Harlequin' and other sketches from Eisenstein's
scenario for *A Poet's Love*, 1946.

Eisenstein's drawings of peons at the Tetlapayac hacienda, 1931.

Two of Eisenstein's drawings from the cycle *'Souvenirs d'enfance'*, 28 November 1942.

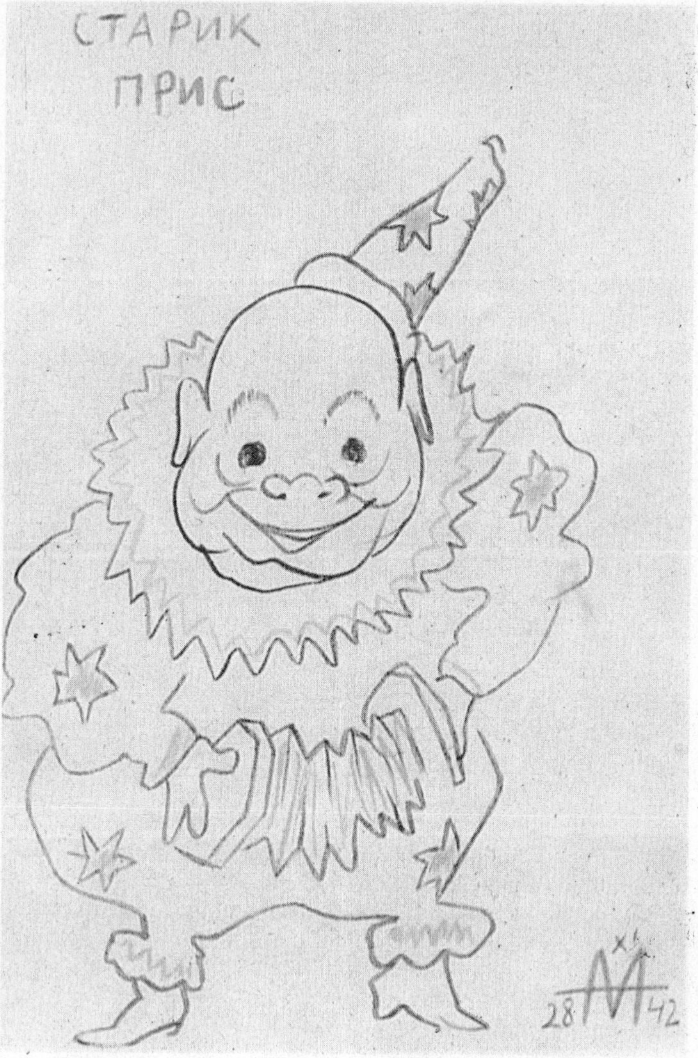
СТАРИК
ПРИС
28 XI 42

Stills from the colour sequence in *Ivan the Terrible*, Part Two.

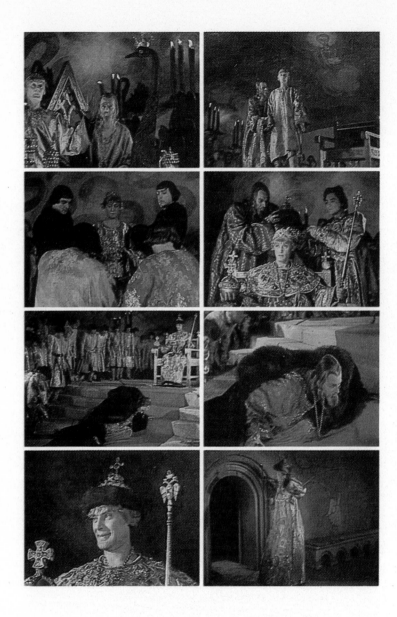

Portrait of Eisenstein by Kiki de Montparnasse (Alice Irine), 1929.

unambiguous of proposals, and suggested they drive off into town together.

That was not so unlikely, from what we knew about this buck-toothed old man with his old woman's bonnet shielding him from the sun on his rides around the fields.

When he lived in Paris, his money had gone like water.

He put money on horses.

He never got out of his tails and tie in Paris; he turned night into day and day into night, in dens of iniquity.

It was easy to believe. He looked a ruin.

But that old Señor Saldivar paid us a special honour.

He was going to Mexico City for a few days and invited us to his house.

Oyster soup, prepared in a silver tureen.

Fish such as the world has not seen.

Lobsters.

The rest of the meal has vanished in a sort of misty vagueness.

There is a combination of the superficiality of Paris with the sensuality of the New World, like the broad avenues of Chapultepec which join the Bois de Boulogne to tropical plants; and the twisting iron architecture from the days of Napoleon III and Maximilian merges with the bronze faces and blue overalls of the contemporary inhabitants of Mexico City.

The old man was transformed.

And if he wore not a dinner jacket but some sort of old man's house-coat, never mind: from the movement of his (albeit enfeebled) hands; from the smile that overcame the flabbiness of his pendulous lips; from his scintillating wit which caught me unawares (his muttering was almost incoherent); from all this it was possible to reconstruct this erstwhile society lion, who was probably as enigmatic and free to dispense largesse as the slightly more implausible Brazilians in Balzac's novels.

. . . But Old English had had enough to drink for all time.

And Arliss played the scene splendidly as his intoxication gradually overtook his arms and legs.

Below the elbows, his arms were immobile.

He checked whether his fingers still moved.

He dropped his forearm on to the table.

The fingers were immobile.

And they knocked like bones against the smooth surface of the table.

The sound of bones in lifeless hands!

How I would like to see that on stage!

Is Arliss so accomplished that a spasm holds the ends of his fingers rigid?! Nothing else could make that noise.

Or was the sound recorded separately?

It had a staggering effect, like a hand knocking on a coffin lid.

I drop my hands on to the table top.

There is a dull thud.

But there is no sound like wood striking against wood.

Darkness again.

Then the lights go up.

Old English was immobile in his chair.

His grand-daughter came in with her companion. They had been to the theatre.

She wanted to show her grandfather her new dress.

She decided against waking him up.

Tiptoed out.

The footman, alarmed, wanted to wake his master.

'Bed-time, sir!'

But Mr Heythorp was not to be wakened . . .

And the maid, Molly, distractedly throwing up her arms over the unusual suicide, cried out: 'Mother o'Jasus! The grand old fightin' gintleman! The great old sinner he was!' Curtain.

In the previous act, an unbalanced and dissolute writer, the mother of his grand-daughter, had sung:

La vie est brève, un peu d'amour,
*Un peu de rêve et puis bonjour.**

The character of one more old sinner who was also a sui-

---

* French: 'Life is short, a little loving,
A little dreaming, then farewell.'

cide blends with Old English, the character created by Arliss and
Señor Saldivar.

He is also from a play.

This time, one by Crommelynck.[34]

From the first act of *Les Tripes d'or* [Golden Tripe], a
strange work by an unusual writer.

The sinner himself does not appear on stage. The play revolves around the money left in his will.

We are dealing here with the question of suicides.

I once attempted a fairly complicated, roundabout method
of suicide.

Curiously, the outcome is still uncertain. Although the case
is very like a fiasco.

Perhaps that was why *The Idiot* was one of the first books I
read again as I lay in the Kremlin hospital after my heart attack.

Not because of its title . . .

But for the scene where Hippolyte tried to commit suicide.

That great writer put his heroes in the most inhumanly
shameful situations, and in *The Idiot* Dostoyevsky surpassed himself.

Nastasia Philippovna, Ganichka and money.

The whole story of Rogozhin's love.

Almost all the situations in which Prince Myshkin found
himself, from the scene of his arrival, to his speech in Aglaya's
house.

And of these scenes perhaps the most tragically humiliating
was the one of Hippolyte's embarrassment after his loudmouthed
exhibitionism—when he read his confession.

. . . I decided to do it not by hanging, or smoking a stick of
dynamite, or eating what my diet forbid, or with a pistol, or by poison.

I decided to work myself to death.

I was deeply struck by the role of fate in Dreiser's *An
American Tragedy*.

In my 'treatment'* of it for Paramount, I emphasised this
tendency in every possible way.

Clyde arranged Roberta's murder perfectly.

---

* In English in the original.

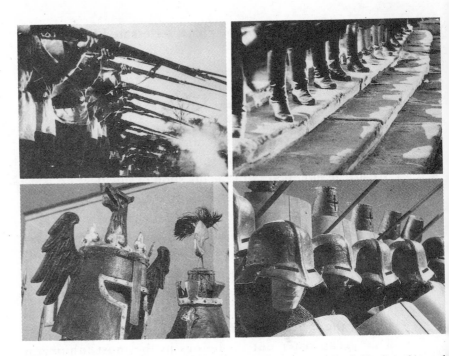

The image of 'impersonal force' in Eisenstein's films: *The Battleship Potemkin* and *Alexander Nevsky.*

The image of 'impersonal force' in Eisenstein's films: *Que Viva México!* and *Ivan the Terrible.*

Then came the notorious 'change of heart': his change of plans when he was in the boat.

And subsequently, the genuinely disastrous occurrence of Roberta's death.

Once the implacable cogs were set in motion, the machine of crime turned everything Clyde had undertaken in his plan for committing the murder into the chain of evidence against him.

Once set in motion, the fatal machine of crime followed its path automatically, like it or not, whether or not he oppose it, or try to escape its criminal intent (once it had been set in motion).

A sort of djinn with a skull and crossbones on its bottle.

Underlying this image, which helped me so much, was a living impression. Of course!

For that was not the first time that I used the image of implacable, automatic, mechanical progress.

Earlier, with exactly the same blind, implacable progress, did the impersonal, faceless (no close-ups!) column of soldiers move down the Odessa steps.

Just boots!

And later—again a faceless, soulless machine—the great-grandmother of General Guderian's [35] hordes of tanks—the press of the iron 'cavalry wedge', the Teutonic Knights in *Nevsky*.

Again faceless. This time the faces were physically covered with helmets and the eye-holes echoed the outline of the slits on the future Tigers and Panthers.

And later—the fatal path Vladimir Andreyevich took to his death, accompanied by the roar of the *oprichniki*, implacably black, again like fate, again with faces masked, like a funeral choir.

. . . I once asked myself, 'What is the most frightening thing?'

And the most frightening thing I vividly remembered were the railway lines at Smolensk during the Civil War.

There were countless lines.

And the number of goods wagons on them was even . . . more countless.

That is ungrammatical. Nevertheless, there were that many.

A giant bottleneck, which those dark red snakes had squeezed into as they strained at the advancing armies.

For the time being in Smolensk they were quiet, but they were ready at a minute's warning to glide further off.

The goods trains lay like vast whales in a backwater, on their cold rails in their sidings.

Look at their backs from this narrow bridge that crosses them.

Both ends vanished into the distance to left and right and blended with the dust of the distant tracks which disappeared into the darkness.

Thus the limitless lights of Los Angeles (it is 55 miles across) disappear into the darkness, as the circling plane drops. A piercing pain in the eardrums. Throbbing temples . . .

And one's temples throb in the same way when you try to comprehend this nocturnal mirage of the trains' scaly backs. The movement back and forth in the darkness.

The hooters sounded funny and hoarse in the darkness.

Was it they who gave me the idea of the waxwings' song in the distance, in the night scene on the eve of the Battle on the Ice in *Nevsky?*

No smaller or less terrifying was this park of inanimate but nevertheless mobile monsters, when I was trying to find my way back to my freight wagon, making my way down between the rails and going under the wheels.

In 1920, I lived in a freight wagon on rails.

Although I was working in the front's Political Administration, Smolensk was so overcrowded that a group of us continued to live in the wagons.

The doors of a wagon slid firmly shut with a bang, coming out of the darkness and going back into it again. Or the pale rectangles of empty wagons glided past like the line of dashes which signify railways on maps.

Hammers banged against axles, as they did in Anna Karenina's nightmares.

The hooters blared in the darkness.

And the points switched, moving over in a measured jump, as if in a strange dance.

The red light turned green.

The green turned red once more.

But this is not the worst thing.

It was not the nocturnal searchings for one's wagon along miles of silent wagons,

nor the terrible heat under the roofs, baked by the midday sun, when I lay ill in bed . . .

But the rear of the train, long, endless; dozens upon dozens of wagons long; the rear of the train as it moved backwards, the blunt nose of the last wagon bearing down on you.

The red rear light glimmering, a single unseeing eye.

Nothing will stop it.

Nothing could hold it back.

The driver was far away at the other end.

He could not see a thing from where he was.

Enemy. Victim. Someone met by chance. Any of these could find themselves on his path.

But nothing could stop the slow movement of the red un-blinking eye which stuck out of the blunt nose of the last wagon as it headed into the darkness.

How many times in the hours of my wanderings along the tracks did those night-time monsters of trains treacherously, with barely a rattle, steal up on me almost furtively, looming out of the darkness; and move past, dwarfing me and then retreating into darkness once more?

I think it was that; their implacable, blind, pitiless movement which migrated into my films: now got up in soldiers' boots on the Odessa steps, now turning their blunt noses into the knights' helmets in Battle on the Ice, now sliding in black robes along the stone flagging in the cathedral, following the candle as it shook in the hands of the stumbling Vladimir Staritsky . . .

This image of the night train migrated from film to film; it has become the symbol of fate.

In An American Tragedy, this was first an image of an un-stoppable crime and then the impersonal automatic process of jus-tice and law . . .

Later I myself ended up in the tenacious claws of the image.

The fuse of my plan was laid in the autumn of 1943.

And the harvest was garnered at the start of 1946.

It was probably the most terrible autumn of my life.

Apart from two catastrophes:

The death of *México*.

And the tragedy of *Bezhin Meadow*.

... Time heals all wounds.

In the rosy haze of the past, unpleasant acts seem like harmless trifles; vicious behaviour becomes irrelevant unpleasantness; and vile actions seem no more than modest viciousness.

Surprisingly, time has not softened my stay in Alma-Ata.

Apart from the satisfaction of the (all too few!) moments of creativity which I gained from my actual work on *Ivan*, everything there was vile.

My stoicism as I endured the move from Moscow was magnificent!

With what self-control, quite unposed (besides, there was no one there to notice it!) did I make this 'act of self-denial' of everything dear that was left to me in my studio in Potylikha!

Manuscripts that had accumulated over the course of twenty years.

Everything concerning my restless path in art for these two decades.

Everything that I thought was a find, a discovery.

Everything I had fought for, made myself ill over, or was mistaken about.

And books, the books—slices of life, my thoughts about them, and quotations which I had yet to transform in unfinished works.

And thoughts ... One huddled in the corner between these shelves. Another hovered near that table. The proximity of these shelves led me to a third; and of those shelves, to a fourth.

The thoughts lived in these four walls were more material than the books.

I sometimes thought I could hold them in my hands— embrace them, nestle up against them ...

They were virtually three-dimensional.

Perhaps, precisely for that reason they are so reluctant to be committed to paper?!

In the terrible *Confession of a Fool*, the psychologically ill Strindberg feels physically inseparable from the other members of his family, the furniture, his surroundings and the walls.

I appear to go further.

I feel (felt?) like Peer Gynt, physically one and the same as the imagined ghosts of thoughts, unthought-out, not fully developed, not fully expounded or written down.

I walk slowly between these invisible inhabitants of my studio.

They stand between the books.

There are many of them.

A kingdom of the unborn.

'You, whose hour has come, are you ready to sail?'[36]

The author of these terrible lines fled from a ruined castle somewhere in Belgium.

He unmoored his little boat on the Channel.

He had a cage on his knees. Inside were two blue birds . . .

Maeterlinck.

. . . 'Are you ready to sail?'

Then it was Eduard Tisse asking me this.

He was making a series of trips from our Sparrow Hills[37] to the distant Kazan Station.

He was taking as much as he could.

Even more than that.

The German[38] had fallen strangely silent.

And the car with her dimmed lamps glided easily through darkened Moscow.

I slowly walked past the books; it was a walk through all my life's experiences.

The renunciation had been effected.

I would have liked to have been able to see myself impartially.

Instead, I took no more than five books with me.

Which?

As always, when about to go off on a journey, detective stories.

Nothing else.

As always, when going on a journey, an expedition, a trip, for a temporary absence.

It is a terrible pose, of course.

A terrible 'theatre for oneself'.

But perhaps this will bestow some sort of Buddhist inner serenity which will last the full twelve days of my mad journey into nothingness.

You remember the train of drunken soldiers, which lost its driver at the end of Zola's *The Rout.*

Our train was not drunk.

But there was plenty of 'loss of face' from seat to seat, from compartment to compartment, from wagon to wagon . . .

Thus began my long journey to Central Asia.

Behind me lay uncertainty.

Ahead of me lay uncertainty.

Some sort of Alma-Ata.

What sort?

Books on the Road[1]

Whether I am going to a sanatorium.

Or from one city to another.

Or to a spa.

Or whether I am going filming, or from place to place, one question bothers me above all others:

What books to take as companions?

A tie that clashes with my socks, or a hat that does not go with the jacket (if it is I who am wearing it, not an actor in the film!), do not trouble me in the least.

But books must go together, just as the flowers in the farewell bouquets must harmonise.

The landscape I am expecting to see also exerts an influence.

But it should contrast rather than harmonise.

The book and the journey.

The journey across the pages and the journey across the mountains, steppes and plains.

I do not understand poetry; I have never bothered with it.

But the rattle of wheels and the rhythm of prose are for me essential complements of each other.

This has long been the case.

Papa and Mama divorced in my early childhood. I stayed with Papa in Riga. Mama was spirited away to Petersburg.

Every Christmas I went to visit Mama in Petersburg.

From my earliest years I would be tucked away one evening in a carriage in Riga and would rub my eyes the next morning in Petersburg.

I always took books to read with me.

The first was *Viy*, by Gogol.

Old Time Landowners, Ivan Ivanovich and Ivan Nikiforovich, A Bewitched Spot.

And of course, *A Terrible Vengeance* published, with illustrations, by Pavlenkov—these were my first railway 'pulp'.

The book would be accompanied by a bag of boiled sweets:

either greenish and transparent like onyx—'Duchesse', or multi-coloured bull's-eyes— 'Malyutka'.

I would often fall asleep with a book in my hands and a fruit-drop between my teeth.

The next morning I would wake up with a funny sensation in my cheek, where the fruit-drop had half-dissolved in the night.

Travelling and reading are inseparable.

I see myself once more with a book, on one of my forays with the military construction division during the Civil War.

For example in Novo-Sokolniki, with Schopenhauer in the shade of a freight wagon, under the carriage awaiting the uncoupling of the train.

A cool breeze blew under the wagon, and the paragraphs on 'parerga and paralipomena' in a small German edition sank deep into my memory.

Kleist's and Immermann's articles on theatre were nearby.

What Kleist had to say about correct organic movement was expressed precisely in the following sentiments: 'true organic movement is possible only for a marionette or semi-god (organic in the sense of mechanical, in accordance with the laws of nature, and the law of gravity most of all).'[2]

Study of Craig's '*Übermarionette*', or the first two or three laws of biomechanics, follows on naturally from Kleist.[3]

. . . And now two barges sailed on their long voyage from Dvinsk to Desna, carrying our military construction division.

I see myself amid the sacks, crates, spades and mattocks, holding a minute book.

This time the author is Bibliophile Jacob (the name Paul Lacroix wrote under) whom we all know so well from his weighty volumes, red and embellished with gold and devoted to customs and the history of costume in France over a certain period.[4]

The reproductions in these books are meagre, poorly re-drawn—for both chromolithographs and wood engravings—and lifeless.

The unique spirit of the epoch, preserved in sculpture, tapestry, embroidery and carved ivory, has been crushed by the costume, the rhythm of the figure's outline and proportions.

Only Racine's countless volumes of the history of costume

are worse than these. They give absolutely no sense of motion or the character of the people, nor how the costume was worn and how the people moved.

You can study costume only from reproductions of real paintings, sculptures, sarcophagi or miniatures, not from these castrated little pictures.

But Lacroix's text is good.

And Bibliophile Jacob has some entertaining stories.

As literature, they are equally as meagre, angular and they fail to convey any of the exuberant liveliness of the past.

Balzac also lambasted him for this . . .[5]

But they are entertaining for their factual content concerning the past.

. . . The barge was gliding along. Our next job was to erect a bridge with defended approaches.

But for the moment, let us read about how the 'Old Bridge' collapsed into the Seine, under the weight of the houses and shops on it (it was then the rule to build on bridges: for instance, the Ponte Vecchio, in Florence).

A new bridge arose on that spot: the romantic, delightful Pont Neuf.

Good heavens! It has so many literary associations!

Dumas' musketeers fenced there with their rapiers.

And Tabarin once shouted from the pavement: 'Why does a dog raise its leg?'[6]

Charlatans pulled teeth there, and faith-healers sold panaceas.

Diagonally opposite stood the Bouridan Tower: recently I fell in love with it in an engraving by Callot.[7]

And in the centre was an equestrian statue of Henry IV.

How many mysterious figures in cloaks and broad hats have met here by moonlight on the pages of novels!

It was there that Arsène Lupin slid past.

That was the heavy tread of Javert.

And there, like an ominous statue, stands Fantômas.

Now—Paul Féval's hero—Rocambole or Captain Fracasse.[8]

Over there, the inhabitants of the Cour des Miracles lurked in their lairs.[9] Later in Paris I was shown the very spot where the

Cour des Miracles once stood: it was then *L'Intransigeant's* editorial offices.

I was still deep in thought about a new bridge to replace the old . . .

. . . but I was already rushing along the bank, levelling the descent to the bridge, which was reaching across the Desna from either bank. The works' manager's boat was floating midstream. And his powerful voice, bursting from his stooped figure, tall boots and roadman's cap, resounded on both banks like a shrapnel bomb of ringing obscenity:

'Oi! That engineer there! . . . Why aren't the . . . approaches ready? . . .'

That engineer was me.

Not up to much as an engineer. Too romantic: my head was full of fifteenth-century Paris—completely the wrong time and place.

But, a few years later, this same engineer will crawl along the supports of the Palace Bridge in Leningrad and talk with the bridge operators about the best way to raise the bridge repeatedly for half an hour, from six o'clock when the bridge was due to be raised, until six-thirty.[10]

The sun was in the right position at ten past six. The bridge had to be down at six-thirty.

Otherwise the trams would be late arriving at Finland Station, and the passengers, streaming in from the dormitory suburbs to the factories and plants, would be correspondingly delayed.

We knew this only too well!

On our last day of work we dodged the vigilant mechanics, who were so engrossed in what they saw going on above that we were able to hold the bridge's maw open for a further ten minutes.

And the rows, the disruption of work, the hold-ups and irritation!

But you can't blame us, for heaven's sake!

We only had twenty minutes a day.

And in those twenty minutes we had to:

kill a white horse, as it galloped, madly pulling a cab;

let drop a golden-haired girl,

let the two halves of the bridge open up,

Stills from the episode 'Bank Bridge' from *October*

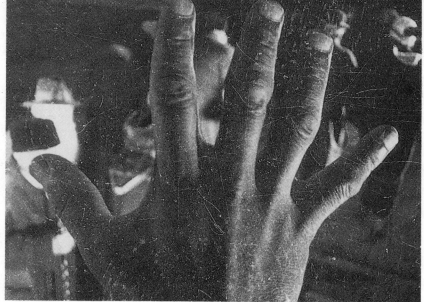

let the golden hair stretch across the bottomless abyss,

let the dead horse and the cab swing from the raised edge of the bridge,

let the cab fall . . .

On screen, this takes a lot less than twenty minutes.

But to film it takes hours!

In daily doses of one twenty-minute spoonful, we knocked out, piece by piece, sections for the montage which crowns the slaughter of 3-5 July 1917, on the corner of Sadovaya Street and Nevsky Prospect.

God knows why I should wake up one morning in the Nicholas Library after filming interior shots for the sequence of the storming of the Winter Palace and see through a window the giant arms of the Palace Bridge, raised heavenwards like the arms of a dying man.

I saw the arms of the bridge almost as in a vision; then the broken cab and the shot horse appeared, and then the golden rays of the sun played upon them before turning into the fair curls of the dying girl . . .

That was why, in order to film one of the most powerful scenes in the film *October*, the one-time engineer was crawling through the mechanical belly of the Palace Bridge and arguing with its operator about the possible rhythm and speed of the rising bridge.

Then the bridge evolved into a symbol: a symbol of the city's split, between its centre and the workers' dormitories during the July Days.

In a direct, tactical sense—but also in the sense that by July 1917 the working masses had not finally rallied around the organisational core of Bolsheviks.

At the start of that day in October, this evoked the idea of another bridge—this time, the one next to Palace Bridge—Nicholas Bridge.

The historic 'Aurora' was moored nearby. She had been lent to us, from Kronstadt, to take part in this historical recreation.

The Nicholas Bridge rotates horizontally.

When it locked to, it linked the outskirts to the centre, so defying the Provisional Government's order to keep the bridges closed on this occasion too and thereby setting in train a series of events that were to have a permanent and dramatic effect on the course of history.

The small Bank Bridge over the Kryukov Canal, with the gilt griffins, also played a part.

It parodied the idea of unity and solidarity.

It was half-way across that bridge that the huge figure of the sailor arose—he was cast in the same mould as those sailors who locked the Nicholas Bridge and was the Baltic equivalent of those sailors in the Black Sea fleet who sailed through the admiral's squadron in *Potemkin*. Simply by raising a powerful arm he scattered the procession of old men: the last bastion of the supporters of reaction, headed by the mayor, Schreider, ran away.

Arrogant and clamorous, they had marched to the Winter Palace in support of their protégés who stood for their ideals: 'the ten capitalist ministers' Kerensky left behind in his haste.

They scarpered, like bedraggled roosters, over the narrow bridge and past the imperturbable griffins, between Kazan Cathedral and the State Bank; just as wretchedly as that bridge pales by comparison with the Troitsky or Liteiny Bridges, or the Palace or Nicholas Bridges which the workers victoriously swept over, an avalanche pouring from the workers' regions on the other side of the Neva.

Thus, a chance glimpse at dawn, the silhouette of the raised bridge, evolved into an image which in turn branched out into a complex of images, ultimately the symbol of two outstretched arms, reaching out to each other in a firm grip. This was of structural importance in my conception of the whole film.

Only the surfeit of details and the haste which prevented a clear and distinct execution of the montage conceal this structure: even those who consider *October* to be a greater work than *Potemkin* fail to notice it.

And this constant rush in filming demolished yet another bridge—the Novgorod bridge in *Alexander Nevsky*.

On that bridge, we filmed the scene of the famous fist fight between the two districts of the old city—Sofiskaya and Torgovaya.

Vaska Buslai and Vasilisa met here for the first time; it was romantic, and provided human interest. Here, in the heat of conflict, Vaska cried out for the first time in delight: 'She's a beaut!' after Vasilisa hit him full in the mouth.

I was very sad to lose the lyrical entrée of the two romantic heroes. And I was very sorry to lose those desperate lads who flew off the bridge into the cold October water of the pond in Potylikha, which was where the bridge 'across the Volkhov' had been built.

Most of all, I missed the whole scene; it was all thrown out.

Rushing full-tilt to meet the deadline, we had no time to spend on finishing the montage or sound recording for this scene.

Will the day ever come in cinema when people come to recognise the importance of time—not only in the seconds on screen, but in the hours of creative labour at the cutting table, the days spent recording the sound; the weeks spent re-recording the finished product?!!

For it is then that the film's most subtle, vivid and animated fabric is woven, the finished film being born in the complicated moves of audiovisual counterpoint.

. . . Oddly enough, it was building bridges that led to my fascination with the principle of counterpoint as a conjunction of innumerable independent sections of action, interwoven into a strict outline through time.

My experience in building bridges while an apprentice at the Izhora camp school. That was also in 1917—not the screen version, but the real thing!

Not long before those months, when we stood one murky night on picket duty with rifles in our hands, the whole school defending one of the approaches to Petrograd against the expected hordes of Kornilov and the 'Wild Division'.

And even then I remember I had in the pocket of my overcoat a small volume of Dürer's sketchbook of his journey to the Netherlands, on the opposite side from my holster.

From time to time we went to warm up in a concealed hut, with something burning and giving off black smoke inside! . . .

In *Alexander Nevsky*, we threw the bridge diagonally across the studio pond, so the length would be right.

And it was not logic that dictated this, but a memory, oddly enough!

There is a bridge like this in real life, thrown without rhyme or reason diagonally across a river. This is in Lucerne.

It is roofed in for its entire length.

With countless oil paintings hanging beneath the roof in each of the bridge's spans, its eccentric path across the river cannot fail to delight the traveller to Switzerland.

I found no explanation for this oddity.

I joked with the Swiss, saying that it looked as though they had built the bridge too long, and that the only way they could fit it all in between opposite banks was to put it diagonally across the river.

I subsequently forgot about it.

And did not think about it again until we were working on *Nevsky*.

. . . However our temporary bridge across the Desna went straight as a die, and if it was slightly uneven in profile, that was only because the piles did not settle uniformly in the different parts of the riverbed.

And small wonder the piles settled!

We were woken one night by a terrible racket.

Gun-carriages, clanking down the slopes.

Ammunition wagons, rumbling.

Field pieces, lurching forwards.

A crack.

Shouts in the darkness.

A blockage.

One span had broken.

It was not designed to allow for retreat.

It was built for advance.

Then, at night-time, it was in tumult.

But we had hand-picked sappers, not conscripts or confused civilians, to do the job.

They rebuilt the span in pitch dark.

There was a fleeting glimpse of backs,

axes,

girders.

And the black stream of retreating soldiers once more crossed the racing waters, which were already faintly reflecting the first light of day.

Sitting on a felled tree, I leafed through Maeterlinck's *Princess Maleine*.

The bridgehead was to be reinforced with another ring of trenches and barbed wire. The local population energetically dug the sand, anxiously awaiting the return of those soldiers who had dashed off to the rear during the night.

Princess Maleine did not interfere with my shouts of encouragement, orders and explanations, nor my hurling of abuse.

But I was sorting out my conscripts very well. Apart from a few refusals to work, there were no conflicts.

Except with a slightly-built young man with brown hair, tinted pince-nez, an antediluvian straw hat with a striped band and a white, striped suit. His cheeks were hollow and he walked with a strange, jumpy motion.

I put him down as a malingerer.

But I gave him some light work, like counting out the planks or something of that sort.

It never occurred to me to mess up his white suit.

My colleagues told me with a laugh that it was accepted practice to give dirty work to anyone wearing a light-coloured suit. Unloading coal, for example, or working with axle grease. Unloading lime or flour would be the job of anyone in a dark suit.

The village idiot was among those sent. He had a beard, short legs, and a tall hat; and, in accordance with all the rules of literary convention, a retinue of jeering boys.

As I did not understand their slang, I could only guess that they were persuading him to jump into the water.

The idiot suddenly jumped, and started imitating a duck flapping its wings. Universal delight.

The people meant no harm, but they were terrified and confused.

In other places it was worse.

Near Dvinsk, for example, all the prostitutes were mobilised. These ladies lifted up their silk skirts as they stood on the trenches, and announced loudly that they had certain 'days' when they could not work.

Vying fiercely with each other, they solicited on the mud

embankments, and led the entire (but not very numerous) contingent of eligible males off into the undergrowth . . .

My men dug among the roots of the pines in an orderly fashion, even thinking about how they might shore up the crumbling sandbanks with planking . . .

Of course, neither Princess Maleine nor little Tintagiles[11] ever dreamed they would end up in such a situation.

Come to think of it, Maeterlinck himself could not have dreamed that in his advanced old age, abandoning everything that he had, he would have to put to sea in a small boat to save himself from the Fascist invasion, taking only a cage holding two little bluebirds.

Hollywood gave sanctuary to the poor fugitive from Belgium and his two little bluebirds.

. . . A few weeks later.

Once again, a barge.

Then a change of boats.

Then Polotsk . . .

This time, the *Memoirs* of Saint-Simon.

Not Saint-Simon the Utopian, but Saint-Simon, the exemplary eighteenth-century stylist and memoirist.[12]

His ironic, malicious, but poetic and uncommonly vivid descriptions and portraits of the nobility and the family of Louis XIV blended curiously with the small, sooty red-brick houses that lined the steep streets of Polotsk.

The only echo came from the tall, baroque Roman Catholic church.

My new foreman was also, apparently, no stranger to literature. But more Boussenard, Stevenson, and Xavier de Montépin.[13]

He spent hours working in the church, digging up the foundations with ferocious energy.

The corridor had a stale smell: water seeped through the walls. The stones were slippery underfoot and there was a feeble sucking sound as the spade worked the sodden earth beneath them. The flickering light of a kerosene lamp. Everything you might see on the cover of a Pinkerton or *The Caves of Leuchtweiss*. Everything, apart from the streams of sweat and the torn shirts. But the treasure, the treasure which one of the citizens had told him of in a terrified whisper, was of course nowhere to be found.

No Polish Cortés or Captain Kidd[14] had buried his booty here. There were no florins, doubloons, goblets or gold candlesticks . . .

There was no time to dig further.

The carts had been loaded up and we had to move on . . .

I blew up the German trenches, abandoned three years ago after Kerensky's ridiculous offensive, while reading Ibsen.

I was in a great hurry. There was a whole battalion of dramatists I had not read.

Rosmersholm and Cardinal Nikolas from *The Pretenders. The Masterbuilder,* Solness and Doctor Stockmann—I knew of these only at second-hand.

On Bones[1]

We were faced by a dead city out of Rider Haggard.[2]

But no epic poem has ever sung of what lay on the approaches to its walls.

No human foot had trodden there for three years.

The Germans had left.

The civilians had not returned.

Farms had been burnt down, or flattened by shells.

We had been commissioned to blow up the Germans' positions, now abandoned, which had been the scene of Kerensky's failed July offensive.

(There was a risk of a fresh Polish invasion.)

They had to be destroyed.

There they were, suddenly before us,

those strange installations!

It was like a dead and deserted Bruges, after the sea had retreated a kilometre, leaving the prosperous maritime town high and dry,[3] a dead Bruges, waist-deep in earth and with its rising chimneys pulled down.

Or like the underground city of Hara-Hoto, when Kozlov, the Russian traveller, discovered it,[4] but a Hara-Hoto sticking out of the Tibetan earth from its waist up, releasing the flights of its galleries.

It had narrow streets, such as you might see in Asia, which intersected with Gothic alleyways.

Taken all in all they were borne aloft by a range of hills, but open spaces had been gouged out of the body of the hills.

Thin wire was stretched along the slopes of the German trenches like a coat of chain mail.

The corrugated iron in the semi-circular vaults of the underground passageways was like curved bands . . .

The rusty rails and trolleys . . .

Concrete blockhouses, with the squeaking visors of shutters over the windows.

Spyholes, glazed with bluish reinforced glass.

Throw a rock at it and the glass shatters into a star of cracks.

But the steel nerves held the fragments of the pane in the frame. The rock bounced off harmlessly at our feet.

A pile of concrete posts lay on the grass like bleached bones.

The broad, rusty, barbed belt wound its triple coils along the sinister mounds.

The furthest, the outermost, lay close to the ground.

The middle one was at chest height, level with the heart.

And the nearest one was the most frightening.

Its immense coils were loops of toothed barbed wire.

No one who escaped being tripped up by the first or lacerated on the second, would find a way out of the embraces of this third lethal belt.

The coils of the rusty snake hissed in the wind.

Not a soul anywhere.

If only a bird would fly overhead.

Or a field mouse scamper by.

Not a soul!

We carefully climbed down through the descending belts of wire.

Something gleamed at the base of this wire cobweb!

It was not concrete posts.

Not metaphors.

Bones . . .

Vesuvius threw torrents of lava down on Herculaneum and Pompeii.

And life in its infinite variety, caught unawares, was frozen in the deep lava. As layer after layer of the petrified river was taken away, a picture emerged of arrested life.

So it was there, beneath the open—too open—sky, in this field near Dvinsk—a frozen picture of an insane offensive: a hysterical maniac sent men to their certain death by a single gesture.

No one had been there for three years.

No bird had flown over this for three years.

Three years of floods and frosts.

The bones lay there.

'Washed by the rains...'[5]

Covered by snow.

Then they reappeared in the spring.

And they were bleached like canvas under the rays of the torrid summer sun.

Flesh and clothing,

tissue and muscle,

eyes and hair, had rotted away, vanished.

The ribs were exposed.

Only bones were left.

And the skeletons lay in a huge fresco of a frozen *danse macabre.*

Belt buckles,

epaulettes,

individual packets of pink bandages,

icons made from tin,

the small shovels sappers use,

even the odd peak from a cap—all those remained intact.

You can go down Death Valley in California and see endless columns of bones—horses, oxen and buffaloes.

They lie in a formless heap, but their general outline marks routes lost among the cracks of the parched earth.

It was a different spectacle here.

Soft green grass covered the earth.

The bones were in exactly the same position as when the bodies fell in the attack, and they lay as if on velvet.

Each skeleton was a drama within the compass of the broader tragedy.

These two, bent up, were trying to dig themselves in; shovels lie near their hands.

But they only had time to cut the turf before falling where they stood.

You can even tell that one was shot in the stomach.

His spine is twisted that way.

Here a skeleton lies on its back, its arms flung wide apart in the St Andrew's cross.

Here is one entangled in the wire.

And another curves to one side. That one is particularly gruesome.

It has no head.

The head lies thirty to forty feet away.

There, half a torso sticks out of a marshy depression, and nearby . . . are the legs.

A water-colour wash of blue-grey mist drifts like cigarette-smoke between these men who are frozen for ever . . .

Few have seen such a field of conflict. Untouched, like a designated area.

Inviolable—like a graveyard.

Imperishable—like the memory of a great drama.

But the next day these strongholds of the German military would vanish forever in a deafening explosion . . . And their enemies would emerge and terrify us even more.

What were those? Carelessly dug-up graves? No.

Those were our trenches, covered with leaf-mould.

At Dvinsk, at Mukden, on the road to Kars and Erzerum, they died like that: robbed, betrayed, but selflessly heroic—our Russian soldiers.

Thus they fell, criminally betrayed, in the folly of 1917.

But I myself suffered a defeat on the Dvinsk field of death.

Did the fuses misfire?

Too small a charge of gun-cotton?

Or were the concrete emplacements stronger than I had calculated?

Nothing of the sort.

The earth flew upwards in a calculated way.

It obligingly filled the trenches, machine-gun nests, and left behind a hopeless mishmash of concrete, rails, netting and wire.

My defeat was not on the field.

But on a sheet of paper, where I was trying to arrange these skeletons at terrible, striking angles.

One thing that tempted me to write these notes was the minimum of stylistic correcting and rewriting that I normally make myself do.

I shuffled and reshuffled the lines of bones, skeletons and ribs like cards, but they still failed to land in a frightening or terrible pattern.

I shuffled, reshuffled . . .

A still from 'The field of death', from the prologue to *Alexander Nevsky*

The field remained indelibly stamped on my memory precisely because of its frozen horror.

But, despite my best efforts, those bones would not lie on the paper to horrifying effect.

It did not work.

Futile . . .

Nor did it work after the hours spent on the churned-up green slope by Lake Pereslavl, rearranging, redigging and scattering the real bones and skulls I requested be brought to me by lorry.

'O field, field, who has scattered upon you . . .'[6]

Having conceived of the prologue to *Alexander Nevsky* as a panorama of fields, strewn with the 'mortal remains' of those who died fighting the Tatars for Russian land, I was bound to remember the battlefield outside Dvinsk.

I ordered a consignment of skeletons, human and horse, and carefully arranged their component parts on the grass: a fresco of a battle, frozen.

I remembered the skeleton with its arms and legs flung apart in the St Andrew's cross.

Another I stuck through with a spear, next to a shield.

One skull lay in its helmet.

Another stuck out of its chain-mail collar.

Hell, none of it worked!

It was revoltingly 'stagey' to look at, and not at all convincing on screen.

On screen, the skeletons looked like white monkeys, parodies of real people.

I scrapped them.

I just left those that happened to stick out of the grass at an angle.

And I spared the first two skulls.

Much to my regret.

Their whiteness was not a case of 'washed clean by the rains'; more that of a porcelain chamberpot.

(The late Alexei Tolstoi snidely remarked that these were not skulls but ostrich eggs!)[7]

But why was this?

The failure can of course be attributed partly to the fact that these carefully separated bones came from a museum of anatomy.

But . . . there were all the bones you could wish for on those pages, and still they refused to combine in a frightening way!!

I have been fascinated by bones and skeletons since childhood.

This fascination is morbid.

(It was skeletons, for example, that made me go to Mexico.)

There is a bundle of motives determining our each and every action.

These motives are not always so clearly defined for us as, for example, Schopenhauer's notes (still extant) which he made concerning the advantages of moving to Mannheim as opposed to staying in Brunswick.

He gave marks out of five in favour of moving to Mannheim.

And also for staying in Brunswick.

He concluded there was everything to gain by moving to Mannheim.

And the philosopher . . . stayed put in Brunswick!

But in this 'bundle' of motives there is always one, typically the wildest, the most impractical, illogical, often absurd and very frequently completely irrational, that decides everything, for all that.

Eisenstein the *Torero*. Photomontage, 1931

My Encounter with Mexico[1]

I well remember sitting in my room in Chistye Prudy, buried in books.

The ceiling had been painted with concentric circles of black and red, with the light-fitting in the centre.

I called it the cupola—the black gave the ceiling depth.

The coloured rings of red and black sometimes seemed to turn and send the room spinning sideways.

I remember holding a German magazine.

And I saw on its pages some striking skeletons and bones.

A human skeleton astride the skeleton of a horse.

He wore a broad-brimmed sombrero, with a bandolier over one shoulder.

There were two other skeletons—a man, judging by the hat and the stuck-on . . . moustache; and a woman, judging by the skirt and pompadour—who were standing in a characteristic dance pose.

And there was a photograph of a hat-shop window—skulls sticking out of collars and ties.

The skulls wore neat straw hats in the latest style—stetsons, with the brims tilted at a killing angle; black and brown bowlers which must have weighed a ton.

What could it be? A madman's delirium, or a modern version of Holbein's *Danse Macabre*?

No! These were photographs of the Day of the Dead, in Mexico City.

The skeletons were . . . children's toys!!

A real one stood in the shop window, decorated the way they are on that day—2 November.

This impression lodged in me like a splinter.

My desperate longing to see this in reality was like a chronic sickness.

And not only this.

But the whole of a country that could take its amusements in such a way!

411

Mexico!

And then the prototype of the Ehrenburg Julio Jurenito, Diego Rivera also appeared (although he appeared in the book itself as the friend and companion of J.J.).[2]

Diego told me not only about the Day of the Dead but also about other fantastic aspects of that amazing country.

My very first work in theatre—my debut—also involved Mexico.

We dramatised and staged a story by Jack London.[3]

I began the production as set designer and then became the co-producer. More of that anon.

Here we need only mention how little the prologue and epilogue of this production (I am referring to the sets) had to do with Mexico.

They both (for some reason we pronounced them 'prólog' and 'epílog') took place in Mexico.

The basic action was set in America.

What saved it of course was the fact that the set was more Suprematist than Cubist (it was 1920) and it was quite hard to spot the incongruity!

Anyway, the swarthy Diego, photographs of his frescoes and his colourful tales all fanned the flames of my longing to get there and to see it all with my own eyes.

And a few years later the dream became reality.

The most unlikely coincidence of circumstances took me there. I went to that country.

Mexico has an amazing effect on most people.

I think that is because, wherever you look, the whole country seems to have just risen from the two oceans that wash her shores—everywhere she seems to be in a state of 'coming into being'.

In that particular dynamic condition that we contrast with the static notion of 'being'.

We know about this mostly from books.

This complex notion about dynamic 'coming into being' means next to nothing to plodding minds.

What is so amazing about Mexico is the vivid sense that there you can experience things which you only know about otherwise from books and philosophical conceptions opposed to metaphysics.

I imagine that when the world was in its infancy it was full of exactly the same supremely indifferent laziness, coupled with the creative potential of those lagoons and plateaux, deserts and undergrowth; pyramids you might expect to explode like volcanoes; palms reaching out to the blue vault of heaven; turtles swimming to the surface not from the bottom of creeks and inlets, but from the depths of oceans that are contiguous with the earth's core.

People who have been to Mexico greet each other like brothers.

For people who have been to Mexico catch the Mexican fever.

Anyone who has ever seen the Mexican plains has only to close his eyes to picture something like the Garden of Eden; of course—Eden was not somewhere between the Tigris and Euphrates, but here, somewhere between the Gulf of Mexico and Tehuantepec!

And this despite the mangy curs licking the dirty cooking pots with food, the universal graft and exasperating irresponsibility of incorrigible sloth, the terrible social injustices and rampantly arbitrary actions of the police force, and agelong backwardness, which coexist alongside highly sophisticated forms of social exploitation.

Time leaches this tragic sediment from memory and, although it remains ineradicable in the consciousness, grains of pure gold are left in one's emotions: the gold of the Mexican dawns and sunsets, the garments of the single madonnas and the columns of carved figures crowding out the altar decorations in a frozen multitude, the inlay work on rifles and embroidery on the sombreros of the *charros* and *dorados*, the stitching on the matadors' capes, the warm bronze of pensive faces, and the succulent fruit with unheard-of names hanging down beneath the dark green, bluish or light grey foliage . . .

We know that our feelings, our consciousness and our frames of reference reflect the real world about us.

Then there is the malicious cardinal from Webster's *The Duchess of Malfi*, whose own reflection played cruel tricks on him.

As he bent down to the water to spear a fat carp with his harpoon, he suddenly saw an enemy rising up from the depths of the water with a spear aimed at his heart.

We also remember the reflection which leaves its owner, as happened to the student of Prague.[4]

Finally there is Wilde's pond which did not mourn the death of Narcissus, because it never did see the youth, in love with himself, as he stooped down; it saw only itself, in the boy's radiant eyes.[5]

There was a similar displacement of reflections between Mexico and me.

I think that it was not that my consciousness and emotions absorbed the blood and sand of the gory *corrida*, the heady sensuality of the tropics, the asceticism of the flagellant monks, the purple and gold of catholicism, or even the cosmic timelessness of the Aztec pyramids: on the contrary, the whole complex of emotions and traits that characterise me extended infinitely beyond me to become an entire, vast country with mountains, forests, cathedrals, people, fruit, wild animals, breakers, herds, armies, decorated prelates, majolica on blue cupolas, necklaces made of gold coins worn by the girls of Tehuantepec and the play of reflections in the canals of Xochimilco.

My atheism is like that of Anatole France—inseparable from adoration of the visible forms of a cult.[6]

Here my passion seemed to surge in the crimson groves of the cardinal's robes, which were gilded by the incense smoke at high mass as autumn gilds the leaf. They bore fruit in the form of amethyst crosses and tiaras, whose split tops looked like overripe pomegranates that had burst open in the sun.

I was intoxicated by the dry asceticism of the writing, the clarity of the drawing; the tormenting severity of a line ripped bloodily from nature's multicoloured body.

The writing seems to have been born from the images of the ropes which stretched the bodies of martyrs; from the weals a whip leaves on the pale surface of skin; from the sound the blade of a sword makes through the air before striking the condemned man's neck.

As even shading destroys the illusion of volume, so a line

414

cuts through colour, so the orderliness of a system dissects the varied chaos of forms.

The tetrahedron of the pyramid of the Moon and Sun in San-Juan-Teotihuacan rose up before me like an implacable razor. The white faces of Popocatepetl's spurs bisected the blue sky. The sharp edge of an agave leaf on the ground. The black wing of a vulture—the *zapilota*—that lives off carrion. The black silhouette of a Franciscan in Pueblo. The black cross of a gravestone, and the black tunic of the *licenciado** who had come to check the fields of an enraged *hacendado*.** The long black shadows of the *tlagiceros*,*** wandering home at sunset with their mules, knowing that no matter who inherits the haciendas, their lot will be the same: to extract the oily juice from the heart of the cruel cactus.

The juice ferments and turns into a stupefying, clear spirit—pulque.

And the wrinkled, sharp-pointed star of the agave, its juice sucked from it, is left to wither beneath the sun's pitiless rays.

Exactly as he is doomed to wither, desiccated, when his life juices have been drained away by the prevailing feudal structure of the landlord-peasant relationship.

Thus graphical severity in Mexico is represented by tragic content as well as by its outward appearance.

The figure of the peon—this combination of a white triangular shirt, an emaciated blackened face and the round outline of a straw hat—is at once a tragic symbol and an almost graphic formula.

Which is how Jose Guadelupe Posada[7] saw them in his incomparable prints. He was the spiritual father of Diego Rivera and Siqueiros, Orozco and Pacheco—setting the peon and the black round spots of his townsfolk and murderers, the generals and the nuns, against one another.

In his prints, social conflict lies in the contrast between black and white: this conflict in another country, another nation, in other latitudes and with shades of a different brutality, gave rise to Breughel's contrasts between 'the fat' and 'the thin'.

---

* Spanish: 'bailiff'
** Spanish: 'landowner'
*** Spanish: 'farm workers'

Stills from the epilogue of *Que Viva México!*

The whips sang through the air.

The acute, cutting pain was succeeded by a warm numbness.

The dry hachure of the blows cut up the body's surface, like flowers; double poppies of wounds opened and blood flowed like rubies. And the line gave birth to colour.

A similarly paradoxical conjunction of dry, leafless stalk and crimson star can be found on the spurs of the Taxco cliffs.

They are called *'sangre de toros'*—bull's blood.

They look like the line which erupts in a flash of colour, the coruscating line that jets blood after the matador's sword has pierced the bull's black hide.

Leaving the sharp brutality of the *charro's* spurs, the silhouette of the old monastery that had been turned into a hacienda after the church's disestablishment, leaving the hoofs of the landowner's horses which pounded the skulls of the peons as they lay buried waist-deep in sand—you head south.

The razor-edged green sail of the agave leaf with its relentlessly sharp tip (formed as the end of the leaf dries) splits up into the green curls of lianas.

There are here none of those strange and surprisingly vicious little red birds which inhabit the central plateau. They disdain raw beetles. They are not much interested in eating beetles or worms straight after killing them. Instead they neatly stick them on to the tip of a leaf and only when the sun's burning rays have dried them out do these red birds fly back to their prey.

Here nature makes things as easy as possible for man.

It was not to camouflage them that she coloured the flocks of parrots in shades of light green.

But so that the eye of the beholder should not have to adjust to any colour outside the green wavelength as it idly roved among the threads of green foliage.

The green, curling lianas loop for miles. There is nothing to breathe.

There is not the perpetually hot, dry heat of the desert to irritate one's lungs here. The hot embraces of the tropics are moist.

Here the whole world is immersed in a hot marshy hollow,

417

its surface coated by a boiling yellow-green mire . . .

I was talking about how when I met Mexico she showed herself in all her contradictions, as though she were a projection of all the various traits and features which I carried and still carry around with me—a knot of complexes.

The simplicity of the monumental, and the extravagance of the baroque—in both its Spanish and Aztec aspects . . .

The duality of these attractions finds echo in the simultaneous fascination with the severity of the peon's white costume—a costume which, in both colour and angularity of silhouette, is like a *tabula rasa* of costume altogether—and with the sculptural quality of gold and silver bas-reliefs, with their excessive use of gold embroidery, which burn above deep blue, or green, or orange and cherry coloured satin beneath the black hats of the protagonists in the *corrida.*

The excess, mirrored in the richness of furs and the black and white lace mantillas of their admirers and the high Spanish pompadours; the fans burning, iridescent and dazzling on Sundays in the searing heat on the tiers of the auditorium surrounding the arena of 'blood and sand'.

They were both close and I valued them.

I found resonances in both.

And both seemed to resonate within me.

And I greedily dug more deeply into the welter of elements of either sort, using the lenses of Eduard Tisse's incomparable film camera.

The tropics responded to a slumbering sensuality.

The latent wanderings of sensuality seemed incarnate in the interweaving of bronzed bodies. It was as if here in the saturated, overgrown rapacity of the lianas which interwove like bodies and of bodies which interwove like lianas, they looked in the mirror and saw how the black almond eyes of the girls in Tehuantepec gazed into the surface of the slumbering tropical backwaters, admiring their floral adornments, which cast a light on the golden surfaces of their bodies.

Washed by moonlight, the regularly breathing abundance of bodies of the *soldaderas* and their husbands—soldiers—held in close embraces seemed embodied in me. They lay scattered in the octagonal yard within the small fortress, which protected the Pacific port of Acapulco (from what? Only the flocks of pelicans which rained like arrows into the amber waters of the Gulf, their heads twisted to one side).

The bodies breathed regularly and in unison; the very earth seemed to be breathing; here and there a white blanket showed up, modestly thrown over a pair lying among the others, black in the moonlight, bodies covered by nothing; bodies not knowing shame; bodies for whom what is natural is natural and naturally needs no concealment.

The sergeant and I slowly walked the length of the narrow parapet with its narrow embrasures; it was like looking down on a battlefield after the trumpets had sounded the attack; a field of death cast in silver, but in essence it was a great cornfield where more and yet more generations of bronze children were being conceived.

Mexico is tender and lyrical, but brutal too.

It has seen pitiless floggings lacerate the golden surface of bare skin. The sharp spines of cactus to which, when the civil war was at its worst, people who survived being shot were tied, to be finished off by the heat from desert sands.

The sharp spines which even today pierce the bodies of those who have bound cacti trunks into a cross and tied them on to their own shoulders and crawled for hours up the pyramids to glorify the Catholic Madonnas—de Guadelupe, Los Remedios, Santa Maria Tonantzintla—Catholic Madonnas who, in the days of Cortés, usurped the positions and places held by pagan goddesses and divinities. The monks avoided changing the routes that pilgrimages had established over the centuries by cleverly erecting statues on those very places—heights, deserts, pyramids—where ancient cults of the heathen Aztec, Toltec and Mayan gods had once held sway. On religious festivals, streams of pilgrims rubbed the skin off their knees as they crawled over the dry dust and prostrated themselves before the statues to press their baked lips to the Queen of Heaven's golden hem or to the sweet-scented remains of the bones of her most faithful past servants (a cheerful, cynical prior of this church-pyramid—Father Figueroa, whose reputation was slightly sullied—fetched them out from under the

419

altar of Los Remedios for us. He was a keen photographer and every Thursday without fail he would race on his motorbike to the brothels of Mexico City, which for some reason were concentrated round a street which bore the most heroic name from Mexico's past—Cuauhtémoc).[8]

This name always springs to mind in connection with brutality and sadism—and who is innocent of these?—and who will cast a stone at me for this, if the fascist-inclined American newspapers met my arrival in the USA with the protest: 'Why allow Eisenstein in, this red dog and sadist?' (Thus wrote the notorious Major Pease;[9] famous in his day, he was later exposed as a German agent, who had unsuccessfully organised underground Fascist detachments—in the shadow of the Statue of Liberty).

It was the regal Cuauhtémoc, the ruler with a hawk-like, Indian profile, who said, 'It's no bed of roses for me, either' when the Spanish Conquistadores tortured him, making him walk on glowing braziers in order to discover where lay the treasure and riches of this country they had enslaved.

The proud Indian addressed these words to one of his comrades-in-arms, who was also enduring torture nearby on a grille and who had dared to let out a groan through clenched teeth.

A bas-relief depicting his heroic sufferings adorns the pedestal of the monument to Cuauhtémoc; his head is thrown back in defiance.

Physical brutality, whether in the 'asceticism' of flagellant monks, or in their torturing of others; in the blood of bull or man, which after mass each week douses the sands of countless Sunday corridas in a sensual communion; or the pages of history telling of the unexampled brutality used to suppress countless uprisings of peons, whipped to a frenzy by enforced unpaid labour; and the brutal reprisals of the leader of the revolt: Villa, who ordered the prisoners to be hanged naked so that he and his soldiers could be entertained by the sight of their last physiological reactions, peculiar to hanged men.

The brutality of the Mexican does not reside only in mutilation and bloodshed, not only in his favourite way of dealing with prisoners, his former slaves: wearing nothing but a top hat, they were forced into a frenzied dance by a haphazard and constant hail of bullets.

There is also, discernible in the ominous *tarantella*, the same malicious humour, irony and that form of Mexican wit which is called *vacilada*. Carlton Beals characterised it in his *Mexican Maze*.[10]

> The *vacilada* is a combination of the ridiculous and the sublime, of vulgarity and purity, of beauty and ugliness, of spirituality and animality, disconcertingly tripping over each other, showering the world with passing glory, like the spray of a rocket flame.
>
> The Mexican's approach to life, death and sex, an approach dominated by the *vacilada*, is shot through with poetic irresponsibility, it defies direct logic, takes serious things lightly, and insignificant things with great gravity. This is a gracious and self-protective distortion, a creative destruction of values cherished by the European mind. (p. 238)

The Mexican's brutal humour is nowhere more in evidence than in his attitude to death.

Mexicans despise death.

Like any heroic people, Mexicans despise both it and those who do not despise it.

Not only that, a Mexican even laughs at death.

The Day of the Dead—2 November—is a day of unbridled revelry, given over to mocking death and its bony symbol, holding a scythe.

In Zurich during the filming of *Women's Misfortune-Women's Happiness* [Frauennot-Frauenglück] Eduard Tisse, 1929

Autobiography[1]

Autobiography?

That means writing about yourself.

I have been writing about cinema for twenty years and, truth be told, most of that has essentially been about myself. More precisely, about what I once happened to do and am still doing on the screen. Then I try to stitch it all together. As Rémy de Gourmont said, 'to formalise the fruits of our own observations is the inevitable aspiration of man, if he is sincere.'[2]

This is not from joy and not from a good life.

Rather from poverty (if we ignore a certain measure of egotism).

True, not from personal poverty, but from the poverty of works of critical analysis. In our cinema, all of the groundwork in research is almost always the job of the creators themselves. Which results in a self-service arrangement, with each of us in his own cafeteria of theories.

You try to write about your work 'with detachment', since few people impartially get into an analysis of what you are doing.

But it always ends up about yourself, from within—unduly personal, too detailed, intimate, and most often . . . triumphant!

I have the same problem now. This time it is at least legitimate and well grounded, since the matter in hand is not an objective, theoretical article, but autobiography.

And autobiography, as everyone knows, means writing about yourself.

'Wie sag ich's meinem Kinde?'*[1]

'*Kinder, seid still—der Vater schreibt seinen Namen!*'*

'Quiet, children—your father is writing his name!' This phrase, written on a postcard with an appropriate scene, was a family joke.

It fitted Papa's character to perfection.

Papa was just as important as the papa in the postcard.

Papa was very vain.

His promotion up the hierarchical ladder and medals, from an Anne to a Vladimir,[2] which his service brought him, were not the only things to cause him endless anxious expectation and joy.

It was not only the fact that his name was to be found in the *Pravitel'stvennyi vestnik* [Official Gazette]: any mention of his name tickled Papa's pride.

For example, Papa never missed a production of the operetta *Die Fledermaus*.[3]

He always sat in the front row and when they came to the famous couplets:

'*Herr Eisenstein! 'Herr Eisenstein!*
'*Die Fledermaus!*'*

he would close his eyes in bliss.

Papa was an exemplary worker and stay-at-home, which probably explains why the nocturnal adventures of his chance operatic namesake—outwardly respectable but actually a profligate playboy —so impressed Mr Eisenstein.

Papa was flattered, even when it was sung at home.

I need not restrain myself in this matter of my father.

I went much further than he did.

I mean, in vanity.

True, I had plenty of scope for exercising this trait, this weighty legacy. The third line of the German was not to be heard at home.

---

* In German in the original.

This was the notorious formula: *'Wie sag' ich's meinem Kind?**
'How do I tell my child?!'

This is every parent's dilemma, when their children begin to fix them with a more than usually inquisitive gaze, and stories about storks and cabbages lose their ability to convince.

'Where do children come from?'

My Mama and Papa never faced the problem of explaining it to their son.

Not because they were ahead of their time and had passed a complete working knowledge on to me at an early age, but because they both simply ducked this ticklish question and contrived to avoid it.

Probably because Mama was, as Americans say, 'over-sexed'.**

Papa in his turn was 'undersexed'.**

Anyway, Papa's and Mama's divorce was probably tied up with that, and the collapse of the Lares and Penates,[4] the familial hearth and the cult of the 'old homestead',** occurred very early on in my life.

This was why I gained an articulate response to this question not from my parents or friends, nor from an experienced matron like the unforgettable Mathildona in Mexico, but . . .

But let us pause for a moment to consider Mathildona.

Address: Mexico City.

More precisely: Cuauhtémoc Street.

He was that heroic Indian king whom Cortés tortured for gold.

He it was who said, 'It's no bed of roses for me, either' when one of his comrades being tortured nearby let out a groan.

This heroic figure, now a tall monument standing on the main road of the city, was then lying on his back.

On a grille like a saint.

Under the grille were coals.

Cuauhtémoc's memory has been honoured by a street in the capital of the Republic of Mexico.

The area of Cuauhtémoc, which resembles a backbone with

---

*   In German in the original.
**   In English in the original.

425

lesser streets branching off it, is the red-light district of Mexico City.

Here at night the ragged tarpaulin booths played gramophones and voices cried out in hoarse falsetto.

How far are these tarpaulin booths from those celebrated by Blok![5]

There too were

Little boys and little maidens,
Little candles, willow wands.[6]

True, there were not any willow wands. But there were candles stuck into the small curved footlights which divided the stage from the benches of the auditorium.

There were boys too—an essential prerequisite of every *carpa*.*

More often than not, they were much more than mere youths.

The pale puffiness of their cheeks showed up beneath the rouge, and their painted lips emitted a broken falsetto, the rhythm echoed by the obscene motions of their fat thighs.

And then, the high-pitched voice of the young girl—really young; small and thin, in a dress of glass beads and gauze—archly singing out *'Mariquita sin calzones*,** a song popular in those days, in those places.

Mathildona lived in the second house from the corner of the main street.

Her name was Mathilda.

Mathildona means the same as Mathilda; but in the superlative.

Just as we would say in Russian Katerinishche for Katerina, Tatyanishche for Tanya, Agrafenishche, Lizavetishche, Matildishche![7]

How to hymn the praises of this massif of bone and firm flesh—Mathildona, you are a landmark of Mexico no less than the

---

    *   Spanish: literally 'carp'.
  **   Spanish: 'Mariquita's got no pants on'

pyramids and cathedrals, the snowy peaks of Orizaba and the dungeons of Veracruz, the palaces of Chapultépec and the bleeding Christ of Tlalmanalco!

I have heard that in the past a woman would accompany a young miner on his first journey down the shaft.

Not accompany, but lead.

She walked ahead.

And showed the way into the mining gallery—the earth's black belly.

The woman took the man's fear into her own chest as he entered the depths of the earth's belly for the first time.

Mathildona was sixty.

And since time immemorial she has led youth after youth into the dark abyss as he took his first steps in life, terrified and horrified at first by the full extent of the mysteries of biology.

I can sense them both, massive and tall, both indomitable in their hour over the capital city at night—the terrifying goddess of death, leaving her gallery in the National Museum, with stone snakes and granite skulls entwining over her, the symbol of finality; and the living massif of the sixty-year-old Mathildona, rising above the region of the *carpas* and the prostitutes of Cuauhtémoc, the symbol of beginning.

Their heads vanish high above in the night sky.

Below they are speckled with the lights of headlamps and trams, cafes and pulque bars.

The light catches the powerful outline of the breast of one, and the other's necklace of stone skulls.

Somewhere in between, all lit up, priests and *licenciados, vaqueros** and doctors, Jesuits and atheists stream like ants.

Mathildona?!

London, Paris, Constantinople—even my native Riga—have their own Mathildonas, I expect.

My parents did not initiate me into the 'secrets'.

I did not know where Riga's Mathildona lived.

I was not allowed to join in my friends' 'exploits'.

---

* Spanish: 'shepherds'

Eisenstein—professor at VGIK, the State Institute of Cinematography of the USSR, 1940.

And my 'Mathildona' turned out to be a weighty tome.

A bookworm—though not a Pharisee, I was bound to learn everything in the first instance from books.

It happened very early, and it was terrible.

The book was not Casanova, Voltaire, or Diderot.

Not even Pushkin; at school, we neatly replaced the asterisks in his 'Cherry' with letters on our school desks.

The book was a solid . . . scientific volume from the library of my grandfather, Doctor Peterson.

I remember the evening when I leafed through that book as I sat in his deep armchair.

The material was set out in its historical, evolutionist context.

From the lowest organisms to the highest.

The successive pages revealed a deeply intriguing path that showed how organisms gradually adapted to increasingly appropriate modes of copulation.

No higher up than spiders, which were relatively highly rational organisms, a distinct picture emerged of what to expect under the heading 'man'.

And my God! O shades of Grécourt, Parny, Chevalier de Boufflers,[8] you will understand my cry—its biological rationalisation was so fascinating that the young reader was more than anything else flabbergasted by the 'deep wisdom' of nature!

Of course a psychoanalyst, quick to make hasty inferences, will now date my passion for books, which I love as though they were living creatures, from this very moment.

I must disappoint him.

My love of books is older.

But I would find it difficult to contest that my almost pathological passion for questions regarding changes of form, evolution, or development is probably very closely connected with the unusual way in which I found out all the ayes and nays from books, before I learned them from personal, practical experience.

In my introductory remarks I wrote that this work was completely amoral.

This holds true not only with the absence of any planned direction, but also with the total absence of any plan at all.

You will agree that in a system which has a planned economy and an ideology, this kind of approach is of course quite amoral . . .

All the chapters start with one thing. They take that reading from a chance recollection, and there then follows, in no particular order, a series of associations. Once I have started a chapter I do not know which way it will turn.

And when I have just finished it, I sometimes begin to suspect that it could have had a 'theme' in the first place.

As has happened for example with the material I have just written.

I genuinely believed that it was about an injured child, whose parents would not take the trouble to explain things as they ought to have done. Something like Steinberg's admirable but unfinished painting.[9]

I had even expected to begin it with the fierce skirmish I had with Papa on this very theme in the summer of 1916.

I remember it as if it were yesterday: we were riding in a cab, driving out of the magnificent Rossi Street, framed on left and right by orange and white walls in finest Empire style.

The architecture of the Alexandrinka is so beautiful that it needs a more important building than a theatre. It darts off into the small streets behind the theatre and takes it over on both sides.

And there for centuries the left and right hand sides have stood, contemplating each other admiringly, as though gazing into a mirror. They have frozen in mutual applause.

The left and right sides of the small street are quite identical. And identically beautiful.

If they were mirrors, girls would be able to put a candle in the middle of the street and see the groom who would emerge from the rear of the theatre which formed the end of the street.[10]

If arms reached out of the façades they could touch each other as in a dance such as a quadrille, and the cabbies would be like the pairs who run, ducking, beneath the raised arms of the couples dancing in two rows.

Papa and I rode in a cab like this when I told my father some bitter home truths.

There were no arms stretching out from house to house.

The arms that were stretched out did not hold gold engagement rings.

Just as there was no gold ring, or arms outstretched in mutual understanding between the two passengers in the cab.

There never were such arms or rings at Flat 7, No. 6 Nicholas Street.[11]

Perhaps that was why the strange architectural fantasy of the most bizarre art nouveau, which Papa was so fixated with, raised similar figures, many storeys high, on the façade of the building on the corner opposite Albert Street in Riga, which Papa had completely covered.[12]

Eight massive maidens made of hollow iron drainpipes lined the façade.

Their hands pointed forwards, at right-angles to the façade.

As if they were doing Sokol gymnastics.[13]

Hands reaching out into the void.

And in order to conceal this fact, they were each given two gold rings to hold.

The void seemed to have been stood on its side and bordered with gold hoops.

In this way, the void became an integral element.

Doughnuts have to have a hole.

Even if the doughnuts were golden and held by eight maidens many storeys high, frozen between the lianas, chrysanthemums and algae of the ornamental design spread across the façade.

Harder to disguise the fact that the actual idea was void.

But, as it happens, the maidens were not destined to live for long.

My memory of their unveiling is vague, but I can clearly remember the day when, bit by bit, they left their lofty pedestals as lengths of guttering.

Rain is very conservative.

It failed to see that the drainpipes were no longer conduits for water; it ignored the artistic arrangement.

The rains beat down on the crowns of the figures' heads, but found no aperture . . .

The hollow Statue of Liberty prancing about in New York Harbour is more fortunate.

431

It has a way in.

Not, it is true, to let the rain come streaming in from the heavens, but to admit the streams of people flooding upwards.

Like white and red blood corpuscles, or a formless lymph satisfying idle curiosity, endless streams of people moved up and down the double-helical staircases whose coils crushed each other like two snakes.

The most interesting thing about this two-fold process of ascent and descent was trying to determine which part of the internal relief of this hollow figure you were at, at any given moment.

Could we already be level with the chest?

Or only as high as the stomach?

There can be no doubt about it—those are the knees!

Thank goodness, this is the nape of the neck.

On the left over there of course is the lowered shoulder. (The right holds the torch aloft.)

. . . The maidens on Papa's façade were sealed top and bottom.

And torrents beat down on the crowns of their heads, unable to force their way inside, to pour through the body and crash down into the drainpipes below.

Heavy downpours coursed all over them.

Their rivulets felt the contours of the body, moving over it like a living hand.

Breasts rose proud above the streams like islands.

Dark currents streamed from under the stomach.

Rain.

Its brief encounter left dark pawmarks on the artificial alabaster of these athletic and senselessly posed figures.

The effect was shocking.

And so one fine day these maidens, reduced to a torso, breasts, arms, thighs and feet, ended their dubious existence.

I could perhaps use them for one thing . . .

It was probably my memory of them that led to my dismembering the giant statue of Alexander III with such mouthwatering excitement, in the opening episode of *October*.

I doubt if I would have seized on the drama of the toppling statue, captured on film, but for memories of Papa's maidens, somewhere at the back of my mind.

And if I add that the dismembered and overturned, hollow figure of the Tsar served as an image for the overthrow of tsarism in February, then it is clear that this start to the film, recalling the defeat of Papa's creation using the image of the Tsar himself, was about my personal liberation from Papa's authority.

The image of Papa's ravaged maidens recurs on two more occasions, in a new variation (the same both times),

in the image of armour.

Actually, not so much the armour itself, as the empty vestments of the armour-clad warriors.

In the epilogue of *Can You Hear Me, Moscow?*[14] at the opening ceremony of the memorial to the sovereign of the small German duchy, the official court poet recites a celebratory poem on the German defeat of the semi-cultured, native population by German armour.

He is himself wearing armour.

He is also on stilts (his poetry is stilted too).

And his knight's costume covers his body and his stilts, so he appears as an iron giant.

At the critical moment the straps break and the empty armour falls away from him with a crash of empty buckets.

And Malyuta Skuratov finds Kurbsky's empty armour in the tent of the traitor prince who had escaped to safety, near Weissenstein Castle (*Ivan the Terrible*, screenplay, 1944).

And the bucket helmet of the Livonian knight echoes hollowly when Vaska Buslai hits it with his harness (*Alexander Nevsky*, 1938).

. . . Papa was a tyrant in his home just like old man Grandet or Mordashev in the vaudeville *A and F.*[15] At least, that was how Mochalov played him, and that was how he won great fame for himself in the role.

A tyrannical Papa was commonplace in the 19th century.

But mine dragged on into the 20th!

This is surely what these pages have been bemoaning—the family's moral depression.

How many times did little Sergei, the exemplary little boy, answer his Papa's questions—weren't his buildings marvellous?—in a studied formula of delight like a learned parrot, even though it ran deeply counter to his ideas and convictions! . . .

Let my protest rage, even if only here, even if only once!

Since my earliest years it was the shackles of cuffs and starched collar instead of torn trousers and ink blots.

Ahead lay the path designated for me, stretching as straight as an arrow.

School. The Institute. Engineering.

Year after year.

From nappies, through my days at the *Realschule*, to end in bronze student epaulettes with the initials of Nicholas I . . .

Well behaved child that I was, it amazes me to think that I sent this whole mapped-out production line to blazes.

It was not social injustice nor material deprivation, nor the ups and downs of my struggle for existence that prepared the ground for my social protest,

but, purely and simply, the prototype of all social tyranny, like the tyranny of a father in his family: a relic from primitive society, when the head of a tribe was a tyrant.

By a circuitous route, Papa and I have come back to our starting-point.

. . . Of course, our cab had long since driven down Rossi Street, through the grey granite and heavy chains of the Chernyshevsky Bridge and our row died down somewhere near Five Dials . . .

But the path of the cab on paper, driving towards the origin of my rebellious activities on its way past the maidens made from guttering, the Statue of Liberty and the dethroned Tsar, to Papa's overturned authority, lies not only in the social subject matter of my films, but also in the form of cinema, which echoes evolution, be it protest against enslavement by the head of the family, or protest against enslavement by a tsar.

And the 'young' Tsar's coronation (meaning Ivan IV) is precisely the emergence of an heir, freed from the ghost of his father, the prototype!

And the commotion around the throne, the fight for the Tsar's caftan and hat, is a depiction, reflected in consciousness, of the same sort of struggle as the one historically played out by generations and entire social strata!

What interests me most of all here is how this whole multitude, from an analysis of atavistic relationships with Papa's authority and the approach to any problem, is always in my case tied up with notions of evolution.

Is it a chance fact (by virtue of which a powerful, emotional factor—at its peak, nothing short of 'mystery'—has firmly attached itself to the picture of evolution) that has so invariably interwoven with the desire and need to see each phenomenon from the viewpoint of its evolutionary emergence?

Another positive circumstance was the fact that this tendency towards a perception of movement was very soon promoted by . . . analytical geometry, the theory of limits and differential and integral calculus.

The curve as a path, not a fact!

Surely it is here that the nerve can be seen with crystal clarity; the principle of development, of emergence, which is so intoxicating in natural phenomena and so poorly understood in the creative processes, in the physiology and biology of forms, styles and works?

I immediately put out feelers whenever anything that has even the faintest hint of this flies into my field of vision.

Etymology: the history of words and how they come to be. I endorse Balzac's words, from *Louis Lambert*, wholeheartedly:[16]

> Isn't this the case with every verb? They are all imbued with a living power which they derive from the soul and which they restore to it through the mysteries of a marvellous action and reaction between word and thought. Might we not say of a lover that he receives as much love from the lips of his mistress as he conveys to her? . . .

Lévy-Bruhl—for want of something better in the way of factual material.[17]

The creation of cinema's own language, its syntax, alphabet, forms and a principle of stylistics which grows out of the schema of a technical phenomenon. The roots and achievements of counterpoint in audiovisual cinema. Finally, the outline of cinema's history, beginning with those arts that preceded it. A history, tracing the emergence of each internal element of cinema as though it were the crowning glory of a tendency a thousand years old; ecstasy as aspiration towards the last zero point, for the individual as well as for the species, etc, etc.

The most staggering thing was that even the limits of the field of research were seemingly set by this same fact. Their limit—the outline of their borders—coincided with that point where understanding of the mechanism for Man's emergence dawned. There, where the white light of discovery dazzled me.

It did not coincide with Man!

Not merely physically—simultaneously with my meeting the object.

But even in books.

'The knowledge of good and evil' as pure knowledge came before knowledge as spontaneous action.

And so my volley of questions found its answer in my astonishment at the wisdom and cohesiveness of the system of the universe and not in a frenzy of spontaneous embraces!

Which is why 'ratio'* comes before 'sex'.

And astonishment is dissipated through circles of investigation that start from a point that does not address the problem: man, not as evolution's highest point, but as Marfa Petrovna, Pyotr Kornilovich, Boris or Lyusya!

Hence too the field of theoretical research and also the tendency of creative limits—a symphony, not a drama, a mass of people as the forerunner of the individual, by music as the birthplace of tragedy *(ce M. Nietzsche n'a pas été si bête!)*** hence too the 'inhumanity' of the system of images used in *Ivan* and hence too my own particular path and style.

Looking closely at this trait of inhumanity in my works and research, you can see at almost every step apparently the same investigative interest, which abruptly fizzles out as soon as it reaches the narrowly human stage of development, somewhere on the level of wise spiders!

Oddly, this is constructive and progressive. For example,

---

* In English in the original.
** French: 'This Mr Nietzsche was not such a fool!'

with regard to Freud: it took years before I realised that the primary reserve of impulses is broader than the purely sexual, which was how Freud saw it—that is, broader than the parameters of the personal, biological adventures of human individuals.

Sex is no more than a concentrate, a tight knot; but through its innumerably repeating spirals it recreates rings of regularity which have an unimaginably large radius.

Which is why I like D.H. Lawrence's conceptions that obliged him to step outside the parameters of sex and into (inaccessible for a limited being) a cosmic, universal confluence.

Which is why I find pre-logic so attractive: it grants the sub-consciousness sensuality, but does not subordinate it to sex.

Which is why the subconscious itself appears first of all as a reflection of one's earliest and most undifferentiated stages of social existence—first of all.

Which is why in analysing the genesis of a principle of form and its different varieties (devices) you go layer upon layer beyond the limits of one ring, as in Dante's *Inferno* (or *Paradise*? Doré[18] imagined Dante's *Paradise* also as passing through rings—of blessedness!) to another. From that, to a third.

Which is why, for example, the widely understood device of synecdoche including its application in poetry, close-up in film and famous understatement* of American practitioners and American anthologists (the majority of which go no further than anthology, avoiding analysis and the subsequent generalisations) is not content with being a pattern of thought of the nature of *pars pro toto* (the limit of ideas in 1935).

Which is why, ten years later, the concept breaks down further into an even earlier, prehuman sphere and argues that this very *pars pro toto* is in fact, at the highest—emotional and sensual—level, a repetition of a purely reflex occurrence: a conditioned reflex which works solely by reproducing a part of the element supplying the stimulus.

Which is why the monstrously ubiquitous and most dramatic—hence, basic—of themes, the theme of revenge, is not content with merely portraying an inevitable counteraction, caused

---

* In English in the original.

by a human, psychological reaction ('tit for tat').*

It interprets this reaction as a partial application of the general law that every action has an equal and opposite reaction, which dictates the pendulum's return swing. (As in the actual conduct of a vendetta, for example, which is based on that law; and also in the exposition of the appropriate structure of a work that echoes this: almost all Elizabethan tragedy arose from the original *Revenger's Tragedy* —remember Shakespeare's tragedies?)

The somewhat Nietzschean title of the article, 'Beyond the Played and the Non-Played' (*Kinogazeta,* 1927)[19,] for example, is surely characteristic.

It begins:

> When there are two contestants it is usually the third who is right. In the ring now: played and non-played.
> That means justice lies with the third.
> *With the extra-played.*

And the actual concept of extra-played cinema, that is a cinema of such principles that stand 'outside' the petty wrangling between 'feature films' and 'documentaries'.

Then, the concept of a non-played cinema was synonymous with documentary cinema.

'Extra-played' cinema talked about the freedom of principles and the all-encompassing nature of the new cinema, whose aesthetic would not be formed according to how the elements which made it up were treated

—by devices used in played or non-played films—

but would emerge primarily from concepts about principles and ideology, for which any treatment of material, real or conceived, is stylistically just as compatible and applicable and equally deserving of inclusion in a synthesised film production and film spectacle.

Another characteristic concept is relevant to that time—in fact, the article quoted refers to it; it is set out in detail in the

---

* In English in the original.

magazine *Iskusstvo* [Art], in an article 'Perspectives'.[20] Only one issue came out (a double, No.1 & 2), as if for the express purpose of printing that article! It then closed down.

It examined intellectual cinema, which developed from the practice of *October* and continued on that path, from the image of the lions in *Potemkin*, to the play of concepts in the former film (the gods, Kerensky on the staircase, etc).[21]

Although the thesis there was also the emotionalisation of intellectual concepts and terms, the very designation placed this variety of cinema beyond emotional cinema—if not entirely, then in any case beyond what is broadly accepted as emotional cinema.

And it is no accident that this watershed of the emotional and the intellectual (if only in name) seems to echo the original 'traumatic' situation in the author's life. My knowledge from books preceded my knowledge from experience and sensation!

It is surely revealing that as recently as a few months ago I came across this idea in a chance note for my autobiography. I chose a sixteenth-century engraving I had fallen in love with long ago for the dust-jacket (and frontispiece for the corresponding part of a book about *Potemkin*—for a foreign publisher). It depicted a monk, a follower of Nicolaus Cusanus, gazing 'beyond the stars'.[22]

For the title 'Beyond the Stars'* meant . . . film stars, meaning by this that the book dealt with problems of cinema—everything, apart from the stars and the spontaneous human (in the primitive sense of the word) participants in film.

Regarding 'human': it is curious again, that the presence of a human (very human!) origin should interest me, again, at its pre-human stage. That is, in all those areas and origins where man is present in art but only latently, not yet manifest.

I am fascinated by someone present in the rhythms of his experience as he . . . produces a work of art.

I am fascinated by 'self-portrait' at the stage of a. . . vessel (as a copy of itself and its receptacle for food and drink).

I find the metaphor of Chinese landscape painting quite fascinating where a flower is not only a flower, but also an allegory for a girl in love (which lends the flower its special intensity and

---

* In English in the original.

quivering lyricism).

And Chinese portraiture of living, natural phenomena, conveyed by different styles of calligraphic shading, take my breath away.

I quote Lin Yutang's book *My Country and My People* (Heinemann, 1936).

The first book of his I read was *The Importance of Living*.

I read it fairly late in life, when I was already familiar with China, Mei Lan-Fan and Marcel Granet's studies.[23]

Lin Yutang's books are shot through with the irresistible charm of the ancient East. I sometimes felt that the ironic, slightly sceptical and infinitely tolerant spirit of the old debauchee, the terribly wise Lao-Tse, had migrated into this contemporary of ours; when he talks of China's traditions and antiquities it is amazing; and he cuts so comical and childishly helpless a figure when he attempts analysis of modern China's destiny, the role of Chiang Kai-Shek or the essence of the Chinese Civil War:

> . . . It seems to me that calligraphy, as representing the first principles of rhythm and composition, stands in relation to painting as pure mathematics stands in relation to engineering or astronomy. In appreciating Chinese calligraphy the meaning is entirely forgotten and the lines and forms are appreciated in and for themselves. In this cultivation and appreciation of pure witchery of line and beauty of composition, therefore, the Chinese have an absolute freedom and entire devotion to pure form as such, as apart from content . . .

> . . . As this art has a history of well-nigh two thousand years, and as every writer tried to distinguish himself by a new type of rhythm or structure, therefore in calligraphy, if in anything, we are entitled to see the last refinement of the Chinese artistic mind . . .

(p.292)

And also:

What is of significance to the West is the fact that not only has calligraphy provided the aesthetic basis for Chinese art, but it represents an animistic principle which may be most fruitful of results when properly understood and applied. As stated, Chinese calligraphy has explored every possible style of rhythm and form, and it has done so by deriving its artistic inspiration from nature, especially from plants and animals, the branches of the plum flower, a dried vine with a few hanging leaves, the springing body of the leopard, the massive paws of the tiger, the swift legs of the deer, the sinewy strength of the horse, the bushiness of a bear, the slightness of the stork, or the ruggedness of the pine branch. There is thus not one type of rhythm in nature which has not been copied in Chinese writing and formed directly or indirectly the inspiration of a particular 'style'. If a Chinese scholar sees a certain beauty in a dry vine with its careless grace and elastic strength, the tip curling upward and a few leaves still hanging on it (haphazardly, and yet most appropriately) he tries to incorporate that into his writing. If another scholar sees a pine tree that twists its trunk and bends its branches downward instead of upward, showing a wonderful tenacity and force, he also tries to incorporate that into his style of writing. We have therefore the 'dry-vine' and the 'pine-branch' style of writing.

A famous monk and calligraphist had practised writing for years without result and one day walking on a mountain path he chanced upon two fighting snakes with straining necks, which showed strength in apparent gentleness. This inspired him to develop a most individual style of writing, called the 'fighting-snakes' style, suggesting the tension and wriggling movement of the snakes' necks. Thus Wang Hsichih (321-379), China's 'prince of calligraphists', spoke about the art of calligraphy in terms of imagery from nature: 'Every horizontal stroke is like a mass of clouds in battle formation, every hook is like a bent bow of the greatest strength, every dot like a rock falling from a high peak, every turning of the stroke like a brass hook, every drawn-out line like a dry wine of great old age, and every swift and free stroke like a runner on his start.'

One can understand Chinese calligraphy only when one's eyes have been opened to the form and rhythm inherent in every animal's body and limbs. Every animal body has a

441

harmony and beauty of its own, a harmony which grows directly from its vital functions, especially the functions of movement...

(pp. 277-8)

The pages from Lin Yutang quoted here were not my 'first discovery'. Personal experience had taught me the mysteries of Chinese calligraphy a long time prior to this.

I was then (1920) studying Japanese and I was learning how to write the characters.

Even then we were struck by the similarity between the stroke and the rhythm of oriental drawing and the calligraphy of outlines; they led to a harmonious blending of the two in pictures, where the drawing could not be separated from the style of the calligraphy used in its compositional execution.

'We' includes two friends who were keen on this, on the same course as me.

One of them was a not very successful artist, half Leftist; he and I did the sets for *The Mexican*—he was called Nikitin.[24] And he even recorded our excited observations, working them into an article in the magazine *Iskusstvo vostoka* [Oriental Art].

The brushwork in a picture of a horse, 'taken' from the crupper, showed the affinity between calligraphic writing and the flight of lines of free drawing.

Do not forget that brushwork in painting is also classified into various styles, in strict correspondence with the subject matter it is to tackle.

Folds of garments are represented by a different set of strokes from those used for steep mountainsides. The stroke used for torrents of cascading water is completely different from that used for capturing the outlines of clouds.

I read and re-read *The Importance of Living* in 1941.

The first summer of the war was over.

The autumn rains had already begun.

Bombing raids made it impossible to go down into the trenches surrounding our building in Potylikha.

No longer could I fall asleep on the ground, watching the beams of the searchlights in the night sky over Moscow.

My neighbours found my imperturbable sleep vexing.

'How can you sleep at a time like this ?!'

I replied that it is perfectly natural for man to sleep on the ground; that millions of people over countless centuries have done exactly that . . .

But then came wet, frosty autumn.

I could not be bothered to go down.

At the first wail of the siren, the building would be evacuated.

Doors slammed in the empty flats but no one had time to lock them as they raced away from the fires and incendiaries which could fly into their homes.

Abandoned cats wandered from flat to flat.

The number of empty flats rose daily.

As did the number of abandoned cats.

Moscow was frantically packing up.

Each day, thousands of Muscovites migrated from Belokamenny Street and Pervoprestolny Street to the Volga; beyond the Volga, to deepest Asia.

Wave after wave of aeroplanes roared past, bang on course above our building in Potylikha (the huge film studio was a fixed landmark for air attacks from the direction of Mozhaisk) and sleep was impossible.

You could not fail to notice the distant explosions across the River Moscow, around the Kiev Station and near the orbital railway bridge separating us from the city.

Somewhere aeroplanes roared.

Somewhere explosions rumbled.

And looking through the crack of the black-out curtain (after of course taking the precaution of switching the light off!), on either side you could see the ominous glow of distant fires . . .

And so—there you have it.*

My odd passion is for teaching.

I devoted many years to teaching in the Institute.

That partly compensated, in those years when I could not make films, for the trauma of Mexico.

---

* In English in the original.

1932-5 was the time when I taught the most intensively.

That was when I 'finished' my book (volume 1, on directing).

But I have been teaching since 1920, when I was myself still learning.

And by 1930 I was even famous abroad.

Colleagues in America were baffled:

'How can you teach others? They will grow up and leave you broke! We don't try to teach others. Over here, if we do ever think about what we do and how, we try to do so when there's nobody else about! But you—you teach, write, publish?!!'

I am not going to go into the social peculiarities of the approach to this question from a Soviet citizen's point of view.

Nor into the fact that there are enough resources here for plenty of directors and that there are too few directors making pictures.

But I will mention the watchword that guided the spirit of my teaching.

Whether I was with students, or writing about the principles which I was able to grasp, or expounding my methods and the peculiarities of those methods of our art and art in general, the motto was, is and probably will be, 'Say it all.'

Hide nothing. Do not mystify.

And the question will immediately arise:

'Wasn't it that watchword, that aim, the same—now ancient —practice which led to the particularly abrupt rejection of Papa?'

Papa, who concealed 'secrets' from me, who never initiated me into them, who let me drift with the tide, to discover these secrets of nature quite by accident.

Of course, that is one way of teaching people to swim.

You just push them in.

But this does not work at all well with . . . puppies.

And the fact that 'puppies' were an Eisenstein family joke before I appeared on the scene and which survived until the beginning of my professional career, is poor justification for applying that method to me!

After my parents' wedding (and they were blessed by none other than Father John of Kronstadt[25]—or 'Giovanni' as he was called in one of the ribald stories published in Shebuyev's papers, *Bich* [The Whip] or *Pulemyot* [The Machine-Gun]) Sasha Fantalov, a distant cousin of Mama's, said to her: 'Well, Yulia; so you're married. And now you'll have Eisenpups . . .'

Sasha Fantalov (I met him somewhat later and had a great affection for him) generally came to mind at the start of each academic year.

The way I said it, it sounded more academic and a little unctuous.

After the usual 'teaching is impossible; one can only learn',

I generally said something about my interest in arming everyone with the facts gained by our experience, so that each could travel his own road. I laid no claims to the stylistics of those who followed my manner. 'It is not my business to rear Eisenpups: far from it.'

This always worked.

And there have indeed been no puppies.

And another phrase of mine, used solely in academic circles and which always went down well, especially when Formalism was in vogue, went:

'It is no more accurate to call someone interested in questions of form, a Formalist, than it would be to call a venereologist a syphilitic!'

Painful childhood experiences can weigh heavily.

And there are many ways of dealing with them.

But I think that Papa's method of educating me as if I were a puppy, is not by itself an adequate explanation for my taking the position I did in educating young people.

The soil had already been well prepared.

And it took one more encounter with that, from a different perspective, for that predisposition to turn into a principle and method.

That is, this would not have happened but for a second encounter with the 'stamp of secret', and that problem I sought a solution to just as fervently as to the one which Papa hid.

Apart from a natural father, there is always a spiritual father going everywhere with you.

Stating this is the most banal truism.

445

But a fact is a fact.

They are sometimes similar, and that is not very satisfactory, but more frequently they differ.

God willed it that with regard to the 'secret', my spiritual father turned out to be the same as my natural father.

On matters concerning art, the answer was that same silence.

Mikhail Osipovich was endlessly evasive when questioned about 'the secrets' of biology.

Vsevolod Emilevich [Meyerhold] was even more evasive on questions about the 'secrets' of the director's art.

Perhaps, to tell the truth, I never felt a particular love for Mikhail Osipovich according to the Biblical code.

But one of the fundamental commands in the Bible is that we 'honour' our parents:

'Honour thy father and thy mother and thou shalt dwell long on the earth.'

A reward that was of dubious value.

And anyway, why should one be grateful to one's parents?

I shall stop here.

In case all this, some day, gets printed.

And such notions might jeopardise an . . . American edition!

Anyway, it was natural to shower all my adoration on my second father.

And I must say that I never loved, adored or worshipped anyone as I did my teacher.

Will any of my pupils ever speak of me like that?

No. And that has less to do with my pupils and myself, than with my teacher and me.

For I am unworthy to undo the laces of his shoes, although he wore felt boots in his unheated workshops on Novinsky Boulevard.

I shall never, even in advanced old age, feel worthy to kiss the dust of his foot-prints; although his human failings have probably erased all trace of him as our greatest theatrical master from the history of our art of theatre.

And it is impossible to live without loving, without worshipping, wholeheartedly and devotedly.

He was a striking man.

Living proof that genius and villainy can reside in one person.

You were lucky if you met him when he was a magus and wizard of theatre.

But woe betide anyone dependent on him as a person.

Lucky the person who could watch him and learn.

And unlucky the person who approached him trustingly with a question.

Once I naively asked him a series of questions about some concealed difficulties.

I suddenly saw Mikhail Osipovich in his aquiline face, with its penetrating gaze and the striking set of the mouth beneath the bent, predatory nose.

A glassy stare which darted left and right and was then utterly transformed, assuming an air of official politeness, a slightly derisive sympathy, before showing ironic surprise at the question: 'Now really, that is curious! M-yes . . .'

I can say precisely where the expression 'I spit in his eye' comes from.

This had no bearing on my love and adoration.

(Buddhists spit out their prayer paper at the statues of their gods!)

But my heart was heavy with great sadness.

I've had rotten luck with fathers . . .

His lectures were like the songs of snakes.

'Whoever hears the songs,

Forgets everything . . .'[26]

As if Sirin sat on his right side,

and Alkonost on his left.[27]

Meyerhold was directing with his hands.

A flashing eye.

Holding a puppet from Java.

The master's deft fingers moved the gilt arms of the doll.

The white face with slanting eyes spun from left to right.

The doll had come to life like Ida Rubinstein; we remember her pose from a painting by Serov.

Photo of Vsevolod Meyerhold with dedication to Eisenstein: 'I am proud of my pupil who has now become a master. I love the master who has now founded a school. I bow to this pupil and master, S. Eisenstein. Moscow, 22 June 1936.'

And it was not a puppet in Meyerhold's hands,
but Ida Rubinstein in *Pisonella.*

And—flinging his hands upwards—Meyerhold directed the cascades of flashing fabrics which fly up in the scene of the market on the shore, on the stage of the Grand Opéra, in Paris.[28]

His hands froze in mid-air . . .

And we had a preview of the 'dead scene' in *The Government Inspector.*[29]

The dolls stood inanimate; and those, which sparkled on stage all evening in their image, danced past them wildly.

The incomparable master stood like Gogol in silhouette.

Then he lowered his arms . . .

You could just hear the faintest ripple of applause; kidskin gloves marking the guests' approval, after Nina's romance in *Masquerade* on the stage of the Alexandrinka, the day before the February Revolution in 1917.[30]

The sorcerer suddenly snapped the cord of enchantment.

He held gold-painted wooden sticks and a piece of coloured cloth.

The king of the elves had vanished.

At the small table sat Lindhorst, the lacklustre archivist.[31]

His lectures were mirages and dreams.

Notes were frantically jotted down.

And on awaking, one's notebooks were covered in 'goodness only knows.'

I can recollect Aksyonov's brilliant analysis of *The Merchant of Venice*, his talk on *Bartholomew Fair* and the Elizabethans' treble intrigue down to their smallest details.[32]

But I cannot remember what Meyerhold talked about.

Flavours, colours, sounds.

A gold haze over everything.

Elusive.

Intangible.

A secret within a secret.

A veil behind a veil.

Not seven.

But eight, twelve, thirty, a half-hundred.

The sorcerer's hands manipulated them around the secret

in a swirl of different hues.

But it was odd:

it was as though the conjurer was being filmed backwards.

The emotional ego was entranced, absorbed and attentive.

The rational ego growled inwardly.

It had not yet been to America and so made no sarcastic comments, such as comparing this dance to an endless strip-tease which should be brought to an end.

Strip-tease is the American version of the 'Dance of the Seven Veils'; an auction, where the public buys the hat, wrap, dress, brassière, panties and frills from a living girl. A first, a second, a third; a bow-tie, a ribbon, the pearl, the last shred of decency. The auditorium is in uproar, shouting, raving.

But beneath the bow-tie—is a bow-tie.

Beneath the ribbon, a ribbon.

Beneath the pearl . . .

The spectacle vanishes in darkness . . .

The third ego is the most tolerant.

The subconscious ego.

That same ego from Yevreinov's play *In the Backstage of the Soul*, which was where I took my first two characters from—the emotional ego, and the rational ego.[33]

Yevreinov's subconscious ego was waiting.

It waited until the emotional ego had finished needling him —stretching the strings at the back of the stage which was framed by the drapes of the lungs with the regularly beating red sac of the heart up near the flies—and suffocated its rational opponent; and the rational ego rang the brain on a little telephone to say:

'In the desk drawer on the right . . .'

A loud report.

Strips of crimson silk, stage blood, hang out of the torn heart.

And a tram conductor walked towards the sleeping ego of the subconscious, holding a torch.

(The lights go down.)

'All change, all change please.'

. . . My subconscious similarly lurked in waiting somewhere while the romantic ego grew drunk on his lectures; and the rational ego sourly grumbled (it had been educated in the Institute of Civil Engineering on differential calculus and integrated differential equations). This was all very well, but when would the 'secrets' be revealed? When would we move on to his method? When would this 'strip-tease à l'envers*' end?

A winter passed in sweetest stupefaction, but nothing concrete remained.

But:

Nezlobin's theatre merged with the First Theatre of the RSFSR.

The concrete Rutkovskaya, the real Sinitsyn, and kind old Nelidov were emblazoned on the Novinsky shields, next to the 'actor of the future' the 'Übermarionette', the young idealists, Hoffmann, Gozzi and Calderón.[34]

Nelidov was a comrade-in-arms.

Nelidov took part in the show *The Fairground Booth*.

And we held *The Fairground Booth* in the same reverence that Ancient Rus had for the Church of the Saviour.[35]

In the evenings, Nelidov told stories about the marvellous evening performances of *The Fairground Booth*, about the gathering of mystics who now look out of Sapunov's sketches in the Tretyakov Gallery, about the première and about how the White Pierrot stood like a stork, one leg behind the other—it was Meyerhold, playing on a thin, treble piccolo.

Not that memories can fill you up. Sinitsyn and Rutkovskaya were no less hungry than Nelidov.

The rest of the company wanted to eat as well.

But he who does not work, may not eat.

And in the theatre, those who do not act, do not eat. (That, at any rate, was the case in 1921!)

So *Nora* was put on after three rehearsals.[36]

I sometimes wonder whether perhaps Meyerhold was simply incapable of talking and explaining?

He certainly could not see and formulate it for himself.

Anyway, whatever it was that hovered elusively and secretively at Novinsky Boulevard in the autumn and winter, it gave itself

---

* In English and French in the original: 'strip-tease inside out'

away completely in the spring.

When you are working, things come out.

You can't fool people completely at work.

When you work, there is no time to weave the invisible golden thread of invention which leads into daydream. When you are working, you have to do things.

And what lay carefully, cannily hidden for two terms was triumphantly laid bare in three days spent rehearsing.

I have seen a few people in my time.

Yvette Guilbert demonstrated her technique for me, for a whole *après-midi*.* I have seen Chaplin filming. I have seen Chaliapin and Stanislavsky, Ziegfeld's shows and the Berlin Admiralspalast, Mistinguette in the Casino de Paris, Katherine Cornell and Lynne Fontanne with Lunt; Alla Nazimova acting in O'Neill and Mayakovsky rehearsing *Mystery-Buffe*; I have spoken with Bernard Shaw about sound cinema, and with Pirandello about ideas for a play; I have seen Montegius in a tiny theatre in Paris— and that same Montegius whom Vladimir Ilyich went all the way across town to see; I have seen Raquel Meller and Reinhardt's productions, rehearsals of *Cuckold*; run-of-the-mill productions of *Hadibuk* and *Erik XIV*, Chekhov's Frazer and Vakhtangov's, Fokine's *Jota Aragonese* and Karsavina in *Chopiniana*; Al Jolson and Gershwin acting in *Rhapsody in Blue*; the three arenas of the Barnum and Bailey circus; flea circuses at fairs; Primo Carnera boxed out of the ring by Schmeling, in the presence of the Prince of Wales; Utochkin's flights and the carnival in New Orleans; I have worked in Paramount with Jackie Coogan, heard Yehudi Menuhin in the Tchaikovsky Hall, lunched with Douglas Fairbanks in New York and breakfasted with Rin-Tin-Tin in Boston; heard Plevitskaya in the Army and Navy Club and seen General Sukhomlinov in the same room in the defendant's box; seen General Brusilov as a witness at the same trial, and General Kuropatkin[37]—my next-door-neighbour—doing his morning jerks; seen Lloyd George in Parliament arguing for the recognition of Soviet Russia, and Tsar Nicholas II unveiling the memorial to Peter the Great in Riga; filmed a Mexican archbishop and adjusted, for the camera, the

---

* French: 'afternoon'

Papal nunciate's, Rosas-y-Flores' tiara; gone for a spin with Greta Garbo; been at a bullfight; and been photographed with Marlene ('Legs') Dietrich.

But not one of these impressions will ever erase from my memory the impressions left by those three days of rehearsals for *Nora* in the gym on Novinsky Boulevard.

I remember shaking the whole time.

Not from cold,

but excitement,

my nerves ready to snap.

The gym was lined with wooden bars, which underline it, as it were.

They were fixed to the walls.

Part of the apparatus.

And every other day, at Lyudmila Gaultier's terse commands, we vigorously loosened our knees and ankles.

Until my legs seemed no longer to belong to me; at forty-eight I can still surprise our esteemed artists by faultlessly raising my legs.

Squashed between the bars and the wall with my back against the window, I looked straight ahead with bated breath.

But perhaps this is where my second tendency comes from.

To rummage, rummage, rummage.

To work my way into every fissure of a problem; to break inside and dig, trying always to penetrate it more deeply, to get ever closer to its core.

I do not look for any help.

But what I find I do not hide; I bring it out into the open— in lectures, books, magazines, newspapers.

And . . . did you know, the most effective way of hiding something is to put it on display?!

Part Two:
The True Paths of Discovery

Monkey Logic[1]

The sucking sound of galoshes slapping against mud.

Our feet slipped out of them.

The mud was a mixture of wet clay and the first snowfall.

A zoo, completely deserted.

Alma-Ata.

Steppe eagles, with bedraggled crests, looked like my companion's aunt.

A deer without antlers and with large moist black eyes looked very like my travelling companion (Kozintsev, the director).[2]

A bear lumbered in aimless circles.

There was an amazing snow leopard.

His terrifying tail twitched at our every movement; it looked like a furry snake distended after a good meal.

The whole body was still, idle.

The eyes were closed one moment . . .

but they would suddenly open wide: fathomless, grey-green.

You can just make out the narrowed pupil, like a second hand on the twelve.

The snow leopard lay utterly still beneath the roof of his cage.

Only the tip of his tail tirelessly, nervously reacted to our every movement.

The snow leopard was like the Japanese military attaché at the Red Army Parade on Red Square.

Bushido—the samurai code of honour—does not permit a Japanese from the élite caste (and this tradition later came to apply to all Japanese in general) to show any change of expression, come what may.

The face of the Japanese attaché was impassive.

But then a new class of combat aircraft cut through the sky.

His expression was set.

His hands were behind his back.

But what they did!

In their yellow gloves they flew like birds.

Fyodor Basmanov in a mask. Eisenstein's drawing for *Ivan the Terrible* Part Two. Alma-Ata, 30 May 1942

Just like the leopard's tail.

While the eye fixed on us did not so much as waver.

The next day I sent Misha Kuznetsov to study this leopard's eye for his role as Fyodor Basmanov.[3]

Kuznetsov's grey eyes were perfect for this.

He had to know how to capture their look.

We went further, into a sheltered enclosure.

There was a strong stench of urine.

A black Great Dane.

Flocks of green parrots—a mass. I saw parrots like that flying among the palms of the Mexican tropics.

Pelicans, too.

The lion smelt of dog.

The tiger smelt of mouse.

We went to see the monkeys.

The baboons were kept separately . . .

I tossed a bit of carrot in.

The monkey stopped what she was doing.

She was, of course, looking for fleas.

Three leaps brought her to the carrot; she did not take her eyes from it.

But then a piece of white paper came into her line of vision, lying not far from the carrot.

The white made a deeper impression on her than did the dull orange.

And the carrot was forgotten.

The monkey moved towards the paper.

But then, just nearby—a penetrating cry and the characteristic chattering of teeth.

The monkey turned away from the paper when she heard the cry.

Her gaze rested on the swaying branch.

A moving object is more eye-catching than a still one.

One jump—and the monkey was already holding on to the branch.

The monkey's mate chattered up above.

The next second, the monkey was already obligingly deep in her mate's fur.

One's living companion is of course a much more attractive proposition than a simply mobile object.

The branch, paper and carrot were all forgotten.

. . . The difference between me and the Alma-Ata monkey is just this one fact:

I jump from object to object in much the same way, as soon as a new object surfaces in my memory.

But, as distinct from the monkey, I still occasionally return to the original object.

I dedicate the progress of the subject matter in these notes to my anonymous sister—the monkey in the Alma-Ata zoo . . .

The History of the Close-Up[1]

A branch of lilac.
>White,
>double-flowered.
>With lush green foliage.
>Hanging heavy in the blinding sun.
>It spilled through the window into my room.
>It swayed above the sill.
>And became the first of my memories of childhood associations.

>A close-up!
>The close-up of white lilac swaying above my cot is my first childhood impression.

>Actually it was not a cot at this stage; it was a small white bed, a nickel sphere crowning each post and a white crocheted net between them to stop me from falling out.

>I was too old for the cot.
>I was all of three or four!
>My parents and I were at our dacha.
>On the Riga coast.
>In modern-day Majori, then called Majorenhof.
>The bough of white lilac, cutting across a ray of sunshine, looked in at my window.

>Swayed above my head.
>My first conscious impression was a close-up.

So it was that my consciousness awoke beneath a spray of lilac.

>Then it began nodding off again, for very many years at a time, beneath that same branch.

>Only the branch was not real but drawn; half painted
>and half embroidered in silk and gold thread.
>And it was on a Japanese folding screen.
>I used to doze off looking at this branch.
>I don't remember when it was placed near the headboard

461

of my bed.

It was as though it had always stood there.

The branch was luxuriant and weighed down.

There were birds on it.

And in the distant background beyond—visible through it—were the traditional features of a Japanese painted landscape.

Small huts.

Reeds.

Streams crossed by little bridges.

Small vessels with pointed prows, drawn with two brush strokes.

But the branch was not only a close-up.

The branch was a typically Japanese foreground, through which the background had been painted in.

And so I was aware of the beauties of foreground composition before I saw Hokusai [2] or was entranced by Edgar Degas.

A small foreground detail can attain such size that it dominates everything else in the painting.

Then somehow a chair was put through the screen in two places.

I remember it had two holes in it.

The screen was taken away.

I think these two branches brought two, organically connected ideas together—the idea of a close-up, and the idea of foreground composition—in one living impression.

And many years later, when I began to look for the historical precursors of the cinema close-up I automatically began searching not in isolated portraits or still lifes but in the fascinating history of how an individual element in a picture begins to move forward from the picture's general make-up and into the foreground.[3] As figures, in a general view of a landscape in which it is sometimes impossible to detect Icarus falling, or Daphnis and Chloë, begin first of all to approach the full height of the painting, and then gradually come so close that they are cut off by the edge of the canvas, as in El Greco's 'Espolio', and later—jumping forward three centuries—the French Impressionists, who were strongly influenced by the Japanese.

For me, it was two Edgars who encapsulated the tradition of

foreground composition.

Edgar Degas and Edgar Poe.

Edgar Poe came first.

The vivid impression of the painted Japanese bough probably accounts for the strong impression left by Poe's story about how
he was gazing out of the window and suddenly saw a gigantic monster crawling up the ridge of a distant mountain.

It then emerges that this is no prehistoric monster, but a little cricket crawling upon the pane.[4]

Only a camera lens can do this, and only a 28 mm lens at
that;[5] it also has an amazing capacity for distorting the close-up,
artificially exaggerating its size and shape.

I have reluctantly decided to set out some proposals concerning Poe's visual imagination elsewhere, in a small work on the
elements of cinema in El Greco's *oeuvre*.

But I think it was probably the conjunction of that branch
of white lilac and the plastic description from Poe's terrifying tale
that decided my more effective and pronounced foreground compositions.

These are the skulls and monks, masks and carousels of the
Day of the Dead in the Mexican film.

The spot of the white lilac branch became a white skull in
the foreground.

And the terrifying element in Poe's story became a group of
monks in black cassocks in the background.

It amounts to the Jesuits' Catholic asceticism, ruling, with a
rod of iron, the sensual magnificence of Mexico's tropical beauty.

The carousels of the Day of the Dead echoed this deeply
tragic theme with irony.

Here were those white skulls once more, flung into the
foreground and almost tangible.

But the skulls were only cardboard masks.

Life-sized carousels and Ferris wheels spun behind them,
flashing through the empty sockets of masks which seemed to say
with a wink that death is no more than an empty cardboard box
that, come what may, the whirlwind of life will punch holes in
without thinking twice.

Another good example is combining the profile of the

Mayan girl with the entire pyramid of Chichen-Itzá, in one and the same frame. But I explored the model of this composition with particular thoroughness in *The Old and The New.*

The incomparable compositions by the second Edgar— Edgar Degas and Toulouse-Lautrec (whose compositions can be even more powerful) bring us back again to the realm of the purely plastic arts.

But the actual interweaving of these descriptive and spontaneously visual impressions meant something quite specific to me.

Here I sensed, probably for the first time, the link between painting and literature, seen as equally plastic.

That gave me my first inkling of how to read Pushkin from a visual, plastic and montage viewpoint and, when I needed an English equivalent, Milton too.[6]

Reading Pushkin and, later, Gogol strengthened my sense of this link.

If Poe showed us an essentially visual picture, described in detail like a visual picture and even as an optical phenomenon, then in Pushkin we find a description of an actual event or phenomenon done with such absolute strictness and precision that it is almost possible to recreate in its entirety the visual image that struck him so concretely.

And I do mean 'struck', which applies to the dynamic of a literary description, whereas an immobile canvas inevitably fails.

Hence it was only with the advent of cinema that the moving picture of Pushkin's constructions could begin to be sensed so acutely.

Tynyanov wrote about the concreteness of Pushkin's lyric poetry, saying that Pushkin's lyric poems were not an interaction of conventionally lyrical formulae, but in all cases were a record of genuine lyrical 'spiritual states' and emotional experiences, always precisely located and having a quite real source.

Analysis of Pushkin's poems (and prose) reveals the same precision in his description of quite real visual images that may be established or recreated from his exposition of them.

Arranging a passage by Pushkin for editing as a sequence of shots is a sheer delight, because each step shows how the poet saw and logically showed this or that event.

Above Eisenstein with his students on the first day of filming *Bezhin Meadow* Moscow, May 1935. (Photo: Jay Leyda) *Below* Stills from the prologue for *Bezhin Meadow* (the first version, 1935-6)

And then as from above inspired
Came forth the ringing voice of Peter
'To the task, in Heaven's name!' And from the tent,
Surrounded by a swarm of favourites,
Comes Peter . . .

The gradual way in which Peter is presented is remarkable. First there is the voice; after it, the crowd, with Peter in the midst of it but still invisible; only then is Peter revealed to us as he is, or rather as 'the thunder of God itself.'

No less original and Pushkinian is the 'micromontage'; i.e. the combination of separate elements within one frame.

Here, the same thing happens in the way the words are deployed within phrases.

And if you take it as read that the consistency with which words are ordered defines their position, as they move from the background of the 'frame' into the foreground (which is natural enough), then almost every phrase of Pushkin's coincides with a scheme of plastic composition, outlined with complete accuracy.

I say a scheme of composition, because the positioning of the words defines the chief and crucial matter of composition: the understood relationship and juxtaposition of the elements of the subject and the other values within the pictures.

This 'essential bone structure' can be dressed up in any type of personal artistic solutions.

And, while following the rigid plan of the author, this enables anyone who might try his hand at literary description in the plastic arts to interpret it in their own way.

The prerequisites and the limit of creative interpretation of a writer's works, as in any aspect of directing, are both to be found here.

A good example of how an author's compositional plan develops, and how failure to notice it can wreck this structure, can be seen by comparing an actual extract from Gogol with a conventional adaptation for cinema. The example comes from Kuleshov's book and is the start of the attack in *Taras Bulba*—the appearance of Andrei:[7]

We have to think, when we are recording the shots for this sequence, how we are going to portray Andrei riding on his horse. If Andrei gallops through the middle distance, the viewer will not be able to see Andrei's face in sufficient detail; the expression in his eyes, the black curls streaming from under his helmet, etc. If Andrei is in the foreground or in close-up, we will then stop the viewer from seeing Andrei for long enough—the horse and rider will no sooner appear on screen than they will vanish off it.

So the frame of Andrei on horseback must be filmed by a tracking shot—moving the camera on a parallel course to the galloping horseman (filming from a truck or a car, etc).

Let us record the shots for this sequence:

4m 3. *Medium shot.* Andrei rides ahead of his regiment. Andrei is the most animated and handsome.

Tracking shot. He is covered in gold.

Sound: Music for the attack. The gleam of the gold.

4m 4. *Close-up.* Waist upwards. His black hair streaming from under his helmet.

Tracking shot. A scarf he treasures is tied about his arm.

Sound: Music for the attack. The gleam of the gold.

6m 5. *Medium long shot.* The walls of the fortress. Out comes the Polish woman.

Sound: Music for the attack. The Polish woman's theme.

3m 6. Close-up: Waist upwards. The Polish woman on the wall.

Sound: Music for the attack. The Polish woman's theme.

'Andrei is the most animated and handsome.'

'The prized scarf, a present from the Polish woman.'

Andrei sees the Polish woman. We show Andrei's good looks and the Pole's scarf.

We say again: '. . . So the black hair flies from under his bronze helmet . . .'

'. . . The prized scarf flutters from his arm . . .'

We show the Polish woman looking at Andrei.

We record the shots:

2m. 7. *Close-up:* Black curls streaming from under Andrei's helmet.

Tracking shot.

Sound: Music for the attack. The Polish woman's theme.

2m. 8. *Close-up:* The scarf fluttering from Andrei's arm.

Tracking shot.

Sound: Music for the attack. The Polish woman's theme.

4m. 9. *Close-up:* From the waist. The Polish woman watches.

Sound: Music for the attack. The Polish woman's theme.[8]

Reading Kuleshov's critique and explanations, you can only agree with his conclusions.

It is all logically correct; all the details are there.

There is however a nagging feeling that you cannot film Gogol in so trivial a way.

Here are these nine shots.

If you take the corresponding passage from the narrative, you will see that it diverges sharply from Gogol in the very first lines; that is to do with principle, rather than mere appearances.

Whereas Kuleshov's chief aim right from the outset is to

show Andrei going into battle (tracking shot, shot 3, close up, shot 4, and so on are specifically so designed), Gogol on the other hand presents him quite differently:

> The gates were opened, and the hussars—the pride of all the cavalry regiments—flew out. Beneath the riders, the brown steppe horses raced as one. In front of the others there rode a knight more animated and handsome than the others. His black hair streamed from under his bronze helmet; his prized scarf fluttered from his arm—it had been embroidered by the hands of the greatest beauty . . . [9]

Where does it say here—where is it indicated, even—that this is Andrei?

Is it accident that Andrei is neither named nor shown at the start?

Of course not.

The next phrase makes the author's intention plain: 'Thus was Taras struck dumb when he saw that this was Andrei . . .' The author's plan was to reveal Andrei's identity as this remarkable knight through Taras's eyes.

So the viewer should be 'dumbfounded' with Taras.

The author's plan was for the foremost, flashing, fabulous soldier to turn out suddenly to be Andrei.

And Gogol does not let Andrei start hacking and chopping immediately. He first devotes many lines of description to his easy and brilliant gallop, using the simile of a young borzoi, before saying how keenly he brandishes his sword.

Whatever impression we have of Andrei in his Polish armour, we gained it a few pages earlier (p. 111), from the description Yankel gives Taras—Yankel had seen him in the town:

> Now he is such an important knight. I almost didn't recognise him! Golden shoulderplates and golden armlets, golden breastplate and golden helmet and gold around his waist and gold everywhere, everything is made of gold. Like the sun in springtime, when all the birds sing in the garden, and there is a scent of grass—that is how he gleams in his gold. . .

469

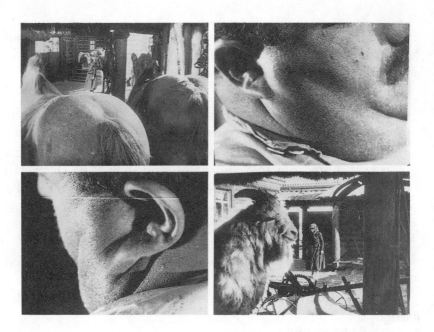

Stills from the episode 'Marfa Lapkina in the kulak's house', from *The General Line*

Long shots from *Que Viva México!*

That is our first impression of Andrei!

Andrei should be shown first as he was when still an un-known knight, shining like the golden sun, before Taras recognised him.

To do this with film shots is extremely simple. Without even having to take the lens cap off!

(Incidentally, this appearance of the radiant knight would make a fine contrast with his death, as told by Taras two pages ear-lier:

'He fell, fell ignobly, like a vile cur!')

Interestingly, the Polish woman is also not 'personified', only indicated: 'The scarf, embroidered by the hands of the great-est beauty . . .'

This type of indirect presentation was a favourite device of Pushkin's, too. That is how Peter leaves his tent in 'Poltava', or Istomina exits in *Eugene Onegin*.

Here he is also concerned that the reader should recognise Andrei at the same time as Taras. This is also connected fundamen-tally to the fact that the viewer must identify right to the end 'with Taras', who in everything he does is the embodiment of the patri-otic idea!

We observe exactly the same thing when we see how one montage group follows the next.

And incidentally, the cross-cut to the woman on the fortress wall is here really a 'silent film' device.

Andrei's 'curls' etc, 'he saw before him'

—she still cannot make up her mind.

And of course the musical leitmotif should have been worked out here, weaving this theme of the drunk, stupefying passion that possesses Andrei in battle and especially in death, when this theme in the music, growing in strength, might cut across the magnified titles, and clearly merge, mixing with Andrei's pronunciation of her name before his death.

This would have been an example of the development of a theme, not only plastically, but also aurally, and finally in an interrelated, audiovisual way.

Of course, the Chinese provide the most interesting exam-ples in this area too: the unity of painting and writing technique, which evolves uniquely from an original visual perception and its specific characteristics and which defines the unexpected characteristics and forms of both painting and writing conventions.

I think that, just as Pushkin's word order turned out to be the ultimate stimulus from my first impressions, so Pushkin himself represented a stepping stone to the theme that absorbed me most—audiovisual counterpoint.

The fact is that Pushkin often splices the intonational and melodic progression of the phrase itself and so creates a visual equivalent to the word order.

The melodic graphics are so distinct and correspond so precisely to the verbally sketched subject of a scene that sometimes it looks like an outline of actual details, or a *mise-en-scène* of events, or a motionless interweaving of everything in view.

Which is one step away from the case where the concrete subject disappears, leaving behind only the outline and the weave of the intonational progression that characterised it.

The melodics of the poetry have merged into music.

The problem of audio-visual combination arises from the possibility of audiovisual correspondence and unity.

(The key part of my only book to date, *The Film Sense*, is devoted to this and there is no point in repeating myself here.)

Here I am interested chiefly in the highways and by-ways that I have travelled on my journey to the central problems and that have excited me in different sectors of my creative practice.

The sweet poison of audiovisual montage came later.

Silent film was primarily concerned with montage and the role of the close-up.

But, curiously, even in silent film I often sought a way of conveying something through a plastic construction composed of purely aural effects.

I remember filming in the Winter Palace one night in October 1927 (for the film *October*). In the Palace rooms I achieved a plastic recreation of the impressions made by a salvo from the 'Aurora's' guns. The echo rolled through the rooms and reached a room where everything had been covered by white sheeting and where members of the Provisional Government were awaiting the fateful moment—the establishment of Soviet Power—wrapped up in fur coats.

A system of 'iris' diaphragms, in a correctly gauged rhythm —an opening and shutting out of views of rooms—attempted to capture the echo's breathing rhythm as it resounded through the galleries. The crystal chandeliers tinkling in reply to the rattle of machine-gun fire on the square was more successful and remained in the audience's memory.

There was also a purely subjective association here apart from the visual and motor equivalent of the swaying crystal pendants. The attempt to capture the graphic equivalent of the echo was, of course, more interesting from the point of view of method!

The close-up in the form that silent pictures handled it—a close-up, that is, which is actually separate from the rest of the picture and no longer connected with it, but entirely abstract in its own right, the *pars pro toto*—is also linked to a vivid impression I had several years before I even began working in theatre!

I associate the close-up of a monosemantic sort, as a part of possible combinations of tempo alone, with a real saraband of noses and eyes, ears and arms, belts held up high by safety pins, earrings and coiffes entwined with flowers and ribbons.

Day-time vision is quite different from night-time.

Day-time, in the sense of being awake.

Night-time, in the sense of dreams.

The interlacing of details and general form is typical of day-time vision and is so harmonious that you need either a highly developed special skill, like Pathfinder's eye,[10] or that of his great-nephew, Sherlock Holmes, or an unusually acute sensitivity of attention, to be able to select at a moment's notice an isolated detail in close-up, from the harmony of the whole.

You need a particularly well-trained analytical visual sense to pick out the detail.

You need a particular aptitude for synthesising thought, to discern among the data of analytical vision the crucial, characteristic detail, the detail which can, as a fragment of the whole, recreate the idea of the whole.

Curiously, when we are asleep, the entirety and the part are blended just as harmoniously, but in such a way that both are equally noticeable.

It is hard to find a better description of this than in . . . Dostoyevsky, in the conversation Ivan Karamazov has with the Devil, where, characteristically, references to the 'highest manifestations' lie next to 'the last button on the shirt-front'. We might also mention Lev Tolstoy in this connection; he is equally at home handling the huge canvases of war or describing 'unexpected details' like the curls of hair against Anna Karenina's neck and it has been said that even 'quite mediocre folk' see similar things in their dreams; that there are such people for whom, in the waking hours, the 'whole' is an amorphous, complex and undifferentiated picture.

But the most rewarding states are those between dream and reality.

The leap from one state to the other seems to splinter both one and the other harmony: fragments of perception or impressions from the perceived object are shaken like dice or shuffled like a pack of cards.

It was at this juncture that I saw the above-mentioned saraband in close-up.

It was not a dance at Bald Hills.

Not on any hill at all, come to that.

It was on a beaten-down space in front of a few large huts somewhere in the old Kholm district, part of what used to be the Pskov guberniya.

This was on another occasion.

During the Civil War I found myself quite unexpectedly thrown into military construction work in the town of Kholm in Pskov, even though this town was ninety-five kilometres from one railway line and seventy from the other . . . We were building defences: trenches, ramparts, blockhouses. Although we had not the faintest idea whom we were defending the town against . . .

It emerged much later that it was a self-interested whim on the part of the sappers' commander that sent us to Kholm; after the retreat from Dvinsk or Polotsk he found himself on the other side of the abandoned positions, and his wife's former estates were somewhere in the Kholm region . . .

This commander was noted for his crazy motorcycling, brilliant expertise as a sapper, and also, perhaps for always doing handstands on his chair whenever you went in to see him with your report each morning.

And at the sappers' amateur dramatics, during our operations around Velikie Luki, this engineer brilliantly acted a taciturn servant with a napkin, in a sketch of *The Double* performed from memory, taken from the repertoire of the prewar theatre of miniatures (on Liteiny Prospekt, I think).

(That was one of my first ever attempts at writing on amateur directing . . .)

And in the rich variety of my terribly vivid impressions of that shifting epoch there resides that small, fleeting memory that had nothing to do with the scale of the epoch and events, but simply emerged somewhere incidental to and remote from the general course of the historical events of those years. In fact it does not even count as an event. The only requirements were a very narrow bench.

An accordion.

With our feet soaking wet, we had 'to warm up' with swigs of home-brew.

Crossing the river to where the girls danced.

Before that, we ate a hearty meal in a peasant's house (yet to be de-kulakised); the family was ready to demonstrate its friendship in any way we asked, just as long as we retained the only son as foreman in the sappers' division, where a student technician was on an equal footing with the other foremen.

We slumbered fairly heavily after the unusually rich meal—I think it was the first one I had ever eaten in a peasant's home—and from the communal round bowl.

There was an amazing sunset.

And an unhealthy sleep at sunset lying on a very narrow bench running the length of the lean-to.

While the girls danced.

And the accordion played uproariously.

And the other members of our 'expedition' kicked out their heels on the beaten square before the spacious hut; below was the silted river, stinking and brackish, where our boat floated (she leaked slightly, hence our wet feet), the rowlocks and chains clinking . . .

I have dozed off many times in my life.

And in all sorts of different situations.

Dying from heat, in a skiff among the pointed-tailed skates in the lagoons in the bird sanctuaries of Campeche.

High up (!) in trees growing in narrow tributaries, their branches trailing in the water and their roots greedily sucking moisture out of those veins which the Pacific Ocean sends, tendril-like, into the impenetrable palm forests of Oaxaca. In the distance, a crocodile's beady eye and upper jaw lay on the surface of the water.

I have been rocked to sleep by an aeroplane flying from Veracruz to Progreso, above the azure waters of the Gulf of Mexico. Flamingoes cut smoothly through the sky like pink arrows, passing between us and the emerald surface of the Gulf.

Sleepiness has overcome me among the sun-scorched bushes around Izamal; bushes which have grown from fissures in the immeasurable expanse of rock with its marvellous carvings, which were once the proud cities of the ancient Toltecs, and which might have been tossed and scattered by an angry giant.

I also felt tired sitting at a red checked tablecloth in a lot of black clubs around Chicago.

My eyelids began drooping in the *bal-musettes*, the Parisian dance halls—'Le Java', 'Boule Blanche', 'Aux Trois Colonnes' . . . young labourers, little older than Gavroche, danced amazing waltzes, holding their partners close and spinning, their feet never leaving the ground.

But for some reason it was only then, long ago, after the rich meal provided by the Pudyakovs, in the cool damp sunset above the unknown stream that I sensed this strange phenomenon, a marvellous farandole before my eyes—now a gigantic nose, the only one of its kind; now the peak of a cap, leading an independent life; now a whole line of dancing faces; now an exaggerated moustache, now just the little crosses embroidered on the collars of a Russian shirt, now the distant view of the village swallowed up by the twilight, now again the too large blue tassel of silk cord hanging around a waist, now an earring entangled in some hair, now a flushed cheek . . .

Oddly, when I embarked upon the theme of peasants and collectivisation for the first time, just over five years later, I did not lose sight of this vivid impression. The kulak's ear, and the fold of skin on his neck filled the entire screen; another's massive nose was as big as a hut; a huge hand hung limply above a jug of kvass; a grasshopper, the size of a reaping machine—all these were constantly being woven intò a saraband of countryside and rural genre pictures, in the film *The Old and The New.*

The last, and perhaps the most purely plastic and also ornamental was the visual impression I experienced in the rarefied, mountain air of Alma-Ata, my entire field of vision suddenly shattering before my exhausted eyes (or brain?) and part of it (the lower left hand side) dissolving into bright zig-zags, like a fan of clearly defined stripes of white, dark blue and dense brown.

Its pattern and range of colour were in precisely the style of Peruvian ceramic painting, and I had found that so overwhelming precisely because its graphic and tonal stylisation made it quite impossible to guess the nature of the external impressions that had given rise to them . . .

Such random, ornamental forms could only have been realised in multiple visual shifts, in dreams in twilight states, whether they were originally visual, or had been initially produced (the laws of weaving transcribed for decorating cylindrical vessels).

Here, on the lowest level, as everywhere where the levels of cultural advancement are still moving upwards, we find this conjoined unity of seeing and perception—a reflection of reality, refracted through consciousness, and a reflection of reality refracted through the prism of sensual thought.

On the lowest rungs of development, this occurs primitively and directly—in the representation itself and in early, stylised attempts at forming that representation. At higher levels, it is more refined, involving that organic dyad of perception in increasingly complex problems of form, until eventually separate chance manifestations of formal solutions and 'discoveries' are synthesised. Individual stylistic mannerisms are even found both to be elements of studying a method of art as it comes together and as elements of the actual method of the arts.

That's Just It[1]

There are some wonderful phrases in Russian.

'It takes all sorts.'

'It's anyone's guess.'

'That's just it.'

The best,

the most versatile, is of course: 'That's just it.'

It comes in handy on all occasions in life.

Such as, when a conversation has to be kept alive but there is nothing to say.

This is akin to Abraham Lincoln's famous judgement on a book: 'People who like this sort of thing will find this the sort of thing they like.'

Saying 'That's just it' has points of similarity.

It is very versatile.

It was particularly versatile during the Civil War, which was where I picked it up, together with the knack of rolling up my puttees quickly, putting on foot bindings and quite disregarding even the most basic creature comforts.

'We've got this Soviet power,' a ruddy peasant might say, his eyes screwed up slyly, 'but we haven't got any salt. Hm?'

'That's just it,' you say brusquely.

'I've heard the south is swarming with Whites,' another says with an innocent expression, but looking at you beadily out of the corner of his eye.

'That's just it,' you sigh.

'You just don't understand our way of life, dragging us off here to dig trenches for you when there's hay to be made.'

'That's just it,' you say, in anguish.

The more ambiguous the remark, the more provocative the question, the more anguished, sensitive or brusque the 'That's just it' will sound.

Try it for yourself; you will find it so.

'That's just it' became a part of my routine in Kholm.

A broad river cut the town of Kholm in two. The Lovat.

Defences were being built along the Lovat's banks; the deep rear passed through this point.

It was so far to the rear that mere strategy cannot explain why we were building reinforcements here.

Like all good Russian rivers, the Lovat has two banks.

One is high, the other low-lying.

Geography textbooks attribute this natural phenomenon to the earth's rotation.

The water is said to flow slowly and cannot catch up with the high bank that is ahead of it.

Just like brother Moon, going to meet his sister the Red Sun.

And the low bank is behind the river and chases the high bank forever.

I expect this is a feature typical of Russian rivers.

I never observed it in Colorado river banks.

In fact, rivers there flow so quickly to bore their bed deep between the sheer walls that they have no time at all for worrying about the differing heights of the banks.

Both rims of the Grand Canyon are extremely high, if you measure from the bottom of the gorge gouged out by the river.

But quite low, if you measure from the average surface of the desert; they do not rise so much as one foot above it.

There was an endlessly long wooden staircase leading to the top of the high bank of the Lovat.

It rose upwards in a series of zigzags and it had railings.

Girls hoisted buckets full of water up the steps, carrying two on a yoke.

Meeting full buckets[2] was hardly a sign that one's life would be a full one. Full buckets were all too frequently met with here.

There was a game the lads would play.

They would let a girl reach the top step.

Then they would tip the bucket over . . .

The aim being to drench the shrieking girl.

The Shelyapins' dwelling ran along the high bank.

It was a big family and their house took up the whole length of the bank.

The Shelyapins were the local grandees.

The joke christening in the separator of Marfa Lapkina's new-born daughter. Moscow, December 1928. (Photo: Dmitri Debabov)

Millers and corn chandlers.

Having said that, they varied enormously.

Some lived in town, others in the country.

Some were well-to-do, others poor.

There were close relatives and distant cousins.

There were masters in their comfortable stone houses and owners of wooden cabins from outlying villages which the town had swallowed up.

The Krasilnikovs lived on the opposite bank.

They were a small family.

A family which ran a certain brewery.

Which also made kvass.

The head of the firm, Krasilnikov, a young man, was the typical outcome of a boy who had been considered an 'awkward' child.

By the time he was twenty he had managed to 'experience all that life had to offer.'

Even the attempt the marshal of the nobility made to abuse him.

He spoke as proudly of this as he did of his success in repaying the debts his parent's brewery had run up: taking advantage of inflation, he used worthless banknotes without even stopping to consider the firm's honour.

His small factory had not yet been nationalised.

But it would be, of course.

Although this was subject to delay because of Eglit, an engineer in our military construction unit.

Eglit was a well-fed Lithuanian with a pinkish grey complexion.

He had a shaved head, grey eyes, and wore a soft brown leather jacket with a velvet collar.

Eglit married Krasilnikov's sister.

The Eglits had a daughter.

They called her their '*dotter*'.

My clerk of works, Sasha Stroyev, lived with the *dotter's*

mother.

I learned the expression 'that's just it' from him.

There was also Grandfather Krasilnikov.

He was seldom to be seen.

He was senile.

And he spent whole days in the grey outdoor privy.

He futilely expended what remained of his masculine energy as he looked through a crack, watching the girls playing in the sun.

Krasilnikov, or his wife, hit him about the hands with nettles a few times a day.

The nettles did not help much.

I expect they even had the opposite effect of heightening his excitement.

'This seems more like a setting for a possible story or novel, wouldn't you say?'

The river.

The Krasilnikovs and Shelyapins on opposite banks.

The Revolution broke out in Kholm.

The military construction corps moved in.

Eglit served under Stroyev.

Stroyev slept with Eglit's wife.

Eglit knew about this.

But Sasha Stroyev stood for the brewery's inviolability. The works made kvass too.

The lads, pouring buckets of water on the girls.

And Grandpa Krasilnikov, looking in his white beard like Father Christmas idle during the summer months, peeping at the little girls through the crack.

'It's a wonderful place, a lovely place—a perfectly Russian place!' Peitsch the sapper sang, throwing a section of the military construction corps into this backwoods.

But I am not writing a novel or a story.

Why have I written all this?

Why?

'That's just it.'

I read Otto Weininger in Kholm.[3]

I had already had a thorough grounding in Freud.

So *Sex and Character* did not produce the effect it otherwise might have done.

I no longer remember when and where it was that I read the funny notion that creation (one's work) was first and foremost a division of oneself, a separation.

This was entertainingly demonstrated by the Lord God's activity in the first week of restless existence, when he created the universe from chaos.

Indeed: he divided light from dark.

Land from sea.

And finally Eve from Adam (Eve was made from Adam).

Chaos began to assume a sort of constant appearance.

Moreover, thanks to that constancy, a certain dynamic necessity for a subsequent reunion was implanted; a necessity for what had been torn asunder, rent in two by divine will, to merge again.

This happened with the most consistent results in the case of Cain, Abel and Seth who (apart from Abel who died at a tender age) triumphantly passed their parents' experience on to their descendants.

Striving as far as possible to blend into a unity, polarised opposites penetrate each other; in the process they create the wealth of forms found in nature, making her powers manifest.

Ancient Jehovah, floating above primeval Chaos before there was this type of activity, was only the humanised embodiment of the remote and mysterious Dao which, (according to Chinese mythology) itself split into two opposing origins. These also always strove to come together, and they gave rise to all natural phenomena, processes and objects in the attempt.

It is highly suspicious that it is none other than Chinese mythology that provides the source of the legend of Adam and Eve; and equally Plato's enthralling legends of living creatures joined by their backs, subsequently to split and doomed to search for their right half in order to complete the cycle of their earthly existence, forming what Rabelais picturesquely described as *'la bête à deux dos**

Using a contrary hypothesis, there is a charming proof that 'halving' is no less important and necessary as 'unifying' in this interesting process.

The horror of indivisibility: a state of permanent bonding or proximity without the means of parting to come together again later.

One of Henri Barbusse's *True Stories* about the atrocities of the Sigurança is *The Two of Them*.[4] People who love one another are tied together, face to face, for an unlimited period. 'Abide with me'. The horror of this position lies in the transition from empathy and sympathy for one another to torment and bestial hatred.

This story seemed incongruous to me then; the others seemed actually realistic.

But the formula reminded me of something I had read long ago in *Mir priklyuchenii* [The World of Adventures], where villainous inquisitors condemned a man to 'be with himself': he was left in a room where all the walls were mirrors. There is a room like this in Gaston Leroux's *The Phantom of the Opera*. In any amusement park in the West. And of course, as a philosophical derivation, by Skovoroda (see the epigraph to *The Hare's Forfeit* by Leskov).[5] But the precursor of this style is of course Edgar Allan Poe in *The Pit and the Pendulum*.

Anyway, I asked Barbusse (we were very good friends) whether this tale was true.

He burst out laughing and said he had of course made it up.

But it is none the worse for that! That makes it a psychological approach to the problem: what would have happened with the striving for unity, had there been no division into two, resolved here with the classically 'primitive' opposition of man and woman.

(Bernard Shaw wrote an ironic passage somewhere about the dream of never parting and remaining forever in each other's

---

* French: 'the beast with two backs'

embraces, and the 'inconveniences' that would ensue if this were to happen.)

Interestingly, the 'horror' when confronting such an 'indivisibility' (depriving you of the opportunity of joining together as opposites!)—but on a cosmic scale—comes from Indian folklore: in the story of the meddlesome jackal, who once wanted to marry, to reunite earth and sky. Luckily, he was persuaded otherwise by the cost of so doing—the cost of everything on earth (as I have said, they arose by division—the halving of the whole, according to oriental mythologies: Taoism, Judaism, Hinduism and Yesidism, etc).

The *contrepart** of this is the Maori myth of the cutting in two of the Sky-Earth, and all her sons rushing out into light and life.

---

* In French in the original.

Monsieur, madame, et bébé [1] *

Mama lived at No. 9 Tauride Street in St Petersburg.

Her front door opened on to a yard.

It had a lift.

There was a white marble fireplace downstairs.

A fire crackling cheerfully in the grate.

For me, it was always winter here.

Year in, year out, I went there only for Christmas.

The fire always crackled cheerfully.

A soft red carpet ran up the staircase.

Mama's boudoir was hung with a pale cream brocade, decorated with tiny garlands of roses.

So were the portières.

The carpet was pale pink to match the roses.

The boudoir was also her bedroom.

Two curtains screened Mama's bed.

Those portières were also decorated with roses.

Many years later, when I was a student living permanently with my mother, I was laid up there with my second attack of measles.

The windows were curtained.

The sun shone through the curtains.

The room was bathed in a bright pink light.

Was it the fever?

Not just the fever: the lining of the curtains was also pink. Sunlight turned pink as it shone through them.

When you turn your head towards the sun and shut your eyes, or hold up your hand in front of a bright light, there is the same pink shining through the skin.

There is the same warm glow when you think of the nine-month-long state of bliss in the womb . . .

The pink light of the room blended with the heat and delirium of my fever.

Grandma's bedroom—I remember being in that room when I was very small—was all light blue.

---

* In French in the original.

Blue velvet on low armchairs and long blue hangings.

Did Grandma have a blue period?

And Mama a pink one?[2]

The hangings and furniture from Mama's boudoir are now in my dacha and coming to the end of their life.

The garlands are barely visible.

The upholstery has turned grey.

The fringe is missing in places on the chairs; at the bottom it looks like an upper jaw with missing teeth.

A grey period?

The divans, settees, couches—whatever they are called!—were littered here and there with books.

Most of them were the yellow books published by Calmann-Lévy.

Library books, taken out by a woman of decisive and independent views.

First of all: *La Nietzschéenne.* [3]

Then the obligatory *Sur la branche,* by Pierre Coulevain.[4]

And of course Bourget's *The Semi-Virgin,*[5] replacing *Twilight* by Dumas *fils.*

I did not open those yellow covers.

But suddenly, breaking the run of books about semi-virgins, I found somewhere a small book called *The Stages of Vice.* [6]

This is nothing less than a sympathetic story of a country girl who 'fell'; first on the Paris 'street'and then in a *maison close.**

Circumstance. Life. Morals.

What makes the book interesting is that it is full of photographs.

Illustrations such as those that, *um die Jahrhundertwende,*** as the Germans say, might fill an edition of Maupassant, Colette and Willy or Gyp. [7]

The ridiculous poses made the pictures charming; they showed these mistresses expecting 'visitors', falling asleep in their wretched mansards after 'work', drinking their morning chocolate, or at their toilette.

And there are a few documentary photographs: luxurious

---

* French: literally 'closed house', meaning 'brothel'
** German: 'at the turn of the century'

beds with cheekily naked, gilt cupids at each corner.

I have loved photographic illustrations of the nineties since I was in nappies. Papa had masses of albums from Paris.

And a particularly large number were to do with the *Exposition Universelle* in 1900.

I knew my *Exposition Universelle* from cover to cover by heart, no worse indeed than I knew the 'Our Father'!

These were probably the first photomontages I ever held.

The principle of these photographs consisted of shooting the models one at a time in different poses, then mounting them all on to a background which was either a photograph, or had been painted.

There was 'Offstage at the *café-chantant*', where the figures represented famous stars, in the extremely revealing costumes of queens of the night, cats with fluffy ears; a jockey, or a marquis.

And of course the fireman—*le pompier*—with a huge false moustache.

Or it was 'Le Foyer de l'Opéra', crowded with men in *hauts de forme* * and high-society ladies in silk wraps, in a sea of lace flounces.

Sometimes it was a carnival; then everyone wore a mask.

Or a general view of a firework display.

Then the characters were enraptured and it was quite clear that the lighting and the source of light did not match and that they were looking in quite a different direction from where one might have expected.

These 'montages' were printed in different tones: pale orange, lilac, sepia, greyish-green.

Perhaps my interest in montage began growing from that point, although the actual type of composite picture is significantly older.

The twenties and thirties of the last century had seen charming patterns of pictures made out of parts of engravings.

Folding fireside screens and flat fireguards were typically decorated in this manner.

Such screens, made in the 'forties, I remember, were still in

---

* French: 'top hats'

use in 1927, in the parts of the Winter Palace that were not a museum.

And Lord Byron once had screens like that—with the portraits of the best English actors playing their best roles.

The fascination with making these composite pictures, together with the art of cutting out silhouettes, began in the middle of the *dix-huitième siècle** with Moreau le Jeune, Eysen and Gravelot.[8]

This pastime was called *découpage* and pictures showing ladies doing this have survived.

Another sort of photo album was constructed on another principle.

As distinct from 'Paris La Nuit', 'Le Moulin Rouge', 'Le Casino', and so on, with Loë Fuller, Jane Avril, the Cake-Walk, the Matchish, Can-Can and so on—the sisters of those contemporaries of photography, the posters and lithographs of Toulouse-Lautrec—some albums had names like 'Le Rêve', or 'Le Rendez-vous', etc, etc.

These albums were as good as cinema.

Page after page of a girl—in bed.

The girl wakes up.

Stretches.

Daydreams.

There she is, washing.

Now she has thrown on a smart blouse.

There she is, doing up her corset.

Etc, etc.

Now she is waiting for her knight in shining armour.

He has not turned up.

The pictures follow each other with the same logical progression as that amazing series of six small canvases by Goya depicting the story of Margorotto, the robber.

Here, the robber is attacking a defenceless monk.

Here the monk suddenly puts up unexpected resistance.

Here, even more unexpectedly, the monk throws the robber.

---

* French: 'eighteenth century'

The robber is put under guard . . .

The photographic illustrations in *The Stages of Vice* followed the second sort of album.

The Stages of Vice is indelibly stamped on my memory.

(There are other books on this principle too, such as *Comment on nous vole, comment on nous tue,** where these studio photographs show '*ces demoiselles*' robbing their clients, as well as elegantly murdering representative types of '*ces messieurs*' with a lump of lead in the heel of a stocking!)

And my imagination was troubled by *The Stages of Vice* until I realised, to my unspeakable surprise, in the Rue Blomet in Paris, chez Madame Aline in Marseilles, or in the Maison des Nations in the Rue Chabanne, that that is how life really is.

More surprisingly still, little has changed over these thirty to forty years.

And in the carved, gilt beds in the Maison des Nations one can discern the twin brothers of the shameless *bambini*** who laughed at you in your childhood from the pages of that book.

In fact, that is not entirely the case.

The corsets have gone, and so have the fluffed-up hairdos with the roller on the forehead.

The dazzling stockings, with the broad strip running round, have also gone.

And the awkward white knee-length *pan-pans**** have vanished forever.

But these are . . . technical details.

Two other books turned up among Mama's settees and divans.

I glanced inside them.

More than once.

But with trepidation.

With a certain excitement.

Mingled with fear.

And these books were carefully wedged between the back and the seat of the chairs and divans.

---

* French: 'How we are robbed, how we are murdered.'
** Italian: 'children'
*** French: 'pantaloons'

To make it seem more natural, cushions were placed on top. Mama's handiwork, richelieu embroidery.

(The patterns were cut out, and held together by a system of very thin strips. How many similar patterns did I stick together for Mama, from magazines! And how many did I later combine, or independently create, myself!)

These books were hidden partly from embarrassment and partly from fear of what was within.

Not because I wanted to be able to put my hands on them at any moment . . .

There was something frightening about these books.

They were *The Garden of Torments* by Octave Mirbeau, and *Venus in Furs* by Sacher-Masoch (the latter was even illustrated).[9]

These were the first pictures of an 'unhealthy sensuality' that I found.

I came across Krafft-Ebing somewhat later.

But I still have a morbid aversion to the first two.

I sometimes wonder why I never play games of chance.

And I do not think it is because I am just not predisposed to gamble.

More likely, the very opposite.

Sometimes you are 'afraid of being scared.'

I used to find that, when I was a child.

I was not afraid of the dark; I was afraid I would wake up in the dark and be frightened!

Which is why I give games of chance a wide berth.

I am afraid that once I start playing, I will not be able to stop.

I remember very clearly being in this pale pink boudoir with the garlands of roses and taking an avid interest in the stock market reports, when Mama decided to stake a smallish sum of 'spare cash' on stocks and shares . . .

I was right to flee Mirbeau and Masoch, who were reaching out for me.

An alarming streak of brutality had been aroused within me even earlier in my life.

Strangely, it was a living impression. But a living impression from the screen!

It was one of the very first pictures I saw. Probably made by Pathé.

In the home of the blacksmith—a billet.

The time: the Napoleonic Wars.

The blacksmith's young wife deceived her husband with a young sergeant of the 'Empire'.

The husband found out.

He caught the sergeant.

Tied him up.

Threw him into the hay loft.

Ripped his coat.

Exposed his shoulder.

And . . . branded him there.

I remember it vividly: the bare shoulder, the huge square iron rod in the muscular hands of the smith with black sideburns and the white smoke (or steam) rising from the burn.

The sergeant collapsed, unconscious.

The smith brought the police.

Before them lay an unconscious man with a bared shoulder.

On the shoulder . . . was a convict's brand.

The sergeant was trussed up like a fugitive.

He was gaoled, in Toulon.

The finale was heroic and sentimental.

The forge caught fire.

The former sergeant saved the smith's wife.

The 'shameful brand' vanished as the flesh burned.

When did the forge burn down? Was it many years later?

Whom did the sergeant save: the smith himself too, or just his wife?

Who pardoned the convict?

I don't remember any of that.

But the scene with the branding still remains ineradicable in my memory.

It gave me nightmares when I was young.

I dreamed about it at night.

Once, I was the sergeant.

Another time, the smith.

I grabbed hold of my own shoulder.

The death of the Grand Princess Yelena Glinskaya. Detail by Eisenstein for the prologue to *Ivan the Terrible*. Alma-Ata, 5 October 1942

Sometimes, I thought it was my own.

And sometimes, someone else's.

And it became uncertain who was branding whom.

For many years, I had only to see fair curly hair (the sergeant was blond) or black sideburns and Napoleonic overcoats for that scene to come to mind. Then I formed a passion for the Empire style.

For a time the ocean of brutalities in which my pictures are steeped could not drown (like the sea of fire which consumed the convict's brand) those early impressions of the vicious film and the two novels from which it doubtless in some way took its source . . .

Nor should it be forgotten that I spent my childhood in Riga during the heat of the events of 1905.

And there are as many terrible and brutal impressions as you could wish for all around: the wild outburst of reaction and repression from men like Meller-Zakomelsky and his accomplices. [10]

Even more important, the brutality in my pictures is indissolubly tied up with the theme of social injustice, and revolt against it . . .

Monsieur, madame et bébé.

Here is yet another title of a book which was very popular in those years.

But I beg your pardon!

I have not only not read or seen this book yet: I do not even know what it is about. I think it was slightly scandalous—at any rate *un peu risqué.*

I only knew it by its title.

I would like to group, under this title, some thoughts that have lately been occupying me a considerable amount.

This title fits them admirably!

But of course, as always, the title of the book brought with it the circle of books from which it was taken.

The books drew in their wake the small tables and chairs which they were scattered upon.

Carpets rolled under the chairs.

Windows appeared at the sides.

Curtains covered them.

The sun shone through them.

And the whole was bathed in the pink, warm opacity of memories.

The pink light between the drawn curtains evoked the image of a mother's bosom.

And strange though it may seem, it is only that and the heading 'Monsieur, madame et bébé' that wholly suit what I want to write about.

But before writing about what I want to—about *Monsieur, madame et bébé* vis-à-vis myself—I want to talk about that in relation to ecstasy.

I came to the subject of ecstasy through that of pathos. [11]

I came to the subject of pathos when trying to rationalise my work on *Potemkin.*

The formula came about readily and of its own accord.

Pathos is when all the component elements are in a state of ecstasy.

In Russian, ecstasy—'ex-stasis' [*is-stuplenie*]—literally means 'stepping outside oneself', 'leaving oneself.'

I was then very interested in 'orthographism'. [12]

I supposed (wholly reasonably) that a true dynamic picture of a phenomenon is typically (very often) reinforced by the verbal definition of the act itself.

This began with the analysis of a mechanical formula for the dynamic of expressive movement. [13]

Here this proposition is proved exactly.

Because a symbol which we are used to considering as figuratively abstract in fact continues to be the symbol of movement which has been stamped by the dynamic process of this expressive movement.

When one has to analyse the motive (the general 'algebraic' formula) that corresponds to a given emotional condition, 'it is enough to read literally' the symbol that man has 'figuratively' reinforced by a verbal symbol for a particular condition.

Because of all the 'arithmetical' nuances of individual cases, 'aversion' [*otvrashchenie*] constitutes a comprehensive 'general' formula of the motive process, which expresses this condition internally: a-version (just as, invariably, *ot-vrashchenie*, *Ab-scheu*), su[b]-spicion, dis-dain, and so on.

The expressive movement that spills out of the 'human system' into space, becomes *mise-en-scène*.

Mise-en-scène is a spatial, metaphorical outline, the sense of which must be read by the viewer.

'Tailing' someone is expressed spatially by preserving the distance between the spy and the object.

The uniformity of the distance conveys the idea of the 'linkage', 'attachment' of one to the other, hence the figurative reading that the second is 'inseparable' from the first.

(N.B. Uniformity of distance may be roughly, crudely literal. But a 'correct' solution here of course will be a dynamically constant distance: that is, a constant average of changing physical intervals:

Not: but:

_____   ____

_____   _____ ___

_____   _____ __

_____   ____

The first way is for analysis.

The second way however is for 'creation': correctly 'naming' the formula, and then 'expanding' it into a construction.)

'Naming' it correctly is only possible when you have sensed it *precisely*, experienced it *precisely*, etc, etc.

All of this has been set out and described in the appropriate place. [14]

And this method later becomes applicable to all questions of form.

Finally, the form itself begins to be read as a 'literal'

reading of the formula of the 'content'.

And I applied this device of etymological analysis—the return of the abstract term to the dynamic picture that gave rise to it—to the range of phenomena such as 'ecstasy' with the greatest excitement.

I tested it in practice.

And the accuracy of this reading (and of the actual mode of reading) was verified at each step.

In pathos, each element stands outside itself.

This has been set out in detail in three sketches 'On the Structure of Things'.[15]

I could here provide a quotation for the order of things:

> Pathos is what makes the viewer leap from his seat. It is what makes him jump. It is what makes him throw up his arms and shout. It is what makes his eyes sparkle in delight, before that same feeling makes him cry. In a word, it is everything that makes the viewer 'come out of himself'.

Put more elegantly, we could say that the effect of pathos in a work is to bring the viewer to ecstasy. Formulating it like that adds nothing new, for in the three lines written above is exactly the same ex-, which means exactly the same as our 'coming out of oneself', or coming out of one's usual state.

All the above-mentioned signs follow this formula faithfully: from sitting to standing; immobility to violent movement; silence to shouting; dullness to brightness; dryness to moisture. All of these are a 'coming out of oneself', 'departure from one state'.

Furthermore, 'leaving oneself' is not 'a departure into the void'. 'Leaving oneself' has to mean entering something different, something of a different quality, something contrasting with what came before (immobility into movement; silence into resonance, etc).

Thus, even from the most superficial description of an ecstatic effect which a pathetic construction may induce, it is clear what must be the basic indication marking the construction of a composition of pathos.

Princess Yevfrosiniya Staritskaya standing over Vladimir, her son who has been murdered. The finale of *Ivan the Terrible* Part Two. (Photo: Viktor Dombrovsky)

In this system, one must be able to observe the condition of 'coming out of oneself' in every instance, and of a constant transition into some different quality.

But this is just a part of the problem—the one I most need—the 'operational' problem.

I call my 'system of aesthetics', which I might eventually assemble, an 'operational aesthetic'.

How to do it.

How to 'do' the pathos clearly.

But for a full picture of ecstasy, you must be clear about the question of the psychological state that constitutes ecstasy.

It is accurate enough to call it the 'behavioural process' connected to ecstasy; that may not be the whole answer, but it points us in the right direction.

The phrase we always use is 'bathed in ecstasy'.

Despite the fact that ecstasy is a state of 'upliftedness', 'exaltation'.

Of course, a purely orthographic analysis is inadequate here.

To understand just how comprehensively precise is the verbal element of this procedural, dynamic symbol which goes with ecstasy, the first thing to do is undertake a huge survey of the works of the great masters who 'immersed' themselves in ecstasy.

There is the psychological repertoire adduced in commentaries for spiritual exercises; the equality between the mechanism of psychic meditation and the basic physical system in the practice of the Khlysts,[16] the dervishes or Mexican *danzantes*. Juxtaposing the Eastern and the Western practices. The Indian ecstatics, Buddha and Nirvana. The ecstasy of the prophets of ancient Judaea and of the mass psychosis at Lourdes, etc, etc.

I soon hit upon the idea of Nirvana and how it might be explained as a psychological state: returning to the embryonic condition.

More time was spent on an all-embracing scrutiny of this than on an assimilation of the phenomenon itself.

My thanks to psychoanalysts who have preceded me on this path.

For here is the key which the verb 'immersed' holds to an

understanding of the phenomenon.

And here is the key for the proper understanding of the verb itself!

A return to the embryonic state!

That accounts for the psychic picture of how one feels when in ecstasy.

But what is interesting is not the inert, lifeless condition induced by ecstasy.

The moment of 'illumination' is what is interesting.

Not the length of the 'stay'.

But the climactic flash.

Emergence.

Ecstasy can be very briefly formulated as participation in the 'emergence', and also as dialectic understands it: the moment of transition from quantity into quality; the moment of a (sensation) of unity arising in a multiplicity, the moment when a unity is formed from opposites.

When does this moment occur, within the parameters of a human individual's experience?

It is that point which, as personal experience, is contained with the whole of its original force, at each moment of analogous situations on later paths of the human individual's emergence and development.

Naturally, that point naturally shoots out at the very first moment of life within the womb—at the lowest threshold and within it.

At the moment when the future human individual is implanted in the womb.

A fair amount has been written about being in the womb (for example, Doctor Alexander on 'Nirvana' in *Imago*).[17]

Rank, in *Das Trauma der Geburt* [The Trauma of Birth], has written beautifully about 'emerging into the light'.

I cannot remember anything of the divinity 'of the first spark'.*

But the 'illumination'—the moment within the limits of personal experience—is of course here.

---

* In English in the original.

And precisely here, in one moment, 'in the moment' . . . *monsieur, madame et bébé.*

According to Hegel, *monsieur et madame* destroy their own selves and their opposite qualities merge into one.

And the physical bearer of this unity—*bébé*—comes into being at this moment.

The question of illumination (and all ecstatics speak of memories of a blinding light) is explained with elegant simplicity.

It is one's first trauma and it always merges in one's conscious (preconscious?), sense (foresense?), memory (pre-memory?) with the second chief trauma—the trauma of birth, the trauma of coming into the light (Rank has written on this exhaustively).

These traumas merge into one: after all, time has no meaning during the nine months spent in the womb! The starting point and the finishing point are the same!

(I omitted earlier to mention a most remarkable author—Ferenczi[18]—who expounded all of this in his *Versuch einer Genitaltheorie* and who also raised at this point the question of the death-wish. And also the regression, through 'aspects' of animate nature, to the level of . . . the inanimate!)

Pathos can be very briefly read as a degree.

Not as something evolutionarily separate from other, less intense aspects of the state of poetic material.

But as something organically integral having differing degrees and an inevitable quality of novelty at a certain level of quantitative intensity.

We can immediately draw conclusions from this.

The pathetic uplift, the explosion of pathos, is momentary —it is only a conjunction of those traits, which, taken *legato** determine the general effect.

And the intensity turns out to be directly proportional to the degree of separation.

A crowd experiences unity at the (pathetic) moment of the outburst—pathetically.

But the unity of the crowd (for instance, the people) can appear gradually, in a leak (as opposed to an explosion!) from the

---

* Italian: 'smoothly'

voluminous work of history.

In both places there will be awareness of the unity.

The emotional coloration of this awareness and sensation will be of one and the same kind.

But the condition will be of a fundamentally different degree.

The same thing happens with means and method.

And the gradual transition, let us say, from opposite to opposite, will be just as essential a basis for exerting influence; but the spirit of the explosive leap will flow not in the appearance (not in the form) in the pathetic work, but will 'fluidly' descend the scale of spontaneous intensity, in forms ranging from novel to short story and chronicle, from tragedy to drama and play . . .

A jump of the multiplier, from normal speed to a deceleration, 'slow motion',* as a dynamic, cinematic means, is a plastic interpretation of the function of this diminishing intensity.

Imagine all three of these types of filming successively applied to one and the same phenomenon—an explosion!—and you will have the full picture.

The same clouds of smoke, the same girders and rails flying upwards, the same clouds of dust.

But an answering explosion of emotions in one (the first case) and fluid, perceptive contemplation in the other (the third).

The questions of the degree of immersion, of the degree of regression and of the degree of return to the 'zero' point, rest in the devices and means used.

And the explosion seems to have been fired with the camera running backwards to the starting point. Because only by returning to this zero can there be a new uplift; and the closer to the zero, the more complete and shattering will be the all-encompassing uplift!

The means of influence are like fragments from yet lower and lower-lying layers of consciousness (preconsciousness).

Neutral form is from the layers of consciousness on today's level.

Works have been deprived of their latent 'grip'* which is

---

* In English in the original.

characteristic of works that do not appeal to the 'lower layers* of consciousness and the emotions.

Orthodox form is like a fragment from the layers of primitive thought.

Pathetic form is buried in the 'profoundest layers',* beyond the limits of sensual thought: instinctive, vasomotive, electrical, chemical and physical phenomena.

*A noter!!** Here, form also embraces the concept of subject —one of the primary ways of realising the desires to be expressed.

The Revenger's Tragedy, for example, can serve as a thematic example of the third case; the realisation of an original, physical law of each action having an equal and opposite reaction. And the scene of the chase is born of instinct—the hunter's instinct.

As Herman Melville puts it so well in *Moby Dick*: '. . . for I believe that much of a man's character will be found betokened in his backbone. I would rather feel your spine than your skull, whoever you are . . .' (from the chapter about the actual extraction of spermaceti from a whale's head). [19]

And it is these very layers of my influence that I attack with my harpoon.

And I try to penetrate them more and more deeply.

But my means are fragments from those layers, for it is only through these fragments that I can make these layers vibrate in unison with my will.

But 'backbone'* and 'spine'* are layers on a par with the embryonic state, repeating the general curve of development, modification and growth of forms and appearances as one grows into the other.

So much for the ways and types of an operational aesthetic.

But maybe it is the same in a psychological sketch?

Perhaps a merging that is legitimate, natural, and crucial— *monsieur, madame et bébé*—at the crucial moment when life's mystery emerges—at the point of the conception—can also reach further; also be observed far beyond the limits of that moment, because of its *legato* reach, in life's slow current?

---

*   In English in the original.
** French: 'N. B.'

Which is what my elaborately expressed discourse has led to.

'That is how I feel!'*

It may be racial.

It may be individual, psychological.

My beloved '*raza de bronce*'—the bronze race of the Mexican Indian is just that.

The masculine frenzy of temper, the feminine softness of outline hiding a steel musculature and the outer muscles flowing around it; and the disposition to forgive coupled with a childish naughtiness—this combination of features in the Mexican Indian makes either him or her—*muchacho* or *muchacha*** forever a continuing unity of *monsieur, madame et bébé*.

Adult men and women seem adolescent in comparison with other races; a race of young people, where the men have not yet lost their early femininity, nor the women abandoned their puerile pranks and both seem charmingly childish.

I mean of course the ideal, pure, collective, synthetic type and the best examples of the women and men, youths and girls, who passed before my camera and before me, during the long months of my wanderings about the strange and wonderful, harsh and tender, childishly delightful Mexico.

I sometimes think that I am, *tout à la fois,**** monsieur, madame et bébé*.

Alas, not only at times of pathetic exaltation.

But even on occasional days of industrious productivity, when, like an inquisitive child, I break into the dense layers surrounding the secrets of my work with a decisive, masterful arm; and then, with the hands of a bustling housewife I try to reassemble the fragments of the broken stratum to insert them block by block into the conception.

Bricks or blocks?

Into a serious matter, or a childish plaything?

But more often I suffer from the melancholy infantilism of an overgrown child, ridiculous and helpless, pitiable and insignifi-

---

* In English in the original.
** Spanish: 'boy' or 'girl'
*** French: 'all at once'

cant in his clashes with life.

Eternally tied to Papa and Mama (again, as I am)—to two people who were sick to death of each other, after living together as husband and wife; spouses whom neither Tsar, God nor any hero could liberate and free from each other; who were not even able to kill each other and were doomed to pay for it eternally with a lacklustre, humdrum existence; the threefold portrait of *monsieur, madame et bébé.* A grotesque caricature of the divine moment when man's threefold nature comes into one, at the very moment of the explosion of ecstasy . . .

Pre-Natal Experience[1*]

Il fut nourri par une chèvre et conserva longtemps des allures brusques et sautillards de sa nourrice . . .[**]

And just think!

None, none of this might ever have happened!

None of the sufferings, searchings, heartaches, or spasmodic moments of creative joy! And all because there was an orchestra playing at the Ogins' dacha at Majorenhof.

Everyone had drunk far too much that evening. A fight broke out and someone was killed.

Papa grabbed his revolver and dashed across Morskaya Street to restore order.

Mama, who was pregnant with me, was scared to death and almost gave birth prematurely.

A few days passed in the fear of possible *fausses couches*.[***]

But that did not happen.

I made my entrance into this world at the allotted hour, albeit three whole weeks early.

And my haste and my love of gunshots and orchestras have remained with me ever since.

Not one of my films goes by without a murder.

It is of course hard to imagine that this episode could have left any impression on me *avant la lettre*.[****]

But a fact is a fact.

My interest in the pre-natal stage of being has always been very strong.

It quickly extended to the invisible aspect of being.

I became interested in the stages of biological development that preceded the stage of man!

---

[*]   In English in the original
[**] French: 'He was suckled by a goat and preserved for a long time the jerky hopping gait of his nanny...' A. Dumas *père*, 'Eugène Sue', *Les Morts vont vite* [The Dead Go Quickly], II, i. (E's reference)
[***] French: 'miscarriages'
[****] French : 'before the event'

In the USA, 1930

More than that, my range of interests took in early forms of social relations; pre-class, primitive society and the forms of behaviour and thought peculiar to it.

It was because they repeated the surviving fragments of all the stages in our consciousness, thought and behaviour that I found these areas so rewarding.

To the Illustrious Memory of the Marquis[1]

'We're having pancakes today.'

   'A soldier came to our house today.'

   'So? We're having pancakes today!'

   'And we had a soldier come!'

The two little boys in the old story boasted to each other long and hard.

   'We're having pancakes today!'

   'Well? We had a soldier!'

They boast long.

They boast hard.

Until one gives in and starts to whine.

Boasting like that is a typically boyish characteristic.

But, as we established at the outset that the little boy in me is still alive, it is only to be expected that all these pages should be full of boasting, either latent or overt.

   I boast on one page that we are having pancakes today.

   On another, that a soldier came to our house.

   I do not only boast about successes and 'merits'.

   But equally about misfortunes and flaws.

   People find all sorts of things to boast about.

   Father's medal.

   A cousin's wooden leg.

   Uncle's sideburns. Grandpa's beard. Aunt Nadya's glass eye.

   A missing finger.

   A pulled tooth.

   An appendectomy.

   And doing yourself down is often of no less value than making an honourable mention.

   This is sometimes done in a calculated way.

   Tom Sawyer for example, who boasted that it was a great honour having to paint the fence.

   He could sell the right to take part in this worthy enterprise to that crowd of gawping, envious onlookers, if the price was high enough.

Sometimes this is the result of a terrible inner compulsion to banish (through boasting) the spectre of personal inadequacy that haunts the majority of us, just waiting for a chance to bite into our souls with a row of small celluloid teeth such as you might find on fur wraps.

I remember the case of Nikita Bogoslovsky, one of our most trenchant satirists, who also wrote music.[2] It was I who delivered him the *coup de grâce*, or better still, *le mot qui tue.*[*]

'Everyone is like an animal of some sort. Some are like bears, others like foxes, some like spiders.

'But Nikita is like a . . . boa.'

This was so close to the mark that he could not even get angry, hurtful though it was.

And I once 'cut' Utyosov with a neat twist.[3]

He once said: 'Eisenstein is a sexual mystic.'

'Better a sexual mystic, than a mystical waiter',[4] I replied (surprising myself with the speed of the retort).

So much for my own wit: I now move on to boast about my 'unrealised proposals'.

These are distinct from 'unrealised productions', that is to say those which were not only conceived and proposed, but even 'given a treatment', to the extent that some of the ideas were developed.

The following list concerns only those subjects and proposals which, at the very most, occupied us for no more than one or two days in proposal meetings and discussions, before being dropped for good.

Some will anyway inevitably come up again as such things do in the most varied of contexts, but it is amusing trying to assemble the most colourful and unusual of them in one place.

Most of them, as is quite logical, begin at the point when we were leaving for Berlin in 1929 on our way to the USA.

The first proposal was also, perhaps, the most extravagant.

We received a visit from a man who was enormously tall, thin and athletic.

---

[*]   French:'the deadly taunt'

511

He was the advertising manager of Nestlé, a Swiss firm, and his area of responsibility was condensed milk.

He had watched *The Old and the New* the previous day, and said that never before had he seen such a heartfelt expression of the essence of milk on screen.

The proposal: an advertisement for his company.

The material: a journey round the world.

The theme: whatever you like—even none at all.

The essential condition: to show that the children of Africa, India, Japan, Australia, Greenland and so on drink Nestlé's condensed milk.

We parted company, as I recall, over the size of the . . . *per diems.*

(But the 'difference' naturally ran much deeper: Soviet power had not made me a film director for that sort of thing!)

Our trade headquarters in Paris was on the Rue d'Astor.

In 1929 there was no film department there.

But there was a sales and distribution office for minerals and diamonds from the Urals.

That department was run by a morose and deadly dull man.

Part of his job included dealing with the sale of our films.

He floundered, utterly helplessly, when it came to the commercial side of our films, although I think he took the credit for exposing one of the most malicious and unusual forms of sabotage to affect his department.

The circumstances, roughly, were these.

Superstition has no place in our country—it was dispelled by our materialist world view and has been banished into the dim and unpleasant past.

But this has nothing to do with the interests of our export trade.

And, if there are peoples and nations who suppose that seven stone elephants in decreasing sizes—even if they come from a society such as ours—can bring them the bloom of bourgeois happiness, then who are we to deny them this? Why stop exporting these *porte-bonheur** bracelets which bring us money? (Particularly in the 1930s, when hard currency was in such short supply that no

---

* French: 'lucky charm'

more than $25 could be taken out of the country for personal purposes, irrespective of the length of the journey. My journey around the world for 28 months on just $25 is a story for another time!)

The seven elephants were carved from malachite, nephrite, chalcedony or topaz.

They were carefully packed.

Then transported world-wide in the unseaworthy vessels of the Soviet Merchant Navy.

But the wretched elephants would not sell.

Why not?

They just did not sell.

First, the customers in the shops did not want them.

Then the shops stopped stocking them.

And at last the wholesalers stopped ordering them.

Perhaps they boycotted them because of their country of origin?

But there was no indication of where they were made!

Perhaps they did not bring good luck?

But they were not bought; the efficacy of their miracle-working powers was not even tested.

They were just not bought.

At the same time, hundreds of sets of seven elephants made in Holland, Germany (Meissen) and Copenhagen were leaving the shelves . . .

What the devil?!

The mountains of carved elephants grew and multiplied.

They filled warehouses and stockrooms.

You could have cobbled whole streets with them.

When suddenly light dawned.

The trunks.

It turned out that only those elephants who carried their trunks jauntily aloft brought good luck.

If the trunk dangled sadly, it could not bring happiness or joy.

And the Soviet elephant was sold in all our overseas markets with its trunk stubbornly lowered.

The ill-starred model had a change of image, being refitted with a triumphantly raised trunk. It more than held its own with the competition from Holland, Copenhagen, Meissen and Dresden in the world markets.

The calibre of the fighting elephants may have dwindled since the days of ·Tamerlane's invasion, but their aggressiveness is undiminished . . .

One fine day the man who traded in diamonds made me an official proposal.

I was considered a specialist in historical pictures.

Belgium had been an independent country for one hundred years.

And the Belgian government would have liked to see a commemorative film of its centenary, made by me.

This of course prepared me for the invitation to go to Venezuela and shoot a commemorative film dedicated to the illustrious memory of the South American freedom fighter, Bolivar.[5]

Oddly, in London, Grierson was asked to pass on an invitation from the Colonial Office that ran the Empire.[6]

It was proposed that I film . . . Africa.

The one stipulation being that I showed that English colonial power led to cultural development and prosperity for the blacks!!!

Grierson was too diplomatic to relay this to me!

I only learned about it later and regretted that Grierson's tact was greater than his sense of humour: to think of what I could have said in reply to such an idea!

When, much later, I was on the border in Nuevo Laredo, between the two countries of Mexico and America (which refused to re-admit me for six whole weeks), I received an invitation to film a history of the state of Texas, with the undertaking that the local ranch owners would let me have as many horses as need be.

(I have given full details regarding that in a more appropriate place, as a digression in my Paris *Epopée*.)

The first subject proposed to me in Hollywood was the martyrdom of the Jesuit missionaries at the hands of the Red Indians; the last themes were *Jew Süss* and Remarque's *Return* [Der Weg zurück].

The talks went no further.

This also happened with *Grand Hotel* and *The Life of Zola*, which Paramount was talking me into while I was still in Paris sign-

514

ing the contract.

And in Paris I was discreetly approached by an intermediary (one of those jewellers on the Rue de la Paix who, like that merchant in the Bible, sold everything to acquire one single stone, a diamond beyond compare,[7] displayed in the window among drapes of dark velvet) with the proposal from Chaliapin that he and I make *Don Quixote*.[8]

'Fyodor Ivanovich is very excited by the idea of working in cinema and would want to try it out with a Russian, at any rate.'

It was Pabst who made the film later, and Fyodor Ivanovich was as unconvincing there as he was once magnificent in this role in the theatre.

When I was in the middle of filming *Que Viva México!* in Mérida, Yucatán, I was sent a proposal by my former Paramount supervisor to go to India and make Kipling's *Kim*!

Poor Mr Bachman had probably never heard of such things as visas or viceroys.

This curious episode reminds me of another.

Our friend Jascha Schatzow lived in Berlin.

As Herr Schatzow, he is a representative for Debrie, the cine camera manufacturers who cover all Europe.

In the autumn of 1929, Schatzow and I debated quite seriously the question of a film for. . . . dogs.

He was interested by this, but it was the commercial possibilities of the venture that first appealed to him, bearing in mind that Berliners of both sexes were very fond of their dogs—and there was a colossal number of dogs in Berlin.

If one of the most picturesque graveyards in Paris is the one for dogs in Auteuil, then why should Berlin not have its own charmingly appointed dogs' cinema?

This thought occupied me, of course, purely from the point of view of a reflex testing of a series of filmic elements (the degree of suggestiveness, questions of rhythm, 'form', which would all be different from our customary system of thinking and imagery, and so on).

The project of course remained just that, going no further than two conversations: one in Schatzow's amazing billiard room in his house, and one in a night club in the west of Berlin.

What could be more extreme?

But even this was not the most unexpected or hilarious thing a film-maker could be offered.

The crowning glory was proposed by Jean C[octeau] the poet, in Paris, in the spring of 1930.

The proposal was to direct and film. Where? Marseilles, itself! And what? 'There is only one sort of film you could make in Marseilles!'

Ça, c'est le comble! *

Oddly, out of all the offers, this one was the most 'feasible' as it had financial backing. The Vicomte de N. was very keen to sponsor it.[9]

Well, in this case, of course, we did not even reach the discussion stage.

I never even met the Vicomte.

Come to think of it, the Vicomte was deeply preoccupied with another matter. Vicomte de N. was a direct descendant of the famous Marquis de S. On either the female or the male side.

And the Vicomte's villa was literally crammed with editions dedicated to the illustrious memory of his ancestor, the Marquis.

In fact, the Marquis' memory was not at all illustrious, but quite the opposite. It was besmirched.

And the Vicomte had set himself the task of . . . rehabilitating the illustrious memory of his great and glorious ancestor.

Which explained the countless editions of *Justine* and *Juliette, The Philosophy of the Boudoir* and *Nights of Sodom* which filled the drawing rooms and bedrooms of the Vicomte's villa.

Maids, wearing white aprons and starched caps, scurried noiselessly among them (as they do in good houses), no doubt catching a sideways glimpse of a few lines of startling text, printed in the large typeface of plush, contemporary editions.

The subject matter of these lines would later form the subject of excited kitchen talk. And I can picture the smooth-shaven servant with bluish cheeks making a penetrating retort to the cries of the cooks and dishwashers: 'So what? In our village . . .'

And even children, it seems, stuck their noses into them, doubtless staggered by the fantastical woodcuts of the eighteenth-

---

* French: 'There's the rub'

century Dutch pocket editions. 'So what? In our school . . . !'

Apropos that, I had a funny experience with one such book on a trip abroad.

At the moment of my departure in 1929, as I stood on the platform, a charming lady—a former opera actress, Rtishcheva—brought me a tiny box—'for your journey'.

Inside was not 'calico and brocade' [10] but a branch of vine and a golden, overripe Duchesse pear.

A tiny volume was concealed beneath the branch and the juicy, bulging fruit.

On the title page Rtishcheva had written 'Just think! Pushkin could once have held this little book!' [11]

And on the half-title page, in a French dialect, was *A New Justine, or Virtue Persecuted.*

This was one volume out of eight, the full edition of *Justine* that sold for many years under the counter, costing an average 2,000 roubles the set.

It had illustrations, which were mostly coffee-stained.

The funniest one was where the hero timed his own release to coincide with the explosion of his boat which he had set on fire, which lent his harmless pastime a unique synchronisation.

But the most *risqué* one absolutely beggared belief.

Oddly, this unorthodox breviary travelled with me on almost all my travels across America and Europe, at the bottom of various suitcases, but I saw it for only the second time when I was in Stolbtsy—a Soviet customs official had taken it out.

You can imagine how my blood ran cold.

But a miracle occurred: the pages of the book obligingly cleaved to each of the illustrations, concealing them as surely as if they were in envelopes or, like the author, trapped in the Bastille. They thus evaded the official's vigilant eye, as his fingers conscientiously flicked through the little book.

In the descriptions of my adventures in Paris, you will find a digression on the miracle of the 'little saint'—St Theresa of Lisieux.

That is the account of how the 'little saint' obligingly provided us with petrol. [12]

Could I call the event at the border town Stolbtsy the

'miracle of St Justine'?!

The atheistic, blasphemous Marquis would have been delighted by such a name!

Jean-Jacques Brousson is of course absolutely worthless, from both a personal and literary point of view.

But his *Anatole France in His Dressing-Gown*, written in the style of Léon Gozlan's *Balzac in Slippers*, is one of the most charming books a reader could hope to find.[13]

I do not agree with the point of the criticism some Frenchman made of this work, although the criticism itself is brilliant in form and style. I quote from memory:

> . . . One man was charged with carrying out another's chamber-pot each night. Instead he carefully stored up the contents. Then, after making his own contribution, he published it. That is what Mr Brousson's *Anatole France in His Dressing-Gown* is . . .

Journey to Buenos Aires was much weaker, but it played so vital a role in the ups and downs of the graph of my life that I will deal with it quite thoroughly elsewhere.

Less famous of course is the collection of small novellas by Brousson. And incidentally they do not deserve special mention.

Only one is amusing, and that is probably a literary retelling of *Boutade* [The Whim] which was once done by the master himself.

(I found the master in Brousson's first work particularly attractive, probably because his nature so strongly resembled that of my own master—Vsevolod Emilevich!)

The hero of this novella is the Marquis: freed from the Bastille and now in his declining years, he vanished into one of the 'Paradises' kept by Madame N. N., and the 'Peyesottes' paid a visit, with their famous ostrich feathers and little *étui de nacre*,* and Mirabeau, famous as the author of *Journal d'un débauché*.[14]

'Teacher! Teach us!' the 'Magdalenes' cried out as one, kneeling—they had been educated by the works of their great and

---

* French: 'mother-of-pearl box'

unexpected client.

The master tried to do so.

But fruitlessly.

He was flung out on to the street in disgrace . . . There was a lot of cerebral anger in this apocrypha, which Brousson had doubtless heard from his master himself . . .

. . . But nothing could stop the Vicomte and Vicomtesse from working on their ancestor's rehabilitation (*de leur illustre an-cêtre*).

I shall leave the poet, the Vicomte and his wife, half pro-tected behind their initials.

The famous ancestor has no need of this.

His works, scattered about the villa, speak for themselves.

The illustrious ancestor of course is the Marquis de Sade.

It could of course transpire that he is only the spiritual forebear of the Vicomte, and the Vicomte himself has in reality an-other title.

But I would like to dwell here less on a description of the unrealised 'creative' meeting with the great-nephew than on the question of my long-lived 'creative partnership' with the 'great-uncle' himself.

Incidentally, Mr Gorman's biography[15] wittily exonerates the Marquis, calling him the learned predecessor of Dr Freud, and explaining his novels as the only available form in the eighteenth century for disquisitions into case histories of psychoses and patho-logical portraits of a particular proclivity!

However, the history of this partnership demands some in-troductory lines of explanation.

Some enthusiasts bequeathe their skeletons to scientific in-stitutes.

'For science.'

Others—the majority—do so for financial gain: the skele-ton is worked to death for a corresponding payment during one's lifetime; the money is spent on living, or more often, in view of the size of the payment, drinking; and, after death, the vendor takes the rap for his bones and instead of a comfortable internment underground, they are fated to stand in a glass case, held together by thin wire clips as an excellent, prepared skeleton.

But underlying both these impulses is a third.

Ex-hi-bi-tio-nism!

Albeit exhibitionism of a most unusual and idiosyncratic variety.

The *ne plus ultra.*

Exhibitionism, to the marrow of one's bones.

Literally.

Come to think of it, there is a greater degree yet.

To set out for inspection, not your 'bone structure', but the ins and outs of your psychical construction.

Not a skeletal, but a psychological exhibitionism!

I would ask all that follows to be ascribed also to that.

There is a reason for my favourite joke not appearing in any collections along the lines of 'The Best-Loved Jokes of Famous People', although of course it is the joke that would best typify the luminaries in the constellations of film stars.

Incidentally, this little story concerns male film stars.

A 'star' once took his charming girlfriend out to dinner.

Having spent all dinner talking only about himself, he remembered himself over dessert and with condescending grace turned attentively and solicitously to his companion and said, inclining his head:

'I have spent all evening talking about myself.

'Let's talk about you.

'What do you think about me?'

Nobody can interrupt my monologue.

Let me take advantage of that.

An unfair advantage!

I shall move brazenly onwards.

I shall be my own horn, gramophone, and record.

Incidentally, talking of gramophones, it—the gramophone —has gone through three distinct phases; three completely different social relationships.

First, with its large, fluted horn, blue, pink, or green, it travelled in triumph through my childhood years as a treasured novelty of technology.

Then it was branded a banal vulgarity; it was only in the cheapest resorts that records of 'ta-ra-ra boom-dee-ay' hoarsely blared out through gramophone horns; spots near Oserki or Pargolovo, which proudly proclaimed themselves Finland, since the train that went there went also to Helsinki, Vyborg, Kelomjakki or Kuokkalu from the Finland Station.

At last the 'third age' dawned, and it took everyday life by storm: a portable, the gramophone's younger brother; it had discarded its brightly-coloured horn like a mammoth freed from its excess of tusk and become a domestic elephant.

My friends from the older generation even now sometimes get the names mixed up.

And my neighbour in Chistye Prudy, a respectable telecommunications engineer who was later given a medal, was not indignant at the noise of the foxtrots which were brought over together with the Flexatone[16] (the *dernier cri*[*] in fashion in 1926) or the portable from Berlin, but the fact of my passion for the 'vulgar amusement of . . . the gramophone.'

And, awesome, exciting, inspiring, frightening, but attracting, too—after the 'isms' in art (Impressionism, Expressionism, Futurism, Dadaism, etc., etc.), a new pack of quite different 'isms' swept across the land, freed from the shackles of inhibitions and unleashed upon a troubled populace by a professor from Vienna and his zealous colleagues and pupils.

Infantilism, narcissism, sadism, masochism, exhibitionism, etc., etc.—these strange words, at first passed on in a whisper down the line, later overran the pages of specialist publishers' specialist magazines to enter the more general sphere of medical and psychological literature. Later still they broke into *belles-lettres* and theatre; replacing the harlequins and columbines of the era of 'reborn theatricality', Hasenclever's[17] *Murder* [Mord] or *Reunion in Vienna* had psychoanalysts running about on stage, and O'Neill's *Strange Interlude* showed us a ponderous, painstaking repeat for the American stage of what had once, long ago, been done wittily, inoffensively and most of all, with a lightness of touch by Yevreinov's Distorting Mirror Theatre, on the Catherine Canal, in the small piece *What They Think, What They Say*.

Strange though it may seem, this came into fashion much

---

[*] French: 'last word'

later in cinema, apart from *Secrets of a Soul* [Geheimnisse einer Seele, Germany, 1926] with Werner Krauss. The real 'vogue'* in cinema for treating this sort of problem on screen coincided with the Second World War, which brought *Spellbound* [USA, 1945] and *The Seventh Veil* [Great Britain, 1945] in the mid-40s and *Lady in the Dark* [USA, 1944], slightly earlier.

Then in the wake of universal recognition came the 'utter rejection' of psychoanalysis and this 'vogue' abruptly ended.

The gains it had made in methods of treatment had been minimal and science had made still fewer advances in understanding inner, psychic life. But nothing at all had been uncovered that shed any light on its application to art.

In 1932, the Vienna Psychoanalytical Publishing House was closed down, and huge quantities of books on this subject were remaindered.

Words ending in 'ism' began to die out and it soon became unfashionable at tea parties to mention the actual 'complexes' that these terms stood for. They ended up on the scrap-heap of vulgarities, somewhere near the fluted pink gramophone horns, corsets from the 1890s, two- and three-seater tandems, and that pastime called 'Diabolo'[18] which everyone raved about until the 1914 war; or skating rinks (where you could smash your kneecaps against asphalt) shortly after the 1905 revolution and the Russo-Japanese War.

I do not know whether one can (or indeed should) expect a widespread 'renaissance' of the principles and ideas of Freud's school, albeit in a revised and purified form.

That school always did seem somewhat 'transitory'; a 'halt' on the way to an attainment of a much wider and deeper grounding, of which sex would be merely one facet among many.

For all that it is particularly accessible and titillating, it is a very limited facet. And this is not only with respect to the 'right' wing, where the socially progressive cycles of human development are given prominence, but also to the 'left'—the biological stages preceding the happy little 'Paradism' of individual erotic bliss, within the limits assigned to 'the human individual'.[19]

---

* In English in the original.

And as regards the actual psychoanalytical 'jargon' of the '20s and the general notions themselves which it signifies, these notions have acquired—through years of use—the 'quaintness' that surrounds everything that has vanished in the past, so I do not shrink from using the jargon in the way that old soldiers breezily talk of redoubts and flèches; old sailors of topgallants; and old ladies about the bustles, *accroche-coeurs*,* bugles** and whalebone, which they grew up with.

Without wishing to boast, I can say that many millions of viewers have seen *Potemkin*.

The most diverse peoples, from the furthest corners of the globe.

And I expect many felt a catch in their throats during the mourning scene over Vakulinchuk's corpse. But I doubt that even one of those millions saw and remembered a tiny piece of montage in some frames of that scene.

Not actually in that one, but the one when the grief turns into anger and the people's fury bursts out at an angry protest meeting around the ward.

An 'explosion' in art, and particularly a 'pathetic' emotional outburst, is constructed according to the very same formulae as a detonation of explosives. I once learned about this in the ensigns' school for engineers in the classes on mines.

There, as here, you need first a build-up of electrical charge (of course the actual means vary, and there is no universal schema!).

Then the constricting framework explodes. And the impact sends the myriad fragments flying.

Oddly, this effect does not take place if you do not interlay, between the build-up and the actual picture of matter flying in all directions, that indispensable 'accentuated' piece which clearly 'signals' the explosion. In a real explosion, this is the role of the detonator cap, just as essential in the rear part of a rifle cartridge as it is in the packets of gun-wadding strapped to the girder of a railway bridge.

---

*   French: 'ringlets'
** i.e. strings of pearls

Filming the sequence 'the death of Aba' for *The Battleship Potemkin*

Such pieces are to be found throughout *Potemkin*.

At the start of the 'Steps' scene there is a large caption: the word 'SUDDENLY!' Then this is followed by the aggressively edited shot of the nodding head, in three different sizes, composed from three short montage-cell pieces.

(This incidentally is a close-up of Olga Ivanovna, Grisha Alexandrov's first wife!) Here, this also gives the impression of a salvo of rifles 'shattering' the silence.

(It was a silent film, and this is one of the ways of creating an effect in silent cinema; a way of representing the first salvo that should roar out 'off camera'!)

The emotional outburst of the finale of the 'Steps' sequence is caused by a shell flying from a gun muzzle—the first explosion which acts as detonator for the purposes of one's perception, before the wrought-iron gates and the pillars of the abandoned dacha at Maly Fontan are blown apart: the second and last 'actual' explosion. (Lions stand between them. These images by themselves illustrate the metaphorical role of compositional construction well enough. And in this regard they have every right to be included in the article 'On the Structure of Objects' which deals with the composition of *Potemkin.*)[20]

There is a similar accent in the leap from the mourning on the shore to the anger of the sailors who come running to a meeting on the deck of the battleship.

It is a very short section, probably not even perceived as a 'subject' but only as a purely dynamic accent—the unambiguous ictus on the frame which is not there long enough to be discerned and for one to make out what is happening. This is what happens: in that very section a young lad tears his shirt in a paroxysm of fury.

This section is like a climax, inserted at the right point between the furious student and the fists—already shaking—flying above the sailors' heads. (In the shot list for *Potemkin,* this section is identified in the third part, No. 761.)

The anger of the people on shore explodes into the anger of the sailors' meeting on deck and now the red flag is hoisted above the 'Potemkin'.

But I am not as interested in the flag as in the section with the torn shirt.

And not as an accent, which is so traditional that it was applied to the rending of the curtain in the temple at the climactic moment of a very ancient tragedy being enacted between the three crosses on Golgotha.[21]

But as an element from my own life.

The point was that, as I said somewhere earlier, sadism for me all comes 'from books'.

I learned about sadism not from children's games as happens, for example, so charmingly with Dostoyevsky's Netochka Nezvanova, which followed the similar 'first impressions' of David Copperfield, Nicolas Nickleby and other children whom the sentimental Dickens made suffer.

My first impressions of sadism were 'from books'; the first situations to suggest themselves to me came not from life or personal experience but were 'reflected' and 'refracted'.

The inseparable companion of the neurosis linked to the illustrious memory of the Marquis de Sade—Jean-Jacques Rousseau's masochism—is said to date from a whipping he received from a certain mademoiselle when he was at that age when, as the Germans put it, *das lustbetonte Gefühl** was making its appearance felt, and not merely as the sensation of pain.

Jean-Jacques described this feeling with ample ex-hi-bi-tionism in his *Confessions*, although he did not have at his disposal even then the whole wealth of nuances that we have.

Anyway, *das lustbetonte Gefühl* did not accompany any pain I may have experienced in an analogous situation.

Although, as far as I recall, I was also given hidings as a child.

Admittedly on only two occasions.

I can hardly recall the first. The main thing I can remember was everything else, apart from the sensation of pain . . . and the offence which led to the hiding.

I was very young, but my memory has retained all the details of the 'encirclement' very vividly.

First, in 'close-up', were Ozols's—Father's messenger's—

---

* German: 'lust-tinged emotion'

green cuffs and buttonholes as he held me by the legs. (I was lying on the bench of my *pupitre**—a recent present.)

I was unused to seeing Ozols doing any sort of work of this nature.

Papa would ensconce himself in an armchair holding a huge register and Ozols would reach up to the top of the wardrobe where the strange rabbit-hutch contraption with the countless pigeon-holes was kept.

The most recent structure of this sort benefiting (or not) from a difference in size, but still providing a full representation of its general character, is the Hotel Moscow, which has completely wrecked the poetry of the Okhotny Ryad of the 'Gribkovs' and the other delicatessens which, during NEP, were still to be found in Moscow, just across from the Iberian Gate and the marvellous Iberia Street (which did a particularly brisk trade in just about anything, from matches and suspenders, to dolls and cocaine).[22]

Each cell of the structure (and there were either twenty-four, thirty-six or forty-eight) held one pair of shiny black boots.

Papa would only wear shiny, black boots with square toes.

He did not acknowledge any other sort.

And he had a huge collection of them, 'for every occasion'.

He even listed them in a register, with any distinguishing features indicated: 'new'; 'old'; 'a scratch'.

From time to time he held an inspection and roll-call.

Then Ozols would slide up and down, opening wide the gates of this boot-garage. But on that occasion these hands held me.

Somewhere between the corridor and the dining-room (the execution was carried out in the dining room), I could hear Salome, the cook, whispering with the maid Minna: they had been admitted too, no doubt to add to my moral humiliation.

The names Salome and Minna are so closely linked in my memory with servants that for many years Lessing's *Minna von Barnhelm* was bound up with eggs and spinach and chicken 'bits' (which was how we used to call that dish made from chicken hearts and stomachs at home).

---

* French: 'writing-desk'

Stills from the scene of 'the demonstration over Vakulinchuk's body, from *The Battleship Potemkin*

It was worse with Salome: it took a supreme effort to divorce the name of our lean, miracle-working cook from the play by Wilde and Beardsley's drawings (I read somewhere recently of the hatred the two felt for each other, to the effect that the latter had done the illustrations for *Salome* as parody!).

My second thrashing came a little later, but before my schooldays began and with much less ceremony.

I remember here being half naked—only my trousers were down.

I remember the 'weapon'—a strap folded three times: normally it went round my little dog's neck when he was taken for walks. He was a little thing, a toy: in those days toy terriers were fashionable.

Mama was the executioner.

And it had absolutely no effect whatsoever.

I laughed cheekily the whole time, although my cheekiness alone deserved punishment.

I had been thoroughly obnoxious to my French (or English?) governess on a walk in Strelkovy Park.

It was worse for Eton schoolboys.

The severity with which this privileged school hardens its young gentlemen was quite monstrous in the very recent past.

There were no sheets or mattresses in the dormitories.

Hordes of rats lived under the floorboards.

In 18** the floors of one building were lifted for repairs. Underneath, a whole layer of bones was discovered.

Nothing alarming about that.

They were not human. They were the bones of animals and birds; the remains of dinners which rats had dragged under the flooring.

The town squares of Novgorod were made with animal bones; in particular, Veche Square,[23] near the Torgovaya district. But we should bear in mind that this was not in Queen Victoria's time, but Alexander Nevsky's—the thirteenth century.

All that remains at Eton of the old arrangement now are the windows of the first class, which have not been glazed since the time of Elizabeth I and have only . . . iron shutters.

I saw this 'system', except using wooden shutters with

unglazed windows, in the homes of poor blacks which lined the wide metalled freeway—'Millionaires' Row'—from New York to Florida, or on those parts of it where it cut through the 'black belt' of the negro states.

But the beams and desks of the building are made from real masts and bowsprits . . . taken from the Spanish Armada which 'Redheaded Bess' donated to this ancient educational establishment.

By working a penknife in between the cracks in one of those pillars, one pupil—on the day before the holidays when we visited the school—drew out a small note in genuine Elizabethan handwriting, written on real Elizabethan parchment . . .

And there is a storeroom with canes too.

Although it seems more for form's sake than a practicality, they are still used at Eton.

And below, in the schoolroom, beneath the iron shutters of one of the unglazed windows, stands a small wooden step-ladder with three rungs.

The victim kneels on it, bending over obediently.

And, as he does so, the ancient rule dictates, 'there shall be nothing between the birch and the body.'

And in accordance with this same rulebook, after the execution the victim's parents are sent a bill for the administration of 'the school's medicine'.

It would seem that the medicine dispensed here was more effective than that which Mama and Papa tried to administer to me: on the whole it failed.

And my first impressions of cruelty were, as I have said, reflections from books.

However, before the true literary impressions—Octave Mirbeau's novel (what did I say?! and now I do not feel like writing out the full title *The Garden of Torments*, just as I prefer to write the subtitle *Venus in Furs*, and when it comes to the outline of the name von Sacher-Masoch, I have first to overcome certain internal inhibitions!)—there came cinematic ones.

But a whole new chain of associations linked Octave Mirbeau to the unhappy fate of the French sergeant on the screen.

I remember three which were especially strong.

The first was an article from the 'Diary of Events'.

I think it came from the *Peterburgskaya gazeta* [The Petersburg Gazette] which Papa took. I was regularly able to read Breshko-Breshkovsky's horrifyingly cheap satirical column, before the paper was sent off to Papa's bedroom.[24]

The article was about the savage revenge a group of butchers took on a shop assistant who had either complained to the manager about their abuses or had threatened to do so.

The drunken butchers dragged him into the back room of the empty shop.

They stripped him. Hung him by his legs from a hook in the ceiling.

Then they began to flay him with a double hook, the sort used for hanging carcases up. Skin came off in chunks.

How this 'event' finished for the young man—whether his screams brought the neighbours running and how these 'monsters' were punished—I have no recollection.

Probably because I simply read no further than that . . .

But the man hanging by his legs and the butcher's hook were still indissolubly linked to images which disturbed me not so much at night as in the daytime.

This picture would suddenly appear before my eyes; the text book, novel or saw (I was still doing fretwork at that time) would fall from my hands.

I would stare fixedly and see before me the drunken butchers (particularly brutal was the ringleader), the hanging body and the terrifying hook.

It is interesting to note that I never 'saw' any blood during this.

Chunks of flesh were torn from the body like wax, leaving bloody strips, but they were not saturated with blood.

I expect it was this image that gave rise to my predilection for St Sebastian.

This St Sebastian—the shop assistant from the 'Diary of Events' hanging upside-down(!)—is a frequent visitor to the pages of my works.

St Sebastian often crops up in drawings I do almost automatically.

The butcher, one of the Black Hundreds. Still taken for *1905*

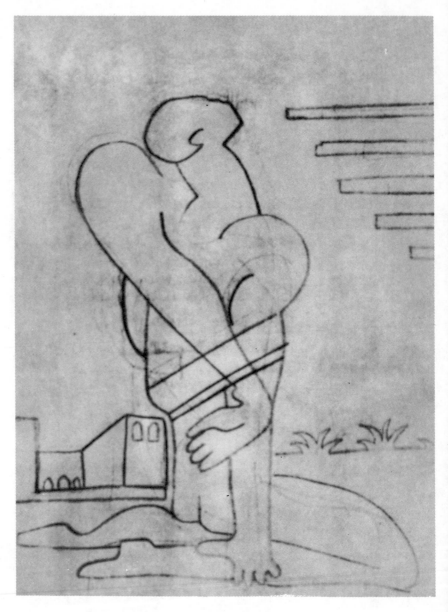

Sebastian. Eisenstein's drawing for *Que Viva México!*

In my Mexican film I named the peon who was martyred in the fields of agave Sebastian; he died in excruciating agony, after suffering all manner of torture, being buried up to his shoulders and trampled beneath the hooves of the *hacendado's* horses.

In *Ivan the Terrible*, the Tatar prisoners were hung on palings like St Sebastian; they were furthermore pierced by what are clearly stage arrows. (However, this episode also has its own peculiar roots, of which more later.)

But before being realised in the scenes of my own works, images taken from a whole series of external, real, visual impressions augmented my inventions of the shop assistant's harrowing fate.

These images were without number . . . fragments of 'Pinkertons', *The Caves of Leuchtweiss*, or the adventures of Nick Carter and Ethel King.[25]

Apart from the news-stands, which sold literature like this on every street corner even in Riga (as was the right of every civilised town in my childhood), there was also a book shop in Riga that had a separate window display for *belles-lettres* of this variety.

The window was horizontal and low down—no higher than a second-year schoolboy of average height, which was far-sighted and expedient!

The *recherché* display of German editions of Pinkertons was changed weekly.

The newspaper salesmen dealt in Russian ones.

The German editions were of a different format and brighter.

The most popular was Nick Carter.

This was at a time when anti-Chinese feeling ran especially high in detective fiction, a reaction to the then famous series of gangland murders in the New York and San Francisco Chinatowns and the all-but-forgotten 'atrocities' of the Boxer Rebellion.

Which was why on the covers almost every week villains with pigtails featured in the various hopeless situations in which Nick found himself.

The covers had a terrifying, magnetic force.

And I remember being unable to take my eyes off those horrors behind the glass, but standing there for ages.

Other covers were worse than the ones with Chinamen.

I remember a shining rainbow-bright cover with a picture of a sarcophagus, filled with molten tin.

Nick Carter was suspended above it, hands and feet tied up in the position of the soldiers about to be put on the rack in Callot's engravings.

On one side was a lady, her dress in disarray, wearing a short skirt (or petticoat?), her bodice undone.

She had one arm stretched out as she took aim.

And the caption read:

'If Nick doesn't tell her what she wants to know, she'll shoot through the rope . . .'

The tin bubbled with hospitality, ready for the doomed Nick.

Another cover was even more fantastical.

It showed an underground park full of various implements of torture. Collars were chained to the walls.

Each collar gripped tightly the neck of a young man who was stripped to the waist.

They all had well-groomed hair with a parting.

And their one item of clothing—their trousers—were perfectly creased.

The cover was pale lilac.

There was also a series of pocket-format magazines about Ethel King, an energetic sleuth who went everywhere at great speed. She was just as popular as Nick Carter.

In one picture she managed to trap the villains near the ant-hill where they buried their victims head down. One was still tied by his feet to a tree trunk.

But the other was already apparently swarming with ants; he was drawing his last breath in one corner of the picture.

Elsewhere, she burst through the ceiling of an operating theatre—this time holding a machine-gun!

The victim was lying on the table, strapped down by a gang of villains while some of them made precise incisions in his bare, athletic torso.

Small rivulets of red blood snaked out from under their knives . . .

This scene recalls the half-believable story of Amaro, the one-eyed general who once came to see us as head of the War Office.[26]

The Mexicans are adept at inventing and embroidering on the truth while looking most sincere—they probably even believe what they say!

Anyway, General Amaro, who had peon blood, was the model for the boy who witnessed the execution of his own father (at the start of the film *Viva Villa!*) and vowed to dedicate his whole life to avenging him and to subject the landlord to the same fate.

In the film, this boy grew up to become the all-powerful and fearsome Pancho Villa.[27]

This actually happened to General Amaro who was promoted to senior command posts during the Civil War and took his revenge on the *hacendado* who had brutally killed his father. They say that, as he swore vengeance, the young Amaro put a metal ring through his ear. He vowed he would not remove it until he had settled the score with the landowner.

Allegedly, after killing the landowner he tore the ring out.

There are people who confirm that this scar on General Amaro's ear can still be seen.

There is a character like him in my Mexican film.

(It was filmed and came out before *Viva Villa!*)[28]

In my Mexican film, the boy witnessed the execution of his older comrades at the end.

The future avenger walked away through the fields of maguey, for the present suppressing his pain, hatred and wish for vengeance . . .

This ending, superficially similar to Chaplin (but essentially diametrically opposed), was linked to the idea that the revolution in Mexico was still unfinished and that the day of reckoning for the peon's situation—no legal rights, miserable living conditions and inferior status—was still a long way off . . .

Incidentally, the young Felix Olvera, who played this boy, used to arrive in a police car during the last period of the filming.

The village policeman would sit in the shade of the agave, lazily smoking cheap tobacco, his rifle carelessly propped up between his knees and at sunset he would take young Olvera back behind prison bars.

Felix was fascinated by the old fashioned sort of large-bore pistol, a 1910 model, which he used in the film.

Young Felix found the temptation irresistible. One day the pistol vanished.

No one would have noticed anything had the unlucky kid not thought of bragging about the pistol to his sister.

There were live rounds in the gun. That day we were filming close-ups of the landlords' lackeys skirmishing with a group of rebellious peons surrounded in an agave bush.

The bullets thudded into the fleshy body of the maguey, which opened its oily lamina like the arms of a crucifix, torn and shot through, and flowed with blood before the cruel lasso and coarse ropes pulled down the doomed fugitives, led by Sebastian.

Felix Olvera shot his own sister.

And, exactly like the peons in my film—who were driven mad by fear—he ran into the limitless expanse of maguey.

A desperate chase ensued.

The landowner's *vaqueros*, raising pillars of dust, were in close pursuit between the bushes.

The old ladies howled for the dead girl.

The girls howled, fearing for the bronzed Felix.

In the slanting rays of sunset, Felix was taken back to the hacienda, roped to the saddle.

Blood streamed from his temple.

Paolino, proudly riding abreast, had knocked him to the ground with a blow from his pistol. His ugly pockmarked mutt, gap-toothed jaws and black sideburns resembled something by Goya.

The wearer of this terrible face, Paolino (the local barber by profession), was a most kindly man but his face, flushed with the excitement of the chase, really looked terrifying in the ruddy rays of the sun.

We did not allow them to shoot Olvera.

But a few days later, when we had 'greased' the *deputado's* palm, we were able to bring poor Felix out with us each day for filming.

This required a few extra pesos for the policeman accompanying him.

On holidays Olvera was not released to us.

According to an ancient custom, he was treated the same as other prisoners on those days . . . he served at table in the house of the omnipotent local administrator, who was the magnate in this tiny region.

Via the *hacendado*, this *deputado* made it clear to us in all seriousness that, if it became necessary ('and the papers all talk of the realism of your films, my señors') for anyone . . . to be shot, a couple of prisoners could be provided for that purpose—from the same prison where our friend Olvera later ended up!

The oddest thing was that we could have taken these criminals and coolly bumped them off and this would never have been of the least concern to anyone.

And this brings us back to the story of General Amaro.

Filming the festival of flowers on the canals between the floating gardens of Xochimilco (there is now some worry that these gardens are beginning to sink), we dressed, in especially valuable headwear and lace mantillas and coats, a certain dazzling, dark-eyed, voluptuously beautiful señorita of not too strict morals.

She was not just any señorita.

She was the one whose name was linked, in a legendary (or perhaps not?) piece of gossip, with General Amaro.

For quite some time she had been Marquise de Pompadour and Madame Dubarry for the all-powerful General.

She then had a secret affair.

The General learned of this.

But he did not let on.

One fine day in an outburst of simulated expansiveness the General presented his favourite with a newly-built country villa set in luxuriant grounds.

Our heroine moved in.

Life went on as before.

The same infidelities.

The same boredom when they—General Amaro and her unlawful lover—were both occupied of an evening.

Then—a walk in the park.

Aimless walks around the house.

And later—as in *Bluebeard*—a little door.[29]

Of course, there was nothing stopping her from looking within.

It was as though her even discovering the door had not been foreseen, never mind her actually going inside.

The door was shut.

Doors do not remain closed for long . . .

And the señorita froze in horror: deep in the cellars of her own house, her eyes took in a perfectly equipped . . . operating theatre.

Gleaming tiles.

A shining tray of surgical instruments.

Chloroform and rubber gloves at the ready. White aprons were near by . . .

What happened next eludes me.

I vaguely remember that the girl fled in panic.

This happened, albeit coincidentally, with perfect timing.

For the General had given the order that both the girl's arms—left and right—were to be amputated at the shoulder that very night! Every possible precaution was to be taken; the very latest surgical techniques were to be employed; absolutely no pain was to be inflicted.

I could not testify to the truth of this story but, given the general conditions in that wonderful country, the details of poor Felix's fate and the *deputado* who so kindly offered me some 'real' prisoners to shoot, the story has a high degree of credibility . . .

(Interestingly, even the episode with the ants later appeared in *Viva Villa!*, when Villa spread honey over Joseph Schildkraut's[30] face—the latter was playing a typically swinish officer from a semi-aristocratic clique in the Mexican military.)

We set out on the deep roadstead off the 'cover town' of San Francisco, on our way towards the real heart of Mexico, away from Ethel King's operating table.

There was a third cover to join those of Ethel King and Nick Carter.

This was one I had at home.

I kept it between the pages of *The Boy's Own Paper Annual*.

And the unhappy butcher's assistant was portrayed here a third way: no longer hanging by his legs, nor chained to the wall by an iron collar, but stretched out on his back by some exotic savages amongst terrifying carved wooden fetishes.

The background consisted of impressions of Chinese executions from Wells's *War of the Worlds,* published at that time in *Mir priklyuchenii* [The World of Adventures], a free supplement in *Priroda i lyudi* [Nature and People] magazine which in those years was taken by families whose young sons were thirsty for Alexandre Dumas.

And perhaps also details of Damiens'[31] execution—he had tried to assassinate one of the Louis—reproduced from old engravings in a large book about crime and punishment.

I unearthed this work from one of Papa's bookcases, behind the stylish editions of Gorbunov, Krylov's *Fables* and *Evenings on a Farm near Dikanka.*[32]

This work, together with Dayot's edition of *The History of the Commune,* became one of the most interesting and intriguing.[33]

The retribution Damiens suffered was shown in full detail.

The special system of straps and chains which bound him permanently to a bed.

And the details of how four horses proved insufficient to tear him into four.

And how his sinews were pounded so that the horses could carry out their task.

And the sulphur and tin being poured into his wounds, etc., etc.

But the strongest impression was the white figure stretched between the exotic idols—a young Englishman, the son of a colonist.

Gradually, visual images failed to soothe these piquant impressions which floated before my consciousness.

The piquancy of the impressions began forcing me to recreate these scenes.

Comrades or partners were not to be drawn into this matter.

So the division between object and subject was erased.

There was no precise 'allocation' of roles.

And, since I was interested in the sensation of pain, I was obliged to inflict it upon myself.

And, since I was, on the other hand, interested in the sensation of causing pain, I could find no other subject than myself.

Anyway, I remember (not in the most illustrious and iridescent period of my childhood) lying stretched out on the floor with my feet stuck into the fireplace (it was not, it must be said, alight) a mixture of the young Englishman and Callot's engraving showing '*chauffeurs** of the 16th century who burned the heels of their victims to extort money. (I was not yet aware of Callot as Callot and I only knew of his work by chance.)

I never recreated the Hindu's bed of nails, probably because I never had enough nails. I was mad about the 'Nuremberg Maiden'.[34] But I was limited in practice by the fact that two or three logs were put beneath one's spine. Three-sided logs, with the apex uppermost. This was done for a purely realistic purpose, giving an otherwise purely decorative situation a certain amount of real pain.

Later another application of these three-sided logs attracted me: it was from trunks hewn exactly like those that they used to make the dolls at Troitse-Sergiev Posad (Zagorsk, as it is now called).[35] The 'Hussar', the 'Lady', the 'Nurse', adhering strictly to the costume and everyday style of the 1820s, also observed the rule whereby a figure's profile should end in a thin wedge—the same wedge that lay in later generations beneath the 'young Englishman's' spine.

I remember at other times hanging myself 'à la Nick Carter', on hooks after I had carefully removed the swing which usually hung in the doorway between the dining room and nursery.

And sometimes of course I hung . . . upside-down, tied to the nickel-plated knob of the family bed which had passed into my hands and been put in my room!

Funnily enough, my first erotic dream came from a Nick Carter-inspired fantasy.

It was a strange being, whose execution I felt very vividly as someone held its pigtail.

I remember the silhouette of the spine, shoulders and head, as it lay half-turned towards me with its pigtail held high up.

There had been some Chinese performers in the circus at

---

* The French in this case indicates people who heated things rather than driving them. [Ed.]

that time; they flew under the big top held by their pigtails and worked as 'catchers' for other members of the troupe.

These flights of course were much more impressive than those on the trapeze and the figure, spreadeagled like a cross of dark blue silk in mid-air and flying round under his almost invisible, black pigtail in the spot light, was a spectacle that held me spellbound.

And I was also at that time fixed on a couplet by Wun-Chi from his *The Geisha*, which also mentioned pigtails:

Chin-Chin
Chinamann
Ist ein armer Tropf.
Jed-jed
Jedermann
Zupft ihn gern am Zopf!*

But my dreams at night—involving a Chinaman, his pigtail and cruelty —probably came from fragments of the covers of such books as *The Dragons of San Francisco*, where the pigtails on the scalps of enigmatic oriental assassins were wound upwards like rattlesnakes, erect from the end of their bodies!

Any exercises in that genre, no matter of what hue, are usually rapidly developed and broadened from the moment when a child starts school.

Typically, schoolfriends are united by common interests; these shared interests and tastes bring them together and forge the bonds of friendship. This was not so in my case.

From that point of view, school was a hollow, unrewarding place.

That was because I was a horribly exemplary little boy.

I studied diligently.

---

* Chin-Chin
Chinaman
Is a wretched mug
Sim-simply
Anyone
Can give his tail a tug!

I did not permit myself 'democratic' friendships.

What was more, in that school there was a blatant national-ist hatred amongst the different sections of the population to which the pupils' parents belonged.

I belonged to the 'Colonists'; the Russian civil-servant class, detested equally by the native Latvian population and by the de-scendants of the first German colonists who had enslaved them.[36]

It should be remembered that Riga had been the residence of Bishop Albert and had been surrounded by knights of the Livonian and Teutonic Orders, whose 'shades from the past' I have been doing battle with on the screen for a good ten years![37]

I did not form a single true friendship in those school rooms.

Although, if I try very hard, I can discern a certain 'supposed' friendship, but it was very short-lived: a sentimental dis-position towards a schoolmate who was younger and more delicate than I; and to one other—a stronger, older boy who was the best gymnast and a desperate hooligan.

The former was brother to a vast number of sisters, all—like their father—of the same height as he, and who went about in woolly, dark green capes fastened by small chain-like buckles.

His mind was of an abstract, theoretical cast; his complex-ion was very pallid.

He was an excellent student, particularly in complex branches of mathematics and in such intricate historical problems as, for example, the derivation of the names of the Dnieper's rapids.

The latter was a muscular, dark-haired athlete. A homeless 'guest' who lodged with two or three others on full board with a French master who taught the younger classes—the ginger-haired Mr Görtchen; he was distinguished by his ginger moustache and a faulty pronunciation of the letter 'y'. (He pronounced the French 'y' like the French 'u'. I can still remember how the title of a typical lesson from the French textbook would grate on my nerves: 'Le Cygne et la cigogne' [The Swan and the Stork] became 'Le Cugne et la Cugogne'.

He was called Reichert and was a great gymnast.

I not only had no aptitude for this skill; I had a strongly

expressed aversion.

I remember, again in my very early childhood, even in my pre-school years, shouting for hours before being compelled (great pressure was brought to bear!) to go to gym classes at the Riga *Turnhalle*.*

A bald, bespectacled German—Herr Engels, lame in one leg—practised with us there and later in the *Realschule* (the gymnasium and the school building shared a yard).

My one clear memory of Herr Engels is that it was he who taught me my first two German palindromes, when I was interested in word-play.

I can vividly recall the term Relief Pfeiler, and the phrase:
*Ein Neger mit Gazelle zagt im Regen nie***

Sergei Sergeyevich Prokofiev was very fond of such word-play; it is to his staggering memory for such things that I am indebted for a whole range of French examples.

As far as music is concerned, I heard a similar palindrome in a work by Meisel, who wrote the faultless score for *Potemkin* and an entirely appropriate one for. *October*.[38]

When he was writing it—and to do so he attended the editing sessions in Moscow—the central heating in the screening-room was being repaired; there was an incredibly loud knocking throughout the building at No. 7 Maly Gnezdikovsky.[39]

I later derided Edmund for writing into the score not only visual effects, but also the plumbers' hammering.

The score fully justified my complaints!

And there was the trick with the 'palindromic' music.

The point is that the film begins with frames which half symbolise the overthrow of the autocracy, depicted by the toppling of the memorial to Alexander III next to the Church of Christ the Saviour.

Both church and statue have long since vanished, but for many years the eagles from the throne's plinth lay scattered about the park in front of the Pushkin Museum.

---

* German: 'grammar school'.
** A palindrome in German which translates literally as: 'A negro with a gazelle never hesitates in the rain.' An English equivalent would be: 'Able was I ere I saw Elba.'

So, in 1927, a *papier mâché* model of the statue was made; it was very funny watching it fall over and disintegrate.

This 'collapse' of the statue was shot 'in reverse' at the same time. The throne, with its armless and legless torso flew up on to its pedestal. Legs and arms, sceptre and orb flew up to join themselves on. Looking dully ahead, the figure of Alexander III sat inviolate on the throne once more.

This was shot for the scene of Kornilov's Petrograd offensive in the autumn of 1917 and these frames showed what all the reactionaries, who associated the General's possible success with the restoration of the monarchy, dreamed about.

The scene went into the film in that form too.

And for that scene Edmund Meisel recorded the music in reverse, the same music that had been played 'normally' at the start.

Visually the scene was a great success. Filming in reverse is always very diverting and I remember how the first old comic films made good use of this device.

Perhaps I recognised my first, early childhood impressions in this disrespectful treatment of the Tsar!

But I do not suppose anyone noticed this musical trick.

Relations between Meisel and myself later soured.

Not of course because of that; nor even because he messed up a public screening of *Potemkin* in London in the autumn of '29, when he ran the speed of the projector to suit the music, without my consent, slightly more slowly than it should have been!

This destroyed the dynamism of the rhythmic correlation to such an extent that people laughed at the 'flying lions' for the first time in the film's existence.

The time allowed for the three, different lions to merge into one was crucial: if it took any longer than that, the artifice would be spotted.

The reason for the split was his wife, Frau Elisabeth; she was unable to hide—indeed, in an inexplicable outburst, confessed to her husband—a certain liaison that had existed between her and the director of the film for which he had written the music.

In all other respects, my lame gym teacher ended badly.

I must confess that to my great satisfaction he ended up no

more and no less than a quartermaster in the German army and, apart from teaching gym, he had a whole series of secondary commitments in Riga to do with the information service.

At the outbreak of World War One, Herr Engels was removed from the gym and so on.

There were all the prerequisites for a genuine friendship with Reichert in my dealings with him, if one could go only by the number of times he and I fought so very furiously.

However, it was not easy for friendship to develop since our time together was confined to school hours, talking on the way home, and in doorways.

I was not allowed to invite a 'nasty boy' home, still less take part in the escapades of a group of boys where he was one of the live wires.

These diversions were of the very sort which I was particularly keen on and which he often invited me to join in, on Sunday mornings in spring.

The kids would divide into two gangs, and play at warring bandits each Sunday, going into the countryside as a matter of course; there was a beautiful spot on the shore of Lake Stint, among the luxuriant pine forests of what then was called Kaiserwald.

Sometimes I even went there for picnics—with Fräulein and my friends from 'good families'—decorously, sedately, with pies and sandwiches.

This place is now called Meza Park; it is there you will find the most prosperous suburbs of Riga.[40]

The game of bandits consisted of the members of one gang taking those of the other prisoner and 'hanging' them mercilessly.

They were not of course hanged by the neck, but were tied to tree-trunks by ropes passed under their arms.

That was the high point of this game of chase and pursuit, fighting and escaping into clumps of bushes on the lake shore, between the uniform trunks of pines.

You can imagine how I would have loved to play at games like these!

You can imagine that even the merest hint at my playing at

such games was *ausgeschlossen** by the strict family régime we had.

It is highly questionable whether this is the best way to bring children up.

Instead of giving instincts free rein and the individual the chance to let off steam, a complex of all sorts of impressions was retained instead of being jettisoned through play or adventure, or being sublimated, without leaving any trace. In the best cases, fleeting memories or impressions—and not only these—settled, or lodged like splinters, or interwove with others. As many years passed they changed their form; they emerged, reworked, in the unexpected shapes, deviations and stylistic peculiarities of an individual outline and genre which led my American hosts to offer, as the first subject for me to tackle in California . . . a biography of those Jesuit missionaries who had died agonising deaths at the hands of Red Indians. And this in turn led to the fascistic descendants of the old Ku-Klux-Klan and the precursors of the Silver Shirts, crying out, in Major Pease's phraseology, for the expulsion of this 'sadist' and 'red dog' Eisenstein from the United States. His presence in America was 'more dangerous even than a massed enemy landing'![41]

However . . .

Any delayed reaction that is not immediately discarded with a triumphant 'Ah!' or some similar spontaneity becomes the very thing which accumulates, builds up and swirls around within us, just waiting for the right external trigger to precipitate a storm, torrent or hailstorm of images, collected by an organising will into the purposeful invincibility of a consciously created work . . .

Was there once a glint of cruelty in my games with my friends outside school?

Of all the 'reconstructions' of Nick Carter covers, I can only very vaguely remember just one case.

It was in Bilderlingshof, on the Riga coast; or even further afield, in Bullen, where the parents of my friend, Baron Tusenhausen, had a dacha.[42]

Near the dacha was another, small house whose boilers and pipes gave it the appearance of a wash-house.

---

* German: 'ruled out'

The Baron's son moved amongst its pipes and boilers, 'in my production', stripped to the waist and wearing a cap; I think he had been taken captive by some hard-hearted villain who was forcing him to print counterfeit banknotes.

But the game came to nothing since, once an outline had been created that followed relatively closely one of the above-mentioned lilac covers, I was quite satisfied with the look of the scene itself. I had never gone into the plot, a scene from which was illustrated on the cover, in any depth—indeed I had not read it at all!

This touches on a feature which is, generally speaking, quite a common one of mine.

I form very sharp pictures of what I am reading or thinking about.

This is where a very big store of visual images is created; an acutely visual memory with a lot of 'day dreaming'* training: I transpose my thoughts or memories into film form and run them past my eyes.

Even now, as I write, my hand essentially is virtually taking in the outline of the pictures that pass before my eyes in a continuous spool of visual images and events.

These acutely visual images cry out intensely and painfully to be expressed on the page.

Once, I was the only means: the object and subject of such reproductions!

Now I have a good 3,000 man-units assisting me in this; I can raise bridges in the city, deploy squadrons at sea, stampede herds of animals and set things on fire.

But a certain hint of 'generality' remains: very often it is quite enough for me to recreate the general visual image that alarms me—albeit not in every detail—for me to rest, contented.

But this often acts as a 'barrier' too against the other elements of expression, which cannot travel the same intensive path of creativity as the visual side of my opera. Music—particularly Prokofiev's or Wagner's—also counts as 'visual' in this taxonomy (or would it be more accurate to term it 'sensual'?).

There is a reason for the quantity of paper, ink and inspira-

---

* In English in the original.

tion I expend on film, searching for a formula to express the relationship between sound and vision![43]

And from another point of view there was a reason for my total dedication to questions of 'sensual' thought and the sensual bases of form. The sharpest focus of my attention rarely alights on the word 'subtext'. It is obvious and axiomatic that the intensity of my interests in different elements of composition and construction fluctuates.

But I prefer such a 'disequilibrium' to a classically strict equilibrium of elements. The beauty of one area's excessive prominence compensates for flaws and shortcomings elsewhere.

But this does not mean that the 'primacy' of audiovisual elements in my works shows a bias towards form at the expense of . . . content, as any idiot might think at this point.

The audiovisual image is the extreme border of self-disclosure around the fundamental motivating theme and the ideas of the work . . .

This corresponds to the classics, where none of the connecting links is ignored: in Gogol for example, the subject extends to the actual verbal fabric of the work; or to the metaphorical system of Shakespeare's texts, as any Shakespeare scholar knows.

Here I remember one more summer when, in the decorous setting of Frau Koppitz's guest-house in Edinburg,[44] where I met Maxim Strauch, I tried to 'bring to life' yet another colourless recreation of my schoolfriends' games: this time it was their game of robbers in the Kaiserwald, where I was not allowed to go.

The external trigger was an uncontrolled 'feudal' war with the neighbouring pension, where another crowd of boys was staying; they were led by a sickly but desperate lout with big ears and the auspicious nickname 'The Jumping Jug'.

In fact it was just before this—in the winter—that I saw a turn at the circus which my memory retained in every detail.

I have liked clowns since my nursery days.

I have always been a little shy about this.

Papa also loved the circus, but he went to see the 'highest class of horsemanship', and William Truzzi's 'group of dressage horses'.

Three clowns: Gorodulin, the fascist (Ivan Pyriev), Joffre, the warmongering general (Alexander Antonov) and Mamayev, the white émigré (Maxim Strauch) in Eisenstein's play *Enough Simplicity for Every Wise Man*. The First Workers' Theatre, Proletkult, 1923.

I assiduously hid my fascination for clowns and pretended to be madly captivated by the horses!

In 1922 I repaid my debt to myself with interest, literally 'flooding' my first, independent show, *Wise Man*, with red and white clowns.

Mother Glumova was a red clown.

Glumov was a white clown.

Krutitsky was a white clown.

Mamayev was a white clown.

All the servants were red clowns.

Turusina also red, and so on.

(Mashenka, the strong-woman act, used a powerfully-built girl who was a relative from Riga—Vera Muzykant.[45]

Kurchayev—a 'trio' of hussars in pink tricots and 'lion-tamer's' dress coats.

Gorodulin, who was played by Pyriev,[46] took three red clowns!)

So there was one 'imported' clown (most turns at that time were brought in from abroad) who worked as the 'fifth' in a troupe on the horizontal bars and did a very funny trick.

He threw a loop over one bar. Then he let it drop to the ground.

He put it over his head so the back of his neck rested against the rope.

Then, with his shoulders resting on the sand, he raised his legs, slightly bending them at the knees (close to the so-called 'grouping' position in acrobatics). Then he took hold of the free end of the rope with both hands and lifted himself, hand over hand, into the air.

When he reached the bar he stretched out to grab hold of it which meant letting go of the free end of the rope, so . . . he plummeted like a stone, landing on his back in the sand.

I found the 'technique' of his elevation fascinating; the descent less so.

Later I simplified the 'technique'. I sat in the loop and, moving my hands up the free end of the rope, I reached the branches of the tree which I had thrown the loop over.

I also remember the way the game was played, vaguely.

There was an 'execution' in it. This entailed lifting the 'condemned' into the tree in the sitting position, but it is not worth dwelling on the details of all this. I think the whole idea came from 'justifying' one's 'ascent' into a tree—it was the first attempt at an external 'projection' of the situation. I can only recall that one governess, after watching our game for some time, shook her head reprovingly, saying:

'That really is a very savage game, children.'

Gradually, moving into work in art, I began to notice that it had one great advantage over other types of 'play'.

Art gave me the chance of giving a much fuller and more logical version of my tormenting dreams.

Part of them was projected externally, independently, as a simple, 'purely artistic' need.

Another part was 'camouflaged' by allegory.

And a third part was physically and spontaneously 'hurled out'.

The *Lustbetontheit** of a great many details goes back to my very earliest experiments in direction.

I learned about the mechanisms of 'sublimation' at some depth from books; but for some reason I hardly applied them to my introspections.

What precipitated that was a shudderingly distasteful impression from the first picture by Abram Matveyevich Room, *Chasing the Moonshine.*[47]

It was a nauseating scene: some ragged workers were devouring tomatoes like pigs, covering themselves and each other with juice . . .

This is of course one of the least appetising approaches by which one may return to the childish state.

Children make awful messes of themselves when they eat, but at that level of development it only serves to . . . endear . . . .

The series 'Our Gang'[48] showed countless close-ups of black women stuffing their faces with watermelons!

Once this behaviour is removed from its appropriate context and transposed into an adult setting, the effect is revolting.

---

*   German: 'tinge of lust'

One of its commonest manifestations, beloved of so many amateurs, is of course the custard pies which the heroes (and other actors) of classical American slapstick* (of the older generation— Ben Turpin, early Chaplin, 'Fatty' Arbuckle, etc) threw in each other's faces.

Here, speed is everything and the parallel 'leading' impression' is a fight, or some comic situation, etc.

In Cambridge, I was introduced to Peter Leonidovich Kapitsa.[49]

He was then a member of Trinity and wore a black gown.

He showed me his laboratory, of which I understood nothing of course except for two things.

First, that there was an electric generator capable of lighting up something like half of London, and that all that energy was directed at an area no more than a few millimetres across.

This machine had something to do with the early attempts at splitting particles of matter, I think.

But the machine and matter are not important here.

What is relevant is one idea of the nature of time which Kapitsa explained to me.

About the shortness of time, as it happens!—which minimises the effects of unbelievably high temperatures which inevitably accompany such a colossal efflux of energy.

The effect of this energy was contained in so brief a moment that only its 'fundamental' effect could be realised—the effect that interested the scientist as he experimented; and any by-products, such as for example a massive temperature increase, did not have any time to take effect.

I may not have described it with complete accuracy, but I grasped the actual principle precisely in that way: neither the researcher's solemnity as I sat at high table* with the professors and the Master, beneath the high Gothic vaulting of the naves which vanished into the gloom, nor the antiphonic prayers, sung in Latin by two voices before the food was served, nor all the other marvels and charming details of my three days in a Cambridge college could erase it from my memory.

---

* In English in the original.

Playing at bandits, Riga 1910

I think that 'timing'* (which comics in American cinema consider the highest virtue in their art) is applicable even here.

This antiphony, the general setting and atmosphere of the whole scene remained so powerful that after many years it could still 'surface', first on the screen of my memories and then in the screen images of *Ivan the Terrible*: in the antiphonic reading of the psalter and the report of the boyars' treachery with the overlying voices of Pimen and Malyuta in the scene with Ivan and Anastasia's coffin.

Switching the structure of the childhood experience on and off, via associations linked with the 'oral zone', happens so quickly that there is no time for 'staleness', 'stagnating' in a mire of psychological detail; the viewer's perception is not allowed *zu schwelgen***—which is how the Germans neatly define a complex of all manner of emotional sensations, in which every pleasurable physiological taste may manifest itself.

It is naturally important to strike a 'balance' and such a dramatic description is only appropriate of course in cases where the artist is completely enslaved by the unique 'behind-the-scenes' motif.

The other extreme—the complete absence, ignoring or 'repression' of any 'behind-the-scenes' motifs—condemns any scene, episode or detail to sterility. The artist will go fatally off the boil.

The only essential is to keep it simmering; if it goes over, you will be bound to scald yourself.

On the other hand, keep it as hot as you can.

As we saw, this element must not be at all limited by images from the narrowly sensual range—that is, tinted by eroticism or infantilism—no matter how much they have been watered down.

If the artist's interlocking with that impression is shown too strongly, that impression will endeavour to 'throw itself into' what the artist is doing, and will prevail, whatever it is.

Which results in the artist falling into an inorganic stylisation; that is, forcibly stretching the material so that it fits another 'true' motif.

---

   *   In English in the original
 ** German: 'to wallow'

I have met with a whole series of such failures in my life.

Situations from the Bible are fundamental. In the minds of impressionable young boys forced to study the Old Testament in their childhood, they remain very distinct images.

The rhetorical manner of Rzheshevsky's writing and the situation surrounding *Bezhin Meadow* were bound to stir up legion similar images and impressions.[50]

They worked their way into the picture in such a thick stream, led, what is more, by the theme of 'father and son' which informs my entire opus, that they completely 'crushed' the objective theme: namely the struggle to establish the collective-farm system. They also buried the theme, subject and stylistics in a welter of purely subjective 'behind-the-scenes' subject matter.

Figures and situations were here 'ossified' in biblical stylisation: Abraham, Isaac, Rustum and Sohrab all came together in one character on screen; and the long-legged adult who overturned the icon stand developed into an echo of the blind strong-man from Gaza.*

And the social value of the film was wholly lost in the alleyways of 'private' subject-matter and the complex of the author's impressions.

Such a mishandling affected, if not the whole, then certainly at least one of the episodes of *October.*

This was the bestial slaughter of the young worker by ladies' umbrellas on the 3-5 July 1917. I have very vivid childhood impressions of the Paris Commune. A splendid album fell into my hands when I was going through Papa's library; I saw reproductions by the great Daumier, and photographs of the smashed columns at Place Vendôme.

To this day I cannot understand what such a seditious work was doing in my father's collection; his devotion to Church, Tsar and Fatherland was genuine.

But a fact is a fact.

I read up on the Paris Commune very early on (presented in the most impressive form—of pictures, sharply underlined caricatures and portraits of the age). Moreover, it brought with it an

---

* i.e. Samson (Ed.)

early and quite detailed knowledge of the Great French Revolution.

I can remember very clearly wearing a cream suit with chevrons—patterns of silvery-white lace—and white shoes, standing near a fir tree radiant with candles and silver and gold tinsel—*Engelshaar**—as those thin strips of gold and silver foil were called. They cascaded in spirals down the tree, crossing over the garlands of sparkling beads or rings of gold paper.

The foot of the tree was hammered home into a grooved piece of iron painted white, and decorated with cotton wool that had been covered with naphthalene (which regularly caused fires).

As the candles burned down they dropped readily into the cotton wool and the dehydrated fir tree instantly became the 'burning bush'!

There were toys around the tree.

It was apparently a Christmas tree.

Before going to 'see the tree' at the Wenzels' house—they had a monopoly of that evening since it coincided with the wife's, Yevgenia Modestovna's, birthday—I had been 'admitted into' the dining-room, which was where the presents were.

There were some masks.

And toy soldiers.

And a circus, comprising a clown, a chair and a donkey. It was called a 'Humpty-Dumpty circus',** distinguished by all the artistes having jointed limbs, so being able to adopt any attitude and combinations of movements.

The original set could be augmented annually: a ring-master, a trainer in tails, an elephant, lion, tiger and horses—all could be bought for it later.

There would also be sure to be one of Wolf's one-volume editions of Pushkin, Lermontov or Gogol.

I also had one of those each year, beginning, I think, with Pushkin.

I remember how many complications there were the next morning when I stumbled upon the poem 'On a Stormy Autumn Evening' when I could not think what 'the fruit of love corrupted',

---

*   German: literally 'angel's hair'
** In English in the original.

which the young woman was tenderly carrying in her arms, could be.

But no clown, mask, no cannon or swords could distract the curly-haired boy from two French volumes in their traditional yellow covers.

These were Mignet's *Histoire de la révolution française.*

One phrase, *le tocsin sonna** became for me the most irresistible call to revolt and was deeply etched upon my memory probably on that evening.

A few years later, romantic pictures of the history I had devoured came to the surface in a romanticised form. In 1913 *Priroda i lyudi* [Nature and People] magazine started bringing its subscribers volumes of the complete works of Dumas; the historical scenes of Mignet were fantastically coloured by *Ange Pitou, The Queen's Necklace* and the full series of *Joseph Balsamo.*

Of the episodes on the Commune, I remember Louise Michel and the *'pétroleuses'* with special clarity and affection.[51] There were also the terrible events at the Versailles concentration camp** where women blinded the imprisoned Communards with their umbrellas.

However, my interest in the Great French Revolution goes back even further.

At the age of eight (in 1907) I was taken to Paris (after the 1905 revolution it was too dangerous to go to the dacha!).

I have only vague memories of Paris and those recollections are what you might expect of a child.

Dark wallpaper and the huge feather pillows in the du Helder Hotel on Rue du Helder!

Lift shafts, probably the first I had ever seen.

Napoleon's grave.

Red-trousered *pioupious *** in the barracks around it.

The bitter taste of hot mulled wine which spoiled my impressions of the Bois de Boulogne (I had dysentery and was given the drink for 'medicinal purposes').

The heavy grey dresses and white headwear of the waitresses

---

* French: 'the alarm sounded'
** E uses this term in Russian: *kontslager'* (Ed.)
*** French :'infantryman' (usually a conscript)

at father's favourite restaurant.

Méliès's films, described elsewhere.

The Jardin des Plantes.

And the black pinafores with sleeves and hoods, which the little girls wore for playing hoopla, in the Tuileries Gardens.

The terrible anger I felt at not being told when we were inside Notre Dame—I raved about the gargoyles I had seen in photographs of this cathedral!

And, of course, above all else, more than anything and more powerful than anything, was the Musée Grévin.

My impressions of the Musée Grévin are even now as fresh as ever.

The triumphant carrying out of the Pope on his throne beneath the ostrich feather fans, the whole scene represented by scores of life-size wax figures which filled the central hall.

Sado-Yakko, sitting life-size among the Japanese fans and countless little tableaux set out on either side.[52]

In another scene Abd-el-Karim was surrendering to the French.[53]

There were dark passageways in which a subterranean archway would suddenly appear out of the darkness on either side, giving a view of early Christians, caught at their various activities in the catacombs.

Some were praying.

Over there, a baptism: you could see the silvery water, frozen in mid-air between the hand holding the cup and the new convert.

In the distance, a panoramic view of the circus.

And in the foreground, terrifying Roman soldiers manhandled some Christians who were huddling in a frightened group around the priest.

And here they lay lacerated beneath the lion's paw, near the iron grille.

We were met on the steps up by Demosthenes holding a lamp; Demosthenes fruitlessly searching for someone.

Higher up, we passed through a Napoleonic epic, set up as a reception at Malmaison.

There was even Josephine, the exotic Rustum, and

Bonaparte himself, dazzling in his coat and stars, and glittering Parisian society.[54]

Standing by a pillar, near the cord which divided the splendour of Napoleon from the humdrum present, stood a grey-haired, moustachioed Frenchman who was tightly holding on to a small black dog.

He could not tear himself away from the spectacle.

We passed him once.

Twice.

The old man was gazing at Josephine's elegant gesture as she handed someone a golden tea cup.

He could not take his eyes off her.

But this old man was by no means a fanatic of the illustrious age of Napoleon. He was one of the wax figures meant to fool the visitors, scattered here and there around the tableaux and seated on benches.

My cousin Modest, claiming he was 'just checking', tugged the plait of a living Frenchwoman . . .

But the section on the 'Terror' was the most impressive of all: it was somewhere above the early Christian 'catacombs', with the clear intention of providing a 'context' in which to view both the tableaux.

Bill Mauldin set up a more successful 'context' for the catacombs.

In one of his marvellous drawings devoted to the American *poilus** on the Italian front in the Second World War, he showed two soldiers in Rome, hopelessly seeking a hotel bed: all were filled with the officer and service corps.

A local stood near by.

'He says we kin git a room in th' Catacombs. They used to keep Christians in 'em'. (Bill Mauldin, *Up Front*, p. 164.)[55] **

In the 'Terror' section, there was even a small, unhappy Louis XVII standing by a drunken cobbler.

And Marie Antoinette in the Conciergerie.

And Louis XVI in a chamber being pursued by the patriots.

---

* French: literally 'hairy men' but the nickname for the common soldier.

** E's reference

And in an earlier tableau 'the Austrian woman' (*l'Autrichienne* = *l'autre chienne**—one of the first puns I really liked!) swooned as she looked out of the window to see a procession bearing aloft a pike with the head of the Princesse de Lamballe.

I moved on from the fates of individuals in the revolution,, as seen in the Musée Grévin, to the life of the masses, as seen in Mignet. But at the same time, to something much greater: to the first notions of historical events conditioned by social injustice and lawlessness.

And the huge white wigs, the figure of Sanson and the aristocrats' jackets, the picturesque *'tricoteuses'* or Théroigne de Méricourt,[56] the swish of the guillotine's triangular blade and even the visual impression of probably the first 'double exposure' which I also saw on the screen in time immemorial—Cagliostro showing Marie Antoinette's ascent to the guillotine in a carafe of water—for all the brightness of the impressions, nothing could displace the image of the hellish society of pre-revolutionary, eighteenth-century France.

One scene of the Paris Commune I cannot forget is the one where the ladies blinded the Communards imprisoned in the camp at Versailles.

The image of these umbrellas gave me no rest until I had included it, 'contrary to reason', in the scene where the young worker was killed, in the July Days of 1917.

In this way I delivered myself of a persistent image, but I overburdened my canvas, quite pointlessly, with a scene whose tone and essence was quite inappropriate for 1917!

Had I had more time for the editing, I would probably have cut that scene much more as it was rather a 'case history of the author's illness' than part of the history of events that make a great epoch!

However . . . I think that the actual umbrellas here were a 'secondary' image.

They tore the poor lad's shirt before executing him.

After the execution, the young man's perforated torso lay on the granite steps, half submerged in the Neva.

---

* French: 'the Austrian woman = the other bitch' (Ed.)

And the ladies wielding umbrellas were not such a far cry from Ethel King with her machine-gun, stooping over the 'martyrs' in exactly the same way, albeit with a different assignment ahead of her.

The paths along which the images converge are strange, unexpected and whimsical.

However . . .

The two halves of the boy's torn shirt lying on the granite steps near the sphinxes of the Egyptian Bridge (which was, in the Petrograd of 1917, opened) bring us back to the start of the article —to the young man who tore his shirt in shot 761 of *Potemkin*.

I tried to argue as convincingly as possible that this was not a mere detail but a *'leitmotif'*.

If we compare the momentary 'sublimated' appositeness of a few parts of *Potemkin* with the 'long drawn-out' episode in *October*, we find further confirmation of how one's *idées fixes* should, or should not, be treated.

What failed in *October* was of the same order as that episode in *Chasing the Moonshine*; and the explosive accent in *Potemkin* belongs to the ranks of 'purified' images.

'Brazenly' shown in their entirety, but at the same time framed by a brutal system of forms of expression and, further, inset into a piquant situation—where they would act on the situation and not vice-versa!—these images defined the very powerful and effective 'Peons' Golgotha'—the execution of the three day-workers in the landlords episode in *Que Viva México!*

The system of plastic images, in which the idiosyncratic 'three bronze youths' played out the tragedy among fields of cruel maguey, was highly praised: references were made to El Greco and Zurbarán.[57]

But what pleased me more was that the stress was not on the similarity, the influence or my recreation of it, but the sense of 'kinship' with the tragic 'spirit' which informed the imagery and the scene.

But here is an example of a sizeable—if not an absolute—fiasco caused by these very images.

The production 'became tongue-tied'.

Still from the episode Xochimilco, from *Que Viva México!*

It did not say all it had to.

It did not say everything.

It failed to put the finishing touches to the system of living bodies for a similar scene in the first reel of *Ivan the Terrible*.

The siege of Kazan.

Kurbsky led the captured Tatars to the front of the palisade.

The half-naked prisoners were roped to posts and palings.

'Shout: "Kazan, surrender!" '

Kurbsky commanded them.

The Tatars were silent.

The iron gauntlet smote them.

The Tatars remained silent.

But two or three gave in.

Their piercing, piteous cry:

'Kazan, surrender!'

'Better you should die at our hands, than at the hands of the uncircumcised infidels!' The mullah cried from the walls of the city.

And a hail-storm of arrows hissed down on the prisoners, throwing them against the walls.

The rush of arrows brought Ivan running out.

He was wearing black armour and was seething with anger.

There was a sun on his black armour.

And a moon on Kurbsky's silver armour.

(Who has seen this film and taken the hint that Kurbsky's glory was only a reflection?)

'This is pointless cruelty—stupidity!' Ivan shouts.

And speaking barely intelligibly, he set out his view that cruelty was only admissible when expediency dictated.

Ivan Vasilievich actually did say that once.

But he did so in quite different circumstances, in a letter to the Emperor Rudolf relating to the St Bartholomew's Night massacre,[58] which he thought was not expedient for so trifling a reason as religious differences . . .

(I think that Ivan saw deeper springs motivating this 'woeful event' and, keeping his own counsel, he disguised his disapproval of the event as 'religious tolerance' although in his own policies the great lord himself stuck to this very same principle whenever doing so might strengthen his multinational, extensive and mixed empire.)

The first part of the scene followed historical traditions.

I found it a very rewarding backdrop for the sharp clash of characters and 'intelligent cruelty' with 'senseless cruelty'.

Seen from the purely human angle, Kurbsky's accusations of Ivan's cruelty on the pages of his letters and history, are abhorrent hypocrisy.

Ivan's actions were born of brutal necessity at a brutal time, during the forging of the autocracy.

Prince Kurbsky's *Life in Volhynia* showed the true character of this 'merciful mercenary' whenever he was guaranteed impunity and absolved from responsibility.

Then Prince Andrei's life was crowned by the episode with the creditors, whom the prince ordered be buried in a pit with leeches. By the time the royal emissaries arrived, they could only obtain a thick gore from it.

This scene is even more rewarding from the purely visual point of view:

The clash between Ivan and Prince Kurbsky at Kazan. Eisenstein's drawing for *Ivan the Terrible,* Part One. Alma-Ata, 17 March 1942

How I Learned to Draw (A Chapter about My Dancing Lessons)[1]

In the first place, I never learned how to draw.

But this is how and why I draw.

Was there anyone in Moscow who had not heard of Karl Ivanovich Kogan, the wizard and magician of stomatology and osteology?

Anyone who did not take their worn-out teeth to him?

Anyone who did not strut about with excellent new jaws made by his hands?

Take Karl Ivanovich.

Make him much thinner.

If this makes his nose too short, stretch it a bit.

Give him a pronounced stoop so that his Madam Situpon—as we said in Riga—sticks out.

Let him wear a railway engineer's frock-coat.

Let him have a wife on one arm—she had the highest hairdo in Riga.

You have just drawn Afrosimov, the greying railway engineer.

I am indebted to Afrosimov for instilling in me the compulsive need and inclination for drawing.

Like all society ladies, Mama was 'at home' on Thursdays.

That aside, Mama and Papa organised monster receptions on their birthdays.

Then all twelve leaves of the round dinner table would be pulled out.

It was as long as the dining room.

It groaned beneath the opulent dinner.

It now stands in my home in Potylikha, circular again, as it was on the day of Creation, in the room I call my library. It was in point of fact a library until my books, bursting their allotted banks, flooded every room and my entire flat was turned into a bookcase!

. . . Near the large table there would be a smaller one, for savouries.

We would have supper after cards and light piano music.

The society was select.

The guest of honour would be the Governor. His Excellency Zvegintsov.

He would preside on Mama's right.

With Papa at the opposite end of the table.

Sometimes, tables were moved into the dining room and set in a horseshoe.

I have forgotten where Papa sat on those occasions, but I do recall that by that time I sat at the table too, on the inside of the horseshoe and straight opposite Mother.

Before that time, I was only wheeled up to the table, nodding off, barely awake.

Even earlier, I would be put to bed before the guests began to arrive.

And I saw only the table, set for dinner, gleaming with silver and crystal.

The maid, Minna, and Ozols, Papa's messenger, would fuss about the table. Ozols wore full dress on such occasions.

First of all, I was only shown the table.

Then I would be regaled with treats from the savouries table.

I loved pickled mushroom. Fresh caviar. I was less keen on salmon. And I did not see the point of oysters.

After Mama and Papa were divorced such receptions ceased: 'the house had fallen.'

Furthermore, Papa's business affairs looked very uncertain.

There was nothing to entertain with, either.

Mama had taken the furniture, which had been her dowry.

I was quite unconcerned—even happy—about all of this.

The unbearable domestic quarrels, which took place mostly at night, ceased.

And I had a whale of a time on my bicycle, racing up and down the empty dining-room and drawing-room.

There was even some sense of triumph.

Father, who was a fearsome man, was very strict with me.

I was simply not allowed into the drawing-room, for instance and, since an arch led from there into the dining-room, a cordon of chairs was put across the archway. I would crawl along those chairs, peeping into the promised land of the drawing-room.

Later I cycled boldly across this room which now resembled a *Niemandsland** after the couches, chairs, tables, lamps and mountains of *Nippsachen*** had been removed (chiefly porcelain from Copenhagen, whose milky-blue colouring, washed-out grey pattern and stream-lined forms delighted lovers of elegance in those happy years).

. . . But the future desert now teemed with people.

The drawing-room was full. So were Mama's boudoir and Papa's study.

At any moment they would all surge into the dining-room for dinner.

But for the time being they sat at the card tables.

I was at that age when I was allowed to meet the guests, but not to sit at table.

I walked among the guests memorising them.

There was the Governor. A head showing good breeding, an aquiline gaze beneath thick eyebrows.

But in all other respects he was what we call a *Tischriese*—a giant at the table.

A giant only as far as the waist, if you begin from the top.

His legs did not match—they were too short.

Just like Lev Tolstoy.

Just like Karl Marx too.

Dollfuss, the late Austrian Chancellor, was a mere dwarf.[2]

He was delightfully called Milli-Metternich, and word had it that they were issuing new stamps in Austria with a . . . life-size portrait of the Chancellor.

The governor's magnificent head was set magnificently, slightly askew, on magnificently broad shoulders.

Just as pelicans in Mexico hold their heads slightly askew when they dive out of the sky like an arrow for fish in the amber bay of Acapulco.

Actual Privy Councillor Zvegintsov's gaze is aquiline.

---

* German: 'no-man's-land'
** German: 'knick-knacks'

569

With bicycle, Riga, 1911

Eisenstein dancing with the ballerina Sara Mildred Strauss, New York 1932. (Photo: Grigori Alexandrov)

Coal-black eyes set beneath grey brows.

He should have soared above the fields of conflict.

At any rate, above the heads of his subordinates and those in his charge.

But this would not have been feasible, even if those in his charge and his subordinates were to bow down almost to the very ground.

As I said, the Governor was very short.

I only remember the ladies who were young, for some reason.

The Vice-Governor's daughter Mademoiselle Bologovskaya.

And that is probably because she—Nadezhda [hope]—was always called by the French translation of her name—Espérance Bologovskaya.

This is like the Spanish, where such widespread names as Incarnacíon, Felicidad or Soledad have retained their meaning.

When Dolores Ibarruri[3] celebrated her fiftieth birthday (in 1945) my greetings card made that point: I said, 'For your next fifty years, may you have a new name: not Dolores, but Victoria Gloria Felicidad.'

As well as Espérance—for some reason, I distinctly remember Mulya Wenzel all in blue, and her sister Tata, all in pink.

My friend Vadim's third sister, Zhuka Wenzel, was too young to be allowed to come.

How did it come about that of that whole galaxy, constellation, I remember only the Wenzels—dressed in the colours of lampshades?

This was not mere chance, it transpires.

In my memory, the sisters (according to all the rules of 'agglutination') have merged with the lampshades. There was no great difference between the lampshades and the ballgowns worn in those years.

The same puffs, frills and flounces.

Suddenly the Wenzel sisters are no longer the Wenzel sisters; they are the Amelang isters.

Two youngish sisters, in their Sunday best. It is virtually impossible to distinguish their dresses from lampshades.

But Papa's drawing-room, full of people, is no longer Papa's drawing-room but a quite different one.

It is empty. Only a dazzlingly polished and horribly empty expanse of parquet.

Convulsed with spasms of fear, I was about to have to dance a waltz across this empty parquet . . .

I was even younger.

And this was my first dancing class.

Little boys and girls, we sat on little chairs and stared at the terrifying parquet.

This huge drawing room was in the house of another railway engineer: Daragan, the head of the Riga-Oryol Railway.

This is where we learned how to dance.

The drawing-room carpets were rolled back and the palms moved up against the windows.

A few years later, the grey-haired Mr Daragan, looking like a saint or a monk in an icon, left Riga.

He was succeeded by the father of another childhood friend, Andrei Melentevich Markov: Melenti Fedoseyevich Markov, who had an official residence in Petersburg, in the building of the Nicholas station itself.

Andrei's father's face was terribly pitted and wrinkled; he wore his hair *en brosse.*

And oddly pale eyes were set against a dark complexion.

And in Andrei's rooms in the mezzanine, near the archway of the left-hand exit from the station, was a colossal electric model railway.

A toy locomotive ran on rails crossing bridges.

There were working signal posts and points.

A landscape of sand surrounded it.

And rivers made from blue paper lay under shiny pieces of glass to add to the effect.

At a certain age, Andrei and I would play here for hours on end.

He was fascinated by the train's workings and operations.

I was fascinated more by some ridiculous toy character—I always made him miss his train and run after it between the rails, and get mixed up between the points.

Not far off, real locomotives whistled and even, occasionally, you could hear the station bell.

The toy railway was synchronised with the noises of real trains and that made the game more life-like.

When we were older, during the war, that same Andrei tried, utterly hopelessly, to teach me cards. And he took me, as his guest (Melenti Fedoseyevich was dead by that time) into the first-class waiting-room of the Nicholas station, and showed me what a prostitute looked like.

The cheapest 'priestesses of love' had made this waiting-room (the station is now called October) their headquarters. They sat there in the buffet making one cup of tea last a whole evening.

Not all evening, come to think of it, but until a client arrived, at least . . .

This is not the case in Mexico.

The girl sits out, in front of a small booth on the street.

Her pimp sits in a bar opposite.

The pimp drinks beer.

As many glasses as the girl has customers.

So he does not lose count, he makes a pile of the beer-mats.

One beer mat for each glass.

In Petersburg the pimps stroll up and down on Ligovka.

. . . However, I am still petrified, confronted by the parquet flooring in Daragan's house.

And I was particularly petrified because of these sisters—the Amelang ladies.

They were significantly older than me.

They were English.

I think they were twins.

And only differed in the colour of their dresses.

They partnered the older boys.

I had dreamy Nina and voluptuous Olga, the Daragan daughters.

But I was in love—utterly, madly—with the unattainable Amelang sisters.

With both at once.

Since they were twins . . .

My dancing classes had no effect on me at all.

trago, the high official. Drawing from a notebook when a child

. . . However, we left Mama's guests when they were about to sit down to a game of cards.

We shall rejoin our guests.

Especially as Mr Afrosimov is seated at one of the tables.

Now Maria Vasilievna Verkhovskaya[4] sat at one table, her silk dress rustling. She had the best snub nose in Riga and her painted eyebrows were as thick as your finger.

I dashed across the drawing room.

Because Mr Afrosimov, using a finely sharpened white chalk wrapped in pale yellow paper with tiny stars upon the dark blue cloth of the card table as he waited for a game . . .

was drawing for me!

He drew wild animals.

Dogs. Deer. Cats.

I remember particularly well what delighted me the most: a fat, bow-legged frog.

The white outline stood out against the dark blue cloth.

The 'technique' does not allow for shading, or the illusion of solidity.

Only an outline.

But never mind that this was a line drawing.

Here, before the eyes of the delighted beholder, this outline took form and started moving.

As it moved, the unseen outline of the object traced a magical path, making it appear on the dark blue cloth.

The line was the track left by the movement.

Years later I still remember this acute sense of line as dynamic movement; a process; a path.

Many years later it made me record in my heart the wise saying of Wang Pi from the third century B.C.: 'What is a line? A line speaks of movement.'[5]

At the Institute of Civil Engineering I came to love Descartes' seemingly arid analytical geometry: it spoke of the movement of a line, expressed by the mysterious formula of an equation.

I devoted many years to my enthusiasm for *mise-en-scène*—to those lines of an actor's path 'through time'.

The dynamics of line and the dynamics of 'movement',

rather than 'repose', remain my abiding passion, whether in lines or in a system of phenomena and their transition from one into the other.

This might explain my tendency towards, and sympathy for, disciplines that announce dynamics, movement and process as their underlying principles.

And on the other hand, I have always liked Disney and his heroes, from Mickey Mouse to Willie the Whale.

Because of their moving figures—again animals and again linear. The best examples had neither shading nor depth (similar to early Chinese and Japanese art) and were made up of outlines that really did move!

The moving lines of my childhood, outlining the shape and form of animals, animated the real lines of the cartoon drawing with real movement.

And perhaps, because of these same childhood impressions, my drawing on the blackboard with chalk in my lectures always gives me the same savour and enjoyment; the sketches fascinate and delight my students and in the process I try to instill in them a perception of line as movement, as dynamic process.

That is probably why it is precisely the purely linear drawing that is my favourite; that is the variety I use to the virtual exclusion of all others, or most of the time.

Dots of colour and shade (in sketches, designed to be shown on screen) are scattered between them almost as a record of the intended effects.

In letters to his brother, van Gogh recorded, on the preliminary sketches, the names of the pigments where he was going to use them.

But it was not van Gogh who dominated my thinking at that time. Incidentally, surely it was the linear drawing of his brush-strokes and their clearly-defined outline on the canvas that first aroused my sympathies towards him?

At that point, I had not seen or heard of van Gogh.

In those early days, it was Olaf Gulbransson's sharp, unadorned outline that had such a beneficial influence.[6]

And the mountains of graphic rubbish, dross like that arid PEM[7] in *Vechernyeye vremya* [Evening Times] and the album War and PEM which drew so much attention to itself during World War One which were full of boring Wilhelms who captivated me for absolutely no reason.

In fact, at this time I began to find Moor's lubok prints fascinating.[8]

By now there is some sense of shading and outline, and very often a solid block of colour fills in the surfaces indicated by this outline.

In this period I did a great deal of drawing and that very badly, muddying the original, true source of the inspiration with a multitude of inferior images and a 'Wanderer'[9] fascination with subjects instead of an 'ascetic' quest for forms (which occupied me later, to the detriment of the former, during my 'artistic' period).

For some reason, I did not study drawing.

And when I had to draw plaster figures, teapots and Dante's mask it came out all wrong . . .

And it now turns out that recollections of my first dancing classes, even though they sneaked in here after the Amelang sisters, are much more relevant than they might appear.

Actually, not so much the classes themselves as my complete ineptitude for learning.

I still cannot manage a waltz, although I was able to pull off a foxtrot with great panache, albeit a jerky, black version in Harlem; and only recently my leaping about caused the heart-attack that has laid me low these past months.[10]

So what is this all about?

Where's the link?

Drawing and dancing are branches of the same tree, of course; they are just two varieties of the same impulse.

Much later, after an initial break from drawing and a subsequent fresh start,[11] after the 'lost and newly-regained paradise' of drawing (which I experienced in Mexico), I was awarded my first (and last!) press review for my skill in drawing.

I also have a one-off review of a performance . . . as an actor.

It makes me desperately proud.

Just think! It did not only say that 'the whole cast (myself included) grossly hammed it', but also that 'they all [and I was moreover the amateur producer] turned into circus clowns'!

This was at the end of 1919 and referred to the amateur show that was put on by the engineers, technicians, and accountants from the army engineering corps, when we were stationed in Velikie Luki.

The notice appeared in Velikie Luki's local newspaper.

The notice my drawings received came fifteen years later and in the . . . *New York Times*.

And this is how it happened and why.

In Mexico, as I said, I began to draw again.

This time in the proper, linear way.

This was influenced less by Diego Rivera[12] who drew with a heavy, broken stroke, or my much-loved 'mathematical' line, which was suitable for the whole diversity of expression which it achieves by the mere variation of its continuous outlines.

In my early films I was also fascinated by the mathematically pure course of montage thought and less by the 'thick' stroke of the accentuated shot.

Fascination with the shot, strange (in fact, quite logical and natural—remember Engels' 'Attention is drawn first of all to *movement* and only afterwards to *what* is moving')[13] though it may be, came later.

It was in Mexico that my drawing underwent an internal catharsis, striving for mathematical abstraction and purity of line.

The effect was considerably enhanced when this abstract, 'intellectualised' line was used for drawing especially sensual relationships between human figures, usually in especially complicated and random situations!

Bardèche and Brasillach believed that a particularly strongly expressed sensualism, coupled with an aptitude for the most removed abstraction, is the basic hallmark of my work; I find this both highly flattering and most apt (see *Histoire du Cinéma*).[14]

The influence here, I repeat, is less Diego Rivera, although he too assimilated (in a way, and to an extent) this synthesis of all the varieties of Mexican primitivism: from Chichen-Itzá bas reliefs, via primitive toys and painted implements, to the incomparable pages of illustrations by José Guadelupe Posada for street songs.[15]

'Before and after exams'. Drawing in a letter to his mother

Here the influence was those primitives which I spent fourteen months greedily palpating with my hands, eyes and the soles of my feet.

And perhaps, even more, the actual, astonishing, linear structure of the stunning purity of the Mexican landscape; the square, white, peon's dress; the round outline of his straw hat; or the felt ones of the *dorados*.

Anyway, I drew a great deal in Mexico.

On my travels through New York, I met the proprietor of the Baker Gallery (Baker himself, I think).

He took quite an interest in the drawings and asked me if I would leave them with him.

Their subject matter was quite fantastical, such as the 'cycles' of Salome, drinking through a straw from the lips of John the Baptist's severed head.

In two colours—I used two crayons.

A 'suite' on the theme of the 'bullfight'. This subject merged with that of St Sebastian in widely varied combinations.

The martyrdom of first the matador, then the bull.

There was even a drawing of a . . . crucified bull, pierced with arrows like St Sebastian.

Do not blame me for any of this.

It was Mexico: in one element of the Resurrection festival they mix the blood of Christ from the morning mass in the cathedral, with the streams of bulls' blood in the afternoon *corrida* in the city's arena. The tickets for the bullfight are decorated with the likeness of the Madonna of Guadelupe, whose four hundredth anniversary is observed not only by the many thousands of pilgrims and scores of South American cardinals in their crimson robes, but even by the splendid *corridas*, 'to the glory of the Mother of God' (*'de la madre de Dios'*).

Anyway, the drawings aroused Mr Baker's (or was it Mr Brown's?) curiosity.

But when the ill-starred, emasculated version of my film, *Que Viva México!* came out in the cinemas, transformed by someone's grubby hands into the pitiful gibberish of *Thunder over Mexico* the 'enterprising Yankees', as our evening paper would call them, exhibited these drawings in a small side-foyer of a theatre.

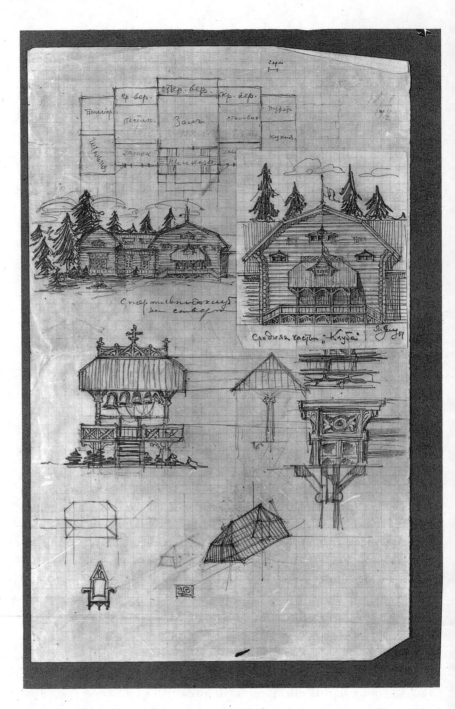

A sports club in the north. Eisenstein's student project.

Which was how an article about my drawings came to appear in a newspaper.

And one picture was actually sold.

And I received . . . $15 in payment.

I strongly suspect that Mrs Isaacs[16] bought it, because later I saw a drawing from the 'bullfight' series in the *Theatre Arts Magazine* (before it dropped *Magazine* from the title).

If I ever find that unique, yellowed review of me as draughtsman among the heap of cinema praise that has been printed, I shall nail it to this spot.

But I remember the chief point it made, and that is what is relevant here.

It was the reference to the lightness of touch: the figures were put on to paper 'as if they were dancing'.

Drawing and dancing, which take their root from the same impulse, here converged.

And the line of my drawing was seen as the trace of a dance.

Here, I think, is also the key to the 'secret' of my double failure in drawing and dancing.

The plaster casts I drew for the entrance examination to the Institute of Civil Engineering, and in my first year there, were even more repugnant than the things I scribbled in the *Realschule*.

I recall with a shudder that stuffed eagle which clawed at me for months at Herr Nieländer's drawing class like the eagle that attacked the bound Prometheus.

Incidentally, the theme of Prometheus and the eagle is one that always returns to my pen or pencil whenever I start filling a series of pages with drawings (for which hotel writing-paper is especially suitable).

(Somewhere I mentioned that it was a matter of principle for Maurice Dekobra to use hotel paper for writing his novels— preferably in Pullmans or other sleeping-cars).[17]

One day I shall have to analyse the 'thematic' course of my drawings

But there are more holes here than cheese.

The most revealing and shamelessly frank drawings are torn into tiny shreds almost straight away, which is a pity: they were drawn almost automatically. But how obscene they were!!

A photograph Eisenstein presented to his mother, with the inscription on the back: 'To my kind, dear mother from her hairy son, in honour of [the play] *Can You Hear Me, Moscow?* Moscow, 20 December 1923'.

Those stubborn, blunt, deathly plastercasts were not at all to my taste!

Perhaps that is because a finished drawing is supposed to have volume, shading, half-tones and reflected light, whereas there is a strict taboo on drawing a graphic skeleton, the line of ribs.

But even more because in drawing from plaster there is an unbreakable, iron law; like the strict set of *pas* in the dance in my childhood and youth—*pas de patineur*, with the arms folded across the chest; *pas d'Espagne*, where one is supposed to 'feel Spanish'. That was the cry of another dancing master at school: Mr Kaulins, a Lithuanian, with his small, dyed beard and moustache, and who wore a dress coat with padded shoulders and satin breeches with black stockings and shoes. Yes, yes, yes—imagine it!

1914. I remember the date well because it was from the windows of his dancing class that I saw my first patriotic torch-light procession, with cheering, shouting and a portrait of the Tsar.

We also danced the Kikapu, Hiawatha (on the basis of *Hacke—Spitze—eins—zwei—drei!*)* and the inevitable Hungarian *csardás*.

Now I know for sure what inhibited me then—it was the dry, rigid formulae and canons both of movements in dance, and of drawing.

And I grasped this in 1921, when I began to learn the fox-trot with Valentin Parnakh, a frail man with a ready smile whom I had invited to our Moscow Proletkult studio to teach it to our actors.[18]

They were also taught the 'technique of comic narrative'; Vladimir Khenkin was moved to tears by my invitation to teach so 'academic' a course.[19]

Acrobatics—techniques of stage flight *y compris***—was taken by Pyotr Kronidovich Rudenko,[20] who ran the incomparable 'Trio Georges'; when I was still a child he held me enthralled as he flew, in his golden yellow *tricot*, under the big top of the Salamonsky Circus on Pauluccistrasse in Riga.

Pauluccistrasse. Pauluccistrasse.

I would not say it was memorable.

---

* German: 'heel—toe—one—two—three'
** French: 'included'

I was born on Nicholas Street.

But . . . my parents spent their honeymoon in Papa's former bachelor flat.

On Pauluccistrasse, next to the Salamonsky Circus (or was it Truzzi? In Petersburg it was the Ciniselli. Where, then, was the Salamonsky?).

At my foxtrot lessons, I understood something very important: unlike the dances of my youth, with the strictly prescribed pattern and sequence of movements, this was a 'free dance', governed only by the regularity of rhythm, which could be used as a peg from which to hang any free, improvised movement.

That was more like it!

I discovered again the free run of a line which so enthralled me; a line, subordinate only to the internal law of rhythm, through the free run of the hand.

To hell with the stiff, fragile plaster—all that was good for was setting broken bones.

This was also the reason why I could not cope with tapdancing. I went over it, repeatedly and conscientiously—but hopelessly— under the guidance of the inimitable Leonid Leonidovich Obolensky—a man of great charm, then still a music-hall dancer, yet to direct the notorious film *Bricks,* and 'involved' with Anna Sten; and yet to become my unfailing assistant at my directing courses at the VGIK (he began at GTK in 1928).[21] He certainly never imagined he would . . . become a monk in Romania, which was where he landed up after escaping from a German concentration camp (he was caught when he tried to jump on to a lorry when our troops were retreating from Smolensk in 1941!).

Only my complete incompetence at penetrating the secret of tap-dancing stops me from reminiscing about how I knocked off a tap-dance as I queued up with the other red-blooded males awaiting admittance to Madame Bruno's bedroom, in a production of *The Magnanimous Cuckold.*

. . . Producers were very free in those years!

I even introduced into a production of *Wise Man* a detail worthy of Aristophanes or Rabelais—something even better than what you might find in an Atellan mime[22]—when I obliged Madame Mamayeva to mount the 'mast of death'—a tightrope—

which stuck out from under General Krutitsky's waist and stretched as far as the balcony of the ballroom of the Morozov villa on the Vozdvizhenka. That was where the mad plays of 'my' Moscow Proletkult theatre were performed.

Many years later—quite recently, in fact—that room was the scene of a banquet, given in joint honour of Priestley, who had just arrived; the anniversary of *The British Ally*, and the departure of the British military mission.[23]

Good grief! I sat at a table with these honoured guests on the very spot where once had stood our small, moveable platforms; my actors would perform before them, on a round carpet sewn with a broad red stripe which was a sort of circus barrier.

And I am sitting on the very spot where the metal cable stretched up from a hook in the stalls, diagonally across the auditorium and finished in the wall of the balcony at the other end of the room.

With an orange parasol to help him balance and wearing a top hat and tails, Grisha Alexandrov ascended the cable in time to the music.

Without a safety net.

It happened once that the upper part of the cable was smeared with engine oil.

(It had dripped from the small pulley which Mishka Eskin held on to as he followed him back down the cable. Mishka died, after he had left our company. He lost both his legs when on the road with the 'Blue Blouse' troupe, which was a terrible end for an acrobat—especially for so brilliant an acrobat and clown as Mishka!)[24]

Grisha, sweating, was going all out and becoming winded. He was wearing thin buckskin shoes, which held the big toe apart for him to grip the cable, but nevertheless he kept sliding inexorably backwards.

Zyama Kitayev—our pianist—began the music from the beginning.

Grisha's feet were sliding.

He could not make it.

Finally, someone worked out what the matter was and held out a walking stick from the balcony.

This time Grisha landed safely on the balcony!

It seems like yesterday.

That only yesterday I was running through the cellars of the Morozov villa, through the blue-tiled kitchen, blocking my ears as I tried not to think about Verka Yanukova who was at that moment flying up the wire, or Sasha Antonov (Krutitsky) who was not entirely sober that evening.[25]

A deathly hush.

Everyone up above had frozen during this deadly trick.

Then the roar of applause, which reached the kitchen, muffled.

That was for Verka—Verochka!—she had completed her turn, and had cried out 'Voilà!' in triumph.

But how long ago that really was!

. . . I tried finding the lighter patch on the parquet under the table: that was where the hook had been for the wire.

I realised just how long ago it was when the General with steely grey temples, the head of the departing British legation who was my neighbour, brought the conversation round to . . . how he educated his children.

'I brought my sons up,' (and one of them, a colossus wearing a funny British Army coat, was dancing nearby on the same parquet flooring where Parnakh once gave me lessons) 'to understand that when it's an uphill slog, he will be glad even of a dry crust of bread . . .'

Hell, was I really so old that I had to endure such talk, at the very spot moreover where I once taught—and utterly differently—a whole crowd of young enthusiasts who ascended wire cables that stretched up as far as the balcony from the very spot where we were sitting, not finding it an uphill slog, as that puritanical motto has it; there, they turned somersaults on the matting; they made love here at night when the carpets were rolled back, under the drying posters for the sets; for one of my plays they even led a . . . camel into this very room, bringing it all the way across Moscow from the Zoo.

It carried Yudif Samoilovna Glizer, the Honoured Artist still doing great things, in one of her first roles—certainly her first grotesque role.[26]

. . . My attempt at eurhythmics was even worse than at tap-dancing.

At eurhythmics—I would call this idle pastime taught by outmoded adherents of Dalcroze's[27] flawed system 'metrics'—I simply and invariably 'came round', at both the entrance and final exams (happy memories!) in Meyerhold's director's studios on Novinsky Boulevard.

Just as well then that I was found to have other qualities which saved me from ending up in the gutter after each examination.

But who will believe this, after someone wrote in America (vis-à-vis *Potemkin*) that I opened the eyes of the world to rhythm in cinema (and rhythm really was and is one of the most powerful devices in my films)?

But who would believe, if he had not seen it for himself, that the miraculous master of rhythm Prokofiev hopelessly missed the beat when dancing (again, dances!) in the drawing room and mercilessly trampled on his partner's toes!

All this talking—or rather writing—has been leading to this: that there is deep within me a long-standing conflict between the free course of the *all'improviso*, flowing line of drawing or the free run of dance, subject only to the laws of the inner pulse of the organic rhythm of purpose (on one hand); and the restrictions and blind-spots of the canon and rigid formula (on the other).

Actually, it is not entirely appropriate or fair to mention formulae here.

The charm of a formula is that, while laying down a general rule, it allows, within the free current which filters through it, 'special' interpretations, special cases and coefficients.

And that is the charm of learning about the functions of theories of limits and differentials.

This touches upon one of the fundamental, pervasive themes, which is also the formula (when taken that way) running through almost all the basic stages of my theoretical searchings, where it always repeats this primordial pairing, and the conflict between its components.

Only the 'special' interpretations change, depending on the nature of the problem.

It may be an expressive movement
or the principle of the form's structure.

And this is not a matter of chance.

For this conflict contains the all-pervasive conflict of relationships between opposites, on which everything that is old, like the world, moves and rests.

Such as the ancient Chinese symbols, the yin and the yang, which I so love.

My work progresses like that too.

By a whimsical, arbitrary flood in my pictures.

And with attempts at stemming this flood later, with the metronome's dry beat, 'to make it regular'.

But even here I am always on the look out for flexibility of method rather than an iron law; my favourite theme and field of research was and remains the initial 'protoplasmic' element in my works and productions, and the role it played in the structure and realisation of the form of phenomena.

This flood overwhelms my theoretical writings, when I submit to it with myriad digressions from the key theme, and banishing it from my pages makes them dry as dust, like the plaster casts in the drawing class, or like the spasms of paralysis when I met the Amelang sisters at Daragan's or Kaulins' dancing lessons.

It was in order to stem this primeval flood that I began writing these reminiscences with the sole (? perhaps, but certainly the chief) purpose of giving myself complete freedom to wallow in the twists and turns of all manner of associations which might crop up during these accounts!

But the corrections and editing of what should be sent to the printers lies nearby, shamefully, criminally and degradingly, like an inanimate plaster cast; all because I do not at all feel like 'tempering' what poured out in wild torrents on to my notebooks, bursting its banks as it did so!

I also derive pleasure from writing this because now I am released from the categories of time and space. I do not have to be consistent in the way I narrate events, nor in the way I order them.

I am also free from their synthesising brother: strict logicality, which carries the principle of consistency over into the field of judgment and disciplined thought.

And again, what can be more diverting than sheer, brazen narcissism, for what are these pages if not an endless array of mirrors for me to see myself in and at any age I like, at that?

Perhaps that is why I have taken such pains always to give the date and place in this mockery of the logic of time, where the scene of action is changing constantly and there is no neat logic of direction or purpose!

Freed from all three at once!

What could be better?!

Surely this is nothing short of heaven, a slice from that happiest stage of our life, even better than carefree childhood: that blessed time when, gently rocked in our sleep, we lay curled up, protected and safe from aggression, in the warm womb of our mothers?!

On Folklore[1]

If only I posed more than I do.

If only I had thought of writing this work in the style of a detective novel.

This is how I would have begun.

It was a wet day in July 1946 in the resort village of Kratovo on the Kazan railway line.

I was sitting, reading a relatively new detective story about Len Wyatt's adventures as he battled against black marketeers and Nazi spies.

The twists and turns of the chase were not so gripping as to divert my attention from the stylistic niceties of such a book as this one by Nicholas Brady—although I doubt if the author himself would make any claims on this score.[2]

But writers of such books either naturally incorporate good examples of genuine 'slang'* or they improvise expressive turns of phrase and coin new words in this style.

Coining slang expressions and turns of phrase is a collective process, at once anonymous and popular, as all other forms of folklore were once anonymous, collective, popular and widespread.

Each individual witticism adds its anonymous weight to the common cause, but the expression that has the most resonance is the one that will continue to enjoy common currency in speech for a long time.

If an image (and expressions are always figurative) resonates with the deepest layers of one's perceptions (and this can only happen to an image when the idiom itself naturally and organically derives its source from the same layers of its 'creator'), then image and idiom have every chance of remaining current and giving great pleasure to the usual audiences and those who take a keen interest in expressions of contemporary popular and poetic coinage.

A broad cross-section of Soviet writers and literati—the in-

---

* In English in the original.

telligentsia—has long been of the opinion that it is good form to admire folklore.

I must confess that I always found this admiration somewhat bewildering.

A small number of zealots apart, it always seemed rather insincere, even a pose, not a genuine understanding. Rather a borrowed admiration with a 'lit-crit' variety of *comme il faut*.

Perhaps this is not entirely fair; maybe this is nothing more than a reflection of my own attitude to this 'fashion'.

I was never terribly keen on images from the 'Kalevala',[3] even though people tried to introduce me to it.

Even after Pushkin had reworked them, neither Bulgarian epics nor the 'Songs of the Western Slavs' ever attracted me.[4]

I must confess that this perplexed me.

Nevertheless it is doubtless from here that the people's soul and spirit take their roots.

Turning to these primary sources had proved fruitful and fertile on so many occasions throughout the history of the arts: like it or not, I had to ponder the question of why my soul remained stubbornly 'unmoved' by the unquantifiable abundance of images from folklore, which was held in such high regard everywhere and was indeed the subject of a great number of books published by Academia when admiration for these works of popular narrative had reached its apogee.

There were of course exceptions as well: *The Lay of Prince Igor* [5] is something I have cherished since my schooldays.

The Miracles of the Mother of God, a medieval folk tale, is a cycle containing some of my favourite stories.

I have loved the *Nibelung* since childhood, before Fritz Lang's films spoiled it for me.[6]

Wagner put things to rights later, but he could not restore my admiration for this Germanicised epic: I found a new admiration for the Nordic *Edda*, the ancient Yggdrasil[7] and the whole wonderful cosmogony in the 'characters' of the extreme Scandinavian North.

I admired more the nameless primitive peoples in Frazer's *The Golden Bough*; so, to a lesser extent, those of Veselovsky, for he turned them into his 'lesser brethren', making them smaller and less colourful than did Sir Joshua.[8]

And in fact, their folklore is like them: be it Bushman, Polynesian, Australian, North American or Mexican; barely noticeable, it is not accorded half the respect shown to more popular folklores that have images people drool over.

But it is these aspects that are much more fascinating; they convey vividly the sense of figurative thought as it is in the process of emerging. You can witness in them ideas that are still in their formative stages; and you can virtually assist in the dynamic of the formation of concepts, while the actual images of the works are sensed as a staging-post in the development of intellect and thought.

More popular—more popular precisely because they are!—more marketable patterns of folklore—even, for example, Dobrynya Nikitich in comparison with Svyatogor![9]—no longer seem a creative lava just boiling over. It is as though the lava has cooled; its intricate patterns have set into a solid mass, formed not forming, and therefore so readily appropriated wholesale as simple forms of inspiration.

And this takes us straight to that unrestrained excitement—fervid turmoil—as I yield to what I find fascinating, when it fascinates me genuinely, profoundly and actively.

It simply never occurred to me systematically to suppose that this was an offshoot of folklore, even though that was how it enthralled and fascinated me.

At a time when the average Soviet intellectual had been exploiting all his 'connections' to be able later to boast of having the complete set of the Academia volumes even though he would never utter one word of popular slang, I very quietly drew volume after volume into my network of books, each of which was full of Paris argot, London cockney and later American slang.

Although the academic interest in French argot forced the publication of a wide range of relevant dictionaries and research a very long time ago, it was much later that fully comprehensive books on slang (I do not mean the highly specialised works that went out of print a long time ago) began coming out (in copious supply, too).

Landmarks like Mencken's *The American Language*, in 1919;

(the *Supplement* in 1945); a *Dictionary of Slang and Unconventional English*, in 1937; and the almost exhaustive *Thesaurus of Slang* only in 1943 (?).

But the first copies of my collection were on the shelves much earlier. *Dictionnaire de la langue verte* is dated 1921.

And Aristide Bruant's dictionaries (*L'Argot parisien*, 1901).[10]

But before I had access to specialised dictionaries and research papers, I had instead a solitary volume by Balzac.

'Une *Instruction criminelle*[11] was part of the *Shine and Poverty of the Courtesans* series, one of my favourite Balzac novels, even including the Corantin and Vautrin cycles. (I suppose that *Cousin Bette* was the best of the others; I tried on several occasions to dramatise it for the stage. I even have somewhere a fairly detailed, overall plan laying out the dramatic and stage solutions.)

This 'Instruction' fell somehow into my hands ages ago and by itself, too. It was not among the other novels (I think it was even before the Revolution).

Then, later, like Isis gathering up the scattered limbs of Osiris,[12] I collected the other novels in the series to gain a full picture of Rubempré, Rastignac, Vautrin, Coralie and Esther.

Perhaps it is the subject matter that makes this novel impressive; taken on its own, with no reference to what comes before or after, the pages devoted to prison slang stand out especially vividly.

Balzac of course delighted in this language for the same sense of living, dynamic emergence.

We should not forget his fascination with etymology (a vice I have long been guilty of!), nor that he wrote a charming passage on that very subject in *Louis Lambert*. He mentions the pleasure to be had from travelling backwards through the history of words, to the roots from which they were formed or evolved.

But it was not Balzac who introduced me to argot.

Nor *Les Mystères de Paris*, which I was lucky enough to acquire in Riga (before 1914) in an edition partly illustrated with 'woodcuts' of drawings by Daumier.

I remember the window of Kumpel's bookshop: it was on a small street. Inside was the book, opened at a page showing the young tramp and a hooligan, Tortillard, the associate of La

595

'The massacre'. Stills from the finale of the film *The Strike*

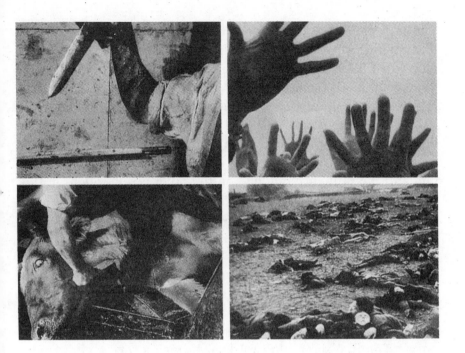

Chouette and the Schoolteacher. These were some of the illustrations by one of Balzac's namesakes—also an Honoré!* It is more than likely that this alone led me to buy this charming masterpiece by Eugène Sue!

Chance does not even come into it, if you bear in mind that Balzac himself wrote *Shine and Poverty* while he was influenced by Eugène Sue's work, which was then very popular.

Balzac envied his success and tried consciously to imitate him and the influence one had on the other is self-evident in this novel; incidentally, this is in its closing sections which, highbrow critics maintained, contribute least to Balzac's reputation as a classic. (*Tant pis*** for his reputation!)

This wonderful 'display'*** of colloquialisms and turns of phrase, vibrant with life, was taken from the fleshpots, prisons and alleyways of Paris—all those *tapis-franc, gouailleuses, chourineurs****—but that was not my first acquaintance with the colourful lowlifers of the French capital, nor their vivid manner of speech.

The first slang phrase I heard which struck a chord were the words: *'Les cognes sont là.'*

They were written on a note which was flung down in Victor Hugo's novel *Les Misérables. Cognes* are policemen.

This terse note serves a complex, dual purpose: it is first the image of what somebody (I have since forgotten who!) was able to write down.

And then it suddenly starts to function as the 'idea' of its content.

Flung at the right moment (by whom?) into an opening in the wall, it saves Jean Valjean from a very tricky situation: two villains were about to satisfy their curiosity with regard to his identity, aided by a heated iron bar . . .

I read *Les Misérables* with utter delight.

My mother sent it to me after she had left us, I think, as I was leaving the second class and entering the third.

The books broke through the exam fever and I managed a

---

*   i.e. Honoré Daumier (Ed.)
**   French: 'so much the worse'
*** In English in the original.
**** French slang: 'low dives', 'drinking dens' and 'cut-throats' respectively.

completely fantastic *tour de force* during a month of revision I not only passed all my exams; I also devoured a vast, multi-volume novel!

L'Abbé Myriel and his candelabras; the noble Javert who vanished at the point of his greatest triumph; the strong arm of the escaped 'hard convict' who helped little Cosette carry the bucket of water; 'Monsieur Madeleine' who put his shoulder under the hay-cart that had toppled on to the old man, and lifted it off him; the wanderings through the labyrinthine Paris sewers—all these cut a swathe through arithmetic problems, history and geography text-books, scripture and Russian during that memorable and, of course, in its way unique school revision period.

The first word that staggered me was *'la veuve',** applied to the guillotine.

I am not sure I grasped the unparalleled precision and 'generality' of this periphrasis at first. It was so merciless a depiction of the perpetual hunger of a woman abandoned.

It would be hard to find a more vivid name for it: the space at the bottom, for the condemned man's head, was like a mouth always hungrily agape.

Perhaps I found this allegory delightful at first because of the more superficial interpretation: simply, widowhood.

But I doubt if that would have been for long.

And of course the most interesting thing is that it was sub-conscious, intuitive: a long time before the real sense of the image became clear.

I expect it was this that made me react so strongly, many years later, to Sadger's conception of a similar derivation for all linguistic formations that had their origins in erotic/symbolic im-ages and to accept it unquestioningly for some time![13]

I found this in the work of Hanns Sachs and Rank, *The Meaning of Psychoanalysis in Science and Spirit.*

I think this book was the first I found that applied psycho-analysis to culture and art. Hitherto, my basic knowledge of psy-choanalysis was derived from 'Leonardo da Vinci and a Memory of His Childhood', and in its application, to the 'early erotic

---

* French: literally 'the widow'

awakening of a child!'[14]

I actually met Hanns Sachs—that marvellous, bespectacled, wise old salamander and his terrifying African mask—a 'symbol of complexes' which hung above his small low patients' couch—in Berlin many years later. We became great friends. He gave me a most interesting book about psychoanalysis, *Versuch einer Genitaltheorie* [Essay in Genital Theory], by Ferenczi, which explained a great deal of things (admittedly *post factum!*) which I had come across on my obsessive quest to penetrate the secrets of ecstasy.[15]

But Sachs and our meeting come in their own time . . .

The text of the note in *Les Misérables*—'*les cognes sont là*'—has a dual meaning, as I have said. It is purely an outline (proof that someone was able to write) and also it conveys a message.

Curiously, the very nucleus of 'argot' word creation is contained in that phrase, or more accurately, in that dual use and interpretation of it.

But, more than that, this is like a formula for what seems the undisputed 'backbone'* of any detective story. More than that again, it is the universal, real, invariable and sole plot of all detective fiction from any age, country or nationality.

Chesterton came close to one general single theme informing all manner of detective fiction.[16]

But he did not touch on it more precisely than with a 'winged phrase'. What was really invariable and eternal appeared to him in the inviolability of Catholic dogma which distracted him from examining systematically what he dropped on the way with the ease of paradox.

The solution to the material basis 'of the mystery story' eluded him.

Blinkered by the mysteries of his attraction solely to the Catholic Church, he could hardly examine this matter, either condescendingly or impartially.

Chesterton progressed from his detective Father Brown to non-detecting fathers—church pastors.

Father Knox (?) or O'Connor has left us with a description

---

* In English in the original.

of Chesterton, on the threshold of the church where he was converted, that has a charming symbol and surprising internal sense.

When he was asked if he had a twopenny catechism (the cheapest edition, probably, as a symbol of meekness), Chesterton searched his pockets feverishly to see whether his customary absentmindedness had got the better of him again.

And the first thing he took out and hastily shoved back into the depths of his pocket was also worth two pennies, but it was a detective story, not a catechism.

The detective novel is built entirely upon a double meaning.

And if all the varieties of peripeteias in the whole, worldwide epic of detective literature (and what makes this folklore less than universal in its sweep—what makes it inferior to the *Odyssey*, the *Divine Comedy*, or the Bible?!) are reduced to their central core, this core is always and invariably a double reading of the evidence: a false one and the true one.

The former is superficial, the second penetrates to the essence.

Or, to use more specialist terminology, the first is spontaneous perception; the second, a mediated response.

Or, to go into the mechanics of both ideas, the first is a 'physiognomical' interpretation, perceived in images; and the second is an 'understood' interpretation revealed conceptually.

But this double interpretation applies not only to different methods.

It also represents different stages, different levels of perception and understanding of phenomena in general.

It is precisely those two stages through which developing mankind passes: every individual's assimilation of nature, through poetry, emotions and images, shifts towards a mastery of it by science, understanding and learning.

So that he can master nature and communicate with it at the highest summits of his relationship with the universe, through a synthesis of the link between science and poetics.

In this sense, any novel about a secret ('mystery')* is a work

---

* In English in the original.

of mystery, treating of the eternal and immutable 'drama' of the emergence of an individual's consciousness; and everyone goes through that drama, irrespective of race, class or nation.

And this of course is the basic reality behind my constant fascination with detective fiction.

Its appeal to that most delicate of processes in the emergence of a personality is invariable, immediate and direct. The individual progressively moves from thinking in images and emotions to the maturity of consciousness; and the synthesis of both in the most sophisticated patterns found in the inner life of creative and artistic people!

And we can see a similar regularity of structure in world folklore and detective fiction as in works by individual, highly gifted artists (and sometimes artists of genius); a universal regularity, which permeates the principle of the whole or any detail to equal degree; and to take it further, the structure of language also (*vide* Shakespeare).[17]

'Argot' and 'slang' are not only for *'couleur locale'*, for establishing a framework within which the 1001 variations of the universal, two-part theme will develop through a double interpretation of the evidence. Every last sequin of the literary apparel which clothes the theme and ideas—its verbal fabric—is coloured with them.

'Argot' and 'slang', like the highest manifestations of poetry, show abstract concept and idea again returning to the primary, sensual charm of an image spontaneously created and expressed.

And when we read the commonplace in what has now become an unusual exposition but which was once uniquely accessible and possible (in terms of method) we travel anew that same path, as we move towards perception and understanding, that we travelled as individuals and as the smallest parts of humanity as a whole; that same path, from thinking in terms of feelings, images and myths, to a really conscious understanding. Moreover, the actual slang image becomes alive and *'irrésistible'* when its word formation is derived from no less original mechanisms; and the structure of its imagery hints at the stages of emergence a human individual himself physically passes through, reflecting the stages of his transition in the early layers of the thought process, just as later, with the first shoots of social organisation and, further, social systems, the individual starts to mould and form his own consciousness, basing it on a reflection of these social systems which now have peculiarities of structure and progressively developing social relations.

Which finally brings us back to that amazing quotation from the book by Nicholas Brady.

It would not be true to say that this quotation gave rise to all the ideas I have mentioned above.

They are very, very, very much older than that.

But the penetrating piquancy of the quotation seemed to resonate not merely in the depths of my brain or spinal cord, but deeper still—in the lymphatic vascular system which has preserved within us the stages corresponding to one-celled life forms and primary protoplasm.

Where in hell's name could a man have taken the image for this idiom from?!

Len Wyatt, the detective, says: '. . . I'm going to have a cold bath, and then start working. But before I make a start, I'm going to wrap myself round a warm breakfast. See you anon . . .'*

This is the very way in which a single-celled amoeba, a ball of living protoplasm, swallows any enemy it may meet, any edible object it may encounter, any breakfast coming its way!

When I come up against imagistic constructions of this kind I feel a jolt like an electric shock.

A responsive reaction is triggered deep within me—beyond the convolutions of the brain, somewhere in the tissue—by the very structures which are my contemporaries from the time when I was an individual on the evolutionary ladder, no more than a child; an embryo, a ball of albuminous protoplasm or a fertile drop, which is all that I once had been.

It is said that a sense of time is instilled beyond all conscious pathways and is connected to the most subtle, structural bases of our tissue—simultaneously the object and the subject of the phenomenon of time in an organic phenomenon of physical development and growth—which only later, later, a great deal later, is able to divide the actual process up as it feels it. Then, on the basis not

---

* p.119, *Coupons for Death*, by Nicholas Brady, Robert Hale Ltd, London, 1944. (E's note in English in the original)

only of the subjective phenomenon, but also of that same phenomenon in the world around us, a sense of time gradually becomes an idea of the movement of a process, in order that, a great deal later, it may be abstracted into a concept of time separate from the process of movement!

I am often struck by such 'basic thrills',* by the most unexpected images and scenes in the most unforeseen works and their unexpected peculiarities, but the ones which remain unequalled and unforgettable.

I remember two brilliantly lucid examples, from Jacques Deval's play *L'Age de Juliette.* (I saw it quite by chance, and it was utterly delightful.) (His *Mol'ba o zhizni* [Prayer About Life] was on in Moscow; the title was a Russian mistranslation from the French: *Prière pour les vivants* [Prayer for the Living].)[18]

I remember the sign that hung above the inn for the torchbearers opposite the entrance to the Père Lachaise cemetery in Paris: it was called 'Au Repos des Vivants'.**

What is particularly salient here is that the play's heroes—who were very young, but about to commit suicide because their parents did not consent to their marriage—lost their innocence, after the boy took a bath when the girl had done so.

Or that after their temporary exit, while electricians were repairing the radio, the audience discovers their relationship has grown deeper when the two go into the next room wearing each other's bath robes—one white, one grey.

But . . .

But I won't repeat myself. I just want to set out an account of this scene as it was, with all the supplementary details, as I did in far-off Alma-Ata, when I was an evacuee, one bitter, gloomy and miserable winter evening. Or when *Ivan* was yet to go into production, or when it ran into difficulties at the production stage, or opposition and squabbling about the way it was being produced.

It would be unreasonable, on the strength of a brief retelling of the plot, to expect the reader's perception to be as entranced by these two fleeting details or rather, two psychological

---

* In English in the original.
** French: 'For the Repose of the Living'

nuances—one in the characters' behaviour and the other in the way the audience is informed of this behaviour—as mine was: I did read the play in its entirety.

I touched on these details at the beginning.

The bathroom scene.

And the scene where the bath robes are swapped, after the electricians have been on.

Why was it precisely these episodes, these details, that held my attention and were so strangely—alogically—emotionally—attractive?

I should have to presuppose remote sources of ideas very deep within me and even more, a social and biological existence that had apparently sprung up in new, ultra-contemporary forms: a couple of bath robes, one white, the other grey, instead of bearskins; and the gleaming tiled bathroom at the Ritz, instead of secret paths and hidden places in tropical forests.

Or so it seems.

Both in the process of the lovers' sensual excitement on stage and even more so when the audience is keying itself up for the young lovers' celebration of their love, Deval makes both the actors and audience think back to the sexual communion of living beings in its oldest form, to touch upon the forms of sexual communion dating from a pre-human age, beyond the limits of one's own human level, human appearance and the forms of these forebears. And among them is the oldest one of all.

Miletta—Deval's touching young heroine—cannot restrain herself from succumbing to the temptation of turning on the gleaming taps in the dazzling bathroom in the Ritz.

And indeed, before departing this life forever, why not allow oneself one bite of a luxury that rich people enjoy daily?

Offstage you can hear first the noise of gushing hot water as the bath runs. Then, the joyous splashing and laughter of Miletta, as she capers beneath the stream.

The noise she makes stops her campanion from writing a farewell note to both their families.

But it does not stop him too from delighting in the elemental hot water, as it covers the dazzling white tiles.

. . . Hot water which Miletta leaped out of, before putting on a white bath robe to run on stage.

Now he comes on stage too.

His bath robe is grey.

A small, theatrical *quid pro quo.*

The radio has broken.

Two electricians come on.

To mend it.

The young people go offstage for a while.

To the bedroom.

The radio is being mended.

The electricians depart.

Miletta comes on, and this time she is wearing the grey bath robe.

And he the white.

What is it?

A cynical device, worthy of a farce?

A smutty trick to tell the audience that during that time the actors had disrobed; then succumbed to the heat of fresh passions; then, once these had been quenched, forgotten in their haste whose was whose?

Or was it something else: to use this detail——the exchange ——to exert influence on whole 'layers'* of early sensual notions, connected with what had happened; an evocation of a whole complex, via the generations who once consecrated and later romanticised this high point of man's biological existence?

All the action unfolds with the utmost purity, romance, romanticisation.

And this detail, supplying the unstated, appears as one of the most subtle and transparent pieces of writing in this play, woven entirely from the wholly mysterious charm of first love and its transition from slumbering emotions to a glorious celebration of love, which the two young beings are introduced to for the first time.

Of course, the detail of the bath robes is for information.

Of course, the slightest false step in the production, or by the actors, and the detail might miss that lyrical note which rang out so clearly; the mother-of-pearl tenderness of the action.

---

* In English in the original.

Shooting *Bezhin Meadow* (the second version). Crimea, 1936. (Photo: Mikhail Gomorov)

I doubt, of course, that Deval ever thought that the outward sign he used to show it, the form he chose to reveal what had happened, could fix in the subconscious the most profound stream of ideas, beliefs, rites and interpretations that have enshrouded marriage throughout all history.

He was probably not aware—did not even suspect—what he was creating when he invested the wedding rite of his young heroes in the outer apparel of the most ancient of customs.

Just opening Frazer's *The Golden Bough*—part two, devoted to Adonis, Attis and Osiris—one can see a long list of examples showing how the exchange of clothing between bride and groom became an obligatory ritual tradition of the wedding ceremony, even among radically different peoples. This list is in the notes, regarding the bride's wedding robes which were worn at some ceremonies by male priests.

Not only the bride and groom exchanged clothing; in some cases, their parents did also.

And the increasing number of participants in such an exchange of clothing, perhaps originating precisely from that point, from that very wedding ritual, led to cross-dressing *en masse* at saturnalia and in whatever forms they have survived—Feasts of Fools, etc. (cf Willson Disher, *Clowns and Pantomimes*, London, 1925).

So we can see that there was a firm basis of fact underlying the young lovers' strange, chance, marriage 'rite' in Deval's play; it dated from ancient times and the present too, temporarily lagging behind at a level of immaturity—the initial stage of future cultural development.

The colossal wealth of factual detail Frazer amassed is equalled by the modesty of his commentary on it.

He goes no further than to suppose that this is some means of keeping out the evil eye and hostile spirits. If this explains, to some extent at least, some of the cases (elsewhere) when, in order to avoid the vengeance of a dead man's soul or a beast, the warrior male hides dressed in women's clothing, that explanation is not valid where the exchange takes place when both the 'persecuted' people are still alive and have simply changed places!

I think this ritual is in fact very closely allied to all those superstitions about the original androgynous being who divides into two discrete aspects—male and female—whose conjugal coupling celebrates a new recreation of the original, initial, single hermaphroditic origin. This situation recreates this point of departure: they are both in communion with this superhuman essence, becoming, at the moment of the ritual, like the original deity; in all cults, this deity unites both male and female origins.

But the worlds which stir beneath the preceding scene are just as deep set: I am referring to that scene where the water brings them close together for the first time. The warm bath, which the young lovers take, the one after the other.

'Have you seen goldfish mating?'

I have not.

The reader may be more fortunate.

But I do not ask the reader this rhetorically; I had once been asked this in all seriousness.

The question came from a strange man with a shaggy ginger beard and a shock of red hair on top. Between these conflagrations, which gazed at each other like the two worlds of the Arcana, there shone a pair of glasses; and behind them his large, penetrating brown eyes looked out with a surprisingly fixed gaze.

That apart, this man was a sapper by calling; he held the position of second-in-command of military construction. I served under him in the Civil War in Velikie Luki as well as in other remarkable towns and small villages of our vast country.

His hair was of an intense colour, despite his age; he would wear army shirts and quilted trousers, a dull brown belt, calf-length boots cut wide, and he was very well disposed towards me.

He was called Krayevich and was a noted eccentric.

He was extremely well-informed.

And about the oddest things. He was an excellent sapper and knew a lot. But he was famous above all for knowing how literally all animals 'do it'.

His short, hirsute figure, which looked like a Konenkov[19] wood sculpture, was wont to stop, fix you with a steady gaze from behind thick lenses and ask abruptly:

'But do you know how . . . ?'

The first half of the phrase was always the same.

Only the species changed, in the second half.

We had kangaroos, camels, giraffes, crocodiles, tortoises and so on and so forth. The list was endless.

Once the question was about goldfish.

And so from the lips—lips surrounded by the luxuriant fiery growth of Krayevich's beard—I learned how goldfish mated. I had never thought about it previously, so it was with considerable astonishment that I heard that there is minimal contact between the two—that it is purely adventitious and takes place solely between their secretions (nothing to do with the word 'secret'!)— in the water and between the two *dramatis personae*—or *pisces*, in this case!

We discussed the pros and cons of sexual communion that way and then parted until the next time; but the strange happiness that is the lot of goldfish was stored away in the deepest recesses of my memory to be recalled when needed, once the right association had been made.

How could I forget Engineer Krayevich, disguised as Neptune and surrounded by darting goldfish, when I read that description of the scene from *L'Age de Juliette?*

True, that scene came fifteen years later; I was even better informed in that area then, though not from any urge to know about each and every variety, but from curiosity about general tendencies and the very definite, evolutionary directions that later forms took. I was curious about the evolutionary changes that the most vital act of any creature underwent.

It was to know more about this (Dr Ferenczi's book *Versuch einer Genitaltheorie*, published in 1924, seemed interesting both from an historical perspective and assessed on its own merits) that I made the acquaintance of our universal forebear, who exists at the lowest level of animal life, and is little more than a vegetable. It looks like a fish, and scientists maintain that it is the official ancestor, the first rung, the beginning of the fascinating truth of evolution that Darwin had deduced.

The founder of all future species which developed by evolution has a beautiful Latin name: *amphyoxus lanceolatus.*

So even if we are not the direct descendants of goldfish, we do at least share the same forebear with the elegant Latin name.

This last would not be at all important, except that we can

610

trace this path (not the social or biological path, but the evolutionary one) back to the ancestor whose mating ritual was identical with the amazing *vita sexualis** of goldfish.

Which made me realise that the element in the two young beings' lovemaking in the Ritz Hotel that excited me without my understanding why, was chosen intuitively and was successful in all respects.

As opposed to Wedekind's fairly crude *Spring Awakening* [Frühlings Erwachen], Deval described this awakening with charming nuances that strike distant chords which reverberate deep within our instinct. And the awakening of emotions involves worlds which are dormant within us; sublimated forms of the emergence of our instincts, as well as of our behaviour, *modus vivendi*, rituals . . .

I don't suppose I can say exactly when I was jolted in that direction—or what by; but whatever it was, that impulse broadened and developed in my personal practice and in my analysis of other people's works, finally to become what I term the *Grundproblem*** of all my conceptions. I set it down, extremely briefly, but with all the detail to be expected of fundamental theories, in 1935, at the conference of the 'great' Soviet cinema.[20]

I can remember one such case very distinctly; it may even be what led me to this.

I had to familiarise myself with how our organs evolved; with the sense organs first of all.

My unfailing adviser, friend and consultant in all such matters—Alexander Romanovich Luria—suggested that I got to grips with a short book by Goldschmidt called *Ascarides*.[21] In a very poetic and populist style (but without compromising the scientific thoroughness), a fascinating picture emerged showing the peripeteias in the emergence of the perfected apparatus of our organism, from the earliest stages and on the lowest rungs of development.

I remember very clearly a passage describing the stillwater

---

  * Latin: 'sex life'
 ** German: 'basic problem', a term frequently used by E. (Ed.)

hydra, which grows new tentacles to replace broken ones.

Clarification was provided by the image of Hercules who wrestled with the Hydra (capital H), in Greek mythology—not this small, defenceless, still-water creature.

But some other early, amazing event was described in images analogous with a marionette, each of whose limbs acquired a life of its own and darted this way and that before being brought in to a whole.

I saw this standard trick—the dancing skeleton, whose arms and legs are flung first wide apart, and then brought close together —in Moscow at that very time. It was during a performance by a wonderful touring puppet company from Vienna, in the premises of the old Music Hall (next to the Tchaikovsky Concert Hall on Mayakovsky Square). That was also the venue where, so many years later, I admired the mastery that gave the puppets a life of their own: stage pieces by 'the magician of the pear orchard', Mei Lan-Fan.[22]

The stout Austrian with his wife and daughter, lit fantastically from below, were seated on a low bench and leaning over the theatre of miniatures' backdrop and hidden by the harlequin of the small mirror of the toy stage.[23] They rhythmically moved their dancing hands which held the wooden crosses, the four ends of which were connected by threads to the puppets' arms, legs and joints. In the capable hands of the Viennese family, they were fantastically alive and limber.

I saw them sideways on, an oblique view from behind the wings.

I saw two rows; living people and dancing figures, spots of light on both and shadows of two sizes—the humans also entering the puppets' dance—conducting sheer Hoffmannesque phantasmagoria amid the sets of the real stage and the toy theatre, piled up on real platforms.

I saw a similar small theatre (but stationary) in an Antwerp cellar in one of the darkest, most crooked alleyways near the port.

The black hulks of depots and houses all around, the pennants of schooners framed by narrow streets. The glimmer of the moon.

And the tiny 'den' with the empty, tiny apron of the stage,

in the depths of a small, dim hall.

There was no performance that evening.

And the next day was to be my last there.

But then the owner of the toy theatre kindly showed me the equipment by candlelight.

The puppets were larger here: they were almost as high as my knees.

And they were crudely fashioned from lumber, their moustaches carved with a few strokes and their cheeks coarsely painted.

But perhaps as they danced in the flickering shadows cast by the candle this incompleteness, roughness made them even more unreal and fantastic than the exquisite workmanship of the Viennese collection, coarse though that was in comparison with Teschner's ultra-aesthetic (and utterly enchanting) puppet troupe.[24]

But to go back to the Ascarides and the actual book on this small and charming vermiform ancestor of all our great-great-great-grandmothers.

It is possible that I will get the details hopelessly wrong—I have not picked the book up in twenty years!

But I remember clearly the idea—a kind of 'inversion': of course the funny picture of the skeleton flying apart and the war-like image of Hercules doing battle with the Hydra, were far from chance analogies, thoughtfully provided by Viennese puppeteers and the Greeks respectively for Herr Goldschmidt to use to illustrate a point.

Both Hercules and the small marionette of a skeleton, with its limbs so horrifyingly independent, are little more than the realisation of 'memories', reminiscences of those early biological and physiological peripeteias and adventures which our revolting species once experienced on its way towards the perfection of today's shape and forms!

And hence the conclusion that self-expression lies at the very heart of works that are genuinely exciting in the types of both subject and forms, within which the subject and even the theme are simply the first stage of the crystallising creative 'urge'. Sometimes even they are omitted (*vide* the group of works that have no subject; or a work which is an adaptation of someone else's, with a preexisting subject).

Any freely selected subject or even one that has been foisted upon me (in either case the interpreter will have to adapt it) is relevant to my vision, understanding and perception; from the inclination to take that very one, right up to breaking the 'received subject' down.

Here it would do no harm to dwell on the high proportion of my works (especially the successful ones) which were 'made to order' with respect to the theme; and in the historical films (that is, in almost all of them!) I was 'blinkered' by the actual events, even though I was at some distance from what really happened!

It would be true to say that I distorted history considerably, with regard to its 'image and likeness', its flavour and the sense of haphazard; but if I sometimes missed the letter I tried at least to catch the spirit; and I immersed myself enough in history for this.

Further, I always tried to pin the situation and the image of an historical event and fact on to the scheme of the primary sensual situation as each element of the form grew and flowed from the language of form—the inexhaustible wealth of means of expression: seams of sensual thought which only inspiration can dislodge, inducing an active trembling of the whole body from head to toe; from the topmost layers of consciousness down to the deepest bases of primary, past, sensual and pre-sensual thought, where the actual terms 'thought', 'memory' and even . . . 'feeling' have almost no place.

But that is precisely what the sighting-point, which my volitional work is aimed at, is like. And it will strike home, with enough all-encompassing inspiration!

P. S. Later, in another 'volute' of these spiralling creative impulses, I will introduce this idea even into the relationship between 'creative associations' born of vivid impressions and the role they play in the imagination (not 'primary' at this point, or 'original'; but even apparently random although I should add an N. B. that the most persistent of those random impressions will of course be those closely connected to the 'deepest layers'* of 'originality'!).

---

* In English in the original.

This will appear in the first edition of my lectures at VGIK ('A Soldier Returns from the Front').[25] While I was devising them, I made a note of the associations and memories which came to life when one link or other had been forged; and by the end I could formulate these associations which arose *post factum*, apparently (and probably actually) comprising the total sum of what my desired plan needs if it is to be realised.

In one example of the so-called *torito* (one of my photographs from Mexico) I was able 'to disentangle'* almost all the elements of previous associations, which were inevitably included in the elements of a natural setting.

To round the whole subject of folklore off, let me say that its value and attraction—from the Bushman to Father Brown and from images from the Bible to the images of Chicago 'slang'—was that it introduced me to early vivid and dynamic ways of grasping the world and the universe with an image that helps us to understand them both, taken together, which is a half-way point to recreating the world.

---

* In English in the original

Inversions[1]

Sometimes, I sum people up well with words.

Especially when I am being malicious.

Comrade E was holidaying with me in Barvikha. I thought he looked like a pink skeleton wearing a lounge suit.

People who know Comrade E can back me up on the 'sensual accuracy' of this description.

Analysing this formula is well worth the effort.

The interesting—realistic!—'core' of this apparently nonsensical image is of a skeleton worn on the outside.

But this is an entirely natural state of affairs, in the case of . . . shrimps, crabs and lobsters.

With crustacea, the outer surface acts as the skeleton; their plates and casings house the soft tissue!

'Crab-like' features are a very popular metaphor for people.

'Crab's eyes' are almost a commonplace.

Why should 'crab's skeleton' be less so?

The 'dénouement' of course came much later.

And led of course to the . . . *Grundproblem*.

The actual description derived from Comrade E's customary bared grin, his smooth, shaven head and his glasses, which exaggerated his eye-sockets considerably.

Also, Comrade E's complexion was an intense pink, like a piglet.

The first thing I saw was the outline of the skull: its structure could easily be discerned behind the flat features of his face.

But what about the pink colouring?

This skull must be made pink.

The pink hue of the skull makes the pink not alive and healthy, but painted and ridiculous.

But a skull pushing through the surface of the skin is an ominous image. No doubt there is an ominous element to Comrade E, especially for those whose articles and plays he cut 'like a censor'! But there is much to be respected in this ominous picture.

But the image must be grotesque.

A skeleton encapsulating a naked body is again a pretty ghastly image.

The 'lounge suit' at once clothes him, makes him normal, taking him out of the symbolic abstraction; and then deflates the whole combination once more.

Furthermore the ominous overtones of a skeleton as a symbol of death are here cancelled out: it is being worn above a jacket, and so is itself no more than an overcoat or a macintosh.

The lounge suit also hints at the 'fullness' of the figure.

The terrifying body with its pink, grinning skull, becomes a joke as you look lower down.

Let us now consider the three 'sources' of the image.

One we have already touched upon.

This sits somewhere in our own ideas physically. With the primary principle of 'ambivalence', which, 'setting' into uncoupled extremes and opposites (a long time before becoming in their apogee the conception of a unity of opposites) it 'recalls' its past ambivalent unity through the device and form of . . . an inversion . . . (which is also funny as a level of development already experienced!)

The dynamic of an ominously living process turns into immobility.

The extreme 'images'—the skull and the face—fragment, and are now put together mechanically and also by the 'deflated' action of dressing.

The pink skull, 'worn over the face', is little more than a farcical device, a crude mask.

Too real!

The fantastic shift is achieved by the shift from the skull-face to the whole skeleton-body.

The 'skeleton' is worn over the body.

In some parts this is not entirely feasible technically and it is slightly awkward.

What would happen to the skeleton's arms and legs?

Would you have to sew stripes on to the sleeves and trousers?

The torso can however be shoved inside the ribcage which surrounds it, one size larger. (Just as galoshes need to be slightly larger than one's shoes.)

It is harder with the pelvis . . .

So, all in all, the expansion of the skeleton, as we see it, stretches the simile.

The 'change of places' between the skeleton and the person's outward appearance is part of that same family of inversions which makes the horse ride the knight in fairy tales. Swift, in his *Gulliver's Travels*, employed this switching of horse and rider, but on a much higher and more sophisticated level.

This is what the broad, general human premises for such an image would have been.

But I myself have two more to add, of a purely personal nature.

One concerns a very subtly worked, figurative canvas of living faces, skulls and cardboard masks, representing skulls, developing from a very remote plan as both 'inversion' and . . . 'double inversion'.

The second premise touches an even deeper past. It is connected not to some figurative association, but to a purely dynamic, figurative interpretation that emerged from a verbal characterisation of the process which makes expressive movements happen.

This was something I thought very deeply about in Moscow in the '20s; the play of masks, faces and skulls came in Mexico in the '30s.

That line written above about 'a skull pushing through the skin' served as a vivid reminder not only of my ideas regarding the principles of expressive movement as a whole, but also of those brief moments of spontaneous practice, where I sketched out the principles in order to understand how mimicry worked.

Another anecdote.

An illustrated one, at that. A Gavarni lithograph, from his series *'Les Enfants terribles'*.

An extremely perplexed subject sits, his eyes fixed on the viewer.

A 'little darling' has climbed on to the arm of the chair.

'Ooh, look what's happening to you. Your head is growing through your hair!'

The dear little boy is looking at . . . a bald patch.

A simple 'inversion'?

Assuredly.

Head and hair have changed place and functions.

But that is not all!

Strange though it may seem, the skull, the layers of skin and the hair really are linked to one another in expressive movement in the most diverse and dynamic relationships.

The link which really exists in nature is applied to a situation which is externally close to but not dependent on that link. That is one of the causes of the comic effect here.

At the same time, there is the sense of some sort of essential correctness in the 'dynamic' picture of the process, as well as the obvious fallacy of applying this process to the given conditions.

(To take an example: if a very tall man stands in cold water, the cold will take at least a fortnight to reach his nose.)

The body, the layers of skin and the follicles are of course linked to one another in expressive movement.

Even the ancients thought that an animal 'bristled' to make itself look larger.

A more scientific point of view would reject this as excessive anthropomorphism and would explain it by saying that when an animal prepares for battle it takes in a large quantity of oxygen which always makes the body expand.

This makes the skin tauten, which in turn pulls each hair into an erect position.

But the hair will do this in precisely the reverse case: when the volume of the body beneath the skin is constant, but the skin's surface rapidly shrinks.

This happens on the head, for example, where of course the volume of the skull cannot change. However the skin contracts convulsively.

It is well known that people instinctively shrink when they experience terror.

Obviously, as far as the head is concerned, this can only affect the scalp.

Which is what happens.

Like the hands, feet and knees, the scalp is 'pulled' towards the 'centre' of the body as a whole, to protect and hug the chest.

Stills from the epilogue for *Que Viva México!*

The head performs a similar action.

It buries itself in the tucked-up knees and the person hides, crouching, in a position of total defensiveness which comes naturally, and in which he spent nine heavenly months utterly relaxed in his mother's womb before emerging into this hostile, unfriendly world which for some reason is thought to be God's own!

But our organism, in the process of expressive movement, is marked by a surprising ability (in some cases) to react as a whole, with one motive.

And conversely, with several motives.

And chief among them are motives which oppose one another.

More accurately, make us react in two contradictory ways to one and the same motive.

And to realise such opposites, the different parts of the organism react in different ways.

Some of them take one line of action.

Others a different one.

In movement, this is no more than the realisation of a contradictory reaction, which is inevitable for a consciousness that responds spontaneously and with mediated reactions in equal measure.

Thus our system is divided, more often than not, into two camps, each trying to realise a contrary plan of action.

Here a basic division occurs between the 'centre' and the 'periphery'. The system's broadly understood 'centre' is linked to a simpler, internal, spontaneous response.

Then, the 'periphery'—the extremities and the mimetic surface of the face—is fundamentally linked to the motor execution mediated by the responsive function which makes the movement . . .

But the 'boundary' between these spheres is by no means fixed.

As one or the other component grows stronger, it seizes more and more elements of the motor system and of the body as a whole, in order to realise its planned movement.

Finally one becomes completely dominant, 'breaking through' into real action and out of that 'struggle between motives', which characterises directly opposing interpretations.

Furthermore, if all groups of muscles are in all cases locked, one should also take into account which muscle of each group is affected first or wholly by innervation, as a result of the impulse to move.

Which is why 'shrinking' in terror, for example, is associated with the opposite image: arms raised upwards and to the side, neck outstretched and eyes wide open.

Assuming that the skin (the extreme periphery) undergoes a rapid contraction, or the whole body rapidly folds in on itself, then there is the same tension of the skin that makes one's hair stand on end.

A division which goes as far as the very limit of the body—the skin—is rare enough and has more to do with the class of phenomena which we ascribe 'to ourselves' as purely physiological, a part of our expressive conditions: tears are forced out; our skin is covered with goosepimples or perspiration and we shiver violently.

Meanwhile, according to how they are realised, all these phenomena are subordinated to those actual formulae, but they are played out at such a peripherally 'remote' spot that they are physically localised at some extreme boundary of our flesh to be registered somewhere beyond the region of a distinct sensual interpretation, not as an 'emotion' this time, but a 'physical condition'.

Exactly the same thing applies to the other extreme, where for example bouts of diarrhoea induced by fear, or 'premature birth' have nothing to do with expressive processes and everything to do with purely physiological phenomena.

The study of 'surface' phenomena is interesting for its links with the distant past; the original, expressive manifestation is the relationship of reciprocal tensions between the inside and outside of amoebae: pseudopodia, where part of the protoplasm alternately protrudes and retracts, as tendency overcomes tendency; endoplasm beats ectoplasm.

And as always, extremes meet.

At the highest level of expressiveness, there is almost the purest reproduction of this first plan (which at its highest level can be sung as a chorus).

623

Which brings us back to the relationship between the whole and its thinnest of coverings. Except that the endoplasm here is the head, as the foremost unit of the body as a whole, and the ectoplasm is the mimetic covering, what we call the face, made up of skin and muscle.

The millimetric seismograph of the face's features which mimetically echo the microscopic vacillations in the struggle between the motives or impulses (and essentially the wearer consequently reacts in opposing ways), is a piece of apparatus that is infinitely refined and perfected, yet it operates according to the same fundamental plan as the pseudopodium.

And it seems no longer wild, strange or absurd to define the principles of mimetic expressiveness as the relationship between facial contractions, as the head tries (precisely tries, rather than succeeds) to push through the surface of the face. Or as the surface of the face tries to run freely over the skull's immobile surface.

When we stand agape in astonishment, what is that if not a spontaneous reaction before the face lights up with comprehension?

A face pinched with grief is a skull, which with the body slides through the thin surface of the face.

And a face bursting with smugness, sleek (that is, the skin tautened) is like a self-satisfied, well-developed chest, ready with the ribcage to pop the buttons of the coat from inside; to blow away the face, the first to carry the impulse of the body and skull!

I can well remember the day when I was doing practical work on expressive movement and a friend and I had a break-through—the realisation of the dynamic of expressive movement came with the verbal formula: 'the skull pushes through the face'.

I have two very close friends.

To me they are virtually two Ajaxes.

I cannot think of one without also thinking of the other.

Actually they were both Aristides, not Ajaxes.

Their surnames sounded similar as well: Bruant and Briand.[2]

One reigned in Montmartre.

The high priest of bars like 'Le Chat Noir' and '[Au] Lapin

Agile'.

This second Montmartre bar was a play on words, in honour of the artist who painted the sign: *l'a peint A. Gill*.[3] *

Just think of Hugo's *Le Pot aux roses* [French: 'The Pot of Roses'], which became *le poteau rose* [French: 'the rose thorn']; or his *'Tu ora'* [Latin: 'You pray'] which became *trou aux rats* [French: 'rat-hole'], which was where Esmerelda found sanctuary when she fell into the hands of the mad old woman.

Or again, that Catholic and reactionary, King Charles X—*le pieux monarque* [French: 'the pious monarch'] whom Travies turned into *le pieu monarque* [French: 'the blockhead monarch'].

My greatest, truest affection was for the former; his soft black hat and red scarf came to stand for all the charm and romance of Paris in the early decades of the century.

The Paris of street songs and argot.

Café-concerts and Yvette Guilbert, Toulouse-Lautrec and Xanrof.

It was some time before I gathered where this strange, apparently abbreviated name was taken from. Its owner wrote songs for Yvette; they were particularly ironic or enchanting.

I think it was Emile Bayard's notes about the Latin Quarter that solved the riddle for me.[4]

A certain young versifier, Fourneau, was looking for a pseudonym.

He was expecting an inheritance from Uncle, but this would not be possible if he were to be identified as the author of frivolous ballads.

Translating Fourneau (*fourneau* means 'stove') into Latin gives *fornax*—but that would be transparently obvious.

But if you then write it back to front—now that's more like it. From Fourneau to Fornax, and thence Xanrof. But anyone who likes Xanrof will have found this out for himself as I did; and those who do not know or care for him will be pretty much indifferent to all this . . .

I love the other Aristide for just one thing he did.

I mention it on every possible occasion.

---

* French: 'painted by A. Gill', but sounding similar to *'Lapin Agile'*

The women in the vanguard, pouring into the Winter Palace. Stills from a scene in *October*.

The women defending the Winter Palace and the Bolshevik envoys.

And I think that this is the best place to mention it.

Briand was famous in his later years as a fervent campaigner for a United States of Europe. It is not that dubious idea that I find attractive, however, but how this idea was born. It struck him, as the saying goes, like a 'winged phrase'.

At some meeting or other he threw out this formula as no more than a rhetorical device contrasting Europe with the United States of America.

It was only later—significantly so—that he began to contemplate what this 'winged phrase' implied—

Of course, when he hurled out these words he could not have been thinking of anything specific; this chance (or maybe not so chance; more a tendency his subconscious encapsulated in a slogan) phrase preceded the formulation and it magically caught on, welding disparate elements of his plan into a programme. That can happen, even in politics.

But good heavens, I am an artist as well.

Not only a researcher.

And the (seemingly) wild, paradoxical (in form) formula will lodge in me without fail, somewhere; even if only as an image ('the skull pushed through the face').

This is bound to appear as a dynamically spontaneous picture.

Not as a figurative description, but as a living image, in which the skull really does come to the surface. The face emerges through the skull. And the face is like a certain image of the skull and the skull like a certain independent face . . .

One, living on top of the other. One hidden beneath the other. One living an independent life through the other.

And one repeating the physical outline of the process via the interplay of face and skull, changing masks.

Masks!

Of course.

Now I can see the masks—now the mask of a skull on a living face, now the mask of a living face on a skull—materialising in this way.

And I have only to surround myself with real\masks for that old forgotten secondary paradoxical formula to come into its own in all the fullness of its figurative form and, in that form, to pick out the formula for the new essence, theme or idea which leaps out of the climactic chords of the whole artistic concept, the whole system of images, the whole picture of the whole film.

The Day of the Dead in Mexico!

I have written elsewhere about precisely how the image of the Day of the Dead took me to Mexico.

That is not the part of the subject that interests me here.

If it was the Day of the Dead that prompted me first to go to Mexico, then it is natural enough that my last word on that country—the ending of the film—should be expressed in images from that same Day of the Dead. The more so as the theme of life and death, expressed ultimately by a living face and a skull, is the key, basic theme which informs the whole film.

The theme of life, death and immortality.

In the crucible of new ideas which were born of the revolution and followed the ruthless purging of old ideas and beliefs, there appeared a new conception even of victory over death, the conquering of death; immortality.

We are mortal, biologically.

Only our social deeds make us immortal; the small contribution we make to social progress, the short distance we run before passing on the baton to the next generation.

This is now a bookish platitude.

Once, people worked out for the first time ever that twice two is four. Many centuries later, the age of relativity gave an innocent problem like that any answer it liked. And this was a new, crucial step towards the threshold of the new, atomic age.

And although we are old enough to remember the time before the October Revolution, we were also sufficiently young when it came to assimilate the ideas that came in its wake.

Now such ideas can be applied to an infinitely wider field than that one-sixth of the world's land mass where they are more than words!

Uncle Sam's recent need for human beings to fly his planes and perish on the battlefield resulted in this new creed of immortality consistently being preached from American screens.

A Guy Named Joe[5] showed dying, dead, smashed-up pilots sitting behind the trainees; pooling their experience paid for with their lives, they led wave after wave of young pilots into the skies.

That says it all.

American inventiveness and skill at extracting from situations a range of possibilities—from lyricism to farce, from low comedy to tragedy—divide the situations into an endless succession of scenes.

But the tenor of the subject rests with the 'General in the Sky' who assigned the smashed-up pilots to the recruits.

And the idea that the hands of each trainee would be guided by the thousands who perished before him attains the height of pathos.

Although Lionel Barrymore uttered this speech in his usual querulous way, and Spencer Tracy as Joe, a dead pilot, listened with his eyes screwed up sceptically as he was commissioned to return to earth and guide the young pilot unseen.

But there is a fundamental difference too. Our idea of immortality is not as a beyond-the-grave cooperation between young and old! We see it as a cause which generations fight and die for.

And that aim is man's freedom, which we supposed our allies were also fighting for.

It was only after the gun smoke had dispersed that we realised that the same words can have completely different meanings in different parts of the world.

Our ideal is to fight for Revolution, to live it, in the name of true freedom; the Allies fought for something quite different.

Time and time again our understanding of immortality was emphatically defined as immortality in the struggle for the revolutionary ideal of freedom.

The bookish platitude for many, for our generation—I say again—was the emergence of a new awareness of life and reality.

But then, as often happens, it is not only a reflection of facts that is repeated in a work's emergence, but also the dynamic of the process; this majestic and magnificent highway leading to a new life, new thoughts and ideas—this very thought—not a formula but a bright and living image—blossomed into the chief subject to emerge from the chaos of countless intersections of episodes and facts, rituals and customs, anecdotes and situations in which the course of life and death intertwine one with another in Mexico as nowhere else,

either in tragic images of death, trampling life underfoot,

or in rich images celebrating life's triumph over death,

or in the fulfilment of one's allotted span,

or in the immensity of an eternal future, engendered by the coming generations that will grow up out of the spilt blood of the dying present.

The interplay of life and death,

as they struggle for the upper hand.

The film starts with the cult of death in ancient Aztec and Mayan civilisations, among the stillness of the ancient stones. And it finishes with the contemptuous *vacilada*, a specific form of Mexican irony which makes the very image of death appear ludicrous, so much liveliness does it generate.

And in between comes the peon, dying beneath the hooves of the *hacendado's* horses; and the Catholic monk, in the blasphemy of self-denial and asceticism as he turns his back on the rich pageant of life in the tropics. And the bull, shedding his blood in the arena to the greater glory of the Madonna; and the country, torn by fratricidal strife and awash with blood, all to the accompaniment of Vatican-inspired shouts of *'Viva Cristo Rey!'**, not *'Viva el Hombre Rey!'*** which is what should have been shouted out in a thunderous roar.

All this comes together in the finale.

The ironic, distorting mirror of the Day of the Dead; the phantom of everlasting death to whom the ancients humbly bowed down in the prologue.

But it is no longer in the form of Aztec and Mayan marble or granite skulls, nor the terrifying image of the Mother of Gods, wearing a necklace of human skulls,

nor even the sacrificial stone of Chichen-Itzá, where the rocks are carved to look like skulls;

no!

Here, a cardboard mask of death dances a rumba, which

---

*   Spanish: 'Long live Christ the King!'
** Spanish: 'Long live Man the King!'

changes into a funeral march among the carousels, fairground stalls and markets to be found on the avenues, squares and boulevards of every town and village, however large or small.

The carousels and Ferris wheels spin.

Some people are dancing a wild rumba.

Skull masks are going in all directions.

There is one, under a peon's straw sombrero;

and there is one under the gold-embroidered sombrero of a charro.

There is one with a lady's hat pinned on top.

There, a topper.

There, a tricorn.

There is one above a workman's overalls; a mechanic, a driver, a smith, a miner.

The carnival is in full swing!

At its climax, masks are flung upwards.

There is one frame filled with cardboard skulls. A gale of laughter blows them away and instead of a white wall of skulls, a bronze wall of peons doubled up with mirth is revealed.

Another frame—also showing explosive laughter—shows a pale mask of cardboard death giving way to the merriment of a day-worker, a mechanic and a driver locked in friendly embrace.

Bronzed, laughing faces.

Eyes glittering like coals; white teeth.

Another group of masks. And wearing the same costumes that they wear throughout the film.

This is what the man who exchanged shots with the *hacendado* was wearing.

This is what he was wearing when he died after being caught.

This is what he wore when he toiled in the fields, or in the cement works.

But the masks spill over into this group of true 'positive heroes' who, in the film, confirm the authority of life; the masks are wearing the clothes of those who, throughout the film, are identified with violence and the enslavement of life (death).

It is they who wear the *hacendados'* suits as they ride their horses over the buried peons.

It is they who wear the shawl and hat that belong to the landowner's daughter.

The same grinning cardboard masks bob between the wing collars, above the stars and ribbons on their dinner jackets and beneath their top hats.

And the general silhouette hints at the president who reviews the firemen's and . . . police parade in the film.

The general's plumage and tricorn hang above another cardboard skull, this time one with a . . . moustache. He elegantly escorts a skull half hidden by a lace fan and wearing a fluttering mantilla, holding castanets.

And he raises his hands to the sky and turns on the spot, mimicking the gestures of the Papal Nuncio and the Archbishop of Mexico on the day of the Madonna de Guadalupe (which is also in the picture). He is an oddity, dressed in his full episcopal regalia; and his gold tiara burns in the sky above that same dull, motionless, cardboard face of death.

This carnival is not derived from Saint-Saens' *'Danse macabre'*, nor Holbein's 'Dance of Death'.

It comes straight from the heart of Mexican folklore: on this day, traders' street stalls are covered with skulls wearing helmets, top hats, caps, sombreros, matadors' berets and bishops' mitres. It comes straight out of the paintings by Mexico's most populist artist José Guadalupe Posada, known as *'Calaveras'*.[6]

On the Day of the Dead, newspapers and special broadsheets are full of pictures on the same subject.

They are all regarded as dead. But if one should only speak well of the dead,

then carnival death demands malicious, heartless, venomous epigrams for each quasi-corpse, to tear off the veneer he sports in life.

And so, in the whirlwind of my screen carnival, after the peon, the mechanic, the driver and the miner have taken off their masks, so too, with a lighthearted flourish, do the dancing *hacendado*, the maiden, the matriarch, the general and the bishop.

And what lies beneath?

Whereas the first case revealed living, bronzed faces, creased with mirth, here one and the same face was exposed.

But it was not a face.

But the yellow bone of a real skull.

Those living people who progressed carrying the seeds of creativity and life beneath the cardboard image of death, had living faces.

Those who carried the seeds of death wore a cardboard grimace to conceal what was even more frightening—the grimace of a real skull.

Historically condemned to death, it carries its emblem on its own shoulders.

This dead face, wrapped in the shreds of an overcoat, or with epaulettes, dinner-jacket and medals, or with surplice and cross, seemingly utters a ghastly warning to those wearing such clothes in the film: it was written above the skull lying at the foot of the crucifix, and addressed to the passer-by:

'I was as you are; you will be as I am.'

Passer-by!

You will not find this description in any versions of the film. They were mutilated and edited by other people even though all the material was ours and indeed had been filmed by us, during our stay in Mexico, the land of miracles. By thoughtless splicing of the material and selling off negative stock for different films, they effectively destroyed the concept and ruined its coherence. Many months' hard work was simply wrecked.

And perhaps I can detect the hand of the Mexican goddess of death in all this, wearing the masks of the obtuse vandals, of the dull-witted American film buyers, taking her revenge for my over-familiar poke in the ribs?

'The Day of the Dead' went out as a separate, independent 'short' without achieving its purpose: to be a tragic and ironic finale to a great poem about Life, Death, and Immortality; I chose Mexico as the material, but the conception was never realised on the screen.

Irony helped me overcome the death of my own child, in whom I had invested so much love, labour and inspiration.

But Comrade E's pink skull has a direct ancestor!

One of José Guadalupe's 'calaveras' has two skulls, both

black.

As a black living in Harlem might picture black angels in his heaven, so the Mexican imagines that blacks have black skeletons!

Long live coloured skeletons.

Colour[1]

Colour. Pure. Bright. Vibrant. Ringing.

When did I come to love it? Where?

Perhaps it was in Vologda.

More accurately, in the Vologda guberniya.

In the little hamlet of Vozhega, to be precise.

I was flung there by Civil War.

Dazzling snow.

Women stood on the snow.

They wore short dun-coloured fur coats with a braid.

And felt boots.

Between the fur and the boots, I could see a strip of a sarafan.

Woollen. Striped.

Relentlessly bright vertical stripes.

Lilac, orange, red and green.

With a strip of white between.

Another one.

Deep blue, yellow, violet and crimson.

Worn through, faded, and moth-eaten.

A pillow on a wicker chair.

A tablecloth, spread out.

A quarter of a century later

and I can still see their patterns just as clearly.

The stripes of the Mexicans' ponchos, equally relentless, intertwine with them.

The inexhaustible heat of the tropics burns within them, while crystals of white frost scintillate in the background.

Voluptuous pink interweaves with pale blue. The yellow mingles with green. White separates brown zigzags from deep indigo.

Perhaps the once pure colours of icons were a prelude to the savage joy of the pure colours on the Vologda sarafans.

Perhaps the penetrating choir of pink flamingoes, standing out against the pale blue backdrop of the Gulf of Mexico, picked

636

up the refrain where van Gogh's canvases in the Hague Museum left off with their whirlwind of colour produced in Arles by the great madman with the missing ear.

Anyway: the green square of the tablecloth in the lemon room flooded with light,

the dark-blue teapot among red cups,

the golden buddha against the azure walls .

or the books in their orange and black binding on the green and gold brocade of the round table.

I always surround myself with such spots of colour. The spines of my books, gold next to purple, draw an ever tighter loop around my rooms like the vertical stripes on a Vologda sarafan.

Dark blue, white, white, orange.

Red, light blue, orange.

Red, light blue, green.

Red, red, white again.

Black. Gold . . .

I find it dull when there is no yellow pencil next to the blue one to set it off; no red and green striped pillow lying on the blue couch;

when the multicoloured dressing-gown fails to dazzle,

when there are no yellow stripes running up the curtains, crossing blue stripes or intersected by crimson ones . . .

And I like it when a bright ribbon of Philippine embroidery meanders across an Uzbek wallhanging. Or a Mongolian stitchwork design sprawls across the dull crimson background of a wall that so advantageously sets off the whiteness of the cardboard emblems of the Day of the Dead, and the Moorish masks black with bloody wounds. These unexpectedly mutate into the semi-ritual dances of the Mexican Indians, which symbolise for them now not the Moorish conquest of Spain, but their own enslavement by the Spanish hordes under Cortés.

The writer Andrei Bely on the day before the evening given in his honour at the Polytechnic Museum. Moscow, 1932

Gogol's Mastery[1]

You could see it from a distance.

    And from beneath.

    It looked like a gate leading into the sky.

    Beyond was the massive vault of the heavens.

    Before us stretched the narrow, steep-sided thoroughfare.

    Going uphill.

    Out of the hollow.

    Along the flat.

    Out of the gulley—

    to the heavenly gates.

    But this was not Tibet.

    We were not climbing up the sacred mountains, where thousands of steps lead thousands of hesitant pilgrims to merge with the heavens.

    Nor was this the pyramids of the ancient Aztecs, heathen temples which wily priests had turned into Catholic cathedrals, fountains of grace which granted the wishes of those who had come to pray.

    It was outside Moscow, of all places.

    A country estate.

    It is now a holiday home.

    Uzkoye.

    It must have been 1932 or '33.

    Winter was ending.

    There were two of us sharing a room.

    It was strange. My room-mate this time was no learned stomatologist or a phytopathologist commissioned to draw the bookworm out of the depths of the Leningrad book depositories, nor even simply a specialist in ancient Greek vases.

    Until you have enough medals and honours to qualify you for a single room, you can count on a short month's holiday to bring you into close contact with someone like that . . .

    This time I shared a room with the editor of a publishing house.

We did not get on particularly well.

For my platonically dry dreams and sighs about my next small book on problems of cinema immediately materialised into the rectangular yoke of a contract which it took me years of bad conscience and inventiveness to wriggle out of, without having to return the advance.

But I heard from him a fair amount of praise for the other clientèle who were foundering in the tentacles of this tenacious book-producing octopus.

A most curious person ended up in its snares.

Bugayev, the writer, took on a new lease of creative life— one last flourish—before he died.

He wrote as Andrei Bely.[2]

Bely was then writing a book on Gogol for publication.

He was going to read extracts from it in the office of the editorial director.

For a small, select circle.

I saw and heard this remarkable old man for the first time, a few weeks later, in the corner room of the editorial office.

He was wearing a professorial hat.

Very fine, silvery hair formed a halo under it.

There was a waxen hue to his pallid features. The wrinkles in his face were of a dull silvery colour, as on an early firearm.

His eyes shone with a rare radiance.

Most biographies look like an ill-considered assortment of facts.

Often haphazard.

Each title seems a flash in the chaos.

They are linked together with biographical details.

But these facts are threaded together without logic.

So the first thing we heard was the element of Gogol's images which seemed arbitrarily to interweave and generally to slip and slide at random through the ins and outs of the author's life.

There is Taras.

And there, Dovgochkhun.

There is Chichikov; and there are Selifan and Petrushka.[3]

There is the bright colouring of *Evenings*.

And here is the quite different key of *Dead Souls*.

And Bugayev suddenly brought this whirlwind (or swarm, as Gogol himself would have said) to a stop.

Forget Taras.

Forget the sorcerer from *The Terrible Vengeance.*

From this point on the line takes another direction.

From Taras to Dovgochkhun.

From Dovgochkhun (less surprisingly) to Peter Petrovich Petukh.[4]

And from the sorcerer to Petro Mikhali in *The Portrait* and from him to Kostanzhoglo in *Dead Souls.*

Bely's brilliant commentary—part bold hypothesis, part indisputable fact and part unexpected quotation—shows the link in its different phases; its modification, rethinking and development into a motif with a new point of departure, the original motif blossoming out into the succeeding one: the historic-heroic motif fades into the mediocrity of the petty land-owning class (from Taras to Ivan Nikiforovich), and what was fantastically frightening with its sheer foreignness, finishes by threatening the old patriarchal and patriotic order with imported industrialism (from Kudesnik to Kostanzhoglo).

And the troika—Selifan, Chichikov and Petrushka—are not just a driver, servant and master in a carriage to which three horses have been harnessed. They are also in their own right a threesome; and as a threesome, a certain complete unit; and Petrushka is not just Petrushka, but the entire unappealing essence of Pavel Ivanovich; that part of him which he hides so diligently behind the thinnest veneer and fragrance and beneath the false bottom of his notorious box . . .

· And then, all of a sudden, Bely hurled a whole series of tables, statistics and figures at us.

What?!

The percentage of different colours which Gogol used at different stages of his work.

The seemingly chaotic assembly of characters in Gogol may be arranged in order of seniority, according to the degree to which the key feature is developed, according to the movement in characterisation towards an even deeper interpretation. And what unexpectedly seems a suddenly self-willed kaleidoscope of colours running through the short stories and novellas, the poems and evenings, the plays and sketches, can also be drawn up in neat ranks showing increases and decreases, surges and abatements, flourishing and fading.

Bugayev's laborious work on every shade of the spectrum, every piece of biographical data, his burrowing between the covers of every work in a considered way, examining every detail, reaffirms his conviction, crucially and conclusively, with the two zeros and oblique stroke of a percentage sign . . .

Quite marvellous.

A marvel of industry and attention.

A marvel of care and respect.

A marvel of insight and poetic affinity with the writer's soul.

Later, as in a dream or a whirl of vision,

I shyly approached the magician.

It transpired that he had known of me for some time, through my films.

I asked him why, in the magnificent roll-call of authors (Gogol and Blok, Gogol and Bely, Gogol and Mayakovsky) there was no entry: Gogol and Joyce. For a long time I had been struck by the similarity in writing styles between the Ukrainian who became one of the greatest Russian writers, and the Irishman who became the pride of English literature.

Bely was not familiar with Joyce's work.

Having linked Gogol with Futurism, why not link him with . . . cinema?

Although he had brilliantly pointed out the 'cut'—everything that happened while Ivan Ivanovich was pushing through the doorway.[5]

We will return to this conversation later.

But for the moment . . .

Bely's brilliantly scathing attack on the Moscow Art Theatre production of *Dead Souls*[6] was launched with Gogol's inimitable palette in his hands. That production was senselessly and unforgivably colour-blind and shortsighted, but the main thing was that it was not dramatic; or more accurately, that it ran counter to the drama of colour and characterisation through colour (which in Gogol are quite inseparable from subject and content) which were here treated obtusely and without meaning.

A Bely evening at the Polytechnical Museum.

I was in the chair . . .[7]

That marvellous evening with Bely at my flat on Chistye Prudy.

Much later in some sort of blur.

A dissolve sequence.

The tragic death of Boris Bugayev, better known by his pseudonym Andrei Bely . . .

The sole memento of those marvellous few months of vivid impressions 'inside Gogol' is the eye-catching yellow binding of *Gogol's Mastery*, published by OGIZ/GIKhL in 1934.[8]

The yellow binding burns on the table like the cover of the Goncourts' *Germinie Lacerteux* in van Gogh's portrait of Doctor Gachet.

Bely's book, yellow as the sun, frames his invaluable observations.

Here they are measured off according to the creative phases.

Into tables and diagrams.

In distinct images and patterns.

By the juxtaposition of quotations which merge into one another like adjacent hues on the spectrum. Or which ring out, a clash of complementary colours.

Gogol's elemental colour courses through them, illuminating the columns and tinting the images.

Yesterday it was different from today.

And tomorrow it will be different again.

First came light.

Light condensed into colour.

Light remained an underlay for colour.

Writing with light underlies writing with colour in the first phase, let us recall: mosaic and stained glass preceded and gave rise to Giotto, the father of modern painting; and the history of painting in Gogol's prose, from the glass landscape in the excerpt from *The Drowned Woman* right up to the description of Plyushkin's room, is analagous to the history of

painting, from the mosaic of Ravenna, through Giotto, to . . .
Rembrandt . . .

(p. 135)

This becomes even clearer under closer scrutiny.

. . . The tendency of painting in its first stage.

The colour spectrum of *Evenings, Taras Bulba* and *Vii* is motley
and bright with few compound colours, like 'translucent
white', 'dark brown', 'fiery violet' and so on. Red is 'red' and it
is dominant (eighty-four references in the tally); 'red as fire'
(ten times); 'as blood, (seven times), scarlet (seven times),
crimson (four times); ruby (once); 'as a buoy', 'as a poppy', 'as
a bullfinch' (its chest). Typical combinations are of gold and
red, red and dark blue, red and green, red and black. In *Vii*
the floor is carpeted with red nankeen; scarlet velvet covers
the body in the coffin; golden tassels and fringes reach the
floor, and the candles have green tracery (red. . . gold . . .
green) . . .

The next most frequent colour is gold, with only thirty-seven
references (11.6%); then come black and dark blue (11% and
10.7%) . . .'

The same thing applies to the people in *The Terrible
Vengeance.*

. . . Gogol studied painting. His manner of dressing out the
scenes in *The Terrible Vengeance* in colour shows the synthesis of
hues in the first phase of his works: red predominates (26%);
after red, only black and dark blue manage more than 10%
(10.6% and 11.5%). The same proportion is observed in *The
Terrible Vengeance,* where there are nineteen mentions of red
for eight of black and blue. Mentions of red include 1) spots
on clothes 2) flashes like red fireworks. These areas are also
mixed with dark blue and green. The sorcerer is cloaked in
red; red is the colour of the boiling blood whose roar fills his
ears and makes him reach for his sword. On the sorcerer, the
red is a patch over a black hole; the black is beneath the red;
the red jacket races through the black forests, cutting the

moonbeams in two in the black boat, appears from under the black mountains as it slowly makes its way towards the black castle . . .

. . . Each of the three main characters is accompanied by his own colour: Danil's colour is gold and dark blue; Katerina's is light blue, pink and silver; the sorcerer is black and red. Red Molyaka prophecies his appearance: a silver willow weeps sorrowfully for Katerina.

Subject matter and colour have been firmly bonded together . . .

(p. 73)

Bely put this particularly well when he wrote about Katerina, depicted in light blue and pink; and the reflected light of Danil's dark blue (and gold) as he approaches her and the red (and black) of the sorcerer . . .

As Gogol's works progress, the spectrum continues to shift.

Especially noticeable is what happens to the red.

From the exuberance of *Evenings on a Farm near Dikanka* to the tragic second volume of *Dead Souls*.

26.6%, 12.5%, 10.3%, 6.4% (p. 121).

The figures speak for themselves.

But here is Bely speaking for them too:

. . . The coloration of the second and third phase.

The spectrum reacts: with a diminishing number of red bits, beginning with *Ivan Fyodorovich Shponka and his Aunt, How Ivan Ivanovich Quarrelled with Ivan Nikiforovich, Old World Landowners* and ending with the comedies, the percentage of red drops: from 26.6% to 12.5%; and it falls lower still in both volumes of *Dead Souls*; 10.3% to 6.4%; in the second volume there are fewer than a quarter of the references to red in *Evenings*; dark blue falls from 10.7% to 6.1% and from 6.1% to 4.9% (in the first volume of *Dead Souls*). Gold falls too, from 11.6% to 8.9%, from 8.9% to 2.8%; silver drops from 7.1 to 3.2 and 2.8 . . .

. . . The shift in vocabulary is matched by a shift in the spectrum too: as the colours glimmer and die, the effect becomes chiaroscuro. In Part One of *Dead Souls*, white, black and grey are foremost. Colours are cast in shadow . . . bluish-grey, like Manilov's wallpaper . . .

. . . At times a lot is shrouded: 'with beauty-spots', 'flies landed on it', 'the sun . . . was shining and . . . flies . . . turned towards it', 'a swarm of flies, borne on a light breeze', 'airborne squadrons of flies . . . scattered . . . pieces', 'an inkwell with a number of flies', in Korobochka's room 'countless flies', a glass 'with three flies' and hence associations with flies: 'flies, not people', 'they died like flies', 'smaller than a fly', and so on.

Corresponding to these specks of black are white parts of women who are chiefly wearing white make-up, but are ironically described as 'shining'. Chartokutsky's wife is shown having white parts (her linen and blouse are white); the governor's daughter in *Dead Souls* is petite and white; the ladies wear dresses 'white as swans', and bootees white 'as smoke' with stockings white 'as snow' . . . there are other white toilet appurtenances . . . 22% white in the first volume, and 17% in the second.

White lies beneath the specks of black.

There is plenty of *'blanc et noir'* here . . .

From the bright flashes of red and blue in a golden setting to black/grey/white, and finally pure *'blanc et noir'*.

This spectrum in Gogol's works was to etch itself into my memory for a long time.

Three Letters about Colour[1]

I began writing these 'memoirs' while I was still bedridden, in the Kremlin hospital, and with only one real reason, of course:

I wanted to prove to myself that I had after all had a life . . .

Then I hastily began to justify my writing by saying that it was an exercise for perfecting my literary style; that, more important, it was a training ground for 'writing easily'—cultivating the skill of spontaneously transferring every idea, every feeling, every image that might occur to me on to the page. This would save time on whatever intervening processes there might be, by pouring it out on to paper then and there.

Another motive prompted me from behind the scenes, which was to give myself a free rein and 'throw out' on to the page the whole gamut of associations which spill out uncontrollably at the least provocation and sometimes apropos nothing at all.

Anyway, I gave myself absolutely free rein for several months.

So far—up to today—I can observe the following:

I have acquired a certain facility for writing,

and have achieved total irresponsibility with regard to what I am writing,

and on a good day I can manage up to thirty-four pages of manuscript (this is in the region of one printer's sheet) at one sitting.

But then again . . . I have completely ruined my style of 'serious writing', highbrow journalism.

My style has not got any lighter; fatally, I am now launching into unrestrained expatiations in all directions, digressing from what is germane to the article.

I had conceived three letters about colour (as an appendix to *Nonindifferent Nature*) before my illness.

Three Letters about Colour.

The Attack on the Cypresses—an exposé of the principled approach to the question of colour. *Andante héroïque. The Springs of Happiness*—scherzo on the theme of *les tribulations*, during the practical realisation of these lofty intentions.

And the third article—*The Letter That Was Not Sent*—consisted of a letter to Tynyanov that I really did not send.

After it had been written, news reached me that this great writer had died an agonising death in hospital (was it in Orenburg?) during the evacuation.[2]

I used to sit and write under the apple-trees at a sanatorium in the hills near Alma-Ata. It was not snowy blossom that weighed down the branches in the spring, but real snow. I spent a winter there, reading Part Three of Tynyanov's *Pushkin*, published in *Znamya* [The Banner].

I learned the details of his last days only recently, from someone who had been in the same ward.

He was unable to lie down; he sat hunched up, his knees up against his chest, suffering unbelievable agony.

The last time we met was in the Central Executive Committee building; I drove him from there in 1939 after we had both been given awards by Mikhail Ivanovich Kalinin himself, who died only a few days later.[3]

Tynyanov could hardly walk; I all but carried him to the car and he told me that my *Mexico* was really an outstanding film. They tried to cure his monstrous illness in Paris, where his doctor told him about the film with great enthusiasm.

And if the doctors in Paris say a work is good, then it really does deserve praise.

Doctors are the greatest connoisseurs, the sternest art critics there. I know that they are particularly fastidious collectors.

Darius Milhaud did not take me to galleries to see the best of French painting; we went to dentists' waiting-rooms. They are the most discriminating collectors of paintings.

. . . A terrible detail:

Tynyanov hunched up on his bed, holding a huge red lobster claw.

The hospital had been hit by an acute food shortage.

They fed the patients with a consignment of huge lobsters from the Far East, which fate delivered up to the city . . .

I am not going to digress here on the subject of lobsters.

I shall avoid mentioning my first encounter with them, in

my childhood, in Houlgate, on the Brittany coast; there were mountains of them—dead, with their muddy orange stomachs uppermost—on the rocks of the bays (*sur les falaises*). At low tide the sea would retreat so far into the distance as to be only a thin dark green strip on the horizon.

I shall not talk about them here, for any reminiscing about them is sure to lead me to my seven-year-old friend Jeanne. I was eight when I was in Trouville and little Jeanne only knew me in my bathing costume.

Once it happened that I met her after lunch, properly dressed (we met each day in the morning when we would sit side by side shrimping).

Little Jeanne walked past without recognising the spruce little boy—her friend she splashed around with in rock pools each morning.

Remembering Jeanne brings me to the big wave.

The vast, towering, headlong waves of the Atlantic, which the broad sweep of the ocean hurls on to the beach as the tide rushes in; a shattering rampart of water thundering on to the emptying shore.

Woe betide the lingerer, lost in thought, who forgets about the tide!

Where a minute before lay the smooth surface of the beach, pools of warm water here and there with a starfish wallowing at the bottom or a family of shrimps, now a gigantic, ominous green-blue wall of salt water rears up.

A short pale figure in a light knitted costume is still splashing about among the shrimps, and the treacherous glaucous swell of the ocean is already swinging round in a broad arc. In a few minutes the foam-flecked crests of giant ridges will crash together with a roar.

If it were not for someone's strong, firm grasp and athletic dash, carrying me to the safety of a distant strip of sand which lay beyond the reach of the sea, then young Jeanne would never again have met her young friend, nor would this pale little boy have grown up to be sitting here now, drawing an idle pencil across a pad of white paper, swallowed up by a sea of memories.

. . . Tynyanov had died and the letter was not sent.

Yuri Tynyanov, writer and literary expert. (Photo: M. Nappelbaum)

Alexander Sergeyevich Pushkin. (Engraving by N. Yutkin, from the portrait by
Orest Kiprensky)

The letter concerned my wish to do the life of Pushkin in colour.

Pushkin, strange to say (for me, not him!), the lover.

On the basis of Tynyanov's theory, which is expounded in *A Nameless Love*.[4]

The fascinating history of the poet's secret love for Karamzin's wife is told here in a much more inspired way and much more acutely, than in the last part of the novel, where he seems to be in a great hurry to finish, frightened that he will not live to see it completed.

The letter was also full of ideas about the colour capacity of film.

The letter was in draft form.

And this gives me now the right to work it up into a more detailed exposition of the way colour was conceived in the film, made in colour.

But I seem to have spoiled my writing style irretrievably: two introductory lines for what became an independent, extensive 'page of memoirs' (instead of the second article *The Springs of Happiness*) itself expanded into an entire fragment of a memoir, with shrimps, lobsters, little Jeanne and the Atlantic Ocean.

And they were only meant as an introductory piece to explain the origin of the pages that follow.

What began as 'a few words' of introduction to the 'second letter about colour' turned into everything except what they were meant to be; and now, instead of an *Anhang** for *Nonindifferent Nature*, they lie in a heap of *freie Einfälle*** with the pompous title *Memoirs*!

They do indeed deal mostly with how, through various associations, key images and impressions and recollections of earlier works, I came to resolve the banquet scene in *Ivan* in the way I did.

---

* German: 'appendix'
** German: 'free ideas'

The Springs of Happiness[1]

Sanin by Artsybashev,
    The Wrath of Dionysus by Nagrodskaya,
    The novels of Lappo-Danilevskaya
    and of course Verbitskaya's *The Springs of Happiness*.[2]
    This is a whole epoch in literature.

An epoch which clearly demonstrated the loss of whatever stability there had been in those echelons of the intelligentsia that had failed to latch on to the Revolutionary movement.

We were still too young to read all that when the books came out.

We learned about them second-hand, from the arguments of grown-ups, from fragments of the polemics linked to their publication, but more from their titles and the authors' surnames.

How long ago it was!

How much has changed: our country has changed its character; the face of Europe has been altered; the whole world has changed over these decades.

How strange it is when chance turns up a photograph of Madame Lappo-Danilevskaya, among the other denizens of the Stage Veterans' Club. I remember her when she was part of the troupe of actors working for the Political Administration of the Western Front in 1920. I myself was working as set-designer in Minsk, just after its liberation.

It comes as a shock to realise that the author of *The Springs of Happiness* had a son who can be seen almost daily—on the stage of the Moscow Art Theatre, acting in *Anna Karenina*, or Gorky's *Enemies*.[3]

This is almost as strange as the thought that Matisse, that old museum piece, is still alive.

Or that Edvard Munch—the father of Expressionism—died only two years ago, in 1944.[4] That movement reached its height and we saw it do so; it passed into oblivion long ago (and we saw it do that, too), supplanted by Constructivism and Surrealism which succeeded it and which have also left the stage.

Yevreinov's 'theatre for oneself'[5] emerged from the turbid whirlpool of these pre-Revolutionary, pre-war years.

It was one of his three small volumes that had model scripts for plays for this theatre which had no audience, critics or auditorium.

I remember one such script.

It is called *The Trying on of Deaths*.

The reader is invited to experience the delightful sensations Petronius felt as he died, his veins cut—a small incision of the auxiliary blood-vessels in his arm in a warm bath—monitored by a concealed accomplice (a doctor) and to the strains of a distant harp.

It is supposed that the first impressions of death from odours is of banks upon banks of flowers . . . etc . . . etc.

. . . The title *The Springs of Happiness* has been explained by contemporaries thus: this is a story about wells or sources of happiness.

The title *Dead Souls* can be read in two ways:

as a literal reference to the serfs on the register who have since died and whom Mr Chichikov wishes to deal in;

or metaphorically, concerning the moribund souls of his clientèle—the representatives of the Russian landowning classes.

Springs of Happiness has a meaning quite different, hidden from the 'wells' idea.

And it is quite cynical: it corresponds fully, in the sphere of love, with the above-mentioned entertainment at the Yevreinov Theatre, *The Trying on of Deaths*.

The 'Springs of Happiness' were a kind of lottery when I was a child.

Every charity fête had one, next to the hoop-la where you had to throw a ring around a stick to win the prize that was hung around it; or the game where you had to throw little balls into coloured bags which were hanging up with sweets and lollipops inside.

The 'Springs of Happiness' consisted of a box standing on a table.

A box, locked up.

Next to the box were twelve keys.

Only one of the twelve would spring the lock.

To 'fit' a key cost one rouble.[6]

When the box opened, its contents would be the prize—ten roubles, I think.

Sometimes it worked first time.

Sometimes, at the second or third attempt.

And sometimes it took twelve keys and the player lost.

Mme Verbitskaya subjected her heroine to such ordeals and quests in the sphere of love.

The title *The Springs of Happiness* is more than just appropriate.

But as far as I recall, the heroine did not come off any the worse.

The Springs of Happiness is not only a method of searching for love. *The Springs of Happiness* is in many respects the method of searching in art.

In those murky periods of its development, when new possibilities that have not been recognised or assimilated suddenly appear; new methods of expression, new means of influence.

Where should we search for our approach? How can we find the right paths? Where should one look for the key that could spring the little box open, revealing wonderful new secrets and possibilities?!

The box could of course simply be smashed open.

'Vandalistic art' aptly describes the thorough-going wrecking of cinema, with regard to what happened to music and dialogue in the talkies.

It is happening again with the practice of colour, which has ransacked oleography rather than painting.

The other way is by fitting the keys to the locks.

For one may have a very distinct idea of one's desires; a very precise set of equations which the unknown—x—must satisfy: new possibilities and a very precise idea of the formulae in which the solutions must be expressed.

But the step from abstract ideas, tangibly exact and close, to their realisation in practice, is sometimes barred by the unbridgeable difficulties of trying to assimilate the peculiarities of the new area of creativity.

In my *Attack on the Cypresses*, I tried to formulate the principles which we brought to bear in our assault on the question of colour in cinema.

The real 'Springs of Happiness' should concern some of those right (but more often wrong) keys we used to attack the Pandora's box of colour film.

I am not sure whether I can say that it was good fortune, or even only chance fortune that led to my first work in colour.

But there was definitely a chain of chance events.

This chain led to the work itself.

And the same chain and the conjunction of the unexpected with chance determined the course I was to take in solving the actual problems of colour.

Colour in cinema had long been a preoccupation of mine.

For so long, in fact, that I regard my entire output in black-and-white to have been in colour too.

In colour, but confined to a limited spectrum of monochrome shades.

But work in colour proper occupied me for a fairly long time too. At least, since the time when I thought that the technical problems had been conclusively solved.

Different pioneers have tackled it differently.

Some worked on mastering the technical possibilities, fascinated by the work on perfecting the new technical phenomenon.

Sound had attracted such vigorous research also—when sound was still not considered an independent element in its own right, to be arbitrarily married to the visual element.

There were the same enthusiasts for mastering colour, which needed a lamp of unprecedented brightness, an optical cube and three films of different tones all running through the same projector, so that one could see on the screen the not particularly fine confetti of different colours (no hues) and tones (no half-tones): reality distorted beyond recognition.

I have had nothing to do with pioneers and enthusiasts of this sort. I am not interested in quests for making a soprano sound as good on film as in reality (in the early days of sound, she was quite indistinguishable from a tenor with a sore throat).

I think that before the present quest should begin, screen

technology should be of a standard able to guarantee accurate re-play of a piano and life-like violin music. So much time and effort has already been spent on this.

Only when that has been established can one start on worthwhile research into audiovisual counterpoint, the *sine qua non* of audiovisual cinema.

It is just the same with colour.

The first, almost incoherent projections of colour film (*Giordano Bruno*), just like my first colour film to be worked out in detail (*Pushkin*), were 'archived' as soon as it became clear that the technology was still in its infancy; that not one formal solution could guarantee success.

And the recurrent theme of *Ivan the Terrible* is the very one that runs the entire gamut of colour in the overwhelming first two-thirds and is quite accessible to black-and-white cinema. Traditional black, grey and white, has the richest variety of textures, from the metallic gleam of the brocade, with its varying quality and style, through the material and cloth, to the soft play of furs, which includes the whole range of shades, from sable and fox to wolf and bear; brown when it is worn, and white for carpets and bedcoverings.

I saw the first models of colour film a very long time ago.

Méliès' magical touch.

It was an underwater kingdom, where bright yellow knights in armour hid in the jaws of green whales and light blue and pink sorceresses were born from the foam of the sea.

Soon afterwards films began appearing with natural colour-ing. I have already forgotten the system and technique used, but they came out in Riga, in about 1910 or 1912.

True, it was in just one cinema—in the Wermann Park, with the portentous name *Kino-Kultura*. This did not stop it from show-ing, after these short colour films of an 'educational' nature, weekly episodes in the *Fantômas* and *Vampire* series.

The films were short and had an overall pink cast and showed white sails of yachts skimming across an azure sea; fruits of different shapes and sizes and flowers which were to be picked by girls with a blaze of ginger hair—or it may be flaxen—and people working the fields in the spring.

My first personal attempts at using colour were: a hand-painted red flag in *Potemkin* and the less well-known montage made from short sections in the scenes surrounding the separator and the 'bull's wedding' in *The Old and The New*.

The question of using colour concretely in film production arose in 1939. In connection with the completion of work on the film *Fergana Canal*, after 'my Tamerlane was amputated', as I used to say at the time.[7]

I conceived the film about the Fergana canal as a triptych about the struggle for water.

Central Asia in a blaze of flowers, thanks to the amazing irrigation system constructed all those centuries ago.

In Tamerlane's fratricidal conflicts and expeditions, man's control over water is destroyed. Sand overruns all.

The poverty of the sandy wastes under the tsars. The fight for one more cup of water from the waterways, where once there had been a perfect irrigation system.

And finally, the miracle of the first collective feat—building the collective farms in Uzbekistan: the Fergana Canal which was an unprecedented project in terms of scale and brought wealth and prosperity to socialist Central Asia.

For reasons not revealed to me, the shooting of the first panel of the triptych was cancelled the very day before we were due to begin work.

The composition of the entire work hung helplessly suspended in mid-air.

The whole plan was dropped very soon afterwards.

I had taken over the production of *Die Walküre* at the Bolshoi Theatre;[8] I devoted the whole conception of the last piece, *Feuerzauber*,* to searching for ways of combining the elements of Wagner's score with a changing play of coloured light on the stage.

Despite the extremely limited technical resources and the far from perfect lighting and the lighting equipment of the Bolshoi's stage, which drastically reduced the range of colours available to us for the fire, we nevertheless achieved an extremely convincing rendering in colour of 'Wotan's Farewell'.

---

* German: 'Magic Fire'

...he scene with Wotan and Brünnhilde, from Richard Wagner's opera *Die Walküre,* in
...senstein's production. The Bolshoi Theatre, Moscow 1940

Perhaps it was from this point, the random cessation of work on *Fergana*, that the series of regular coincidences began, that led in practice to working with colour.

With only a limited spectrum of colours to play idly from the flies above the stage of the Bolshoi, on to the *Feuerzauber* of Wagner's *Die Walküre*, no more than two tonal qualities were possible.

Allow me to set all the tints of this Magic Fire into play and alternate the purple-crimson and blue lights which are all the colours you have under your control at the console.

It is as well also that before this, in the scene of 'Wotan's Farewell', you have managed to retrieve for the colour-change square lights as large as the whole of the backstage.

Here it is, metallic bronze to begin with.

Now it fluidly changes into silver.

And now, with the embrace in the music, it suddenly changes into the deepest, lyrical blue . . .

Wagner's score is not too rich in its coloration, but it flares up, burns, bathed in light, organically and in the spirit of movement within the music.

In the Magic Fire, Loge's theme runs like a thread of blue through the purple of fire, the underlying element.

Now that theme melts in the fire.

Now it seems to have smothered the fire.

The perspiring and begrimed face of the electrician looks up, tired and plaintive, from beneath the lid of the lighting box. Only he is able to match the knife-switches and rheostats to the movements of the assistant director's finger as it twitches in time to the score, synchronously with the frenzied orchestra, now wailing, now seething, now roaring, now mellifluous as it reaches the finale of the last act of the second opera in the Ring cycle.

One way or another, I take the first practical steps in chromophonic—a synthesis of sound and colour—counterpoint, on the stage of the Bolshoi, for myself.

I must also mention my other 'firsts' in my work which for some reason have always so uncannily linked me to this building.

It was here that a fragment of my first, independent work as director was shown. It was some anniversary connected to the theatres of the 'Left', in 1923.[9]

It was here that for the first time I was on a poster, identified as the 'director' and 'producer'.

And here for the first time, before a flabbergasted spectator from the edge of the pit, came the whistle and roar of the percussion band that answered my hoot of the football siren as I leaped out of my red velvet seat and a young actress of my then Proletkult theatre performed in her dazzling yellow costume the first circus trick in the whole history of the Bolshoi Theatre, ascending a six-metre-long pole . . . the mast of death!

And it was here, two years later, that the white rectangle of a cinema screen was unrolled: again for the first time. Making its own evocative entrance, it cast those ancient, deep-rooted and rigid traditions to the four winds.

The waves of the Black Sea, the surge of the revolt and the firing on the Odessa Steps burst out of that projection box, somewhere near the old 'royal' box; they lashed the screen, hit the audience and the prow of the victorious battleship broke into the auditorium, the red pennant fluttering above.

The première of *Potemkin* took place on the anniversary of 1905, within these very walls.[10]

In 1940, silver horses rose up into the lighting rig above the stage, as if soaring into the clouds.

There was no dazzling sunlight to hasten the joyous song of love into the audience; instead a yellow spotlight shone from behind a curtain, saturating the auditorium with light.

And the wind machines beneath the stage always failed to blow—they never once fanned the tongues of fire, which hung limply in the blue and scarlet light, looking more like streamers above a butcher's shop than the play of fire which was supposed to protect Brünnhilde's sleep, until Siegfried came to wake her . . .

The chromophonic combination of streams of music and light. The play of the beams of light.

The magic, when links are found . . .

That is not so much,

but what I derived of infinite emotional value from this work, with its burning aspirations, inspired strivings and tragic achievement, was condemned by insuperable technical difficulties to crawl where it should have burst into the heavens . . .

But where, among the warlike maidens' unruly steeds leaping into the heavens, lay the chief object of our quest—the life-story of Alexander Sergeyevich Pushkin?

Right in the middle.

I had still not finished arranging *Die Walküre* by May 1940.

It went on until the autumn.

And I devoted the summer to Alexander Sergeyevich.

I reached the point where I felt I knew my hero well enough to call him by his first names.

That is how historians speak of great figures in the past.

I remember some historians discussing the screenplay of *Alexander Nevsky* and debating the various theories about how he was poisoned when he was being entertained by the Khan.

'In my view,' one of them said, 'it was perfectly simple. Alexander Yaroslavich simply had tuberculosis. Nor should you forget that he had had a difficult journey, which would have lowered his resistance . . .'

And that somehow brought Alexander Yaroslavich five hundred years closer.

And that same scholar demolished the remaining interval completely when he—or was it another?—tried to describe my future hero in more detail and said he had a beard 'a bit like Nekrasov's'.[11]

Work on Pushkin began after I had suspended my experiments on chromophonic counterpoint in the *Die Walküre*—experiments that I was bang in the middle of.

But, before going into that, I should say a few words about my work on Wagner.

In my production at the Bolshoi, which again was more a sketchy idea than a complete picture, Wotan's appearance was preceded by toppling pine trees.

Then, near the curtain, they rose up from the ground once more, joining the Valkyries' final upward flight and their divine father's furious departure.

I had identified the Valkyries with pine trees.

Probably because I first heard their frenzied flight on someone's piano among the giant pines in the forests of Finland.

The chords carried the warrior maidens off up to the crowns of the trees at Raivola station.

And I came to know the structure of leitmotif and counterpoint among the bases of even greater trees—the famous redwoods around San Francisco.

I rested for a week in their cool shade, far from the heat and commotion of Hollywood; I gnawed the sweet fruits of knowledge and drank the subtle poison of Joyce's *Ulysses* and the commentary by Stuart Gilbert.

Autumn 1930.

It was from . . . literature that I mastered the obvious tangibility of the technique of musical counterpoint.

This was probably not only correct, but natural too.

Because I came to it after mastering visual counterpoint.[12]

I needed the bare bones of counterpoint, separated from what was customary and usual—the world of sounds.

In a form in which they could become the backbone of what was new, unprecedented.

And it was very appropriate that they were encased in a literary form.

The more so as I was holding a quite remarkable piece of literature.

Which was devised not simply as 'music', but in strict accordance with musical canon: exactly on the principle of *fuga per canonem*.

The Sirens' episode from *Ulysses*.

Tiny squirrels hopped about gnawing nuts at the feet of these gigantic trees.

The crowns of the giant redwoods vanished in the blue sky.

And the multiple passages of regular, intricate constructions from the chapters of this novel's exceptionally musical prose whispered the secrets of these melodic structures in my ear one by one.

The chapter begins with bronze by gold: two heads of hair, Miss Lydia Douce's and Miss Minna Kennedy's.

It takes place in the Ormond Bar.

The girls are working in the bar.

Above Eisenstein, Williams & Shpiller during the production of *Die Walküre* in the Boshoi Theatre. *Below* Rehearsal for *Die Walküre*

But our interest in what happens here goes beyond the girls, the visitors and potential drama of premonitions.

It lies in the way this complex network of different personal experiences and personalities dissolves in a strict pattern of musical writing.

Stuart Gilbert, one of the most reliable commentators on Joyce, said:

> . . . The episode of the Sirens opens with two pages of brief extracts from the narrative which follows. These fragmentary phrases appear almost meaningless to the reader till he has perused the chapter to its end; nevertheless they should not be 'skipped'.

In a footnote, Gilbert wrote:

> So curious is the language of this episode that, when it was sent by the author from Switzerland to England during the Great War, the Censor held it up, suspecting that it was written in some secret code. Two English writers (it is said) examined the work, and came to the conclusion that it was not 'code' but literature of some unknown kind.

What are these two pages?

> . . . They are like the overtures of some operas and operettas, in which fragments of the leading themes and refrains are introduced to prepare the hearer's mood and also to give him, when these abridged themes are completed and developed in their proper place, that sense of familiarity which, strangely enough, enhances for many hearers their enjoyment of a new tune . . .

Another expert and devoted follower of Joyce, Professor Curtius, reacted with critical disapproval to these attempts by Joyce, when he underscored the link between the structure of this chapter, and Wagner's way of working:

. . . These two pages of seemingly meaningless text form in reality an extremely carefully calculated composition, which can only be understood when the reader has perused the whole chapter and perused it with the greatest attention. The literary technique employed is an exact transposition of the musical technique. To be more precise, the technique of Wagner's leitmotif. But there is this difference, that the musical motif is complete in itself and more satisfying; I can listen with delight to a Wagnerian leitmotif, even if I cannot place the allusion (Valhalla theme? Walsungen theme?). But the word motif, unintelligible in itself, acquires meaning only when I relate it to its context . . . Joyce has deliberately ignored the essential difference between sounds and words, and for this reason his experiment is of questionable value . . .*

Stuart Gilbert met this objection by suggesting that in music too the first notes of a theme are equally fragmentary and supply no more than do the initial, 'truncated' phrases of Joyce's text.

More important of course is the fact that this section too, like all the other chapters of Joyce's *Ulysses*, is immensely exaggerated.

Everything that subtly informs (to a lesser or greater degree) the style of this or that variety of literary writing, is here a *ne plus ultra*, the peak of material tangibility and clarity.

That same hyperbole that led to 735 pages of narrative being devoted to the events of one day in the life of an exceptionally modest, insignificant Dubliner—the advertisement canvasser, Leopold Bloom!—is also manifest in the technical devices and the method of writing.

Stuart's research into the nature of music and the observance of the laws of music in the writing of this chapter is compelling and scrupulous.

It probes every essential element of 'strict writing'. And it takes delight in each essential encounter with the most unlikely features and canonical figures.

---

* Ernst Robert Curtius, *James Joyce und sein Ulysses* (Verlag der Neuen Schweizer Rundschau, Zurich, 1929), pp. 54-5. (E's reference)

It traces the path of music, from the structure of the chapter as a whole, to its influence on all the particularities within the writing; and it discovers verbal correspondences to *fermata* in music and explains how, by using abridged names, he achieves the effect of simultaneity, which corresponds to what is called *stretto* in a fugue. Etc, etc.

There would of course be no point in enumerating all these now.

I will confine myself to purely general notions.

. . . The language and content of this episode (its technique is the *fuga per canonem*) are throughout handled in a characteristically musical manner. The theme is rarely simple; there are generally two, three or four overlapping parts, which, synchronised by intertwinement in the same sentence, or closely juxtaposed, produce the effect of a chord of music. He who reads such passages as certain cultured concert-goers prefer to hear a fugue—with the parts kept mentally distinct in four, or fewer, independent horizontal lines of melody—will miss much of the curious emotive quality of Mr Joyce's prose in this episode. For most of the sensuous value of music, the enthralment of the Sirens' song, is missed by the musical 'high-brow' who forces himself to analyse the sounds he hears and separate the music into independent lines of horizontal parts. To enjoy to the full the emotion of symphonic music, the hearer should be aware of it as a sequence of chords, listen vertically as well as horizontally. And this holds good not only for the romantics such as Beethoven and Wagner, who (especially the latter) 'think in chords', but also, though in a somewhat less degree, for counterpoint fuguists like Bach . . .

This is all elementary stuff for musicians, of course.

For people who study literature, it is the very limit of compound structural writing.

But I am writing a traveller's notebook, not a textbook; it is my aim to map the crossroads, the highways and byways I travelled on as I sought to master the different means of influence outside my amazing art.

667

And at these crossroads I thought that the bases of musical rhythm could be applied to architecture; the shifts in tonality taking the place of the Gothic arches of Chartres Cathedral, the *plein-chant** perceived through moonlight shining through the 13th-century stained glass, counterpoint which I adored in the work on the pontoon bridge and the harmony of movements in space and in time, and the fugue, shown in the paradoxes of Joyce's prose. All these enriched and expanded my films, giving them a breadth of expression that they would never have acquired from a familiarity with the classicism of Bach or Taneyev alone.[13]

The last notion to enter my memory positively as I sat with the squirrels busy cracking nuts while the trees rustled high above my head, was the concluding paragraph of Stuart's chapter:

> . . . In no other episode, perhaps, of *Ulysses* has Mr Joyce attained such a complete 'atonement' between subject-matter and form. To Professor Curtius the experiment appeared 'of questionable value', and if it were a mere *tour-de-force,* an artificial grafting of musical on verbal idiom, musicoliteral virtuosity, his doubt would be well-founded. But here the musical rhythm, the sonority and counterpoint of the prose are evocative of the theme itself, the Sirens' 'song of enthralment'. This episode differs from most examples of 'musical prose' in that the meaning does not lose but is, rather, intensified by the combination of the two arts; sense is not sacrificed to sound but the two are so harmonised that, unless his ears, like the Achaeans', are sealed with wax against the spell, the reader, hearkening to 'the voice sweet as the honeycomb and having joy thereof, will go on his way the wiser'. (*Odyssey*, XII, 186-8)

The great Bach understood the interplay of separate passages within the seemingly highly abstract composition of a fugue in a way that was profoundly humanistic.

He heard the 'voices' of living people.

Together, these voices sounded like an excited confabula-

---

* In French in the original.

tion on a matter of great mutual interest.

When someone had nothing to contribute, he remained silent.[14]

'Uncle Vanya'—Ivan Lebedev[15] is the legendary wrestling referee, and hero of my (and many others'!) childhood—would 'line up' all his 'alumni'.

Murzuk and Lurikh.

Zbyszko-Cyganewicz and Cyclops.

Aberg and 'Black Mask'.[16]

They all passed before the cheering crowd, before grappling with each other in bridges and double-nelsons and turning into an indissoluble counterpoint of overstrained muscles, arched spines and bloody necks with the dull thud of skulls thrown back against the matting.

Some Japanese came.[17]

They were led by Sadanji, the 'Stanislavsky of Tokyo'.

The classical canon of his acting gradually became disturbingly innovative.

The concentrated beam which transmitted the plot according to the canon was sometimes diffused by an unexpected, unforeseeable and inappropriate psychologism.

In plays which were written in a more orthodox way, however, he was more strict.

Such as the performance of *Narukami*.

But, taken as a whole, the plays preserved the sheen of classical perfection.

They were also preceded by a line-up.

Here it was called *kumadori*.

To do it, the audience had to be introduced to a number of essential ideas about the play which would later develop into satin raiments embroidered with silk, knots of tightly-coiled black wigs which spilled out of their bronze bases, which lay on the actor's shaven head (turquoise enamel was a fair representation of the bluish stubble; it filled the area between the white painted face and the silhouetted horse's mane, bound in a headband).

This was similar to the way the cast of characters in Elizabethan theatre disported themselves before the tragedy began, supplying the audience with details about themselves.

'King Maximilian' and his rebellious son 'Adolf' were presented to the audience.[18]

And the individual cogs of their complicated manoeuvres, Scribe and Labiche, Dumas *fils* or Sardou, were introduced by the leader of the chorus.

This is just the same as Joyce's juggling with truncated phrases to introduce the tonic characters of the Sirens' episode into the emotional fabric of verbal counterpoint.

And I, the youngest offspring of these glorious old lines, threw spots of colour, the first dancing colour frames of a dance in the Alexandrov sloboda—abstractly, like a dance of colours—into the beginning of the episode so that the golden horde of *oprichniki* could later arise from the gold and change into the theme of golden majesty and the wisdom of heavenly azure; shirts would develop out of the red and blood, in the candle-light; the spots of black would quench, like ash, the light of progress, reinstating the darkness once more.

And this was much later.

But then my telephone rang.

And I consented over the phone to a production of *Die Walküre* in the Bolshoi . . .

Children sometimes ask: 'Why is there a light?'

Equally valid would be the question: 'Why *Die Walküre?*'

'Because.' It is hard to think of a more logical answer.

I think it must have been the most unprepared, on-the-spot response I have ever professionally given.

Made while Williams and Samosud,[19] who had decided to butter me up for some reason with this production, were speaking on the phone.

Their flattery paid off.

I could not of course stand in the way of 'The Ride of the Valkyries'.

But this apparently chance, subsidiary exercise then became, of sheer necessity, a part of a solution to audiovisual matters which I had been obsessed by since my experience with audiovisual work on *Alexander Nevsky*, which concluded what Meisel and I had been working on in the score for *Potemkin* all those years ago.

(Not to mention even earlier quests on the same lines in the Proletkult theatre.)

In any event, at almost the same time as the work on Wagner, I was offered the chance of working seriously in colour, for colour cinema.

As was only to be expected of course, the proposal stipulated a natural 'wide spectrum of colours'.

The best subject, in that it had the widest range of colours, and was, at the same time, interesting and acceptable ideologically for the leadership, was the highly-colourful (!) Giordano Bruno.[20]

Italy, of course . . .

Renaissance dress . . .

A fire . . .

Two other themes were taken on board at the same time.

One presented itself.

Colonel Lawrence and the Arab revolt in the Middle East.

The psychological aspect of Lawrence is bound to interest the reader familiar not only with *Revolt in the Desert*, but also the terrible inner confession of nihilism, moral bankruptcy and the Dostoyevskian character of the *Seven Pillars of Wisdom*—his record of his wartime exploits.[21]

True, the only colour here is in the green of the Prophet's flag and the green turbans of the generals.

And also the remarkable description of the old Arab woman, who had never seen blue eyes before and asked the intelligence officer whether his eyes were blue because the sky shone through them.

In fact, the green turban comes not from the Colonel's writings but from an English novel with a similar theme.

And in order to treat the material more freely, the film was not to be too factually biographical; the setting had to be a different, but no less popular, base for the mysterious colonel's activities —Iran.

Again history was a different theme.

Invariably, the colourful past would be looked for on the cusp between the Middle Ages and the Renaissance.

One of the reviewers for the Committee on Cinema Affairs came to me with this theme like a fox terrier carrying a slipper, all because of the bright colours of the costumes.

The theme was . . . the plague.

Why the plague?

Why the plague, rather than cholera, smallpox or typhoid?

In fact, it was not the colourfulness of this theme that appealed, but something quite different, although the appeal lasted only for a short period, until I had finished the graphic sketch.

It was the possibility of devising a film showing how the 'variety of colour', so dear to the leadership's heart, could be consumed by blackness as the plague spread.

Using different material, another aspect of this theme of the sensual (and colourful!) wealth of life being consumed, turning into stone, excited me for quite different reasons. That was how I solved the knotty problem of gold in my planned film (and completed screenplay) of Blaise Cendrars' novel *Sutter's Gold*.

I had wanted to produce a romanticised version of Captain Sutter's life for Paramount, while I was in America.

And also the destruction, caused by the discovery of gold on his Californian estates: it led to his prosperous farms being ravaged and to his own death. I wanted to express this with the vivid impression which the drags of the Californian gold prospectors have left on me to this day.

Mountains of spoil still stand where they were flung up from the half-excavated mines; as in Sutter's time, they bury the lush greenery of the fields around the mines.

Beneath the soulless layer of stones lay once-verdant orchards, fields, pastures and meadows.

Implacably, constantly and inexorably the wall of stone advanced, encroaching on the green and ruthlessly crushing living, vital shoots for the sake of gold.

The 1848 Gold Rush sent hundreds of thousands of prospectors to California in search of the valuable metal which so amply rewarded the effort of extracting it.

It is difficult to imagine how it was; to picture oneself in the throes of this maddening fever.

But a modicum of personal experience makes it easy to see how this elemental pursuit of gold must have raged like a typhoon, a hurricane, a welter of passions.

Considerably later, I happened to wind up in the mountains in the Kabardino-Balkarian Republic, at places which had only just been discovered by the prospectors.

A narrow gorge.

A rivulet.

A few home-made, rickety, shallow vats.

My travelling companion and guard (no doubt on the payroll of the Republic's NKVD!)[22] stooped to gather a handful of muddy earth.

The clods were put in a tin, bowl-like vessel.

The earth was carefully washed by rocking the vessel.

And suddenly some small specks appeared at the bottom.

Gold!

The ground seemed to shake underfoot, opening up to its depths; and through the surface of dark mud, overgrown with turf, I could see millions of barely detectable grains of gold-dust!

You can easily imagine how people might fling themselves to the ground with arms outstretched, trying to amass it in their hands; people, made drunk by their contact with this wealth lying scattered under the soles of their boots; people ready to kill anyone who dared to walk on this sea of gold lying beneath the topsoil; people quite prepared to pan this amoral and lecherous rich earth in the warm blood of any rival trespassing on excavated grains of gold which were invisible to the naked eye . . .

The feet of thousands of such madmen trampled over Sutter's land; thousands of hands ran through it and turned it over; thousands of people raced towards this spot, coming from all corners of the globe and ready to tear each others' throats out for the sake of a tiny clod of this earth which bears so strange a crop in its core . . .

The flourishing paradise of Captain Sutter's Californian groves and pastures was trampled underfoot and crushed by filthy crowds lusting for gold.

Sutter was ruined . . .

But then, with fresh determination, the proud old man threw thousands of writs at these dirty invaders who had appropriated and occupied his land.

Sutter's estates at that time were extensive and prosperous.

Over the course of a few years, San Francisco grew up on those estates, expanding from a small mission into a large and bustling city.

The town grew in an unexpected and strange way.

You can see how it happened from old engravings.

Flotillas of barges and boats blocked up all the available moorings and clogged the bays.

The boats dropped anchor and remained in the bays thereafter.

The gaps between the boats were bridged with gangways and ultimately silted up.

Shacks were built on the decks.

Bungalows at first; then two- and three-storeyed dwellings.

The holds became cellars.

The decks dovetailed together, forming streets and alleyways.

The intruding holds and decks absorbed the surface of the bays as the slagheaps had done; the greenery of the gulf was buried by the secretly whispering sand which turned the once lush paradise into a saltmarsh hinterland, such as you might find in Central Asia.

When suddenly, one man, old and decisive, threw down the gauntlet before this town of boats and barges, which had worked its tentacles deep into the fissures of the coastline like an octopus and frantically dug into the shore and surrounding hills.

And another swarm gathered over California.

This time, a black one.

The attorneys' dress was a long jacket and tall, long-fibred topper—as we know from photographs of Lincoln and his colleagues in the legal profession.

Thousands of black jackets and toppers swooped down on San Francisco, like a flock of ragged crows.

An unprecedented battle was imminent: one man against an entire city.

And a third flock, black and ghastly, silhouetted between the yard-arms and lanterns in the coastal fog and blackness of the Californian night, spread itself over the once fertile, flourishing soil of Captain Sutter.

The image of a black flock is a vivid one which continues to attract me.

Perhaps because it is essentially a living impression.

Where would you have to go now (or even before the war) to see scores, if not hundreds of black toppers, wandering among the old low houses, vanishing into the twilight and then suddenly reappearing, lit by pinpricks of yellow light from small barred windows?

Does such a place exist outside Daumier's engravings—in real life, can you see such a fantastic sight?

Oddly enough, yes.

True, you won't see any beards or moustaches beneath the hats.

There is little more than down on upper lips, in fact.

True, the people who wear them are unlikely to be of mature years.

I shouldn't think the oldest is as much as twenty.

But the mysterious twilight hides their age: only the general outline is visible and the figures of the younger, juvenile, top-hat wearers in these alleys and mysterious pools of light only serve to intensify the fantastical element. They might be gnomes spirited from a Hoffmann story, or strange inhabitants of Poe's terrible stories.

But they are just whippersnappers.

Or more accurately, young gentlemen, scions of privileged families with the means to send them to Eton.

I did not mention Windsor Castle, nearby; or the white, round turned-down collars and morning-trousers: that would have given the game away too soon.

After our tour of Windsor Castle, where da Vinci's notebooks and Holbein's paintings are kept, my friend Professor Isaacs —with the bowler, red sidewhiskers and inevitable brolly—and I visited neighbouring Eton. This is the first link in the chain of English education; its discipline and atmosphere knocking the fragile, degenerate or excessively plump and indulged boys into stern and implacable, soulless and callous gentlemen, who do not go about bragging that they rule the world as the less prudent Germans do, but firmly believe that they do nevertheless and act with unwavering wholeheartedness for the glory of Britannia, Ruler of the Waves.

This type of gentleman, first sketched in the paradoxical silhouette of a young Etonian in his top hat, is refined still further in the chilly rooms of Cambridge and Oxford which are clad in the masonry of Tudor (and earlier) times, in refectories, where the ceilings vanish in the darkness, in the towering naves of the chapels, but also in the best-equipped physics, chemistry and electromagnetics laboratories,

And in the third link of a career which almost always stretches from Eton to Parliament via Oxford or Cambridge, this fully-fledged gentleman displays to the world the strange spectacle of the permanency of Cadogan's policies, irrespective of whether the springs of happiness have revealed a Tory or a Labour government in the ballot boxes . . .

The avalanche of blackness consuming colour remains an enduring image of mine, one of my favourite ideas.

It is fed, from time to time, by new, associative impressions such as the trip to Windsor, a page from Cendrars' novel, a slagheap near Sacramento, or even a flock of black eagles—zapilotes—circling above the carcasses of horses in Mexico who died in bullfights and were dragged out into the yard at the back.

The eagles perched decorously on the fence around the yard to the rear of the arena in Mérida, capital of Yucatán.

They were waiting . . .

However, Giordano Bruno, Lawrence and the plague promptly made way for another candidate on the list of projects I was to undertake.

The hero was virtually calculated mathematically.

In the same way, I think, that a displacement in the orbits of other luminaries postulated *a priori* the presence of another planet—Uranus[23]—long before ultra-powerful telescopes enabled man to see it.

What was the order of the day when sound came to cinema?

The lives of musicians.

And when colour arrived, what then?

The lives of . . . painters.

What should one not attempt with both colour and sound?

676

Neither of these!

So what should one do?

Neither.

There is a third.

Not the life of a painter,

nor the life of a musician,

but the life of a . . . poet!

Which was how I hit upon the idea of making a film about Pushkin.

I intend to devote this third letter about colour to other and of course basic and crucial motives that led to this idea.

'The Letter That Was Not Sent' will use concrete examples to show how I envisaged the composition of the whole, according to the idea of a film entirely shot in colour.

Here I shall just say that *Pushkin* shared the fate of the *Plague, Bruno* and *Lawrence.*

He remained in the 'ideas' section of my archives.

Front-line intelligence revealed that colour film was not yet ready.

There were problems that were for the time being insurmountable.

Colour was not an obedient servant, running to do the bidding of the questing craftsman: it was a terrible and savage tyrant who demanded so much light that it damaged the actors' costumes and melted their make-up; it was a scoundrel who wrung the heart of the colour idea dry; a vulgarian who rode roughshod over perceptions of colour; an idler who was unable to achieve even one per cent of the idea, the fantasy, the flight of what had been imagined in colour.

Then *Ivan* appeared.

Then war came.

Then victory.

And out of conquered Germany came an avalanche of the colour abominations of German cinema.

Then came three-layered colour film.

And this marked the beginning of a new chain of chance happenings which, after the war, took up a series of plans for colour which had been compiled before the war.

Of course, the yearning for colour arose spontaneously from my work on audiovisual counterpoint.

And of course only colour, colour and again colour is really capable of solving the problem of commensurability, of finding a common denominator for sound and vision.

Enthusiastically greeting the arrival of sound (Pudovkin and Alexandrov signed the article 'Statement On Sound' with me),[24] I once wrote very condescendingly about colour and three-dimensionality in cinema, believing they could contribute nothing new in principle to the mastery of cinematic form.

People could then only guess at the possibilities of audiovisual counterpoint in cinema.

What was then being portrayed on the screen had only begun to be mirrored by the sound.

Now, the practice of audiovisual cinema has made a real contribution to the development of cinema.

And sound, striving to find a visual image, beats powerfully in the confines of black-and-white, where it is forced to blend entirely with what is being portrayed.

The highest forms of organic kinship between the melodic pattern of the music and the tonal structure of a system of successive colour frames are only possible with the advent of colour.

But it is time to move from general phrases to the matter in hand,

from the manifesto, to a plan of action,

from loud declamations, to the practicalities.

From a tirade, to a history of those ups and downs, which were comic and sad, enjoyable and maddening, exciting and joyous (but more frequently infuriating) which we experienced during our actual work with colour on the two scenes in Part Two of *Ivan the Terrible*!

Was anything here not left to chance?!

The fact that Prokofiev left Alma-Ata before me.

But *Ivan the Terrible's* feast and the dancing could not be filmed without the music, composed and taped.

Which meant that we had to film the feast and the dancing in Moscow.

But Prokofiev fell ill and he was unable, working as he was

678

to meet deadlines for *War and Peace* and *Cinderella*, to give me the score I needed that summer.

Autumn came, winter was not far off.

The set had been ready since the summer.

The score was further delayed.

Meanwhile, Dom Kino held a conference on colour.

No spectacle is less enjoyable than arguments and debates about things which no one has actually experienced first-hand.

It is futile, irksome.

But what irritated even more was the free supplement:

watching specimens of colour work by Americans, Germans and the few other courageous types who pushed the pre-war two- and three-film system beyond its limits and then had the gall to strut before us, amazed that we could show on our screens 'that wretched colouring of costume' and 'those fake complexions'.

Anger is a very good creative stimulus.

Unexpectedly among all this shoddy tat from abroad, we saw a documentary.

Filmed in colour.

The Potsdam Conference.[25]

The colour in this film was terrible and inconsistent.

Faces changed from brick-red,

to violet.

Green fluctuated from spring onions,

to the oxide on old bronze coins.

Two-thirds of the spectrum were impossible.

No!—Perhaps half.

But next came a series of interiors at Cecilienhof.

And some rooms.

A vivid red carpet filled the whole screen.

A row of white easy-chairs picked out in red formed a diagonal.

So, red could be done!

More than that—we saw a few shots of the Chinese pavilion at Sanssouci.

When I was looking over it once, I saw Potsdam and some other relics of Frederick the Great's reign in real life.

The Chinese gilt figures also came out well.

More than that, there were also a green cast and reflections from the white marble steps.

Red was possible. Gold worked.

If I could assume that blue would work . . .

I could always risk it . . .

The set for Ivan's feast had been up since the summer.

The feast had to be an explosion, between the dark scene of the plot against the Tsar and the murky scene of his attempted murder.

Why not resolve this explosion in colour?!

The colours would burst into dance.

And fade at the end of the feast, imperceptibly resolving into black-and-white photography . . . the tone of the tragic and chance death of Prince Vladimir Andreyevich at the hands of the murderer sent by his mother to kill the Tsar.

This was perfectly in keeping with my style and mood! In the preceding episode, in colour, the black of the cassocks first engulfed the gold of the robes of the *oprichniki*; then *oprichniki* in their black robes covered the gold of Vladimir's mantle; and finally the whole mass of black *oprichniki* swamped the inside of the cathedral. In its dark belly, they—and their even darker shadows—were swallowed up in the night; among them, was Vladimir, pitiable and helpless, his groan barely audible.

The Prize for *Ivan* [1]

. . . Khmelyov's coffin stood on stage.

He was once in one of my films—*Bezhin Meadow.*[2]

And later, in 1942, he burst into my hotel room hurling drunken accusations at me for not casting him as Ivan in my picture.

Now he was in a coffin.

The corpse had already been cleaned of make-up; the beard had been peeled off, the costume of Ivan the Terrible—robes, ring, wig and crown—had been taken away.

He had died during a rehearsal.

In the midst of the vicissitudes of Ivan's fate, Alexei Tolstoi died on the stage.

Yuzovsky recently came to visit me in the Kremlin hospital.[3]

He recalled with horror a telephone conversation we had had, on 1 February.

We had laughed as we talked of the fateful danger facing people working on *Ivan.*

Tolstoi was dead. Khmelyov was dead.

'"But I'm still alive!" You laughed into the receiver,' Yuzovsky told me the next evening . . .

At the height of the banquet in Dom Kino, these vehicles had come for me, from the hospital.

My arms and legs had gone.

I remembered Arliss's *Old English,* except my arms had gone limp, instead of stiff.[4]

I did not go in an ambulance.

I walked to my car.

Perhaps it was subconscious? Perhaps, for reasons I could not understand, I remembered another evening. Also in winter.

The year before.

In Barvikha.

When another of Ivan's victims was being borne out of a neighbouring building.

I had never liked the Count.[5]

681

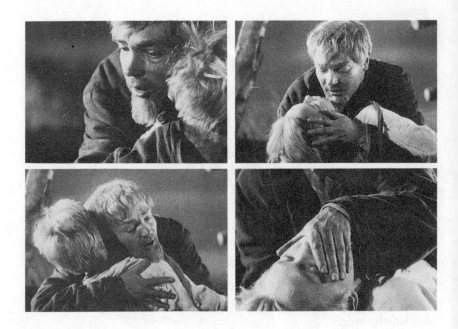

Nikolai Khmelyov playing the father in *Bezhin Meadow* (Second version, 1936-7)

Neither as writer,

nor as a person.

It is hard to say why.

Perhaps, for the same reason that Quakers and Sybarites instinctively avoid each other, or Colas Breugnon and the ascetics?[6]

And, although I would hardly lay claim to the title of St Anthony, I felt something of an old maid when I was in the company of the Count. . .

The vast, white, dusty and completely flat, salt surface of land, somewhere near the aerodrome near Kazalinsk, or Aktyubinsk.

I flew back to Alma-Ata in 1942 and the Count accompanied me as far as Tashkent.

There were no bushes. Not even a blade of grass. Not a fence. Not so much as a stump.

We managed without a stump, then, a short distance from the plane.

We returned.

'Eisenstein, you are a pessimist,' the Count told me.

'In what way?'

'There is something in your face . . .'

We were somehow, tacitly, alien, even antagonistic to each other.

So it was with complete indifference that I looked at his body, lying in the small bedroom off his hospital room.

His jaw was bound up in bandages.

His arms were folded across his chest.

The white of cartilage in his pinched, bruised nose.

His wife and sister were crying.

Also present was a general with two ladies.

More interesting than the dead Count were the details.

Such as the coffee.

His sick-nurse continually poured coffee out for all who wanted it, and all who did not as well.

They were about to take the body out.

Clear the ward.

And that night the body was flown to Moscow.

The next morning, the room would have a new occupant.

Esfir Shub

There was no need to worry about the tablecloth.

The coffee was poured out quite carelessly.

As if to splash the cloth deliberately, so liberally was it be-spattered with pools of the dark liquid.

A smashed jug of cream lay under the table: a jarring note.

But the nurses had arrived.

They covered the body with a grey army blanket.

With half his head sticking out from beneath it; deep-sunk eyes.

They got it wrong, of course.

They tried to carry him out head first, of course.

The legs stuck up, comically, until one of the elderly nurses intervened.

They turned the trolley so that his feet faced the exit.

They were still on the first flight of stairs when someone turned on a tap in the bathroom, breaking the silence.

And a cleaner, with bucket and mop, almost bumped into the trolley as she squelched about in her bare feet . . .

Day and night, mattocks and spades scraped away in the belly of Moscow.

They were building the metro.

Girls dressed as miners walked evocatively across Theatre Square.

Underground Moscow had its own life.

It was at this period that I met Pasternak.[7]

He lived on the Arbat.

He lived above the tunnelling.

He wrote by night.

And the subterranean scrapes, cracks, clanks and squeals distracted him.

Urbanism was burrowing its way beneath the poet.

One morning he could not leave his flat.

The building had subsided.

It had started to bow.

And this prevented the door from opening.

Pasternak leant out with his elbows on the broad win-dowsill.

It was evening.

And we were somewhere high above Moscow, visiting someone.

In the night air you could hear the piercing and plaintive whistling of the trains.

'Trains,' Pasternak remarked, 'are the only honest people around. They're having a hard time, but they don't try to conceal it.'

He looked at me with his wide brown eyes above his negroid lips.

'Eisenstein, you are like an undecorated church . . .'

In those years, the years of *Counterplan* [Vstrechnyi, 1932] and *The Happy Guys* [Veselye rebyata, 1934], *Petersburg Night* [Peterburgskaya noch', 1934] and *The Storm* [Groza 1934], my position in cinema was just that.

But now what?

Churches have been resurrected and the domes of the Kremlin cathedrals have been gilded.

Chiaureli,[8] with *The Vow* [Klyatva, 1946] took his place among the patriarchs of cinema.

I am last, apart from Simeon the Stylite![9]

We all, in some way at some time, play at being great historical figures.

I have described somewhere my and Pudovkin's first meeting with Dovzhenko, whose career was just beginning.

And I related how we assigned to ourselves the roles of various titans of the Renaissance. Pudovkin got his teeth into Raphael. Dovzhenko was allotted Michelangelo. And I was Leonardo . . .

In her relations with me in the 1920s, Esfir Ilyinichna Shub[10] probably saw herself as some kind of enigmatic George Sand.

Although it would be difficult to find anyone bearing a fainter resemblance to Chopin or de Musset than me, short-legged and corpulent as I am. But why else would she have advised me to read Tynyanov's *A Nameless Love*, when I was struggling to find the dramatic kernel of the plot for my already prepared general, lyrical conception for my film biography of Pushkin? Did she really, in the spring of 1940, see herself playing Karamzina to my . . . Pushkin?

But why did I instantly, with burning, unreserved resolve, latch on to that very notion? It was as though I had just seen that very drama being screened before my eyes.

A picture of such a love.

A love hidden and illicit. But illicit rather than hidden.

But of such strength.

And inspired.

A love which strove to immerse its unattainability in the flourishes of the endless Don Juan catalogue, which could catch up with Pushkin's, and even outstrip it.[11]

Charlie Chaplin!!

'In the purple rays of sunset.'

Hollywood . . .

Candles burning down after dinner.

1930.

However . . .

I have not yet explained how the conception of making a film about Pushkin came about.

How I wrote a screenplay on just one theme without even having the time to find a subject. How Tynyanov suggested a plot for the screenplay.

Marion[1]

I have already written of my great capacity for envy.

Further, this envy takes the strangest forms.

For example, I was terribly envious of a famous joke about Deburau.

A tall, thin, pale person, seized by a terrible melancholia, went to the doctor.

The doctor advised him to go out and have a good time.

Have some laughs.

'Go and see Deburau.'

'I am Deburau . . .'

Yesterday, a very similar thing happened to me.

My heart is very weak.

The doctor advised me to take a break from my usual activities and mental pursuits.

'Take up photography!'

Ha, ha, ha!

Some diversion: at the very roughest guess, I must, during my lifetime, have taken some 15,000 photographs, counting each sequence—never mind the ones between them!—as a separate photograph.

Apropos the melancholy of jokers.

I know one pretty closely.

The very greatest of his time.

Charlie Chaplin.

It is now hackneyed to say that his films are a mixture of smiles and tears.

As he is in life.

I remember a terrible evening in Beverly Hills.

As ever, we were playing tennis.

Apart from us, the three Russians, on that occasion there were also three Spaniards.

And Ivor Montagu.[2]

The Spaniards were somehow importunate and suspicious. The Russians were boring.

Ivor was a particularly outspoken Englishman from Cambridge. Chaplin was doing his best to keep his end up in a 'highbrow English conversation'.* Then he started clowning around.

That day he was especially animated and mischievous.

Especially playful, especially entertaining.

When you are with him, he is not still for one moment.

He has a medieval *horror vacui*: he is scared of the empty moment, a second of unoccupied time, intervals in the endless succession of *lazzi*, 'practical jokes'* or puns.

One moment he dances to the radio, parodying oriental dances.

And the next he impersonates the King of Siam, whose nose would barely reach the table top.

When they came to administer extreme unction to Rabelais, he tossed the blanket back and lay there dressed as Harlequin.

Of course Chaplin's Harlequin does not conceal a dying body.

But a spirit deeply affected by the long, cold fingers of the winged angel of melancholy, as depicted sitting sorrowfully, cheek on hand, in Dürer's woodcut.

This angel is Marion Davies.[3]

Marion Davies is Charlie's one and only real, long-lasting love.

But Marion belongs to Hearst. And, once Hearst has his hands on something, he will not let anyone else have it . . .

This evening Chaplin's playfulness is especially highly-wrought: the Harlequin costume has been pulled on with even more nervousness than usual, to hide as much as possible of the sad little figure who has borne such unconsolable sadness since his Whitechapel childhood.

When he was at the Nezhin secondary school, Gogol began writing humorous stories to dispel the melancholia that afflicted his brother and himself.

Chaplin is afraid of solitude.

He grabbed his guests.

---

* In English in the original.

He was like a child scared of being alone in the dark.

He asked us to stay for dinner.

His man Kono[4] and the other Japanese glided through the dining room.

Superficially, it looked like an improvised feast.

'The purple light of sunset' played on the silverware.

Then the sun set and candles were brought.

And a strip of purple sky led Chaplin to reminisce.

Three Russians and three Japanese sat facing each other like wooden figures on the right and left.

The Englishman from Cambridge sat opposite the host.

The laughter died away.

The sunset and the motionless figures reminded Charlie of something.

The same sunset.

The same still figures.

Except wrapped up in red blankets, coats, sarapes.

The small church in a rocky hinterland near the small desert station in Mexico.

The still figures were there as witnesses.

Before the altar stood the priest, impatient.

Chaplin stood in one corner of the church.

And in the other was a young maiden with her mother.

The priest held a bible.

The dying rays of the blood-red sunset shone through the roundel above.

Inside the church was the deep blue of twilight.

The groom was Charlie.

And the bride was Miss Grey.[5]

The priest impatiently shifted his weight from one foot to the other like a horse trampling the ground.

The bible banged against the worn red velvet screen. At home, a rich red-pepper soup was awaiting him. The witnesses wore red sarapes.

The last rays of the blood-red sunset in the round window above.

A Study in Scarlet?

Why not?

A photo presented to Eisenstein by Chaplin.

A photograph sent to Pera Atasheva with the inscription 'To my best friend in USSR together with my best friend in USA' (Hollywood, September 1930).

That was the first detective story by Conan Doyle that I read.

It was my first encounter with Sherlock Holmes.

But you do not have to be Sherlock Holmes to deduce that a marriage is about to take place.

Everyone was at their place.

The priest.

The groom.

The bride.

The two rings.

The Bible.

The two Mexicans, silent witnesses.

Why did the ceremony not begin?

From deep within the church came the harsh, persistent sound of an argument.

Everyone listened attentively.

With the possible exception of the Madonna and the two Mexicans who were supremely indifferent to it.

All they cared about was the handful of pesos they would take home for their wasted time.

The voices belonged to two attorneys.

They were very angry, forgetting where they were.

They waved their arms about as if they were in their own offices.

In the twilight, the two pairs of pince-nez glinted aggressively as they jumped up and down.

The rays of light intersected as the two pince-nez wearers pounced on each other.

And it seemed sometimes that it was not rays of light, but the sparks that fly when blades are crossed.

At night, the shadows were like crêpe. In English, shooting crap means playing with marked cards.

In this game, the two attorneys tried to beat each other: faithful guard-dogs defending the interests of their respective clients.

Charlie sighed.

Charlie the narrator.

Probably, Charlie uttered sighs like that when he was taking part in that ridiculous ceremony.

Chaplin looked at a crucifix and probably found much in common between the life of the protagonist in the Bible and his own.

He almost met his Calvary, on any number of occasions . . .

The Madonna sank into the darkness.

There was just enough light to make out the face on the crucifix above.

The man on the cross looked reproachfully at the money-changers in the temple.

His hands were nailed to the wood.

He could not take a knotted cord and drive both attorneys out on to the street as they blasphemously raised their voices in the temple.

Two documents lay beneath the prominent noses of the perspiring attorneys:

A marriage document.

And a divorce document.

Both were drawn up for the same people.

For Charles Spencer Chaplin and Miss Lita Grey.

Then the priest pronounced a short prayer and bound the couple, who at that moment were exchanging rings before him, together for all time, for this world and the next.

They signed the first document.

And a moment later, the second.

Joined by God for all time, they would now be torn asunder by the hands of these two lawyers.

Prince Louis Bonaparte, after his first unsuccessful coup, was sentenced to life imprisonment in a fortress—for ever.

'How long does eternity last for, in France?' The Prince asked and escaped from the fortress to pull off a successful coup.

Eternity is even shorter here.

And it would have been shorter still but for some clause in the document regarding money which obliged those zealous attorneys to lock antlers once more.

But this too was settled.

They all bowed their heads.

Hastily the priest said all that he had to.

Two signatures on one document.

695

The marks of witnesses in confirmation.

The ink was barely dry on the first document when the signatures were put to the second.

Which annulled it.

Nevertheless St Peter has been given the prerogative to tie and untie.

'And what is tied on earth shall be tied in Heaven.

And what is untied . . .'

Nobody has ever said anything about the interval between these two procedures.

I forgot to clarify just one detail: whether the same witnesses put their marks to both documents, or whether there were two pairs of witnesses.

And when they said their congratulations.

In the middle of the ceremony.

Or at the end.

Or twice.

The scene before the altar is always the traditional 'happy end'.*

So it is now.

This is the happy end of a long and cunning intrigue.

The ending cost Universal's best comic roughly 1,000,000 dollars.

Chaplin may have regretted this million as he told us all about it in the dining-room, with the candles, many years later in Beverly Hills.

This drama extends further back.

There was a similar reverse narrative in a novella by Flammarion, I seem to remember: *Lux*.[6]

The premise is that the speed at which particles of light from Earth travel to a planet increases at a constant rate.

So that what happens on Earth appears, to the observer on another planet, to happen in reverse.

With delightful Gallic brilliance, Flammarion introduced all manner of bizarre happenings which might result from this.

He made human life flow backwards before the eyes of the

---

* In English in the original: the form *kheppi-end* is used in Russian for 'happy ending'.(Ed.)

observer.

Events acquired a new, engaging logic.

People, attired in mourning black, sob at the graveside, which torchbearers of gloomy aspect dig up in order to condemn someone to life in this Vale of Tears.

Husbands and wives, having annoyed each other for a great many years, embrace fondly and with a tender 'first kiss', thank each other for their newly restored freedom. After a phase of friendship and a first meeting, they part joyfully.

And on reaching his life's end, man vanishes in a strange way, with the help of a . . . midwife.

Ves' klass
prosit vas
v poslednii raz
prochest' rasskaz.*

These immortal lines are chalked on the blackboard, twice a year without fail.

Before the end of the second and fourth quarters of the school year—the end of the first and second terms.

A school tradition allows—nay, insists—that the last lesson of each term be devoted to a story read by the teacher.

I remember the reverse action of Flammarion's novella having heard it just once, in one of the junior years at the Institute in Riga, where I first tasted the fruits of knowledge.

It made a strong, indelible impression, despite the fact that all the others were completely forgotten about—no amount of cudgelling my mind can recall them.

Why?

I think because Flammarion's plot is not the only one of its kind.

The device of reverse action is a very popular one in a certain new art form, whose first impressions only take the form of

---

* Russian: The whole class
Says you must
Read the story
For the last time . . .

697

running pictures (and I do mean running and bobbing up and down) jumping on a white canvas hung in flats with knocked-through walls—the first 'bioscopes'.[7]

Apart from Méliès, whose work I saw in Paris when I was eight, my first impressions of cinema came from short films in 'The Royal Bio' in Riga.

The first, which was memorable for its repulsiveness, was of Mounet-Sully's acting; he was filmed as Oedipus reciting a monologue and jam flowed thickly from his eyes.[8]

The second, which came before Max Linder, Pockson and Prince, was of races and it looked as though the projectionist was drunk.[9]

The horses took the fences.

Then they came to an abrupt halt in mid-air (the projectionist was staring at a girl).

Then the horses were madly transported in the opposite direction—backwards.

(While staring at the girl, the projectionist had absent-mindedly begun cranking the apparatus in the other direction.)

He saw everything back to front.

In a restaurant, the patrons carefully removed sausage sandwich after sausage sandwich from their mouths and also carefully replaced a succession of leaves back on the branches as the leaves flew obligingly up from the gravel path and into their hands.

And then suddenly a grand vista of crazy 'traffic'* on a city street, all hurtling backwards.

I was for a time denied admission to the bioscope then.

*Die Damen werden aus dem Café gehoben.***

I remember this last subtitle as if it were yesterday; it was not on the screen, but read out by a special announcer attired as a circus ringleader, standing to one side and explaining the action as it unfolded.

I was hurriedly taken by the arm and led out—the subject matter was not for one of my years.

The women rebelled and did what the men had done.

They began to frequent cafés.

---

* In English in the original.
** German: 'They are carrying the ladies out of the café'.

Talk politics.

Smoke cigars.

While their husbands sat at home doing the washing.

And went for walks in an endless chain of prams.

Then the men rebelled.

They burst into the cafés.

They grabbed the ladies and triumphantly bore them out on to the street.

Die Damen werden aus dem Café gehoben.

'They are carrying the ladies out of the café,'

announced the man in the uniform.

I was (all but) carried out of the cinema.

I held on to a chair. I did not want to leave. My eyes were glued to the screen.

To no avail.

I shall never know what finally happened to the poor women.

A Man's Fate in Yevreinov's Distorting Mirror Theatre, the ancient Greek buffonade by John Erskine and finally [. . .], the author of *Tonner*, later put the finishing touches to the fantastical situation of lords changing places with their ladies, although it becomes difficult henceforward to trace the line of my interest in the question of bisexuality, when it enters clearly the area of ecstasy.[10] Huysmans wrote of Sainte François and Saint Thérèse, thinking that this designation was more appropriate to the psychological cast of mind of a saint, who acts more like someone of the opposite sex.

Some of St Theresa's admonitory letters to nuns make amusing reading: domestic and administrative instructions are interspersed with frequent ripostes and earthy, Rabelaisian, red-blooded humour!

The film about the liberated women's ill-fated escapade (it took place at the same time as the 'suffragettes'' public displays and only just anticipated the fashion for ladies' *jupes-culottes*)* is in one respect immediately linked to films where sequences run in reverse order.

There is the same inversion of opposites.

The women take the place of their partners, just as here

---

* In French in the original.

forward motion became backward motion.

Both films prepared the ground for Flammarion's story.

Sterne's novel (*Tristram Shandy*) is written from start to finish.[11] Alice's adventures through the looking-glass.

Poe's doctrine that novellas, if they do not actually start at the end and work backwards, are nevertheless written that way and ought to be written that way.[12] It is all so much flowers and ribbons, interwoven into a wreath of first impressions, which end up with the actual principle of the comic structure being that same 'reverse', the simplest comic effect, broadened, heightened and then applied to any philosophical concept that is dominant at a particular historical period.

A hotel is burgled.

The police cordon the building off. The commissioner has all the exits covered.

The criminal has vanished.

'Might he have left by one of the . . . entrances?' A policeman hazards.

Surely this 'unexpectedness' negates the unassailable status quo, the fixed predictability of Kant's metaphysical universe, which made him find funny even the premise that there could be something funny?

Surely the illogical negates logic (the dominant principle of one epoch) and is considered the basis of comedy, in exactly the same way that the period of *élan vital* supposed mechanicism to be the basis of what is funny (because it negated the basic doctrine)?[13]

Are they not simultaneously equal and inverse; as a door is both an entrance and an exit, representing two different approaches from two different directions, to the same phenomenon—even the yawning gape of an aperture in the flat surface of a wall?

And is it not just the same in the simplest comic trick of reversing the motor in cinematography, consolidating a favourite psychological 'game' from one's childhood into a technical device?

A rider galloping under his horse.

An axe using the carpenter to chop.

Fish pulling anglers out of the river.

And other such delights from the embellishments and

folklore of childhood, collected in Grandville's *un autre monde* in order to spill out in a cascade of unexpected results from between the covers of that mad book.

However, the principles of comedy have their own place in their own book.

And I only mention them here, *en passant*, because it is precisely here and now that the two elements—reverse filming and the nature of the actual principle—have joined together to make one whole inversion.

The unity of the nature of tickling, the physiological mechanism of laughter, the structure of wit, the principle of humour, were all felt much earlier.

However . . .

In the best traditions of primitive comic film, like the racehorse frozen in flight above a fence, we have left Chaplin and his young bride—bride and divorcee—hanging in mid-air, beneath the vaults of the little church in Mexico.

We set the wheels in motion.

In reverse, as we said.

And now there is no longer a church before us, but a small railway halt.

A long passenger train at the platform.

The staid Kono strolled officiously along the platform.

He had evidently got off the train to have a breath of fresh air.

Such was the general verdict of the hundred-odd reporters who did not let him out of their sight as they stayed on board.

A whistle.

He climbed back on board.

And the train pulled out.

Further into the heart of Mexico.

Away from Los Angeles.

The reporters sank back into their seats and made themselves comfortable once more.

Not here, then . . .

Busy watching Kono as he got off the train, they did not notice what was happening under the carriages.

The endless corridor between the wheels of the train.

701

Stretching in both directions.

A lady with her daughter ran in one direction, bent double.

And, pressed to the ground on all fours, a great comic actor made his way in the other direction in a degrading farce, this time not on the screen but for real.

Traditionally the groom and bride arrive at the church from different directions.

Here, both had to run away in different directions before meeting at the altar, which in this case involved a hasty separation of the newly-weds, forever, as in Flammarion's novella!

They had to avoid meeting reporters and journalists before the affair could be made lawful; before the affair could be recognised by a *de jure* marriage; before the divorce could be processed.

No one should know when the second followed the first and that 'both the two' after the marriage are *de facto.*

This *de facto* could cost Chaplin not only a paltry million.

But . . . a lifetime of hard labour.

The girl, the 'victim', was only sixteen.

And the rape case could also be treated as the seduction of a minor.

'You must understand me!' Chaplin said, anguished by the mere memory of it. 'Imagine, a blossoming young girl, as tall as a grenadier.

'And me, next to her . . .'

We vividly pictured this puny little manikin next to a larger-than-lifesize Venus de Milo.

'Can you see me as a rapist?

'Can you imagine me with her in my arms?!'

We agreed it was not easy.

And the mystery of Venus's missing arms, this time at least, seems a perfectly apt image for the embraces which so easily swept the little man up in the air as he stood enraptured in the web of his own sensuality.

But this case involved not only the two deft arms of the young Venus herself.

There is a third arm too and it played a key part: it was the protagonist.

Charlie sighed.

'Her documents said she really was sixteen . . .'

The hand of Moscow!

To this day, Anglo-Saxons, on either shore of the ocean which lends its name to a certain treaty, look for the 'hand of Moscow' everywhere.

As happened earlier too.

Moscow, involved in this??!

Yes—the hand of Moscow.

But a friendly hand, which Anatoli Vasilevich Lunacharsky[14] extended across the seas and oceans.

The invitation to drop everything and come to the Soviet Union.

Here, as always, the hand of Moscow opposed the Hearsts, giving them a rap across the knuckles.

It was Hearst who obligingly set the sixteen-year-old adventuress Lita Grey on a collision course with Chaplin.

It was they who helped ensnare Chaplin in the web of intrigue.

The boycott of his films had just begun.

'The Daughters of the American Revolution', a term that is for women what 'sons of bitches' is for men, were already blowing their trumpets of Jericho, which resounded across all America, carrying the message that the little man with the bowler and the moustache was breaching the citadel of American morality.

He could see even at this early stage the rippling mirage of scandal: a court-case and penal servitude.

The sluice-gates of filth were opened, ready to ruin and drown this diminutive character who made the whole world laugh, feel happy, and cry.

At the last minute, Hearst himself threw the lever of his all-destroying machinery and called off his pack of newspapers and newshounds.

Chaplin slid out from under the looming court-case which would have spelt ruination and ignominy.

Money and the press are omnipotent in America.

Hearst runs the press.

Chaplin holds the money.

A million or so.

Nothing!

'This will teach the boy to forget about Marion Davies . . . '

Hearst thought.

Chaplin slid off his chair.

Ran upstairs.

We waited a little while.

Then we left.

We didn't see Chaplin again that evening.

We saw him then as few people see him.

Pale, suffering, his face crumpled.

He remembered a lot that was difficult and painful.

But it takes even more pain and hardship to forget about something . . .

I cannot undertake to confirm all the above details on oath.

Whether both the attorneys wore pince-nez.

Whether there was a velvet screen before the altar.

Or if there was, if it was worn.

Whether the priest was in a hurry to get back to his red-pepper soup.

And exactly how Randolph Hearst expressed his thoughts about Chaplin and Marion Davies.

And I am quite sure that Charles Chaplin did not look at the crucifix.

I am just retelling a story.

And an impression received from a story, at that.

Furthermore, a story I heard all of sixteen years ago.

But one thing I can guarantee:

The atmosphere of the story.

And the atmosphere of the setting where it was told.

Chaplin's heart-rending melancholy, which took the upper hand in the farcical situations between Charlie and the 'grenadier', the two haggling lawyers or Kono's air of concentration which distracted the reporters.

And the purple rays of sunset which played on the silverware and triggered Charlie's reminiscences of this whole epic.

[Now around me is the dazzling gold of the midday sun. Yet I am burdened by melancholy.

We all have our Marion Davieses . . .]

The Dollar Princess[1]

I have never had a good ear. I have always found it difficult to remember a tune so that I could recognise it again.

And as for remembering it well enough to be able to sing it myself—that was out of the question.

But there have been exceptions.

I remember rocking on my bed all night after *The Tales of Hoffmann*—which I had seen and heard for the first time in Riga—and singing the 'Barcarolle' over and over again.[2]

And even now of course I can sing the waltz from *The Dollar Princess*, if not aloud, then to myself; it amazed me when I heard it for the first time, also in Riga, probably aged about twelve.

I remember the words:

> *Das sind die Dollarprinzessen,*
> *Die Mädchen von vie-ie-lem Gold*
> *Mit Schätzen u-u-unermessen . . .* *

But these pages will not deal with my first impressions of operas or operettas.

I shall set out elsewhere the details of my first encounter with *Eugene Onegin* at the amateur dramatic society in Riga, where all the usual 'romance' of the sets in Act One looking now through the colonnades on to the endless fields (Rabinovich at the Bolshoi)[3] were summarily replaced with a green garden seat pushed against the back of the stage.

Similarly I shall talk of the first theatre comics to fascinate me—Fender, Kurt Busch and Sachsl[4]—in the German Theatre and Opera House in Riga, the scene of my introduction (at a tender age) to the repértoire from *Hansel and Gretel*, to *Götz von*

---

* German: These are the dollar princesses,
The girls with lots of gold
And treasures beyond measure . . .

Berlichingen and from *Wallenstein's Death* to *Der Freischütz* and *Madame sans gêne* (the unforgettable Fender played the cobbler and had three words to say; and to this day I can still recall the floating arabesque as he uttered the phrase *'Wie eine Fee',** referring to the imminent entrance of the Marshal's wife!), *Around the World in Eighty Days*, and the operetta *Feuerzauberei*.

I also saw the latter before the war (I mean the war of 1914!). But I cannot be more precise than that, since, as I recall, after 1914 another of my favourites, Sachsl, who played Bonaparte himself in *Madame sans gêne* and here the part of an actor playing Bonaparte in a film who rode a white horse on to the stage towards a model film camera (this was the first film sequence that I saw)— was suspected of spying and interned!

Before that scene, Fender sang

Und die Mühle
*Und sie dreht sich...***

against a backdrop of a landscape, with a model windmill.

The vanes of the windmill began turning in the background, in time to the music . . .

The *Schlager**** dominated the whole scene:

In der Nacht, in der Nacht
*Wenn die Liebe erwacht . . .*****

and

Kind ich schlaf' doch so schlecht
*Und ich träum' doch so schwer . . .******

I repeat:

---

    *   German: 'Like a fairy'
   **   German: And the windmill,
                     How it turns . . .
  *** German: 'hits'
 **** German: At night, at night,
                     When love burns bright . . .
***** German: Child, I sleep so badly,
                     Tormented by terrible dreams . . .

I remember *The Dollar Princess* from a quite different occasion.

When I met a real dollar princess very many years later.

Principally because this meeting quite unexpectedly opened my eyes to the cause of the age-long trauma of the ugly duckling, which I mentioned earlier.[5]

And it certainly went a little way towards overcoming this trauma.

When I realised what it was, it was already late. But in the final analysis, an abstract structural schema frequently held as much pleasure for me as did an actual fact.

Katerinki[1]

We will try to fictionalise one's tragic romantic experience.

Let's see how the symbolising machinery works.

Millionaire's daughter made . . . princess (*notez: Die Dollarprinzessin*).

The movie director builder of 'Canvases' made—Cathedral Builder.

His inability to talk and to make conversation we transform into a literally swallowed tongue.

He swallowed his tongue and talked through his cathedrals.

Now elaborating this image we set:[*]

Les piliers de ses cathédrales fûrent ses consonnés.
Les rosaces—ses voyelles.
Les battements de son coeur—les roulements de l'orgue.
L'étendue de sa pensée—le dome recouvrant sa nef.
Les sons des cloches—la voix de son message.[**]

And, hiding somewhere in the foundations of the crypts of cathedrals he had made, he sent into the world an ever-increasing number of arches, gallery after gallery; enfilade after enfilade of vaults; and he spoke through the coloured patterns of the glass.

Through the spires of his belfries he summoned people to elevated thought.

His organ music drew people to feel the majesty of emotions.

He himself was mute
and without a tongue.

And so he became the guardian of his own works which

---

[*] The basic language of the text so far has been English. (Ed.)
[**] French: The pillars of his cathedrals were his consonants.
            The stained glass windows were his vowels.
            The beating of his heart was the peals of organ music.
            The breadth of his thoughts was the dome above his nave.
            The ringing from the belfry was the voice of his message.

spoke on his behalf.

As dancers are the slaves of their own feet, girls slaves of their own voices accompanied by the lute and, as those whose expertise lies in plucking the strings of a harp become slaves to their hands, he himself spent some time in the darkness, whispering to himself or writing in the dust with an unsteady finger:

'Who am I? No more than the steward of my thoughts, the resigned servant of my works . . . A bell-shaped vessel through which the people—my brothers—speak. I myself am nothing.'

And once a Little Princess came to the last cathedral that he had built.

She walked along the vaulted galleries.

And through the rays shining through the stained glass.

And she glanced into the crypt.

She took him by the hand and led him to a great feast.*

The Little Princess and the Great Cathedral Builder Who Swallowed His Tongue

Once upon a time there lived the richest little princess in the world.

Never married,

afraid,

and so she whored around and especially with a red-headed lad of the lowest grade,

famous for his voice that carried over the oceans,

and by his force that could overturn anything in the world.

On the other end of the great big world there lived the famous Cathedral Builder who had swallowed his tongue and talked through the edifices he built.

At high table were the greatest Grands of the world at that time.

The Chinese prince besides her father,

Earl Venceslas with his fair haired spouse—Pearl of the East.

---

* The basic language of this section was Russian but the rest is in English (Ed.)

Sir Archibald native of Schottland.

They drank the health of the Builder, but he couldn't say a word since ['and' in Russian] he had no Arches, Pillars and Counterforts.

So he was mute.

Then the Princess asked him to deliver her of a drunken beastly baron trying to seduce her by his love proposals.

Asking her to dance with him.

So he delivered her and explained that there remained no need for dancing.

'Let us drink to springtime in the Great Builder's heart,' said her Father the King, but being a Magician and not being it enough he couldn't break at once the spell resting on the poor little Great Builder.

But time went on, and the Magician's words like seeds began to flourish.

And the poor little Builder saw that his spell and the spell on the little princess were nearly the same.

When somebody looked at him, he thought they looked at his Cathedrals.

When somebody looked at her, she thought they were hunting for her millions.

So he ran to her and wanted to tell her—sister, don't we suffer of the same?

And shouldn't we go together?

Aren't we really worth nothing at all, you for yourself, and me for mine?

But never, never could he get in touch with her. Fate was against them. And so she went away with her Fatum. And he remained muter than ever*.

---

* This section in English.

A Poet's Love (Pushkin)[1]

. . . I was looking for material for a colour film.

For a film with music, one would 'naturally' pick a biography of a composer.

And for a film in colour, doubtless the story of a painter.

Which is why, for a film uniting colour and music, I chose neither one nor the other.

I chose the life of a man of letters. Pushkin.

But of course, there were other reasons.

Because it was precisely a colour film of Pushkin that could impart the same moving drama of colour, the same movement of the chromatic spectrum, to the tone of the poet's fate as it unfolded; just as Gogol's creativity may be discerned not through his life, but in the succession of his works.

A curious colour-shift occurs throughout the entire corpus, which includes the entire range of tones at the start with *Evenings on a Farm Near Dikanka* and ends with the second part of *Dead Souls*.

If the author's tragic history emerges through the fabric of his works, his youthful wholehearted dedication to a full life, shifting towards an ascetic darkening, represented by a shift away from the rich fullness of colours towards a severe monochrome, such as we see on a screen,—then the same dramatised shift in colour could reflect the environment in which the poet's fate so tragically unfolded; from the carefree, wide-open spaces of Odessa, to the cold shroud of snow by the Black Brook.[2]

Images from his life intermingled with ideas represented in colour.

Here is the rich palette of oils, at the most auspicious of beginnings.

Tsar Boris, clad in thick gold, with flecks of silver in his black beard.

Here is Tsar Boris's monologue, which could be portrayed cinematically as a nightmare ('beholding the blood-soaked infants').[3] The red carpets of the cathedral. The red candlelight. And, illuminated by it, seemingly splashed with blood, the icon frames.

The Tsar rushes about his apartments.

Dark blue. Cherry red. Orange. Green.

They rush to meet him.

The multicoloured brightness of the apartments and towers of the Kremlin palace burst upon the Tsar, a nightmare of colour, as the camera lunges this way and that.

The poet saw the character of the Tsar-cum-regicide, Alexander, in Boris.[4]

In the fireplace at Mikhailovskoye, smouldering embers flare up.

Nicholas seems to be looking out at the poet from the fire (superimposition, quite permissible in film).

The poet's hand doodles on a sheet of paper.

A gallows.

Gallows, gallows, gallows.

'And perhaps, I . . . me also . . .'—nervously written between these recollections of the Decembrists.

Staring into the fireplace.

The vision of Nicholas, returning his gaze from the flickering embers.

The paper is crumpled in his fist.

Like Luther's inkwell hurled at the devil, the ball of paper flies at the ominous vision.

The vision fades.

The paper, with the ominous gallows, flares up, devoured by the last tongues of flame in the dying hearth.

In a burst of light, there comes the startling knock of a policeman's sword.

The first bloody highlight—the newly-kindled flame—gleams on the policeman's helmet . . .

Summoned by Nicholas, Pushkin gallops to Moscow.

The theme of blood is identified with the colour red. In 'The Requiem', it is Danzas's red cap-band.[5]

The animated flow of skaters moving towards the islands.

Although 'flow' is a bad metaphor, as this is in winter, on snow and in sleighs.

No one pities him.

Nor, of those who were to see him a few hours later when

his blood formed a red wreath on the snow, would there be many to mourn.

No one feels any sorrow for him.

And he is satisfied.

He politely exchanges bows with those he passes in his sleigh; he caustically tells his companion [. . .][6]

His companion can hardly hear him.

He fidgets on the seat of the sleigh.

He is preoccupied by a strange, thankless task.

He is trying to attract the attention of those he passes to what he is holding in his hands.

But in such a way that his companion does not notice.

The object is a flat case, for carrying pistols.

But the people he meets, though unfriendly, are invariably attracted to his companion's curls which flow from beneath his top hat.

One more unsuccessful attempt to attract attention to the case in the officer's hands.

And one more caustic comment from his curly-haired companion.

No one pities him.

And he is satisfied.

He is going to a duel.

And he is delighted that no one stands in his way.

A very smart sleigh passes by.

Inside, a well-dressed lady.

But she is shortsighted and does not recognise the curly gentleman.

Although the curly poet is her husband.

But did I say that the gentleman going to a duel was a poet?

I have always pictured Pushkin's duel, like all duels, as taking place in the morning.

Like the duel between Onegin and Lensky, in the opera version.

This duel though takes place in the afternoon; between four and five o'clock, to be more precise.

And Pushkin and Danzas (he is the nervous officer doing

all he can to draw people into the affair, since he cannot openly tell them of the impending tragedy) are proceeding to their rendezvous through the glitter of elegant skaters, among the islands of St Petersburg.

Bah! All the faces are familiar.

There is not one person one could stop at.

Not one person one could stop . . .

Danzas testified that Natalya Nikolayevna was among those who met Pushkin.

Because of her poor sight, she did not see or recognise the poet.

The sounds of dancing, the cream of Petersburg society happily skating, ring out with greater urgency.

And the strains of Prokofiev's 'Requiem', as yet distant, will mingle with it, an increasingly ponderous and gloomy musical sub-text.[7]

For Pushkin is travelling to his death, through the round dance of Petersburg's elite.

The 'Requiem' swells . . .

It is intensified by the dancing.

It diminishes, fades. The external motif is the pale blue chill in the air, which dulls all colour; hoarfrost, which tones down the ruddy glow of moustaches and sideburns, the snow falling from the branches, and hangs like a new kind of lace before the fire-works, deadening their colours.

The flickering light of the cherry satin, Natalya Nikolayevna's muffler—she is 'the madonna with a squint.'[8]

The final range of colours is misty grey.

And harsh black-and-white.

Snow.

The duellers in silhouette.

One spot of colour.

Bloody.

Red.

Not on his chest.

Not on his shirt.

Not on the poet's waistcoat.

In the sky!

The blood-red disc of the sun.

Natalya Pushkina-Goncharova. (Watercolour by Karl Bryullov)

Baron George d'Anthès-Heeckeren, who killed Pushkin in a duel.

Not radiant.

But that same dark red colour as it shines low above the horizon, visible on frosty days among the black silhouettes of trees, the Empire-style palings of Petersburg, the outline of lamp-posts behind the spire of the St Peter and St Paul Fortress . . .

A red diamond of light shines through the particoloured pane of the door in the mezzanine and falls on Natalya Nikolayevna's fingers, which are white with dread.

The poet has been brought home.

And the first woman he wanted to see was not her, his wife.

The first woman he called for was . . . Karamzina, the historian's wife.[9]

The red diamond could be blood.

Natalya Nikolayevna hides her hands.

But now her magnificent white dress is covered in a cascade of diamonds—now of all the colours of the rainbow.

And Natalya Nikolayevna's pure white dress (which she wears in all the pale violet scenes of her love affair, courtship and marriage, including the inauspicious omen of the dropped ring) suddenly becomes the motley costume of Harlequin.

As she jumps up from her seat to admit Karamzina, dressed entirely in severe black, Natalya Nikolayevna is lit up by all the colours of the glass panes as the light filters through them.

And her white dress suddenly becomes something resembling that masquerade costume of a lady Harlequin, which she wore when Pushkin was experiencing pangs of particularly acute jealousy at the masked ball, when he and d'Anthès were consumed by jealousy of a third man.

But the blood-red velvet of the royal box and the black, still guardian angel, Benckendorff's spy, maintain an enigmatic silence above the stage, which has been arranged according to Lev Tolstoy's observations on Nicholas I's amorous encounters . . .[10]

Thus the colour leitmotifs of the themes were woven into the subtleties of the action.

And also scenes began to wind themselves around a certain central core.

This core for me had to be the most beautiful, strict and magnificent, of all possible themes using the material of the poet's life—Yuri Tynyanov's theory about the 'nameless love' Pushkin had for Karamzin's wife.

I do not know how much of this is fact and how much fiction.

But I know that this theory holds great possibilities for the plot.

And I think the theory holds the key (Tynyanov does not write about this) to understanding that thoroughly incomprehensible, inexplicable and blind love Pushkin felt for Natalya Nikolayevna.

The key to the bewildering number of Pushkin's escapades.

Donjuanism (after all, did not Pushkin write *Don Juan?*) is often interpreted as unsuccessful attempts to find the one woman who is inaccessible.[11]

The line of women is varied.

Laura, with the flaming hair.

Donna Anna, beneath her severe veil.

But not even the thousand and three (*mille e tre* on Don Juan's list) can provide an exhaustive variety of shades of hair, timbres of voice, waistlines, or angles of the arms.

And one woman is sought for among all these.

Is this one like her?

But they are all different.

Yet nevertheless.

This one's hair. That one's walk. A third has dimples. A fourth, full lips. A fifth, wide-set eyes, at a slight angle. There, well-rounded legs. Here a curious waist. Voice. Way of holding a handkerchief. Favourite colours. Laughs easily. Or eyes which always fill with tears at the same harpsichord music. The same cascading ringlets. Or a similar flash of earrings, reflecting crystal chandeliers.

The chains of associations which enable one suddenly to substitute one being for another, purely on the strength of the similarity of a microscopic feature, or on the basis of a fleeting community to replace someone with somebody else—even sometimes to change two people around because of a barely noticeable trait— are complete mysteries.

And probably only this can explain his blind, incomprehensible and monstrously misplaced attraction to Natalya Nikolayevna.

It is doubtless true that Natalya Nikolayevna embodied to a very considerable degree those features of the older woman which had left an indelible impression on the unbridled, impassioned emotions of the lycéeist. He was in love with the wife of a much respected man, who read to him, in his wife's presence—and I think, even with her participation—an ironic lecture on the inappropriateness and absurdity of his fascination.

And later, many many years later, in his apartment in Tsarskoye Selo, Karamzin showed Count Bludov the cushion on the divan where, as a a pupil at the lycée, the now universally famous writer and poet had sat sobbing . . .[12]

Key periods in the romantic peripeteias of Pushkin the man and Pushkin the writer are slotted into this central pivot of his secret, lyrical drama, which was to last all his life, but which had been hidden behind his debauchery and turbulent Donjuanism and the final tragic story of his marriage.

The periods indissolubly appeared not only in bright colours, according to a strict spectrum; they even seemed painterly in their execution.

After the brief prologue around the divan at Tsarskoye Selo, which assembled around a bouquet the passionate young lycéeist, the cold, ironic man who was to be the official historian of the Russian state and Yekaterina Andreyevna Karamzina. with her unexpected and unfinished outburst of regret . . . (this lady apparently lived by the motto 'but I belong to another and will always be true to him').[13]

Alexander Sergeyevich reappeared in the south.

Among the tents of 'The Gypsies'.[14]

It was he who left their intimate canopy when Aleko returned unexpectedly with the bear in the pale dusty water-colour softness of the terrain of the southern steppes and plunged into the gaudy, Bryulovian brightness of oriental watercolours at the start of the nineteenth century, in teeming, polyglot Odessa ('a sandpit in summer and an inkwell in winter').[15]

The spurs of Tatyana's husband from the forthcoming *Onegin* were on Vorontsov's boots.

Emperor Nicholas the First

'The locusts flew, flew . . .'[16]

Pushkin was 'an Arab devil'.[17]

A murkiness spread over the potentially colourful water-colours of the south . . . The golden grape, the robes, striped turbans and yellow silks . . .

The grey and milky blue motif of the blizzard and the devils, which musically and visually anticipated the future blanket of snow of the duel and the pandemonium of high-society loathing, harmonised with the bells on the carriage which brought Pushkin at full tilt to his incarceration at Mikhailovskoye.

As the bright flame in the grate follows the darkness of a blizzard, so the period of artistic maturity was painted with thick strokes of rich colour: Boris succeeded Ruslan.

The spectrum is full, saturated with colour. The texture of the oily sheen.

The southern haze has lifted.

Maturity.

There is a similar richness in the people around.

The senior priest of the Svyatogorsk monastery—the future Varlaam.

Arina Rodyonovna.

His affecting, rustic love for her niece.[18]

Kern.

(I am not setting down the plot. This is not how the biography would develop. It is not rigidly consistent. It is just certain areas, how I would resolve them.)

A summons to Moscow.

Istomina from *Eugene Onegin*.

A fateful meeting with Natalya Nikolayevna.

Entrancement, leading to the poet's ensuing pale violet courtship.

A discordant note is struck (beyond the shot) by the click of the abacus in the Linen Factory[19] which was expecting to be able to balance its books, at the expense of the poet's inspiration if need be.

The discord peaks, drawing the violet and white into the silvery top of an iconostasis, orange-blossom, wedding veil and the ominous dropping of the ring . . .—and the line leading from the

Linen Factory, to the hasty note (the day before the marriage!) requesting money (nothing to pay for the carriage to ride to church in).

St Petersburg.

The deep blue and indigo which consumes the colourful sportiveness of the full range of colours.

By degrees.

With jealousy mounting with each turn of the plot and inseparable from the scorn of society and his worries about money.

As once—in my earliest sketches for colour projects—I had an idea for a film about the plague in which gradually the blackness spread and overran the joyfully coloured landscapes, the costumes of those dining, the luxuriance of the gardens and the radiant sky itself.

Jealousy is the plague, in this case.

And the frames are dark rectangles with one or two spots of colour torn from the darkness. The green baize and the yellow candles in the casino where, in the mirror, fingers held up behind the poet's head look like horns.

The blackness of the night surrounding Golytsina's orange apartment—she had turned night into day after being told that she would die in the middle of the night. Meeting his rival.

The line—Pushkin—d'Anthès—Nicholas.

The bronze horseman.

The circle of the moon in the raven-black night.

Nicholas's bronze face.

'You just wait!'[20]

The theme of Othello.

More gypsies. Not in the unconstrained south, but in a poor gypsy apartment by the Black Brook.

Pancakes in the morning.

The gypsies sing Pushkin his song from 'The Gypsies'.

'Old husband, grim husband . . .'[21]

As they sang songs to Ivan in his old age; epic tales and stories about him and Kazan which he captured.

Now he himself is the 'old husband' (despite being only thirty-seven), the 'grim husband'.

The Order of the Cuckolds.[22]

The duel theme develops, gathering momentum.

The sleigh ride, as narrated.

The colours fade.

The blanket of snow.

Silhouettes of trees standing like symbols of death.

Like a spot of blood on the blanket is the dead, crimson disc of the sun, against a dull winter sky above the rimed tree tops.

The flat blackness of the coffin, stolen from the burial service and driven off into the night.[23]

Watercolour has a soft register. Oil has a rich one. Again the soft, pale and lyrical register. Then high-society dazzle. The black-and-white woodcut with its spot of colour. A reprise of the high-society dazzle. A sharp black line against the whiteness of the background. Strips of light against the blackness at the ending . . .

A haywire, unsystematic retelling of a screenplay and the ideas a director had about colour, for a theme that was never to be realised.

We are said to be still technically incapable of making colour films.

My next film was also made in colour and in black-and-white—*Ivan the Terrible.*

After Thursday's Shower[1]

This small, ridiculous woman died today, Thursday evening.

She was seventy-two.

And for forty-eight of those seventy-two years she was my mother.

She lay in a room downstairs.

I was upstairs.

And it would have been hard to say which of us was the more dead.

She and I were never close.

Our family broke up when I was very young.

It was one of those breaks that take years to heal.

The sort of break that destroys natural bonds, natural instincts, the feeling of family closeness.

When we were alive, we got on badly.

I hardly ever went to see her.

Now that she was dead, I was drawn towards her room.

And in death we were both at peace and close to one other.

The barrier, which when we were alive kept our too similar natures apart, no longer stood between us.

She was eccentric.

I was eccentric.

She was ridiculous.

I was ridiculous.

Now we were both silent.

And we understood each other as if for the first time.

And nothing held us apart: we were as we had been once; before she was a mother, before I was a child.

I read somewhere that the gulf between mankind and the higher primates is narrower than the gulf separating the primates from common monkeys.

I was somehow remote from the living: that distance was greater than the one separating the living from the dead.

Hence, both were equally close . . . or distant from me.

And perhaps the dead were even closer than the living.

Little Sergei with his mother in Riga.

With his mother, 9 May 1932, the day of his return to the USSR after working abroad.

But there was no difference between them.

The living seemed ghostly.

Ghosts seemed to be alive.

And in life—three days earlier—Yulia Ivanovna had perhaps been less real than she was now in imagination and memory.

The late Khmelyov was somewhere with me, although when he was alive we barely acknowledged each other.

Vsevolod Emilevich, Nemirovich, Khazby or Kadochnikov, Stanislavsky and Yelizaveta Sergeyevna . . .[2]

The remoter, the less real, the less tangible they were, the nearer they seemed; and those whom I did see, appeared unreal.

I remember travelling in a narrow berth, from Moscow to Vladikavkaz.

I had just been separated from a little child, a Mexican.[3]

And the sobbing in my chest: schizophrenia, most likely.

For my heart cannot distinguish between an objective image and an image in my imagination.

So they revolve around me, the shades of the living and the dead, intermingling, possessing equal weight, all seemingly just as alive (or just as dead).

Yulia Ivanovna groaned continually.

Her pulse beat more slowly, then stopped.

The groans came muffled through the floor of my room on the first floor.

Our dog howled in the distance.

Zholtik.

He had bitten someone.

So in those days he was on a leash.

I went out into the garden.

Yulia Ivanovna was a great believer in planting bushes and trees, but she had no overall plan.

We argued a lot.

In her siting of shrubs, there was no consideration of how they would look together. We agreed on one thing.

We both liked bushes in thick clumps.

Especially at the back, near the fence.

Yulia Ivanovna planted this area with clumps of rudbeckias.

These have yellow spherical flowers in autumn, at the end of a very tall stem.

Why did my hand want to reach out and snap them off? . . .

I returned.

The porch was rotten and sagged.

Yulia Ivanovna dreamed of converting it into a verandah.

There was not enough money that year.

I sat down heavily on a straw-filled chair on the porch.

The chair had lost its sheen. It was discoloured.

It had always been left out in the rain.

I looked at the flowers in my hand.

There were seven, as it turned out.

Seven fatal yellow globes.

Seven.

I listened hard.

And there . . .

Quietly, quietly—almost silently, the door slowly opened.

That had never happened before.

The door slowly opened—unusual for a door opening of its own accord, more usual if someone is pushing it.

Behind it was the plain white surface of the second door.

Who came through that area of white and opened the outer door?

An aspen stood near the rotten porch.

It was once an unprepossessing bush; but it had grown into nothing short of a tree during the war.

Yulia Ivanovna had wanted it felled.

I had wanted it left.

Then, just as mysteriously as the door opening and taking just the length of time needed to go those three steps, between her and the aspen, a branch began to rustle, long and eloquently.

The branch was saying something—a rushed farewell, then silence.

Where did that breath of wind come from, on that still day?

Wotan spoke through such a rustle, in the branches of the ancient ash: words of approval and farewell to Sigmund, his son.

729

Yulia Ivanovna as a young lady

Photo presented to her son after the première of *The Battleship Potemkin,* inscribed: 'My pride. Mama. 1926'

And so Yulia Ivanovna took her leave of me, walking unseen through the doorway and rustling something distinctly and hurriedly, as if someone was already waiting for her at the gate, through which a small bird flew a minute or so later.

Was it really over?

I went through the doorway.

In the distance, indistinct moans.

I held the yellow flowers.

And in front of me were feathers, feathers, feathers.

Black ones.

Ostrich.

They lay everywhere.

On armchairs. On the divan. On the beds.

Little Sergei, playing, had scattered a collection of black ostrich feathers, torn out of a hat and boa from the 1890s . . .

I went into Yulia Ivanovna's room.

She was holding out a hand towards me.

Her speech was rapid, but it was already incoherent, without words.

All in the same rhythm, forced out in starts where once there might have been an intonation.

For her distinct words had already flown, rustling the branch above the porch.

Her eyes were probably sightless.

Although only half covered by her eyelids.

She could not see, but she sensed my immediate presence.

And her muttering was just her worrying about me.

I put her hand on her cold forehead.

She grew quiet . . .

I took it away.

And suddenly, then, for the first time, I felt something in my heart, my throat . . .

I went down to Yulia Ivanovna's room a second time . . .

I looked round to see that the room was not entirely empty.

The first time it looked as if everything had been taken out.

But now I could only see the couch; it took up the middle of the room.

She slept on this couch once, when I had measles.

Yulia Ivanovna Eisenstein as an old lady.

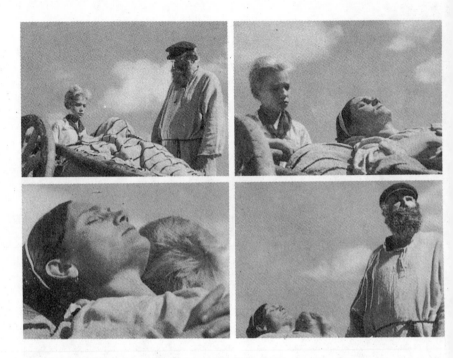

Stills of the episode 'the mother's death' from *Bezhin Meadow* (first version).

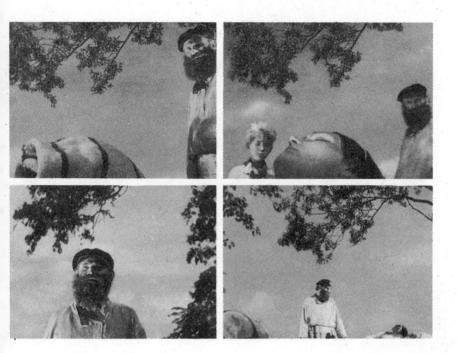

I pulled back the blanket.

The tip of her nose was slightly darker.

I looked at the coins on her eyes.

For some reason, I thought they were British pennies, with Britannia on one side and the characteristic profile of the young Queen Victoria on the other.

I used to play with old coins like that once.

But these were not pennies.

But five-kopek pieces.

On the right eye—darkened by oxidation—was the number five, a sickle and the year 1940 underneath.

I pulled the blanket down further.

She was cold, even through the dress.

A cushion had been placed between her chin and her chest.

It was embroidered.

Once I had copied a pattern for her to sew.

Richelieu stitching.

Now the cushion was to stop her jaw hanging open.

Below were her hands.

Yulia Ivanovna's hands.

I never saw them stop moving, all month.

Carrying a tray, at morning, afternoon and night.

Or darning.

Or moving deftly between the raspberry canes as she picked the fruit.

Or getting her accounts book muddled—Yulia Ivanovna got hopelessly lost with that.

Or measuring out my medicine drops.

They were once the hands of a lady.

With manicured nails.

Pale.

That month I saw them sunburnt, but strangely soft, not coarsened as they moved before me.

Only their outline had been broken.

There was some disfigurement (from gout?).

Going down to see her the first time, I kissed her forehead.

Now I kissed her hand . . .

A small, white, old lady lay before me.

In some ways very distantly reminiscent of Grandmother, as I remember her.

Yulia Ivanovna always dreamed about Grandmother, whenever some disaster or unpleasantness was in the offing.

Now Yulia Ivanovna was quiet, severe, still.

Eternally serious, with the dark spots of coins on her eyes.

The coins blurred and looked like the dark shadows of eye sockets above white lips clamped severely shut.

I had, to my horror, known all month that Yulia Ivanovna was dying . . .

Doing exercises in style for my forthcoming memoirs, I jotted down a page.

There it is, later on.

It contains a fateful slip of the pen.

'Of how to say simple things in a complicated manner.'*

Leonardo da Vinci would have put it thus:

People throw off the pelts which they put on, and bury them in the ground.

But the pelts become animals once more, and hide from people, when those people (after some years have elapsed) dig the ground up again.

Before the evacuation, Yelizaveta Sergeyevna had buried her new sealskin coat somewhere near the verandah of Olga Ivanovna Preobrazhenskaya's dacha.[4]

When Ye. S. died, Yulia Ivanovna wanted to dig it up again, but it was not to be found.

Olga Ivanovna Preobrazhenskaya's caretaker knew about this sealskin coat, buried near the verandah . . .

'The gentle art of saying simple things in complicated ways.'*

I suddenly came to, crossed the name out and inserted the right one.[5]

---

* In English in the original.

The late Yelizaveta Sergeyevna.

But I felt that I could not erase what had come out on to the paper of its own accord. Death was waiting for Yulia Ivanovna.

And when, exactly three days later, completely out of the blue, she told me that she had had a small fit, I knew deep down that it was only the first.

And there would be a fatal one . . .

Life's 'Formulae'[1]

Among the stories, myths and plays which I not only loved when young, but which went on to form a set of ideas, aspirations and 'ideals', I remember very distinctly three that undoubtedly had a profound effect on me.

The first was not so much a story or a legend, but a line of thought perhaps from Marie Corelli's *Grief of Satan*, or one of Victoria Cross's novels (she wrote *Six Chapters of a Man's Life*).[2]

A notion about philosophy: philosophy is like cocaine—it can deaden your joy, but at least it stops you feeling pain.

For me, this had fateful repercussions. The feeling of joy was rigorously killed off, but philosophy proved inadequate defence against the feeling of pain.

And heavens! Only I know the full depth of the feeling of pain, and the bitterness of suffering, through which, as through the rings of hell, my personal, all too personal inner world moves from year to year.

The second impression which struck me very early on (and very deeply, at that) was some legend or other, I think from a national Persian epic.

It concerned a certain strong man who would become a hero and who had felt, since childhood, a calling to accomplish some very great task.

Preparation for this future accomplishment meant conserving his strength until he had attained his full might.

He went to a bazaar, where some tanners, as I recall, pressed around him. 'Get down on your knees before us and lie in the filth of this bazaar, so that we can walk over you,' they jeered.

And the hero-to-be, saving his strength for the future, humbly lay at their feet in the filth.

This is said to have happened as many as three times.

Later the hero reached manhood, attained the full mastery of his unprecedented strength and performed all the feats of unheard of difficulty that lay before him.

I found this episode with the tanners utterly captivating: his unheard of self-control and sacrifice of everything, including his self-esteem, as he readied himself for the achievements to come, where he would accomplish what had already been primordially ordained and decreed.

This motif emerges clearly on two occasions in my work.

In the unrealised part of my screenplay for *Alexander Nevsky*, where, after the Germans had been routed on Lake Peipus, the Tatar horde advanced on Russia once more, to exact vengeance.

The victor, Nevsky, hastened to meet them.

He walked submissively between the purifying fires in front of the Khan's pavilion and humbled himself on one knee before the Khan. His meekness gained the time needed to build up strength so that later this enslaver of our land could be overthrown too, although not by Nevsky's hand this time, but by the sword of his descendant, Dmitri Donskoy.

The prince died on his way back from the hordes, poisoned, looking at the field—Kulikovo Field—lying before him. Pavlenko[3] and I had our holy warrior make a detour for this purpose, leaving the historic route which Alexander Nevsky actually took on his way back and so he did not reach his own home.

It was not my hand that drew the red pencil across the page after the scene where the German masses were put to flight.

'The screenplay ends here', I was told. 'A prince as good as that cannot die!'

But, if my hand humbled a prince and a saint in the name of a higher purpose, Tsar Ivan the Terrible did not escape the same fate either.

Immediately after reaching the height of his glory in the thundering of kettle-drums, against a background of racing clouds and the roar of cannon over the victors' heads, the victor of Kazan attained an even greater degree of glory in the next scene. Griefstricken, he abased himself, falling down before the gold brocade hems of the boyars' furs, tearfully beseeching the stony cohort not to hack Rus up after his, the first god-crowned autocrat of the Russian state's, imminent, feverish death . . .

In my personal, too personal history I have had on several occasions to stoop to these levels of self-abasement.

The last photo of Eisenstein.

And in my personal, most personal, hidden personal life, this was perhaps rather too frequently, too hastily, and almost too willingly done—and also to no avail.

But then, 'in the course of time', I too was able to chop heads off as they stuck out of their fur coats; Ivan and I rolled in the dust before the gold-stitched hems but accepted this humiliation only in the cause of our most passionate longings . . .

For my part of course this chopping was metaphorical.

And more frequently, as I wielded the sword above someone's head, I would bring it crashing down on my own instead.

The third impression was Bernard Shaw's *The Chocolate Soldier*. This was in my very tender, romantic, heroically-inclined years: by a merciless twist of irony, it would seem, I had cooled my youthful bent for pathos permanently.

And then I spent my whole life in heroic-pathetic drudgery, with screen 'canvases' in the heroic style!

Let a description of my visit to Bernard Shaw in London, 1929, follow here. This happened after he had sent me a cablegram which overtook me exactly half way across the Atlantic Ocean when I was sailing to America. He proposed that I film *The Chocolate Soldier*, 'on the condition that the entire text be altered not one jot.'[4]

Hence, retrospective interpretation of that tireless atmosphere of persuasive charm, which he showed me throughout my stay. The great honour of this proposal, coming as it did point-blank, and from someone who had never, for any sum, sold anyone the right to film one of his works.

On a par with Maxim Gorky, another major writer whose proposal to film one of his works I 'turned down'.[5] *

And here naturally I must describe my trip to Gorky to see Gorky, to hear the screenplay he wanted filmed by my own hands.

And even before his death the old man could not forgive or forget this 'outrage'*—and I saw him several times in the interval.

---

* In English in the original.

The True Paths of Discovery[1]

Torito

It is seldom an easy matter to untangle the knot of secondary associations, early impressions and the facts of a previous experience which are found in the plot that inspired me and which assist in the realisation of the composition.

To give an example: take one of the shots in our Mexican film. It is recognised, by people who have a thorough knowledge of Mexico, to be one of the more successful photographic recreations; to have captured the physiognomy of the country particularly profoundly. Probably because of the impression these compliments have had on me, I immediately attempted to analyse it, to see what made the substance of this photograph so typically Mexican—how it captured the country's style, spirit and physiognomy so well.

I still have a diary entry for 16 August 1931, with my notes on that theme which I had made almost on the day of filming.

(I must note in passing that the style of shot composition was one of the basic problems of form in our Mexican film. For despite the piquancy and typicality of things Mexican, it was extremely difficult to find ways of showing them so that they would convey the style and spirit of Mexico. But this comes elsewhere. The point has been made that we worked long and hard over problems of style.)

And so Martin Fernandez, playing Sebastian, stood before us in the straw hat and white sarape of the peons. 'Torito' is the traditional firework on Mexican national holidays. It is worn on the head, parodying the bullfight. It shoots rockets (the really powerful ones are fired from horns). In the background was the portico of the same hacienda where pulque—Mexican vodka—was distilled in huge bullhide vats. Everything was purely Mexican. But what was it that led to all the elements being together, in that combination, within the frame of a single photo? (It should further be noted that the scene itself is intermediary. The chief subject—with the *torito*, which the rebellious peons used to burn the hacienda down—went further. This was simply the first encounter with it.)

743

The still of the _torito_ from the film _Que Viva México!_

Venice, St Mark's Square

The key compositional combination for *torito* and the hacienda block at Tetlapayac turned out to be a reconstruction of a very old, plastic memory from childhood.

I remember when I was a young child that my room was hung with tinted photographs. Father brought them back from his travels abroad: Venice with the Doge's Palace and the Lion of St Mark.* Somehow, when I was young, they formed a familiar pattern. So much so that even twenty-five years later I had only to see a lancet window, a portico and a cardboard bull, with a vague semblance of wings on his back, to feel an insuperable longing to combine them all into a single composition. Characteristically, there was even a stone barrier in the foreground, reminiscent of an embankment. This is a clearly 'Venetian' motif: the buildings rising up sheer on the edge of the embankment. This inevitably made me want to place the *torito* at the top—it had to break the skyline. This new exigency was dictated by the Lion of St Mark, silhouetted against the sky.

The plastic positioning of the portico itself in precisely that compositional arrangement was based on another 'irritant'. More precisely, it was based on that same childhood memory which had been taken up by a new visual impression.

Indeed, why had those landscapes, typical of de Chirico,[2] affected me so strongly, when I saw them in Paris in the previous year?

I saw them as some sort of link between the real Mexico and the Venice I remembered from childhood. They (or landscapes like them) proved so memorable because of the Venetian motifs which I remembered because of the specifically Italian shade, which so closely resembled the spots of colour and the outlines of shadows on sunny days in Mexico. (Some frames in the film were based on this too.)

One more plastic notion from that series was woven into the complex. I can remember seeing most clearly on Boulevard Montparnasse, in a bookshop window, a recently published album of Max Ernst's Surrealist montages (*La Femme aux 100 têtes* par Max

---

* Sadly I no longer possess these photographs; they were destroyed in Riga during the occupation. But the attached photos of the same subjects give a very good impression of them. (E's note)

Ernst). It was open at a page showing a portico with skeletons, which was the backdrop to a tall lamp with butterflies. Again that compositional pattern: a portico and something with wings! (Incidentally, the composition of this illustration coincided almost completely with mine.) But here a new motif also had been included: death and skeletons. (And this gallery of skeletons is very similar to a gallery on the cover of one of the earlier Pinkertons which also made a powerful impression on me in my delicate childhood). And this motif of doom and death links this montage directly with my theme. The sensation recurred a year and a half later in the composition of a particular frame, for the fate of the peons who had revolted and their deaths were essential to the plot of the film.

According to the screenplay, the peon Sebastian took Maria, his bride (seen at the back of our screen) to the *hacendado* for his permission to marry her. A disagreement flared up over the ancient *ius primae noctis* which still obtained in Mexico before the 1910 revolution (!!!) and this led to the peons' revolt and their flight. Ambushed in a field of agave, they were caught and suffered a bloody retribution. A sense of doom hung over Sebastian and a group of his friends. And under the influence of this motif, from the entire rich variety of colours and styles of Mexican dress, I chose . . . white: the white sarape. This theme—the link between white and death and also mourning—dates from my earliest sensitivities and memories. I was once astonished to learn that the Chinese wear white, not black, for mourning. More significantly, I recalled that in the last act of the opera *Khovanshchina*, all the Old Believers who had been condemned to death and who burnt down their hut while still inside, wore white shirts.[3] And from somewhere came a fragment of religious verse (possibly from the same opera, or a romance): 'Clothe yourself in white raiment'. At least this fragment was never far off, during all of my immersion in things Hispano-Aztec-Toltec, when we were deciding which costumes the doomed peons should wear.

I distinctly remember also another 'key' moment, which seemed to influence the return to the white shirts of *Khovanshchina*, redesigned into long sarapes. I saw in Mexico a flier advertising subscription to Webster's *Encyclopedia Americana*. Every means of attracting subscribers was resorted to: from the astronomical number of words and illustrations contained within, to the etymological derivations of words. And there it turned out that the well-known word 'candidate' comes from Roman times and is closely connected with the concept of purity and innocence (what irony!). In the pre-election practice of those days, that quality was represented by the candidates' wearing togas of dazzling white. It symbolised their probity, honesty and purity. The white of Chinese mourning. The white shirts of the doomed Old Believers. The white togas showing the purity and honesty of the Roman candidates. Each idiosyncratic quality merged with the others, into the white sarape of the Mexican peon—far from 'formalistically', as we can see, but in a way that was connected with sense and subject to a profound degree.

(Incidentally, white sarapes in Mexico, although not unheard of, are nevertheless few and far between, chiefly because of their impracticality and tendency to stain. And the light grey sarape, as seen in the frame, was far from being my first 'impressionistic' adaptation, but it was something that was fundamentally 'emotionally charged', demanded by circumstances, but as I remember, hard to find and not a simple solution!)

There was another moment in the peons' tragic fate that was linked to Paris and my childhood. The rebellious peons fled from their pursuers into the agave fields that stretched far to the horizon; they were caught and taken to be executed. How to show the exchange of fire? Should they be filmed among the bushes of agave, defending themselves? A proper siege?

I see on the pages of my director's notes the terse note: 'Sebastian and his comrades are in a giant maguey plant . . . Fort Chabrol.'

That's a great help!

Not many people have seen maguey. And by now, probably, no one can remember what Fort Chabrol was. One thing I can say in advance, and that is that it has nothing to do with Mexico, maguey, peons or agave. Strictly speaking, I did not know Fort Chabrol proper; I only found it in phrases like 'the Fort Chabrol of such-and-such a street' (like the Lady Macbeth of such-and-such a district).[4] The matter led to a small page of a pre-Revolutionary edition of *Ogonyok* [The Torch], or *Sinii zhurnal* [The Blue Paper], with touching descriptions of a besieged house on a 'certain' street which bandits had occupied. For three whole days, armed with guns, they fought off all attempts the police made to seize them. 'Fort Chabrol' became firmly welded, in my imagination, with the valour (naturally valour!) of the three men surrounded by *force majeure* and heroically returning fire. My notions about Fort Chabrol were tinted with heroism . . .

At the right moment, a pencil mark introduced the complex of these touching sentiments into the screenplay, linked as they were to a heroic spirit I had long held in awe. It was not the 'Fort' that was of importance, but the fact that the entire complex of emotions associated with this exotic name should emerge here, in the scene which really proved to be one of the most powerful and heartrending.*

As regards the heroism of Fort Chabrol—the grandfather of that scene which I filmed under that name in the heroic episode of Mexico, an 'irony of fate' decreed that it should be absolutely, utterly and completely . . . the reverse.

I learned the details of the history of Fort Chabrol much later. It turned out that the real Fort Chabrol was one of the last rumblings of the storm precipitated by the . . . Dreyfus affair. It was a challenge by a clique of antisemites and monarchists, who were quartered in a villa on the Rue Chabrol and who were resolved to defend the president of the . . . Antisemitic League, a Jules Guérin. Guérin was meant to testify before the Supreme Court, as was Déroulède,[5] who appeared in court before Guérin, on 12 August 1899, charged with treason. The militant antisemites and monarchists withstood a drawn-out siege, and caused Paris much mirth at the expense of the police, who seemed unable to sort them out. More accurately, the police would have treated this affair much more seriously had it been a group of revolutionary workers. The entire history of this scandal and its dramatic conclusion have been dramatically described in Paul Morand's book, *1900*.[6]

---

* In this respect, it is characteristic that the associations followed this line rather than superficial, situational and perhaps more spontaneous and immediate lines—Bancroft, who shot at the police (a film I saw much later) or the ruined fort of Vaux near Verdun. (E's note)

The rebellious peons in the maguey undergrowth. Still from *Que Viva México!*

In any event, these compositional associations, diametrically opposed though they were in form and content, merged quite seamlessly with the Mexican models. I ask you to bear in mind that the hacienda building, Sebastian, the *torito*, the stone barrier and the time of day for filming all had to be assembled and composed. They were composed directly, according to some vague, unwritten code. One integral picture was arranged with an utterly brutal regularity, with all the details pinned on to it until the hoped-for effect was achieved; and only in that form could it liberate all those impressions which, as can be seen, had been shelved for years, their energy accumulating in my consciousness and creative stock.

The success of this episode, which despite all the antisemites, Old Believers, Surrealists and skeletons was purely Mexican in its resolution, can of course be explained by the fact that the associations were not deployed mechanically but as the principal point, the chief, fundamental idea—in Goethe's words, 'opportunely'.[7]

Of course, one cannot always have those essential supporting elements at one's fingertips: the essential 'scaffolding', made up of a stock of resonances, compositional schemes, or templates for working from. Sometimes there is nothing for it but to cast about, searching hurriedly for such elements which have the right resonances, or templates. This happens in those cases where there is an agonisingly acute desire and a thematic need to express an idea plastically with precision; that idea which at a given moment possesses you, but which is absent from the stock of essential material. Off you go to find it. Not in search of the 'unknown', but of that which definitely and concretely accords with the vague image which hovers before your consciousness and emotions.

The Tale of the Vixen and the Hare

An example.

In *Alexander Nevsky* there is the charming figure of Ignat, the linkmail maker.

751

It would have seemed natural for this representative of the artisan class to have been present right at the start of a depiction of 13th-century Rus in its most diverse aspects.

Perhaps, according to an *a priori* sociological scheme, Pavlenko and I had such a representative. I do not remember! But, if that was the case, then it was so abstracted that I do not even remember it and that would have been impossible if this had been a living image.

So he can be taken as someone who never existed: either factually, or 'in essence'—if he existed in rough drafts as 'a space allocated to the artisan class'.

In either case, how he came into being was exactly as follows.

Athena was supposed to have been born from the skull of Zeus. Ignat, the armourer, had a similar fate.

With just this difference: that here it was Alexander's skull.[8]

And not so much the skull as Nevsky's thoughts of a strategy.

I had an insuperable desire to make Alexander a genius.

In everyday thought, genius is always (and wrongly) linked to something like Newton's apple, or Faraday's mother's jumping teapot lid.[9]

Wrongly, because the ability to extrapolate a universal law from an individual case and subsequently to find a useful application for it, in derivative spheres of every kind of activity, is really connected to one of the features which comprise the complex psychological apparatus of a genius.

In an everyday context—in its obvious aspect—it is believed to be simpler: the ability to apply conclusions about something chance and insignificant to something unexpectedly different and weighty.

Something concerning a falling apple, to something concerning . . . the globe and the law of universal gravity.

If the hero does something like that in the film, then the viewer will very rapidly 'reflexively' come to find the associations which usually surround the question of genius.

And the stamp of genius is as clearly marked on this prince as a halo.

Ignat tells 'The Tale of the Vixen and the Hare'. Scene from *Alexander Nevsky*

Dmitri Orlov as Ignat. Scenes from *Alexander Nevsky*.

We had only one opportunity in the film for his genius to dazzle—that was in the strategy of the Battle on the Ice, the famous pincer movement in which he crushed the 'iron swine'*—the Teutonic Knights—the pincers entirely surrounding the enemy. This is a manoeuvre all generals throughout history have dreamed of; it brought unfading glory to the first person to employ it (apart from Alexander): Hannibal, at the battle of Cannae.[10] It brought hundred-fold more glory to the generals of the Red Army, who employed it even more brilliantly in the battle of Stalingrad.

Hence the film's business is clear: a 'Newton's apple' had to be found which would reveal to Alexander, as he deliberated on the imminent battle, a picture of the strategy for the Battle on the Ice.

Situations like this for showing inventive cunning are extraordinarily difficult. It is harder than anything to 'invent' an image, when the spontaneous need for it has been strictly formulated. Here is the formula for what we need: now go and find an image for it.

The procedure advances organically and especially conveniently: a figurative sense of the theme and the gradual crystallisation of the formula of an idea (thesis) move, as though merging together and being wrought into one, at the same time.

But when such a formula is already complete and articulated, it can be very difficult to steep it in a soup thick with images of spontaneous, primary, 'inspired' emotional feeling.

This is what causes many dramatists and writers, past and present, great misery. Having made problematic plays, plays à thèse, their speciality; or plays designed to demonstrate, through the fate of the characters and performance of the actors, a ready-coined thesis, or 'clause', the natural life of the play itself is suffocated; the thesis is not polished smooth to come across as a particularly acute coining of the theme's overall sense, nor the ideas which gave rise to the thing. Moreover, sometimes posing the question in this way can lead to clearly preconceived 'discoveries' which in essence are purely mechanical.

---

* This is a manoeuvre known as a cavalry wedge, which aims to force its way through the enemy lines and make the breach increasingly wide. The Russian word *svin'ya* also means 'pig' or 'swine'. (Trans.)

There was nothing to be done: that was how it happened. The formulation of the copy-book 'order' preceded the natural evolution of the scene itself, owing to the spontaneity of the internal need; it bypassed the formula and immediately demanded that a figurative form be found for it.

There was nothing for it!

I had to 'seek solutions', 'try them on', and conduct consciously the play of 'proposals and selection' that happens almost uncontrollably, when you take both horses of a pair of bays—conscious and figurative thought—in one, levelly tightened bridle and make them gallop abreast towards the one common goal—the wise imagery of the whole.

You begin with trial and error, measuring for size.

What did Alexander have to see on the eve of battle that could enable him to conceive a plan of action for the easiest destruction of the Germans?

Furthermore, the plan was well-known, *a priori*.

Not to allow a wedge to break through the army.

To make the wedge stick fast.

Then to fall upon it from all sides and the rear.

And strike, strike, strike.

A wedge. A wedge, sticking . . .

Pavlenko thought of an 'image' instantaneously: the night before the battle. There would be campfires, of course. Logs, of course. Chopped, of course.

An axe strikes a knot. It is wedged . . . and sticks fast.

The lively beginning grew cooler and cooler. It was so dull, so lacking in visual appeal. So wrong, too. You can imagine Russian camp fires in a forest, piled up with well chopped logs, like the ones we placed on the tiled stove in Pavlenko's flat, which was in an outbuilding of the house which, according to tradition, belonged to the Rostov family. It now houses the Writers' Union. In the very same wing where, according to tradition, Andrei Bolkonsky lay severely wounded . . .[11]

We were embarrassed; we immediately made our excuses. One of us had quite forgotten that he was expected somewhere else and the other really had to be going.

The next day, no one mentioned firewood.

Perhaps, Alexander's thoughts should not turn to a wedge stuck fast? Perhaps, he should think about ice being too thin to bear the weight of the knights? (Alexander's plan took account of this circumstance also. And the ice did indeed crack when the knights retreated, panic-stricken, sealed inside their heavy armour, just when they were piled up against the high bank of Lake Peipus.)

Well now, let's see.

An 'image' is instantly ready: at the edge of the ice walks a . . . cat.

Ice is thinnest at its edge.

The ice . . . shatters . . . beneath . . . a cat . . .

This proposal was so cretinous we almost choked.

Again, we had both completely forgotten. Pavlenko was already very late . . . I had to be making my way . . .

A few more days.

And more of the same. I do not know about Pavlenko, but I could not sleep at night.

Everywhere axes were sticking in logs, cats slipped on ice; then axes shattered the ice and cats were wedged into logs.

To hell with it!

All sorts of mad ideas come to mind when you cannot sleep and lie tossing from side to side.

I reached out for the bookcase.

I needed something to take my mind off things.

I picked a collection of 'cherished', 'adult' Russian folk tales.[12]

Almost the very first was 'The Vixen and the Hare'.

Well now!

How ever did I come to forget my favourite story?

One jump took me to the telephone.

I roared triumphantly down the receiver:

'Got it!

'Someone begins telling the story of 'The Vixen and the Hare' by the camp fire.'

How the Hare jumped between two birches.

And the Vixen chased after him and got stuck, wedged between those two birches . . .

After half an hour or so of great exertion, the fable took on the form that it has in the film.

['So the Hare jumped into a gully and the Vixen, she came after him. Then the Hare jumped between two birches. And the Vixen, she came after him—and stuck fast! Try as she might, she was wedged between the birches and could not move an inch. It was all up for her. Then the Hare, who was standing close by, he looked at her seriously and said, "Perhaps I'll bust your maidenhead, now . . ."

'The soldiers around the camp fire laugh. Then Ignat continues:
'"Oh, don't do that, I could never bear the shame. Have pity!"
'"You had no pity for me," said the Hare, and he bust it.']

Alexander hears the story being told at the campfire. (The Prince's mingling with his troops will look good. The proximity between the general and his soldiers.)
He interrupts to ask:
'Stuck between two birches?'
'And he bust it!' answered the story-teller, jubilantly, to much laughter.
Of course, Alexander had long borne in mind the image of an encirclement.
Of course, he did not learn this wise strategy from a fable.
But the distinct dynamic of the situation in the story provided Alexander with the trigger necessary for him to deploy his actual fighting force.
Buslai lets the swine's snout snuffle around.
The snout sinks in . . .
Gavril Olexich's troops secure the flanks . . .
And the irregulars strike at the rear!
Inspired now, quickly, precisely and covering every contingency, Alexander sketches in the outline for the next day's battle.

759

Eisenstein enacting the moment of Ignat's death (Mosfilm, 1938).

Alexander says to Gavril and Buslai:

[Drawing himself up, Alexander turns to the soldiers and says: 'We will fight them on the ice . . .

'There, by Raven Rock, will be the vanguard . . . You, Gavril, take the regiments on the left. I'll take my men on the right, and the Prince's Regiment. And you, Mikula, take the peasants and the ambush force. We know the Germans will strike in a wedge, there, by Raven Rock, and the vanguard will bear the brunt of that.'

Buslai asks:
'Who will take the van?'

Alexander answers:
'You will. You have run all night, now you can rest for a day. And bear the full brunt, giving no quarter, until Gavril and I press them in on the sides, from left and right. Got it? Let's go.'

Alexander leaves.]

In the satisfaction with what has just been achieved there is a passing recognition that a general rule might be deduced from what has just occurred.

All our attempts were unsuccessful so long as we tried to find a similar plastic prototype for a plastic image of the battle: logs, a cat, etc.

The key material was supplied by another dimension: narrative, story-telling.

I suspect a certain natural truth underlies all this. It is the dynamic outline which fits the fact or subject, rather than the details themselves, that should lead to the conception.

And, if the fact or subject is of a different order—for

761

example, not plastic, but auditory—then the sensation of this dynamic schema is more acute as the brain can transpose it into another area—more acute, and much more efficacious.

Perhaps we are dealing here with a law characteristic of inventiveness as a whole?

And my own 'representative' case, showing how Alexander 'invented', sheds light on the mechanism of inventiveness in general?

Surely everyone knows that, according to Gutenberg's testimony, the complex invention of book-printing by means of setting each letter separately, came about as a result of three completely and absolutely indirect impressions; the dynamic essence of each of these was abstracted and then 'mixed' with another area and another set of actions.

How was this remarkable art invented?

We know about this from the letters Gutenberg wrote from the banks of the Rhine, in the middle of the 15th century, to monks of the Cordelliers' Brotherhood[13] (*Histoire de l'invention de l'imprimerie par les monuments*, Paris, 1840).*

I shall quote extracts from them, pedantically preserving their idiosyncratic form, their repetitiveness and tone, at once artless and passionate. The anomalies in the way he set down his thoughts convey beautifully the inventor's inner turmoil; at every step, he is tortured by an impatient longing to succeed.

We can follow these stages in his quest and the gradual development of his discovery.

a) First—the burning desire, 'the *idée fixe*': to shorten the copyists' lengthy labours.

Gutenberg was burning with longing to achieve this.

For a month, my head has been hard at work; thought must emerge from my skull fully-armed like Athena . . .

I want to inscribe with one action of my hand, one movement of my fingers, in one go, with one expulsion of my thought

---

* E's reference.

everything a large sheet of paper can take in terms of lines, words and letters, that the most industrious of clerks could accomplish in one day (or in many).

(From the first letter.)

But what method should be used? Playing cards and small pictures of saints suggest the method to be tried first:

b) The first thing that led me to the method was playing cards and small pictures.

You have seen, as I have, playing cards and pictures of saints . . . These cards and pictures have been engraved on small wooden blocks and below are words, whole lines, which are also engraved . . . A layer of viscous ink is put on top of this engraving; a sheet of slightly dampened paper is put on this layer of ink, and that paper is rubbed and rubbed until it begins to shine. Then the sheet is lifted clear and you will see on the other side a picture which looks as if it has been drawn on, with words which look written on. The ink was transferred to the paper, leaving the engraved block, drawn by the paper's elasticity and held by its dampness . . .

Renewing the ink on the block and repeating the process, you can make hundreds and thousands of identical prints.

So. What you have done for a few words, a few lines, you must learn how to reproduce on to whole, large sheets printed sheets; large sheets, covered with letters on both sides, making whole books and the first book of all: the Bible.

How? There is no point in thinking about how to engrave 1,300 pages on these boards; no point in attempting to obtain these prints by rubbing the reverse side of the paper, since the second side can only be covered with words at the expense of the first side, which will have to be rubbed . . .

How to proceed? I do not know, but I know what I want to do: I want to copy the Bible; I want the impressions ready for the pilgrimage to Aix-La-Chapelle . . .

(From the first letter.)

And so, the urgent desire usefully to serve religion is also expressed in his letter. But there now emerges a second phenomenon which led him to the means of realising his wish: minting.

c) Minting is the second key phenomenon.

Each coin starts off as a stamp (die). The stamp is a small steel rod with one engraved end which takes the form of a letter, a few letters, all the symbols that are to appear in relief on the coin.

It is dampened and driven into another piece of steel, giving it depth (*un coin*). Small gold discs (blanks) are set into these, also wetted, and when they are hit hard they become coins.

(From the second letter.)

d) The third key phenomenon: a press and printing.

But the idea of minting gave rise to the idea of pressure, as the die is pressed into the steel. Two memories—of a wine-press and printing—complete the picture, combining an additional principle of repetition. Gutenberg wrote:

I attended a wine-making, and I saw how the grape juice runs. Working backwards from effect to cause, I was preoccupied with the press's strength, which nothing could resist.

One could create such pressure using tin. A simple substitution, and light dawned. The pressure which the tin exerted would have to leave a mark behind on the paper. The inventor exclaims triumphantly:

'So that's it! God has revealed a secret to me, as I had besought him . . . I ordered a great quantity of tin be brought to my room: that was the pen I was going to write with.

'But the handwriting, engraving and pattern: how would they look?'

Then he had the idea of the possibility of repeated use.

The big monastery seal which the monks affix for a signature was what prompted him.

'Does your seal not enable you to produce these signs and letters as often as you require?'

They had to produce similar ones for this new technique:*

We must melt, forge, make a countersunk die, like your brotherhood has on its seal. A mould, such as that used for the casting of your chalices . . .

First, a relief made of steel; a *poinçon*—a rod with the letter proud on one end, then an incision made by a blow of the rod into brass. This is the mother's breast of the letter— the matrix . . .

Finally the letters themselves:

A sharp tap sends the molten metal into the very bottom of the matrix . . . you open the mould, take out the image of the steel rod realised in tin—a small tin rod with a delicate relief on one end, and the residue on the other, which you will need to file away. They are as alike as sisters, these letters: they all bear the likeness of the *poinçon*, their father.

(Fifth letter)

Hence: independent letters, all alike:

. . . Movable letters. That they can be moved is of course the real treasure I have discovered while seeking the unknown via the unknown. From these letters and blanks between to establish the spacing, I can make words, etc.

(Letters eight and nine)

The full picture of the invention is just the same as the one we traced just before as I went through all the phases of our search

---

* At that time, seals were engraved, to give a raised image on wax, like those that we use for sealing wax. They were like negatives of what is today a simple resin stamp, where letters stand out in relief, on the actual stamp. (E's note)

for a composition.

First, the most acute desire to realise a definite idea, which has possessed the inventor. The needs of his like-minded associates—making the Bible more widely accessible—were concentrated in this idea. (There was also a more circumscribed and precise task: to contribute, morally and economically, to the success of the pilgrimage to Aix-La-Chapelle.)

The seeker's personal inspiration turned out to be the expressed command of a social group whose interests he shared.

The elements that could enable the invention to be realised practically, but represented only in vague outline, were sought feverishly.

When possessed by a theme, consciousness only registers those features of a chance phenomenon that can, one way or another, lead to the realisation.

To sum up, we have found three basic characteristics of this invention: the results of the future apparatus will resemble the reproduction of engravings. The future apparatus will print, by applying pressure to paper (the technique of printing for preparing a pictorial engraving was then unknown—see above); the apparatus will be able to reproduce the image of the actual letters by a method completely new to woodcut printing at that time (it will not be necessary to engrave each letter afresh, as is the case with engraving blocks: using a mould, each letter can be reproduced as often as needed).

These three crucial moments arose from his own experience and the principles of three analogous technical situations: playing-cards and images of saints gave him the idea of the woodcut printing technique for drawing the letters; the wine-press and the monastery seal gave him the idea of the using tin as the material for the letters; finally, money and minting inspired a similar apparatus for forming letters. And the principal features of these three partially analogous phenomena merged into a new, independent invention.

Then there is the famous case of Otto von Guericke, who made the Magdeburg hemispheres.[14] It was a rose, whose scent he drew in through his nostrils (that is, he created an artificial vacuum which nature rushed in to fill—bringing the scent with it!), that led him to the idea of a pump that could extract air.

Surely the same thing happens in art?

The painter, Repin, heard Rimsky-Korsakov's *Vengeance*[15] and his response was not an imitative piece of music, but a painting: Ivan the Terrible standing over his murdered son: the colour and actions of the characters embodied the same dynamic of emotions that he felt in the music.

And the encounter with the squadron in *The Battleship Potemkin,* is *sui generis* a new version of the traditional 'chase' sequence, taken from a quite different point of view, and interpreted according to the subject of the material, observing precisely the rules which generally govern the traditional build-up of suspense and dynamic! . . .

. . . But there is no time for meditating here.

We have more work to do on the screenplay.

The first thing that emerged from the above-mentioned resolution was an order to the wardrobe department.

In order to 'drive' the link between the plan of battle and the story into the consciousness, the peasant irregulars would wear giant hare-fur ear-muffs as they drove a wedge into the Germans' rear.

But a 'chain' reaction of inventiveness is hurtling off with particular impetuosity in another direction.

How the image of the story-teller was formed.

The fable had to be told well, dramatically.

Who was our best actor for narrative and story-telling?

Who?

Dmitri Nikolayevich Orlov, of course.[16]

No one who has listened to his inimitable rendering of Dogada can be in any doubt about that.

Orlov had all the wisdom, archness, seeming naivety and calculating cunning that you would expect to find in a Russian peasant of the middle orders; an artisan, or craftsman . . .

Stop!

We had in our list of *desiderata* for the film a vacancy for just such a person.

By that point he was faceless.

That is, not counting the face of one of the figures with a

767

funny basin-crop on the Korsun Doors of St Sophia in Novgorod.

The style of the story and Orlov's particular arch innuendo with his eyes screwed slyly up, breathed life into the outline of this representative of Novgorod craftsmen, a social category indicated in the cast list by the general heading *desiderata*.

Orlov was to be a linkmail maker.

More shrewd than the simple young soldiers.

No wonder he teaches them, albeit with crude fables.

And so that the fable should not stand out from the general flow of his talk, the style of his talk should be in character: from embellishment, to his patois; from folk sayings, to proverbs.

And so that the story would not sound simply crude, but crude only in the way it was told, it was important that Ignat (his name had already been found, but goodness knows where it came from!) should be a truly Russian man and patriot.

And so when arguments broke out on the town square about 'whether it was worth fighting for some kind of unified Rus'—which is how the conservative propertied classes of Novgorod viewed the national business, it fell to none other than Ignat to summon the people of Novgorod to fight the Germans.

And now Ignat comes forward with a call to arms.

But so that it should not sound mere rhetoric, he must be a patriot in deed as well as word.

And he leads the town's metal-beaters day and night, forging swords, lances and mail. But his 'activism' must not be confined to his professional work.

It must fill the breadth of his soul.

He makes presents ('take them all') of everything that has been made, forged and wrought.

And so this does not leave the aftertaste of a banal, theatrical gesture, we will earth him with a gentle irony, which begins to make its presence felt in his sayings. Let his tongue run away with itself in his generosity; let him be too extravagant.

Let the metal-worker end up without any mail, because he has given it all away.

Let him be left with nothing.

('The defenceless armourer' is such an innovation that it would not be proper for the traditional 'barefoot cobbler' to pose too.

We will not leave Ignat without boots, therefore; we have already learned something about the methods of 'transplanting' situations—not for nothing did that cat of ours dive under the ice!)

But perhaps that would be overstated.

We shall not leave him without mail. Better, more amusing, to give him a coat the wrong size.

'It is too short!' He will say, slightly perplexed, rather distressed and confused; he will be left with a short coat after giving all the others out.

But then, looking at the dramatic necessities from another angle, the viewer's hostility towards the Germans must be assured.

A positive hero had to die.

When Pskov was sacked, the only people who died were those who had done nothing to win the viewer's sympathy: they were merely his compatriots—Russians—people from Pskov.

The sack of Pskov did not strike the viewer with sufficient emphasis—there was no element of personal fate to involve the audience closely.

'The coat is too short! The coat is too short!' It has a good ring to it, it stands repetition.

A refrain.

All the rules governing refrains dictate that there must be a new light cast on the subsequent repetition—it must be interpreted differently.

On one hand, 'the coat is too short!'; on the other, one of the film's heroes must die.

Not Alexander.

Nor Buslai.

Gavril Olexich almost dies, as it is.

But both must be alive at the end.

'The coat is too short! . . .'

But the coat could offer insufficient protection in other places than at the bottom.

It might not cover the throat properly . . .

Comedy can turn into tragedy.

And if what is tragic echoes what was comic, the grief is deepened, and anger mounts at the cause of that grief . . .

And the funny 'the coat is too short!' is said first self-consciously and then with dramatic urgency as he pulls the collar up higher than the murderer's knife . . . whose knife?

Of course, the most treacherous of the enemy host: Tverdilo, the turncoat Governor of Novgorod.

'The coat is too short! . . .' is repeated as a refrain, the second time as the last breath of this likeable character—this witty, sly, selfless servant of Russia; this ardent patriot and martyr of the common cause.

So, out of the needs of the whole, the live features and necessary qualities of a new character develop organically within the work; just as the situation and unique conditions of an historical event stir up the people's hearts, calling them to action, throwing up unexpected heroes and revealing those traits of character and deeds which bathe the people in the rays of undying glory . . .

And the actor Orlov walked around the huge Mosfilm hangar on Potylikha, from episode to episode, following the dramatic fate of his chainmail maker, continually bending over to the tip of Ignat's boot.

There was a crumpled and greasy bundle at the end of the boot: this was the verbal tissue that fleshed out his role.

Orlov would stoop down to add a new saying to the list:

'Birds of a feather . . .'

One more for his stock.
He had read it somewhere.
And something had reminded him of it.
He had learned it from someone.
Or he would stoop down to pull out an apposite saying—he had found the part in his role where he could slip it in.

One would be most appropriate before his death: overconfident talk. His guard was down. He missed the ominous glint of a knife.

Orlov walked around Mosfilm, croaking and bending over, arguing with himself as Ignat about which lines fitted best where.

Constantly and conscientiously. .

What a shame I did not find this one saying earlier:

The mushrooms have eyes:
They put them in pies
And eat them alive
In Rya-a-zan . . .

I can almost hear you saying that.
But it is too late.
Hard to believe though it is, we made that picture eight years ago . . .

Layout

In real creative work, of course, this progress is far from gradual and intelligible.

The plastic perception of the parts, the calculation of the correlations, the possibilities for the spatial coordinates, the points where the juxtapositions of *mise-en-scène* are particularly expressive—all these hit you from all sides, in a highly dramatic manner.

It is like lava which hurls itself at you, surging up from all sides—part of the calculation for the finale, a convenient aspect of the climax, the dynamic flourish of a chance sequence, the angle of a certain grouping.*

What comes first, what follows, what comes earlier, what later—it is impossible to establish any of this as the first, general, chaotic sketch of the whole spills out on to the page.

When it settles on the paper with its platforms, bridges and staircases, the environment of the conceived scene is like an 'impress' formed by the whirlwind of activity which fashions for itself a pedestal and supporting sides; crossbeams holding the action

---

* Many of the scenes in *Ivan the Terrible* were drawn up before being written. If it is done normally,
1 theme
2 content
3 subject
4 layout
  then the commonest procedures are: 1-4-3-2; 3-2-4-1; and even 4-3-2-1.
(E's note)

together; surfaces, for the broad scope of the action; or slopes, along which it might develop upwards, or which it can gradually descend.

Sometimes even in this mad gallop, a cavalcade of the future 'acting workshop' as it is formed in your senses, its separate elements which have just settled can anticipate you and introduce changes to situations, calling for new, unexpected episodes: inset platforms intensify the drama of conflicts. Bare surfaces, created for the essential parts of a certain scene, beg to be used differently elsewhere. A detail that seems to have arisen quite by chance becomes the place for applying successive, unforeseen changes of direction in developing scenes, as they come together in counterpoint.

It is more or less impossible to establish such a 'flight' in one's notes.

And the cascade of notes on the following pages is an attempt to record (if not completely) a wholly improvised initial outline in the form in which I tried demonstrating it at one of my lectures.

I had tried to switch on the 'whirlwind' at once, 'at all points'; that is, to give free rein to the new 'urges' that each new element of the scene, the *mise-en-scène* and the situation includes and provokes: these influenced each other in turn; so the dynamic of the situation grew, illuminated at the same time by the growth of the static component of *mise-en-scène*—the picture of the scene in relief, as if it had taken its shape from the forms underpinning the whirlwind dashes of *mise-en-scene* as they race after each other sequentially.

First of all.

The chaotic dynamic formula of the key whirlwind.

The invariable 'primordial element'.

Someone speaks to his followers.

The opposition bursts in.

The speaker is quietened.

No more for the time being.

So:

A high point.

Its base.

Something for them to rush out from.

Towards the speaker. His audience. The supporters. The opposition.

The Plan of the Battle on the Ice on Lake Peipus, sketched by Eisenstein.

Diagram 1:

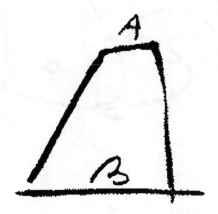

So, A.

And its base, B.

How best to burst in?

'Bursting in' means through an opening.

A round opening is an extreme case.

Round gates of Chinese palaces?

No! They would not be of use to the running crowd, because of the lower section.

Retain the idea of a round opening, but adjust the lower part to make it easy for the people to run through.

Diagram 2:

An arch!
A—He is talking
B—They are listening
C—They burst in
Next—The overthrow

Diagram 3:

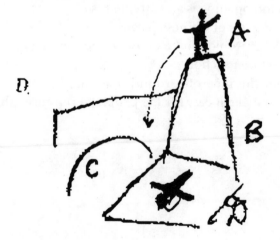

So. He is lying down.

Lying is materially important.

He must be seen.

D—The platform at the base needs to be raised.

Diagram 4:

In order for it to be seen distinctly, an arrow will have to be affixed.

As on posters:

What have you done for
the common cause?

Diagram 5:

Fix it scenically, with a 'look'.

She (who?) should come out after his fall.

Obtain the maximum effect from this by having the sight-
lines on a diagonal.

Diagram 6:

She has to come out.

She needs her own small arch. (If the first, gently sloping,
then large; or if vertical, small.)

Arch C is narrower than the bridge.

More precisely, she enters—that's the first thing. Then she
sees him.

There are two points on the bridge, a and c.

The tug towards him grows stronger.

They draw near.

A look.

Diagram 7:

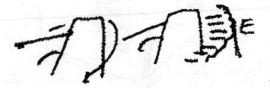

It only remains for her to descend.

Their look is direct.

The descent towards him must be circuitous.
The line in the air needs to be underpinned.
So a staircase down comes into being.

Diagram 8:

She has made the descent.
She lies over him.
They form a cross.
The platform, D, is inclined.
The outward appearance is beautiful. They need to be in differently coloured clothing, to emphasise that they are lying across each other.
Take an extreme case: *blanc et noir.*
He is in black.
She is in white.

Diagram 9:

Is he a monk? Savonarola. Campanella. Bruno.
Is she a convert? St Genevieve? Beatrice?
The platform is clearly ideal for an audience.
They listen, en masse.
Not chance bystanders, but adherents.
One mass, forged from many people.
The outward appearance is good: those nearer the back
(from the viewer's position) are higher.

Diagram 10:

Those who are to overthrow him race up staircase E
This is preceded by a brief struggle.
His adherents are scattered.

Diagram 11:

The *mise-en-scène* is destroyed.
The opponents burst in, forming a ring around the followers.
The opponents press in, taking over the platform.
The followers turned round on the spot. Their attention was focused on the speaker, at the back—high up. Now it is on the 'footlights'—on the opponents.

Diagram 12:

The opponents break in from the right, throwing the followers down off the platform.

Diagram 13:

The followers are scattered.
Necessity demands some details of construction in the
foreground, on the left and right. Steps down into the pit, or
a barrier running the length of the footlights.

Diagram 14:

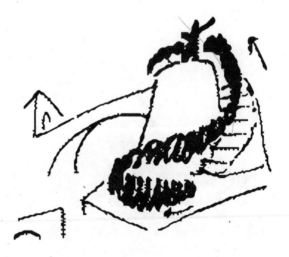

The left flank of those bursting in rushes towards the
speaker (the left route is greater—more clearly
distinguished). Those on the right may be occupied with
ending the fight.

Diagram 15:

The end of the tail—those on the right cross over to the left—
catches the defeated man. This is how the overthrow happens:
1: the platform is surrounded
2: they climb on to the platform and surround him
3: they lift him up
4: they throw him down
5: raised arms emphasise the fall
The Speaker vanishes in the pile of captured people.

Diagram 16:

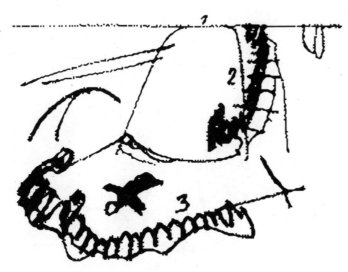

He is thrown up out of the crowd.

They run this way and that as he falls.
Some have remained at the top and on the staircase.
Those at the base throng around the platform, a ring of black.

Diagram 17:

She appeared in the archway. She is seen in sequence by
1) those at the top; 2) those on the staircase; 3) those at the
bottom.
Those in black—who burst in—apprehensively back away
from her.

Diagram 18:

Perhaps she is . . . blind?

Her unseeing eyes are even more terrible when she 'feels', up above, that he is somewhere down below in the deathly silence?

Perhaps it is his mother?

She appears at point b the moment after everyone gathered in a crowd in the right (struck by a superstitious horror).

Diagrams 19 and 7:

When she stops at point b—the wild rushing back of those in black, under the arch (19)

After their escape, her descent towards him (19 and 7)

Diagram 20:

Two possible ways for her to approach him: A and B.

B of course is better. Falling on her knees, and then falling across him—in front of the audience. This is visible. This bypasses the 'exchange of looks' (or, if she is blind, the sensation of his presence. Perhaps, she bent over at an angle, perhaps she is on her knees, feeling, probing . . .)

Diagram 21:

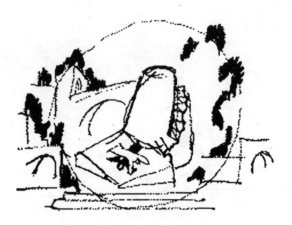

Here she has fallen on to her knees.
Stretching out.
And the black ring of the enemy looks like a funeral ring (wreath) around her.

Diagram 22:

Obviously, the black figures on the right will need to be

surrounded by details of a city: porticoes, loggias, flat roofs, windows and so on.

Diagram 23:

But now she rises up.
And her mute call is answered: from every corner, her followers begin to return, gathering in strength.

Diagram 24:

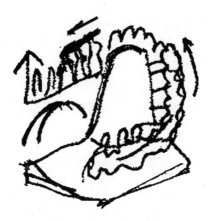

And now their arms are raised in anger.
And the black ring of their enemy hides, cowardly.
And the funeral procession bears off the body of the dead man.
The Speaker.

Diagram 25

And only she, she alone is left, sobbing at the base.
Deep in shadow . . .
Or she stands at the top end of the platform of the tower,
her arms raised in anger; the scarlet rays of sunset bloody
her white clothing.

Cast dark silhouettes of sails against the backdrop, or the
funeral crosses of mournful pennants, and you will be ready to write
a play around the central scene we have just prepared . . .

The Author and His Theme[1]

Twenty Years Later (1925-45: from *Potemkin* to *Ivan*)

Twenty years have passed . . .

Two decades.

That is twice the time allowed for by the law of prescription: after that period, a guilty man is freed from any obligations before the law and anyone seeking justice no longer has a valid claim.

I think this entitles me to talk about *Potemkin* and the author in the third person, as I would of any extraneous object, of an object and person with an objective existence outside myself. It is only thanks to happy (?) chance that I know of them, more or less and in greater detail, than do many other researchers.

I will therefore speak of the author and film impartially, not fighting shy of the affection I feel for them both. And I shall take advantage of my access to a significant amount of material unknown to anyone else—after all, no one else had any access to it.

And as I have already resolved to write of the author of *The Battleship Potemkin* as I would of someone I did not know, I will try to do so according to the criterion which none other than . . . Belinsky insisted upon:

> Contemporary criticism should reveal and lay bare the poet's soul in his works. It should follow his dominant theme, the thought governing his whole life, his whole existence. It should observe and elucidate his inner contemplation and his spirit . . .
>
> (*The Poetry of Baratynsky,* 1842)*

Of all the questions which lend themselves too readily to disorganised screeds of writing, a very popular one is:

the author and his theme.

Whether authors have such a theme running 'through' all their works, or not; whether it always exists; what relationship does

---

* E's reference.

an evolving series of works bear towards it; etc, etc. All of this is certainly not very well known, and so it is an unbelievably rich vein for endless inferences and guesses.

But there is one thin element of truth, however.

Some researchers find this confirmed even in the simple comparison of titles.

Thus for example Krzhizhanovsky, author of *The Poetics of Titles* (now long out of print), adduced a list of examples of this from Russian and foreign literature.[2]

Jack London's basic theme is family and stock; the overwhelming majority of his titles are precisely to do with this.

With regard to Goncharov, the author goes even further, holding that Goncharov's theme is even linked to a particular auditory symbol—'Ob'.[3]

This sound symbol recurs in a series of the author's key works (*Ob-ryv* [The Precipice]; *Ob-lomov; Ob-yknovennaya istoriya* [A Common Story], and one work which should, in its inner workings, have broken the run of this series (and which was not realised) would have had an exceptional title too: *Ne-ob-yknovennaya istoriya* [An Uncommon Story].

Similar examples are titles which adhere closely to a given formula. This is the case with one of the best and most prolific writers of detective fiction, from the golden age of the genre in America: S.S. Van Dine (in the 1930s).[4]

All the titles are variations on one theme: *The Canary Murder Case, The Dragon Murder Case; The Kennel Murder Case* and so on.

But there is more to it than that: in each title, the one word which defines the distinguishing incident has no more and no fewer than . . . six letters. Canary, dragon, kennel, garden, scarab, casino, Benson (a surname), Greene (ditto), Bishop (a complex pun which throws red herrings the detective's way, as it can be read as 'Primate', a surname and finally as the chess piece) and so on.

In one article, the author of these novels (a middling art-critic and a failure at serious literature, but who went on to make a fortune from detective fiction) commented on this circumstance.

He explained it as superstition: the first such title brought him good luck and he clung fervently to the formula of his first literary success!

Eisenstein editing *October,* 1928

Of course, this discourse on titles only covers the superficial aspect of the question, the heart of which probably lies very deep.

I am not about to solve this question. And I want to limit myself to just one example of a theme running 'through' my work, as I am already beginning to find it fascinating and tempting to analyse the case of an author who was responsible for such works as *The Battleship Potemkin* and *Ivan the Terrible*, whose themes are seemingly incompatible.

What could be more startlingly different than the themes and treatment of those two works, separated by an interval of twenty years?

The first had a collective and a mass of people.

The second, an autocratic individual.

In the first, there was something resembling a chorus, a monolithic and united collective.

The second was about a sharply defined character.

The first showed a desperate struggle with tsarism.

The second showed tsarist rule being established for the first time.

If here, at these extremes, the themes appear divergent, polarised, then what lies between seems, at first glance, unimaginably chaotic: themes thrown together haphazardly.

It would seem funny to think that this author could have a unified theme, one that ran 'through' his works; it would be naive to talk of it in that way.

Indeed!

If we consider my planned work as well as the work I achieved, there are: a short story about one, unique strike (*The Strike*); a wreath of exotic novellas situated in a Mexican landscape (*Que Viva México!*); there is the epic exposition of the October Revolution, 1917 (*October*) and—an odd juxtaposition—*An American Tragedy* (based on Theodore Dreiser's novel); the history of a black ruler of Haiti—Henri Christophe, the liberator-turned-despot of his island; Alexander Nevsky's heroic struggle against the Teutonic interventionists who invaded in the 13th century—'the German dogs'; the introduction of a collective economy into a backward rural setting (*The Old and The New*); the history of Captain Sutter, on whose Californian estates gold was first discovered in 1848; the history of a mutiny on a battleship; a screenplay about the building of the Fergana Canal (1939), an idiosyncratic historical triptych (Part One included episodes from Tamerlane's campaigns, printed in *Iskusstvo kino* [The Art of Cinema], in 1939); there is in my files a detailed treatment of a screenplay about Pushkin in colour, an intimately personal view of the poet's life. It took as its theme Tynyanov's brilliant article mentioned for the first time: 'Bezymennaya lyubov'' [A Nameless Love] (*Literaturnyi kritik* [The Literary Critic], no. 5, 1939) and then significantly less interestingly developed in the third part of *Pushkin* . . . And finally a film about a historical colossus—Ivan the Terrible and the establishment of autocracy in 16th-century Muscovy!

The most casual observer could tell at a glance that this resultant mass is composed of irreconcilable and incompatible elements.

Only the most driving obsession could force you to look for a unity of theme in this particoloured mixture; to look for the one theme which informs this whole disparate variety.

To palpate the author's one pervasive thought which 'dominated his entire life' (well, perhaps not all, but a twenty-five-year-long section of it at any rate: 1920-45).

Let us remember for the time being this tendency—to look for that one thing in this many-coloured variety. We shall find those things that concern a driving obsessiveness repaid with interest later on.

We shall now avail ourselves of a little patience and look at what each of these works was examining, in greater detail.

As we do so, we shall distinctly remember that this has nothing to do with the different costumes and robes, historical situations or the stance of this or that film, nor with chance ethnographic variations. In each and every case, it has to do with those elements within the theme which emotionally drew the author to deal with this or that subject, the majority of which were his free choice. There was always a 'personal turn' within the theme anyway and, in every case, the actual material of the film was written independently.

This is irrespective even of whether the film was commissioned by the State—for in that case, the episode on the

'Potemkin' is an episode from *1905*—or whether the film was an adaptation from a book, in which case the author would have to have been very keen on it, either for the way the events unfolded (Blaise Cendrars' *Sutter's Gold*), or for the psychological actuality of a thing (indicated by Tynyanov in *Pushkin*); or whether the choice of theme was entirely free (*Que Viva México!*).

Unity

If I were an impartial researcher, I would say of myself: this author appears to be constantly fixated with one idea, one theme, one subject.

Everything he has thought up and done, not only within the different films but through all his plans and films, is in each and every case one and the same thing.

Almost invariably, the author uses different periods (13th, 16th or 20th centuries), different countries and peoples (Russia, Mexico, Uzbekistan, America), different social movements and processes within the shift towards different social forms, as different masks covering one and the same face.

This face is the realisation of the ultimate goal - the attainment of unity.

With Russian revolutionary and socialist material, this is the problem of national and patriotic unity (*Alexander Nevsky*) or state unity (*Ivan the Terrible*), or collective or mass unity (*The Battleship Potemkin*) or socio-economic unity (*The Old and The New*), or Communist unity (*Fergana Canal*).

Abroad, this is either the same theme, in a different guise suiting the national aspects, or the seamy side (which is always tragically coloured) of the same theme, which sets off the positive side of the whole opus. This happened in *Nevsky* too: the bright theme of patriotism is underscored by the darker episodes of the Germans' reprisals at Pskov, which represented Russian unity.

The tragedies of individualism, planned during our tour of the West, were: *An American Tragedy*, *Sutter's Gold* (the paradise of primitive patriarchal California being destroyed by the curse of gold—which had completely corrupted the moral and ethical system of Captain Sutter—who opposed the gold), *Black Majesty* (hero of the Haitian revolutionary wars of independence, fought by the Haitian slaves of French colonists, and who was a comrade-in-arms of Toussaint L'Ouverture and who became the emperor of the island: Henri Christophe, who perished after an individualistic split from his own people), *Fergana Canal* (another 'hymn' to collectivist unification through socialist labour) the only means of bridling the forces of nature—water and sand—which were unloosed by the human discord of Tamerlane's wars in Central Asia. When his state collapsed, the desert came into its own. The peoples of Asia languished under the tyranny of nature as well as under the tyranny of tsarist Russia, and this first tyranny was overthrown too.

Finally, *Que Viva México!* This was the history of cultural changes, but not presented vertically—in years and centuries—but horizontally: as utterly diverse stages of culture, coexisting in the same geographical area, next to each other. This is what makes Mexico such an amazing place. Some provinces (Tehuantepec), built on a matriarchal system, lie next to provinces which virtually achieved Communism by revolution in the second decade of this century (Yucatán, Zapata's programme, etc). The central episode of Mexico concerned the idea of national unity—historically, the 'United Entry' into the capital—Mexico. This was the combined forces of Villa, who came from the north, and Emiliano Zapata, who was from the south. The central figure in the plot was a Mexican woman—a *soldadera*—who moved, with the same concern for her man, from faction to faction of the Mexican soldiery that were fighting each other and riven with the contradictions of civil war. It was as if she physically embodied the image of the one, nationally united, Mexico, working against the international intrigues which were attempting to carve the nation up and to play the different sections off against each other.

At this point, you will retort all the more fiercely that this only goes to show that all the observations made relate only to me, the author, who is now absolutely *toqué*,* fixated on a single, albeit respectable, idea—and that one only.

And I must answer all the more truculently that this is not at all the case; and again, 'in the case we have examined', we have only an example of a particularly, perhaps, emphasised feature, which is absolutely general.

And again, perhaps, only more glaringly obvious . . .

The process of assimilating material, i.e. making it 'one's own', happens at the moment when, coming into contact with reality, it begins to set itself out according to a grid of outlines and sketches of the same special structure as that in which one's consciousness was formed.

It makes no difference whether this encounter is with a new land and milieu; with a picture of a bygone age; or happens face to face with one's own epoch, the present.

I became acquainted with all the aspects of such encounters: with an unknown land which suddenly appeared before me; with a past age which suddenly unfolded before me; or face to face with my own times.

I also encountered different possibilities within these encounters. With imaginary coincidences of my matrix with the outline of the phenomenon I met, and with the morbid streak in my works; with still unresolved meetings and the great feeling which accompanies an absolute coincidence. I speak of this from personal experience.

There is in each of us something like those complex knots that Leonardo designed for the Milan Academy and that he drew on the ceilings.

We encounter a phenomenon.

And the plan of this knot seems to be laid over this phenomenon.

The features of one coincide, or otherwise.

They coincide partially.

Here and there.

They do not coincide.

They clash with one another, striving for coincidence.

---

* French: 'touched'

Sometimes breaking the structure and the outlines of reality, in order to satisfy the contour of individual desire.

Sometimes violating individualities in order to 'synchronise' with the demands of what they have clashed with.

I cannot actually remember any examples of the latter from my own personal practice; but then I could give plenty of examples illustrating the former . . .

Eisenstein, October 1930

P. S.¹

P.S. P.S. P.S.

Of course,—P.S.!

On 2 February this year, a heart muscle ruptured. There was a haemorrhage. (An infarction.) By some incomprehensible, absurd and pointless miracle, I survived.

All the facts of science dictated that I should die.

For some reason, I survived.

I therefore consider that everything which happens from now on is a postscript to my own life . . .

P.S. . . .

And indeed, who, at the age of forty-eight, has read this about himself:

'. . . *un des plus fameux metteurs-en-scène de son temps . . .*'* (The monthly magazine of the Institut des hautes études cinématographiques, Paris 1946, in the section *Critique des critiques,* on *Ivan the Terrible.*)

Or (from *La Revue du cinéma,* 1 October 1946):

. . . La présentation d'un nouveau film d'Eisenstein suscite le même étonnement que ferait naître la création d'une nouvelle pièce de Corneille. On s'est tant appliqué à donner au cinéma une histoire qu'a force de traiter les metteurs-en-scène de classiques qu'il semble qu'ils soient d'un autre age . . . on pardonnerait volontiers à Eisenstein d'être encore en vie, s'il était content de refaire Potemkine *ou* La Ligne générale. *Mais* Ivan le Terrible *vient de bouleverser*

---

*   French: 'One of the most famous directors of his time'

*toutes les idées saines et simples que la critique avait facilement dégagées de l'étude des grands auteurs du muët.**

I never imagined that this sort of thing would be written about me—certainly not before I had reached my seventies—and I thought I simply would not live that long!

And here, at forty-eight—

P.S.

P.S.

P.S.

---

* French: 'The showing of a new film by Eisenstein provokes the same astonishment that would meet a new play by Corneille. So much effort was used to invest cinema with a history, that it seems as if directors, proclaimed as classics, come from a different age.

One could readily forgive Eisenstein for still being alive, if he were content with remaking *Potemkin* or *The General Line.* But *Ivan the Terrible* has just overturned all the healthy, simple truths that criticism had easily drawn from studying the experience of the great *auteurs* of silent film.

Notes

Eisenstein's own notes, and indications of those passages where English is the language of the original, are placed at the end of the relevant page.

Throughout the notes Eisenstein is referred to as E and frequently cited works are abbreviated as follows:

ESW 1   S. M. Eisenstein, *Selected Works*: vol. 1: *Writings, 1922-34* (ed. & trans. R. Taylor), (London & Bloomington, Indiana, 1988)

ESW 2   S. M. Eisenstein, *Selected Works:* vol. 2: *Towards a Theory of Montage* (ed. & trans. M. Glenny; co-ed. R. Taylor) (London, 1991)

The History of Eisenstein's Memoirs

1. Stanislavsky's *My Life in Art* was published in London in 1925.
2. Quotation from a manuscript in Eisenstein's archive.
3. See *ESW 1*, pp. 33-8.
4. See below, p. 183
5. H. Marshall (ed.), *Nonindifferent Nature* (Cambridge, 1987).
6. S. M. Eizenshtein [Eisenstein], *Izbrannye proizvedeniya v shesti·tomakh* (Moscow, 1964-71).
7. They have not been included in the present edition. They have however been included in the German translation: N. Kleiman and W. Korschunowa [Korshunova] (eds), *Yo. Ich selbst. Memoiren* (Berlin, GDR, and Vienna, 1984), vol. 2, pp. 974-1106.The titles of the pieces translate as: *The Greatest Uprightness in Artistic Creativity, Visits to Millionaires, 25 and 15, Nemchinov-Post Railway Station, V. V., An Evening with Craig, The Birth of a Master, We Have Met, Judith, P-R-K-F-V, and The Treacherous Telephone Number.*

About Myself

1. Written in Moscow on 10 September 1944 as an introduction to the autobiographical notes.
2. Italian: literally, 'I lived, I wrote, I love . . .' E has got the tense of the last word wrong. Stendhal was the pseudonym of Marie Henri Beyle (1783-1842), French novelist who accompanied Napoleon's armies during the Russian campaign in 1812 and later spent several years in Italy. His best-known works are *The Red and the Black* [Le

Rouge et le noir] and *The Charterhouse of Parma* [La Chartreuse de Parme].

Foreword

1. Written in May 1946.
2. Paul Gavarni (1804-66) was a French graphic and water-colour artist. Honoré Daumier (1808-79) was a painter, graphic artist and caricaturist who specialised in caricatures of the contemporary middle classes and their pretensions.
3. Jules (1830-70) and Edmond (1822-96) Goncourt were French writers.
4. Louis Ferdinand Celine (1894-1961), French writer and poet; Jean-Paul Sartre (1905-80), French writer, philosopher and polemicist, leading light of Existentialism.
5. E suffered his first heart attack on 2 February 1946, while attending the official celebrations at Dom kino [Cinema House] in Moscow for the award of the Stalin Prize to *Ivan the Terrible* Part One .
6. Maurice Maeterlinck (1862-1949), Belgian playwright and poet. Arthur Schopenhauer (1788-1860), German philosopher.
7. *The Clansman* was written by the American T. Dixon in 1905. D. W. Griffith filmed *The Birth of a Nation* in 1915.
8. E first visited Paris with his parents in 1906 and saw his first film, Georges Méliès' *Les Quatre cent farces du diable* [The Devil's Four Hundred Tricks] there two years later.
9. Vassa Zheleznova was the main character in the play of the same name by Maxim Gorky, first written in 1910 and revised in 1935. E's maternal grandmother, Iraida Konetskaya, had inherited a barge company carrying freight on the Marinsky canal system, which linked the Baltic Sea and the River Neva to the River Volga.
10. The silver shrine of Alexander Nevsky, who had been canonised by the Russian Orthodox Church, was moved in 1724 on the orders of Peter the Great from the old religious centre of Vladimir to the new capital St Petersburg, where it is now to be found in the Hermitage Museum.
11. Edward Gordon Craig (1872-1966), English stage director and theorist.
12. Stefan Zweig (1881-1942), Austrian author, met E in Moscow in 1928.
13. Theodore Dreiser (1871-1945), American writer, who met E first in Moscow in 1927 and then in the USA in 1931, when E was planning

to film his novel *An American Tragedy*.

14. Chistye Prudy is the street in central north-east Moscow where E lived from 1920 to 1934.

15. Josef von Sternberg (1894-1969), Vienna-born film director best known for the six films he made that starred Marlene Dietrich, including *The Scarlet Empress* [USA, 1934], in which she played Catherine the Great. He also completed the project for a film version of Dreiser's *An American Tragedy*: see below, n. *Otto H. and the Artichokes*, n. 7.

    Erich von Stroheim (1885-1957), also Vienna-born, directed in Hollywood *Foolish Wives* [1922], *Greed* [1923-5], *The Merry Widow* [1925] and *Queen Kelly* [1928, unfinished] but never completed a sound film. He also acted: for example in Renoir's *La Grande illusion* [France, 1937].

    Ernst Lubitsch (1892-1947), German-born Hollywood director whose films were characterised by a blend of subtle humour and visual wit that became known as 'the Lubitsch touch'.

    King Vidor (1894-1982), American film director, whose major silent films included *The Big Parade* [1925] and *The Crowd* [1928].

16. Sergei D. Merkurov (1881-1952), one of the leading Soviet sculptors of the Stalin period, director of the Pushkin Museum 1945-50.

17. The novel *The Song of Bernadette* [1942] by the Austrian writer Franz Werfel (1890-1945) was filmed by Henry King in 1944.

18. Yoshiwara was the Tokyo equivalent of London's Soho. E describes the similar quarter of Monterrey in 'Friends in Need': see p.224.

19. Vladimir Mayakovsky (1893-1930), Futurist and 'poet of the Revolution', took his own life.

The Boy from Riga (An Obedient Child)

1. Written 5-7 May 1946 in the Kremlin hospital.

2. Douglas Fairbanks Sr (1883-1939), American stage and screen actor, and Mary Pickford (1893-1979), actress known as 'America's sweetheart', saw *The Battleship Potemkin* in Berlin in 1926 and came to Moscow, not just to 'shake the hand of the boy from Riga', but also, since they were co-owners with Charles Chaplin of United Artists, to invite him to make a film in Hollywood. In 1928 the invitation was renewed by the President of United Artists Joseph Schenk but, by the time E did reach the USA in 1930, he was under contract to Paramount. see *Charlie Chaplin*, n. 4.

3. *The Film Sense*, edited and translated by Jay Leyda, was published by Harcourt & Brace, New York, and Dennis Dobson, London in 1942. It included the theoretical essays 'Montage 1938' and 'Vertical Montage', which are also included in *ESW2*, pp. 296-401.
4. Alfred de Musset (1810-57), French writer, poet and playwright.
5. Yuri Tynyanov (1894-1943) wrote this article in 1939 suggesting that the real nameless love of Pushkin's life had been Yekaterina Karamzina (1780-1851), the wife of the famous Russian historian Nikolai Karamzin (1766-1826). E took Tynyanov's hypothesis as the basis for his project *A Poet's Love*, see pp. 712-24.
6. A reference to the 'list' of lovers that Pushkin apparently kept, and to the many women in Chaplin's life.
7. In Pushkin's poetic novel *Eugene Onegin* there is no diary as such but, among the papers relating to Chapter Seven there are notes for 'Onegin's Diary', which would have reflected his inner thoughts. Here E is therefore postulating an imaginary diary reflecting the character's egotistical self-absorption.

Why I Became A Director

1. Probably written in 1944 as a draft for a collection entitled *Kak ya stal rezhisserom* [How I Became a Director] (Moscow, 1945), although the text eventually printed there was quite different.
2. E's longer writings on montage are gathered in English into *ESW2*.
3. Izhora is a river near St Petersburg which has given its name to several settlements along the bank. This was one area where E did his military service during the Civil War that followed the 1917 Revolution.
4. *Masquerade* by the 19th century Russian poet and dramatist Mikhail Lermontov was directed by Meyerhold at the Alexandrinsky Theatre in Petrograd in 1917. He directed Molière's *Don Juan* in the same theatre in 1910 and Calderón's *The Constant Prince* in 1915.
5. Jacques Callot (1592/3-1635), French etcher whose masterpiece, completed in 1633, was entitled *'Les Grands Misères de la guerre'* [The Great Miseries of War].
6. Andrei Belyi, *Masterstvo Gogolya* [Gogol's Mastery] (Moscow, 1934). See also: *Gogol's Mastery*, n. 2.
7. Lindhorst was an acquaintance of E. T. A. Hoffmann and the butt of many jokes and fantastic stories among his circle of friends. Hoffmann also gave the name to the hero of his play *Der goldene*

Topf [The Golden Pot] and E's reference here is to that work.

8. E wrote the script for a satirical comedy *MMM*. At one point, according to this script, E the director was to play chess against E the scriptwriter, i.e. against himself. The script was published in *Iz istorii kino 10* [From the History of Cinema 10] (Moscow, 1978), pp. 98-156.

9. Immanuel Lasker, German, was world chess champion from 1894 to 1921. José Raoul Capablanca, Cuban, was champion from 1921 to 1927.

10. In 1819 Pushkin was warned by the St Petersburg clairvoyant Kirchhof that he 'would live for a long time if he did not suffer a misfortune in his thirty-seventh year in connection with a white horse, a white head, or a white person'. The man who killed Pushkin in a duel, Baron Georges d'Anthès-Heeckeren, had blond hair and belonged to the Cavalry Guard whose parade uniform was white. Thus was the prophecy fulfilled.

11. Lev Tolstoy included an ironic chapter 31 entitled 'The Ideal of *comme il faut*' in his *Youth*.

12. Nikolai N. Yevreinov (1879-1951), theatre director, dramatist, scholar, founded the Starinny Theatre in St Petersburg and from 1910 to 1917 was chief director of the Distorting Mirror Theatre, a theatre of miniatures in the same city. See also *The Springs Of Happiness*, n.2

13. Rémy de Gourmont (1858-1915), French writer.

14. The reference to Jacob's struggle with the angel is from Genesis 32, 25-6.

Souvenirs d'enfance

1. Written in fragments on 27 February 1945 and 7 May 1946 in the sanatorium at Barvikha.

2. Farce by S. I. Turbin, much performed by both professional and amateur groups at the turn of the century.

3. Luigi Pirandello (1867-1936), Italian playwright whose international reputation is based on his play *Six Characters in Search of an Author*.

Otto H. and the Artichokes

1. Written in Alma-Ata on 15 October 1943.

2. There is a play on words here. *The Fiery Angel* was a novel by the

Russian Symbolist poet Valeri Bryusov published in 1908, which Sergei Prokofiev turned into an opera in 1922. E is here using the assonance between Pirandello, the playwright's name, and the words πυρ [Greek: fire] and *angelo* [Italian: angel].

3. Rabindranath Tagore (1861-1941), Indian poet.

4. The reference is to Otto H. Kahn (1867-1934), the American banker and patron of the arts, chiefly opera. He was responsible for the reorganisation of New York's Metropolitan Opera and for attracting Arturo Toscanini to the United States. He would therefore have been seen as a potential patron for E.

5. A punning reference to Pirandello's best-known play *Six Characters in Search of an Author.*

6. The reference is to Horace B. Liveright (1886-1930), co-publisher of 'The Modern Library' series of significant works in popular format, stage producer and virulent opponent of censorship in all its forms. He promoted the careers of younger writers, including Dreiser, and produced the stage version of *An American Tragedy* in 1926. After that he worked in Hollywood.

7. *An American Tragedy* by Theodore Dreiser (1871-1945) was re-worked for Paramount as a film script by E and Ivor Montagu. Their version was rejected and the project handed over to Josef von Sternberg (See *Foreword*, n. 15.).

8. Josef von Sternberg's film of *An American Tragedy* was released in 1931. E's dim view of this version is exemplified by his comments in the article 'Help Yourself!', *ESW1*, pp. 219-37, but especially the caption to the illustration on p. 237.

9. Grigori V. Alexandrov né Mormonenko, nickname: Grisha (1903-83), began his career as E's assistant in the First Proletkult Theatre and was his assistant director on his four completed silent films from *The Strike* to *The Old and the New.* After their return from Mexico Alexandrov became the founder and leading director of the new genre of popular musical comedies, beginning with *The Happy Guys* [Veselye rebyata, 1934].

10. Ellis Island, the US Immigration Service station in New York harbour, where immigrants from Europe were processed.

11. Reference to the poem by Byron in which the 'Prisoner of Chillon' is incarcerated in a dungeon below the water level of Lake Geneva.

Millionaires I Have Met

1. Undated, but probably written in early May 1946.

2. The reference is to the somewhat ungainly statue of Alexander III sculpted by Paolo Trubetskoy and erected in St Petersburg. E misquotes the first line of Demyan Bedny's poem 'The Fearful Ghost': 'My son and my father have been executed' - the son being Nicholas II, executed by the Bolsheviks in Yekaterinburg in 1918, and the father Alexander II, assassinated in 1881 in St Petersburg on the spot where the Church of the Sacred Blood was subsequently erected.

3. E means the four sculpted groups of horses on the Anichkov Bridge that takes Nevsky Prospect over the Fontanka Canal in St Petersburg. These were removed during the blockade from 1941 to 1944.

4. Valentin A. Serov (1865-1911), Russian painter and graphic artist, member of the Wanderers group of socially conscious artists. E discusses his portrait of the actress Maria Yermolova in *ESW 2*, pp. 82-105.

5. Rumours abounded that Rasputin (Grishka) was exercising his undue influence at Court through an illicit affair with the Tsarina (*not* the Tsaritsa) Alexandra (Sashka) Fyodorovna.

The Christmas Tree

1 Undated, but marked 'MEM'.

2 Auguste Mignet (1796-1884) was one of the leading French historians of his time. His *Histoire de la Révolution Française* was published in 1824.

3 Ange Pitou and Joseph Balsamo are the eponymous principal characters of novels by Alexandre Dumas *père*.

An Unremarked Date

1. Probably written before 1945, but the manuscript lacks both title and date.

2. Arkadi T. Averchenko (1881-1925), Russian humorist, was editor of the journals *Satirikon* [Satyricon] and *Novyi Satirikon* [New Satyricon] from 1908 to 1917.

3. This is an error. The attempt on the German ambassador Count Mirbach took place in July 1918. E probably means the murder of Linde, a Commissar in the Provisional Government, who was in favour of a continuation of the Russian war effort.

4. Sergei N. Khudekov (1837-1927), journalist, historian of the

Russian ballet and editor of *Peterburgskaya gazeta*.

5. Gostiny Dvor is the largest department store in St Petersburg, situated on Nevsky Prospect.

6. 9 January 1905 was the date of Bloody Sunday, when a peaceful group of demonstrators, attempting to petition the Tsar and led by Father Gapon, were shot by soldiers. The event helped to spark off the tumultuous events of the so-called 1905 Revolution. 14 December 1825 (Old Style: 26 December, according to the Gregorian calendar) was the date of the Decembrist Uprising by a group of noblemen against Tsar Nicholas I.

7. This was the pseudonym that E used for his early published drawings.

8. Jean Moreau (1741-1814), French, painter, engraver and graphic artist.

9. For Callot see *Why I Became a Director*, n. 5.
Stefano della Bella (1610-64), Florentine graphic artist.
William Hogarth (1697-1764), English painter, noted for his satirical engravings.
Francisco Goya (1746-1828), Spanish painter.

10. This filming was for *October* in 1927.

Le Bon Dieu

1. Written in the Barvikha sanatorium on 19 May 1946.
2. Religion was in fact E's best subject at school in Riga.
3. The historical figure of Pimen died in 1571 and was Bishop of Novgorod.
4. Joseph of Volotsk (the monastic name of Ivan Sanin, 1439/40-1515) headed a movement, called the Josephites after him, that promoted the role of the church in political and social life.
5. Nil of Sora (the monastic name of Nikolai Maikov, 1433-1515) preached that the path to moral perfection lay in asceticism and lived as a recluse.
6. Serafim of Sarova (1760-1833) was a monk at the Sarova monastery. Tikhon of Zadonsk (1724-83), Bishop of Voronezh, was known for his asceticism.
7. Domenikos Theotokopoulos, known as 'El Greco' [The Greek] (1541-1614) was a Cretan-born painter active in Spain who specialised in religious scenes.
8. The Le Nain brothers were all painters of the French school: Antoine (1588-1648), Louis (1593-1648) and Mathieu (1607-77).

9. Boris M. Zubakin (1894-1938) was a professor of archaeology and writer of improvised poems.

10. Konstantin S. Stanislavsky (1863-1938), co-founder in 1898 of the Moscow Art Theatre, was the leading exponent of both the theory and practice of psychological realism and naturalism on stage. See E's discussion of Stanislavsky's 'Method' in *ESW 2*, especially pp. 138-46, and *The History of Eisenstein's Memoirs,* n.1.

11. Part of the old city of Moscow east of the Kremlin. Before the Revolution second-hand booksellers used to set up their stands along the city wall surrounding Kitai-gorod.

12. Eliphas Levi (pseudonym of Alphonse Louis Constant, 1810-75) was the founder of modern Occultism in France.

13. Mikhail Chekhov (1891-1955) was a stage and screen actor and a theatre scholar. Valentin S. Smyshlyayev (1891-1936) was a theatre producer, director and scholar. He co-directed *The Mexican* with E at the First Proletkult Theatre in 1921. See *ESW 1*, p. 33.

14. Rudolf Steiner (1861-1925), German philologist and founder of Anthroposophy.

15. Yelena P. Blavatskaya (1831-91), Russian writer and philosopher, founded the Theosophical Society in New York in 1875.

Novgorod—Los Remedios

1. Written on 24 May 1946.
2. The widow of Fyodor Dostoyevsky.
3. The monastery of the Trinity and St Sergius at Zagorsk (now Troitse-Sergiyev Posad) was a centre of toy-making in Russia. The Museum of Russian Toys is now open next to the monastery.

The Citadel

1. Written on 23 May 1946.
2. A. J. Cronin's (1896-1981) novel *The Citadel* was written in 1937 and filmed the following year.

'The Knot that Binds' (A Chapter on the Divorce of Pop and Mom)

1. Written in Barvikha on 23 May 1946. 'Divorce of Pop and Mom' is in English in the original.
2. The version of *Pinocchio* by Alexei N. Tolstoi (1882-1945) was

published in the USSR under the title *The Little Golden Key* and in 1939 Alexander Ptushko made an animated film based on Tolstoi's adaptation and with the same title. Disney's cartoon film *Pinocchio* was released in the same year.

3. Charles D. Gibson (1867-1944) was an American artist and illustrator who contributed regularly to the weekly *Life*, where his 'Gibson girls', modelled on his wife, appeared and attracted widespread popularity because they defined the contemporary ideal of American femininity.

Alfredo Vargas (sic) was an artist whose 'Vargas girls' appeared in the American magazine *Esquire* between October 1940 and March 1946. His drawings were collected into calendars, which proved very popular with the G.I.s sent to the front line. After the war Vargas was given a citation by President Harry S. Truman for his contribution to the upkeep of forces' morale.

4. The rest of this piece was written on different paper and may therefore have been composed at a different date.

5. *Levyi front iskusstv* [Left Front of the Arts] was a group of radical artists, founded in 1922, who produced the journals *LEF* (1923-5) and *Novyi LEF* [New LEF] (1927-8).

6. Anatole France (1844-1924), French author; see also *The Road to Buenos Aires*, n. 2.

'A Family Chronicle' (Stefan Zweig, Ernst Toller, Babel. About Freud. Meyerhold and K. S.)

1. Written 29-30 May 1946 and corrected on 30 June 1946.

2. Presumably this is an affectation: *Gazette littéraire* being the French for *Literaturnaya gazeta* [Literary Gazette], then the organ of the Union of Soviet Writers.

3. John Dos Passos (1896-1970), American writer.

4. Dreiser visited E on 16 November 1927. In his book *Dreiser Looks at Russia* (London, 1928), p. 206, he describes his impressions:

On entering, I remarked that he had the largest and most comfortable looking bed I had seen in Russia, and I envied him the same, I having thus far seen only narrow and most uncomfortable looking ones. He smiled and said he had bought this magnificent thing from an American farming commune near Moscow where he had been taking pictures.

5. Zweig's 'Heroism of the Intelligentsia' has not been translated into English.

6. The essays on Dostoyevsky and Dickens appeared in *Drei Meister* [Three Masters], that on Nietzsche in *Der Kampf mit dem Dämon* [The Battle with the Demon], and on Stendhal in *Drei Dichter ihres Lebens* [Three Poets of Their Life].

7. *Verwirrung der Gefühle* had been published in 1926.

8. Zweig's trilogy of essays *Die Heilung durch den Geist* dealt with all three of these and was first published in German in 1931 and translated into English as *Mental Healers* in 1933.

9. E is mistaken: it was the Wednesday Psychological Society that Stekel initiated in 1902

10. 'The School of Athens' is a fresco by Raphael in the Vatican that shows the wise men of Plato's Academy in discussion. The 'Wagnerian name' refers to Freud's first name, Sigmund, which is also the name of the hero of Wagner's opera *Die Walküre.*

11. E's mistake: Merope was Oedipus's adoptive mother. The wife of Laius, King of Thebes, was Jocasta : she later became the wife of her natural son Oedipus, who had killed his father, hence the 'Oedipus complex'.

12. Vsevolod E. Meyerhold (1874-1940) was the innovative theatre director, with whom E had worked briefly in the early 1920s. His role in Soviet theatre was somewhat akin to E's role in cinema and it is no coincidence that E later refers to Meyerhold as 'my spiritual father'.

13. Igor V. Ilyinsky (1901-87), stage and screen actor, from 1920 to 1935 at the Meyerhold Theatre, where he acted, *inter alia,* in the original production of Mayakovsky's *Mystery-Bouffe* [Misteriya-buff] in 1921. Major film appearances included *Aelita* [1924], *The Festival of St Jorgen* [Prazdnik sv. Iorgena, 1930] and the archetypal bureaucrat Byvalov in *Volga-Volga* [1938].

14. Maria I. Babanova (1900-83), actress who worked at the Meyerhold Theatre from 1920 until 1927.

15. Meyerhold staged the play in 1904/6.

16. Meyerhold left the Moscow Art Theatre in 1902 because he was dissatisfied with the repertoire and production style of the Theatre.

17. The image of the 'Demon' appeared frequently in the work of the Symbolist painter and graphic artist, Maximilian A. Vrubel (1856-1910), inspired by the poem written by Mikhail Lermontov between 1829 and 1841 and by a professional interest in Slav mythology. The best known of these pictures are 'Sitting Demon' (1890) and 'The Demon Downcast' (1902).

18. When Meyerhold's Theatre was closed in 1938 Stanislavsky

employed him as a director in the Opera Theatre, which he was then in charge of.

19. Vladimir I. Nemirovich-Danchenko (1858-1949), theatre director, playwright and scholar, was co-founder of the Moscow Art Theatre.

20. Stanislavsky's death in 1938 deprived Meyerhold of his protector and exposed him to the full force of the purges, to arrest and death.

21. Zweig's *Amok*, the second part of *Die Kette. Ein Novellenkreis* [The Chain. A Cycle of Novels], was first published in 1922.

22. Isaak Babel (1894-1941), Soviet Jewish writer. His Civil War experiences as a Chekist and political commissar provided the material for the collection of short stories entitled *Red Cavalry* (1926) and his knowledge of the Jewish criminal underground informed his *Odessa Tales* (1931). He assisted E with the revision of the script for *Bezhin Meadow* and was arrested in 1937 after production of the film was stopped. He is thought to have died in 1941.

23. Nina F. Agadzhanova-Shutko (1889-1974) was E's co-author on the original script for *The Year 1905*, one episode of which eventually became *The Battleship Potemkin*. She also wrote the scripts for Kuleshov's *The Two Buldis* [Dva-Buldi-Dva, 1930] and Pudovkin's *The Deserter* [Dezertir, 1933]. The script for *The Career of Benya Krik* was based by Babel on his own *Tales of Odessa* and was filmed by V. Vilner in 1926 for VUFKU's Odessa studio.

24. Mikhail Ya. Kapchinsky was director of the First Goskino Factory [i.e. studio] in Moscow in 1924-5, while E was making *The Strike* and *The Battleship Potemkin*.

25. Kazimir S. Malevich (1878-1935), Russian painter and founder of Suprematism.

26. *The Bazaar of Lust*, found among E's papers after his death, was a script for a satirical tragicomedy dealing with a brothel at the front line during the First World War.

27. Babel wrote his play *Maria* in 1934/5.

28. Zweig's *Joseph Fouché* was first published in Leipzig in 1929.

29. Ernst Toller (1893-1939), German Expressionist playwright, best known for his *Masse Mensch* [Mass Man] and *Hoppla, wir leben!* [Hurrah, We're Alive!, 1927].

30. Elisabeth Bergner (1897-1986), German-born actress who was one of the most popular stars of the Berlin stage in the 1920s. She first came to prominence in the plays of Frank Wedekind but was catapulted to international fame by her portrayal of Shaw's *St Joan* in 1924. After the Nazi takeover in 1933 she and her husband, the

film director Paul Czinner, emigrated to Great Britain, where in 1934 she played the title role in his film of *Catherine the Great*.

31. Pyotr L. Kapitsa (1894-1984), Soviet physicist, who worked with Rutherford at Cambridge.
32. Ernest Rutherford (1871-1937), British physicist.
33. Literally 'clothed fleas', the reference is to traditional Mexican handicraft models of miniature scenes of landscapes and 'clothed' insect corpses displayed in nutshells!
34. José Guadalupe Posada (1851-1913), Mexican graphic artist.

Toys

1. Written on 29 May 1946.
2. Now the Moscow Station in St Petersburg.

Names

1. Draft dated 29 May 1946.
2. Kornei I. Chukovsky (1882-1969), literary critic and historian and best known Soviet children's author. The reference translated here as 'euphonious nonsense' is to the *zaum* or 'trans-sense' poetry of Alexei E. Kruchenykh (1886-1968).
3. Maka and Viba Strauch were E's childhood friends: Maxim M. Strauch [also Shtraukh] (1900-74) was a Soviet actor and director who also worked under E at the First Proletkult Workers' Theatre in Moscow and then as one of his 'iron five' associates in film in 1925-8. Viba was his sister Nina Maximovna.

Muzis

1. Manuscript dated 18 July 1946.
2. The houses are still there, having been recently restored, and the street is now called *Alberta iela*.

Madame Guilbert

1. This is the earliest of the chapters, written on 10 July 1942.
2. Yvette Guilbert (1867-1944), French cabaret singer, and Victorien Sardou (1831-1908), French dramatist.
3. Rocambole is the principal character in a multi-volume detective novel by the French writer Pierre Alexis Ponson du Terrail (1829-71).

4. The *Microrobert* dictionary of the French language defines the *bal musette* as 'a popular dance-hall, where people dance, usually to the accompaniment of the accordion, the java, the waltz, the foxtrot, in a particular style known as *le musette'*.
5. Caroline Otero (1868-1965), French variety artiste, singer and dancer. Cléo de Mérode (1881-1966), French dancer.
6. The Empress Maria was involved in charitable activities.
7. Konstantin Ye. Makovsky (1839-1915), Russian painter.
8. See *Why I Became a Director*, n. 11.
9. Naum Kleiman reports anecdotal evidence that E paid for flowers to be placed on his father's grave in Berlin from the time of his first visit in 1926 until his own death in 1948.

MilEngers

1. The manuscript is undated, but probably written at the end of May or beginning of June 1946.
2. Gatchina: town with a former tsarist palace near St Petersburg; Dvinsk, now Daugavpils in Latvia; Kholm, a small old town near Novgorod; Nyandoma, a district capital in the Arkhangelsk region. .

Dead Souls

1. Probably written at about the same time as *MilEngers*.
2. E is here mistaken: in Poe's story the orangutan enters the room through the window.
3. From February until May 1920 E acted as director and set designer in the drama studio he helped to found in the cinema in Velikie Luki after the garrison club had been destroyed during the fighting.
4. Victor Henri de Rochefort (1831-1913) who published *La Lanterne* was in fact a *marquis* and not a *comte*. The play on words in the first issue, published on 31 May 1868, was as follows: 'La France contient, dit l'*Almanach impérial*, trente-six millions de sujets, sans compter les sujets de mécontement' [France, according to the *Almanach impérial*, contains thirty-six million subjects, without counting the subjects of their discontent].

    Nikolai I. Rochefort was a *Russian* count and engineer and the author of a tract on the documentation relating to piece work published in 1913.

Dvinsk

1. Dated 11 May 1946.
2. Groucho Marx's *Beds* has not been traced.

A Night in Minsk

1. The manuscript is undated but written on the reverse side of a draft plan for E's introduction to his projected book on *Method*.
2. In 1920 E had worked, with the artist Konstantin Yeliseyev, on painting the coaches of the 'Red Army Soldier' *[Krasnoarmeets]* agit-train. The collapsible stage, an idea which they had developed for the Red Army's mobile theatre productions, was resurrected by E in 1921 for the Moscow Proletkult's Studio Theatre when he designed a stage 'for shows either in the open air or in an enclosed space'.

Nuné

1. Both *Nuné* and *'The Twelve Apostles'* were written at the same time in April 1945 in the form of a single essay for a collection to celebrate the twentieth anniversary of *The Battleship Potemkin*. Publication of the collection was abandoned but the single essay was published in abridged form for the twenty-fifth anniversary of the film. Both are here reproduced in their full original form.
2. The words written by Byron in his diary following the success of his *Childe Harold's Pilgrimage*.
3. George Antheil (1900-59) was an American composer and pianist. His piano and orchestral music was heavily influenced by jazz, and after 1936 he concentrated on film music.
4. Details of the struggle surrounding the censor's attempts to ban *Potemkin* and of its eventual success in Berlin are to be found in: G. Kühn, K. Tümmler & W. Wimmer (eds), *Film und revolutionäre Arbeiterbewegung in Deutschland, 1918-1932* [Film and the Revolutionary Workers' Movement in Germany, 1918-1932] (Berlin GDR, 1975), pp. 323-69.
5. Max Reinhardt (1873-1943), probably the most celebrated theatre director in Europe, director of the Deutsches Theater, closely associated with the Salzburg Festival, known for his insistence on maintaining illusion in theatre.
6. Asta Nielsen (1883-1972), legendary Danish-born superstar of silent cinema.

813

7. Julio Alvarez del Vayo (1891-1975), Spanish diplomat and politician, was the ambassador of the Spanish Republic to Mexico in 1931-33, during which time he supported E's film expedition. In 1936-45 he was Foreign Minister in the Spanish Republican government in exile.

8. See *A Family Chronicle*, n. 23.

9. Grigori M. Kozintsev (1905-73) and Leonid Z. Trauberg (1902-90), began their collaboration in the early 1920s with the Factory of the Eccentric Actor (FEKS) and went on to make the Maxim trilogy in the 1930s.

10. E's dispute with Proletkult over the authorship of the script for *The Strike* led to a bitter polemic, which is translated by Alan Upchurch in: J. Leyda (ed.), *Eisenstein 2: A Premature Celebration of Eisenstein's Centenary* (Calcutta, 1981), pp. 1-8.

11. Proletkult, the Proletarian Culture organisation, aimed to produce a specifically proletarian culture for post-Revolutionary Soviet audiences, but its ideas and its growing mass membership were seen by Lenin and others as a challenge to the authority of the Party and in December 1920 it was subjugated to Lunacharsky's People's Commissariat for Enlightenment. E clearly also regarded the Proletkult's ideas on art as extreme: he left the organisation after a dispute over the authorship of the scenario for *The Strike* in the winter of 1924-5. See n. 10 above.

12. The Strastnoy Monastery (or Monastery of Christ's Passion) was torn down in 1930 as part of the campaign against religion and later replaced by a large heated outdoor swimming pool.

13. Doctor Aibolit, a free re-working of Doctor Doolittle, is the hero of a series of children's stories by the Soviet writer and translator, Chukovsky: see *Names*, n. 2.

14. From 1923 to 1926 Malevich headed the State Institute for Artistic Culture [GINKhUK] in Leningrad.

15. RAPP was founded as a proletarian literary pressure group in 1925 but laid aggressive claim to sole legitimacy and hegemony in artistic matters in the name of the proletariat. It attacked and attempted to discredit and hound from office and influence those who did not agree with its dogmatic positions. It was dissolved by decree of the Communist Party Central Committee on 23 April 1932 and its dissolution paved the way for the creation of the Union of Soviet Writers as an all-embracing umbrella organisation in 1934.

16. The term 'ironclad screenplays' *[zheleznye stsenarii]* was used in the mid-1920s and reflected the ideas of those who felt that the

screenplay should encompass every detail of a film, before it went into production, and that in production the screenplay should be strictly adhered to. E counterposed to this his own notion of an 'emotional screenplay' or libretto, which would confine itself to the broad outlines of the film and permit the director a very considerable degree of scope for innovation and creative freedom.

'The Twelve Apostles'

1. See *Nuné*, note 1.
2. Baron Pyotr N. Wrangel (1878-1928), a general in both the tsarist and White armies: it was his defeat in the Civil War that finally brought the War to an end in 1921.
3. The 'drama at Tendra' is the title of the second 'act' of *The Battleship Potemkin* in which the ship's captain attempts to punish the group of leading mutineers. These historical events took place on 14 June 1926 in Tendra Bay, by the island of Tendra in the Black Sea close to Odessa.
4. 'And so till death itself' [*Hasta la muerte*] is one of the savagely satirical etchings in Goya's series *Los Caprichos*, offered for sale in 1799.
5. Yuri K. Olesha (1899-1960), prose-writer, dramatist and poet, a native of Odessa.
6. 'But Russians can overcome any obstacle' is a line from an eighteenth-century ode which has become a popular saying.
7. The 'Black Hundreds' was the popular name for the right-wing nationalist groups, the Union of the Russian People [*Soyuz russkogo naroda*] and the Union of Michael the Archangel [*Soyuz Mikhaila Arkhangela*], both formed in 1905 to combat the emerging Revolutionary movement. The Black Hundreds were responsible for pogroms and other attacks upon the Jews and other non-Russian minorities.
8. Goskino was the cinema organisation covering the Russian Federation and some of the smaller Republics, while VUFKU controlled production and distribution in the Ukraine. E worked for Goskino; Dovzhenko and Vertov for VUFKU.
9. After 1926 scriptwriters and directors in Soviet cinema received a legally determined percentage of the takings from every performance of their work, by analogy with the way in which dramatists were paid for every performance of their plays. E had campaigned for this after his dispute with Proletkult over the script

for *The Strike* (see *Nuné* n. 11). Towards the end of the 1930s this system was replaced by a one-off fee.

10. Konstantin I. Feldman (1881-1968), who took part in the filming of *Potemkin*, had been one of the delegates from the city of Odessa to the ship in 1905.

11. The member of the Anniversary Commission concerned was in fact Meyerhold (see '*A Family Chronicle*', n. 12), but, by the time he arrived in Paris, Prokofiev had already left, so that the invitation was never delivered.

12. Eduard K. Tisse (1897-1961) was E's cameraman from *The Strike* right through to *Ivan the Terrible*, although for this last film he shot only the exteriors.

    For Alexandrov, see *Otto H. and the Artichokes*, n. 9.

13. Alexander A. Levitsky (1885-1965) one of the most senior Soviet cameramen, had begun filming *The Year 1905* with E in Leningrad. Differences of artistic principle had led to a rupture in their collaboration before E moved to Odessa, and Levitsky was replaced by Tisse. After *Potemkin* had been completed, E wrote: 'Lost a month and a half because of a personality clash with Levitsky... It is difficult to make a contemporary revolutionary piece when your cameraman nurtures a philistine antipathy and enmity towards cranes, wharves and locomotives, and his ideal is represented by Catholic churches made out of cardboard.' ('Tezisy k vystupleniyu v ARK' [Theses for a Speech to ARK, 1926]). The last phrase is a reference to Vladimir Gardin's film *Cross and Mauser* [Krest i mauzer, 1926], which Levitsky was filming in Odessa after his replacement on *Potemkin* by Tisse.

14. See *ESW 1*, pp 183-6.

15. 'Le Duc' [the Duke] is the popular name in Odessa for the statue at the top of the Steps of the one-time Governor-General Duke Armand-Emmanuel Richelieu, sculpted by Ivan Martos in 1826.

16. Reference to the poem 'An Unusual Adventure that Happened to Vladimir Mayakovsky One Summer at His Dacha' [Neobychainoe priklyuchenie, byvshee s Vladimirom Mayakovskim letom na dache], written in June/July 1920 by Mayakovsky, in which he describes a conversation with the sun while drinking tea.

17. The reference is to Joshua, 10, vv. 12-13. The Battle on the Ice sequence for *Alexander Nevsky* was filmed in the baking summer sun in July 1938, using salt to re-create the impression of ice.

18. For Kapchinsky, see '*A Family Chronicle*', n. 24.

19. A play on the refrain of the three sisters in Chekhov's play of that

name, 'To Moscow, to Moscow, to Moscow!'

20. *Seeds of Freedom* was directed in 1942-3 by Hans Bürger from a script by Albert Maltz, with music by Paul Abraham.

21. H. D. Glance, 'The Second Birth of a Classic Film', *Theatre Arts,* August 1943.

22. 'Dickens, Griffith and Ourselves' [Dikkens, Griffit i my], published in: *Materialy po istorii mirovogo kinoiskusstva. Tom I: Amerikanskaya kinematografiya: D. U. Griffit* [Materials on the History of World Cinema. Vol. I: American Cinema: D. W. Griffith] (Moscow, 1944); translated as 'Dickens, Griffith and the Film Today' in: J. Leyda (ed.), *Film Form: Essays in Film Theory* (New York and London, 1949), pp. 195-255. See also *The History of the Close-Up,* n. 3.

23. Nikolai Bauman, one of the leaders of the Revolutionary movement in Moscow, was assassinated by tsarist agents on 18 October 1905. His funeral procession became a mass demonstration and a significant event in the 1905 Revolution.

24. For 'Bloody Sunday' in 1905, see *An Unremarked Date,* n. 6. When the news of 'Bloody Sunday' reached Baku the city was torn by inter-ethnic massacres by roaming bands of both Azerbaijanis and Armenians. This massacre took place on 6-9 February 1905.

25. See *Nuné,* n. 4.

A Miracle in the Bolshoi Theatre

1. The manuscript is undated and difficult to read. It is possible that it is in some way connected to E's plan of May 1946 for a chapter entitled 'The Bolshoi Theatre', in which he intended to relate his 'incursions' on to the boards of the celebrated Moscow theatre: the scene from *Wise Man* shown as part of a jubilee evening for Meyerhold in 1923; his participation in the celebrations of the fifteenth anniversary of Soviet cinema in January 1935; his production of Wagner's opera *Die Walküre* in 1940, etc. This chapter would also have mentioned the première of *Potemkin* on 24 December 1925 at an evening devoted to the celebration of the twentieth anniversary of the 1905 Revolution.

Mémoires posthumes

1. Written in Alma-Ata on 17 October 1942.

Epopée

1. The cycle of essays with this general title was written at Barvikha at the end of May 1946, with some additional material inserted shortly afterwards.

2. Friedrich [also Fridrikh] M. Ermler (1898-1967), né Vladimir Breshov, was one of the leading film directors in Leningrad. His works included: *Katya's Reinette Apples* [Kat'ka—bumazhnyi ranet, 1926], *A Fragment of Empire* [Oblomok imperii, 1929], *Counterplan* [Vstrechnyi, 1932, with Sergei Yutkevich], *Peasants* [Krest'yane, 1935] and the two-part *A Great Citizen* [Velikii grazhdanin, 1937-9].

3. James Ensor (1860-1940) was a Belgian painter and graphic artist.

4. *New Babylon* [Novyi Vavilon] was the title of the film made by Grigori Kozintsev and Leonid Trauberg in 1929 about the Paris Commune. The film took its title from the name of a large department store.

5. The Chemin des Dames was the scene of prolonged fighting between French and German troops in the First World War.

6. The British Board of Film Censors was set up by the film industry as an act of self-preservation in 1912. The 1909 Cinematograph Act had given local authorities the power to license buildings for use as cinemas. This had been intended as a fire prevention measure but the Act had been so loosely worded that it could also have been interpreted as conferring powers of censorship. Since there were more than seven hundred local authorities, the possibility that they might separately exercise censorship powers was seen as a threat to the commercial viability of the industry. A centralised self-regulating body was thus seen by the industry as preferable to a system of chaotic state-backed censorship.
See: J. Richards, *The Age of the Dream Palace. Cinema and Society in Britain 1930-1939* (London, 1984), pp. 91-2.

7. Jean Chiappe (1878-1940), perfect of the Paris police from 1927, sacked in 1934 for his extremist sympathies. The quotation is from the Symbolist poet, konstantin Balmont (1867-1942).

8. Léon Moussinac (1890-1964) was a French writer, theatre and film scholar, friend of E, and later author of *Sergei Eisenstein. An Investigation into His Films and Philosophy* (New York, 1970; original French edition, Paris, 1964). Dr René Allendy was a French doctor and psychoanalyst, who was also an art collector.

9. In articles such as 'Our *October*. Beyond the Played and the Non-Played' (1928), 'Perspectives' and 'The Dramaturgy of Film Form

(The Dialectical Approach to Film Form)' (both 1929), and 'An Attack by Class Allies' (1933), in *ESW 1*, pp. 101-6, 151-80, 261-75.

10. Cf. *ESW 1*, p. 199, where E writes 'From image to emotion, from emotion to thesis'.

11. One of the questions put to E in the Sorbonne discussion was: 'What do you think of Surrealism?'; see: *ESW 1*, pp. 201-2.

12. Alexander P. Dovzhenko (1894-1956), Ukrainian Soviet film director.
Vsevolod I. Pudovkin (1893-1953), Soviet film director and actor, closely associated with Lev Kuleshov, co-signatory with E of the 'Statement on Sound', *ESW 1*, pp. 113-14.

13. Jacques-Bénigne Bossuet (1627-1704), Bishop of Meaux, was a proponent of the reunification of the Christian church.
Léon Gambetta (1838-82) was a French politician, in 1881-2 Prime Minister and Foreign Minister of France.
For Rochefort, see *Dead Souls*, n. 4.
Gavroche is the name of a Parisian street urchin, a character in Victor Hugo's novel *Les Misérables*.

14. A quotation from St Paul's Epistle to the Colossians, 3, v. 11.

15. ESW 1, p. 201.

16. In the original manuscript E refers to 'Rue Grenelle' but this is an error. The Rue de Grenelle runs through the left bank area of Paris from near Saint-Sulpice through the Place des Invalides almost to the Champ de Mars.

17. The reference is to Kutuzov's tactics in defeating Napoleon in 1812.

18. At the beginning of 1930 one of the leaders of the White émigré organisation, General Kutepov, disappeared in mysterious circumstances for which the Soviet government was widely held responsible.

19. André Tardieu (1876-1945), French Prime Minister 1929-30 and 1932.

20. A paraphrase of Voltaire's famous remark, 'If God did not exist, we should have to invent him.'

21. Léonard Rosenthal's *Faisons fortune* [Let's Be Rich!] was published in Paris in 1924. Rosenthal was also the author of *The Kingdom of the Pearls* (London, 1920) and *L'Esprit des affaires* [The Business Spirit] (Paris, 1928).

22. In late 1929 E travelled twice from Paris to England. On 18/19 November he lectured to the London Film Society on film, and on 8 and 13 December he spoke at Cambridge University and the Society for Cultural Relations with the USSR. It was during one of

these visits that Grigori Alexandrov made the acquaintance of Léonard Rosenthal and Mara Gris.

23. The film *Romance sentimentale* was twenty minutes long. It was directed by Alexandrov, with Tisse as cameraman. For advertising reasons E was named as director, although he only played a minor part in editing the sound track.

24. Jean Painlevé (b. 1902), French director of popular scientific films.

25. Renaud de Jouvenel was the youngest son of Henri de Jouvenel (1876-1935), French statesman, senator, diplomat and journalist, editor of *Le Matin* (see also below, n. 81). Renaud later fought with the French Resistance.

26. Anatole de Monzi (1876-1947), French statesman, senator and former minister.

27. Roland Tual, writer and critic, was close to the Surrealists until 1928, then founded the journal *Revue du cinéma* with Jean-Georges Auriol. After the Second World War, this was re-established by André Bazin as *Cahiers du cinéma*. See *Pages from Literature* n. 8.

28. E explored the concept of 'ecstasy', as the psychological and aesthetic phenomenon of *ex-stasis* in a number of works, but especially 'On the Structure of Things' in *Nonindifferent Nature* (Cambridge, 1987), pp. 3-37.

29. St Theresa of Lisieux (1873-97) was canonised only in 1925.

30. E had been interested in Lourdes and the phenomenon of mass ecstasy since reading Zola's novel *Lourdes*, published in 1894, as a child.

31. Reference to the legend that the French King Charles IX, a fanatical opponent of the Huguenots, had shot some of them himself during the St Bartholomew's Night massacre of 24 August 1572.

32. André Breton (1896-1966), French poet, writer and aesthetic theorist, one of the founders of Surrealism.

33. André Malraux was to meet E again in Moscow in 1934, where he attended the First Congress of Soviet Writers. After the Congress E and Malraux worked together in the Crimea on a screenplay based on Malraux's novel *La Condition humaine*, about the revolutionary movement in China, which was to be made into a film by the young director Albert Gendelstein.

34. Germaine Krull (1897-1985), French photographer.

35. Joris Ivens (1898-1989), Dutch-born documentary film-maker.

36. The building that then housed, and hence also the popular name for, the French Foreign Ministry. It is now the museum of nineteenth-century French art, the Musée d'Orsay.

37. Tristan Tzara (1896-1963), French poet and dramatist, was first a theorist of Dada and later one of its critics.

38. Gertrude Stein (1874-1946), American writer who lived in France.

39. Filippo Tomaso Marinetti (1876-1944), Italian writer and theorist of Futurism and later a supporter of Mussolini. Among other things Marinetti preached the principles of 'Tactilism'—a belief in the importance of touch and texture—in art.

40. Max Ernst (1891-1976) was one of the most important German Surrealist painters. Luís Buñuel (1900-83), Spanish film director made *Un Chien andalou* [An Andalusian Dog] in France in 1928 and *L'Age d'or* [The Golden Age] in 1930.

41. Alexandre Millerand (1859-1943) was President of France from 1920 to 1924.

42. The lavish Parisian restaurant Maxim's and the dancers in its exotic floor-show feature prominently in both the plot and the staging of Franz Lehár's operetta *The Merry Widow* (1905).

43. Henri Guernioux was a deputy in the National Assembly and Victor Basch (1863-1943) was Professor of Aesthetics at the Sorbonne, and chairman of the French League for Human Rights, in which Guernioux, as E has already mentioned, was also active.

44. Georges Clemenceau (1841-1929), French statesman and twice Prime Minister, with Zola a defender of Dreyfus (see below, n. 53), nicknamed the 'Tiger' because of his caustic tongue. E is mistaken about the year of his death.

45. Maurice Dekobra, pseudonym of Maurice Tessier (1885-1973), French writer of detective stories, including *La Madonne des sleepings* [The Madonna of the Sleeping Cars, 1925].

46. Clemenceau advocated Allied intervention in the Russian Civil War to provide Western Europe with a *cordon sanitaire* against the spread of Bolshevism. Edward M. House was President Woodrow Wilson's principal adviser at the Peace Conference that led to the signature of the Treaty of Versailles in 1919.

47. *Wilson* [USA, 1944]: see L. J. Leff & J. Simmons, '*Wilson*: Hollywood Propaganda for World Peace', *Historical Journal of Film, Radio & Television*, vol. 3, no. 1 (1983), pp. 3-18.

48. Gustav Stresemann (1878-1929), German Foreign Minister 1923-9, associated with the policy of fulfilment of the reparations clauses of the Treaty of Versailles and with Franco-German reconciliation.

49. Reference to Hamlet's words in Shakespeare's play, Act 1, Scene 5: 'There are more things in Heaven and Earth, Horatio, than are dreamt of in your philosophy.'

50. Silvio Pellico (1789-1854), imprisoned for fifteen years in 1820 for his political beliefs.

Vera Figner (1852-1942), Russian revolutionary and leading member of the Narodnaya Volya [People's Will] terrorist branch of the Populist movement: imprisoned for twenty years from 1884.

Nicola Sacco (1891-1927) and Bartolomeo Vanzetti (1888-1927), Italian immigrant workers, were condemned to death in Massachusetts in 1921 and finally sent to the electric chair in 1927, although widely believed to be innocent. The case became a *cause célèbre* at the time and was widely reported in the Soviet press as an instance of the failings of US justice.

51. Reference to the play *The Dreyfus Affair* [Die Affäre Dreyfus] by Hans José Rehfisch and Wilhelm Herzog, premièred in Berlin in 1929, which took Zola's well-known *J'accuse* as the basis for an attempt to deploy the social forces of the Third Republic as a dramatic device.

52. William Dieterle (1893-1972) made *The Life of Emile Zola* in 1937 with Paul Muni playing the title role.

53. References to the principal events in the Dreyfus affair. After his first trial in 1894 found him guilty of treason Dreyfus was transported to 'Devil's Island' off French Guiana. At a second trial in 1898 the court martial cleared the real spy, Esterhazy. The third trial in 1898/9 found Dreyfus guilty with extenuating circumstances and significantly reduced his sentence, whereupon he was pardoned by the President. Zola's letter defending Dreyfus, '*J'accuse!*' was cited in court and its author was forced to flee to Great Britain. The 'enigmatic *bordereaux*' were the forged documents that formed the basis for the case against Dreyfus. In July 1906 the verdict of the court-martial was quashed: Dreyfus was exonerated, restored to his rank in the army and awarded the *Légion d'honneur*.

54. Reference to the comedy *Le Voyage de M. Perrichon* [Mr Perrichon's Journey] by Eugène Marie Labiche (1815-88).

55. Eugène Klopfer was a French film distributor.

56. Nuevo Laredo is the name of the small border town where E and his team were forced to spend a month from 17 February to 14 March 1932 waiting for their transit visas for the USA.

57. Gabrielle Réjane (1856-1920), French actress.

58. See *Foreword*, n. 18.

59. The title given to an anthology of plays by Prosper Mérimée, which he published under the pseudonym of Clara Gazul, the name of a

Spanish actress.

60. *Pointillisme* is the method deployed by the Neo-Impressionists of using small dots of intermingled primary colours to achieve a brighter and clearer secondary colour which relies on distance to make an 'optical' mixture in the spectator's eye.

Alfred Sisley (1839-1939), French-born Impressionist painter of British parentage.

Georges Seurat (1859-91), French painter most closely associated with the Neo-Impressionists and the technique of *pointillisme*, whose best-known painting is probably 'Sunday on the Island of Grande Jatte' (1886).

61. Etienne de Beaumont was a French art patron, stage designer and balletomane.

62. Name of a character in Marcel Proust's *A la recherche du temps perdu*.

63. Carl Dreyer (1889-1968), Danish film director, made *The Passion of Joan of Arc* [La Passion de Jeanne d'Arc] in France in 1928.

64. Abel Gance (1889-1981), French film director, playwright and actor, whose monumental film *Napoléon* [France, 1927] used split and multiple screens to portray the scale of its hero's achievements.

65. The film was in fact titled *The End of the World* [La Fin du monde, France, 1931] and was premièred in January 1931, although unfinished and mutilated by others. It was one of the earliest French sound films and Gance had pioneered a stereophonic sound system for it. E's meeting with Gance took place on 25 February 1930.

66. The Bois de Vincennes lies on the right bank of the Seine to the south-east of Paris. Joinville lies in the same direction.

67. Paul Féval (1817-87), French novelist, dramatist and author of boulevard novels.

For Ponson du Terrail see *Madame Guilbert*, n. 3.

68. E is mistaken. After his conviction in 1945 for collaboration with the Nazis Pétain was imprisoned at Portalet and later on the Île d'Yeu. E may have confused this with the fact that General Gamelin, French Commander-in-Chief in 1940, had his headquarters in the Château de Vincennes and was consequently accused of cutting himself off from the outside world and from the real problems that beset the French Army and led to the fall of France in June 1940.

69. Mata Hari, pseudonym of Margaretha Zelle (1876-1917), Dutch-born dancer executed during the First World War as a German spy. There are several screen versions of her life. Marlene Dietrich

(1901-92) played the role of an agent code-named X27 in von Sternberg's *Dishonored* and Greta Garbo played the title role in George Fitzmaurice's *Mata Hari* [both USA, 1931].

For Sternberg's role in *An American Tragedy*, one of the reasons for E's barbed remarks, see *Foreword*, n. 15, and *Otto H. and the Artichokes*, nn. 6-8.

70. *Hold Back the Dawn* [USA, 1941] starred the French-born actor Charles Boyer (1899-1978).

71. Reference to the national quotas which governed immigration into the USA at the time.

72. E's chronology is wrong here. Herbert Hoover (1874-1964) was the Republican thirty-first President of the USA from 1929 until his defeat by the Democrat, Franklin D. Roosevelt (1882-1945), in the November 1932 elections. Hoover had reacted to the Wall Street crash in October 1929 with a reluctance to extend federal government intervention in the economy and a belief that natural economic forces would bring about a revival of trade. Roosevelt's 'New Deal' offered 'direct, vigorous action' against the Depression through such measures as public works, farm support and improved labour relations.

73. Since 1634 the inhabitants of this Bavarian (*not* Austrian) village have staged a regular passion play as a thanksgiving for their ancestors' deliverance from the plague.

74. Pudovkin (see above, n. 12) did some camera tests for the role of Pimen, the Archbishop of Novgorod, but the role was eventually played by Alexander Mgebrov and Pudovkin appeared as Nikolai, a beggar simpleton.

75. Alberto Cavalcanti (1897-1982), Brazilian film director: attended the congress at La Sarraz and worked in Britain from 1934 until 1949, first with John Grierson at the GPO Film Unit and later for Ealing Studios.

76. Fyodor Chaliapin [also Shalyapin] (1873-1938), famous Russian bass singer and actor who emigrated to France in 1921.

77. Georg W. Pabst (1885-1967), German film director whose film *Don Quichotte* was made in 1933. His other films included *Pandora's Box* [Die Büchse der Pandora, 1929], *The Threepenny Opera* [Die Dreigroschenoper] and *Kameradschaft* [both 1931].

78. *The Maid of Pskov* [Pskovityanka, 1915] was in fact made by Alexander Ivanov-Gai, specifically to film Chaliapin in Rimsky-Korsakov's opera in his greatest role, Ivan the Terrible. Chaliapin's unhappy memories of this episode are cited in J. Leyda, *Kino. A*

History of the Russian and Soviet Film (London, 1960), pp. 77-8. He also sang the role at the first performance of the opera in London at the Drury Lane Theatre in 1913.

79. Colette was the pen name of the French writer Sidonie Gabrielle Colette (1873-1954).

80. Willy was the pen name of Henri Gauthier-Villars (1859-1931), French theatre and music critic to whom Colette was married from 1893 to 1906. She published her first novels under his pen name.

81. Renaud's father was Henri de Jouvenel (see above, n. 25). He was married to Colette from 1912 to 1924.

82. See above, n. 8.

83. *La Comédie humaine* was the generic title given by Balzac to his cycle of novels. Gérard de Nerval, pseudonum of Gérard Labrunie (1808-55), French poet, forerunner of Surrealism.

84. Philibert Louis Debucourt (1755-1832), French painter and graphic artist.

85. Camille Desmoulins (1760-94) represented Paris in the National Convention and was an ally of Danton.

86. Philippe Egalité, Duke of Orléans (1747-93)—a member of the Bourbons, the French royal family—took on the name 'Egalité' during the French Revolution and was a member of the National Convention.

87. At this point in the manuscript there is an outline for the rest of *Epopée*: 'I'm lionized in the salons on the boulevard. Mara is persuaded to invite me. The cartoon about my expulsion in *Izvestiya*. Monsieur Muzard's remark that I shall never be let in anywhere again. The secret of Monsieur Tardieu's bed.' (In English in the original.) The last topic is developed in the next chapter. The cartoon, by Boris Yefimov, was ironically headed: 'A Great Victory for Democratic France'; see p. 256.

88. Jean Cocteau (1889-1963), French poet, essayist, artist, film-maker and playwright: his films include *Beauty and the Beast* [La Belle et la bête, 1945], *Orphée* [1950] and *Le Testament d'Orphée* [1960].

89. Reference to Maupassant's novella *La Maison Tellier* and thereby to brothels.

90. *The Hands of Orlac* [Orlacs Hände, Austria, 1925] starred the German actor Conrad Veidt (1893-1943) in the leading role. His other film roles included Cesare in *The Cabinet of Dr Caligari* [Das Kabinett des Dr Caligari, Germany, 1919], Ivan the Terrible in *Waxworks* [Das Wachsfigurenkabinett, Germany, 1924], the title role in *The Student of Prague* [Der Student von Prag, Germany,

1926], Count Metternich in *Congress Dances* [Der Kongress tanzt, Germany, 1931] and his last part was as Major Strasser in *Casablanca* [USA, 1943].

91. Mary Marquet (1895-1979) was born Micheline Marie Marquet in St Petersburg.

92. *La Voix humaine* [The Human Voice] was a one-act monologue for the female voice, first performed at the Comédie Française in 1930 by Berthe Bovy.

93. See above, n. 59.

94. *Les Mariés de la Tour Eiffel* [The Eiffel Tower Wedding Party] was a satirical 'spectacle play with music' first performed at the Comédie Française in 1921 with sets and costumes by Pablo Picasso.

95. In May 1922 E and Sergei I. Yutkevich (1904-85) wrote the libretto and some sketches for the pantomime *Columbine's Garter* for a production planned for MASTFOR [Masterskaya Foreggera], the experimental workshop theatre run by Nikolai M. Foregger. (né Greifenturn, 1892-1939). The inspiration for this 'Constructivist' pantomime was Arthur Schnitzler's play *Beatrice's Veil* with music composed by Ernő Dohnányi, which had been produced by Meyerhold in 1910 as the pantomime *Columbine's Scarf* and by Alexander Tairov (1885-1950) in 1916 as *Pierrette's Shawl*.

96. Louis Aragon (1897-1983), French writer associated with the Surrealists.

97. Paul Eluard (1895-1952), French poet, also associated with the Surrealists.

98. See *Epopée*, n.32

99. Enrico Prampolini (1894-1956), Italian painter, sculptor, stage designer and director, early member of the Italian Futurist movement and co-author, with Marinetti (see above, n. 39) of many of its major manifestoes.
    The first Congress of Independent Film-Makers was held at the château of La Sarraz, near Lausanne, Switzerland, from 3 to 7 September 1929 at the invitation of its wealthy owner, Mme Hélène de Mandrot. E was expelled from Switzerland immediately afterwards. For details of the films shown at the Congress, see *Comrade Léon*, n. 4.

100. Reference to the poem 'Kachalov's Dog' (1925) by Sergei A. Yesenin (1895-1925).

101. French: 'a carcass'. A pamphlet with this title, directed against Anatole France, had been published by a group of radical left-wingers in 1924.

102. E must be referring to his first visit to Paris in 1906 since Eiffel died in 1923.

103. See above, n. 92.

104. Jean Desbordes (1906-44) was a rising French novelist and at that time Cocteau's boyfriend. For details of their meeting see: E. Sprigge & J.-J. Kihm, *Jean Cocteau: The Man and the Mirror* (London, 1968), pp. 106-11; the incident at *La Voix humaine* is described on pp. 117-18. Desbordes's first novel *J'Adore* [I Love] was published in Paris in 1928 and in 1936 his two-act play *La Muse* was performed at the Comédie Française. He was murdered by the Gestapo during the Liberation.

105. A remark from Alexander Griboyedov's (1795-1829) comedy *Woe from Wit* [Gore ot uma, 1824], referring to the burning of Moscow in 1812; it has since become a Russian saying.

106. Constant Coquelin (1841-1909), French actor who made his debut at the Comédie Française in 1860 in a Molière play but was mainly associated with the role of Cyrano de Bergerac. His younger brother, Ernest, was also an actor.

107. Jean-Gaspard Deburau, pseudonym of Jan Kaspar Dvořák (1796-1846), Bohemian-born French mime who developed the secondary character of Pierrot into a pale, elongated hero of mythic proportions at the Théâtre des Funambules in Paris. He was reincarnated as Baptiste, played by Jean-Louis Barrault, in Marcel Carné's film *Les Enfants du Paradis* [France, 1945].

108. Kiki was the stage name of the model Alice Irine, famous as a cabaret artiste in the 1920s.

109. For Alexandrov, see *Otto H. and the Artichokes*, n. 9. His musical comedy *The Happy Guys* [Veselye rebyata] was made in 1934 and proved to be one of the most popular Soviet films of the 1930s.

110. Cocteau also wrote the script for the film version of his 1920s novel *Les Enfants terribles*, directed by Jean-Pierre Melville [France, 1950].

111. E is mistaken with his chronology again. The basilica of Sacré Coeur was built after a design by Paul Abadie (1812-84) in 1876-1910, and *not* in the reign of Napoléon III.

112. Aristide Bruant (1851-1925), French poet and cabaret artiste who wrote numerous songs in Parisian *argot* which he performed in this bar. In 1901 he published a *Dictionnaire de l'argot au XXme siècle* [Dictionary of 20th Century Slang]. He was also the subject of a famous work by Toulouse-Lautrec.

113. Les Halles, now redeveloped, was the part of the Marais district of Paris where the warehouses, slaughterhouses and principal food

markets of the city were situated. The nickname 'the belly of Paris' was given to it by Zola.

114. At this point in the manuscript there is a comment in the margin: 'Rendezvous with Berthelot at night in the Quai d'Orsay. Briand's arrived.' For some reason E confined himself to a description of Berthelot's outward appearance and never returned to the story.

115. See above, n. 34.

116. Man Ray (1890-1976), American painter, photographer and film-maker associated with Surrealism and the avant-garde.

Eli Lotar (1905-69), French photographer, cameraman on Luís Buñuel's film *Land without Bread* [Las Hurdes, Spain, 1932].

André Kertész (1894-1985), French photographer of Hungarian extraction.

117. The query is E's. The Rue Notre-Dame-des-Champs runs between the Boulevard du Montparnasse and the Jardin du Luxembourg on the left bank.

118. Reference to the red document dated 14 March 1930 abrogating E's residence permit for Paris, which is preserved in the archives in Moscow.

119. Erich Maria Remarque's novel *Im Westen Nichts Neues* had been published in 1928.

120. Joris Karl Huysmans (1848-1907), French writer of Huguenot descent who converted to Catholicism in 1892.

121. *The Abyss* (1891) and *Saint Lydwina of Schiedam* (1901) were both works by Huysmans.

122. E left France on board the 'Europa' on 8 May 1930 for the USA.

123. At this point the main text for *Epopée* breaks off. In the manuscript there is a note: 'The balance of power at this moment: *Les 12 stations* [the twelve Stations of the Cross] of Monsieur Tardieu's progress at the sitting of the Chamber.' The published fragments that follow are written on separate sheets of paper. The first (in square brackets) derives from a draft for a conclusion to *Epopée*, dated 2 July 1946. In addition to an account of the last visit to the Préfecture, mention is made in this draft of the following subjects: a journey through France and the signing of a contract with a representative of Paramount; 'A journey to the South of France with Moussinac. The French radicals. Vaillant has his own island. Barbusse a villa in Cannes . . . The Promenade des Anglais (Nice— a colour photograph in my nursery). A call from Paris. Mr Lasky. A chase after a train *à l'américaine*. Plantations of roses for perfume. A crocodile and alligator farm. We miss the train by one minute. I read Blaise Cendrars' *L'Or* [Gold]. Pencilled comments like the

lashes of a whip. Pleyel's grand piano hauled across the prairie by a dozen oxen. The invasion of the metalled road. The saw of Sutter's sawmill in Frisco. Sutter's death. Interwoven impressions. Hôtel Edouard VII. Mr Lasky.'

The description of the project for *Sutter's Gold* is to be found in the chapters entitled *The Works of Daguerre* and *The Springs of Happiness.*

124. Cf *Epopée*, n. 20.

The Lady with the Black Gloves

1. Written on 14 October 1943 in Alma-Ata. In 1946 E pondered how best to integrate this essay into the *Memoirs*. At first he thought of including it in *Epopée* but then remarked: 'Yvette after Berthelot'. There is an echo in the title chosen of Anton Chekhov's short story 'The Lady with the Lapdog'.

2. E is almost certainly mistaken here on two counts: first, on the attribution of the poetry to Goethe and, second, on the title. The reference is almost certainly to Ludwig van Beethoven's (1770-1827) Lieder cycle *An die ferne Geliebte* [To the Distant Beloved], a setting of poems by Aloys Jeitteles (1792-1858).

3. i.e. Toulouse-Lautrec.

4. F. W. Murnau (1888-1931) filmed his version of *Faust* in 1926.

5. *The Distant Princess*, a three-act verse drama by Edmond Rostand (1868-1918) who also wrote *Cyrano de Bergerac*. In the original production in 1895 Sarah Bernhardt played the title role.

6. Stéphane Mallarmé (1842-98), French Symbolist poet.
   Albert Robida (1848-1926), French illustrator and humorous writer.

7. In her book *La Passante émerveillée (Mes voyages)* [The Wondrous Passage (My Travels)] (Paris, 1929), p. 2, Guilbert describes her first transatlantic voyage: '. . . and so I embarked upon the 'Etruria', belonging to an English company. Oh, I shall never forget that first crossing!!! My chambermaid and I thought we could hold out . . . It was December, a stormy month. The doctor, who was perpetually in my cabin, was shocked at my condition. I think that is when I must have dislocated my liver, because for ten days and nights I did nothing but vomit! I held the doctor's arms with my sweat-drenched hands and cried: "Ten thousand francs for the captain, monsieur, if he will consent to stop for an hour! . . . One hour of respite, monsieur, I'm dying, I'm dying . . ."'

8. Leopold von Sacher-Masoch (1836-95), Austrian writer of erotic novels involving self-abuse, from whom the phenomenon of

'masochism' takes its name.

9. Leopold von Sacher-Masoch, *Russische Hofgeschichten* [Stories of the Russian Court] (1873-4).

10. Shaw's comedy *Great Catherine* was published in 1913.

11. Francisque Sarcey (1827-99), French writer and theatre critic.

12. Xanrof, pseudonym of Léon Fourneau (1867-1953), French humorist, playwright and songwriter who also wrote songs for Yvette Guilbert.
Théophile Steinlen (1859-1923), French graphic artist, etcher and lithographer of Swiss descent.

13. Konstantin M. Miklashevsky (1866-1944), Russian theatre scholar, film director and actor. It was at a lecture given by Miklashevsky in Moscow that E first met his future 'spiritual father', Meyerhold (see 'A Family Chronicle', n. 12.)

14. Meyerhold, in a section of his *On Theatre* [O teatre] (St Petersburg, 1913) written in 1911-12, recalled the opening scene of his 1906 production:

In the first scene of Blok's *Fairground Booth* there is a long table covered with a black cloth reaching to the floor and parallel to the footlights. Behind the table sit the 'mystics', the top halves of their bodies visible to the audience. Frightened by some rejoinder, they duck their heads, and suddenly all that remains at the table is a row of torsos minus heads and hands. It transpires that the figures are cut out of *cardboard* with frock-coats, shirt-fronts, collars and cuffs drawn on with soot and chalk. The actors' hands are thrust through openings in the cardboard torsos, and their heads simply rest on the cardboard collars.

Cited from the translation in E. Braun (ed.), *Meyerhold on Theatre* (London; 1969), p. 141.

The Teacher

1. Dated 16 October 1943, this text follows on directly from *The Lady with the Black Gloves*, even though *Otto H. and the Artichokes* was written in between on 15 October.

2. A counter-relief was an abstract composition of metal, wire and wood that had been developed since 1915 by the Russian Constructivist artist, Vladimir Ye. Tatlin (1885-1953) from his earlier three-dimensional painterly reliefs.

3. Russian abbreviation for *proizvodstvennaya odezhda* [literally: 'working clothes'], a term used by the Constructivists to describe the uniform costume of blue linen designed by Lyubov Popova (see below, n. 8) in 1922 and first used by Meyerhold in his production of *The Magnanimous Cuckold* [Le Cocu magnifique/Velikodushnyi rogonosets] by the Belgian dramatist, Fernand Crommelynck (1888-1930). It was Meyerhold's intention that 'against the bare constructions of the set surfaces young actors in blue linen overalls would demonstrate their mastery without make-up, in pure form, as it were, without the aid of theatrical illusions'.

4. Zinaida Raikh, also Reich (1894-1939), Meyerhold's second wife and a member of the Meyerhold Theatre troupe from 1921 until its closure in 1938. She was found brutally murdered with her throat cut on 17 July 1939, a month after her husband's arrest. See R. Leach, *Vsevolod Meyerhold* (Cambridge, 1989), p. 29.

5. NEP, the New Economic Policy, adopted at the end of the Civil War in March 1921, allowed a partial restoration of private enterprise in order to restore the shattered economy to pre-1914 levels. In the cultural sphere the policy gave rise to commercially-orientated activities aimed at entertaining the re-emerging urban middle class, who were characterised as 'Nepmen'.

6. 'Theatrical October' was the programme for the revolutionary renewal and political activisation of theatre proclaimed by Meyerhold on his appointment in November 1920 as head of the Theatre Department [TEO] of Narkompros, the People's Commissariat for Enlightenment, a post he held until May 1921.

7. Ivan A. Aksyonov (1884-1935), Soviet poet, translator and critic, Meyerhold's closest associate in the early 1920s and head of GVYTM, the State Higher Theatre Workshops, in 1922-3. He was also the author of the first biographical essay on E, eventually published posthumously as *Sergei Eizenshtein. Portret khudozhnika* [Sergei Eisenstein. Portrait of an Artist] (Moscow, 1991). See also *'Wie sag ich's meinem Kinde?'*, n. 32.

8. The *budyonovka* or 'Budyonny helmet', introduced into the Red Army in 1919 and named after Semyon M. Budyonny (1883-1973), commander of the First Cavalry Army during the Civil War of 1917-21. The cloth cap was shaped like the ancient Russian metal helmet with a pointed peak, hence the reference in the text to 'the ancient . . . helmet'. E played on this similarity in his drawings for *Alexander Nevsky* in order to underline the topical relevance of his thirteenth-century subject matter.

9. Lyubov S. Popova (1889-1924), Russian Constructivist artist, set and costume designer, responsible for the overalls mentioned above.

10. Isadora Duncan (1878-1927), American dancer who married the Russian poet Sergei A. Yesenin and lived in the USSR from 1921 to 1924. See also n. 15 below.

11. These were the basic slogans of the 'Theatrical October' proclaimed by Meyerhold in 1920 with the intention of 'revolutionising' everyday life in particular.

12. In 1920 these weekly meetings were held on Mondays at the RSFSR Theatre No 1 (as Meyerhold's theatre was then called) to discuss the 'show-meeting' of *The Dawn* [Les Aubes], based on the play by the Belgian dramatist Emile Verhaeren (1855-1916).

13. Nikolai P. Ulyanov (1875-1945), Russian painter and graphic artist who worked with Meyerhold from 1905 till 1935.

14. Konstantin N. Nezlobin (1857-1930), Russian theatrical entrepreneur, director and actor, who owned theatres in Riga and other cities in the Baltic provinces before the Revolution. He worked in Moscow from 1909 to 1917.
Anatoli P. Nelidov (1879-1949), Russian actor who worked in several of Meyerhold's theatres.

15. In his production of Lermontov's *Masquerade* for the Alexandrinsky Theatre in St Petersburg in February 1917 Meyerhold introduced the figure of a blue Pierrot who, during the masquerade of the title, intrigues Nina, the heroine of the play, with the lost bracelet (the motive on which the plot is constructed). Thus a character from the *commedia dell'arte*, integrated into the romantic tragedy through the device of the masked ball, became one expression of the theme of Fate which lay at the base of Meyerhold's conception of the production.
Alexander Ya. Golovin (1863-1930), Russian painter and stage designer who made the sets for Meyerhold's most important pre-Revolutionary productions.

16. Nina G. Kovalenskaya (1888-?) worked at the Alexandrinsky Theatre from 1908 to 1917 and played Nina in *Masquerade* and Fernando in *The Constant Prince*, both in Meyerhold's productions.
Alexander Ya. Zakushnyak (1879-1930) acted with Meyerhold in 1906-7 and again in the 1920s.

17. Ceuta and Oppidomagne are the scenes for the action in Calderón's *The Constant Prince* and Verhaeren's *The Dawn* respectively.

18. From 1914 to 1916 at No. 6 Borodinskaya Street in St Petersburg the Meyerhold Studio produced small-scale experimental

pantomimes, interludes and études.

The Forest, by the Russian dramatist Alexander N. Ostrovsky (1823-86) was however not produced by Meyerhold until 1924, so E is here mistaken.

19. The 'World of Art' [Mir iskusstva] was a group of artists founded in 1898 by Alexander Benois and Sergei Diaghilev. It promoted the aesthetic ideals of *art nouveau* and Symbolism.

20. Boris Ye. Zakhava (1896-1976) acted at the Meyerhold Theatre in 1923-5 but was based from 1913 until his death at the Vakhtangov Theatre.

21. Ludmila Gautier was a choreographer and teacher who worked at GVYTM and with the Proletkult studios. Her husband Alexander F. Gautier (1894-1937) taught boxing at GVYTM.

22. The Battle of Pharsalus was the scene of Caesar's decisive victory in 48 BC.

23. GVYRM: the State Higher Directors' Workshops.

24. Reference to the lost film version of Oscar Wilde's *The Picture of Dorian Gray,* produced by the Thiemann and Reinhardt Company in 1915, which Meyerhold scripted and directed and in which he also played the part of Lord Henry Wotton.

Farewell

1. Written in Moscow on 10 September 1944 (the same day as the chapter *About Myself*) for the collection *Kak ya stal rezhisserom* [How I Became a Director]. This chapter describes a visit by E and Meyerhold to 'the heart of Moscow'—i.e. the Kremlin—at an unknown date.

2. A line from the second couplet of the arietta 'The Purple Negro' by the Russian song-writer Alexander Vertinsky (1889-1957):

    The last time I saw you that close to,

    A car swept you off into the streets

    And I dreamt that somewhere in San Francisco

    A purple negro is handing you your mantle.

3. Viktor B. Shklovsky (1893-1984), in his *Zametki o proze Pushkina* [Observations on Pushkin's Prose] (Moscow, 1937), pointed out that in the epigraphs to *The Captain's Daughter* it is not just the actual lines that are important, but also the preceding and succeeding lines, where significant characteristics forbidden by the tsarist censorship are concealed.

4. In his set designs (especially for the 1901 production of Rimsky-

Korsakov's opera *The Maid of Pskov*) Alexander Golovin (see *The Teacher*, n.15) depicted Russian cathedrals from a truncated upward-looking perspective, reinforced by cupolas that seemed to vanish into the distance, thus creating the effect of monumental architecture.

The Treasure

1. Also written on 10 September 1944, this piece recalls E's rescue of Meyerhold's archive in 1941. There is another account of this in a subsection entitled 'The Treasure' of K. Rudnitskii, 'Krushenie teatra' [The Destruction of a Theatre], *Ogonek* [The Torch], 1988, no. 22 (May), pp. 10-14.
2. Nikolai Raikh, Meyerhold's father-in-law through his second marriage.
3. Maria, Meyerhold's granddaughter by his first marriage.
4. The premises of GVYRM: see *The Teacher*, n. 23.
5. One of Meyerhold's last productions was of the play *The Lady of the Camellias* by Alexandre Dumas *fils*, which had its première on 19 March 1934 with Zinaida Raikh as Marguerite Gauthier. It was also the production with which the Theatre closed in January 1938. Many critics considered the production to be Meyerhold's finest.

Me Too

1. Dated 9 June (or July) 1946.
2. Maxim M. Litvinov (1876-1951), Soviet state and Party functionary and diplomat, People's Commissar for Foreign Affairs from 1930 to 1939. His wife Ivy, née Low (1889-1977) was an English-born writer.
3. Goethe used as a pretext for his departure from the theatre the fact that one of the actors at the Weimar Court Theatre had brought a dog on stage without Goethe's permission.
4. See *Epopée*, n. 100.

The Road to Buenos Aires

1. Undated, but most probably written in June 1946.
2. Jean-Jacques Brousson was secretary to Anatole France (see '*The Knot that Binds*', n. 6) from 1902 to 1909. His second book on the author is entitled *Itinéraire Paris-Buenos Aires*. Albert Londres' book about the recruitment of European women for prostitution in

Brazil was called *The Road to Buenos Aires:* in 1929 E discussed with French film studios the possibility of making a film based on this book.

3. The relevant passage appears to have been lost, if indeed it was ever written.

4. David Alfaro Siqueiros (1898-1974), Mexican painter and political activist, one of the founders of the Mexican school of monumental painting.

5. Jesse L. Lasky (1880-1958), the US film producer who invited E to Hollywood.

6. Vicky Baum's novel was filmed by Edmund Goulding in 1932 and starred Greta Garbo.

7. *Chang* [USA, 1927], documentary film made by Merian Cooper and Ernest Schoedsack about elephants in the Siamese jungle.

8. See *Otto H. and the Artichokes*, pp. 48-9.

9. Major Frank Pease, self-styled 'professional American patriot', led the campaign against E's presence in the USA, denouncing him as part of a 'Jewish Bolshevik conspiracy' to 'turn the American cinema into a communist cesspool'. See: M. Seton, *Sergei M. Eisenstein* (revised edn, London, 1978), especially pp. 167-8.

10. The Hays Office was set up in 1922 as the Motion Picture Producers and Distributors of America, a voluntary censorship organ to ward off the prospect of legislative control: in 1930 it published the Hays Code, which imposed a strict moral framework on American cinema and remained in effect until 1966. The Fish Committee, the forerunner of the post-war McCarthyite House UnAmerican Activities Committee, was responsible for cinema matters and visited Hollywood in October 1930, at Maj. Pease's instigation, to investigate Communist infiltration of American cinema.

11. B. P. Schulberg (1892-1957), American film producer, worked for Paramount from 1925 to 1932.

12. Carl Laemmle (1867-1939), American film tycoon who founded Universal studios in 1912. His son, Carl Jr (b. 1908) was put in charge of Universal production in 1929.

13. Irving Thalberg (1899-1936), US film production executive, Vice-President and supervisor of production at MGM, who provided the model for the hero of Scott Fitzgerald's *The Last Tycoon*.

14. Sylvia Sidney (b 1910) and Clara Bow (1905-65)—known in the 1920s as 'the "It" girl'—were American film actresses.

The Works of Daguerre

1. Undated, with the title written in Pera Atasheva's hand. The numbering of the pages in the manuscript begins with 26 but the other 25 have not been identified, although they may come from one of his theoretical works from the period 1943-6.
2. Mack Sennett (1880-1960), American actor, director and producer. Gordon Craig: see *Foreword*, n. 11.
3. Jean Harlow (1911-37), American film actress and archetypal platinum blonde.
4. See *ESW 1*, pp. 203-5.
5. Reference to the unrealised project for *Sutter's Gold*, based on the novel *Gold* by Blaise Cendrars (1887-1961): see *Epopée*, n. 123. The script has been published in: I. Montagu, *With Eisenstein in Hollywood. A Chapter of Autobiography* (Berlin GDR, 1968), pp. 149-206.
   John August Sutter, a Swiss immigrant, founded his New Helvetia settlement in 1839 and gold was discovered there in 1848.
6. Louis Jacques Mandé Daguerre (1787-1851) and Joseph Nicéphine Nièpce (1765-1833) were French pioneers of photography.
7. Henri Rousseau (1844-1910), French naive painter, known as 'Douanier' because he worked for the Parisian municipal customs service.
8. The most important Russian public library before the Revolution, now forming part of the State Lenin Library in Moscow.
9. Hervey Allen's *Anthony Adverse* was published in 1934.

My Encounter with Magnasco

1. Undated, but probably written in June 1946. It is the only one of a projected series of chapters on 'Encounters with Painting'.
   Alessandro Magnasco (1667-1749) was an Italian painter of melodramatic landscapes.
2. Reference to the Moscow Museum for Modern Western European Painting founded in 1918 on the basis of the nationalised collection belonging to the merchant and art patron Sergei Shchukin. The works are now exhibited in the Pushkin Fine Arts Museum in Moscow and the Hermitage in St Petersburg.
3. This painting, from the year 1889, is reproduced in the book by the Russian art historian Yakov Tugendhold, *Zhizn' i tvorchestvo Polya Gogena* [The Life and Times of Paul Gauguin]: a copy of the second

edition, published in 1918, has been preserved in E's library.

4. Reference to the Expressionist and Fauvist pictures painted before the First World War by the Dutch artist Kees van Dongen (1877-1968).

5. The book by the German art historian, Julius Meier-Graefe, *Die spanische Reise* [Spanish Journey] (Berlin, 1910), played an important part in the recognition of the international significance of El Greco's work.

6. Reference to the five-volume *Geschichte der Malerei* (5 vols, Leipzig, 1902) by the German art historian Richard Muther (1860-1909), translated as *The History of Painting from the Fourth to the Early Nineteenth Century* (2 vols, London & New York, 1907) and to *Geschichte der Kunst aller Zeiten und Völker* [History of the Art of Every Period and People] (3 vols, Leipzig & Vienna, 1900-11) by another German art historian, Carl Woermann (1844-1933).

7. Additional material for the second version of *Bezhin Meadow* was being shot at the Yalta studios in the Crimea in the summer and autumn of 1936. Production was stopped in March 1937, ostensibly because E had run well over budget.

8. Vakulinchuk is the murdered sailor in *Potemkin.* The mourning scenes surrounding his 'lying-in-state' in a tent by the harbour spark off the Odessa Steps massacre.

9. See *The Twelve Apostles*, n. 15.

10. Alexander N. Benois (1870-1960), Russian artist, critic and art historian, leading member of the 'World of Art' group (see *The Teacher*, n. 19).
    Viktor E. Borisov-Musatov (1870-1905), Russian painter.

11. Wilhelm Busch (1832-1908), German poet, caricaturist and illustrator.
    Zinaida Ye. Serebryakova (1884-1967), Russian artist, member of the 'World of Art' group.

12. For Serov, see *Millionaires I Have Met*, n. 4.
    Mstislav V. Dobuzhinsky (1875-1957), Russian graphic artist and set designer, member of the 'World of Art' group. E discusses his 'October Idyll' in *ESW 2*, pp. 125-9.

13. E is mistaken once more about the time scale: no more than ten years had elapsed between the events described and the time of writing.

14. Nikolai K. Cherkasov (1903-66) played the title roles in both *Alexander Nevsky* and *Ivan the Terrible* and is the author of *Notes of a Soviet Actor* (Moscow, n.d.).

837

Museums at Night

1. Undated, but analysis of the paper used suggests 1943-4, rather than 1946. It is possible that E wanted to make use of a text that was originally intended for *Method*.
2. The 'Mona Lisa' was stolen from the Louvre in 1911 and returned two-and-a-half years later after being found in Florence.
3. Jacob Isaacs, known as Jack (1896-1973), lecturer in English Literature at King's College, London and Professor of English Language and Literature at Queen Mary College, London, from 1952 to 1964, and one of the leading members of the London Film Society during its early years.
4. E may have seen 'The Triumph of Caesar' by the Italian painter Andrea Mantegna (c. 1431-1506) during his visit to Hampton Court. It is not clear what the reference to 'The Rape of Ganymede' means. The original painting that E describes is by Rembrandt and is in the Zwinger Gallery in Dresden: E may have seen it exhibited in Moscow in 1945. There is a copy by Rubens in the Prado in Madrid, but E never went there. It is possible that there is another copy somewhere in England, or that the Prado copy was there on temporary loan. At Windsor E may have seen a drawing by Michelangelo on the same subject. Pushkin mentions the Rembrandt painting in his *Journey to Erzerum* (1835) mentioned below.
5. See *The Springs of Happiness*, pp. 674-6.
6. See *An Unremarked Date*, n. 2.
7. What is conventionally known as the Hermitage Museum actually consists of three interlinked buildings: the Winter Palace, the Hermitage proper and the New Hermitage.
8. It is actually in *Boyhood*, Chapter 2 'The Storm'.

Colleagues. (Hospitals. Grosz. Sternberg. Jannings. Supervisors)

1. Dated 16 July 1946, Kratovo, but this was written in the same pink crayon as the corrections and the original text may therefore have been written earlier. The title has been provided by the Russian editors.
2. Reference to Walt Whitman (1819-92), American poet, and the American Civil War.
3. George Grosz (1893-1959), German painter and draughtsman best

known for his savage satirical sketches of the Weimar Republic.

4. See *'The Knot that Binds'*, n. 3.

5. See *The Boy from Riga*, n. 2.

6. *The Scarlet Empress* [USA, 1934] was Sternberg's film version of the life of Catherine the Great, with Marlene Dietrich in the title role.

7. In fact, Rudolf Belling (1886-1972), German-born sculptor.

8. See *Foreword*, n. 15.

9. *The Salvation Hunters* [USA, 1925] was Sternberg's first film as director. It was based on his own script and starred George K. Arthur, who financed the film's budget of $4,800, and Georgia Hale.

10. George Bancroft (1882-1956), American actor, starred in a number of Sternberg's American films, including *Underworld* [1927], *The Docks of New York* [1928] and his first sound film *Thunderbolt* [1929].

Emil Jannings (1884-1905), German actor who played opposite Marlene Dietrich in *The Blue Angel* [Der blaue Engel, Germany, 1930].

Karl Huszar, a.k.a. Mr Charles Puffy, Hungarian film comedian who lived in the USA in the 1920s. He played the minor role of the publican in *The Blue Angel*.

11. Jackie Coogan (1924-84) became famous at the age of seven for his role in Chaplin's *The Kid* [USA, 1921]. In 1930 Paramount contracted him to play Tom Sawyer in the film directed by Norman Taurog.

12. Directed by William Desmond Taylor in 1917.

13. See *The Boy from Riga*, n. 2.

14. Phillips Holmes played Clyde in Sternberg's *An American Tragedy* [USA, 1931] with Sylvia Sidney as Roberta. E's view of the film is conveyed in 'Help Yourself!' [1932] in *ESW 2*, pp. 219-37.

15. Jannings played Mephistopheles in F. W. Murnau's *Faust* [Germany, 1926].

16. Reference to *The Playboy of Paris* [USA, 1930]—the French release title was *Le Petit café*—made by the German director Ludwig Berger (1892-1970), best known for his versions of operettas and his collaboration with Michael Powell and Tim Whelan on *The Thief of Bagdad* [UK, 1940].

17. See *Otto H. and the Artichokes*, n. 6.

18. See *Otto H. and the Artichokes*, n. 4.

19. Greta Garbo, née Gustafsson (1905-90), Swedish-born superstar of Hollywood cinema.

Charlie Chaplin

1. Written in April 1939 for Chaplin's fiftieth birthday but not published at that time. The authorised typescript is marked *Memoirs*. The text has been edited slightly: a passage on Sternberg identical to that in *Colleagues* has been removed, as have the birthday greetings that concluded this piece in its original form.
2. An ironic reference to the criticisms of *Bezhin Meadow* in 1937 when E had been accused of 'Formalism'. See the critique by Boris Shumyatsky, the head of the Soviet film industry, in his 'The Film *Bezhin Meadow*' (19 March 1937), translated in R. Taylor & I. Christie (eds), *The Film Factory. Russian and Soviet Cinema in Documents, 1896-1939* (London & Cambridge, Massachusetts, 1988), pp. 378-80.
3. Douglas Fairbanks had starred in *Robin Hood* in 1922: the world-wide success of the film had led him to add the name of the legendary 'noble robber' to his visiting card. It was in fact *Robin Hood* that replaced *Potemkin* on the two occasions in 1926 when attempts were made to show E's film at a first-run cinema in central Moscow: See R. Taylor, *The Politics of the Soviet Cinema, 1917-1929* (Cambridge, 1979), p. 95. Fairbanks' other films mentioned by E are: *The Mark of Zorro* [1920] and *the Thief of Bagdad* [1921].
4. Joseph M. Schenk (1878-1961), Russian-born Hollywood executive producer, at this time with United Artists but later with 20th Century-Fox. Schenk produced all Buster Keaton's films as well as some of the later works of D. W. Griffith. For Jack Pickford, see *Colleagues*, n.12.
5. Reference to the purpose-built studios constructed from 1927 onwards at Potylikha, in the Sparrow Hills south-west of Moscow, now the headquarters of Mosfilm.
6. Pola Negri, née Apollonia Chatupiec (1894-1987), Polish-born stage and screen actress, associated with the films of Ernst Lubitsch (See *Foreword*, n. 15), especially *Madame Dubarry* [Germany, 1919] in which she starred with Emil Jannings. Her tempestuous affair with Chaplin during the filming of *A Woman of Paris* [1923] lasted nine months and is documented in: D. Robinson, *Chaplin: His Life and Art* (London, 1985), pp. 324-31.

Comrade Léon

1. Written on 15 December 1946, evidently as an introduction to the

Russian translation of Léon Moussinac's *L'Age ingrat du cinéma*
[Cinema's Awkward Age] (Paris, 1946). The translation was not·
published and the essay was included in the memoir materials
under its original title *Comrade d'Artagnan*. It was first published by
Pera Atasheva in the journal *Znamya* [Banner] in 1960.

2. See *Epopée*, n. 8.
3. See *Epopée*, n. 99.
4. Buñuel: see *Epopée*, n. 40.
   Dreyer: see *Epopée*, n. 63.
   Three French films by Cavalcanti (see *Epopée*, n. 75) were shown:
   Rien que les heures [Nothing but Time, 1926], *En rode* [Sea Fever,
   1927] and *Le Petit chaperon rouge* [Little Red Riding Hood, 1929], as
   was one by Man Ray (see *Epopée*, n. 116): *L'Etoile de mer* [Sea Star,
   1928].
   Hans Richter (1888-1976), the German painter and film-maker,
   showed three of his so-called 'absolute films': *Inflation* [1927],
   Vormittagsspuk [Ghosts before Breakfast, 1928]—in which he also
   acted with the composers Paul Hindemith and Darius Milhaud—
   and *Etudes de formes* [Studies in Form, 1929].
   Walter Ruttmann (1887-1941), the German documentary film-
   maker, showed his *Berlin—die Symphonie einer Großstadt* [Berlin.
   Symphony of a Big City, 1927].
   Horizontal-Vertikal Messe [Horizontal-Vertical Mass] by Richter's
   associate, the Swedish painter and animated film-maker Viking
   Eggeling (1880-1925) was also shown.
   Ivens (see *Epopée*, n. 35) was represented by *De Brug* [The Bridge,
   Netherlands, 1928] and *Regen* [Rain, Netherlands, 1929].
5. See *Epopée*, n. 99.
6. The Hon. Ivor Montagu (1904-84), 3rd son of the 2nd Baron
   Swaythling and leading light in British table-tennis between the
   wars, also a film-maker and writer, accompanied E on his travels in
   the West in 1929-30, and was co-author with E of the script for *An
   American Tragedy*. See also *The Works of Daguerre*, n. 5.
7. Georgi Dimitrov, also Dimitroff (1882-1949), Bulgarian Communist
   tried and acquitted on charges of complicity in the February 1933
   Reichstag fire. His trial was held at the Reich Supreme Court in
   Leipzig.
8. Jean-Georges Auriol (1907-50), French critic, founder and editor of
   the journal *Revue du cinéma*, the forerunner of *Cahiers du cinéma*.
   See *Epopée*, n. 27.
9. Béla Balázs (1884-1949), Hungarian author, critic and film theorist,

whose views were the subject of E's riposte 'Béla Forgets the Scissors' (1926) in: *ESW 1*, pp. 77-81.

10. Henri Barbusse (1873-1935), French writer.

11. Paul Vaillant-Couturier (1892-1957), French politician and editor-in-chief of the Communist Party newspaper *L'Humanité*.

12. A paraphrase of Pimen's words in Pushkin's *Boris Godunov* (1825). The collection of Moussinac's articles is *Le Cinéma soviétique* (Paris, 1928).

Pages from Literature

1. This chapter consists of three fragments illustrating the biographical theme *Encounters with Literature*. The untitled first, handwritten fragment is dated 19 August 1944 and was intended as the preface to a projected book on *Montage in Literature*, which was never written. The epigraph is from the collection *Moloko kobylits* [Foals' Milk] (Moscow, 1914) by the Futurist poet Velimir Khlebnikov (1885-1922).

2. Reference to the popular series published by the M. O. Wolf Co. in St Petersburg.

3. Quotation from Pushkin's poem 'Romance' (1814).

4. See also *Novgorod—Los Remedios*, p. 85 and *The Works of Daguerre*, p. 290.

5. The title of a romantic poem by Mikhail Lermontov (1840). *Mtsyri* is the Georgian word for a novice in a religious order.

6. Maxim Gorky, pseudonym of Alexei Peshkov (1868-1936), Russian Realist writer and playwright, returned from self-imposed exile in 1928 and became first president of the Union of Soviet Writers at the time of its founding congress, which adopted the doctrine of Socialist Realism in 1934.

7. Dmitri D. Shostakovich (1906-75) completed the opera *Lady Macbeth of the Mtsensk District* in 1933. It had its première in Leningrad under that title in 1934 but was staged in Moscow by Nemirovich-Danchenko in the same year under the title *Katerina Izmailova*. It was initially a phenomenal success but, when Stalin went to see it, he walked out in a rage and the opera was famously denounced by *Pravda* on 28 January 1936 under the headline 'Muddle instead of Music'. Shostakovich revised it as *Katerina Izmailova* in 1956.

8. Shostakovich's *The Nose* was performed in 1930. Sergei S. Prokofiev (1891-1953) wrote *The Gambler* in 1929 and *War*

and Peace in 1941-2: it was first produced in 1946.

9. Shostakovich's 7th Symphony, the 'Leningrad', op. 60, was first performed in 1942.

10. From a conversation with Ilya Ye. Repin (1844-1940), the Russian painter associated with the 'Wanderers', which was published in *Russkoe slovo* [The Russian Word] on 17 January 1913. E analysed Repin's portrait of Lev Tolstoy: see *ESW 2*, pp. 93-105.

11. Reference to the nineteenth century controversy over Russia's historical destiny between the Slavophiles, who believed in Russia's unique spiritual mission and therefore rejected Peter the Great's reforms, and the Westernisers, who believed in the necessity of those reforms and saw Russia's future in a rapprochement with Western culture and civilisation.

12. The Alexander Nevsky monastery, at the far end of Nevsky Prospekt from the Admiralty in St Petersburg, encompasses the cemetery where many leading figures from Russian cultural life are buried, including Dostoyevsky, Tchaikovsky and many other composers.

13. Mstyora and Palekh are centres for lacquer-work and other crafts in rural Russia. For Sergiev Posad, later Zagorsk and now Troitse-Sergiev Posad, see *Novgorod—Los Remedios*, n. 3.

14. See '*A Family Chronicle*', n. 34.

15. Ahab is the one-legged captain obsessed with his pursuit of the whale in Herman Melville's novel *Moby Dick.*

16. Reference to Konstantin M. Stanyukevich (1843-1903), author of several collections of maritime stories.

17. Like the 'Potemkin', the 'Ochakov' was involved in the events of 1905. In November the crew, led by Lieut. Peter Schmidt, took part in the uprising in Sebastopol.

Encounters with Books

1. The text of this chapter was written with interruptions. The first page is inscribed 'Barvikha, 1 June 1946. Night'. The last part (with the working title *Lawrence. Melville. 'The Love for Three Oranges'* is dated 12 June 1946, but may have been written in May. The sections in between are incomplete, especially the passage about quotations.

2. G. K. Chesterton (1874-1936), English writer and critic.

3. Gottfried Wilhelm Leibniz (1646-1716), German philosopher, mathematician and physicist, who argued that monads were the substances that constitute the real world.

4. Reference to Jonathan Swift's *Gulliver's Travels*, Part 3, Chapter 5.

5. E quotes this in his 'Draft of "Introduction" ', *ESW 2*, p. 7, where he attributes the remark to Gabriel Nandé.

6. The reference to Kurbsky and Ivan is ironic: the Prince betrays Tsar and country but criticises the Tsar's punctuation.

7. A play on words: 'lebeda' is the Russian for 'goose-foot', a weed eaten only by the starving.

8. Otto Rank (1880-1939), Austrian psychologist and psychotherapist, and Hanns Sachs, German psychoanalyst, published *Die Bedeutung der psychoanalyse zur Geisteswiseenschaften* (Wiesbaden, 1913).

9. Isidor Sadger, Austrian philologist.

10. This section was never written.

11. Harry Houdini, né Erich Weiss (1874-1926), Hungarian film actor who became a world-famous escapologist.

12. Archduke Maximilian of Austria, a member of the Habsburg family, was made Emperor of Mexico in 1863, as part of an attempt to spread French influence in Central America, and he and his wife Carlotta were shot by revolutionaries in 1867.

13. Benito Juarez (1806-72), Mexican republican leader: Chief Minister 1855-7 and President 1861-72.

14. Reference to William Dieterle's film *Juarez* [USA, 1939], based on Franz Werfel's play *Juarez und Maximilian.*

15. See the discussion in *ESW 2*, especially pp. 138-46.

16. Primo Carnera (1906-67), Italian world boxing champion.

17. E intended to expand on the theme of pre-logic in *Method*. See also: H. Lövgren, 'Trauma and Ecstasy' in: L. Kleberg & H. Lövgren (eds), *Eisenstein Revisited. A Collection of Essays* (Stockholm, 1987), pp. 93-111.

18. Rockwell Kent (1882-1971), American painter and graphic artist.

19. John Barrymore (1882-1942) did in fact play the part twice on screen: in the silent *The Sea Beast* [1926] and the talkie *Moby Dick* [1930].

20. Lillian Hellman (1905-84), American scriptwriter and dramatist.

21. Most of the studio shots for *Ivan* were filmed at night because in 1943-4 electricity was used in the daytime to keep the armaments factories in Alma-Ata in production. E fell seriously ill with exhaustion: it was his first minor heart attack, which led two years later to his myocardial infarction.

22. Cf. J. Leyda (ed.), *Eisenstein on Disney* (Calcutta, 1986).

23. See 'A Family Chronicle', n. 12.

24. This is a reference to Meyerhold's journal, which he edited under

the pseudonym of Dr Dapertutto, and *not* to Prokofiev's opera, based on Gozzi's fantastic comedy, which was in fact first performed in Chicago in 1921: its first Soviet performance took place in Leningrad in 1927.

25. Fyodor F. Komissarzhevsky (1882-1954), Russian director, scholar and theorist of theatre, was in 1911 a director at Nezlobin's theatre in Moscow (see *The Teacher*, n. 14). He emigrated permanently in 1919.

    Yevgeni B. Vakhtangov (1883-1923), Russian theatre director who tried to reconcile the theoretical differences between Stanislavsky and Meyerhold through his system of fantastic realism. His production of Gozzi's *Princess Turandot* was staged in 1922.

26. Vladimir Veidle (1895-1979), Russian poet.

27. See *Nuné*, n. 9.

28. See *The Teacher*, n. 15.

Bookshops

1. The title derives from the rough plan of 8 June 1946. The first fragment in the manuscript is undated but entitled 'Books': since this word appears elsewhere, it would seem that it was intended as part of a cycle. The second fragment (beginning 'There are town squares that look like halls') bears the dates 13 June and 13 July and the heading *Rue de l'Odéon. Sylvia Beach* crossed out by E. The original plan envisaged an account of a series of bookshops in Moscow and St Petersburg, of encounters with various books, booksellers and bibliophiles, and then of the various theatre stages E had stood on, as theatre-lover or director. This section was never written.

2. Ernest Antoine Aimé Léon, baron Seillière (1866-1955), French sociologist, journalist and critic.

3. Rochefort: see *Dead Souls*, n. 4.

    L'Eclipse (1868-1919) and *L'Assiette au beurre* (1901-36) were French satirical papers.

4. Kuno Fischer (1824-1907), German Idealist philosopher, author of the ten-volume *Geschichte der neueren Philosophie* [History of Modern Philosophy].

5. In fact these stations are now, respectively, the Moscow station in St Petersburg and the Savelovsky station in Moscow.

6. A play on the word 'Aurora': as the name of the cruiser that fired the shot signalling the storming of the Winter Palace on the night

of 25 October 1917; as the heroine of Tchaikovsky's ballet *Sleeping Beauty*; and as the Roman goddess of the dawn.

7. Characters from the *commedia dell'arte*. Harlequin (Arlecchino) was dim-witted and famished; the Captain (Capitano) a braggart soldier; and Brighellà crafty and unscrupulous.

8. Lev (also Léon) S. Bakst (1866-1924), painter and member of the 'World of Art' group, principally a set and costume designer (e.g. for Diaghilev's *Ballets russes*) but also highly regarded for his book illustrations, which were published in very expensive editions.

9. Giovanni Battista Piranesi (1720-78), Venetian architect who recorded the antiquities of Rome in hundreds of etchings. The reference here is to the series of etchings of imaginary and megalomaniac prisons, the *carceri d'invenzione* [prisons of invention], dating originally from 1749-50 and re-worked in 1761.

10. Darius Milhaud (1892-1974), French composer, conductor and critic.

11. See *Epopée,* n. 21.

12. Otto H. Kahn: see *Otto H. and the Artichokes*, n. 4.
    George Romney (1734-1802), English portrait painter.

13. Adrienne Monnier (1892-1955), French poetess, memoirist and Paris bookshop owner.
    Sylvia Beach (1887-1962), publisher and owner of the 'Shakespeare & Co.' bookshop in Paris, publisher of Joyce's *Ulysses*.
    Jean-Paul is in fact Léon-Paul Fargue (1898-1947), French poet.

14. Cited in English from: A. Monnier, 'In the Land of Faces', *Verve*, 1939, no. 5-6. A copy of this issue reached E only on 22 April 1946.

15. Paul Verlaine (1844-96), French Symbolist poet. *Hombres* was banned because of its homoerotic content.

16. Harris: see : *Foreword*, p. 4.

17. Thineas T. Barnum (1810-91), founder and owner of America's greatest circus, Barnum and Bailey; see *'Wie sag ich's meinem Kinde?'*, n. 37.

18. See *Le Bon Dieu*, n. 13.

19. See *ESWI*, p.33.

20. See *Nuné*, n. 3.

21. Carry A. Nation, née Carry Amelia Moore (1846-1911), American political activist. Jay Leyda has pointed out that Carlton Beals, who lived in, and wrote numerous books on, Latin America, was not her son, but her god-son.

22. The original idea for the film project *Black Majesty* (about the black uprising at the end of the 18th century against French rule and, in

E's words, the 'tragedy of the transformation of a leader into a despot') came to E in the summer of 1930 in Hollywood and was rejected by Paramount. A year later in Mexico E did a series of drawings on the subject. He returned to the theme back in Moscow in both his lectures at VGIK, the Film Institute, and his writings. One of the May sketches for the *Memoirs* devoted to unmade films contains this line: 'The "Black Predecessor" (Henri Christophe as forerunner * for Ivan)' [* in English].

Paul Robeson (1896-1976), the black American singer and actor, visited E in Moscow in December 1934 to discuss the project, which never came to fruition.

23. John Reed (1887-1920), American journalist, remembered for his coverage of the Mexican and Russian revolutions, the latter in his *Ten Days that Shook the World.*

    Ambrose Bierce (1842-1914), American writer and humorist, who went missing during the Mexican civil war.

24. Francisco Villa, nicknamed Pancho (1877-1923) and Emiliano Zapata (1877-1919) were leading figures in the Mexican Revolution of 1910-17.

    Viva Villa! [USA, 1934] was directed by Jack Conway.

25. See *Dead Souls*, n. 4.

26. See *Foreword*, n. 11.

27. See *Epopée*, n. 107.

    Louis Péricaud (1835-1909), French art historian, actor and playwright. His book about the Théâtre des Funambules appeared in 1897.

28. Diego Rivera (1886-1957), Mexican painter and muralist much inspired by traditional folk motifs.

29. Edward Lear (1812-88), author of *The Book of Nonsense* (1846).

    Lewis Carroll, pseudonym of Charles L. Dodgson (1832-98), author of *Alice in Wonderland* and *Alice through the Looking-Glass.*

    Sidney J. Perelman (1904-79), American writer and cartoonist.

    James G. Thurber (1894-1961), American writer and caricaturist.

    Jessy A. Stagg, American painter and graphic artist.

    Saul Steinberg (b. 1914), American caricaturist.

30. George Arliss (1868-1946), English stage and screen actor, starred in *Old English* [USA,1930].

31. Louis N. Parker's play *Disraeli* was twice filmed in Hollywood with Arliss in the title role: by Henry Kolker in 1921 and Alfred Green in 1929. E saw the latter version in London.

32. Paul De Kruif, American bacteriologist and author of popular

scientific books.

33. Dzhambul Dzhambayev (1846-1945), popular Kazakh poet.

34. See *The Teacher*, n. 3.

35. General Heinz Guderian (1888-1954), German tank general in charge of the Panzer divisions in the Second World War.

36. Quotation from the play *The Blue Bird* [L'Oiseau bleu] (1908) by Maurice Maeterlinck (see *Foreword*, n. 6), which had its première in Moscow.

37. The site of the Mosfilm studios at Potylikha.

38. The nickname for Tisse who, like E, was born in Latvia.

Books on the Road

1. The plan for this chapter was sketched out on 8 June 1946 in Barvikha and the text written later after *Bookshops*.

2. A paraphrase of the passage in Heinrich von Kleist's (1777-1811) *'Über das Marionettentheater'* [On the Marionette Theatre], *Sämtliche Werke* [Collected Works] (Leipzig, n.d.), pp. 134ff: 'At its purest grace is apparent in a human body whose consciousness is either non-existent or unending, i.e. in a marionette or god.'

3. Gordon Craig (see *Foreword*, n. 3), in support of his theory of the 'sole will of the director', argued that the ideal representation of the director's conception could be guaranteed by a 'hypermarionette', i.e. by a larger-than-life-size doll like those used in cult worship in the ancient Orient and Greece.

4. Paul Lacroix (1806-84), French author of historical novels and books on the history of costume in France, such as *XVIIIme Siècle: Institutions, usages et costumes, France 1700-1789* [The 18th Century: Institutions, Customs and Costumes, 1700-89] (Paris, 1875).

5. At this point in the manuscript there is a hiatus and reference to a quotation. In the Russian translation the review of Balzac's 'Two Fools: A Story from the Time of François I' by P. L. Jacob the Bibliophile, Member of Every Academy, E partly underlined this passage:

. . . it is sad to see how life, which could be better used to be of more use to society, is wasted on childish imitation of archaic turns of phrase and the usage of words that have long disappeared from our vocabulary . . . In a more progressive era he resurrects archaic forms which do not correspond to new view or new data on ancient times . . . This means giving memory preference over thought.

Recollection has significance only for prediction.

Bal'zak ob iskusstve [Balzac on Art] (Moscow & Leningrad, 1941), pp. 476-7. Balzac's position corresponds to E's own stylistic conception during the making of *Ivan*.

6. Tabarin, pseudonym of Antoine Girard (1584-1633), French actor who performed on the streets of Paris in short scenes that he wrote himself.

7. See *Why I Became a Director*, n. 5.

8. Arsène Lupin was the gentleman thief who was the hero of works by the French author Maurice Leblanc (1864-1941).

Javert was a police informer, a character in Victor Hugo's *Les Misérables*.

Fantômas was the main character in the eponymous adventure stories by Marcel Allain and Pierre Souvestre and the subject of a five-part film serial [France, 1913-14], which they scripted and Louis Feuillade directed.

Paul Féval: see *Epopée*, n. 67.

Rocambole is the hero of the novel by Ponson du Terrail (see *Madame Guilbert*, n. 3).

Captain Fracasse is the eponymous hero of the novel by Théophile Gautier (1811-72).

9. Old quarter of Paris, once the refuge of beggars and cripples, depicted by Victor Hugo in his novel *Notre-Dame de Paris*.

10. This was to film the sequence with the white horse for *October*.

11. The hero of Maeterlinck's play *La Mort de Tintagiles* [The Death of Tintagiles].

12. Claude, Comte de Saint-Simon (1760-1825), French Utopian Socialist.

13. Louis-Henri Boussenard (1847-1910), French author of popular adventure stories

Robert Louis Stevenson (1850-94), Scottish author whose works include *Treasure Island, Dr Jekyll and Mr Hyde* and *The Master of Ballantrae*.

Xavier de Montépin (1823-1910), French author of numerous historical novels, some of which were dramatised.

14. Capt. William Kidd (1680-1701) was hanged as a pirate in London. Legend has it that he buried stolen treasure in various places around the world.

On Bones

1. Undated, but it is clear from the text that it was written immediately after the previous chapter.
2. Henry Rider Haggard (1856-1925), English author of historical and adventure stories.
3. From the 13th to the 18th centuries the Flemish port of Bruges [Brugge] was a centre of world trade but it lost its importance as the estuary silted up. E was familiar with the novel by the Belgian writer Georges Rodenbach *Bruges la morte* [Bruges the Dead].
4. Hara-Hoto was the ruins of a city in the Gobi Desert discovered in 1907 by the Russian explorer Pyotr K. Kozlov (1905-73).
5. A line from Pushkin's poem 'The Ballad of Oleg the Wise' (1822).
6. Quotation from Pushkin's poem 'Ruslan and Ludmila' (1817-20).
7. See *'The Knot that Binds'*, n. 2.

My Encounter with Mexico

1. The manuscript of this chapter has either been lost or not yet found. In E's archive there is a typewritten copy of the first part of the text without date or title. It is possible that the ending is missing since the text ends abruptly: 'Here the whole world is immersed in a hot marshy hollow, its surface coated by a boiling yellow-green mire (p.417).' The second part is taken from a manuscript of 1943 belonging to the book on *Method*. The Russian editors have decided to include it because of the numerous references to other texts in the *Memoirs*.
2. Reference to the hero of the novel *Neobychainye pokhozhdeniya Khulio Khurenito i ego uchenikov* [The Unusual Adventures of Julio Jurenito and His Apprentices], written in 1920-1 by Ilya G. Ehrenburg (1891-1967).
3. Reference to the production of *The Mexican*: see *Le Bon Dieu*, n. 13, and *ESW 1*, p. 33.
4. Reference to the fantasy *The Student of Prague*, devised by Hanns Heinz Ewers and Paul Wegener for their 1913 film, the first German 'art' film. The story was re-made as a film by Henrik Galeen [Germany, 1926] and Arthur Robitz [USA, 1935] and re-worked into a novel by Ewers.
5. Reference to Oscar Wilde's poem 'The Disciple'.
6. See *'The Knot that Binds'*, n. 6.
7. See *'A Family Chronicle'*, n. 34.

8. Cuauhtémoc (1495-1522), the last Aztec king, led the resistance against the Spanish Conquistadores and was forced to surrender his capital. On the orders of Cortés he was tortured and hanged.
9. See *The Road to Buenos Aires*, n. 9
10. In the manuscript there is space for a quotation. In E's copy of *Mexican Maze* these two paragraphs are underlined.

Autobiography

1. Undated.
2. See *Why I Became a Director*, n. 13.

'Wie sag ich's meinem Kinde?'

1. This chapter was written in several parts: the manuscript of the first is dated 13 June 1946, the second 14 June, the insertion ('The somewhat Nietzschean title...) 3 July, and the last part ('And so...'), 18 June 1946. There are in addition notes (dated 18 and 27 June) for possible additions and amendments.
2. The honours system in tsarist Russia was almost as complicated as the system of ranks of the nobility. The four-class Order of St Vladimir was instituted in 1782 for service to the country, bravery in battle or long service. It was second only to the order of St Andrew the First-Named and among the distinguished recipients were Derzhavin and Karamzin. The Order of St Anne joined the statute of Russian decorations in 1797 and later had four classes: it was principally a military award for junior officers.
3. In the operetta *Die Fledermaus* [The Bat, 1874] by Johann Strauss (1825-99) the leading male character is called Eisenstein. The *dénouement* described here, when Eisenstein is unmasked as the eponymous 'Bat', takes place in the final act.
4. In ancient Rome the Penates were the household gods, while the Lares were the souls of virtuous dead ancestors who acted as guardians of the family and of those who lived in the family home.
5. Reference to Blok's play *The Fairground Booth* (1906), in which the fate of the actors in the booths symbolises the fate of the theatre and of art in general. See also *The Lady with the Black Gloves*, n. 14.
6. The opening lines of Blok's poem 'Willow Wands' (1906).
7. The ending *'ishche'* in Russian denotes something very large.
8. Jean-Baptiste de Grécourt (1683-1743), French abbot and author of frivolous verses.

851

Evariste Désiré de Parny (1753-1814), French poet.

Stanislaw Jean, Marquis de Boufflers (1738-1814), French officer and writer of gallant verses.

9. See *Bookshops*, n. 29.

10. Reference to the old Russian custom of fortune-telling on Christmas Night when unmarried girls would try, with the aid of mirrors and candles, to find out who their future husband was going to be.

11. The flat where E was brought up in Riga: now *Kr. Valdemara iela*.

12. Now *Elizabetes iela*, 10a/10b. The buildings designed by E's father are discussed in J. A. Krastiņš, *Stil' modern v arkhitekture Rigi* [Art Nouveau in Riga Architecture] (Moscow, 1988).

13. A Czech gymnastics system developed by M. Tyrš and popular in Russia at the beginning of the twentieth century.

14. Play by Sergei M. Tretyakov (1892-1939) produced by E at the Proletkult First Workers' Theatre in 1923.

15. *A and F* or *Ace and Fop* was a vaudeville written by P. S. Fyodorov. The role of the domestic tyrant Mordashev was played by A. Martynov and not, as E asserts, the great Russian actor P. Mochalov.

16. There is a space here in the manuscript for E's favourite quotation from p. 2 of his copy of *Louis Lambert*, included here.

17. In the early thirties E had closely studied the works of Lucien Lévy-Bruhl (1857-1939), French ethnographer and psychologist and author of studies of pre-logical thought and used many of his observations in the context of his work on the *Grundproblematik*. E was particularly interested in *La Mentalité primitive* [Primitive Thought] (1922) and *Le Surnaturel at la nature dans la mentalité primitive* [The Supernatural and Nature in Primitive Thought] (1931).

18. Gustave Doré (1832-83), the most celebrated French designer of wood-engraved book illustrations of the nineteenth century.

19. E is mistaken: the original manuscript was dated 8 March 1928 and the article 'Our *October*. Beyond the Played and the Non-Played' appeared in two parts in *Kino* in the issues dated 13 and 20 March 1928, and not in *Kinogazeta* in 1927; translated in *ESW 1*, pp. 101-6. This quotation opens the second part of the article.

20. This attribution is correct! Translated in *ESW 1*, pp. 151-60.

21. E discusses these episodes in both *ESW 1* and *ESW 2*.

22. Nicolaus Cusanus (1401-64), German philosopher, mathematician and cardinal, trusted adviser to Pope Pius II.

23. Lin Yutang (1895-1976) published a number of books designed to introduce the Orient to the Western reader, such as *My Country and*

My People (London, 1936) and *The Importance of Living* (London, 1938).

Mei Lan-Fan: See: *On Folklore*, n. 22.

Marcel Granet (1884-1940), French Sinologist and sociologist.

24. Leonid A. Nikitin collaborated with E on the sets for both *The Mexican* and *Lena* for Proletkult.

25. Father John of Kronstadt, popular name for Ioann I. Sergiev (1829-1908), was a well-known priest and bishop in the Orthodox Church.

26. Quotation from the aria sung by the Hindu merchant in the opera *Sadko* (1898) by Nikolai A. Rimsky-Korsakov (1844-1908). The aria portrays India as a land of gems and mystery, a dream world.

27. Sirin is a fabulous bird and Alkonost a human face from old Slav mythology.

28. Ida L. Rubinstein (1885-1960) appeared in 1913 in Meyerhold's production of *Pisanella* by the Italian poet and dramatist Gabriele d'Annunzio (1863-1938) at the Théâtre du Châtelet, and *not* at the Opéra.

29. At the end of his play *The Government Inspector* Gogol envisaged a 'dumb scene' when the officials are paralysed at the news that the real inspector has arrived. In his 1926 production Meyerhold turned this into a 'dead scene', in which live actors were suddenly replaced by enormous dolls.

30. Meyerhold's lavish production of Lermontov's *Masquerade* had its first performance on 25 February 1917, the eve of the February Revolution. See: E. Braun, *The Theatre of Meyerhold. Revolution on the Modern Stage* (London, 1979), pp. 135-44.

31. For Lindhorst, see *Why I Became a Director*, n. 7.

32. For Aksyonov, see *The Teacher*, n. 7. In his copy of Aksyonov's book *Shakespeare* (Moscow, 1937), pp. 310-11, E has marked off a paragraph that obviously reminded him of the author's lecture at GVYRM:

In his true tragedies, the cycle which begins with *Hamlet*, Shakespeare invariably constructs the action around the opposition between three characters. The first is the complete embodiment of a false principle (the old, the feudal or the archaic - the amoral); the second tries to master the means of overcoming the dictates of the old world; the third stands firmly on the ground of a new consciousness. It is, of course, the middle character who is the principal figure in the tragedy, the focus for the conflict. His inner victory over the contradictions in his own consciousness unlocks the tragedy, turning Hamlet, let us say, who overcomes the Laertes within himself, into Fortinbras, or elevating Macbeth to a Macduff, Othello to Desdemona.

33. The monodrama *In the Backstage of the Soul* [V kulisakh dushi] by Nikolai Yevreinov (see *Why I Became a Director*, n. 12) was first staged in 1911.

34. Bronislava I. Rutkovskaya (1880-1969 and Vladimir A. Sinitsyn (1893-1930) both acted in Nezlobin's theatre (see *The Teacher*, n. 14) in the 1920s.

35. Nikolai N. Sapunov (1880-1912) painted the sets for Meyerhold's production of Blok's *The Fairground Booth* in 1906 (see *The Lady with the Black Gloves*, n. 14).
   The Church of the Transfiguration of the Saviour on the Nereditsa Hill near Novgorod, constructed in 1198, was one of the masterpieces of mediaeval Russian architecture and fresco painting. It was destroyed during the Second World War.

36. Meyerhold's production of Ibsen's *Nora* was first staged on 20 April 1922 at the Actor's Theatre in Moscow, so that E's chronology is once again misleading.

37. Florenz Ziegfeld (1867-1932), American theatre impresario, founder of the 'Ziegfeld Follies' in New York.
   Mistinguette, pseudonym of Jeanne Bourgeois (1873-1956), French cabaret artiste.
   Katherine Cornell (1898-1974), American actress, director and theatrical impresario.
   Lynne Fontanne (1887-1983), British-American stage and screen actress, wife of Alfred Lunt (1892-1977), American stage and screen actor.
   Alla A. Nazimova (1879-1945), Russo-American actress who studied with Stanislavsky at the Moscow Art Theatre and later became a leading interpreter of Ibsen on the Broadway stage and one of the major silent film stars.
   Montegius, pseudonym of Gaston Brounswick (1872-1952), French *chansonnier*.
   Raquel Meller, Spanish singer, actress and revue star, who appeared in the title role in Jacques Feyder's film *Carmen* [France, 1926].
   Max Reinhardt, see *Nuné*, n. 5.
   Mikhail M. Fokine (1880-1942), Russian dancer and choreographer who created the ballet movements for *The Firebird* (1910) and

Petrushka (1912) by Igor Stravinsky (1882-1971).

Tamara P. Karsavina (1889-1978), Russian ballerina, member of Diaghilev's Ballets Russes company.

Al Jolson, pseudonym of Joseph Rosenblatt (1883-1950), Russian-born American variety singer and actor who appeared in the first talkie *The Jazz Singer* [USA, 1927].

James A. Bailey (1846-1906), American circus entrepreneur, associate of and successor to Barnum (see *Bookshops*, n. 17).

Primo Carnera: see *Encounters with Books*, n. 16.

Sergei I. Utochkin (1876-1915/16), pioneering Russian aviator who established the first public flights between various Russian cities in 1910-11.

Jackie Coogan: see *Colleagues*, n. 11.

Yehudi Menuhin (b. 1916), American-born British violinist of Russian parentage.

Nadezhda V. Plevitskaya, née Vinnikova (1884-1941), Russian *chanteuse*.

Vladimir A. Sukhomlinov (1848-1926), Russian general and, from 1909 to 1915, War Minister. Tried in 1916 for inadequately preparing the Russian Army for the First World War and sentenced to life imprisonment; died in emigration.

Alexei A. Brusilov (1883-1926), Supreme Commander of the South Western Front during the First World War.

PART TWO: The True Paths of Discovery

Monkey Logic

1. Written on 22 June 1946 in Barvikha.
2. See *Nuné*, n. 9.
3. Mikhail A. Kuznetsov (b. 1918) played this part in *Ivan the Terrible.*

The History of the Close-Up

1. E began this on 26 June 1946 in Barvikha but never completed it. He left gaps for quotations from examples that he had used elsewhere. Some of these quotations have been included where they are essential for an understanding of the general sense of the text. The final part, beginning with 'This was on another occasion', is taken from the manuscript for *Method*.

2. Kazusika Hokusai (1760-1849), Japanese painter and engraver particularly noted for his views of Mount Fuji, a considerable influence on the French Impressionists. See also *ESW 1*, pp. 211-12, and *ESW 2*, pp. 120-1.

3. E is referring to his work on 'The History of the Close-Up in the History of Art', which was completed in draft form in 1943 but which he continued working on until October 1947. Part of it was published as 'Dikkens, Griffit i my' [Dickens, Griffith and Ourselves]; see '*The Twelve Apostles*', n. 22

4. The insect in Poe's story is in fact a death's-head moth.

5. The 28 mm wide-angle lens was the widest available in E's time. It preserved considerable depth of focus and therefore made it possible to pass from medium close-ups to deep-focus *mise-en-scène* shots.

6. E used examples from Pushkin's 'Poltava' in 'Pushkin the Montageur' and 'Montage 1938', translated by Michael Glenny in *ESW2*: the extract following in the text is from p. 222.
   E also used examples from Milton's 'Paradise Lost' for the first English publication of 'Montage 1938' under the title 'Word and Image' in J. Leyda (ed.), *The Film Sense* (London, 1943), pp. 52-7.

7. The following extract contrasting a scene from Gogol's *Taras Bulba* (1839) with Kuleshov's treatment is taken from E's unfinished 'Montage in Literature' (1941).

8. Lev V. Kuleshov (1899-1970), Soviet film director and theorist who first developed the notion that montage was central to the specificity of cinema. This quotation is from his *Osnovy kinorezhissury* [The Foundations of Film Directing] (Moscow, 1941), pp. 66-7.

9. N. V. Gogol, *Polnoe sobranie sochinenii* [Complete Collected Works] (Moscow, 1937), vol. 2, p. 142. (E's reference)

10. Pathfinder was the eponymous hero of stories by James Fenimore Cooper.

That's Just It

1. This chapter consists of three fragments, the first of which is dated 28 June 1946.

2. A Russian omen.

3. Otto Weininger (1880-1903), psychologist of sex and author of *Geschlecht und Charakter* (1903), translated as *Sex and Character* (1906)

4. The Sigurança was the secret police in the Kingdom of Romania. For Barbusse, see *Comrade Léon*, n. 10.

5. Grigori S. Skovoroda (1722-97), Ukrainian philosopher, poet and scholar. The epigraph is taken from his 'Dialogue or Talk about the Ancient World' and misquoted by Leskov: 'Stand, if you will, on level ground and have a hundred mirrors placed around you. Then you will see that your body mass has a hundred aspects but, when the mirrors are taken away, all the copies disappear. Our body mass is however just like a shadow of the real person. This creature represents, like an ape, the visible presence of the invisible and individual strength and divinity of the person, of whom all our body masses are but shadowy reflections.'

Monsieur, madame, et bébé

1. This text was written in two or three drafts. The date on the first page—14 July 1946, Kratovo—probably relates to the date of editing.
2. A jocular reference to the 'blue'and 'pink'periods in the early work of Pablo Picasso.
3. *La Nietzschéenne* was a popular novel published in 1907 under the nom-de-plume of Daniel Lesueur, the pseudonym of Henry Lapauze (1865-1927), Curator of the Petit Palais gallery in Paris, and his wife, Jeanne Loiseau.
4. Pierre Coulevain was the pseudonym of Augustine Favre de Coulevain (1888-1913). Her novel *Sur la branche* [On the Branch] was published in 1904.
5. E's mistake: *The Semi-Virgins* was written by Marcel Prévost.
6. *The Stages of Vice* [Les Etapes du vice] is incorrect. The proper title of this work by the Marquis de Sade is *Histoire de Juliette ou Les Prospérités du vice* [The Story of Juliet, or the Joys of Vice].
7. Gyp was the pseudonym of the French woman writer Sibylle-Gabrielle-Marie-Antoinette de Riquetti de Mirabeau, Comtesse de Martel et Janville (1849-1932), who wrote popular and somewhat salacious novels.
8. Moreau (see *An Unmarked Date* n. 8) illustrated the works of Molière, Voltaire and Rousseau.
   Charles Eysen (1720-78), French graphic artist.
   Gravelot, pseudonym of Hubert François Bourguignon (1699-1773), French painter, graphic artist and engraver.
   All three are represented in Lacroix: see *Books on the Road*, n. 4.
9. Octave Mirbeau (1850-1917), French writer of erotica.
   For Sacher-Masoch, see *The Lady with the Black Gloves,* n. 8.

10. Meller-Zakomelsky was the Governor-General of the Baltic provinces who brutally suppressed the revolutionary events of 1905 in that region of the Russian Empire.

11. The problem of 'pathetic construction' began to interest E particularly after the success of *Potemkin*. In *The General Line* he set out to introduce pathos into 'inherently non-pathetic' (rural) material. His first attempt to generalise theoretically from this experience was his unfinished essay 'How Pathos Is Created' (1929), later re-worked into 'Pathos' (1945-7), part of *Nonindifferent Nature* (Cambridge, 1987), pp. 38-199.

12. E's ironic term for the analysis of the derivation of words in the history of art.

13. Cf 'The Montage of Film Attractions' (1924) in *ESW 1*, pp. 39-58.

14. At its fullest in the first part of *Direction* in 'The Art of *Mise-en-scène*' (as yet unpublished).

15. Cf *Nonindifferent Nature*, p. 27. We have preferred our own translation.

16. The Khlysts were a mid-17th century Russian religious sect who believed that, by ecstatic rituals, including 'zealous whipping' (with a whip known as a *khlyst*—hence the sect's name) and 'running around in circles', they could drive evil spirits from their bodies and effect the resurrection and reincarnation of Christ in Man.

17. Frank Alexander (1891-1964), American psychologist, head of the Chicago school of psychoanalysis. *Imago* was the journal founded by Freud in 1912.

18. Sandor Ferenczi (1873-1933), Hungarian neurologist and pupil of Alexander. His *Versuch einer Genitaltheorie* (1924) has been translated as *Thalassa: A Theory of Genitality* (1949).

19. From Chapter 80, 'The Nut'.

Pre-Natal Experience

1. Written on 5 July 1946 and probably intended as an introduction to part of *Method*.

To the Illustrious Memory of the Marquis

1. Almost certainly written on 15 and 16 July 1946 and probably initially intended as an insert into *Monsieur, madame et bébé* but later grew into a separate chapter.

2. Nikita V. Bogoslavsky (b. 1913), Soviet composer.

3. Leonid O. Utyosov (1895-1982), leading Soviet jazz musician.

4. There is an untranslatable pun in Russian which plays on the two meanings of *polovoi*—'sexual' and 'waiter'.

5. Simon Bolivar y Ponte (1783-1830) led the struggle for the independence of Latin America from Spain.

6. John Grierson (1898-1972), British documentary film-maker, theorist and producer.

7. See: Matthew, 13, 45-6: 'Again, the kingdom of heaven is like unto a merchant man, seeking goodly pearls: Who, when he had found one pearl of great price, went and sold all that he had, and bought it.'

8. See *Epopée*, n. 77.

9. Vicomte Mathieu de Noailles, husband of the poet Anna-Elisabeth de Noailles (1876-1933), whose salon was frequented by Cocteau and Colette.

10. A play on Nekrasov's poem 'The Pedlars' which became a popular Russian song: 'Oh, my basket is full, full of calico and brocade.'

11. Margarita I. Rtishcheva, Russian popular entertainer who specialised in imitating singers of different nationalities. The actual inscription read: 'Here's a little book for your journey! Perhaps you'll be bored enough to read it and smile. It's eighteenth century. Who knows? Perhaps Pushkin held it in his hands and leafed through these yellowing pages! 19.8.29'

12. See p. 209

13. See *The Road to Buenos Aires*, n. 2.

14. The German translation of E's autobiography attributes this work to Victor Mirabeau, but he was an eighteenth-century French economist. The reference is almost certainly to Sibylle-Gabrielle-Marie-Antoinette de Riqueti de Mirabeau: see *Monsieur, madame et bébé*, n. 7. In 1905 she published *Journal d'un casserolé* [The Diary of a Man Betrayed]. She is *not* to be confused with Octave Mirbeau (see *Monsieur, madame et bébé*, n. 9).

15. Herbert S. Gorman, American literary historian, author of *The Incredible Marquis* (1929).

16. Flexatone was a trade mark.

17. Walter Hasenclever (1890-1940), German Expressionist dramatist and poet.

18. 'Diabolo' was an early twentieth-century game in which a two-headed top was spun, tossed and caught on a string attached to two sticks, held one in each hand.

19. E often makes metaphorical use of the terms 'left'—to denote an

earlier, more primitive stage—and 'right' to denote a later, more developed stage. These usages possibly derive from his interest in graphology.

20. H. Marshall (ed.), *Nonindifferent Nature* (Cambridge, 1987), pp. 3-37.

21. Cf. Matthew, 27, 51: 'And, behold the veil of the temple was rent in twain from the top to the bottom; and the earth did quake and the rocks rent.'

22. The Iberian Gate contained a chapel where the tsar always worshipped when arriving from outside Moscow before entering the Kremlin. It was destroyed in the reconstruction leading to the building of the Hotel Moscow between Manège Square and Okhotny ryad in 1930.

23. The *veche* was the popular assembly through which Novgorod was governed in the thirteenth century.

24. Nikolai N. Breshko-Breshkovsky (1874-1943), Russian journalist.

25. Nat Pinkerton was the fictitious hero of serial detective stories by anonymous authors. The character's name was widely used by the Russian avant-garde in the 1920s, especially as a generic term.
    The Caves of Leuchtweiss was a historical novel which also appeared anonymously.
    Nick Carter and Ethel King were the main characters in popular adventure stories.

26. General Joaquim Amaro, Mexican War Minister in the 1920s.

27. See *Bookshops*, n. 24.

28. Materials for *Que viva México!* were edited without E's consent into *Thunder over Mexico*, which was premièred in May 1933. *Viva Villa!* was released in 1934.

29. The action of Béla Bartók's opera *Duke Bluebeard's Castle* revolves around the mysteries concealed behind seven doors.

30. Joseph Schildkraut (1895-1964), American stage and screen actor of Austrian descent.

31. Robert François Damiens (1715-57) attempted to kill Louis XV with a knife and was hanged in a particularly gruesome manner.

32. Ivan F. Gorbunov (1831-95), Russian actor and writer.
    Evenings on a Farm near Dikanka was a series of stories by Nikolai Gogol which included *Sorochintsy Fair*, *Christmas Eve* and *A Terrible Revenge*.

33. Armand Dayot (1857-?), French art historian whose works include *L'Invasion. Le Siècle 1870. La Commune 1871* [Invasion. The Century 1870. The Commune 1871].

34. By 'Nuremberg Maiden' [*Nürnberger Jungfrau*] E means the 'iron maiden', an instrument of torture used by the Inquisition. It consisted of a kind of iron cupboard in the shape of a townswoman of the sixteenth century lined on the inside with long sharp nails which pierced the incarcerated victim when the door was closed. One of the most famous of these 'iron maidens' was kept in Nuremberg, hence the reference.

35. See *Novgorod—Los Remedios*, n. 3.
The 'Hussar', the 'Lady' etc. were standard toy designs from this town.

36. At the turn of the century Riga was predominantly a German-speaking port with a Latvian-speaking native population in the agricultural hinterland and a governing class of Russian civil servants.

37. Reference to the battle scene in *Alexander Nevsky* and to the third part of *Ivan the Terrible*, a significant part of which was to deal with the war between Ivan and the Livonian Order (1558-83) to secure an outlet for Russia on to the Baltic Sea.

38. Edmund Meisel (1874-1930), Austrian-born musician and composer who wrote scores for the German performances of these films.

39. The headquarters of the state cinema organisations Goskino and Sovkino in the 1920s and indeed still the headquarters of the State Committee for Cinema (by then once more called Goskino!) at the time of the dissolution of the USSR in 1991.

40. Now Mezaparks to the north-east of Riga.

41. See *The Road to Buenos Aires*, n. 9.

42. Now Bulduri, part of the town of Jūrmala.

43. Especially in the articles 'Vertical Montage' (1939-40), *ESW 2*, pp. 327-99, and 'Nonindifferent Nature' (1945-7) in *Nonindifferent Nature*, pp. 216-396.

44. Edinburg is now Dzintari.
For Strauch, see *Names*, n. 3.

45. Vera G. Muzykant was an actress who worked at the Proletkult First Workers' Theatre.

46. Ivan A. Pyriev (1901-68), Soviet film director who acted in the First Workers' Theatre and the Meyerhold Theatre. He acted in E's production of *Wise Man* and his first film *Glumov's Diary*.

47. *Chasing the Moonshine* [Gonka za samogonkoi, 1924] was a short film made by Abram M. Room (1894-1976).

48. 'Our Gang' was the name of an American comedy group consisting of six children and a dog, the heroes of a very popular series of

films produced by Hal Roach.

49. See *A Family Chronicle*, n. 31.

50. Alexander G. Rzheshevsky (1903-67), who wrote the screenplay for *Bezhin Meadow*, was a firm believer in the notion of the 'emotional scenario'. The plot was based upon a real event: the murder of a Young Pioneer, Pavlik Morozov, by his relatives in September 1932 in the northern Urals because he had denounced his father to the village soviet for speculating with false papers for kulaks who had fled. In Rzheshevsky's version Stepok prevents the kulaks from setting light to the crop fields of the collective farm and is murdered by his father. In his film E elaborated on this basic theme with emotionally powerful metaphors, such as Abraham's sacrifice of Isaac in the Old Testament, the New Testament collision between God the Father and God the Son, and a number of examples from Greek mythology. Mythological figures were also deployed, somewhat paradoxically, in the scene in which the church is converted into a club.

51. Louise Michel (1830-1905) was an active participant in the Paris Commune and the *pétroleuses* were the women who, following her call, preferred to set Paris alight rather than surrender.

52. Sado-Yakko was a Japanese actress.

53. E is mistaken: the reference is to the Arab Emir Abd el Kadir (1807-83), who led the Algerian resistance to the French between 1832 and 1847.

54. Joséphine Beauharnais, Napoleon's first wife. Roustum was his servant.

55. *Up Front* by William H. Mauldin (b. 1921) was published in Cleveland and New York in 1948.

56. The *tricoteuses* (literally: 'knitting women') were the women who knitted while watching the executions during the revolutionary terror.
   Théroigne de Méricourt (1762-1817), actress and courtesan who sided with the Girondins during the French Revolution.

57. Francisco Zurbarán (1598-1664), Spanish painter.

58. See *Epopée*, n. 31.

How I Learned to Draw (A Chapter about My Dancing Lessons)

1. Dated 17 July 1946.

2. Engelbert Dollfuss (1892-1934), Austrian Chancellor from 1932,

was assassinated by the Nazis.

3. Dolores Ibarruri (1895-1987), known as 'La Pasionaria', was one of the Communist leaders in the Spanish Civil War. After Franco's victory in 1939 she emigrated to the USSR, where E met her.

4. Maria Verkhovskaya was a prominent social figure in pre-Revolutionary Riga. Her salon was frequented by leading musicians and theatre people and E visited the house during his youth.

5. Wang Pi (226-149 BC), Chinese philosopher. The quotation is from his *Basic Principles of the Book of Transformations*.

6. Olaf Gulbransson (1873-1966), German caricaturist of Norwegian extraction who contributed to the satirical journal *Simplicissimus*.

7. The pen name of P. P. Matyunin, a Russian caricaturist. *Vechernyeye vremya* was a newspaper that supported the tsarist régime and later the Provisional Government.

8. Dmitri Moor, pseudonym of Dmitri S. Orlov (1883-1941), poster and graphic artist and painter. The lubok that inspired his work was a traditional Russian woodcut that told a story.

9. For the 'Wanderers', see *Millionaires I Have Met,* n. 4.
   There is a play on words here between *'Peredvizhniki'* [the Wanderers] and *'podvizhniki'* [ascetics].

10. See *Foreword*, n. 5.

11. The rough draft for this chapter contained a plan for an insert entitled 'On the Break in My Drawing': 'There was an interruption—and quite rightly so!—in 1916. Minna Ivanovna and the painter Tyrsa: giveaway price. I abandoned it.' But in 1917 he began drawing again: at first, political caricatures and sketches for costumes and stage sets, later still real set designs. The big break in his drawing began in 1924, when he started to make *The Strike,* and he only began again seven years later in Mexico.

12. See *Bookshops*, n. 28.

13. A paraphrase of part of the introduction to Engels' *Anti-Dühring*.

14. M. Bardèche and R. Brasillach, *Histoire du cinéma* (Paris, 1935), p. 285:

All this matters little: nobody has aimed a more accurate and self-willed camera at the world. No Romantic (and he is a Romantic) has been more severe with himself, no sensualist (and he is cinema's greatest sensualist) has been more profoundly intelligent. In him abstraction and sensuality merge as they do in the greatest creative artists.

15. See *A Family Chronicle*, n. 34.

16. Edith Isaacs was the editor of *Theatre Arts Monthly*, as it was actually called. E met her in New York in April 1932 on his return from Mexico.

17. See *Epopée*, n. 45.

18. Valentin Ya. Parnakh (1891-1951), Russian poet, translator and choreographer, published a collection entitled *Introduction to the Dance* in 1925.

19. Vladimir Ya. Khenkin (1883-1953), Russian actor.

20. Pyotr K. Rudenko, alias Georges, Russian circus artiste and acrobat.

21. Leonid L. Obolensky (b. 1902), pupil of Kuleshov who later became E's assistant at VGIK. His film *Bricks* [Kirpichiki, 1925], a light comedy, was made for the commercially orientated Mezhrabpom studio.
    Anna P. Sten (1910-93) played the leading role in Boris Barnet's *The Girl with a Hatbox* [Devushka s korobkoi] in 1927. In 1930 she moved to Germany and starred in *Der Mörder Dimitri Karamasoff*, directed in 1931 by her husband Fyodor Otsep. From 1934 she worked first in Hollywood and then in Britain.
    The State Film School in Moscow was known as GTK from 1925 to 1930, then as GIK till 1934, and subsequently as VGIK, which it still remains.

22. The mimes of the Atellans were popular comedies in ancient Rome in the first century BC.

23. The Morozov villa (coincidentally just across the street called Vozdvizhenka from the cinema where *Potemkin* had its first run) was used by Proletkult in the early 1920s and it was here that E staged his production of *Enough Simplicity for Every Wise Man*. It had belonged to Ivan Morozov, one of the leading art collectors in pre-Revolutionary Russia. His home was sequestrated after the Revolution and his collection transferred to state galleries. The villa was later the headquarters of the Society for Cultural Relations with Foreign Countries. The reception E refers to took place in August 1945 when J. B. Priestley (1894-1984) was in Moscow for the world première of his play *An Inspector Calls* at the Kamerny Theatre.
    The British Ally was a Russian-language paper published by the British Embassy in Moscow during the Second World War.

24. Mikhail M. Eskin (1903-25) acted with Proletkult. The 'Blue Blouse' was the name of a popular troupe of travelling actors who performed agitational plays on current political topics in the early 1920s.

25. Vera D. Yanukova (1895-1939) played the role of Mme Mamayeva in E's production of *Wise Man.*
    Alexander P. Antonov (1898-1962) was one of E's 'iron five' group of assistants and also acted in *Glumov's Diary, The Strike* and *Potemkin.*

26. Yudif S. Glizer (1904-68), wife of E's life-long friend and collaborator, Maxim Strauch (see *Names,* n. 3), became a leading stage actress, notably at the Theatre of the Revolution. In E's production of *Wise Man* she rode a camel. Her memoir, 'Eizenshtein i zhenshchiny' [E and Women], was published in *Kinovedcheskie zapiski* [Cinematic Notes], no. 6 (1990), pp. 120-30.

27. Emile-Jaques Dalcroze (1863-1950) was the Swiss musician who originated eurhythmics.

On Folklore

1. Dated 19 July 1946, Kratovo. In accordance with E's intentions a shortened extract from *Method* has been inserted in the middle of this chapter.

2. Nicholas Brady, pseudonym of John Victor Turner, American thriller writer.

3. The Kalevala is the Finnish national epic, gathered together in the mid-nineteenth century from songs and folk tales.

4. The 'Songs of the Western Slavs' are a cycle of sixteen poems written by Pushkin in 1833 and published in 1835. Most of them are free versions of texts in Prosper Mérimée's volume of poetry *La Guzla,* supposedly based on Serbian and Croatian folklore. In addition, Pushkin included a number of authentic songs and themes from Serbian, Croatian and Czech folklore and two poems of his own.

5. Epic battle poem and classic of mediaeval Russian verse. Academia was a Leningrad publishing house.

6. The German director Fritz Lang (1890-1976) made his film version of the Nibelungen saga in Germany in 1924 in two parts: *Siegfried's Death* [Siegfrieds Tod] and *Kriemhild's Revenge* [Kriemhilds Rache].

7. The *Eddas* were the Icelandic sagas; Yggdrasil is the cosmic ash of German mythology, the tree of knowledge in which Odin/Wotan sacrificed himself to himself.

8. *The Golden Bough* is a study of early magic and religion by the Scottish anthropologist Sir James G. Frazer (1854-1941).
    Alexander N. Veselovsky (1838-1906) was a Russian literary

historian.

The reference to 'Sir Joshua' is presumably either a misnomer for Sir James Frazer or a reference to the English painter, Sir Joshua Reynolds.

9. Characters from Russian epic songs dating back to the eleventh century.

10. For Bruant, see *Epopée*, n. 112.

11. The original title for the third part of the novel. In the first published edition in 1846 Balzac called this part 'Where Bad Paths Lead'.

12. In Egyptian mythology Osiris is killed by his brother Seth and dismembered, only to be re-assembled by his sister-wife Isis.

13. See *Encounters with Books*, n. 9.

14. E is here referring to the essay by Freud on da Vinci's recollection of a childhood dream. The correct details are: *Leonardo da Vinci: A Psychosexual Study of Infallible Reminiscence* (New York, 1916).

15. For Sachs, see *Encounters with Books*, n. 8, and for Ferenczi, see *Monsieur, madame et bébé* n. 18.

16. See: G. K. Chesterton, 'Defence of the Detective Story' in *The Defendant* (London, 1901).

17. Reference to a book that E valued highly and often cited: C. F. E. Spurgeon, *Shakespeare's Imagery and What It Tells Us* (Cambridge, 1935). See *ESW2*, pp.187-91.

18. Jacques Deval, pseudonym of Jacques Boularon (1894-1972), French author of comedies in the style of Sacha Guitry.

19. Sergei T. Konenkov (1874-1971), Soviet sculptor whose figures were based on folklore, myth and fairy tale.

20. The proceedings of the January 1935 Conference of Soviet Film Workers, including E's contribution, were published under the title *Za bol'shoe kinoiskusstvo* [For A Great Cinema Art] (Moscow, 1935).

21. Alexander R. Luria (1902-77), Soviet psychologist and pioneer of neuropsychology.

The actual title of Goldschmidt's book is: *Ascaris. Eine Einführung in die Wissenschaft vom Leben für jedermann* [Thread-Worm. An Introduction to the Science of Life for Everyman].

22. Mei Lan-Fan (1894-1961) was a Chinese classical actor with the Peking Opera whom E met in Moscow in 1935. In his 1935 article 'To the Magician of the Pear Orchard' E explained: '"Pupils of the Pear Garden" is an ancient title given to Chinese actors who are trained in the appropriate part of the Imperial Palace. Mei Lan-Fan's official title—First in the Pear Orchard—means that he

occupies first place among China's actors.'

23. The harlequin (actually *manteau d'Arlequin*) is a curtain attached to a fixed wing and soffit painted to look like an open curtain. It hangs directly behind the main curtain and serves to restrict the view from the auditorium into the stage works. Mirror is the name given to the vertical front surface of the stage between proscenium and apron.

24. Richard Teschner (1879-1948), Austrian painter, graphic artist, set designer and puppeteer.

25. E is referring to the first volume of his planned textbook on *Direction* to be entitled *The Art of Mise-en-scène*, the bulk of which was devoted to a detailed treatment of the theme 'A soldier returns from the front and finds his wife with a babe-in-arms'. The situation was treated successively from the standpoint of melodrama, pathos and comedy, and the different versions were analysed for the concrete solutions they offered and the associations they employed.

Inversions

1. This chapter was produced on 30 July 1946. There was a note attached to the manuscript with a list of the basic themes and two remarks 'for myself'. One of these concerns the place the chapter should occupy in the *Memoirs*: 'Probably to follow *Skeletons*' [in English in the original], i.e. after *On Bones*. However the text is closely linked to the *Grundproblematik* and, for this reason, the Russian editors have elected to include it in the cycle of chapters from July 1946. E's second remark reflects his dissatisfaction with the literary quality of the text: 'Run out of steam—pretty bad—a lot of stylistic corrections'. The manuscript has no title and the Russian editors have selected this one from a reference in one of the drafts.

2. Aristide Briand (1845-1932), French statesman, Prime Minister, Foreign Minister and advocate of a United States of Europe. See also *Epopée*, n. 114.
   For Bruant, see *Epopée*, n. 112.

3. André Gill (1845-85), French caricaturist.

4. E. Bayard, *Quartier latin, hier et aujourd'hui.* (Paris, 1924). Bayard also wrote *Montmartre, hier et aujourd'hui* (Paris, 1925).

5. *A Guy Named Joe* [USA, 1943].

6. See *'A Family Chronicle'*, n. 34.

Colour

1. This text was probably written in early August 1946. The final sentences were written on a separate sheet of paper under the heading 'First Encounter' and at a different time. They were possibly intended as a link between the text and the cycle of chapters on the 'mastery of colour'.

Gogol's Mastery

1. Undated and untitled. Possibly written as early as 1940 for the unfinished article 'Montage 1940' but more probably written in early August 1946.
2. Andrei Bely, pseudonym of Boris N. Bugayev (1880-1934), Russian writer and, in the pre-Revolutionary period, one of the leading figures in Russian Symbolism. His best known work is the novel *Petersburg*: see also *Why I Became a Director*, n. 6.
3. Taras is the Cossack hero of the story *Taras Bulba*.
   Dovgochkhun is Ivan Nikiforovich, one of the two principal characters in *The Story of How Ivan Ivanovich Quarrelled with Ivan Nikiforovich*.
   Chichikov is the charlatan who is the central figure of the novel *Dead Souls*. Selifan and Petrushka are his coachman and servant respectively.
4. Petukh (literally in Russian: 'cockerel') is a landowner in Part Two of *Dead Souls*.
5. A. Belyi, *Masterstvo Gogolya* [Gogol's Mastery] (Moscow, 1934), p. 159.
6. The novel was dramatised by Mikhail Bulgakov and directed by Stanislavsky, and the production opened on 28 November 1932.
7. E chaired an evening in Bely's honour at the Polytechnical Museum in Moscow in 1933.
8. The State Publishing House for Literature.

Three Letters about Colour

1. Written on 20 August 1946 in Kratovo after *The Springs of Happiness*.
2. Yuri Tynyanov (see *The Boy from Riga*, n. 5) died of multiple sclerosis on 20 December 1943 in Moscow. In 1941, already seriously ill, he had been evacuated from Leningrad to Perm, where he had continued to work on his biographical novel *Pushkin*

despite intense pain.

3. Mikhail I. Kalinin (1875-1946), Soviet head of state from March 1919 until his death, which was six years later than suggested here by E.

4. The title of Tynyanov's study of Pushkin: see *The Boy from Riga*, n. 5.

The Springs of Happiness

1. The first part of this chapter is dated 3 July 1946, the second 3 August 1946, and the insert on E's work on *Die Walküre* was probably written even later.

2. These boulevard romances were all published at the turn of the century. The authors are: Mikhail P. Artsybashev (1878-1927), Yevdokia A. Nagrodskaya (1866-1930), Nadezhda A. Lappo-Danilevskaya (1875/6-?) and Anastasia A. Verbitskaya (1861-1928).

3. Vsevolod A. Verbitsky (1896-1951), son of Anastasia Verbitskaya, acted with the Moscow Art Theatre for many years.

4. Edvard Munch (1863-1944), Norwegian painter, one of the principal inspirations for German Expressionism.

5. In his three-volume theoretical work *The Theatre for Oneself* (1915-17) Yevreinov (see *Why I Became a Director*, n.12) argued that every individual was capable of metamorphosis and role-playing: everyday life could therefore be metamorphosed in theatre so that every individual could simultaneously be actor and spectator.

6. There is an untranslatable pun here: the Russian word *klyuch* can mean both 'spring' and 'key'. Similarly the Russian word *schast'e* can mean either 'happiness' or 'fortune', so that what is here translated as 'The Springs of Happiness' would have a variety of alternative meanings to a Russian.

7. E's unfinished project for *Fergana Canal* dates from May to October 1939: see W. Sudendorf, *Sergej M. Eisenstein. Materialien zu Leben und Werk* (Munich, 1975), p. 228.

8. The production opened on 21 November 1940.

9. On 2 April 1923 in the Bolshoi Theatre an evening celebrating twenty-five years of Meyerhold's theatrical activity included an extract from E's production of *Wise Man* entitled 'Joffre off to Campaign'.

10. See *A Miracle in the Bolshoi Theatre*, pp. 180-2.

11. Nikolai A. Nekrasov (1821-78), Russian poet, writer and dramatist.

12. See *ESW 2*, passim.

13. Apart from Bach's 'The Art Of Fugue', E had in mind the

theoretical work by the Russian composer and scholar Sergei I. Taneyev (1856-1915) *Podvizhnoi kontrapunkt strogogo pis'ma* [The Moveable Counterpoint of Strict Style].

14. In 'On the Structure of Things' E quotes from the book by E. K. Rozenov, *I. S. Bakh i ego rod* [J. S. Bach and His Kind] (Moscow, 1911), p. 72:

. . . According to testimony coming to us from Bach's pupils, he taught them to look at the instrumental voice as they would a personality, and at the polyphonic instrumental composition as a conversation between these personalities, while setting up a rule that each of them 'speak well and in time, and if they have nothing to say, it would be better to remain silent or wait their turn . . .'

Quoted from *Nonindifferent Nature* (Cambridge, 1987), p. 4.

15. Ivan V. Lebedev (1879-1950), Russian athlete, referee and circus artiste.

16. These were all wrestlers at the turn of the century. Cyclops and Aberg also appeared in circus acts. 'Black Mask' was the popular name for a wrestler whose identity was not known.

17. Reference to the visit by the Kabuki theatre to the USSR in August 1928 with Itakawa Sadanji (1880-1940), director, actor and dramatist. See *ESW 1*, especially pp. 115-22, 181-94.

18. Characters from the popular mediaeval Russian *Play of King Maximilian* which had its roots in Byzantine mystery plays.

19. Pyotr V. Williams [Vilyams] (1902-47), Russian painter and set designer, principal stage designer at the Bolshoi Theatre from 1941 until his death.
Semyon A. Samosud (1884-1964), principal director at the Bolshoi from 1936 to 1943.

20. E proposed a film on the Italian painter Giordano Bruno (1548-1600) to the Committee on Cinema Affairs in 1940 but the idea was rejected; see Sudendorf, p. 228.

21. The proposal for a film about Lawrence of Arabia envisaged a script written by Lev R. Sheinin (1906-67), who had written the play *The Prestige of the Empire* about the Beilis affair in 1913, which E submitted as another film project at roughly the same time. On Sheinin's connections with the secret police, see: L. Kozlov, 'The Artist and the Shadow of Ivan', in: R. Taylor & D. Spring (eds), *Stalinism and Soviet Cinema* (London & New York, 1993), p. 244, n. 13.

22. The NKVD was the People's Commissariat for Internal Affairs, synonymous with the secret police, which formed one part of its organisation.

23. E's mistake: Levernier's calculations predicted the existence of Neptune, not Uranus.

24. *ESW 1,* pp. 113-14.

25. The first Soviet colour documentary film, made with Soviet three-colour stock and directed by Sergei Gerasimov in 1945.

The Prize for *Ivan*

1. This chapter consists of three fragments written at different times. The first section, dealing with the deaths of Khmelyov and Tolstoi, was written in mid-June 1946 as part of another chapter from which it was subsequently removed. The text presented here is preceded in the manuscript by a few words from that chapter. The second section, entitled *The Prize for 'Ivan',* is dated 28 June 1946. The third section, with neither date nor title, links the other two with the theme of the search for a colour concept for *A Poet's Love.*

2. Nikolai P. Khmelyov (1902-45), Russian actor and director, part of the Moscow Art Theatre troupe from 1924 until his death. He played the role of the Father in the second version of *Bezhin Meadow* (1936-7), replacing Boris Zakhava, who played the part in the first version (1935-6).

3. Khmelyov died on 1 November 1945, shortly before the première of *Difficult Years,* the second part of the two-part drama *Ivan the Terrible* (1941-3) by Alexei N. Tolstoi, who had died on 23 February 1945 during the rehearsals for the first part of the drama *Eagle and Eagle-Woman* on the stage of the Maly Theatre.
   Iosif Yuzovsky, pseudonym of Iosif Ilyich (1902-64), was a literary and theatre scholar and critic.

4. See *Bookshops,* pp. 373-80.

5. i.e. Alexei Tolstoi

6. The eponymous hero of Romain Rolland's novel *Master Breugnon* [French title: *Colas Breugnon*].

7. Boris L. Pasternak (1890-1960), Nobel Prize-winning Russian poet, translator and writer, author of the novel *Dr Zhivago.*

8. Mikhail E. Chiaureli (1894-1974), Georgian film director responsible for such key films of the Stalin cult as *The Vow* and *The Fall of Berlin* [Padenie Berlina, 1949].

9. Simeon the Stylite (390-459) was the first of the pillar ascetics,

spending the last thirty-six years of his life at the top of a pillar in northern Syria, ostensibly to avoid contact with the mass of pilgrims who came to see him.

10. Esfir I. Shub (1894-1954), compilation documentary film-maker. E worked with Shub on the re-editing of Fritz Lang's *Dr Mabuse der Spieler* [Germany, 1921/2] from two parts into one for Soviet distribution. It was on this film that E cut his cinematic teeth.

11. Late in 1829 Pushkin wrote in the poetry album of his lady friend in Moscow, Yelizaveta Ushakova, a list of names of the women who had been the 'objects' of his passions: this later became known as Pushkin's 'Don Juan list'.

Marion

1. Written on 28 June 1946 in Barvikha. The final sentences, deleted from the manuscript, have been reconstructed, as they provide a transition to the following chapter. The last sentence probably read: 'And at midday I (?) feel the sensation of a flaming (?) sunset.

2. See *Comrade Léon*, n. 6.

3. Marion Davies (1898-1961), American actress, protégée of the newspaper magnate William Randolph Hearst (1863-1951).

4. Toraichi Kono was Chaplin's valet and general assistant from 1916 to 1934.

5. Lita Grey (b. 1908), American child film extra who appeared in Chaplin's *The Kid*. From 1924 to 1927 she was Chaplin's second wife, the mother of his two eldest sons. E's account of the wedding in this chapter is therefore erroneous.

6. Camille Flammarion (1842-1925), French writer, publisher and astronomer.

7. One of the many early words for cinema theatres: see Yu. Tsivian, *Early Cinema in Russia and its Cultural Reception* (London & New York, 1994).

8. Jean Mounet-Sully (1841-1916), French actor who worked from 1872 at the Comédie Française.

9. Max Linder (1883-1925), French comedian, one of the leading comic actors of the silent cinema.
   Pockson, pseudonym of John Banny (1863-1915), American film comedian.
   Prince, pseudonym of Charles Prince Rigadon (1872-1933), French film actor.

10. For Yevreinov, see *Why I Became a Director*, n. 12.

872

John Erskine (1879-1951), American novelist and scholar, wrote *The Private Life of Helen of Troy* in 1925.

The title *Tonner* has not been traced and E has left the author's name blank, but the reference may be to Louis Delluc's film *Thunder* [Le tonnerre, France, 1921].

11. What E meant to indicate here was that in Sterne's *Tristram Shandy* the hero/narrator is carried away by so many digressions that the novel ends with his birth.

12. E. A. Poe, *Marginalia*: 'I cannot help thinking that romance-writers in general might now and then find their account in taking a hint from the Chinese, who, in spite of building their houses downwards, have still sense enough to *begin their books at the end*.'

13. Reference to the ideas expressed in *Le Rire. Essai sur la signification du comique* [Laughter. An Essay on the Signification of the Comic] by Henri Bergson (1859-1941).

14. Anatoli V. Lunacharsky (1875-1933), Soviet People's Commissar for Enlightenment from 1917 until 1929, also wrote scripts for popular film melodramas often featuring his actress wife Natalia Rozenel.

The Dollar Princess

1. Dated 28 June 1946 but unfinished. A few days later E returned to the main theme of this chapter in *Katerinki*.

2. Cf *ESW 2*, pp. 255, 373-3, 413 n. 262.

3. Reference to the sets designed by Isaak Rabinovich for the 1933 production of Tchaikovsky's opera *Eugene Onegin*.

4. Hans Fender, German theatre and opera actor, worked in Riga at the turn of the century.

   Kurt Busch (1879-1954), German opera actor and director, worked in Riga from 1905 to 1911, as did the actor Fritz Sachsl.

5. This chapter was never written but a plan for it, dated 8 May 1946, does survive. It is headed in English 'The case of the ugly duckling who never really became a swan (never to become a man)'.

Katerinki

1. Dated 8 August 1946 and written in English, French and Russian. This chapter marks E's third attempt to give an account of his tragic love for an unknown girl. The first was *The Dollar Princess*, which he never completed. A week later, on 4 July 1946, he began a chapter entitled *From Katrinka to Katlinka*, but gave up almost

immediately. More than a month later he returned to the subject and gave his memoir the form of a 'discovery' of a romantic love story. As is clear from the text, he wrote his 'fairy tale' in two attempts. Next to the date he wrote: 'At the top of the page a facsimile of an old hundred-rouble note.' These pre-Revolutionary notes were known colloquially as *katerinki* because they bore a portrait of Catherine the Great. This remark is probably less a reference to the wealth of the 'Dollar Princess' than an allusion to her name and to the name of the girl whom the 'Cathedral Builder' had fallen in love with (according to the draft of 4 July) seventeen years previously.

A Poet's Love (Pushkin)

1. Undated and untitled. It is very probable that it was written as early as 1944-5 for *Method* or *Nonindifferent Nature*, but later removed for the 'Third Letter on Colour'. Comparison with the unsent letter to Yuri Tynyanov shows that this text is a re-working and fuller exposition of the ideas expressed in that letter in late December 1943. This chapter concludes the cycle dealing with the 'discovery' of the dramaturgy of colour film.

2. Pushkin's sojourn in Odessa in 1823/4 was the last stage in his 'southern exile', which preceded his 'northern exile' on his mother's estate at Mikhailovskoye in the Pskov province. The Black Brook is near St Petersburg and was the scene of the duel that killed Pushkin on 27 January 1837 (Old Style).

3. E was planning a film version of Pushkin's *Boris Godunov* in 1940 but this never came to fruition. Some of his ideas for the use of colour were later deployed in *Ivan the Terrible* Part Two. See also: 'Pushkin the Montageur', *ESW 2*, pp. 203-23.

4. Alexander I ascended the throne in 1801 after the murder, with his knowledge, of his father Paul I. The boyar Boris Godunov was elected tsar in 1598 after the death of Ivan the Terrible's son, Fyodor. Rumours abounded that Boris had been responsible for the murder of Fyodor's brother and legitimate heir, Dmitri. Pushkin used this version of events as the basis of his drama, thus raising the issue of succession to the throne through murder without actually incurring the wrath of the censors.

5. Konstantin K. Danzas (1801-70), school friend of Pushkin and his second for the duel with d'Anthès.

6. At this point E left space for a quotation, probably from Danzas'

recollections of the duel.

7. The project for the Pushkin film envisaged a score by Prokofiev in which the 'Requiem' was part of a sequence entitled 'Pushkin Travelling to the Duel'.

8. Pushkin jokingly referred to his wife in this way.

9. See *The Boy from Riga*, n. 5.

10. Reference to Chapter 15 of Tolstoy's *Khadzhi Murat*.

11. Reference to Pushkin's 'minor tragedy' *The Stone Guest*, written in 1830. See also *The Prize for 'Ivan'*, n.11.

12. Tsarskoye Selo, also the site of one of the royal summer palaces, was the settlement south of St Petersburg where Pushkin and his family lived.

13. Tatyana's last remark to Onegin in Chapter 8 of Pushkin's *Eugene Onegin*.

14. E has his chronology confused again here: the poem 'The Gypsies' was begun in Odessa and completed in October 1824 in Mikhailovskoye.

15. A jocular remark by Pushkin.

16. Quotation from a report in verse by Pushkin to Governor General Vorontsov who had sent the poet on a pointless expedition to combat locusts.

17. An untranslatable pun: the Russian term *Bes arabskii* literally means 'an Arab devil' but also alludes to his negro ancestry, since Russians at that time did not distinguish between Arabs and negroes.

18. During his exile at Mikhailovskoye, Pushkin was placed under the supervision of the local priest, who provided a model for the monk Varlaam in *Boris Godunov*.
Arina Rodyonovna was a serf and Pushkin's nanny.
Olga Kalashnikova, a serf who bore Pushkin a son, was *not* Arina Rodyonovna's niece.

19. Owned by Pushkin's in-laws, the Goncharovs.

20. The well-known rebellious and prophetic cry by Eugene, the hero of Pushkin's poem 'The Bronze Horseman', addressed to the awesome statue of Peter the Great on the Senate Square next to the Admiralty and the River Neva in St Petersburg. E's Pushkin project envisaged a scene in this square, where the Decembrist Uprising took place in 1825, as 'the poet's rebellion'.

21. Lines from Zemfira's song, which affirms the right to free love.

22. The ostensible cause of the first challenge to a duel to d'Anthès was the anonymous and libellous 'diploma' sent to Pushkin and his friends which 'elected' him a 'Co-Adjutant (Deputy) to the Grand

Master of the Order of Cuckolds, and Historian of the Order'.
23. Fear of popular reaction to Pushkin's untimely death meant that the funeral arrangements were changed at the last minute.

After Thursday's Shower

1. Dated 8 August 1946, this chapter is essentially a diary entry written immediately after the death of E's mother. The Russian title *'Posle dozhdika v chetverg'* means literally 'After Thursday's Shower' but the phrase is used colloquially to denote procrastination.
2. Vsevolod Emilevich is Meyerhold: see *A Family Chronicle*, n. 12.
   Nemirovich: see ibid., n. 19.
   Khazby was one of E's pupils.
   Valentin I. Kadochnikov (1911-42), Soviet film director and animation artist, one of E's pupils at VGIK.
   Stanislavsky: see *Le Bon Dieu*, n. 10.
   Yelizaveta S. Telesheva (1893-1943), actress, director at the Moscow Art Theatre, worked as E's assistant for acting on *Bezhin Meadow* (second version), in which she also appeared, and *Alexander Nevsky* and at VGIK.
3. i.e. *Que Viva México!*
4. Olga I. Preobrazhenskaya (1881-1971), Soviet film director and actress whose best-known work is probably *Women of Ryazan* [Baby ryazanskie, 1927].
5. In the manuscript E had originally and absent-mindedly written his mother's name Yulia but then crossed this out and substituted Telesheva's initials 'Ye. S.', hence the sense of premonition.

Life's 'Formulae'

1. Roughed out on 15 August 1946, this chapter ends in outline form.
2. Marie Corelli (1864-1924) and Victoria Cross, pseudonym of Vivian Cory, were British and American popular writers respectively.
3. Pyotr A. Pavlenko (1899-1951), Soviet scriptwriter who collaborated with E on the screenplays for *Alexander Nevsky* and *The Great Fergana Canal.*
4. *The Chocolate Soldier* was an operetta, first performed in New York in 1909 with music by the Austrian composer and conductor, Oskar Straus (1869-1954), based on the Viennese operetta *Der tapfere Soldat* [The Brave Soldier], which was in turn an unauthorised version of Shaw's play *Arms and the Man*, first performed in 1894—

hence Shaw's insistence on fidelity to his text.

5. See *Pages from Literature*, n. 6.

The True Paths of Discovery

1. On 14 October 1946 E wrote two texts. One, entitled 'The True Paths of Discovery' (here called 'The Tale of the Vixen and the Hare') was written as a memoir and dealt with work on *Alexander Nevsky*. The other, 'Layout', was an illustrated exercise demonstrating the process of creative improvisation. E's notes indicate the links between these 1946 texts and the 'Torito' section written for the first volume of *Direction* in 1934. For this reason the Russian editors see the pieces grouped here as constituting a cycle of three chapters in the *Memoirs*, rather than an expansion of the textbook, and they have therefore taken the title of the reminiscence about *Nevsky* as the title for the chapter as a whole.

2. Giorgio de Chirico (1888-1978), Italian painter who lived in France and was one of the founders of Surrealism.

3. *Khovanshchina* was written by Modest P. Mussorgsky (1839-81) between 1872 and 1880 but left unfinished. It was completed by Nikolai A. Rimsky-Korsakov (1844-1908). The opera ends with the Old Believers, realising that their cause is lost, burning themselves on a funeral pyre of their own making.

4. Reference to Nikolai Leskov's story *Lady Macbeth of the Mtsensk District*, on which Shostakovich based his opera: see *Pages from Literature*, n. 7.

5. Jules Guérin, member of the *Ligue des Patriotes*.
Paul Déroulède (1846-1914), French writer and politician, founded the *Ligue des Patriotes* in 1882.

6. Paul Morand (1889-1976), French writer and diplomat of right-wing persuasion, published *1900* in Paris in 1925.

7. Goethe maintained that his works were 'opportune', as was the creative impulse itself.

8. Cf 'The Two Skulls of Alexander the Great' (1926), *ESW 1*, pp. 82-4.

9. It was in fact, or so the anecdote goes, James Watt who was inspired to develop the steam engine from observing the way that steam made the lid on his mother's kettle jump.

10. During the Second Punic War at the Battle of Cannae in 216 BC Hannibal and his Carthaginian cavalry outflanked the Roman army and inflicted the worst defeat on the Romans in history: almost

50,000 out of a total of 86,000 men were lost.

11. The headquarters of the Soviet Writers' Union occupied a former masonic lodge between Herzen and Vorovsky Streets in west-central Moscow, next door to the town house that was supposedly the model for the Rostov family mansion in Tolstoy's *War and Peace.*

12. Reference to the volume *Zavetnye rasskazy* [Cherished Tales], compiled by the Russian historian and anthropologist Alexander Afanasiev (1826-71) and published anonymously in Geneva in the 1860s. E had been given this book by Viktor Shklovsky.

13. Franciscan friars of the strict rule. The correspondence was not genuine.

14. Otto von Guericke constructed the Magdeburg hemispheres, two cups held together by atmospheric pressure once the air has been pumped out from between them and a vacuum created.

15. The reference is to the opera *The Maid of Pskov* [Pskovityanka], also known as *Ivan the Terrible,* by the Russian composer Rimsky-Korsakov, which received its first performance in St Petersburg in 1873.

16. Dmitri N. Orlov (1892-1955), stage actor who narrated fairy tales on Soviet radio.
    Dogada is a character in a Russian fairy tale.

The Author and His Theme

1. This chapter is composed of two texts dating from different periods. The first is an unfinished autobiographical essay dated 27 October 1944 and the second is an extract from *Method* dealing with the same problem. The Russian editors have included them here because of E's repeated intention to demonstrate the continuity of his subject matter.

2. Sigismund D. Krzhizhanovsky (1887-1950), Soviet literary scholar.

3. Ivan A. Goncharov (1812-91), Russian civil servant and censor who became a writer. The three novels cited were in fact written in the reverse order: *A Common Story* in 1847, *Oblomov* in 1859 and *The Precipice* in 1869.

4. See *Dead Souls,* p 128.

P. S.

1. Written in December 1946. With this piece E broke off work on his *Memoirs.*

Index